THE RIGHT TO KEEP AND BEAR ARMS

A Collection of Historical Documents Relating to the Second Amendment

THE RIGHT TO KEEP AND BEAR ARMS

A Collection of Historical Documents Relating to the Second Amendment

HARWOOD W. LOOMIS

ELDERSLIE PRESS

The Right to Keep and Bear Arms

A Collection of Historical Documents
Relating to the Second Amendment

ISBN: 978-1-7364434-3-9 (Paperback Edition)

Library of Congress Control Number: 2021909660

Published by:
ELDERSLIE PRESS
172 Peck Hill Road
Woodbridge, Connecticut 06525
United States of America

I have ancestors on both the maternal and paternal side of the family going back to the American Revolution who played roles in the founding of the United States of America. History, ultimately, will decide whether they did well or poorly. The results of my research into the history of the documents that led up to the drafting of our Constitution, as well as significant laws and Supreme Court decisions that followed it, show that the Constitution is not perfect but that, overall, the Framers did a remarkable job.

This book is dedicated to the memory of my patriotic ancestors and all their contemporary patriots who created the United States of America and our Constitution, as well as to the memory of my grandparents, Thomas III and Eleanor Wallace, who ingrained in me an appreciation for our Constitution.

"I have little patience with people who take the Bill of Rights for granted. The Bill of Rights, contained in the first ten amendments to the Constitution, is every American's guarantee of freedom."

— President Harry S. Truman, 1956, *Years of Trial and Hope*

CONTENTS

FOREWORD

"Since 1789 the average life span of national constitutions world-wide has been 19 years, according to scholars at the University of Chicago (https://www.uchicago.edu/features/20100920_constitution/?mod=article_inline). Meanwhile, "We the People of the United States" are now well into the third century under our Constitution. We've lived under the same written charter longer than any people on earth. We've had regular federal elections every two years, uninterrupted even by the Civil War...." (Joseph Tartakovsky, "The Culture That Sustains America's Constitution," *The Wall Street Journal*, 2 July 2018).

I've known Harwood Loomis for some fifteen years — going back to our days as moderators on ForumM1911.org — as an advocate for the right to keep and bear arms and as a New Englander whose family history is intertwined with the early history of our Nation. And we can all, now, through this volume explore with Mr. Loomis some of the philosophical and conceptual foundations of our Democratic Republic.

On one hand we see the evolution of limitations on the power of the sovereign by subjecting sovereign power to civil authority and better definitions of certain individual rights. On the other hand, we come to understand the right to keep and bear arms to be a personal, individual, and fundamental right.

The notion that the "divine right" of a monarch could be subject to the constraint of civil, political processes is fundamental to the development of the western, democratic nation-state. And, as is apparent from the comments (pp 159-162) of the Founders regarding the right to keep and bear arms, the private possession of weapons was considered significant — both politically and privately.

Enjoy the book. I did. And I plan to keep it handy for reference.

Frank Ettin, J. D.
May, 2021, Lafayette, CA

PREFACE

As a U.S. Army veteran, when I enlisted I swore an oath to support and to defend the Constitution of the United States of America against all enemies, foreign and domestic. I took that oath seriously, and in the years since I was released from active duty and discharged from the U.S. Army it has been my view that nothing in my discharge papers released me from my vow to support and defend our Constitution.

The Bill of Rights is an integral part of the Constitution. As I look at the world and read the news today, it strikes me that the Constitution I swore to support and defend, especially the Second Amendment, is under attack from enemies within. Our public media, whose role is supposed to be that of objective reporter, have become a mouthpiece for the enemies of the Constitution. The truth about the origins, the history, and the intent of the Second Amendment have been stricken from our educational system, and the populace are being misled, duped, deceived, and hoodwinked as to the meaning and intent of the Second Amendment.

I have spoken or exchanged correspondence with a great many people who understand this and who continually ask, "What can I do to help people understand the truth about the Second Amendment and the Right to Keep and Bear Arms?" In 1597, Francis Bacon wrote, "Knowledge is power." Thomas Jefferson used that phrase multiple times in his writings. I believe that the answer to people who question the meaning and the intent of the Second Amendment is to show them where it came from, and show them what the men who wrote it said it meant at the time they wrote it.

The problem is that the many documents that show us that history and meaning are available, but they are not in one place and they often aren't easy to find. My purpose in compiling this book is to bring together as many of those documents as possible in one place, under one cover, so that anyone who has a sincere interest in understanding the Second Amendment has at his or her fingertips all the references they need to fully and objectively explore the question of the origins and the meaning of the Second Amendment.

Harwood Loomis
May, 2021, Woodbridge, Connecticut

ACKNOWLEDGEMENTS

This book would not have been possible without help, advice, and encouragement from a large number of people over a prolonged period of time. It isn't possible for me to name them all because, to be honest, I asked so many people questions along the way that I am certain that I have forgotten some. Without intending to omit anyone, I would like to express my thanks to John Caradimas, Paul Acampora, and Spyros Georgilidakis for on-going advice and for their patience in responding to innumerable "Hey, what do you think about ___?" questions. Thanks also to Spyros and his wife, Evi Thomakou for reviews and constructive criticism in regard to the book layout and the cover design.

I also want to thank Matthew H. Lucas, Esq., for being available as a sounding board when I had questions about how to address certain legal questions, and also for helping me know if I had covered them adequately

It is not my intention that this book should in any way be regarded as a legal text; it is not. It is merely a collection of historical documents, but the documents by themselves would be useless without some introduction and explanation. Since I am not an attorney, any errors or inaccuracies in my descriptions of the legal importance of these documents are my errors, not those of my resources.

ACKNOWLEDGMENTS

INTRODUCTION

I attended junior high school in the late 1950s. At that time, there were no classes titled "Civics," which is where I suppose whatever is taught today about the Constitution and the Bill of Rights is offered. In my day the class was called "Social Studies," and it was taught in the seventh and eighth grades. When I took Social Studies, we learned that we have a Constitution and that the Bill of Rights was not originally a part of the Constitution — and that's about all we learned. We were not taught that there was a constitution — the Articles of Confederation — before the Constitution. We were not taught that there was considerable debate over whether or not our federal government should be a strong federal government, we were not told about *The Federalist Papers* or *The Anti-Federalist Papers,* and we were not taught anything about the origins of the several personal/civil rights enshrined in the Bill of Rights. We certainly were not taught that the Constitution passed and was ratified only when the Federalists agreed to add a Bill of Rights to the Constitution.

My daughter has been out of high school for several years but, even so, she followed me by roughly half a century. It is my impression, from her and from looking at some of her high school text books, that American students today are being taught even less about our Constitution and the Bill of Rights than what was taught in my high school years.

One of the (perhaps inevitable) results of the lack of education regarding the Constitution and the Bill of Rights is the wide-spread misunderstanding among the populace today regarding what the Second Amendment says, what it means, and what it meant to the Framers who wrote it. Even in my junior high school Social Studies classes, the impression was conveyed that the Framers of our Constitution were somewhat akin to Moses when he went up the mountain to receive the Ten Commandments — we were given the distinct impression that the Constitution of the United States was something entirely new and unprecedented in history. In fact, all the history I was taught about the American Revolution in junior high school and high school talked about the King of England; we were not taught that much of what the American colonies rebelled against was not the King, but the Parliament — in which the colonies were not represented. I was not taught anything about the fact that, at the time of the American Revolution, Great Britain was not an absolute monarchy but, rather, it was a constitutional monarchy — and had been for more than a century. I was also not taught that the British had a Bill of Rights dating to 1689, a century before the drafting of the American Bill of Rights, and that the Framers of our Constitution, being British subjects prior to the Declaration of Independence and many of them being lawyers, certainly were well aware of the English Bill of Rights and other documents preceding it.

I often encounter people who have an interest, on one side or the other, in the debate over gun control. The question, "Why doesn't anyone understand what the Second Amendment means?" is a common theme in these discussions. The answer is, "Because they don't teach us that in the schools."

The road to the Constitution of the United States and the Bill of Rights is a long one, which arguably begins with the *Magna Carta* (if not before). In the interest of making these discussions more informed, rather than simply two ill-informed sides trading uninformed opinions, I have undertaken to collect in one volume the text of as many of the milestone documents leading up to our Bill of Rights as possible. Also, in the furtherance of informed discussion regarding the Second Amendment, I also include several significant documents that followed the adoption of the Bill of Rights.

Most Americans are completely unaware that a joint subcommittee of the Congress concluded in 1982 that:

> The conclusion is thus inescapable that the history, concept, and wording of the second amendment to the Constitution of the United States, as well as its interpretation by every major commentator and court in the first half-century after its ratification, indicates that what is protected is an individual right of a private citizen to own and carry firearms in a peaceful manner.

The 1982 Congressional report is included in this volume. Following that, in 2004, the Attorney General of the United States commissioned a second report on the meaning and intent of the Second Amendment. That report concluded:

> For the foregoing reasons, we conclude that the Second Amendment secures an individual right to keep and to bear arms. Current case law leaves open and unsettled the question of whose right is secured by the Amendment. Although we do not address the scope of the right, our examination of the original meaning of the Amendment provides extensive reasons to conclude that the Second Amendment secures an individual right, and no persuasive basis for either the collective right or quasi-collective right views.

This report is also included in the following pages.

* * * * *

Many of the documents I have included in this collection are transcriptions. However, Supreme Court decisions can be lengthy; the *Heller* decision is 154 pages, and the *McDonald* decision is 203 pages. When citations are given to a particular sentence or passage from a Supreme Court decision, they include not just the name and number of the case but also the page number. For this reason, in the following pages I have elected not to transcribe Supreme Court decisions but to reproduce them as they appear in the federal government's archives. This preserves the pagination and footnotes, but it also reduces the size of each page by approximately five percent. I believe the retention of pagination to allow finding citations is worth the inconvenience created by the reduction in size.

THE RIGHT TO KEEP AND BEAR ARMS

A Collection of Historical Documents
Relating to the Second Amendment

The Magna Carta

In the beginning ...

The journey to understand the American Bill of Rights (and its Second Amendment) rightly begins in England, in the year 1215, with the signing of the first *Magna Carta*. Written in Latin, the document's full name is *Magna Carta Libertatum* ("Great Charter of Freedoms"). The web site of the Encyclopedia Brittanica has this to say about it:

> **Magna Carta**, English **Great Charter**, charter of English liberties granted by King John on June 15, 1215, under threat of civil war and reissued, with alterations, in 1216, 1217, and 1225. By declaring the sovereign to be subject to the rule of law and documenting the liberties held by "free men," the Magna Carta provided the foundation for individual rights in Anglo-American jurisprudence.
> [*Source: https://www.britannica.com/topic/Magna-Carta*]

In the early 13th century, King John of England was not only the King of England, he was also Duke of Normandy (in France), Duke of Aquitaine (in France), Count of Anjou (in France), and Lord of Ireland in 1199. At the time of his ascension to the throne in England, John was more powerful in France than the King of France. This changed, however, in 1204 when the King of France wrested Anjou and Normandy from John's control. Because those provinces had been under his family's rule for centuries, John wished to regain control and, to that end, he engaged in a costly war against France. In order to finance the war he imposed taxes that were significantly higher than had been the norm in England prior to that time.

Leading English nobles resented the higher taxes, and the high-handed way in which the taxes were collected. When the English forces suffered a humiliating defeat at Bouvines in 1214, the nobles' dissatisfaction came to a head, leading to a confrontation with the King. The result of the confrontation was the *Magna Carta*.

The text of the *Magna Carta* document on the following pages is a translation from the Latin, with the individual clauses numbered (as is evident in the image preceding the text, the provisions were not numbered in the original, nor were they neatly separated into paragraphs). In this document we can see an enumeration of individual rights that could not be violated ("infringed") by the

Crown (the government). Some of the many rights enumerated in the *Magna Carta* foretell rights specified in the Bill of Rights in the Constitution of the United States. For example:

- Number 38 sounds a lot like our Fifth Amendment, which says that a person cannot be compelled to testify against himself.
- Number 39 is a likely candidate as the inspiration for our Sixth Amendment, which guarantees us the right to a speedy and public trial before an impartial jury.

Although King John agreed to the provisions of the *Magna Carta*, it is unlikely that he had any intention of honoring them. At that time, England was still a Roman Catholic country, and the Church wielded considerable authority. Within three months following the issuance of the *Magna Carta*, John applied to the Pope and had the *Magna Carta* declared invalid, on the grounds that it interfered with the rights of the King. The rebellious nobles then renounced their fealty to John. When John died on October 16, 1216, much of England was under the control of France. The English nobles agreed to make John's young son, Henry III, king–under the guidance of a committee of regents until he reached majority. Consequently, the *Magna Carta* was reissued in late 1216, signed by Henry III, with most of the original provisions intact.

Although it is tempting to consider the *Magna Carta* as the start of the constitutional monarchy in England, historical sources generally concur that this actually occurred in the 17th century and that the *Magna Carta* was a first step in a process leading up to the creation of a constitutional monarchy, rather than the foundation itself. The transformation of the English form of government to that of a constitutional monarchy was accomplished as a result of the Petition of Right in 1627; the English Revolution, which culminated in the English Bill of Rights of 1689; and the Act of Settlement of 1701.

A number of the Founding fathers of the United States were lawyers or, at least, learned men. They were obviously familiar with these documents, because those documents formed the basis of English common law and that's the law the American colonies were under. Consequently, reading these documents provides an insight into where the Founders got some of the ideas they incorporated into our Constitution and Bill of Rights.

Full-text translation of the Magna Carta (1215)

Clauses marked (+) are still valid under the charter of 1225, but with a few minor amendments. Clauses marked (*) were omitted in all later reissues of the charter. In the charter itself the clauses are not numbered, and the text reads continuously. The translation sets out to convey the sense rather than the precise wording of the original Latin.

JOHN, by the grace of God King of England, Lord of Ireland, Duke of Normandy and Aquitaine, and Count of Anjou, to his archbishops, bishops, abbots, earls, barons, justices, foresters, sheriffs, stewards, servants, and to all his officials and loyal subjects, Greeting.

KNOW THAT BEFORE GOD, for the health of our soul and those of our ancestors and heirs, to the honour of God, the exaltation of the holy Church, and the better ordering of our kingdom, at the advice of our reverend fathers Stephen, archbishop of Canterbury, primate of all England, and cardinal of the holy Roman Church, Henry archbishop of Dublin, William bishop of London, Peter bishop of Winchester, Jocelin bishop of Bath and Glastonbury, Hugh bishop of Lincoln, Walter bishop of Worcester, William bishop of Coventry, Benedict bishop of Rochester, Master Pandulf subdeacon and member of the papal household, Brother Aymeric master of the knighthood of the Temple in England, William Marshal earl of Pembroke, William earl of Salisbury, William earl of Warren, William earl of Arundel, Alan of Galloway constable of Scotland, Warin fitz Gerald, Peter fitz Herbert, Hubert de Burgh seneschal of Poitou, Hugh de Neville, Matthew fitz Herbert, Thomas Basset, Alan Basset, Philip Daubeny, Robert de Roppeley, John Marshal, John fitz Hugh, and other loyal subjects:

+ (1) FIRST, THAT WE HAVE GRANTED TO GOD, and by this present charter have confirmed for us and our heirs in perpetuity, that the English Church shall be free, and shall have its rights undiminished, and its liberties unimpaired. That we wish this so to be observed, appears from the fact that of our own free will, before the outbreak of the present dispute between us and our barons, we granted and confirmed by charter the freedom of the Church's elections - a right reckoned to be of the greatest necessity and importance to it - and caused this to be confirmed by Pope Innocent III. This freedom we shall observe ourselves, and desire to be observed in good faith by our heirs in perpetuity.

TO ALL FREE MEN OF OUR KINGDOM we have also granted, for us and our heirs for ever, all the liberties written out below, to have and to keep for them and their heirs, of us and our heirs:

(2) If any earl, baron, or other person that holds lands directly of the Crown, for military service, shall die, and at his death his heir shall be of full age and owe a 'relief", the heir shall have his inheritance on payment of the ancient scale of 'relief". That is to say, the heir or heirs of an earl shall pay £100 for the entire earl's barony, the heir or heirs of a knight 100s. at most for the entire knight's 'fee', and any man that owes less shall pay less, in accordance with the ancient usage of 'fees'.

(3) But if the heir of such a person is under age and a ward, when he comes of age he shall have his inheritance without 'relief' or fine.

(4) The guardian of the land of an heir who is under age shall take from it only reasonable revenues, customary dues, and feudal services. He shall do this without destruction or damage to men or property. If we have given the guardianship of the land to a sheriff, or to any person answerable to us for the revenues, and he commits destruction or damage, we will exact compensation from him, and the land shall be entrusted to two worthy and prudent men of the same 'fee', who shall be answerable to us for the revenues, or to the person to whom we have assigned them. If we have given or sold to anyone the guardianship of such land, and he causes destruction or damage, he shall lose the guardianship of it, and it shall be handed over to two worthy and prudent men of the same 'fee', who shall be similarly answerable to us.

(5) For so long as a guardian has guardianship of such land, he shall maintain the houses, parks, fish preserves, ponds, mills, and everything else pertaining to it, from the revenues of the land itself. When the heir comes of age, he shall restore the whole land to him, stocked with plough teams and such implements of husbandry as the season demands and the revenues from the land can reasonably bear.

(6) Heirs may be given in marriage, but not to someone of lower social standing. Before a marriage takes place, it shall be made known to the heir's next-of-kin.

(7) At her husband's death, a widow may have her marriage portion and inheritance at once and without trouble. She shall pay nothing for her dower, marriage portion, or any inheritance that she and her husband held jointly on the day of his death. She may remain in her husband's house for forty days after his death, and within this period her dower shall be assigned to her.

(8) No widow shall be compelled to marry, so long as she wishes to remain without a husband. But she must give security that she will not marry without royal consent, if she holds her lands of the Crown, or without the consent of whatever other lord she may hold them of.

(9) Neither we nor our officials will seize any land or rent in payment of a debt, so long as the debtor has movable goods sufficient to discharge the debt. A debtor's sureties shall not be distrained upon so long as the debtor himself

can discharge his debt. If, for lack of means, the debtor is unable to discharge his debt, his sureties shall be answerable for it. If they so desire, they may have the debtor's lands and rents until they have received satisfaction for the debt that they paid for him, unless the debtor can show that he has settled his obligations to them.

* (10) If anyone who has borrowed a sum of money from Jews dies before the debt has been repaid, his heir shall pay no interest on the debt for so long as he remains under age, irrespective of whom he holds his lands. If such a debt falls into the hands of the Crown, it will take nothing except the principal sum specified in the bond.

* (11) If a man dies owing money to Jews, his wife may have her dower and pay nothing towards the debt from it. If he leaves children that are under age, their needs may also be provided for on a scale appropriate to the size of his holding of lands. The debt is to be paid out of the residue, reserving the service due to his feudal lords. Debts owed to persons other than Jews are to be dealt with similarly.

* (12) No 'scutage' or 'aid' may be levied in our kingdom without its general consent, unless it is for the ransom of our person, to make our eldest son a knight, and (once) to marry our eldest daughter. For these purposes only a reasonable 'aid' may be levied. 'Aids' from the city of London are to be treated similarly.

+ (13) The city of London shall enjoy all its ancient liberties and free customs, both by land and by water. We also will and grant that all other cities, boroughs, towns, and ports shall enjoy all their liberties and free customs.

* (14) To obtain the general consent of the realm for the assessment of an 'aid' - except in the three cases specified above - or a 'scutage', we will cause the archbishops, bishops, abbots, earls, and greater barons to be summoned individually by letter. To those who hold lands directly of us we will cause a general summons to be issued, through the sheriffs and other officials, to come together on a fixed day (of which at least forty days notice shall be given) and at a fixed place. In all letters of summons, the cause of the summons will be stated. When a summons has been issued, the business appointed for the day shall go forward in accordance with the resolution of those present, even if not all those who were summoned have appeared.

* (15) In future we will allow no one to levy an 'aid' from his free men, except to ransom his person, to make his eldest son a knight, and (once) to marry his eldest daughter. For these purposes only a reasonable 'aid' may be levied.

(16) No man shall be forced to perform more service for a knight's 'fee', or other free holding of land, than is due from it.

(17) Ordinary lawsuits shall not follow the royal court around, but shall be held in a fixed place.

(18) Inquests of novel disseisin, mort d'ancestor, and darrein presentment shall be taken only in their proper county court. We ourselves, or in our absence abroad our chief justice, will send two justices to each county four times a year, and these justices, with four knights of the county elected by the county itself, shall hold the assizes in the county court, on the day and in the place where the court meets.

(19) If any assizes cannot be taken on the day of the county court, as many knights and freeholders shall afterwards remain behind, of those who have attended the court, as will suffice for the administration of justice, having regard to the volume of business to be done.

(20) For a trivial offence, a free man shall be fined only in proportion to the degree of his offence, and for a serious offence correspondingly, but not so heavily as to deprive him of his livelihood. In the same way, a merchant shall be spared his merchandise, and a villein the implements of his husbandry, if they fall upon the mercy of a royal court. None of these fines shall be imposed except by the assessment on oath of reputable men of the neighbourhood.

(21) Earls and barons shall be fined only by their equals, and in proportion to the gravity of their offence.

(22) A fine imposed upon the lay property of a clerk in holy orders shall be assessed upon the same principles, without reference to the value of his ecclesiastical benefice.

(23) No town or person shall be forced to build bridges over rivers except those with an ancient obligation to do so.

(24) No sheriff, constable, coroners, or other royal officials are to hold lawsuits that should be held by the royal justices.

* (25) Every county, hundred, wapentake, and tithing shall remain at its ancient rent, without increase, except the royal demesne manors.

(26) If at the death of a man who holds a lay 'fee' of the Crown, a sheriff or royal official produces royal letters patent of summons for a debt due to the Crown, it shall be lawful for them to seize and list movable goods found in the lay 'fee' of the dead man to the value of the debt, as assessed by worthy men. Nothing shall be removed until the whole debt is paid, when the residue shall be given over to the executors to carry out the dead man's will. If no debt is due to the Crown, all the movable goods shall be regarded as the property of the dead man, except the reasonable shares of his wife and children.

* (27) If a free man dies intestate, his movable goods are to be distributed by his next-of-kin and friends, under the supervision of the Church. The rights of his debtors are to be preserved.

(28) No constable or other royal official shall take corn or other movable goods from any man without immediate payment, unless the seller voluntarily offers postponement of this.

(29) No constable may compel a knight to pay money for castle-guard if the knight is willing to undertake the guard in person, or with reasonable excuse to supply some other fit man to do it. A knight taken or sent on military service shall be excused from castle-guard for the period of this service.

(30) No sheriff, royal official, or other person shall take horses or carts for transport from any free man, without his consent.

(31) Neither we nor any royal official will take wood for our castle, or for any other purpose, without the consent of the owner.

(32) We will not keep the lands of people convicted of felony in our hand for longer than a year and a day, after which they shall be returned to the lords of the 'fees' concerned.

(33) All fish-weirs shall be removed from the Thames, the Medway, and throughout the whole of England, except on the sea coast.

(34) The writ called precipe shall not in future be issued to anyone in respect of any holding of land, if a free man could thereby be deprived of the right of trial in his own lord's court.

(35) There shall be standard measures of wine, ale, and corn (the London quarter), throughout the kingdom. There shall also be a standard width of dyed cloth, russet, and haberject, namely two ells within the selvedges. Weights are to be standardised similarly.

(36) In future nothing shall be paid or accepted for the issue of a writ of inquisition of life or limbs. It shall be given gratis, and not refused.

(37) If a man holds land of the Crown by 'fee-farm', 'socage', or 'burgage', and also holds land of someone else for knight's service, we will not have guardianship of his heir, nor of the land that belongs to the other person's 'fee', by virtue of the 'fee-farm', 'socage', or 'burgage', unless the 'fee-farm' owes knight's service. We will not have the guardianship of a man's heir, or of land that he holds of someone else, by reason of any small property that he may hold of the Crown for a service of knives, arrows, or the like.

(38) In future no official shall place a man on trial upon his own unsupported statement, without producing credible witnesses to the truth of it.

+ (39) No free man shall be seized or imprisoned, or stripped of his rights or possessions, or outlawed or exiled, or deprived of his standing in any way, nor will we proceed with force against him, or send others to do so, except by the lawful judgment of his equals or by the law of the land.

+ (40) To no one will we sell, to no one deny or delay right or justice.

(41) All merchants may enter or leave England unharmed and without fear, and may stay or travel within it, by land or water, for purposes of trade, free from all illegal exactions, in accordance with ancient and lawful customs. This, however, does not apply in time of war to merchants from a country that is at war with us. Any such merchants found in our country at the outbreak of war shall be detained without injury to their persons or property, until we or our chief justice have discovered how our own merchants are being treated in the country at war with us. If our own merchants are safe they shall be safe too.

* (42) In future it shall be lawful for any man to leave and return to our kingdom unharmed and without fear, by land or water, preserving his allegiance to us, except in time of war, for some short period, for the common benefit of the realm. People that have been imprisoned or outlawed in accordance with the law of the land, people from a country that is at war with us, and merchants - who shall be dealt with as stated above - are excepted from this provision.

(43) If a man holds lands of any 'escheat' such as the 'honour' of Wallingford, Nottingham, Boulogne, Lancaster, or of other 'escheats' in our hand that are baronies, at his death his heir shall give us only the 'relief' and service that he would have made to the baron, had the barony been in the baron's hand. We will hold the 'escheat' in the same manner as the baron held it.

(44) People who live outside the forest need not in future appear before the royal justices of the forest in answer to general summonses, unless they are actually involved in proceedings or are sureties for someone who has been seized for a forest offence.

* (45) We will appoint as justices, constables, sheriffs, or other officials, only men that know the law of the realm and are minded to keep it well.

(46) All barons who have founded abbeys, and have charters of English kings or ancient tenure as evidence of this, may have guardianship of them when there is no abbot, as is their due.

(47) All forests that have been created in our reign shall at once be disafforested. River-banks that have been enclosed in our reign shall be treated similarly.

*(48) All evil customs relating to forests and warrens, foresters, warreners, sheriffs and their servants, or river-banks and their wardens, are at once to be investigated in every county by twelve sworn knights of the county, and within forty days of their enquiry the evil customs are to be abolished completely and irrevocably. But we, or our chief justice if we are not in England, are first to be informed.

* (49) We will at once return all hostages and charters delivered up to us by Englishmen as security for peace or for loyal service.

* (50) We will remove completely from their offices the kinsmen of Gerard de Athée, and in future they shall hold no offices in England. The people in

question are Engelard de Cigogné, Peter, Guy, and Andrew de Chanceaux, Guy de Cigogné, Geoffrey de Martigny and his brothers, Philip Marc and his brothers, with Geoffrey his nephew, and all their followers.

* (51) As soon as peace is restored, we will remove from the kingdom all the foreign knights, bowmen, their attendants, and the mercenaries that have come to it, to its harm, with horses and arms.

* (52) To any man whom we have deprived or dispossessed of lands, castles, liberties, or rights, without the lawful judgment of his equals, we will at once restore these. In cases of dispute the matter shall be resolved by the judgment of the twenty-five barons referred to below in the clause for securing the peace (§61). In cases, however, where a man was deprived or dispossessed of something without the lawful judgment of his equals by our father King Henry or our brother King Richard, and it remains in our hands or is held by others under our warranty, we shall have respite for the period commonly allowed to Crusaders, unless a lawsuit had been begun, or an enquiry had been made at our order, before we took the Cross as a Crusader. On our return from the Crusade, or if we abandon it, we will at once render justice in full.

* (53) We shall have similar respite in rendering justice in connexion with forests that are to be disafforested, or to remain forests, when these were first afforested by our father Henry or our brother Richard; with the guardianship of lands in another person's 'fee', when we have hitherto had this by virtue of a 'fee' held of us for knight's service by a third party; and with abbeys founded in another person's 'fee', in which the lord of the 'fee' claims to own a right. On our return from the Crusade, or if we abandon it, we will at once do full justice to complaints about these matters.

(54) No one shall be arrested or imprisoned on the appeal of a woman for the death of any person except her husband.

* (55) All fines that have been given to us unjustly and against the law of the land, and all fines that we have exacted unjustly, shall be entirely remitted or the matter decided by a majority judgment of the twenty-five barons referred to below in the clause for securing the peace (§61) together with Stephen, archbishop of Canterbury, if he can be present, and such others as he wishes to bring with him. If the archbishop cannot be present, proceedings shall continue without him, provided that if any of the twenty-five barons has been involved in a similar suit himself, his judgment shall be set aside, and someone else chosen and sworn in his place, as a substitute for the single occasion, by the rest of the twenty-five.

(56) If we have deprived or dispossessed any Welshmen of land, liberties, or anything else in England or in Wales, without the lawful judgment of their equals, these are at once to be returned to them. A dispute on this point shall be determined in the Marches by the judgment of equals. English law shall apply to holdings of land in England, Welsh law to those in Wales, and the

law of the Marches to those in the Marches. The Welsh shall treat us and ours in the same way.

* (57) In cases where a Welshman was deprived or dispossessed of anything, without the lawful judgment of his equals, by our father King Henry or our brother King Richard, and it remains in our hands or is held by others under our warranty, we shall have respite for the period commonly allowed to Crusaders, unless a lawsuit had been begun, or an enquiry had been made at our order, before we took the Cross as a Crusader. But on our return from the Crusade, or if we abandon it, we will at once do full justice according to the laws of Wales and the said regions.

* (58) We will at once return the son of Llywelyn, all Welsh hostages, and the charters delivered to us as security for the peace.

* (59) With regard to the return of the sisters and hostages of Alexander, king of Scotland, his liberties and his rights, we will treat him in the same way as our other barons of England, unless it appears from the charters that we hold from his father William, formerly king of Scotland, that he should be treated otherwise. This matter shall be resolved by the judgment of his equals in our court.

(60) All these customs and liberties that we have granted shall be observed in our kingdom in so far as concerns our own relations with our subjects. Let all men of our kingdom, whether clergy or laymen, observe them similarly in their relations with their own men.

* (61) SINCE WE HAVE GRANTED ALL THESE THINGS for God, for the better ordering of our kingdom, and to allay the discord that has arisen between us and our barons, and since we desire that they shall be enjoyed in their entirety, with lasting strength, for ever, we give and grant to the barons the following security:

The barons shall elect twenty-five of their number to keep, and cause to be observed with all their might, the peace and liberties granted and confirmed to them by this charter.

If we, our chief justice, our officials, or any of our servants offend in any respect against any man, or transgress any of the articles of the peace or of this security, and the offence is made known to four of the said twenty-five barons, they shall come to us – or in our absence from the kingdom to the chief justice – to declare it and claim immediate redress. If we, or in our absence abroad the chief justice, make no redress within forty days, reckoning from the day on which the offence was declared to us or to him, the four barons shall refer the matter to the rest of the twenty-five barons, who may distrain upon and assail us in every way possible, with the support of the whole community of the land, by seizing our castles, lands, possessions, or anything else saving only our own person and those of the queen and our children, until they have secured such redress as they have determined upon. Having secured the redress, they may then resume their normal obedience to us.

Any man who so desires may take an oath to obey the commands of the twenty-five barons for the achievement of these ends, and to join with them in assailing us to the utmost of his power. We give public and free permission to take this oath to any man who so desires, and at no time will we prohibit any man from taking it. Indeed, we will compel any of our subjects who are unwilling to take it to swear it at our command.

If one of the twenty-five barons dies or leaves the country, or is prevented in any other way from discharging his duties, the rest of them shall choose another baron in his place, at their discretion, who shall be duly sworn in as they were.

In the event of disagreement among the twenty-five barons on any matter referred to them for decision, the verdict of the majority present shall have the same validity as a unanimous verdict of the whole twenty-five, whether these were all present or some of those summoned were unwilling or unable to appear.

The twenty-five barons shall swear to obey all the above articles faithfully, and shall cause them to be obeyed by others to the best of their power.

We will not seek to procure from anyone, either by our own efforts or those of a third party, anything by which any part of these concessions or liberties might be revoked or diminished. Should such a thing be procured, it shall be null and void and we will at no time make use of it, either ourselves or through a third party.

* (62) We have remitted and pardoned fully to all men any ill-will, hurt, or grudges that have arisen between us and our subjects, whether clergy or laymen, since the beginning of the dispute. We have in addition remitted fully, and for our own part have also pardoned, to all clergy and laymen any offences committed as a result of the said dispute between Easter in the sixteenth year of our reign (i.e. 1215) and the restoration of peace.

In addition we have caused letters patent to be made for the barons, bearing witness to this security and to the concessions set out above, over the seals of Stephen archbishop of Canterbury, Henry archbishop of Dublin, the other bishops named above, and Master Pandulf.

* (63) IT IS ACCORDINGLY OUR WISH AND COMMAND that the English Church shall be free, and that men in our kingdom shall have and keep all these liberties, rights, and concessions, well and peaceably in their fullness and entirety for them and their heirs, of us and our heirs, in all things and all places for ever.

Both we and the barons have sworn that all this shall be observed in good faith and without deceit. Witness the abovementioned people and many others.

Given by our hand in the meadow that is called Runnymede, between Windsor and Staines, on the fifteenth day of June in the seventeenth year of our reign (i.e. 1215: the new regnal year began on 28 May).

* * * * *

Source: G.R.C. Davis, *Magna Carta* (London: British Museum, 1963), pp. 23–33.

The Provisions of Oxford
(1258)

The 13th century was a turbulent time for England. Kings Henry III and his son, Edward I, both saw rebellions against what the nobility viewed as excessive taxation and excessive interference in the way the feudal lords administered their holdings. The nobles' dissatisfaction resulted in the Provisions of Oxford in 1258, which were quickly followed by the Provisions of Westminster in 1259. The former made reference to "parliaments," using the word in a fairly direct translation from its French roots as a term referring to the coming together of a formal group to talk (from the French *parler*: to speak; to talk) and establishing periodic (three times per year) parliaments as a vehicle for conducting the business of government.

An interesting footnote is that, although original copies of the *Provisions* were distributed throughout the country in three languages–Latin, French, and Middle English (representing one of the first recognitions of English in any official capacity–no original copies have survived, in any of the languages. The text reproduced on the following pages is not a transcription of the original text but, rather, a transcription of what the *Provisions of Oxford* were reported to have said.

The following historical note pertaining to the Provisions of Oxford is taken from the web site of the English Parliament.

* * * * *

The Provisions of Oxford were created in 1258 by a group of barons led by Simon de Montfort. The provisions forced King Henry III to accept a new form of government. Written confirmations of the Provisions of Oxford were sent to sheriffs in all of the contemporary counties of England.

Why were the Provisions of Oxford important?

The 'Provisions of Oxford' placed the king under the authority of a Council of Fifteen, to be chosen by twenty-four men made up of twelve nominees of the king, and twelve nominees of the reformers. The chief ministers, the Justiciar and

Chancellor were to be chosen by and responsible to the Council of Fifteen, and ultimately to the community of the realm at regular parliaments to be held three times a year. This was revolutionary. It was the most radical scheme of reform undertaken before the arrest and execution of King Charles I in the 1640s.

In addition to controlling the central government, the reformers, urged on by swelling discontent among the lesser aristocracy, townsmen, merchants and freemen in the localities, began an investigation into abuses of local officials and a reform of local government. These reforms show the growing power of social groups beyond the major barons, who though still leading the reform, evidently felt they could not ignore popular discontent. In this regard they introduced reforms that were even harmful to their own local interests.

Full-Text Reconstruction of the Provisions of Oxford (1258)

It has been provided that from each county there shall be elected four discreet and lawful knights who, on every day that the county is held [i.e. the county court], shall assemble to hear all complaints touching any wrongs and injuries inflicted on any persons by sheriffs, bailiffs, or any other men, and to make the attachments that pertain to the said complaints until the first arrival of the chief justiciar in those parts: so that they shall take from the plaintiff adequate pledges for his prosecution, and from the defendant for his coming and standing trial before the said justiciar on his first arrival; and that the four knights aforesaid shall have all the said complaints enrolled, together with their attachments, in proper order and sequence—namely, for each hundred separately and by itself—so that the said justiciar, on his first arrival, can hear and settle the aforesaid complaints singly from each hundred. And they shall inform the sheriff that they are summoning all his hundredmen and bailiffs before the said justiciar on his next arrival, for a day and a place which he will make known to them: so that every hundredman shall cause all plaintiffs and defendants of his bailiwick to come in succession, according to what the aforesaid justiciar shall bring to trial from the aforesaid hundred; also as many men and such men—both knights and other free and lawful men—as may be required for best proving the truth of the matter, in such a way that all are not troubled at one and the same time; rather let as many come as can be tried and concluded in one day.

Also it is provided that no knight of the aforesaid counties, by virtue of an assurance that he is not to be placed on juries or assizes, shall be excused by a charter of the lord king or be exempt from this provision thus made for the common good of the whole kingdom.

Those chosen from the Lord King's side

The lord bishop of London [Fulk Basset]; the lord bishop elect of Winchester [Aymer de Lusignan]; the lord Henry, son of the king of Germany; the lord John, earl de Warenne; the lord Guy de Lusignan; the lord William de Valence; the lord John, earl of Warwick; the lord John Mansel; Brother John of Darlington; the abbot of Westminster; the lord Henry of Hengham.

Those chosen from the side of the earls and barons

The lord bishop of Worcester [Walter de Cantilupe]; the lord Simon, earl of Leicester; the lord Richard, earl of Gloucester; the lord Humphrey, earl of Hereford [Humphrey de Bohun]; the lord Roger Marshal; the lord Roger de Mortimer; the lord John Fitz-Geoffrey; the lord Hugh Bigod; the lord Richard de Gray; the lord William Bardulf; the lord Peter de Montfort; the lord Hugh

Despenser. And if it should happen that of necessity any one of these cannot be present, the rest of them shall elect whom they please in place of the absentee, namely, another person needful for carrying on that business.

Thus the community of England swore at Oxford

We make known to all people that we have sworn on the holy gospels and are held together by this oath, and promise in good faith, that each one of us and all of us together will help each other, both ourselves and those belonging to us against all people, doing right and taking nothing that we cannot take without doing wrong, saving faith to the king and crown. And we promise on the same oath that none of us will ever take anything of land or movables whereby this oath can be disturbed or in any way impaired. And if any one so acts contrary to this, we will hold him as a mortal enemy.

This is the oath of the twenty four

Each one swore on the holy gospels that he for the glory of God and in loyalty to the king and for the benefit of the kingdom will obtain and treat with the aforesaid sworn persons upon the reform and improvement of the condition of the kingdom. And that he will not fail for gift or promise, for love or hatred, for fear of any one, for gain or loss, loyalty to act according to the tenor of the letter that the king has given on this and his son likewise.

Thus swore the chief justiciar of England

He swears he will well and loyally according to his power do what belongs to the justiciars office of dispensing justice to all men and for the profit of the king and the kingdom, in accordance with the provision made and to be made by the twenty four, and by the king's council and the magnates of the land, who will swear to help and support him in these things.

Thus swore the chancellor of England

That he will not seal any writ except a writ of course without the order of the king and of the councillors who are present. Nor will he seal a gift orf great wardship or of a large sum of money or of escheats without the assent of the full council or of the greater part of it. And that he will not seal anything that is contrary to what has been and will be ordained by the twenty four or by the greater part of them. And that he will not take any reward otherwise than is agreed for others. And he will be given a companion in the way that the council will provide.

This is the oath taken by the wardens of the castles

That they will keep the king's castles loyally and in good faith for the use of the king and his heirs. And that they will give them up to the king or his heirs and to no other and through his council and in no other way, that is to say, through men of standing in the land elected to the council or through the greater part of them. And this form above written is to last full twelve years. And henceforth they shall not be prevented by this establishment and this oath from being able to give them up freely to the king or his heirs.

These are the men sworn of the king's council.

The Archbishop of Canterbury, The bishop of Worcester, the earl of Leicester; the earl of Gloucester, the earl Marshal, Peter of Savoy, the count of Aumale, the earl of warwick, the earl of Hereford, John Mansel, John Fitz-Geoffrey, Peter de Montfort, Richard de Gray, Roger Mortimer, James Audley.

The twelve on the king's side have chosen from the twelve on the side of the community the earl Roger Marshal and Hugh Bigod. And the party of the community has chosen from the twelve who are on the side of the king the earl of Warwick and John Mansel. And these four have power to elect the council of the king; and when they have made the election, they shall designate those to the twenty-four. And that shall hold on which the majority of these four agree.

These are the twelve who have been elected by the barons, on behalf of the whole community of the land, to consider common needs along with the king's council at the three annual parliaments:

The lord bishop of London, the earl of Winchester, the earl of Hereford, Philip Basset, John de Balliol, John de Verdun, John de Grey, Roger de Sumery, Roger de Mohaut, Hugh De spencer, Thomas de Gresley, Giles d'Argentein.

These are the twenty-four appointed by the community to consider aid for the king:

The bishop of Worcester, the bishop of London, the bishop of Salisbury, the earl of Leicester, the earl of Gloucester, the earl Marshal, Peter of Savoy, the earl of Hereford, the count of Aumale, the earl of Winchester, the earl of Oxford, John Fitz-Geoffrey, John de Grey, John de Balliol, Roger Mortimer, Roger de Sumery, Roger de Mohaut, Peter de Montfort, Thomas de Gresley, Fulk of Kerdiston, Giles d'Argentein, John Kyriel, Philip of Basset, Giles of Erdington.

And if any one of these cannot or will not be present, those who are present shall have power to elect another in his place.

Concerning the state of Holy Church

It should be remembered that the state of Holy Church is to be amended by the twenty-four chosen to reform the state of the kingdom of England—at what time and place they think best, according to the powers that they hold by writ of the king of England.

Concerning the chief justice

Furthermore that a chief justice—or two—shall be appointed; also what power he shall have; and that he shall be for only one year, so that at the end of the year he shall render account of his term before the king and the royal council and before the man who is to follow him.

Concerning the treasurer and the exchequer

The same with regard to the treasurer; so that he shall render account at the end of the year. And according to the ordinance of the said twenty-four, other good men are to be appointed to the exchequer, whither all the issues of the land are to come, and not elsewhere. And let that be amended which seems in need of amendment.

Concerning the chancellor

The same with regard to the chancellor; so that he shall render account of his term at the end of the year, and that merely by the king's will he shall seal nothing out of course, but shall do so by the council that surrounds the king.

Concerning the power of the justice and of the bailiffs

The chief justice has power to redress the misdeeds of all other justices, of bailiffs, of earls, of barons, and of all other people, according to the rightful law of the land. And writs are to be pleaded according to the law of the land in the proper places. And the justices shall accept nothing unless it is a present of bread and wine and like things: namely, such meat and drink as have been customarily brought for the day to the tables of the chief men. And this same regulation shall be understood for all the king's councillors and all his bailiffs. And no bailiff, by virtue of his office or of some plea, shall take any fee, either by his own hand or in any manner through another person. And if he is convicted, let him be punished; likewise the man who gives. And the king, if it is suitable, shall give fees to his justices and to his people who serve him, so that they shall have no need of taking anything from others.

Concerning the sheriffs

As sheriffs there shall be appointed loyal persons, good men who are landholders; so that in each county there shall be as sheriff a feudal tenant of the same county, who shall well, loyally, and justly treat the people of the county. And he shall take no fee; that he shall be sheriff for no more than a year in all; that during the year he shall render his accounts at the exchequer and be responsible for his term; that the king, from the royal income, shall make allowance to him in proportion to his receipts, so that he may rightly keep the county; and that he shall take no fees, neither he nor his bailiffs. And if they are convicted, let them be punished.

It should be remembered that, with regard to the Jewry and the wardens of the Jewry, such reforms are to be established as shall carry out the oath in this respect.

Concerning the escheators

Good escheators are to be appointed. And they shall take nothing from goods of deceased persons whose lands ought to be in the king's hands; but that, if a debt is owing to him, the escheators shall have free administration of the goods until they have carried out the king's wishes—and this according to the provision in the charter of liberties. Also inquiry shall be made concerning the misdeeds committed there by escheators, and that redress shall be made for such. Nor shall tallage or anything else be taken, except as it should be according to the charter of liberties.

The charter of liberties is to be strictly observed.

Concerning the exchange of London

It should be remembered to establish reforms touching the exchange of London; also touching the city of London and all the other cities of the king, which have been brought to shame and ruin by tallages and other oppressions.

Concerning the household of the king and queen

It should be remembered to reform the household of the king and queen.

Concerning the parliaments, as to how many shall be held annually and in what manner

It should be remembered that the twenty-four have ordained that there are to be three parliaments a year: the first on the octave of St. Michael, the second on the morrow of Candlemas, and the third on the first day of June, that is to say, three weeks before St. John [this means 6th October, 3rd February and 3rd June]. To these three parliaments the chosen councillors of the king shall come, even if they are not summoned, in order to examine the state of the kingdom and to consider the common needs of the kingdom and likewise of the king; and by the king's command also at other times, whenever it is necessary. So too it should be remembered that the community is to elect twelve good men, who shall come to the three parliaments and at other times, when there is need and when the king and his council summon them to consider the affairs of the king and the kingdom. And the community shall hold as established whatever these twelve shall do—and this is to reduce the cost to the community. Fifteen are to be named by these four men—that is to say, by the earl Marshal, the earl of Warwick, Hugh le Bigot, and John Mansel—who have been elected by the twenty-four to name the aforesaid fifteen, who are to form the king's council. And they are to be confirmed by the aforesaid twenty-four, or by the majority of those men. And they shall have the power of advising the king in good faith concerning the government of the kingdom and concerning all matters that pertain to the king or the kingdom; and of amending and redressing everything that they shall consider in need of amendment or redress. And [they shall have authority] over the chief justice and over all other people. And if they cannot all be present, that shall be firm and established which the majority of them shall enact.

These are the names of the principal castles of the king, and of those who have charge of them

Robert de Neville	Bamburgh
	Newcastle upon Tyne
Gilbert de Grant	Scarborough
William de Bardolf	Nottingham
Ralph Basset of Sapcote	Northampton
Hugh Bigod	Tower of London
Richard de Grey	Dover
Nicholas de Moels	Rochester
	Canterbury
	Winchester
Roger de Samford	Porchester
Stephen Longsepee	Corfe
Matthew de Bexil	Gloucester
Henry de Tracy	Exeter
Richard de Rochele	Haldesham
John de Grey	Hereford
Roger Walerand	Salisbury
Hugh Despencer	Horston
Peter de Montfort	Bridgewater
The earl of Warwick	Devizes
John son of Bernard	Oxford

The Provisions of Westminster (1259)

Like the *Magna Carta*, the *Provisions of Oxford* did not long survive their execution. The year following saw the drafting of a new document, the *Provisions of Westminster*, which had the effect of defining and limiting the powers and authority of the barons in response to growing unrest among the tenant landholders. Henry III, the king, was influenced in this by his son and heir, Edward I. In turn, Edward was influenced by Simon de Montfort, who had also been central to the creation of the *Provisions of Oxford.*

While the *Provisions of Oxford* were aimed primarily at curbing the excesses of the Crown against the nobility, the *Provisions of Westminster* were noteworthy as the beginning of recognition of the rights of tenants and commoners against the excesses of the nobility in the administration of their lands and holdings. The *Provisions of Westminster* were drawn up by the twenty-four lords appointed pursuant to the *Provisions of Oxford* the year before. The *Provisions of Westminster* largely replaced and supplanted the *Provisions of Oxford*, with the addition of new provisions intended to define the mutual responsibilities between lords and their tenants, as well as reforms to the Crown courts.

Ultimately, supported by a Papal bull in 1261, King Henry III repudiated the sections of the *Provisions of Westminster* that limited the powers and authority of the Crown, but the portions pertaining to the courts and laws were affirmed in the *Statute of Marlborough* in 1267.

Some sources consider the *Provisions of Westminster* to be the most important document in the history of English legislation since the reissue of the *Magna Carta* in 1225.

Full Text of the Provisions of Westminster (1259)

In the year 1259 from the Incarnation of the Lord, the forty-third of the reign of King Henry, son of King John, at a meeting of the lord king and his magnates at Westminster on Michaelmas fortnight, the provisions hereinunder written, by the common counsel and consent of the said king and his magnates, were enacted and published by the same king and his magnates in this form:

With regard to the performance of suit to the courts of the magnates and of other lords who have such courts, it is provided and established by general agreement that no one who is enfeoffed by charter shall henceforth be distrained to perform suit to his lord's court, unless he is specifically obliged by the tenor of his charter to perform the suit; with the sole exception of those whose ancestors were accustomed to perform suit of this kind, or who, before the first crossing of the said lord king into Brittany—after the time of which crossing twenty-nine and a half years had elapsed down to the time that this constitution was made.

If anyone distrains1 his tenant contrary to this provision let quick justice be done about it in the king's court as is subsequently provided.

If it happens that an inheritance is divided between several parceners (like an inheritance that arises as from one heir), the other parceners [someone who takes an equal share] shall help with the cost of doing the suit reasonably. And if tenants are enfoeffed with the same inheritance the lord many no longer demand more than one suit as is aforesaid.

If any lords distrain their tenants contrary to this provision, than at the complaint of the tenant let them be attached to come to the king's court at an early date to answer them; on which day they shall have one excuse for nonappearance if they are in the realm and the beasts in this connection are to be released immediately to the plaintiff and so remain until the action between them is terminated. And these who have levied the distress do not appear on the date that was given them by way of essoin [a legal excuse for non attendance] [to seize property], or on the first date if they were not essoined, then shall the sheriff of the district be ordered to cause them to appear on another date, and if they do not appear the sheriff shall be ordered to distrain them by all that they possess in his bailiwick, and he be answerable to the king for the issue therefrom and that he produce them in person in court on another day. And then on that day if they do not appear the plaintiff shall go away without day[i.e. without any liability] and the beast shall stay released, so that the lords henceforth shall not be able to distrain them on that account until they have their deraignment [i.e. their suit or case] by and action in the king's court, saving to the lords their rights in respect of the suits whatever they dare to institute legal proceedings about them. And the lords are to come to the court of the king to answer. And the plaintiffs can have their plaints; then by judgement of the court they shall recover the damages they have had by reason of this distress.

On the other hand let lords distrain their suit by the same speedy justice tenants who withhold from their lords suits which they owe and which they have done since the aforesaid term, and recover their damages just as their tenants do from them. As to suits which were withheld before the aforesaid term the common law shall run as usual.

With regard to the sheriff's tourn, it is provided that, unless their presence is specially demanded, archbishops, bishops, abbots, priors, earls, and barons, or other men of religion, or women, shall not of necessity come thither. But tourns are to be held in the way they were held in the time of the predecessors of our lord king who now is. And if any have lands in several hundreds they are not to be distrained or to attend tourns except where they live. And the tourns shall be held according to the form of the king's Great Charter, and as they were customarily held in the time of the kings John and Richard.

It is also provided that neither on the eyres of the justices nor in the counties nor in the courts of barons nor in a liberty or elsewhere shall fines henceforth be taken from anybody for miskenning [i.e. a mistaken citation], or on condition that people are not molested.

Furthermore it is provided that in a plea of dower that is before the bench one should give four days in the year at least, namely one day each term. And if one can give more, one should give more.

Like is essoins of darcin presentment and or quarteimpedit [i.e. whoever made the last appointment to a church benefice] of churches that are vacant one should give a day every fortnight or every three weeks according to whether the district is a long way off or near. And if anyone who is impleaded by quare impedit does not come on the first day and does not have himself essoined, on another day if he does not come let him there be distrained by all his lands and his chattels by the great distress, as said above.

Moreover, with regard to charters of exemption and liberty, that those securing them are not to be put on assizes, juries, or recognitions, it is provided that, if their oath is so essential that without it justice cannot be administered as in the grand assize or in a perambulation or where they are witnesses, by name either in charters in writing, in attaints or in other case which cannot be decided without the oaths of knights, in such cases they shall be forced to swear, saving to them their aforesaid liberty and exemption in other respects.

No one except the king is in future to levy a distress outside his own fee or on the king's highway where everybody can come and go.

In addition, if it happens that the lord after his tenant's death takes his lands into his hand becuase the heir is under age and then when the heir comes of age will not surrender his land without being sued, that the heir get back his land into his hand by writ of mort d'ancestor together with the damaged he has sustained on account of the detention after his full age. And likewise if the heir is of age when his ancestor dies and in as the heir apparent who is regarded and accepted, that the chief lord may not evict him, or take anything or remove anything, except take a simple seisinonly. And if the chief lord keeps him out, so that he is allowed to obtain a writ of mort d'ancestor or of cosinage [a writ to recover land], he may recover his land and his damages as by writ of novel disseisin.

On wardship of socage it is so provided that if land which is held in socage is held in wardship by his kinsmen because of the heir who is under age, the guardian cannot do waste, sale or any destruction of the land that is in his wardship, but shall safely keep it for the benefit of the heir so that when he comes of age the guardian shall answer to him loyally for the issues and the profits of the thing, saving to him his reasonable outlay. Nor can he sell or give the marriage except to the advantage of the minor.

In addition it is provided that the escheators, those appointed to hold inquests, justices assigned to take assizes and justices assigned to hear and determine pleas of trespass, or any other bailiff, have no power to amerce for failure to obey a common summons, except the chief justice and the justices in eyre for all pleas.

It is likewise provided that no man of religion can buy any land without the agreement of the lord, namely that lord who is nearest except for the mesne lord.

It is likewise provided on essoins that no one henceforth is to be distrained to take an oath in warranty of the essoin either in county court or elsewhere. Hereafter no one but the king shall hold in his court a plea concerning false judgment rendered in a court of his tenant; for pleas of this sort especially pertain to the crown and dignity of the king.

It is provided that if anyone is distrained and his beasts are kept against gage and surety, the sheriff when complaint has been made can freely release the beasts in accordance with the law of the land, if they are taken outside a liberty, without contradiction and without hindrance from him who took them. And if they are within a liberty and the bailiff will not release them the sheriff shall release them for default on the part of the bailiff of the liberty.

Without the king's writ, no one may henceforth distrain his free tenants to respond concerning their free tenements or anything that pertains to their free tenements. Nor may he cause his free tenants against their will to take oaths; so that no one may do this without the king's precept.

It is provided that no bailiff who ought to render account is to take himself off away from his lord. And if he will not render his account and has no land or tenement whereby he can be distrained he is to be attached in person, so that the sheriff in whose bailiwick he is found shall make him come to render account if he is in arrears.

It is provided that no farmers during the period of their farm shall do sale or exile of woods, houses, men or other things belonging to the tenement which they have at farm, unless they have special permission in writing to make the sale. And if they do it and are convicted, they shall render the damages for it.

Hereafter itinerant justices shall not amerce vills on their eyres because particular twelve-year-old persons do not come before sheriffs and coroners for inquests concerning a man's death or other matters pertaining to the crown; so long as, nevertheless, enough men come from those vills for satisfactorily carrying out such inquests.

No coroner or sheriff or other bailiff from now on shall amerce townships because they do not come to inquests. But when they find a default, let it be put in the coroner's roll and presented before the justices in eyre who have power to amerce townships and no one else.

No judgment of murder shall henceforth be rendered before the justices in a case that is adjudged merely one of accident; but murder shall be proper in the case of a man feloniously slain, and not otherwise.

No justice or sheriff or other bailiff is from now on to amerce townships for hue and cry raised and not followed up if it is not raised for reasonable cause, such as for the death of a man, robbery, wounding or similar case with pertains specially to the crown.

Furthermore is any one is vouched to warranty in a plea of land in the eyre of the justices he is not from now on to be amerced for not being present, inasmuch as no free man ought to be amerced for default except on the first day of the coming of the justices. But if he who is vouched to warranty is then within the same county, then it is for the sheriff to cause him to come on the third day or the fourth according to whether he is far away or near, as is the practice in the eyre of the justices. And if he is living in another county he shall have a reasonable summons of 15 days in accordance with the common law.

Furthermore than justices are provided to go through the land. And there is to be one of the 12 or others of the community to see that justice is done to plaintiffs and to all others. And so they are to see that order is sent to the counties that establishments made for the benefit if the realm, those that are made and those that will, are to be kept.

Likewise that the provisions that have been made since the beginning of these establishments are to be upheld and maintained.

Furthermore the rolls of these establishments are to be read and affirmed. And the charters of liberties and of the forests are to be kept and maintained. It is likewise provided that no one is to come and attend parliament with horses or with arms, or armed, unless he is specifically ordered by the king or by his councillor by writ for the common business of the land.

Where itinerant justices were lately on circuit, good men and sage are to be appointed to hear and inquire into all complaints that could have been terminated without writ during the last seven years; similarly that if anyone has not made plaint before the seven years and has not had justice he is to recover to get it. And they are to have the power to inquire concerning the sheriffs and their bailiffs, how they have behaved towards the district since their establishment.

They are to enquire also concerning the bailiffs of the rich men of the land and concerning the rich men themselves.

Itinerant justices are to have the same power as sheriffs in their eyre; in addition they are to have their own power throughout their eyre. And there are to be provided from the less important people of the council two or three who are to be constantly in attendance on the king between parliaments. And they are to be changed at each parliament and others appointed. And their action is to be viewed at each parliament. And if there is anything in it to be amended, it is to be amended by those of the council. And if any important business arises between parliament that cannot be settled by the aforesaid two or three, or can not well be delayed until the next parliament, all those of the council are to the summoned by writ to settle this business. And there is to be put in the writ the occasion of the summons, if this is not secret. And if any of the others of the council, or of the aforesaid two or three, comes to king's council as long as the business lasts both as to their own business and as to the king's business for which they are summoned.

It is to be remembered that two good men are to be provided to sell the wardships that are now of right in the king's hand.

Furthermore that two good men are to be provided to ordain equally with the council of the exchequer concerning sheriffs and counties.

Furthermore people are to be provided to go with the king to France. And who shall stay in the land with the Justiciar.

And that an answer is to be given to the envoys from Wales. And it is to be provided how the writs of the provisions and of the establishments shall issue from the chancery without delay. And likewise about the envoys who shall go to Rome.

For selling the wardships the Justiciar, the treasurer, Mr Thomas of Wymondham, Sir Roger of Thirkleby and Sir Henry of Bath are to be appointed immediately. And that these same are to ordain and provide on what items the queen ought to get gold.

It is provided that these same are to come to the exchequer and view the sums of all kinds of tallages that have been imposed since the king's accession. And that they are to estimate how much each one can raise. And these same are to provide how one ought to proceed in pleas about customs and about services. And these same are to provide how one ought to proceed in escheats and in wardships.

It is to be provided which people ought to go to correct trespasses and wrongs done, which can be determined without writ.

The Justiciar is to provide this with the others. And which are to be at the bench with the justices, and which at the exchequer.

It is provided that four knights are to be appointed in each country [*sic*] to observe the wrongs which sheriffs do; that if it happen that they do wrongs, these four are to admonish the sheriffs to have them corrected. And if they will not correct them, let them enter the wrongs done onto a roll, and show them to the chief justices at the end of the year when he asks for them; or earlier if he asks for them, if so be that the plaintiffs to who the wrongs have been done are willing to prosecute. And that these aforesaid four knights are not to have any authority to interfere with the performance by the sheriffs of their office.

If a clerk is accused of the death of a man, of robbery, or larceny or other crime that concerns the crown, then it is by command of the king delivered on bail to 12 good men that they have him before the justices or released by pledges without command of the king if the aforesaid 12 or the pledges have his person before the justices on the first day, they are not in future to be amerced, even though the clerk will not answer or stand his trial in the king's court, insomuch as they were not pledged or going surety for anything other than to produce the clerk's person in court.

The justiciar, the treasurer Sir Henry of Bath, Sir Roger of Thirkleby and the barons of the exchequer are to provide this year instantly which good men, upright and sage, are to be sheriffs this year. And they are to be vavasours [i.e. tenant, landholder, vassal] in the shire they are sheriffs of. On the other hand, next year at the last county court before Michaelmas there are to be chosen in full county court four good men, upright and who will be advantageous to the king and to the shire in this office. And they are to be at the exchequer at Michaelmas. And the barons are to pick out the most sufficient in their estimation

Furthermore good men are to be chosen by the Justiciar and the treasurer to provide during this advent and the festival days, against the next parliament, what is to be amended at the great exchequer and at the exchequer of the Jews. And by the same reasonable sustenance is to be provided for those who are at either exchequer.

It is provided that Sir Thomas de Gresley, justice of the forest, is to take Nicholas of Ramsey and three knights from each county and they are to enquire into the condition of the forests, of vert and venison, and of sales and destructions, and by whom they are done. And they are to enquire about malpractices in connection with forest pleas and by whom they were established and from what time; and when he has done this he is to make it known to the king and his council.

It is to be done the same way with the forests beyond the Trent; that the chief justice provide four knights and enquire about all the forests beyond Trent in the way aforesaid.

The archbishop, the bishop of Worcester, the earl marshal, the earl of Warwick are to be with the Justiciar to deal with the important business of the kingdom as long as the king is out of England. And all those of the council and the community's twelve who stay in England are to be summoned if needs be. Sir Philip Basset and Sir Roger Mortimer are to be constantly with the Justiciar.

It is provided that the Justiciar is to provide that the castellans are to have reasonable sustenance for keeping the king's castles and maintaining them. It is provided to put two good men from the community for from the community's twelve or from others with the justices at the bench. And that they are to see that justice is done. And in the same way two good men from the community or from the community's twelve or from others are to be put at the exchequer.

These are the provisions and the establishments made at Westminster at the Michaelmas parliament by the king and his council and the twelve chosen by the common counsel before the community of England which then were at Westminster in the forty third year of the reign of Henry the son of king John.

* * * * *

[*Source: "The Provisions of Westminster, 1259," from The History of England web site at https://thehistoryofengland.co.uk/resource/the-provisions-of-westminster-1259/*]

The Dictum of Kenilworth
(1266)

Following the ratification of the *Provisions of Oxford* in 1258 and the *Provisions of Westminster* in 1259, King Henry III obtained support from the Pope and in 1261 annulled his agreement to those provisions. Rebellious nobles thereupon engaged in open warfare against Henry and those nobles who remained loyal to him. The rebels were initially successful. However, Simon de Montfort, the *de facto* leader of the rebellious barons, was killed in battle in 1265 by Price Edward (son of Henry III and later King Edward I). Although the remaining rebel barons continued their resistance in the face of harsh repercussions under Henry and Edward, eventually more moderate voices prevailed upon the Crown and less punitive penalties were agreed upon and set down in the *Dictum of Kenilworth* in 1266.

The Dictum of Kenilworth was, in essence, a peace treaty with the rebels following the death of Simon de Montfort. The document marks the end of the reform movement and the restoration of royal power, although many of the reforms passed by Simon de Montfort were accepted by the king. Dated 30 October 1266 (E 164/9).

* * * * *

The original document was written in Latin. The following descriptive passage, and the translation of the full text of the Dictum of Kenilworth on the following pages, are courtesy of The [British] National Archives and are reproduced here in accordance with the terms and conditions of the Open Government Licence. The National Archives discussion of the Dictum of Kenilworth can be found at:
https://www.nationalarchives.gov.uk/education/resources/magna-carta/dictum-of-kenilworth/

Full Text of the Dictum of Kenilworth (1266)

In the name of the Holy and Undivided Trinity, amen. To the honour and glory of Almighty God, the Father, the Son, and the Holy Ghost, of the glorious and most excellent Mother of God the Virgin Mary, and of all saints by whose merits and intercessions we are governed on Earth. To the honour of the Holy Catholic and Apostolic Roman Church, which is the mother and ruler of all the faithful; to the honour of the Most Holy Father and out lord Clement, ruler of that universal Church; to the honour and good prosperous and peaceable estate of the most Christian prince, lord Henry, illustrious king of the whole realm of England, and of the English Church. We, Walter, bishop of Exeter, Walter, bishop of Bath and Wells, Nicholas, bishop of Worcester, and Richard, bishop of St David's, Gilbert de Clare, earl of Gloucester and Hertford, and Humphrey de Bohun, earl of Hereford, Philip Basset, John Balliol, Robert Walerand, Alan de la Zuche, Roger de Somery, and Warin de Bassingbourne have been given full power from the lord king, from other nobles, counsellors of the realm, and from the leading men of England according to the terms enrolled in letters published and sanctioned by the seals of the king and others, to provide for the state of the realm especially in the matter of the disinherited, favouring no person in this matter, but having God alone before our eyes, doing all things as in the sight of Almighty God and in order, rightly preferring the Head to the Members.

(1) We declare and provide that the most serene prince, lord Henry, illustrious king of England, shall have, fully receive, and freely exercise his dominion, authority, and royal power without impediment or contradiction of anyone, whereby the royal dignity may be offended contrary to approved rights, laws, and long established customs, and that full obedience and humble attention be given to the same lord king, to his lawful mandates and precepts, by one and all, greater and lesser men of the king-dom. And one and all shall, through writs, seek justice and be answerable for justice at the court of the lord king as was the custom before the time of the disorder.

(2) Furthermore, we ask the same lord king, and with reverence urge him in his piety, that he appoint, for doing and rendering justice, such men as, seeking not their own interests but those of God and right, shall justly settle the affairs of subjects according to the praiseworthy laws and customs of the kingdom and thereby strengthen the throne and royal majesty with justice.

(3) Likewise we ask and urge the lord king that he fully protect and observe the liberties of the Church, and the charters of liberties and of the forest, which he is expressly bound to keep and hold by his own oath.

(4) Also the lord king shall provide that the grants which, up to the present, he has made freely and not under compulsion shall be observed; and he will establish firmly other necessary measures which are devised by his men at his pleasure. Furthermore, the English Church shall be fully restored to its liberties and customs which it had and should have had before the time of such dis-orders, and shall be permitted to exercise them.

(5) We declare and provide that the lord king shall completely excuse and pardon each and all of those who, from the beginning and up to the present time, because of the present disorders of the realm, have offended against or done any injury to him or the royal crown and who return to his peace within forty days after the publication of this our ordinance. The lord king shall in no way for any cause or reason, because of these past injuries or offences, bear any vengeance against these offenders nor shall he inflict any penalty or revenge against them in life, limb, imprisonment, exile, or fine. Excluded are those mentioned below in this our present ordinance.

(6) We also declare and provide that all places, rights, goods, and all other things pertaining to the royal crown shall be restored to that crown, and to the lord king, by those who detain them in their possession unless they can show that hold them by reasonable warrant from the lord king or from his ancestors.

(7) Also, we declare and provide that all bonds, deeds, and instruments which the lord king, his eldest son the Lord Edward, or other faithful subjects have hitherto made or drawn up by reason of the Provisions of Oxford or because of the disorder present in the realm, at the instance of the late Simon de Montfort, earl of Leicester, and his accomplices, are absolutely nullified and destroyed and shall be held completely annulled and valueless. The injurious and damnable acts of the said Simon and his accomplices, together with the agreements about land made by them when he exercised power, are nullified and have no force.

(8) Humbly begging both the lord legate and the lord king that the lord legate shall absolutely forbid, under distraint of the Church, that Simon, earl of Leicester, be considered to be holy or justs as he died excommunicate according to the belief of the Holy Church. And that the vain and fatuous miracles told of him by others shall not at any time pass any lips. And that the lord king shall agree strictly to forbid this under pain of corporal punishment.

(9) We reverently and humbly beseech our venerable father Lord Ottobono, cardinal deacon of St. Adrian and apostolic legate of the Holy See, that, since he knows it expedient for the king, he should announce that benefit of absolution may be given both to the lord king and to other men of the realm both great and small, who have made little effort to observe the sworn charters, to the observation of which all are bound by the sentence of excommunication pronounced against all who do not observe the said charters.

(10) Likewise we beseech and urge, saving the approved customs of the realm, that no man of any condition shall take corn or any manner of victual, or any other goods under guise of borrowing or provision of future payment, without licence of those who own the things or goods.

(11) We commend London and urge and beseech the lord king that he provide, by his council, for the reform of the state of the city in the matter of lands, rents, power, and liberties, and that provision of this kind be made immediately.

(12) Concerning the condition and business of the disinherited, among other things which we have ordained and established, wishing to proceed in the way of God and the path of equity, we have been led to provide, by assent of the venerable father Ottobono cardinal deacon of St. Adrian and apostolic legate of the Holy See and by assent of the noble Henry of Almain, having similar power, that there be no disherison but rather ransom, as follows. Those who fought at the start of the war and are still in arms ; those who violently and maliciously held Northampton against the king ; those who fought against and assailed the king at Lewes; those captured at Kenilworth after having sacked Winchester; those who have in other ways opposed the king and have not been pardoned; those who fought at Evesham; those who were in the battle at Chesterfield; those who freely and of their own will sent their followers against the king or his son; the bailiffs and officers of the earl of Leicester who robbed their neighbours and caused murder, arson, and other evils to be committed shall pay five times the annual value of their lands. If they pay this redemption they shall recover their lands. Furthermore, if any one shall be forced to sell land, only he who holds it by gift of the lord king may buy it, if he offer as much as any other buyer and on the same terms. Similarly, if he who wishes to redeem his lands be forced to place the land to farm no one shall have greater right to farm the land than he who holds it of the gift of the lord king, and he shall have it on these terms that he be willing to give as much as any-one else to hold it at farm. He who gives satisfaction for all his land shall have full possession ; if satisfaction be given for a half or a third part he shall immediately have a half or a third part. If the person redeeming his lands has not fulfilled his obligations at the last appointed term, half the remaining land shall remain with those to whom the land has been granted by the lord king. The person redeeming the land shall be free, within the said term, to see all or part of the land in the manner above mentioned, and similarly he may place the land to farm.

(13) If anyone has woods and wishes to sell them for his ransom, he who holds them by gift of the lord king shall appoint a trustworthy representative who shall receive the money while the disinherited tenant, who sells the woods, shall name a representative whom he trusts. These two receivers shall, in their presence, pay the money which they have received for the woods to those to whom the ransom is due.

(14) Be it noted that earl Ferrers shall be punished by a ransom of seven times the annual value of his lands. Knights and squires who were robbers and collaborated with the leading robbers in skirmishes and plundering raids, if they have no lands but have goods shall pay as ransom one half of their goods. Further-more they shall find a trustworthy surety that they will henceforth preserve the peace of the king and of the realm. Those who have no possessions shall swear on the Holy Gospel of God, and find a trustworthy surety that henceforth they will preserve the peace of the king and of the realm. Furthermore, they shall suffer fitting and satisfactory penance under judgement of the Church. Excepted are the banished whom the king alone may remit.

(15) The lords of heirs under age and in ward shall pay ransom for them to the grantee. When the heirs attain their majority they shall pay the ransom to their lords according to the terms under which others pay in two or three years. The lords of such lands shall have custody of the heirs with rights of marriage until the majority of the heirs. If, however, the lords of the lands refuse to pay the ransom to those to whom the lands were given by the lord king, these shall have custody of the heirs with rights of marriage with-out disparagement until the full age of the heirs who should then pay ransom to the grantee as others have paid and on the same terms.

(16) Wardships which belong to the lord king shall remain with those to whom they have been given by the lord king. When the heirs shall come of full age they shall pay ransom at the same terms as others and no waste shall be made by those who have custody. If such waste be made justice shall be enforced against them as is contained in Magna Carta.

(17) All persons in the castle shall be in the common way and form of peace, except Henry de Hastings and those who mutilated the king's messenger. These shall be punished by a ransom of seven times the annual value of their lands or they shall place themselves at the king's mercy.

(18) The king shall by just award pronounce his pleasure concerning any one who supported the lord king before the battle of Lewes and was disinherited after the battle because he was unwilling to support the king's son and come to his aid.

(19) Woods shall not be sold or wasted in any way by those who hold them now except after failure to make payment at the last term. Those to whom the lands have been given by the lord king shall have necessaries for the maintenance or restoration of dwellings. If they act otherwise they shall be severely punished.

(20) If there be anyone about whom it is feared that he wishes to cause or wage war the legate and the lord king shall provide for themselves such security as they shall deem expedient, sending him out of the realm for a fixed time or otherwise as they shall see fit. Nevertheless if it so happens that such a person be hindered from paying his ransom he shall not on this account be dis-inherited.

(21) If there be anyone (who is dissatisfied) with this ordinance let him submit to the judgement of the court of the lord king before the feast of St. Hilary [13 January 1267]. If any man be out of the kingdom he shall have the respite granted to those across the sea according to the law and custom of the land, provided he remain in peace, otherwise he shall not be in this form of peace.

(22) As the king is bound to many who have aided him and have faithfully stood by him, for whom he has provided no lands, and some have more than they should have, the king shall provide for them from the ransoms which are collected, lest this be a cause of further unrest.

(23) Furthermore let the legate, the king, and Henry of Almain stipulate that there be chosen twelve who will diligently and faithfully execute these things and let the lord king and his heirs cause them to be firmly observed and maintained. Let them examine and fulfil the ordinances made by the twelve selected, in the manner of the regulations which have already been enacted. Otherwise they shall make true and reasonable estimates according to what the twelve executors shall provide.

(24) Those holding lands at farm, who were against the lord king, shall lose the farms; those who keep the farms, saving the rights of the lords of e lands, shall pay an annual rent and at the end of the term the lands shall revert to the true lord.

(25) Concerning castles which were built by charter, and by consent of the lord king, without the consent of the disinherited. We ordain that the lord of the land pay the cost, which was imposed before the proclamation by consent of the king or make reasonable exchange of land.

(26) Laymen who openly supported the interests of the earl and his supporters, gaining followers by lies and false tales, rousing them to the side of the earl and his accomplices and withdrawing them from supporting the lord king and his son, shall be punished by the payment of twice the annual value of their lands.

(27) Those who were coerced or driven by fear to battle but who neither fought nor did evil; weaklings who because of force or fear sent their military following against the king or his son; those who were coerced or driven by fear to be robbers and made plundering raids with the leading robbers but who, when possible, ceased plundering and returned to their homes, remaining there at peace, shall pay a ransom of one year's value of their lands.

(28) Those who knowingly bought the goods of others shall restore the value of the things which they bought. They are at the mercy of the lord king for they did this unjustly, as the lord king forbade this six months ago.

(29) Those who, at the command of the earl of Leicester, entered Northampton but neither fought nor did harm, if they fled to the church when they saw the king coming and this is proved by lawful men; those who did not hold lands of the earl of Leicester but obeyed his command shall pay a half year's

value of their lands. Those who held lands of the earl are in the mercy of the king.

(30) Powerless people and others who did no harm shall immediately recover their lands and receive their damages in the court of the lord king. Let the accuser so be punished so that henceforth the king will not easily believe them and let them be punished as were those who unjustly caused the king's faithful subjects to be disinherited, nevertheless without danger of mutilation or disherison. Those who are maliciously accused shall immediately have their lands and recover their damages in the king's court, as mentioned above.

(31) Women shall have their heritages and dowers of their first husbands. They shall have the lands of their husbands in the manner in which the king has ordained, and the lands shall be ransomed.

(32) The ransom of those who opposed the king shall be paid. No ransom shall be paid by those who were not against the king, instead they shall immediately recover their lands and recover damages as mentioned above.

(33) Mention has been made of those maliciously accused, and receivers shall be punished as mentioned above. Submission has been made to the king, either by the other lords through you or let it prevail in its own right through a friendly or imposed peace.

(34) We say nothing of Simon de Montfort, the countess, and the sons of the earl, as the lord king has placed their case in the hands of the king of France

(35) All those who have been received in peace by those so appointed shall remain in the condition in which they were so received. All who have been ransomed shall not be bound to answer for damages and for trespasses committed by them against those whom they fought at the time of the unrest. Mutual damages and trespasses are excused, saving, nevertheless, the right of action of each man who was not involved in the unrest and saving, as far as he is concerned, that which pertains to the Church.

(36) Furthermore, as it is considered to be most dangerous that castles be in the control of those who acted evilly against the king, we award and ordain concerning the castles of Eardisley [Herefordshire], Bytham [Lincs.], and Chartley [Staffs.] that a reasonable exchange be given for them.

(37) Henceforward all shall keep a firm peace and none shall commit murder, arson, robbery, or any other violation of the peace. He who shall do this and shall be convicted shall have judgement and law according to the custom of the realm.

(38) Furthermore all of those whom it concerns shall swear on the Holy Gospels that they will not, on account of the disorders, take revenge nor procure, consent to, nor support such action. If anyone takes revenge he shall be punished by the court of the lord king and let those who have harmed the Church make satisfaction to it.

(39) Furthermore, he who does not consent to this decision shall be a public enemy of the king, of his sons and of the community. Laymen and clergy,

allowed by canon and lay law, may prosecute him as an enemy of the peace of the church and of the realm.

(40) Those who are imprisoned or in custody, having found a sufficient and reasonable surety, shall be liberated by pledge or by another competent and reasonable surety according to the ordinance of the legate and of the king.

Given and published in the castle at Kenilworth, on the second day before the kalends of November [31 October], in the year of grace 1266, the fifty-first year of the reign of the lord Henry, king of England.

* * * * *

Full transcript taken from RE Treharne and I.J Sanders (eds), *Documents of the Baronial Movement of Reform and Rebellion, 1258-1267* (Oxford, 1973).

The Petition of Right
(1628)

With the Dictum of Kenilworth in 1266, stability was restored to the fractious relationship between the English monarchy and the nobility, and there matters remained for a period of more than 300 years. The Parliaments established by the Magna Carta, the Provisions of Oxford, the Provisions of Westminster, and the Dictum of Kenilworth met regularly. By the 14th century, the Parliaments had come to an arrangement under which burgesses and knights conducted their business in one chamber (or "house"), which came to be called the House of Commons, and the nobility conducted their business in another chamber, which was called the House of Lords.

In the early 17th century, King Charles I was engaged in a costly war against Spain. Charles I also believed strongly in the doctrine of the Divine Right of Kings, meaning that he thought his authority to rule came directly from God, and that he did not require permission or agreement from the Parliaments for his policies and practices. In order to raise money to finance the war, the King went against the agreements established centuries before by the Magna Carta, the Provisions of Oxford, the Provisions of Westminster, and the Dictum of Kenilworth, and he began to unilaterally impose taxes and demand contributions (which the Crown called "loans") from the people in excess of the taxes established by the Parliaments. He also required the citizens to house the soldiers of his army in their homes, at their expense. Those who resisted or who refused to pay were imprisoned.

The House of Commons, in particular, chaffed under the imposition of these additional taxes and impositions, which they considered to be unlawful. In 1628, the Parliament (the House of Commons) sent a petition to the King, demanding that the Crown recognize four basic principles:

- There would be no taxes imposed without the consent of the Parliament;
- There would be no imprisonment without cause;
- The people would not be forced to quarter soldiers in their homes; and
- There would be no martial law during times of peace.

The King had no recourse other than to agree to these provisions if he wished to continue to receive funding for the war, so he nominally accepted the terms of the Petition. In practice, he ignored it to the greatest extent possible.

Despite its limited effectiveness, the Petition of Right is generally regarded as an important document in the history of England as a constitutional monarchy.

Beyond that, some of these same complaints would subsequently find their way into the American colonies of Great Britain. The complaints the colonies had against rule by the home country included similar issues:

- Taxation without representation in the Parliament;
- Unjust imprisonment without cause;
- Citizens were required to quarter soldiers in their homes; and
- The imposition of martial law during times of peace.

Full Text of the English Petition of Right (1628)

The Petition exhibited to his Majesty by the Lords Spiritual and Temporal, and Commons, in this present Parliament assembled, concerning divers Rights and Liberties of the Subjects, with the King's Majesty's royal answer thereunto in full Parliament.

To the King's Most Excellent Majesty,

Humbly show unto our Sovereign Lord the King, the Lords Spiritual and Temporal, and Commons in Parliament assembles, that whereas it is declared and enacted by a statute made in the time of the reign of King Edward I, commonly called Stratutum de Tellagio non Concedendo, that no tallage or aid shall be laid or levied by the king or his heirs in this realm, without the good will and assent of the archbishops, bishops, earls, barons, knights, burgesses, and other the freemen of the commonalty of this realm; and by authority of parliament holden in the five-and-twentieth year of the reign of King Edward III, it is declared and enacted, that from thenceforth no person should be compelled to make any loans to the king against his will, because such loans were against reason and the franchise of the land; and by other laws of this realm it is provided, that none should be charged by any charge or imposition called a benevolence, nor by such like charge; by which statutes before mentioned, and other the good laws and statutes of this realm, your subjects have inherited this freedom, that they should not be compelled to contribute to any tax, tallage, aid, or other like charge not set by common consent, in parliament.

II. Yet nevertheless of late divers commissions directed to sundry commissioners in several counties, with instructions, have issued; by means whereof your people have been in divers places assembled, and required to lend certain sums of money unto your Majesty, and many of them, upon their refusal so to do, have had an oath administered unto them not warrantable by the laws or statutes of this realm, and have been constrained to become bound and make appearance and give utterance before your Privy Council and in other places, and others of them have been therefore imprisoned, confined, and sundry other ways molested and disquieted; and divers other charges have been laid and levied upon your people in several counties by lord lieutenants, deputy lieutenants, commissioners for musters, justices of peace and others, by command or direction from your Majesty, or your Privy Council, against the laws and free custom of the realm.

III. And whereas also by the statute called 'The Great Charter of the Liberties of England,' it is declared and enacted, that no freeman may be taken or imprisoned or be disseized of his freehold or liberties, or his free customs, or be outlawed or exiled, or in any manner destroyed, but by the lawful judgment of his peers, or by the law of the land.

IV. And in the eight-and-twentieth year of the reign of King Edward III, it was declared and enacted by authority of parliament, that no man, of what estate or condition that he be, should be put out of his land or tenements, nor taken, nor imprisoned, nor disinherited nor put to death without being brought to answer by due process of law.

V. Nevertheless, against the tenor of the said statutes, and other the good laws and statutes of your realm to that end provided, divers of your subjects have of late been imprisoned without any cause showed; and when for their deliverance they were brought before your justices by your Majesty's writs of habeas corpus, there to undergo and receive as the court should order, and their keepers commanded to certify the causes of their detainer, no cause was certified, but that they were detained by your Majesty's special command, signified by the lords of your Privy Council, and yet were returned back to several prisons, without being charged with anything to which they might make answer according to the law.

VI. And whereas of late great companies of soldiers and mariners have been dispersed into divers counties of the realm, and the inhabitants against their wills have been compelled to receive them into their houses, and there to suffer them to sojourn against the laws and customs of this realm, and to the great grievance and vexation of the people.

VII. And whereas also by authority of parliament, in the five-and-twentieth year of the reign of King Edward III, it is declared and enacted, that no man shall be forejudged of life or limb against the form of the Great Charter and the law of the land; and by the said Great Charter and other the laws and statutes of this your realm, no man ought to be adjudged to death but by the laws established in this your realm, either by the customs of the same realm, or by acts of parliament: and whereas no offender of what kind soever is exempted from the proceedings to be used, and punishments to be inflicted by the laws and statutes of this your realm; nevertheless of late time divers commissions under your Majesty's great seal have issued forth, by which certain persons have been assigned and appointed commissioners with power and authority to proceed within the land, according to the justice of martial law, against such soldiers or mariners, or other dissolute persons joining with them, as should commit any murder, robbery, felony, mutiny, or other outrage or misdemeanor whatsoever, and by such summary course and order as is agreeable to martial law, and is used in armies in time of war, to proceed to the trial and condemnation of such offenders, and them to cause to be executed and put to death according to the law martial.

VIII. By pretext whereof some of your Majesty's subjects have been by some of the said commissioners put to death, when and where, if by the laws and statutes of the land they had deserved death, by the same laws and statutes also they might, and by no other ought to have been judged and executed.

IX. And also sundry grievous offenders, by color thereof claiming an exemption, have escaped the punishments due to them by the laws and statutes of this your realm, by reason that divers of your officers and ministers of justice have unjustly refused or forborne to proceed against such offenders according to the same laws and statutes, upon pretense that the said offenders were punishable only by martial law, and by authority of such commissions as aforesaid; which commissions, and all other of like nature, are wholly and directly contrary to the said laws and statutes of this your realm.

X. They do therefore humbly pray your most excellent Majesty, that no man hereafter be compelled to make or yield any gift, loan, benevolence, tax, or such like charge, without common consent by act of parliament; and that none be called to make answer, or take such oath, or to give attendance, or be confined, or otherwise molested or disquieted concerning the same or for refusal thereof; and that no freeman, in any such manner as is before mentioned, be imprisoned or detained; and that your Majesty would be pleased to remove the said soldiers and mariners, and that your people may not be so burdened in time to come; and that the aforesaid commissions, for proceeding by martial law, may be revoked and annulled; and that hereafter no commissions of like nature may issue forth to any person or persons whatsoever to be executed as aforesaid, lest by color of them any of your Majesty's subjects be destroyed or put to death contrary to the laws and franchise of the land.

XI. All which they most humbly pray of your most excellent Majesty as their rights and liberties, according to the laws and statutes of this realm; and that your Majesty would also vouchsafe to declare, that the awards, doings, and proceedings, to the prejudice of your people in any of the premises, shall not be drawn hereafter into consequence or example; and that your Majesty would be also graciously pleased, for the further comfort and safety of your people, to declare your royal will and pleasure, that in the things aforesaid all your officers and ministers shall serve you according to the laws and statutes of this realm, as they tender the honor of your Majesty, and the prosperity of this kingdom.

The Fundamental Orders of Connecticut (1639)

The reign of King Charles I of England was a period during which the original colonies that later became the United States of America were established and grew in size and importance. Although most of the individual colonies drew up documents that spelled out how they would be governed (at least at the local level), in 1639 three separate settlements along the Connecticut River (Hartford, Wethersfield, and Windsor) came together to draft a constitution (of sorts) under which the three colonies would function together.

The document was known as the Fundamental Orders of Connecticut. Because I attended middle school and high school in Connecticut, perhaps it is not surprising that I was taught that the Fundamental Orders of Connecticut constituted an important basis for the later Constitution of the United States.

Prior to this compact, cities and towns in the region that now encompasses Connecticut had fallen generally under the auspices of the Massachusetts colony, although Rhode Island also claimed jurisdiction over some of the same areas. Massachusetts prevailed over Rhode Island, however, and the government of the Massachusetts colony established a commission to oversee the functioning of the three towns. Although the commission's charter expired in 1636, the towns continued to pursue a cooperative agreement thereafter.

The result was the Fundamental Orders of Connecticut, which was finalized in January of 1639. It should be noted that New Haven colony, located only twenty-five miles to the south of Hartford, also created a "constitution" of sorts, which was adopted in June of 1639. Despite the proximity in time and in location, it is the Fundamental Orders of Connecticut that some sources and authorities regard as an important document precedent to the drafting of the Constitution of the United States.

One notable difference between the Fundamental Orders and the constitution of the New Haven Colony is that the Fundamental Orders do not impose any religious test for citizenship, whereas the New Haven constitution was predicated on membership in the [Protestant] church, under which the colony was founded, for admission as a planter and citizen.

Full Text of the Fundamental Orders of Connecticut (1639)

For as much as it hath pleased Almighty God by the wise disposition of his divine providence so to order and dispose of things that we the Inhabitants and Residents of Windsor, Hartford and Wethersfield are now cohabiting and dwelling in and upon the River of Connectecotte and the lands thereunto adjoining; and well knowing where a people are gathered together the word of God requires that to maintain the peace and union of such a people there should be an orderly and decent Government estab-lished according to God, to order and dispose of the affairs of the people at all seasons as occasion shall require; do therefore associate and conjoin ourselves to be as one Public State or Commonwealth; and do for our-selves and our successors and such as shall be adjoined to us at any time hereafter, enter into Combination and Confederation together, to maintain and preserve the liberty and purity of the Gospel of our Lord Jesus which we now profess, as also, the discipline of the Churches, which according to the truth of the said Gospel is now practiced amongst us; as also in our civil affairs to be guided and governed according to such Laws, Rules, Orders and Decrees as shall be made, ordered, and decreed as followeth:

1. It is Ordered, sentenced, and decreed, that there shall be yearly two General Assemblies or Courts, the one the second Thursday in April, the other the second Thursday in September following; the first shall be called the Court of Election, wherein shall be yearly chosen from time to time, so many Magistrates and other public Officers as shall be found requisite: Whereof one to be chosen Governor for the year ensuing and until another be chosen, and no other Magistrate to be chosen for more than one year: provided always there be six chosen besides the Governor, which being chosen and sworn according to an Oath recorded for that purpose, shall have the power to administer justice according to the Laws here established, and for want thereof, according to the Rule of the Word of God; which choice shall be made by all that are admitted freemen and have taken the Oath of Fidelity, and do cohabit within this Jurisdiction having been admitted Inhabitants by the major part of the Town wherein they live or the major part of such as shall be then present.

2. It is Ordered, sentenced, and decreed, that the election of the aforesaid Magistrates shall be in this manner: every person present and qualified for choice shall bring in (to the person deputed to receive them) one single paper with the name of him written in it whom he desires to have Governor, and that he that hath the greatest number of papers shall be Governor for that year. And the rest of the Magistrates or public officers to be chosen in this

manner: the Secretary for the time being shall first read the names of all that are to be put to choice and then shall severally nominate them distinctly, and every one that would have the person nominated to be chosen shall bring in one single paper written upon, and he that would not have him chosen shall bring in a blank; and every one that hath more written papers than blanks shall be a Magistrate for that year; which papers shall be received and told by one or more that shall be then chosen by the court and sworn to be faithful therein; but in case there should not be six chosen as aforesaid, besides the Governor, out of those which are nominated, than he or they which have the most writen papers shall be a Magistrate or Magistrates for the ensuing year, to make up the aforesaid number.

3. It is Ordered, sentenced, and decreed, that the Secretary shall not nominate any person, nor shall any person be chosen newly into the Magistracy which was not propounded in some General Court before, to be nominated the next election; and to that end it shall be lawful for each of the Towns aforesaid by their deputies to nominate any two whom they conceive fit to be put to election; and the Court may add so many more as they judge requisite.

4. It is Ordered, sentenced, and decreed, that no person be chosen Governor above once in two years, and that the Governor be always a member of some approved Congregation, and formerly of the Magis-tracy within this Jurisdiction; and that all the Magistrates, Freemen of this Commonwealth; and that no Magistrate or other public officer shall execute any part of his or their office before they are severally sworn, which shall be done in the face of the court if they be present, and in case of absence by some deputed for that purpose.

5. It is Ordered, sentenced, and decreed, that to the aforesaid Court of Election the several Towns shall send their deputies, and when the Elections are ended they may proceed in any public service as at other Courts. Also the other General Court in September shall be for making of laws, and any other public occasion, which concerns the good of the Commonwealth.

6. It is Ordered, sentenced, and decreed, that the Governor shall, either by himself or by the Secretary, send out summons to the Constables of every Town for the calling of these two standing Courts one month at least before their several times: And also if the Governor and the greatest part of the Magistrates see cause upon any special occasion to call a General Court, they may give order to the Secretary so to do within fourteen days' warning: And if urgent necessity so required, upon a shorter notice, giving sufficient grounds for it to the deputies when they meet, or else be questioned for the same; And if the Governor and major part of Magistrates shall either neglect or refuse to call the two General standing Courts or either of them, as also at other times when the occasions of the Commonwealth require, the Freemen thereof, or the major part of them, shall petition to them so to do; if then it be either denied or neglected, the said Freemen, or the major part of them,

shall have the power to give order to the Constables of the several Towns to do the same, and so may meet together, and choose to themselves a Moderator, and may proceed to do any act of power which any other General Courts may.

7. It is Ordered, sentenced, and decreed, that after there are warrants given out for any of the said General Courts, the Constable or Constables of each Town, shall forthwith give notice distinctly to the inhabitants of the same, in some public assembly or by going or sending from house to house, that at a place and time by him or them limited and set, they meet and assemble themselves together to elect and choose certain deputies to be at the General Court then following to agitate the affairs of the Commonwealth; which said deputies shall be chosen by all that are admitted Inhabitants in the several Towns and have taken the oath of fidelity; provided that none be chosen a Deputy for any General Court which is not a Freeman of this Commonwealth.

   The aforesaid deputies shall be chosen in manner following: every person that is present and qualified as before expressed, shall bring the names of such, written in several papers, as they desire to have chosen for that employment, and these three or four, more or less, being the number agreed on to be chosen for that time, that have the greatest number of papers written for them shall be deputies for that Court; whose names shall be endorsed on the back side of the warrant and returned into the Court, with the Constable or Constables' hand unto the same.

8. It is Ordered, sentenced, and decreed, that Windsor, Hartford, and Wethersfield shall have power, each Town, to send four of their Freemen as their deputies to every General Court; and Whatsoever other Town shall be hereafter added to this Jurisdiction, they shall send so many deputies as the Court shall judge meet, a reasonable proportion to the number of Freemen that are in the said Towns being to be attended therein; which deputies shall have the power of the whole Town to give their votes and allowance to all such laws and orders as may be for the public good, and unto which the said Towns are to be bound.

9. It is Ordered, sentenced, and decreed, that the deputies thus chosen shall have power and liberty to appoint atime and a place of meeting together before any General Court, to advise and consult of all such things as may concern the good of the public, as also to examine their own Elections, whether according to the order, and if they or the greatest part of them find any election to be illegal they may seclude such for present from their meeting, and return the same and their reasons to the Court; and if it be proved true, the Court may fine the party or parties so intruding, and the Town, if they see cause, and give out a warrant to go to a new election in a legal way, either in part or in whole. Also the said deputies shall have power to fine any that shall be disorderly at their meetings, or for not coming in due

time or place according to appointment; and they may return the said fines into the Court if it be refused to be paid, and the Treasurer to take notice of it, and to escheat or levy the same as he does other fines.

10. It is Ordered, sentenced, and decreed, that every General Court, except such as through neglect of the Governor and the greatest part of the Magistrates the Freemen themselves do call, shall consist of the Governor, or some one chosen to moderate the Court, and four other Magistrates at least, with the major part of the deputies of the several Towns legally chosen; and in case the Freemen, or major part of them, through neglect or refusal of the Governor and major part of the Magistrates, shall call a Court, it shall consist of the major part of Freemen that are present or their deputiues, with a Moderator chosen by them: In which said General Courts shall consist the supreme power of the Commonwealth, and they only shall have power to make laws or repeal them, to grant levies, to admit of Freemen, dispose of lands undisposed of, to several Towns or persons, and also shall have power to call either Court or Magistrate or any other person whatsoever into question for any misdemeanor, and may for just causes displace or deal otherwise according to the nature of the offense; and also may deal in any other matter that concerns the good of this Commonwealth, except election of Magistrates, which shall be done by the whole body of Freemen.

In which Court the Governor or Moderator shall have power to order the Court, to give liberty of speech, and silence unseasonable and disorderly speakings, to put all things to vote, and in case the vote be equal to have the casting voice. But none of these Courts shall be adjourned or dissolved without the consent of the major part of the Court.

11. It is Ordered, sentenced, and decreed, that when any General Court upon the occasions of the Commonwealth have agreed upon any sum, or sums of money to be levied upon the several Towns within this Jurisdiction, that a committee be chosen to set out and appoint what shall be the proportion of every Town to pay of the said levy, provided the committee be made up of an equal number out of each Town.

14th January 1639 the 11 Orders above said are voted.

* * * * *

[Source: *The Federal and State Constitutions Colonial Charters, and Other Organic Laws of the States, Territories, and Colonies Now or Heretofore Forming the United States of America* Compiled and Edited Under the Act of Congress of June 30, 1906 by Francis Newton Thorpe Washington, DC : Government Printing Office, 1909.

As cited by The Avalon Project, Yale Law School, https://avalon.law.yale.edu/17th_century/order.asp]

The English Bill of Rights
(1689)

Although King Charles I of England nominally agreed to the demands set forth in the Petition of Right in 1628, he continued to believe that he was not subject to any limitations established by the Parliament, and that he ruled by the Divine Right of Kings. His reign was characterized by continued injustices and disagreements with the Parliaments. In addition, his wife (Henrietta Maria of France) was a Roman Catholic, and many of Charles' English subjects feared and suspected that he would reintroduce Catholicism to England.

The years 1642 through 1645 saw actual armed warfare between Royalist forces loyal to the monarchy and forces aligned with the Parliament. Charles was defeated and surrendered in 1645. He subsequently escaped from captivity, was recaptured, and after years of negotiations he was eventually put on trial in 1649. Although he maintained that the court had no jurisdiction to try a king, he was convicted of high treason and executed by beheading on January 30, 1649.

Upon the death of his father, Charles II became the king of Scotland, but England (under Oliver Cromwell) declared itself a commonwealth and a republic, and was governed by Cromwell and his cohort until Cromwell's death in 1658. Following Cromwell's death, England decided to restore the monarchy. In exchange for promises by Charles II of leniency toward most of the people who had deposed and executed his father, and a promise that he would rule in cooperation with the Parliament, in 1660 Charles II was crowned King of England, Scotland, and Ireland.

In 1662, Charles II married a Portuguese princess, Catherine of Braganza (a Roman Catholic). Although they remained married until Charles' death in 1685, Catherine was never able to produce a child as heir to the throne. When Charles died unexpectedly in 1685, because he had no legitimate offspring the monarchy went to his brother James, who ruled as James II of England and James VII of Scotland.

James converted from the Anglican religion to Roman Catholicism before the death of his brother, Charles II. Although James and his first wife had eight children, six of the children died young, with the only two who survived into adulthood being the princesses Mary and Anne. Although Charles II did not prevent James' conversion to Catholicism, he did require that Mary and Anne be raised as Anglicans.

By the late 17th century, James had alienated a large segment of the populace and had disbanded the Parliament. His eldest surviving daughter, Mary, was married to the Dutch prince, William of Orange — who was a Protestant. In 1688 a group of English Protestant nobles encouraged William of Orange to invade England. In November of 1688 he did so. Much of James' army defected to the Protestant invaders, and James faced a numerically superior attacking force. Rather than risk engaging in battle, James threw the Great Seal into the Thames River and attempted to flee to France. He was captured but, not wanting to make him a martyr, William subsequently allowed him to escape, whereupon he made his way to France and the protection of his cousin, Louis XIV.

Victorious without having engaged in battle, William called a new Parliament in January of 1689. This Parliament ruled that, having discarded the Great Seal and fled the country, James had *de facto* abdicated, leaving the throne vacant. Because James had no living sons, his eldest heir was Mary — who was married to William of Orange, who had just succeeded in routing James. The Parliament declared that Mary would become Queen, and the she would co-rule with her husband, William of Orange. The Scottish Parliament followed suit in April of 1689.

Along with declaring William and Mary as co-rulers, the English Parliament of 1689 also enacted a Bill of Rights. Among other provisions, this Bill of Rights established that no future monarch of England could be Roman Catholic, and no English monarch could marry a Roman Catholic.

The Bill of Rights is important because it firmly established, for the first time, that England's monarchs did not rule by the Divine Right of Kings but, rather, by the consent of the governed. The Bill of Rights codified limitations on the power of the monarch, and it spelled out the rights of the Parliament.

The Bill of Rights also contained other provisions that later found their way into the Constitution of the United States and its Bill of Rights, including:

- A prohibition against cruel and unusual punishment;
- A prohibition against taxation without the approval of Parliament;
- A guarantee of freedom of speech (although this was limited to the Parliament);
- A requirement for free elections;
- A right for citizens to petition the king; and
- A guarantee that Protestants could have arms for their own self-defense.

Thus, in addition to being a critical document in the path of England and Great Britain to being a constitutional monarchy, the English Bill of Rights of 1689 is likewise significant as a precursor to the Constitution of the United States. In it we can see several provisions that presage provisions set forth in the Bill of Rights that constitute the first ten amendments to the Constitution of the United States.

Full Text of the English Bill of Rights (1689)

An Act Declaring the Rights and Liberties of the Subject and Settling the Succession of the Crown

Whereas the Lords Spiritual and Temporal and Commons assembled at Westminster, lawfully, fully and freely representing all the estates of the people of this realm, did upon the thirteenth day of February in the year of our Lord one thousand six hundred eighty-eight [old style date] present unto their Majesties, then called and known by the names and style of William and Mary, prince and princess of Orange, being present in their proper persons, a certain declaration in writing made by the said Lords and Commons in the words following, viz.:

Whereas the late King James the Second, by the assistance of divers evil counsellors, judges and ministers employed by him, did endeavour to subvert and extirpate the Protestant religion and the laws and liberties of this kingdom;

By assuming and exercising a power of dispensing with and suspending of laws and the execution of laws without consent of Parliament;

By committing and prosecuting divers worthy prelates for humbly petitioning to be excused from concurring to the said assumed power;

By issuing and causing to be executed a commission under the great seal for erecting a court called the Court of Commissioners for Ecclesiastical Causes;

By levying money for and to the use of the Crown by pretence of prerogative for other time and in other manner than the same was granted by Parliament;

By raising and keeping a standing army within this kingdom in time of peace without consent of Parliament, and quartering soldiers contrary to law;

By causing several good subjects being Protestants to be disarmed at the same time when papists were both armed and employed contrary to law;

By violating the freedom of election of members to serve in Parliament;

By prosecutions in the Court of King's Bench for matters and causes cognizable only in Parliament, and by divers other arbitrary and illegal courses;

And whereas of late years partial corrupt and unqualified persons have been returned and served on juries in trials, and particularly divers jurors in trials for high treason which were not freeholders;

And excessive bail hath been required of persons committed in criminal cases to elude the benefit of the laws made for the liberty of the subjects;

And excessive fines have been imposed;

And illegal and cruel punishments inflicted;

And several grants and promises made of fines and forfeitures before any conviction or judgment against the persons upon whom the same were to be levied;

All which are utterly and directly contrary to the known laws and statutes and freedom of this realm;

And whereas the said late King James the Second having abdicated the government and the throne being thereby vacant, his Highness the prince of Orange (whom it hath pleased Almighty God to make the glorious instrument of delivering this kingdom from popery and arbitrary power) did (by the advice of the Lords Spiritual and Temporal and divers principal persons of the Commons) cause letters to be written to the Lords Spiritual and Temporal being Protestants, and other letters to the several counties, cities, universities, boroughs and cinque ports, for the choosing of such persons to represent them as were of right to be sent to Parliament, to meet and sit at Westminster upon the two and twentieth day of January in this year one thousand six hundred eighty and eight [old style date], in order to such an establishment as that their religion, laws and liberties might not again be in danger of being subverted, upon which letters elections having been accordingly made;

And thereupon the said Lords Spiritual and Temporal and Commons, pursuant to their respective letters and elections, being now assembled in a full and free representative of this nation, taking into their most serious consideration the best means for attaining the ends aforesaid, do in the first place (as their ancestors in like case have usually done) for the vindicating and asserting their ancient rights and liberties declare

That the pretended power of suspending the laws or the execution of laws by regal authority without consent of Parliament is illegal;

That the pretended power of dispensing with laws or the execution of laws by regal authority, as it hath been assumed and exercised of late, is illegal;

That the commission for erecting the late Court of Commissioners for Ecclesiastical Causes, and all other commissions and courts of like nature, are illegal and pernicious;

That levying money for or to the use of the Crown by pretence of prerogative, without grant of Parliament, for longer time, or in other manner than the same is or shall be granted, is illegal;

That it is the right of the subjects to petition the king, and all commitments and prosecutions for such petitioning are illegal;

That the raising or keeping a standing army within the kingdom in time of peace, unless it be with consent of Parliament, is against law;

That the subjects which are Protestants may have arms for their defence suitable to their conditions and as allowed by law;

That election of members of Parliament ought to be free;

That the freedom of speech and debates or proceedings in Parliament ought not to be impeached or questioned in any court or place out of Parliament;

That excessive bail ought not to be required, nor excessive fines imposed, nor cruel and unusual punishments inflicted;

That jurors ought to be duly impanelled and returned, and jurors which pass upon men in trials for high treason ought to be freeholders;

That all grants and promises of fines and forfeitures of particular persons before conviction are illegal and void;

And that for redress of all grievances, and for the amending, strengthening and preserving of the laws, Parliaments ought to be held frequently.

And they do claim, demand and insist upon all and singular the premises as their undoubted rights and liberties, and that no declarations, judgements, doings or proceedings to the prejudice of the people in any of the said premises ought in any wise to be drawn hereafter into consequence or example; to which demand of their rights they are particularly encouraged by the declaration of his Highness the prince of Orange as being the only means for obtaining a full redress and remedy therein. Having therefore an entire confidence that his said Highness the prince of Orange will perfect the deliverance so far advanced by him, and will still preserve them from the violation of their rights which they have here asserted, and from all other attempts upon their religion, rights and liberties, the said Lords Spiritual and Temporal and Commons assembled at Westminster do resolve that William and Mary, prince and princess of Orange, be and be declared king and queen of England, France and Ireland and the dominions thereunto belonging, to hold the crown and royal dignity of the said kingdoms and dominions to them, the said prince and princess, during their lives and the life of the survivor to them, and that the sole and full exercise of the regal power be only in and executed by the said prince of Orange in the names of the said prince and princess during their joint lives, and after their deceases the said crown and royal dignity of the same kingdoms and dominions to be to the heirs of the body of the said princess, and for default of such issue to the Princess Anne of Denmark and the heirs of her body, and for default of such issue to the heirs of the body of the said prince of Orange. And the Lords Spiritual and Temporal and Commons do pray the said prince and princess to accept the same accordingly.

And that the oaths hereafter mentioned be taken by all persons of whom the oaths have allegiance and supremacy might be required by law, instead of them; and that the said oaths of allegiance and supremacy be abrogated.

I, A.B., do sincerely promise and swear that I will be faithful and bear true allegiance to their Majesties King William and Queen Mary. So help me God.

I, A.B., do swear that I do from my heart abhor, detest and abjure as impious and heretical this damnable doctrine and position, that princes excommunicated or deprived by the Pope or any authority of the see of Rome may be deposed or murdered by their subjects or any other whatsoever. And I do declare that no foreign prince, person, prelate, state or potentate hath or ought to have any jurisdiction, power, superiority, pre-eminence or authority, ecclesiastical or spiritual, within this realm. So help me God.

Upon which their said Majesties did accept the crown and royal dignity of the kingdoms of England, France and Ireland, and the dominions thereunto belonging, according to the resolution and desire of the said Lords and Commons contained in the said declaration. And thereupon their Majesties were pleased that the said Lords Spiritual and Temporal and Commons, being the two Houses of Parliament, should continue to sit, and with their Majesties' royal concurrence make effectual provision for the settlement of the religion, laws and liberties of this kingdom, so that the same for the future might not be in danger again of being subverted, to which the said Lords Spiritual and Temporal and Commons did agree, and proceed to act accordingly. Now in pursuance of the premises the said Lords Spiritual and Temporal and Commons in Parliament assembled, for the ratifying, confirming and establishing the said declaration and the articles, clauses, matters and things therein contained by the force of law made in due form by authority of Parliament, do pray that it may be declared and enacted that all and singular the rights and liberties asserted and claimed in the said declaration are the true, ancient and indubitable rights and liberties of the people of this kingdom, and so shall be esteemed, allowed, adjudged, deemed and taken to be; and that all and every the particulars aforesaid shall be firmly and strictly holden and observed as they are expressed in the said declaration, and all officers and ministers whatsoever shall serve their Majesties and their successors according to the same in all time to come. And the said Lords Spiritual and Temporal and Commons, seriously considering how it hath pleased Almighty God in his marvellous providence and merciful goodness to this nation to provide and preserve their said Majesties' royal persons most happily to reign over us upon the throne of their ancestors, for which they render unto him from the bottom of their hearts their humblest thanks and praises, do truly, firmly, assuredly and in the sincerity of their hearts think, and do hereby recognize, acknowledge and declare, that King James the Second having abdicated the government, and their Majesties having accepted the crown and royal dignity as aforesaid, their said Majesties did become, were, are and of right ought to be by the laws of this realm our sovereign liege lord and lady, king and queen of England, France and Ireland and the dominions thereunto belonging, in and to whose princely persons the royal state, crown and dignity of the said realms with all honours, styles, titles, regalities, prerogatives, powers, jurisdictions and authorities to the same belonging and appertaining are most fully, rightfully and entirely invested and incorporated, united and annexed. And for preventing all questions and divisions in this realm by reason of any pretended titles to the crown, and for preserving a certainty in the succession thereof, in and upon which the unity, peace, tranquility and safety of this nation doth under God wholly consist and depend, the said Lords Spiritual and Temporal and Commons do beseech their Majesties that it may be enacted, established and declared, that the crown and regal government of the said kingdoms and dominions, with all and singular the premises thereunto belonging and appertaining, shall be and continue to their said Majesties and the survivor of them during their lives and the life of the survivor of them, and that the entire, perfect and full exercise of the regal power and government be only in and executed by his Majesty in the names of both their Majesties during their joint lives; and after their deceases the said crown and premises shall be and remain to the heirs of the body of her Majesty, and for default of such issue to her Royal Highness the Princess Anne of Denmark and the heirs of the body of his said Majesty; and thereunto the said Lords Spiritual and Temporal and Commons do in the name of all the people aforesaid most humbly and faithfully submit themselves, their heirs and posterities for ever, and do faithfully promise that they will stand to, maintain and defend their said Majesties, and also the limitation and succession of the crown herein specified and contained, to the utmost of their powers with their lives and estates against all persons whatsoever that shall attempt anything to the contrary. And whereas it hath been found by experience that it is inconsistent with the safety and welfare of this Protestant kingdom to be governed by a popish prince, or by any king or queen marrying a papist, the said Lords Spiritual and Temporal and Commons do further pray that it may be enacted, that all and every person and persons that is, are or shall be reconciled to or shall hold communion with the see or Church of Rome, or shall profess the popish religion, or shall marry a papist, shall be excluded and be for ever incapable to inherit, possess or enjoy the crown and government of this realm and Ireland and the dominions thereunto belonging or any part of the same, or to have, use or exercise any regal power, authority or jurisdiction within the same; and in all and every such case or cases the people of these realms shall be and are hereby absolved of their allegiance; and the said crown and government shall from time to time descend to and be enjoyed by such person or persons being Protestants as should have inherited and enjoyed the same in case the said person or persons so reconciled, holding communion or professing or marrying as aforesaid were naturally dead; and that every king and queen of this realm who at any time hereafter shall come to and succeed in the imperial crown of this kingdom shall on the first day of the meeting of the first Parliament next after his or her coming to the crown, sitting in his or her throne in the House of Peers in the presence of the Lords and Commons therein assembled, or at his or her coronation before such person or persons who shall administer the coronation oath to him or her at the time of his or her taking the said oath (which shall first happen), make, subscribe and audibly repeat the declaration mentioned in the statute made in the thirtieth year of the reign of King Charles the Second entitled, _An Act for the more effectual preserving the king's person and government by disabling papists from sitting in either House of Parliament._ But if it shall happen that such king or queen upon his or her succession to the crown of this realm shall be under the age of twelve years, then every such king or queen shall make, subscribe and audibly repeat the same declaration at his or her coronation or the first day of the meeting of the first Parliament as aforesaid which shall first happen after such king or queen shall have attained the said age of twelve years. All which their Majesties are contented and pleased shall be declared, enacted and established by authority of this present Parliament, and shall stand, remain and be the law of this realm for ever; and the same are by their said Majesties, by and with the advice and consent of the Lords Spiritual and Temporal and Commons in Parliament assembled and by the authority of the same, declared, enacted and established accordingly.

II. And be it further declared and enacted by the authority aforesaid, that from and after this present session of Parliament no dispensation by _non obstante_ of or to any statute or any part thereof shall be allowed, but that the same shall be held void and of no effect, except a dispensation be allowed of in such statute, and except in such cases as shall be specially provided for by one or more bill or bills to be passed during this present session of Parliament.

III. Provided that no charter or grant or pardon granted before the three and twentieth day of October in the year of our Lord one thousand six hundred eighty-nine shall be any ways impeached or invalidated by this Act, but that the same shall be and remain of the same force and effect in law and no other than as if this Act had never been made.

The Act of Settlement
(1701)

King James II (who also ruled Scotland as James VII) ascended to the throne in February of 1685. James was Roman Catholic, which was not popular with his subjects but he was crowned out of respect for his position as the next in line to his older brother, Charles II. Very soon after he took the throne, however, two problems began to manifest. James believed in the Divine Right of Kings, which meant that he rejected the concept that he needed to respect and to work with the Parliament. When he was unable to persuade the parliament to enact his proposals, he attempted to impose them by royal decree, without the consent of the Parliament.

James had a daughter, Mary, who was a Protestant and who was married to William III of Orange. At the time, William and Mary resided in the Netherlands. In 1688, a son was born to James, raising concern that Great Britain might be seeing the start of a Roman Catholic dynasty. (At that time, Great Britain's line of succession to the throne followed the principle of *primogeniture*, which meant that the crown was inherited by the eldest son even if there were daughters who were older.) In addition, James tried seven Anglican bishops for seditious libel, a trial which was viewed by the citizens and by the Parliament as an attack on the Church of England.

The bishops were acquitted. Riots followed, and an invitation was extended to William of Orange to intervene. William arrived in England in late 1688. The army deserted James, whereupon he escaped and took refuge in France. In early 1689 the Parliament declared that James had abdicated the throne, and the Parliament installed William and Mary as joint rulers of Great Britain. In doing so, the Parliament established that the monarch ruled by the will of the Parliament rather than by the Will of God. The document installing William and Mary as monarchs and establishing (among other things) that the monarch should be Protestant was the English Bill of Rights of 1689.

It was thought at the time the Bill of Rights was enacted that the question of Protestant succession to the throne had been settled. However, a decade later, the situation looked a lot less settled. Queen Mary died in 1694, leaving no children. Her Protestant sister, Anne, had 17 children, all of whom had died by 1694. Thus, when King William was nearing death in 1700, the most direct heir to the throne was Anne's half-brother James — who was a Roman Catholic, and whose birth to King James II had been the cause of the Glorious Revolution that deposed King James and brought William and Mary to the throne.

The Parliament then enacted the Act of Settlement in 1701. The Act of Settlement codified the requirement that the monarchy must pass to a Protestant heir. At that time, the closest Protestant relation was Sophia, Electress of Hanover. Sophia was a granddaughter of James I and a first cousin to Chares II and James II.

The Act of settlement also established new prerequisites for future monarchs of Great Britain:

- Future monarchs would have to be "in communion with" the Church of England. By excluding Roman Catholics and those of other faiths, this established that the Princess Sophia, of Hanover, was next in the line of succession after Anne, the younger sister of Mary. However, Sophia died before Queen Anne, setting the stage for the next King of England to be George, Elector of Hanover.
- If a future monarch was not English by birth, Great Britain would not be obligated to go to war to protect the monarch's native country. This provision was included because the next in line for the throne after William's sister-in-law, Anne, was a granddaughter of James I and a native of Hanover (Germany), as was her son, who became King George I.
- Judges were appointed to serve as long as they exhibited good behavior. They were no longer subject to recall at the will of the ruling monarch.
- Impeachments issued by the House of Commons could no longer be pardoned by the monarch.

William of Orange died in 1702, at which time Anne ascended to the throne. She ruled until her death on August 1, 1714. Upon the death of Queen Anne, the throne passed to Sophia's son, George, who became King George I.

* * * * *

While the Settlement Act was primarily intended to ensure that the ruling monarch of England and Great Britain would always be a Protestant, the Act also reinforced the principle that the monarch served by the grace of the Parliament rather than by the Grace of God.

Full Text of The Act of Settlement (1701)

An Act for the further Limitation of the Crown and better securing the Rights and Liberties of the Subject
[Assented to 1701.]

Recital of *Bill of Rights 1689*, Section 2, and that the late Queen and Duke of Gloucester are dead; and that His Majesty had recommended from the Throne a further Provision for the Succession of the Crown in the Protestant Line. The Princess Sophia, Electress and Duchess Dowager of Hanover, Daughter of the late Queen of Bohemia, Daughter of King James the First, to inherit after the King and the Princess Anne, in Default of Issue of the said Princess and His Majesty, respectively and the Heirs of her Body, being Protestants

I. Whereas in the first year of the reign of Your Majesty, and of our late most gracious sovereign lady Queen Mary (of blessed memory), an Act of Parliament was made, entitled, *An Act Declaring the Rights and Liberties of the Subject and Settling the Succession of the Crown*, wherein it was (amongst other things) enacted, established, and declared that the crown and regal government of the Kingdoms of England, France, and Ireland, and the dominions thereunto belonging, should be and continue to Your Majesty and the said late Queen, during the joint lives of Your Majesty and the said Queen, and to the survivor: and that after the decease of Your Majesty and of the said Queen, the said Crown and regal government should be and remain to the heirs of the body of the said late Queen; and for default of such issue, to Her Royal Highness the Princess Anne of Denmark, and the heirs of her body; and for default of such issue to the heirs of the body of Your Majesty. And it was thereby further enacted, that all and every person and persons that then were, or afterwards should be reconciled to, or shall hold communion with the see or Church of Rome, or should profess the popish religion, or marry a papist, should be excluded, and are by that Act made for ever incapable to inherit, possess, or enjoy the Crown and government of this realm, and Ireland, and the dominions thereunto belonging, or any part of the same, or to have, use, or exercise any regal power, authority, or jurisdiction within the same: and in all and every such case and cases the people of these realms shall be and are thereby absolved of their allegiance: and that the said Crown and government shall from time to time descend to and be enjoyed by such person or persons, being Protestants, as should have inherited and enjoyed the same, in case the said person or persons, so reconciled, holding communion, professing or marrying, as aforesaid, were naturally dead: After the making of which statute, and the settlement therein contained, your majesty's good subjects, who were restored to the full and free possession and enjoyment of their religion, rights, and liberties, by the providence of God giving success to your majesty's just undertakings and unwearied endeavours for that purpose, had no greater temporal felicity to hope or wish for, that to see a royal progeny descending from Your Majesty, to whom (under God) they owe their tranquillity, and whose ancestors have for many years been principal assertors of the reformed religion and the liberties of Europe, and from our said most gracious sovereign lady, whose memory will always be precious to the subjects of these realms: and it having since pleased Almighty God to take away our said sovereign Lady, and also the most hopeful Prince William, Duke of Gloucester (the only surviving issue of Her Royal Highness the Princess Anne of Denmark) to the unspeakable grief and sorrow of Your Majesty and your said good subjects, who under such losses being sensibly put in mind, that it standeth wholly in the pleasure of Almighty God to prolong the lives of Your Majesty and of Her Royal Highness, and to grant to Your Majesty, or to Her Royal Highness, such issue as may be inheritable to the Crown and regal government aforesaid, by the respective limitations in the said recited act contained, do constantly implore the divine mercy for those blessings: and Your Majesty's said subjects having daily experience of your royal care and concern for the present and future welfare of these Kingdoms, and particularly recommending from your throne a further provision to be made for the succession of the Crown in the Protestant line, for the happiness of the nation, and the security of our religion; and it being absolutely necessary for the safety, peace, and quiet of this realm, to obviate all doubts and contentions in the same, by reason of any pretended title to the Crown, and to maintain a certainty in the succession thereof, to which your subjects may safely have recourse for their protection, in case the limitations in the said recited act should determine: therefore for a further provision of the succession of the Crown in the Protestant line, we Your Majesty's most dutiful and loyal subjects, the Lords Spiritual and Temporal, and Commons, in this present Parliament assembled, do beseech Your Majesty that it may be enacted and declared, and be it enacted and declared by the King's most excellent majesty, by and with the advice and consent of the Lords Spiritual and Temporal, and Commons, in this present Parliament assembled, and by the authority of the same, That the most excellent Princess Sophia, Electress and Duchess Dowager of Hanover, daughter of the most excellent Princess Elizabeth, late Queen of Bohemia, daughter of our late sovereign lord King James the First, of happy memory, be and is hereby declared to be the next in succession, in the Protestant line, to the imperial Crown and dignity of the said Realms of England, France, and Ireland, with the dominions and territories thereunto belonging, after His Majesty, and the Princess Anne of Denmark, and in default of issue of the said Princess Anne, and of His Majesty respectively: and that from and after the deceases of His said Majesty, our now sovereign lord, and of Her Royal Highness the Princess Anne of Denmark, and for default of issue of the said Princess Anne, and of His Majesty respectively, the Crown and regal government of the said Kingdoms of England, France, and Ireland, and of the dominions thereunto belonging, with the royal state and dignity of the said Realms, and all honours, styles, titles, regalities, prerogatives, powers, jurisdictions and authorities, to the same belonging and appertaining, shall be, remain, and continue to the said most excellent Princess Sophia, and the heirs of her body, being Protestants: and thereunto the said Lords Spiritual and Temporal, and Commons, shall and will in the name of all the people of this Realm, most humbly and faithfully submit themselves, their heirs and posterities: and do faithfully promise, that after the deceases of His Majesty, and Her Royal Highness, and the failure of the heirs of their respective bodies, to stand to, maintain, and defend the said Princess Sophia, and the heirs of her body, being Protestants, according to the limitation and succession of the Crown in this act specified and contained, to the utmost of their powers, with their lives and estates, against all persons whatsoever that shall attempt anything to the contrary.

The Persons inheritable by this Act, holding Communion with the Church of Rome, incapacitated as by the former Act; to take the Oath at their Coronation, according to *Coronation Oath Act 1688*

II. Provided always, and be it hereby enacted, That all and every person and persons, who shall or may take or inherit the said Crown, by virtue of the limitation of this present act, and is, are or shall be reconciled to, or shall hold communion with, the See or Church of Rome, or shall profess the popish religion, or shall marry a papist, shall be subject to such incapacities, as in such case or cases are by the said recited act provided, enacted, and established; and that every King and Queen of this Realm, who shall come to and succeed in the imperial Crown of this Kingdom, by virtue of this act, shall have the coronation oath administered to him, her or them, at their respective coronations, according to the act of Parliament made in the first year of the reign of His Majesty, and the said late Queen Mary, intituled, *An Act for establishing the Coronation Oath*, and shall make, subscribe, and repeat the declaration in the act first above recited mentioned or referred to, in the manner and form thereby prescribed.

Further Provisions for securing the Religion, Laws, and Liberties of these Realms

III. And whereas it is requisite and necessary that some further provision be made for securing our religion, laws and liberties, from and after the death of His Majesty and the Princess Anne of Denmark, and in default of issue of the body of the said Princess, and of His Majesty respectively; be it enacted by the King's most excellent majesty, by and with the advice and consent of the Lords Spiritual and Temporal, and Commons, in

Parliament assembled, and by the authority of the same,

That whosoever shall hereafter come to the possession of this Crown, shall join in communion with the Church of England, as by law established;

That in case the Crown and imperial dignity of this Realm shall hereafter come to any person, not being a native of this Kingdom of England, this nation be not obliged to engage in any war for the defence of any dominions or territories which do not belong to the Crown of England, without the consent of Parliament;

That no person who shall hereafter come to the possession of this Crown, shall go out of the dominions of England, Scotland, or Ireland, without the consent of Parliament;

That from and after the time that the further limitation by this act shall take effect, all matters and things relating to the well governing of this Kingdom, which are properly cognizable in the Privy Council by the laws and customs of this Realm, shall be translated there, and all resolutions taken thereupon shall be signed by such of the Privy Council as shall advise and consent to the same;

That after the said limitation shall take effect as aforesaid, no person born out of the Kingdoms of England, Scotland, or Ireland, or the dominions thereunto belonging (although he be naturalized or made a denizen, except such as are born of English parents) shall be capable to be of the Privy Council, or a member of either House of Parliament, or to enjoy any office or place of trust, either civil or military, or to have any grant of lands, tenements or hereditaments from the Crown, to himself or to any other or others in trust for him;

That no person who has an office or place of profit under the King, or receives a pension from the Crown, shall be capable of serving as a member of the House of Commons;

That after the said limitation shall take effect as aforesaid, judges commissions be made quamdiu se bene gesserint, and their salaries ascertained and established; but upon the address of both

Houses of Parliament it may be lawful to remove them;

That no pardon under the Great Seal of England be pleadable to an impeachment by the Commons in Parliament.

The Laws and Statutes of the Realm confirmed

IV. And whereas the laws of England are the birthright of the people thereof, and all the Kings and Queens, who shall ascend the throne of this Realm, ought to administer the government of the same according to the said laws, and all their officers and ministers ought to serve them respectively according to the same: the said Lords Spiritual and Temporal, and Commons, do therefore further humbly pray, That all the laws and statutes of this Realm for securing the established religion, and the rights and liberties of the people thereof, and all other laws and statutes of the same now in force, may be ratified and confirmed, and the same are by His Majesty, by and with the advice of the said Lords Spiritual and Temporal, and Commons, and by authority of the same, ratified and confirmed accordingly.

* * * * *

[*Source: https://en.wikisource.org/wiki/Act_of_Settlement_1701*
This work is in the public domain worldwide because the work was created by a public body of the United Kingdom with Crown Status and commercially published before 1971.]

A Summary View of the Rights of British America
(1774)

The preceding documents constitute the major documents in the progression of England from an absolute monarchy to a constitutional monarchy, and from an assemblage of individual kingdoms to Great Britain. They also illustrate and document the gradual establishment of specific rights for all citizens of Great Britain, not only the royal family and the nobility.

The 18th century saw considerable expansion throughout the British colonies in North America. Although the first successful British colony in North America (Jamestown, Virginia) was settled in 1607, throughout the 17th century and into the 18th century the North American continent was colonized by England, France, Spain, and Holland. France controlled what is now eastern Canada and the western part of what is now New York state. What now constitutes the New England states was under English control, encompassing the Massachusetts Bay Colony (which included present-day Maine), Vermont, New Hampshire, Rhode Island, and Connecticut. What is now New Jersey and the eastern part of New York state was controlled by the Dutch. Eastern Pennsylvania, Maryland, Virginia, Carolina, and Georgia were under English control. Finally, to the south, Florida was controlled by the Spanish.

Through a succession of skirmishes, wars, and treaties, by the 18th century the entire eastern portion of the North American continent from present-day Maine through Georgia was under British control and rule. The citizens of all these colonies regarded themselves as subjects of the English Crown. However, as the 18th century progressed the citizens of the colonies increasingly chaffed under restrictions that applied to them but not to British subjects in England.

The stage was now set for politically cataclysmic events in the British colonies on North America. Although by the middle of the 18th century Great Britain was a constitutional monarchy and British citizens living in Great Britain had certain rights guaranteed to them, such as the right to a representational form of government, the right to maintain arms for self-defense, and a guarantee that they would not have the King's soldiers quartered in their homes, the loyal British subjects in the colonies were denied many of the same rights enjoyed by their counterparts in Great Britain.

As one example: a major export of the colonies around the Chesapeake Bay, notably Virginia, was tobacco. The colonies produced far more tobacco than could be consumed in Great Britain. But the colonies were not allowed to sell their produce anywhere other than to Great Britain. The result was that the American tobacco growers were forced to sell to wholesalers in Great Britain at extremely low prices, whereupon those British wholesalers would, in turn, sell the tobacco at great profit in the markets which were prohibited to the American colonies. In Massachusetts, colonial importers of tea were heavily taxed while the British East India Company could import tea into the colonies without paying the same taxes, which allowed the company to undercut the colonial merchants. The colonists objected to these taxes, because the taxes were imposed on them by the British Parliament and the colonies were not represented in the Parliament.

Late in 1773 the British East India Company sent seven ships loaded with tea to the colonies. One ship was destined for each of the cities of New York, Philadelphia, and Charleston, while four were destined for Boston. The colonists resisted the importation. The consignee in Charleston resigned rather than confront the opposition, the tea was unclaimed, and was eventually seized by customs. The consignees in New York and Philadelphia likewise resigned, and those ships returned to England with their cargoes of tea.

On the night of December 16, 1773, the colonists of Boston took decisive action by boarding the four ships in Boston Harbor and throwing the entire cargo of tea overboard. The incident came to be known as the Boston Tea Party. The act of resistance was viewed by the Crown as an act of insurrection, and the government of Great Britain responded in a heavy-handed manner by sending large numbers of soldiers to Boston to enforce British law on the colonists. Whatever degree of self-government the Massachusetts colony had enjoyed was cancelled, and rule by a British governor was imposed.

From the Petition of Right in 1628 onward it had been established that the citizens of Great Britain would not be required to quarter soldiers in their homes, yet the citizens of the colonies were required to do so. The Petition of Right also established that citizens had a right to petition the government for grievances; when the representatives of colonial governments attempted to petition for relief from grievances, the colonial legislatures were closed down by order of the Crown.

Finally, in 1774 Thomas Jefferson drafted a lengthy exposition of his views of the rights of the colonies and the citizens of the colonies. His draft, *A Summary View of the Rights of British America*, which was discussed and debated at the First Continental Congress, held that the colonies were independent of the authority of Great Britain and that they should be governed by their own legislative bodies rather than by the British Parliament. Jefferson was not present at the Congress when his draft was debated. Ultimately, the First Continental Congress decided on a less radical statement to the government of Great Britain. Friends of Jefferson then had copies of his draft printed and distributed in Philadelphia, New York, and London.

Of particular note is that, although he himself owned slaves, in his draft Jefferson introduced the idea that slavery was wrong and should be abolished in America. He points out that slavery in America was not introduced by the colonists but imposed on them by Great Britain, and that efforts by the colonies to abolish the importation of slaves had been quashed by the Crown.

Full Text of A Summary View of the Rights of British America (1774)

Resolved, that it be an instruction to the said deputies, when assembled in general congress with the deputies from the other states of British America, to propose to the said congress that an humble and dutiful address be presented to his majesty, begging leave to lay before him, as chief magistrate of the British empire, the united complaints of his majesty's subjects in America; complaints which are excited by many unwarrantable encroachments and usurpations, attempted to be made by the legislature of one part of the empire, upon those rights which God and the laws have given equally and independently to all. To represent to his majesty that these his states have often individually made humble application to his imperial throne to obtain, through its intervention, some redress of their injured rights, to none of which was ever even an answer condescended; humbly to hope that this their joint address, penned in the language of truth, and divested of those expressions of servility which would persuade his majesty that we are asking favours, and not rights, shall obtain from his majesty a more respectful acceptance. And this his majesty will think we have reason to expect when he reflects that he is no more than the chief officer of the people, appointed by the laws, and circumscribed with definite powers, to assist in working the great machine of government, erected for their use, and consequently subject to their superintendance. And in order that these our rights, as well as the invasions of them, may be laid more fully before his majesty, to take a view of them from the origin and first settlement of these countries.

To remind him that our ancestors, before their emigration to America, were the free inhabitants of the British dominions in Europe, and possessed a right which nature has given to all men, of departing from the country in which chance, not choice, has placed them, of going in quest of new habitations, and of there establishing new societies, under such laws and regulations as to them shall seem most likely to promote public happiness. That their Saxon ancestors had, under this universal law, in like manner left their native wilds and woods in the north of Europe, had possessed themselves of the island of Britain, then less charged with inhabitants, and had established there that system of laws which has so long been the glory and protection of that country. Nor was ever any claim of superiority or dependence asserted over them by that mother country from which they had migrated; and were such a claim made, it is believed that his majesty's subjects in Great Britain have too firm a feeling of the rights derived to them from their ancestors, to bow down the sovereignty of their state before such visionary pretensions. And it is thought that no circumstance has occurred to distinguish materially the British from the Saxon emigration. America was conquered, and her settlements made, and firmly established, at the expence of individuals, and not of the British public. Their own blood was spilt in acquiring lands for their settlement, their own fortunes expended in making that settlement effectual; for themselves they fought, for themselves they conquered, and for themselves alone they have right to hold. Not a shilling was ever issued from the public treasures of his majesty, or his ancestors, for their assistance, till of very late times, after the colonies had become established on a firm and permanent footing. That then, indeed, having become valuable to Great Britain for her commercial purposes, his parliament was pleased to lend them assistance against an enemy, who would fain have drawn to herself the benefits of their commerce, to the great aggrandizement of herself, and danger of Great Britain. Such assistance, and in such circumstances, they had often before given to Portugal, and other allied states, with whom they carry on a commercial intercourse; yet these states never supposed, that by calling in her aid, they thereby submitted themselves to her sovereignty. Had such terms been proposed, they would have rejected them with disdain, and trusted for better to the moderation of their enemies, or to a vigorous exertion of their own force. We do not, however, mean to under-rate those aids, which to us were doubtless valuable, on whatever principles granted; but we would shew that they cannot give a title to that authority which the British parliament would arrogate over us, and that they may amply be repaid by our giving to the inhabitants of Great Britain such exclusive privileges in trade as may be advantageous to them, and at the same time not too restrictive to ourselves. That settlements having been thus effected in the wilds of America, the emigrants thought proper to adopt that system of laws under which they had hitherto lived in the mother country, and to continue their union with her by submitting themselves to the same common sovereign, who was thereby made the central link connecting the several parts of the empire thus newly multiplied.

But that not long were they permitted, however far they thought themselves removed from the hand of oppression, to hold undisturbed the rights thus acquired, at the hazard of their lives, and loss of their fortunes. A family of princes was then on the British throne, whose treasonable crimes against their people brought on them afterwards the exertion of those sacred and sovereign rights of punishment reserved in the hands of the people for cases of extreme necessity, and judged by the constitution unsafe to be delegated to any other judicature. While every day brought forth some new and unjustifiable exertion of power over their subjects on that side the water, it was not to be expected that those here, much less able at that time to oppose the designs of despotism, should be exempted from injury.

Accordingly that country, which had been acquired by the lives, the labours, and the fortunes, of individual adventurers, was by these princes, at several times, parted out and distributed among the favourites and followers of their fortunes, and, by an assumed right of the crown alone, were erected into distinct and independent governments; a measure which it is believed his majesty's prudence and understanding would prevent him from imitating at this day, as no exercise of such a power, of dividing and dismembering a country, has ever occurred in his majesty's realm of England, though now of very antient standing; nor could it be justified or acquiesced under there, or in any other part of his majesty's empire.

That the exercise of a free trade with all parts of the world, possessed by the American colonists, as of natural right, and which no law of their own had taken away or abridged, was next the object of unjust encroachment. Some of the colonies having thought proper to continue the administration of their government in the name and under the authority of his majesty king Charles the first, whom, notwithstanding his late deposition by the commonwealth of England, they continued in the sovereignty of their state; the parliament for the commonwealth took the same in high offence, and assumed upon themselves the power of prohibiting their trade with all other parts of the world, except the island of Great Britain. This arbitrary act, however, they soon recalled, and by solemn treaty, entered into on the 12th day of March, 1651, between the said commonwealth by their commissioners, and the colony of Virginia by their house of burgesses, it was expressly stipulated, by the 8th article of the said treaty, that they should have "free trade as the people of England do enjoy to all places and with all nations, according to the laws of that commonwealth." But that, upon the restoration of his majesty king Charles the second, their rights of free commerce fell once more a victim to arbitrary power; and by several acts of his reign, as well as of some of his successors, the trade of the colonies was laid under such restrictions, as shew what hopes they might form from the justice of a British parliament, were its uncontrouled power admitted over these states. History has informed us that bodies of men, as well as individuals, are susceptible of the spirit of tyranny. A view of these acts of parliament for regulation, as it has been affectedly called, of the American trade, if all other evidence were removed out of the case, would undeniably evince the truth of this observation. Besides the duties they impose on our articles of export and import, they prohibit our going to any markets northward of Cape Finesterre, in the kingdom of Spain, for the sale of commodities which Great Britain will not take from us, and for the purchase of others, with which she cannot supply us, and that for no other than the arbitrary purposes of purchasing for themselves, by a sacrifice of our rights and interests, certain privileges in their commerce with an allied state, who in confidence that their exclusive trade with America will be continued, while the principles and power of the British parliament be the same, have indulged themselves in every exorbitance which their avarice could dictate, or our necessities extort; have raised their commodities, called for in America, to the double and treble of what they sold for before such exclusive privileges were given them, and of what better commodities of the same kind would cost us elsewhere, and at the same time give us much less for what we carry thither than might be had at more convenient ports. That these acts prohibit us from carrying in quest of other purchasers the surplus of our tobaccoes remaining after the consumption of Great Britain is supplied; so that we must leave them with the British merchant for whatever he will please to allow us, to be by him reshipped to foreign markets, where he will reap the benefits of making sale of them for full value. That to heighten still the idea of parliamentary justice, and to shew with what moderation they are like to exercise power, where themselves are to feel no part of its weight, we take leave to mention to his majesty certain other acts of British parliament, by which they would prohibit us from manufacturing for our own use the articles we raise on our own lands with our own labour. By an act passed in the 5th Year of the reign of his late majesty king George the second, an American subject is forbidden to make a hat for himself of the fur which he has taken perhaps on his own soil; an instance of despotism to which no parallel can be produced in the most arbitrary ages of British history. By one other act, passed in the 23d year of the same reign, the iron which we make we are forbidden to manufacture, and heavy as that article is, and necessary in every branch of husbandry, besides commission and insurance, we are to pay freight for it to Great Britain, and freight for it back again, for the purpose of supporting not men, but machines, in the island of Great Britain. In the same spirit of equal and impartial legislation is to be viewed the act of parliament, passed in the 5th year of the same reign, by which American lands are made subject to the demands of British creditors, while their own lands were still continued unanswerable for their debts; from which one of these conclusions must necessarily follow, either that justice is not the same in America as in Britain, or else that the British parliament pay less regard to it here than there. But that we do not point out to his majesty the injustice of these acts, with intent to rest on that principle the cause of their nullity; but to shew that experience confirms the propriety of those political principles which exempt us from the jurisdiction of the British parliament. The true ground on which we declare these acts void is, that the British parliament has no right to exercise authority over us.

That these exercises of usurped power have not been confined to instances alone, in which themselves were interested, but they have also intermeddled with the regulation of the internal affairs of the colonies. The act of the 9th of Anne for establishing a post office in America seems to have had little connection with British convenience, except that of accommodating his majesty's ministers and favourites with the sale of a lucrative and easy office.

That thus have we hastened through the reigns which preceded his majesty's, during which the violations of our right were less alarming, because repeated at more distant intervals than that rapid and bold succession of injuries which is likely to distinguish the present from all other periods of American story. Scarcely have our minds been able to emerge from the astonishment into which one stroke of parliamentary thunder has involved us, before another more heavy, and more alarming, is fallen on us. Single acts of tyranny may be ascribed to the accidental opinion of a day; but a series of oppressions, begun at a distinguished period, and pursued unalterably through every change of ministers, too plainly prove a deliberate and systematical plan of reducing us to slavery.

That the act passed in the 4th year of his majesty's reign, intitled "An act for granting certain duties in the British colonies and plantations in America, &c."

One other act, passed in the 5th year of his reign, intitled "An act for granting and applying certain stamp duties and other duties in the British colonies and plantations in America, &c."

One other act, passed in the 6th year of his reign, intitled "An act for the better securing the dependency of his majesty's dominions in America upon the crown and parliament of Great Britain;" and one other act, passed in the 7th year of his reign, intitled "An act for granting duties on paper, tea, &c." form that connected chain of parliamentary usurpation, which has already been the subject of frequent applications to his majesty, and the houses of lords and commons of Great Britain; and no answers having yet been condescended to any of these, we shall not trouble his majesty with a repetition of the matters they contained.

But that one other act, passed in the same 7th year of the reign, having been a peculiar attempt, must ever require peculiar mention; it is intitled "An act for suspending the legislature of New York." One free and independent legislature hereby takes upon itself to suspend the powers of another, free and independent as itself; thus exhibiting a phoenomenon unknown in nature, the creator and creature of its own power. Not only the principles of common sense, but the common feelings of human nature, must be surrendered up before his majesty's subjects here can be persuaded to believe that they hold their political existence at the will of a British parliament. Shall these governments be dissolved, their property annihilated, and their people reduced to a state of nature, at the imperious breath of a body of men, whom they never saw, in whom they never confided, and over whom they have no powers of punishment or removal, let their crimes against the American public be ever so great? Can any one reason be assigned why 160,000 electors in the island of Great Britain should give law to four millions in the states of America, every individual of whom is equal to every individual of them, in virtue, in understanding, and in bodily strength? Were this to be admitted, instead of being a free people, as we have hitherto supposed, and mean to continue ourselves, we should suddenly be found the slaves, not of one, but of 160,000 tyrants, distinguished too from all others by this singular circumstance, that they are removed from the reach of fear, the only restraining motive which may hold the hand of a tyrant.

That by "an act to discontinue in such manner and for such time as are therein mentioned the landing and discharging, lading or shipping, of goods, wares, and merchandize, at the town and within the harbour of Boston, in the province of Massachusetts Bay, in North America," which was passed at the last session of British parliament; a large and populous town, whose trade was their sole subsistence, was deprived of that trade, and involved in utter ruin. Let us for a while suppose the question of right suspended, in order to examine this act on principles of justice: An act of parliament had been passed imposing duties on teas, to be paid in America, against which act the Americans had protested as inauthoritative. The East India company, who till that time had never sent a pound of tea to America on their own account, step forth on that occasion the assertors of parliamentary right, and send hither many ship loads of that obnoxious commodity. The masters of their several vessels, however, on their arrival in America, wisely attended to admonition, and returned with their cargoes. In the province of New England alone the remonstrances of the people were disregarded, and a compliance, after being many days waited for, was flatly refused. Whether in this the master of the vessel was governed by his obstinancy, or his instructions, let those who know, say. There are extraordinary situations which require extraordinary interposition. An exasperated people, who feel that they possess power, are not easily restrained within limits strictly regular. A number of them assembled in the town of Boston, threw the tea into the ocean, and dispersed without doing any other act of violence. If in this they did wrong, they were known and were amenable to the laws of the land, against which it could not be objected that they had ever, in any instance, been obstructed or diverted from their regular course in favour of popular offenders. They should therefore not have been distrusted on this occasion. But that ill fated colony had formerly been bold in their enmities against the house of Stuart, and were now devoted to ruin by that unseen hand which governs the momentous affairs of this great empire. On the partial representations of a few worthless ministerial dependents, whose constant office it has been to keep that government embroiled, and who, by their treacheries, hope to obtain the dignity of the British knighthood, without calling for a party accused, without asking a proof, without attempting a distinction between the guilty and the innocent, the whole of that antient and wealthy town is in a moment reduced from opulence to beggary. Men who had spent their lives in extending the British commerce, who had invested in that place the wealth their honest endeavours had merited, found themselves and their families thrown at once on the world for subsistence by its charities. Not the hundredth part of the inhabitants of that town had been concerned in the act complained of; many of them were in Great Britain and in other parts beyond sea; yet all were involved in one indiscriminate ruin, by a new executive power, unheard of till then, that of a British parliament. A property, of the value of many millions of money, was sacrificed to revenge, not repay, the loss of a few thousands. This is administering justice with a heavy hand indeed! and when is this tempest to be arrested in its course? Two wharfs are to be opened again when his majesty shall think proper. The residue which lined the extensive shores of the bay of Boston are forever interdicted the exercise of commerce. This little exception seems to have been thrown in for no other purpose than that of setting a precedent for investing his majesty with legislative powers. If the pulse of his people shall beat calmly under this experiment, another and another will be tried, till the measure of despotism be filled up. It would be an insult on common sense to pretend that this exception was made in order to restore its commerce to that great town. The trade which cannot be received at two wharfs alone must of necessity be transferred to some other place; to which it will soon be followed by that of the two wharfs. Considered in this light, it would be an insolent and cruel mockery at the annihilation of the town of Boston.

By the act for the suppression of riots and tumults in the town of Boston, passed also in the last session of parliament, a murder committed there is, if the governor pleases, to be tried in the court of King's Bench, in the island of Great Britain, by a jury of Middlesex. The witnesses, too, on receipt of such a sum as the governor shall think it reasonable for them to expend, are to enter into recognizance to appear at the trial. This is, in other words, taxing them to the amount of their recognizance, and that amount may be whatever a governor pleases; for who does his majesty think can be prevailed on to cross the Atlantic for the sole purpose of bearing evidence to a fact? His expences are to be borne, indeed, as they shall be estimated by a governor; but who are to feed the wife and children whom he leaves behind, and who have had no other subsistence but his daily labour? Those epidemical disorders, too, so terrible in a foreign climate, is the cure of them to be estimated among the articles of expence, and their danger to be warded off by the almighty power of parliament? And the wretched criminal, if he happen to have offended on the American side, stripped of his privilege of trial by peers of his vicinage, removed from the place where alone full evidence could be obtained, without money, without counsel, without friends, without exculpatory proof, is tried before judges predetermined to condemn. The cowards who would suffer a countryman to be torn from the bowels of their society, in order to be thus offered a sacrifice to parliamentary tyranny, would merit that everlasting infamy now fixed on the authors of the act! A clause for a similar purpose had been introduced into an act, passed in the 12th year of his majesty's reign, intitled "An act for the better securing and preserving his majesty's dockyards, magazines, ships, ammunition, and stores;" against which, as meriting the same censures, the several colonies have already protested.

That these are the acts of power, assumed by a body of men, foreign to our constitutions, and unacknowledged by our laws, against which we do, on behalf of the inhabitants of British America, enter this our solemn and determined protest; and we do earnestly entreat his majesty, as yet the only mediatory power between the several states of the British empire, to recommend to his parliament of Great Britain the total revocation of these acts, which, however nugatory they be, may yet prove the cause of further discontents and jealousies among us.

That we next proceed to consider the conduct of his majesty, as holding the executive powers of the laws of these states, and mark out his deviations from the line of duty: By the constitution of Great Britain, as well as of the several American states, his majesty possesses the power of refusing to pass into a law any bill which has already passed the other two branches of legislature. His majesty, however, and his ancestors, conscious of the impropriety of opposing their single opinion to the united wisdom of two houses of parliament, while their proceedings were unbiassed by interested principles, for several ages past have modestly declined the exercise of this power in that part of his empire called Great Britain. But by change of circumstances, other principles than those of justice simply have obtained an influence on their determinations; the addition of new states to the British empire has produced an addition of new, and sometimes opposite interests. It is now, therefore, the great office of his majesty, to resume the exercise of his negative power, and to prevent the passage of laws by any one legislature of the empire, which might bear injuriously on the rights and interests of another. Yet this will not excuse the wanton exercise of this power which we have seen his majesty practise on the laws of the American legislatures. For the most trifling reasons, and sometimes for no conceivable reason at all, his majesty has rejected laws of the most salutary tendency. The abolition of domestic slavery is the great object of desire in those colonies, where it was unhappily introduced in their infant state. But previous to the enfranchisement of the slaves we have, it is necessary to exclude all further importations from Africa; yet our repeated attempts to effect this by prohibitions, and by imposing duties which might amount to a prohibition, have been hitherto defeated by his majesty's negative: Thus preferring the immediate advantages of a few African corsairs to the lasting interests of the American states, and to the rights of human nature, deeply wounded by this infamous practice. Nay, the single interposition of an interested individual against a law was scarcely ever known to fail of success, though in the opposite scale were placed the interests of a whole country. That this is so shameful an abuse of a power trusted with his majesty for other purposes, as if not reformed, would call for some legal restrictions.

With equal inattention to the necessities of his people here has his majesty permitted our laws to lie neglected in England for years, neither confirming them by his assent, nor annulling them by his negative; so that such of them as have no suspending clause we hold on the most precarious of all tenures, his majesty's will, and such of them as suspend themselves till his majesty's assent be obtained, we have feared, might be called into existence at some future and distant period, when time, and change of circumstances, shall have rendered them destructive to his people here. And to render this grievance still more oppressive, his majesty by his instructions has laid his governors under such restrictions that they can pass no law of any moment unless it have such suspending clause; so that, however immediate may be the call for legislative interposition, the law cannot be executed till it has twice crossed the atlantic, by which time the evil may have spent its whole force.

But in what terms, reconcileable to majesty, and at the same time to truth, shall we speak of a late instruction to his majesty's governor of the colony of Virginia, by which he is forbidden to assent to any law for the division of a county, unless the new county will consent to have no representative in assembly? That colony has as yet fixed no boundary to the westward. Their western counties, therefore, are of indefinite extent; some of them are actually seated many hundred miles from their eastern limits. Is it possible, then, that his majesty can have bestowed a single thought on the situation of those people, who, in order to obtain justice for injuries, however great or small, must, by the laws of that colony, attend their county court, at such a distance, with all their witnesses, monthly, till their litigation be determined? Or does his majesty seriously wish, and publish it to the world, that his subjects should give up the glorious right of representation, with all the benefits derived from that, and submit themselves the absolute slaves of his sovereign will? Or is it rather meant to confine the legislative body to their present numbers, that they may be the cheaper bargain whenever they shall become worth a purchase.

One of the articles of impeachment against Tresilian, and the other judges of Westminister Hall, in the reign of Richard the second, for which they suffered death, as traitors to their country, was, that they had advised the king that he might dissolve his parliament at any time; and succeeding kings have adopted the opinion of these unjust judges. Since the establishment, however, of the British constitution, at the glorious revolution, on its free and antient principles, neither his majesty, nor his ancestors, have exercised such a power of dissolution in the island of Great Britain; and when his majesty was petitioned, by the united voice of his people there, to dissolve the present parliament, who had become obnoxious to them, his ministers were heard to declare, in open parliament, that his majesty possessed no such power by the constitution. But how different their language and his practice here! To declare, as their duty required, the known rights of their country, to oppose the usurpations of every foreign judicature, to disregard the imperious mandates of a minister or governor, have been the avowed causes of dissolving houses of representatives in America. But if such powers be really vested in his majesty, can he suppose they are there placed to awe the members from such purposes as these? When the representative body have lost the confidence of their constituents, when they have notoriously made sale of their most valuable rights, when they have assumed to themselves powers which the people never put into their hands, then indeed their continuing in office becomes dangerous to the state, and calls for an exercise of the power of dissolution. Such being the causes for which the representative body should, and should not, be dissolved, will it not appear strange to an unbiassed observer, that that of Great Britain was not dissolved, while those of the colonies have repeatedly incurred that sentence?

But your majesty, or your governors, have carried this power beyond every limit known, or provided for, by the laws: After dissolving one house of representatives, they have refused to call another, so that, for a great length of time, the legislature provided by the laws has been out of existence. From the nature of things, every society must at all times possess within itself the sovereign powers of legislation. The feelings of human nature revolt against the supposition of a state so situated as that it may not in any emergency provide against dangers which perhaps threaten immediate ruin. While those bodies are in existence to whom the people have delegated the powers of legislation, they alone possess and may exercise those powers; but when they are dissolved by the lopping off one or more of their branches, the power reverts to the people, who may exercise it to unlimited extent, either assembling together in person, sending deputies, or in any other way they may think proper. We forbear to trace consequences further; the dangers are conspicuous with which this practice is replete.

That we shall at this time also take notice of an error in the nature of our land holdings, which crept in at a very early period of our settlement. The introduction of the feudal tenures into the kingdom of England, though antient, is well enough understood to set this matter in a proper light. In the earlier ages of the Saxon settlement feudal holdings were certainly altogether unknown; and very few, if any, had been introduced at the time of the Norman conquest. Our Saxon ancestors held their lands, as they did their personal property, in absolute dominion, disencumbered with any superior, answering nearly to the nature of those possessions which the feudalists term allodial. William, the Norman, first introduced that system generally. The lands which had belonged to those who fell in the battle of Hastings, and in the subsequent insurrections of his reign, formed a considerable proportion of the lands of the whole kingdom. These he granted out, subject to feudal duties, as did he also those of a great number of his new subjects, who, by persuasions or threats, were induced to surrender them for that purpose. But still much was left in the hands of his Saxon subjects; held of no superior, and not subject to feudal conditions. These, therefore, by express laws, enacted to render uniform the system of military defence, were made liable to the same military duties as if they had been feuds; and the Norman lawyers soon found means to saddle them also with all the other feudal burthens. But still they had not been surrendered to the king, they were not derived from his grant, and therefore they were not holden of him. A general principle, indeed, was introduced, that "all lands in England were held either mediately or immediately of the crown," but this was borrowed from those holdings, which were truly feudal, and only applied to others for the purposes of illustration. Feudal holdings were therefore but exceptions out of the Saxon laws of possession, under which all lands were held in absolute right. These, therefore, still form the basis, or ground-work, of the common law, to prevail wheresoever the exceptions have not taken place. America was not conquered by William the Norman, nor its lands surrendered to him, or any of his successors. Possessions there are undoubtedly of the allodial nature. Our ancestors, however, who migrated hither, were farmers, not lawyers. The fictitious principle that all lands belong originally to the king, they were early persuaded to believe real; and accordingly took grants of their own lands from the crown. And while the crown continued to grant for small sums, and on reasonable rents; there was no inducement to arrest the error, and lay it open to public view. But his majesty has lately taken on him to advance the terms of purchase, and of holding to the double of what they were; by which means the acquisition of lands being rendered difficult, the population of our country is likely to be checked. It is time, therefore, for us to lay this matter before his majesty, and to declare that he has no right to grant lands of himself. From the nature and purpose of civil institutions, all the lands within the limits which any particular society has circumscribed around itself are assumed by that society, and subject to their allotment only. This may be done by themselves, assembled collectively, or by their legislature, to whom they may have delegated sovereign authority; and if they are alloted in neither of these ways, each individual of the society may appropriate to himself such lands as he finds vacant, and occupancy will give him title.

That in order to enforce the arbitrary measures before complained of, his majesty has from time to time sent among us large bodies of armed forces, not made up of the people here, nor raised by the authority of our laws: Did his majesty possess such a right as this, it might swallow up all our other rights whenever he should think proper. But his majesty has no right to land a single armed man on our shores, and those whom he sends here are liable to our laws made for the suppression and punishment of riots, routs, and unlawful assemblies; or are hostile bodies, invading us in defiance of law. When in the course of the late war it became expedient that a body of Hanoverian troops should be brought over for the defence of Great Britain, his majesty's grandfather, our late sovereign, did not pretend to introduce them under any authority he possessed. Such a measure would have given just alarm to his subjects in Great Britain, whose liberties would not be safe if armed men of another country, and of another spirit, might be brought into the realm at any time without the consent of their legislature. He therefore applied to parliament, who passed an act for that purpose, limiting the number to be brought in and the time they were to continue. In like manner is his majesty restrained in every part of the empire. He possesses, indeed, the executive power of the laws in every state; but they are the laws of the particular state which he is to administer within that state, and not those of any one within the limits of another. Every state must judge for itself the number of armed men which they may safely trust among them, of whom they are to consist, and under what restrictions they shall be laid.

To render these proceedings still more criminal against our laws, instead of subjecting the military to the civil powers, his majesty has expressly made the civil subordinate to the military. But can his majesty thus put down all law under his feet? Can he erect a power superior to that which erected himself? He has done it indeed by force; but let him remember that force cannot give right.

That these are our grievances which we have thus laid before his majesty, with that freedom of language and sentiment which becomes a free people claiming their rights, as derived from the laws of nature, and not as the gift of their chief magistrate: Let those flatter who fear; it is not an American art. To give praise which is not due might be well from the venal, but would ill beseem those who are asserting the rights of human nature. They know, and will therefore say, that kings are the servants, not the proprietors of the people. Open your breast, sire, to liberal and expanded thought. Let not the name of George the third be a blot in the page of history. You are surrounded by British counsellors, but remember that they are parties. You have no ministers for American affairs, because you have none taken from among us, nor amenable to the laws on which they are to give you advice. It behoves you, therefore, to think and to act for yourself and your people. The great principles of right and wrong are legible to every reader; to pursue them requires not the aid of many counsellors. The whole art of government consists in the art of being honest. Only aim to do your duty, and mankind will give you credit where you fail. No longer persevere in sacrificing the rights of one part of the empire to the inordinate desires of another; but deal out to all equal and impartial right. Let no act be passed by any one legislature which may infringe on the rights and liberties of another. This is the important post in which fortune has placed you, holding the balance of a great, if a well poised empire. This, sire, is the advice of your great American council, on the observance of which may perhaps depend your felicity and future fame, and the preservation of that harmony which alone can continue both to Great Britain and America the reciprocal advantages of their connection. It is neither our wish, nor our interest, to separate from her. We are willing, on our part, to sacrifice every thing which reason can ask to the restoration of that tranquillity for which all must wish. On their part, let them be ready to establish union and a generous plan. Let them name their terms, but let them be just. Accept of every commercial preference it is in our power to give for such things as we can raise for their use, or they make for ours. But let them not think to exclude us from going to other markets to dispose of those commodities which they cannot use, or to supply those wants which they cannot supply. Still less let it be proposed that our properties within our own territories shall be taxed or regulated by any power on earth but our own. The God who gave us life gave us liberty at the same time; the hand of force may destroy, but cannot disjoin them. This, sire, is our last, our determined resolution; and that you will be pleased to interpose with that efficacy which your earnest endeavours may ensure to procure redress of these our great grievances, to quiet the minds of your subjects in British America, against any apprehensions of future encroachment, to establish fraternal love and harmony through the whole empire, and that these may continue to the latest ages of time, is the fervent prayer of all British America!

The Declaration of Independence
(1776)

In retribution for (among other acts of civil disobedience) the Boston Tea Party, the British Parliament enacted a series of laws labeled by the colonists in Massachusetts as "the Intolerable Acts." The governor appointed by the Crown over the Massachusetts Bay Colony was also a military officer, General Thomas Gage. By 1775, Gage commanded a force of approximately 3,000 regular army troops, all headquartered in Boston.

Gage exercised effective control over Boston, but not over the remainder of the colony. Throughout the colony, in anticipation of armed action by the British army, the colonists had been forming and training militias. They had also begun stockpiling arms in two locations outside of Boston, one at Concord and another in Worcester. General Gage was aware of this and, with the concurrence of his superiors in Great Britain, he decided on a strategy of quick raids to seize the militias' arms, hoping thereby to neutralize opposition to British rule. Colonial sympathizers in Boston, however, were aware of the plans and arranged a system to notify the outlying areas of when a raid was expected to occur.

The crucial date was April 19, 1775. By that date, the colonials had removed most of the arms stored at Concord to various other locations where they hoped they would be safe from British confiscation. However, another concern was that the British wanted to arrest John Adams and John Hancock, two influential member of the opposition to the British repression of colonial rights. Both Adams and Hancock had fled from Boston and were deemed by the British as fugitives. They were living in Lexington, Massachusetts.

General Gage planned a secret expedition to Concord on the date of April 19. 1775. Spies in Boston learned of the plan and, on the night of April 18, Paul Revere and William Dawes set out on horseback by two different routes to warn the colonists between Boston and Lexington of an impending expedition by the British. Adams and Hancock were removed to a safer location, but the colonials felt that the number of troops reportedly being readied for the raid was far more than would be needed to arrest two men, and they correctly concluded that the objective was probably the arms the British believed were still stored at Concord.

Approximately 700 British regulars set out from Boston early on the morning of April 19, 1775. They crossed the Charles River by boat, then set out on foot for Lexington and Concord in the middle of the night. While the British were marching, messengers were spreading out throughout the countryside around

Boston to call out the local militias. The response was overwhelming; by late in the day, more than 4,000 militiamen had responded to the call.

Early on the morning of April 19, as the first elements of the British expedition approached Lexington, the colonials did not have a large number of armed men. The captain of the local militia ordered his men to muster on the town common but not to engage the British unless the British fired first. What happened as the British entered Lexington has never been determined with any degree of certainty. *Someone* (it is still not known if it was a British soldier, a militiaman, or someone who was not among the forces facing one another, fired a shot. This caused the British to open fire, and then to charge the colonials with fixed bayonets. The final tally was that the British killed eight men and wounded another ten. The British suffered only one casualty.

The British force then proceeded to Concord, in search of the colonists' arms supplies. When they first arrived at Concord, the British outnumbered the militia forces and the militiamen fell back to a location from which they could observe the British activities. The British found and heavily damaged a few cannons, but most of the arms they had expected to confiscate had already been moved and hidden. However, during the time the British were conducting their search, additional militiamen continued to arrive from surrounding towns, eventually amounting to a force of approximately 4,000 men.

The initial fire fight between the British and the militia at Concord resulted in several people from both sides being killed or wounded. The unexpected resistance–and its effectiveness–caused the British to withdraw into the town of Concord itself, and then to begin the march back to Boston. By this time, however, the number of colonial defenders had grown significantly. Various groups of militia staged ambushes all along the route from Concord back to Lexington, and additional groups of militia continued to ambush and harass the British all the way back to Charlestown. The final tally was 49 killed, 39 wounded, and 5 missing on the colonial side, compared to 73 killed, 174 wounded, and 53 missing on the British side.

The next day, Boston was surrounded by a force of 15,000 armed militiamen from as far away as Rhode Island and Connecticut.

The American Revolution had begun.

* * * * *

In the aftermath of the Boston Tea Party, the colonies had convened the First Continental Congress, which had drafted a petition to the King of England asking for relief from their grievances. That petition was ignored. Following the battle of Lexington and Concord, a Second Continental Congress convened in May of 1775, in Philadelphia. The Second Continental Congress drafted another petition to the King, again seeking relief from what the colonists viewed as unconstitutional infringements on their rights as subjects of the British Crown. That petition was also rejected by the King. The King responded on August 23, 1775, by issuing a Proclamation of Rebellion. The Second Continental Congress replied to this on December 6, 1775, arguing that they were loyal subjects of the Crown but that the Parliament had no authority over the colonies because the colonies were not represented in the Parliament.

The Second Continental Congress continued to meet through the end of 1775 and into 1776. Initially, although a relatively small number of colonists and of delegates to the Continental Congress favored separating entirely from England, the Congress did not have the authority to go to that extreme. Some of the thirteen colonies had not given their delegates authority to do more than attempt to negotiate with the British government, and some of the colonies had expressly instructed their delegates not to engage in discussions of independence from Great Britain.

The British, on their part, failed to understand their adversaries. King George increased the number of soldiers in the colonies, attempting to crush what he regarded as a rebellion by sheer force of numbers. Parliament, on its part, adopted in late 1775 a new law called the Prohibitory Act. The Prohibitory Act included two provisions that had the effect of virtually ensuring that the colonies would sever their relationship to the Crown.

First, the Act established an economic blockade of the colonies. Americans were forbidden to conduct trade with any nation, and the British navy was ordered to seize any American merchant ship found to be carrying trade goods. Under the provisions of international law at the time, this amounted to a declaration of war. Secondly, the Prohibitory Act declared that the colonies were thereafter "outside the King's protection." In other words, the colonies were outlaws.

From that point forward, the colonies had no reason to continue their efforts to remain loyal to the Crown. The view among the colonies and at the Continental Congress was that they had not asked for independence, but that independence had been forced upon them. John Adams (the future President of the United States) wrote: "It throws thirteen colonies out of the royal protection, levels all distinctions, and makes us independent in spite of our supplications and entreaties.... It may be fortunate that the act of independency should come from the British Parliament rather than the American Congress."[1]

During the early months of 1776, many of the colonies modified their instructions to their delegations at the Continental Congress, authorizing a vote in favor of independence from Great Britain. By late June of 1776 the only colony that had not voted to declare independence was New York. In New York, the military occupation of New York forced their Provincial Congress to adjourn and to escape from the city. This left New York without binding instructions to its delegation; New York did not expressly approve the concept of a declaration of independence until after the document had been finalized.

In June of 1776 the Continental Congress appointed a committee to draw up a draft of a document declaring the colonies independent of Great Britain.

---

[1] John Adams to Horatio Gates, March 23, 1776.
https://founders.archives.gov/documents/Adams/06-04-02-0023

Although the committee consisted of five people (John Adams, Benjamin Franklin, Thomas Jefferson, Robert Livingston, and Roger Sherman), it was Thomas Jefferson who was given the task of writing the first draft. His first draft was reviewed within the committee, revisions were suggested and made, and a revised draft was completed and presented to the Continental Congress on June 28, 1776.

After revisions proposed by the full assembly and considerable political maneuvering, the Declaration of Independence was approved by the Second Continental Congress on July 2, 1776. New York abstained because its delegates had not yet received authorization to vote for independence, but the authorization was issued a week later, making the vote unanimous.

The Declaration of Independence is now associated with the date of July 4, 1776, not because that was the date it was initially approved but because July 4 was the date the declaration, with some final revisions by the assembly, was formally issued.

* * * * *

Reading the itemized tabulation of complaints against England, it is impossible not to observe that many of the complaints echo similar complaints found in earlier documents from the history of England, such as the Petition of Rights and the English Bill of Rights.

The Full Text of the Declaration of Independence (1776)

In CONGRESS, July 4, 1776
The unanimous DECLARATION of the thirteen united STATES OF AMERICA

When in the Course of human events, it becomes necessary for one people to dissolve the political bands which have connected them with another, and to assume among the powers of the earth, the separate and equal station to which the Laws of Nature and of Nature's God entitle them, a decent respect to the opinions of mankind requires that they should declare the causes which impel them to the separation.

We hold these truths to be self-evident, that all men are created equal, that they are endowed by their Creator with certain unalienable Rights, that among these are Life, Liberty and the pursuit of Happiness.–That to secure these rights, Governments are instituted among Men, deriving their just powers from the consent of the governed, –That whenever any Form of Government becomes destructive of these ends, it is the Right of the People to alter or to abolish it, and to institute new Government, laying its foundation on such principles and organizing its powers in such form, as to them shall seem most likely to effect their Safety and Happiness. Prudence, indeed, will dictate that Governments long established should not be changed for light and transient causes; and accordingly all experience hath shewn, that mankind are more disposed to suffer, while evils are sufferable, than to right themselves by abolishing the forms to which they are accustomed. But when a long train of abuses and usurpations, pursuing invariably the same Object evinces a design to reduce them under absolute Despotism, it is their right, it is their duty, to throw off such Government, and to provide new Guards for their future security.–Such has been the patient sufferance of these Colonies; and such is now the necessity which constrains them to alter their former Systems of Government. The history of the present King of Great Britain is a history of repeated injuries and usurpations, all having in direct object the establishment of an absolute Tyranny over these States. To prove this, let Facts be submitted to a candid world.

He has refused his Assent to Laws, the most wholesome and necessary for the public good.

He has forbidden his Governors to pass Laws of immediate and pressing importance, unless suspended in their operation till his Assent should be obtained; and when so suspended, he has utterly neglected to attend to them.

He has refused to pass other Laws for the accommodation of large districts of people, unless those people would relinquish the right of Representation in the Legislature, a right inestimable to them and formidable to tyrants only.

He has called together legislative bodies at places unusual, uncomfortable, and distant from the depository of their public Records, for the sole purpose of fatiguing them into compliance with his measures.

He has dissolved Representative Houses repeatedly, for opposing with manly firmness his invasions on the rights of the people.

He has refused for a long time, after such dissolutions, to cause others to be elected; whereby the Legislative powers, incapable of Annihilation, have returned to the People at large for their exercise; the State remaining in the mean time exposed to all the dangers of invasion from without, and convulsions within.

He has endeavoured to prevent the population of these States; for that purpose obstructing the Laws for Naturalization of Foreigners; refusing to pass others to encourage their migrations hither, and raising the conditions of new Appropriations of Lands.

He has obstructed the Administration of Justice, by refusing his Assent to Laws for establishing Judiciary powers.

He has made Judges dependent on his Will alone, for the tenure of their offices, and the amount and payment of their salaries.

He has erected a multitude of New Offices, and sent hither swarms of Officers to harrass our people, and eat out their substance.

He has kept among us, in times of peace, Standing Armies without the Consent of our legislatures.

He has affected to render the Military independent of and superior to the Civil power.

He has combined with others to subject us to a jurisdiction foreign to our constitution, and unacknowledged by our laws; giving his Assent to their Acts of pretended Legislation:

For Quartering large bodies of armed troops among us:

For protecting them, by a mock Trial, from punishment for any Murders which they should commit on the Inhabitants of these States:

For cutting off our Trade with all parts of the world:

For imposing Taxes on us without our Consent:

For depriving us in many cases, of the benefits of Trial by Jury:

For transporting us beyond Seas to be tried for pretended offences

For abolishing the free System of English Laws in a neighbouring Province, establishing therein an Arbitrary government, and enlarging its Boundaries so as to render it at once an example and fit instrument for introducing the same absolute rule into these Colonies:

For taking away our Charters, abolishing our most valuable Laws, and altering fundamentally the Forms of our Governments:

For suspending our own Legislatures, and declaring themselves invested with power to legislate for us in all cases whatsoever.

He has abdicated Government here, by declaring us out of his Protection and waging War against us.

He has plundered our seas, ravaged our Coasts, burnt our towns, and destroyed the lives of our people.

He is at this time transporting large Armies of foreign Mercenaries to compleat the works of death, desolation and tyranny, already begun with circumstances of Cruelty & perfidy scarcely paralleled in the most barbarous ages, and totally unworthy the Head of a civilized nation.

He has constrained our fellow Citizens taken Captive on the high Seas to bear Arms against their Country, to become the executioners of their friends and Brethren, or to fall themselves by their Hands.

He has excited domestic insurrections amongst us, and has endeavoured to bring on the inhabitants of our frontiers, the merciless Indian Savages, whose known rule of warfare, is an undistinguished destruction of all ages, sexes and conditions.

In every stage of these Oppressions We have Petitioned for Redress in the most humble terms: Our repeated Petitions have been answered only by repeated injury. A Prince whose character is thus marked by every act which may define a Tyrant, is unfit to be the ruler of a free people.

Nor have We been wanting in attentions to our Brittish brethren. We have warned them from time to time of attempts by their legislature to extend an unwarrantable jurisdiction over us. We have reminded them of the circumstances of our emigration and settlement here. We have appealed to their native justice and magnanimity, and we have conjured them by the ties of our common kindred to disavow these usurpations, which, would inevitably interrupt our connections and correspondence. They too have been deaf to the voice of justice and of consanguinity. We must, therefore, acquiesce in the necessity, which denounces our Separation, and hold them, as we hold the rest of mankind, Enemies in War, in Peace Friends.

We, therefore, the Representatives of the united States of America, in General Congress, Assembled, appealing to the Supreme Judge of the world for the rectitude of our intentions, do, in the Name, and by Authority of the good People of these Colonies, solemnly publish and declare, That these United Colonies are, and of Right ought to be Free and Independent States; that they are Absolved from all Allegiance to the British Crown, and that all political connection between them and the State of Great Britain, is and ought to be totally dissolved; and that as Free and Independent States, they have full Power to levy War, conclude Peace, contract Alliances, establish Commerce, and to do all other Acts and Things which Independent States may of right do. And for the support of this Declaration, with a firm reliance on the protection of divine Providence, we mutually pledge to each other our Lives, our Fortunes and our sacred Honor.

Georgia
Button Gwinnett
Lyman Hall
George Walton

North Carolina
William Hooper
Joseph Hewes
John Penn

South Carolina
Edward Rutledge
Thomas Heyward, Jr.
Thomas Lynch, Jr.
Arthur Middleton

Massachusetts
John Hancock

Maryland
Samuel Chase
William Paca
Thomas Stone
Charles Carroll of Carrollton

Virginia
George Wythe
Richard Henry Lee
Thomas Jefferson
Benjamin Harrison
Thomas Nelson, Jr.
Francis Lightfoot Lee
Carter Braxton

Pennsylvania
Robert Morris
Benjamin Rush
Benjamin Franklin
John Morton
George Clymer
James Smith
George Taylor
James Wilson
George Ross

Delaware
Caesar Rodney
George Read
Thomas McKean

New York
William Floyd
Philip Livingston
Francis Lewis
Lewis Morris

New Jersey
Richard Stockton
John Witherspoon
Francis Hopkinson
John Hart
Abraham Clark

New Hampshire
Josiah Bartlett
William Whipple

Massachusetts
Samuel Adams
John Adams
Robert Treat Paine
Elbridge Gerry

Rhode Island
Stephen Hopkins
William Ellery

Connecticut
Roger Sherman
Samuel Huntington
William Williams
Oliver Wolcott

New Hampshire
Matthew Thornton

The Articles of Confederation
(1777)

The original version of the document Americans now known as the Constitution of the United States was not, in fact, the first agreement among the colonies in their quest to establish self-government, independent of Great Britain and the Parliament. The first attempt, the Articles of Confederation, was drafted in 1777 but was not adopted until almost four years later, being ratified on March 1, 1781.

The problem then was the same problem faced by the drafters of the second United States Constitution: the struggle to balance the rights and independence of the individual states against the need for some functions of the government to be centralized. During the later debates over adoption of the United States Constitution, this debate played out in print in the forum of the Federalist Papers and the Anti-Federalist Papers. At the time of the drafting and ratification of the Articles of Confederation, however, the debate simply meant that the process took a long time.

The Articles of Confederation went through six drafts, with the first being written by Benjamin Franklin in 1775. A year later, after two other drafts had failed to gain significant support, a fourth draft was written, by John Dickinson of Pennsylvania. The Dickinson draft was presented to the Congress in June of 1777. His first draft went through revisions in July and August of 1777, resulting in a second draft that was presented to the full Congress. After additional debate and more revisions, a final draft was created and printed in November of 1777. This final draft was approved for submission to the states for ratification.

Ratification of the Articles of Confederation was delayed due to conflicting land claims. Several of the states claimed that their lands extended as far west as the Mississippi River or the western ocean. Other states' western limits were restricted to a few hundred miles west from the Atlantic Ocean. Maryland was landlocked, with no possibility of westward expansion. Because of this, Maryland declined to ratify the Articles of Confederation because of a [justifiable] concern that other states westward expansion could potentially dwarf Maryland's significance in the confederation.

There was no way for Maryland to expand to the west because Virginia already extended northerly along the western border of Maryland, forming an absolute block to any possibility of westward expansion for Maryland. Consequently, Maryland and the other states whose western expansion was limited by their charters feared the potential future inequity of allowing some states virtually unlimited westward expansion.

The deadlock was broken in 1781 when Thomas Jefferson proposed a compromise, under which Virginia would surrender its westward expansion claims if the other states would do likewise, and all lands lying west of the original colonies/states would belong to the United States—with the understanding that the western lands could eventually be formed into new states, which would then be allowed to enter into the confederation. This compromise was successful, and the Articles of Confederation was finally ratified and became effective as of March 321, 1781.

The Articles of Confederation were a start, but an imperfect start. The document was flawed in several important respects. First, it made no provision for a national executive branch or for a national judiciary. The only branch of the federal government was the Congress, and the Congress had no authority to impose taxes or to regulate interstate commerce. The Congress itself was to serve as the arbitrator in disputes between or among the individual states.

The Articles of Confederation did provide for the federal government to mint money, to establish a postal service, to raise and army and a navy, and to enter into treaties with other nations.

The Articles of Confederation were as much a contract as they were a constitution. By this, it means that the nature of the new government was explicitly one of a collective of individual states, and the Articles made clear that the Congress held no powers other than those expressly established and granted to it under the provisions of the Articles of Confederation. The intent of this was carried through into the Constitution of the United States of America in 1788.

While the Articles of Confederation did not address an individual or collective right to keep and bear arms, they did provide precursors to several other provisions which subsequently found their way into the Constitution of the United States, such as:

- Article IV includes a full faith and credit clause, which is also found in Article 4, Section 1 of the Constitution.
- Article IV also includes a rights and privileges clause, which is found in Article 4, Section 2 of the Constitution.
- Freedom of speech is address in Article V of the Articles of Confederation, but only with respect to debates in the Congress.
- Article IX, paragraph 5 addresses raising, equipping, and paying for military forces but does not address the militias of the several states, or individual rights to keep and bear arms.

As imperfect as they were, the Articles of Confederation were the first constitution of the United States.

Full Text of the Articles of Confederation (1777)

To all to whom these Presents shall come, we the undersigned Delegates of the States affixed to our Names send greeting.

Whereas the Delegates of the United States of America in Congress assembled did on the fifteenth day of November in the Year of our Lord One Thousand Seven Hundred and Seventyseven, and in the Second Year of the Independence of America agree to certain articles of Confederation and perpetual Union between the States of Newhampshire, Massachusettsbay, Rhodeisland and Providence Plantations, Connecticut, New York, New Jersey, Pennsylvania, Delaware, Maryland, Virginia, North-Carolina, South-Carolina and Georgia in the Words following, viz.

"*Articles of Confederation and perpetual Union between the States of Newhampshire, Massachusettsbay, Rhodeisland and Providence Plantations, Connecticut, New-York, New-Jersey, Pennsylvania, Delaware, Maryland, Virginia, North-Carolina, South-Carolina and Georgia.*

ARTICLE I. The stile of this confederacy shall be "The United States of America."

ARTICLE II. Each State retains its sovereignty, freedom and independence, and every power, jurisdiction and right, which is not by this confederation expressly delegated to the United States, in Congress assembled.

ARTICLE III. The said States hereby severally enter into a firm league of friendship with each other, for their common defence, the security of their liberties, and their mutual and general welfare, binding themselves to assist each other, against all force offered to, or attacks made upon them, or any of them, on account of religion, sovereignty, trade, or any other pretence whatever.

ARTICLE IV. The better to secure and perpetuate mutual friendship and intercourse among the people of the different States in this Union, the free inhabitants of each of these States, paupers, vagabonds and fugitives from justice excepted, shall be entitled to all privileges and immunities of free citizens in the several States; and the people of each State shall have free ingress and regress to and from any other State, and shall enjoy therein all the privileges of trade and commerce, subject to the same duties, impositions and restrictions as the inhabitants thereof respectively, provided that such restrictions shall not extend so far as to prevent the removal of property imported into any State, to any other State of which the owner is an inhabitant; provided also that no imposition, duties or restriction shall be laid by any State, on the property of the United States, or either of them. If any person guilty of, or charged with treason, felony, or other high misdemeanor in any State, shall flee from justice, and be found in any of the United States, he shall upon demand of the Governor or Executive power, of the State from which he fled, be delivered up and removed to the State having jurisdiction of his offence. Full faith and credit shall be given in each of these States to the records, acts and judicial proceedings of the courts and magistrates of every other State.

ARTICLE V. For the more convenient management of the general interests of the United States, delegates shall be annually appointed in such manner as the legislature of each State shall direct, to meet in Congress on the first Monday in November, in every year, with a power reserved to each State, to recall its delegates, or any of them, at any time within the year, and to send others in their stead, for the remainder of the year.

No State shall be represented in Congress by less than two, nor by more than seven members; and no person shall be capable of being a delegate for more than three years in any term of six years; nor shall any person, being a delegate, be capable of holding any office under the United States, for which he, or another for his benefit receives any salary, fees or emolument of any kind.

Each State shall maintain its own delegates in a meeting of the States, and while they act as members of the committee of the States.

In determining questions in the United States, in Congress assembled, each State shall have one vote.

Freedom of speech and debate in Congress shall not be impeached or questioned in any court, or place out of Congress, and the members of Congress shall be protected in their persons from arrests and imprisonments, during the time of their going to and from, and attendance on Congress, except for treason, felony, or breach of the peace.

ARTICLE VI. No State without the consent of the United States in Congress assembled, shall send any embassy to, or receive any embassy from, or enter into any conference, agreement, alliance or treaty with any king, prince or state; nor shall any person holding any office of profit or trust under the United States, or any of them, accept of any present, emolument, office or title of any kind whatever from any king, prince or foreign state; nor shall the United States in Congress assembled, or any of them, grant any title of nobility.

No two or more States shall enter into any treaty, confederation or alliance whatever between them, without the consent of the United States in Congress assembled, specifying accurately the purposes for which the same is to be entered into, and how long it shall continue.

No State shall lay any imposts or duties, which may interfere with any stipulations in treaties, entered into by the United States in Congress assembled, with any king, prince or state, in pursuance of any treaties already proposed by Congress, to the courts of France and Spain.

No vessels of war shall be kept up in time of peace by any State, except such number only, as shall be deemed necessary by the United States in Congress assembled, for the defence of such State, or its trade; nor shall any body of forces be kept up by any State, in time of peace, except such number only, as in the judgment of the United States, in Congress assembled, shall be deemed requisite to garrison the forts necessary for the defence of such State; but every State shall always keep up a well regulated and disciplined militia, sufficiently armed and accoutered, and shall provide and constantly have ready for use, in public stores, a due number of field pieces and tents, and a proper quantity of arms, ammunition and camp equipage.

No State shall engage in any war without the consent of the United States in Congress assembled, unless such State be actually invaded by enemies, or shall have received certain advice of a resolution being formed by some nation of Indians to invade such State, and the danger is so imminent as not to admit of a delay, till the United States in Congress assembled can be consulted: nor shall any State grant commissions to any ships or vessels of war, nor letters of marque or reprisal, except it be after a declaration of war by the United States in Congress assembled, and then only against the kingdom or state and the subjects thereof, against which war has been so declared, and under such regulations as shall be established by the United States in Congress assembled, unless such State be infested by pirates, in which case vessels of war may be fitted out for that occasion, and kept so long as the danger shall continue or until the United States in Congress assembled shall determine otherwise.

ARTICLE VII. When land-forces are raised by any State for the common defence, all officers of or under the rank of colonel, shall be appointed by the Legislature of each State respectively by whom such forces shall be raised, or in such manner as such State shall direct, and all vacancies shall be filled up by the State which first made the appointment.

ARTICLE VIII. All charges of war, and all other expenses that shall be incurred for the common defence or general welfare, and allowed by the United States in Congress assembled, shall be defrayed out of a common treasury, which shall be supplied by the several States, in proportion to the value of all land within each State, granted to or surveyed for any person, as such land and the buildings and improvements thereon shall be estimated according to such mode as the United States in Congress assembled, shall from time to time direct and appoint.

The taxes for paying that proportion shall be laid and levied by the authority and direction of the Legislatures of the several States within the time agreed upon by the United States in Congress assembled.

ARTICLE IX. The United States in Congress assembled, shall have the sole and exclusive right and power of determining on peace and war, except in the cases mentioned in the sixth article—of sending and receiving ambassadors—entering into treaties and alliances, provided that no treaty of commerce shall be made whereby the legislative power of the respective States shall be restrained from imposing such imposts and duties on foreigners, as their own people are subjected to, or from prohibiting the exportation or importation of any species of goods or commodities whatsoever—of establishing rules for deciding in all cases, what captures on land or water shall be legal, and in what manner prizes taken by land or naval forces in the service of the United States shall be divided or appropriated—of granting letters of marque and reprisal in times of peace—appointing courts for the trial of piracies and felonies committed on the high seas and establishing courts for receiving and determining finally appeals in all cases of captures, provided that no member of Congress shall be appointed a judge of any of the said courts.

The United States in Congress assembled shall also be the last resort on appeal in all disputes and differences now subsisting or that hereafter may arise between two or more States concerning boundary, jurisdiction or any other cause whatever; which authority shall always be exercised in the manner following. Whenever the legislative or executive authority or lawful agent of any State in controversy with another shall present a petition to Congress, stating the matter in question and praying for a hearing, notice thereof shall be given by order of Congress to the legislative or executive authority of the other State in controversy, and a day assigned for the appearance of the parties by their lawful agents, who shall then be directed to appoint by joint consent, commissioners or judges to constitute a court for hearing and determining the matter in question: but if they cannot agree, Congress shall name three persons out of each of the United States, and from the list of such persons each party shall alternately strike out one, the petitioners beginning, until the number shall be reduced to thirteen; and from that number not less than seven, nor more than nine names as Congress shall direct, shall in the presence of Congress be drawn out by lot, and the persons whose names shall be so drawn or any five of them, shall be commissioners or judges, to hear and finally determine the controversy, so always as a major part of the judges who shall hear the cause shall agree in the determination: and if either party shall neglect to attend at the day appointed, without showing reasons, which Congress shall judge sufficient, or being present shall refuse to strike, the Congress shall proceed to nominate three persons out of each State, and the Secretary of Congress shall strike in behalf of such party absent or refusing; and the judgment and sentence of the court to be appointed, in the manner before prescribed, shall be final and conclusive; and if any of the parties shall refuse to submit to the authority of such court, or to appear or defend their claim or cause, the court shall nevertheless proceed to pronounce sentence, or judgment, which shall in like manner be final and decisive, the judgment or sentence and other proceedings being in either case transmitted to Congress, and lodged among the acts of Congress for the security of the parties concerned: provided that every commissioner, before he sits in judgment, shall take an oath to be administered by one of the judges of the supreme or superior court of the State where the cause shall be tried, "well and truly to hear and determine the matter in question, according to the best of his judgment, without favour, affection or hope of reward:" provided also that no State shall be deprived of territory for the benefit of the United States.

All controversies concerning the private right of soil claimed under different grants of two or more States, whose jurisdiction as they may respect such lands, and the States which passed such grants are adjusted, the said grants or either of them being at the same time claimed to have originated antecedent to such settlement of jurisdiction, shall on the petition of either party to the Congress of the United States, be finally determined as near as may be in the same manner as is before prescribed for deciding disputes respecting territorial jurisdiction between different States.

The United States in Congress assembled shall also have the sole and exclusive right and power of regulating the alloy and value of coin struck by their own authority, or by that of the respective States.—fixing the standard of weights and measures throughout the United States.—regulating the trade and managing all affairs with the Indians, not members of any of the States, provided that the legislative right of any State within its own limits be not infringed or violated—establishing and regulating post-offices from one State to another, throughout all the United States, and exacting such postage on the papers passing thro' the same as may be requisite to defray the expenses of the said office—appointing all officers of the land forces, in the service of the United States, excepting regimental officers—appointing all the officers of the naval forces, and commissioning all officers whatever in the service of the United States—making rules for the government and regulation of the said land and naval forces, and directing their operations.

The United States in Congress assembled shall have authority to appoint a committee, to sit in the recess of Congress, to be denominated "a Committee of the States", and to consist of one delegate from each State; and to appoint such other committees and civil officers as may be necessary for managing the general affairs of the United States under their direction—to appoint one of their number to preside, provided that no person be allowed to serve in the office of president more than one year in any term of three years; to ascertain the necessary sums of money to be raised for the service of the United States, and to appropriate and apply the same for defraying the public expenses—to borrow money, or emit bills on the credit of the United States, transmitting every half year to the respective States an account of the sums of money so borrowed or emitted,—to build and equip a navy—to agree upon the number of land forces, and to make requisitions from each State for its quota, in proportion to the number of white inhabitants in such State; which requisition shall be binding, and thereupon the Legislature of each State shall appoint the regimental officers, raise the men and cloath, arm and equip them in a soldier like manner, at the expense of the United States; and the officers and men so cloathed, armed and equipped shall march to the place appointed, and within the time agreed on by the United States in Congress assembled: but if the United States in Congress assembled shall, on consideration of circumstances judge proper that any State should not raise men, or should raise a smaller number than its quota, and that any other State should raise a greater number of men than the quota thereof, such extra number shall be raised, officered, cloathed, armed and equipped in the same manner as the quota of such State, unless the legislature of such State shall judge that such extra number cannot be safely spared out of the same, in which case they shall raise, officer, cloath, arm and equip as many of such extra number as they judge can be safely spared. And the officers and men so cloathed, armed and equipped, shall march to the place appointed, and within the time agreed on by the United States in Congress assembled.

The United States in Congress assembled shall never engage in a war, nor grant letters of marque and reprisal in time of peace, nor enter into any treaties or alliances, nor coin money, nor regulate the value thereof, nor ascertain the sums and expenses necessary for the defence and welfare of the United States, or any of them, nor emit bills, nor borrow money on the credit of the United States, nor appropriate money, nor agree upon the number of vessels of war, to be built or purchased, or the number of land or sea forces to be raised, nor appoint a commander in chief of the army or navy, unless nine States assent to the same; nor shall a question on any other point, except for adjourning from day to day be determined, unless by the votes of a majority of the United States in Congress assembled.

The Congress of the United States shall have power to adjourn to any time within the year, and to any place within the United States, so that no period of adjournment be for a longer duration than the space of six months, and shall publish the journal of their proceedings monthly, except such parts thereof relating to treaties, alliances or military operations, as in their judgment require secresy; and the yeas and nays of the delegates of each State on any question shall be entered on the journal, when it is desired by any delegate; and the delegates of a State, or any of them, at his or their request shall be furnished with a transcript of the said journal, except such parts as are above excepted, to lay before the Legislatures of the several States.

ARTICLE X. The committee of the States, or any nine of them, shall be authorized to execute, in the recess of Congress, such of the powers of Congress as the United States in Congress assembled, by the consent of nine States, shall from time to time think expedient to vest them with; provided that no power be delegated to the said committee, for the exercise of which, by the articles of confederation, the voice of nine States in the Congress of the United States assembled is requisite.

ARTICLE XI. Canada acceding to this confederation, and joining in the measures of the United States, shall be admitted into, and entitled to all the advantages of this Union: but no other colony shall be admitted into the same, unless such admission be agreed to by nine States.

ARTICLE XII. All bills of credit emitted, monies borrowed and debts contracted by, or under the authority of Congress, before the assembling of the United States, in pursuance of the present confederation, shall be deemed and considered as a charge against the United States, for payment and satisfaction whereof the said United States, and the public faith are hereby solemnly pledged.

ARTICLE XIII. Every State shall abide by the determinations of the United States in Congress assembled, on all questions which by this confederation are submitted to them. And the articles of this confederation shall be inviolably observed by every State, and the Union shall be perpetual; nor shall any alteration at any time hereafter be made in any of them; unless such alteration be agreed to in a Congress of the United States, and be afterwards confirmed by the Legislatures of every State.

And whereas it has pleased the Great Governor of the world to incline the hearts of the Legislatures we respectively represent in Congress, to approve of, and to authorize us to ratify the said articles of confederation and perpetual union.

Know ye that we the undersigned delegates, by virtue of the power and authority to us given for that purpose, do by these presents, in the name and in behalf of our respective constituents, fully and entirely ratify and confirm each and every of the said articles of confederation and perpetual union, and all and singular the matters and things therein contained: and we do further solemnly plight and engage the faith of our respective constituents, that they shall abide by the determinations of the United States in Congress assembled, on all questions, which by the said confederation are submitted to them. And that the articles thereof shall be inviolably observed by the States we re[s]pectively represent, and that the Union shall be perpetual.

In witness whereof we have hereunto set our hands in Congress. Done at Philadelphia in the State of Pennsylvania the ninth day of July in the year of our Lord one thousand seven hundred and seventy-eight, and in the third year of the independence of America.

On the part & behalf of the State of New Hampshire

Josiah Bartlett

John Wentworth, Junr.
August 8th, 1778.

On the part and behalf of the State of Massachusetts Bay

John Hancock
Samuel Adams
Elbridge Gerry
Francis Dana
James Lovell
Samuel Holten

On the part & behalf of the State of Rhode Island And Providence Plantations

William Ellery
Henry Marchant
John Collins

On the part & behalf of the State of Connecticut

Roger Sherman
Samuel Huntington
Oliver Wolcott
Titus Hosmer
Andrew Adams

On the part & behalf of the State of New York

Jas. Duane
Fra. Lewis
Wm. Duer
Gouv. Morris

On the part & behalf of the State of New Jersey Novr. 26, 1778

Jno. Witherspoon
Nathl. Scudder

On the part & behalf of the State of Pennsylvania

Robt. Morris
Daniel Robardeau
Jonah Bayard Smith
William Clingan
Joseph Reed, 22d July, 1778

On the part & behalf of the State of Delaware

Tho. M'Kean Feby. 12, 1779
John Dickinson May 5, 1779
Nicholas Van Dyke

On the part & behalf of the State of Maryland

John Hanson March 1, 1781
Daniel Carroll March 1, 1781

On the part & behalf of the State of Virginia

Richard Henry Lee
John Banister
Thomas Adams
Jno. Harvie
Francis Lightfoot Lee

On the part & behalf of the State of No. Carolina

John Penn
July 21st, 1778
Corns. Harnett
Jno. Williams

On the part & behalf of the State of South Carolina

Henry Laurens
William Henry Drayton
Jno. Mathews
Richd. Hutson
Thos. Heyward, Junr.

On the part & behalf of the State of Georgia

Jno. Walton
24th July, 1778
Edwd. Telfair
Edwd. Langworthy

The Anti-Federalist Papers
(1787–1788)

The Articles of Confederation were ratified in 1781 and by the mid-1780s were already demonstrating the inherent weaknesses in the document and in the new government. In reality, there was essentially no central government, *per se*. The original United States of America was not a nation, but a federation of independent, sovereign states that had agreed to allow the Congress to perform certain, limited functions with respect to matters that affected more than one of the member states.

Notably, the central Congress had limited power to regulate interstate commerce, and no power to regulate international commerce. Although the British Crown had reconciled itself to the reality that the American colonies were no longer British possessions, the individual states found that they could not negotiate favorable terms for trade with England because they were not a nation, but a collection of thirteen independent states—none of which would commit to being bound by any treaty or trade agreement negotiated by the Congress in the name of the United States.

By 1786 affairs in some of the states had deteriorated sufficiently that citizens resorted to armed intervention. The most serious of these incidents occurred in Massachusetts where, in 1786, a group of former Revolutionary War veterans attempted to prevent a circuit court from conducting business. The incident was quickly put down, but it provided notice to influential men in all the states that something had to be done.

In September of 1786 a constitutional convention was convened in Annapolis, Maryland, for the purpose of amending the Articles of Confederation to better address issues pertaining to interstate commerce. Only five of the thirteen states attended. (Four others sent delegates, who arrived too late to participate.) Lacking a quorum, the delegates of the five states in attendance did not hold formal discussions on amendments to the Articles of Confederation; instead, they issued a report calling for a constitutional convention, proposed to be held in Philadelphia in 1787. This call was echoed by the Congress, resulting in a constitutional convention being scheduled for May of 1787.

Although the express purpose of this convention was to amend the Articles of Confederation to correct specific flaws and weaknesses, some of the delegates attended the convention with the broader goal of replacing the Articles of Confederation entirely, replacing them with an all-new constitution that would create a much stronger national ("federal") government. Those who favored a strong national, central government were known as "Federalists."

Others, who argued that the United States had just fought a war to get rid of a king and a national government, favored a weaker central government and stronger states' rights and individual rights. Advocates against a strong central government became known as "Anti-Federalists."

The convention opened on May 25, 1787, with a minimum quorum of seven states attending. Delegates from additional states arrived as the discussions proceeded. The discussions and negotiations of the convention were carried out in secret, so that each delegate would feel empowered to speak freely.

After considerable debate and negotiation, a final draft of an all-new constitution was approved and adopted by the convention on September 8, 1787. The final draft was submitted to the Congress, which approved it on September 28,1787. After the document had been approved by the Congress, it was submitted to the states for ratification.

The debate between the Federalists and the Anti-Federalists then changed to a propaganda campaign to influence the votes of the states for or against ratification of the new documents. Several notable personalities wrote articles either for or against the proposed new constitution for publication in the newspapers of the day. Some wrote under their own names, while others (on both sides of the debate) wrote under pen names to preserve their anonymity. Although these essays can now be found in organized collections, they were not published as such at the time. The various essays were collected and organized many years later by historians. The collection of essays arguing against a strong national government has come to be known—collectively—as the Anti-Federalist Papers.

The first major collection of Anti-Federalist Papers was assembled by Professor Moton Borden of Columbia University. He selected 85 essays, which corresponded to and contrasted with the 85 essays that comprise the opposing Federalist Papers. A more comprehensive collection, entitled *The Complete Anti-Federalist*, was compiled by Professor Herbert Storing and graduate student Murray Dry of the University of Chicago. This work was begun in 1961 and was completed by Dry in 1981, after the death of Professor Storing. Published by the University of Chicago Press, this collection takes up seven (7) volumes and occupies 1840 pages.

Of these, few pertain directly or closely to the Right to Keep and Bear Arms. The following pages reproduce the text of those that do so:

- No. 7: Argues that a strong central government will become an oppressor of the people, and may lead to civil war.
- No. 8: Expresses both a concern that the federal government may impose burdensome taxes, and that a federal standing army may be used against the citizens of the individual states.
- No. 9: Expresses the concern that an overly-powerful central government will become oppressive, and will forget that the agents

thereof are elected to serve the interests of their constituents rather than their own interests.

- No. 10: Expresses a concern that when one political party becomes too powerful, it is the people who suffer.
- No. 29(1): Argues in favor of a citizen militia rather than a standing army, except in times of actual war.
- No. 29(2): Argues that a standing army under a national government may be used to oppress the people and to suppress individual rights.
- No. 51: Expresses a concern that the constitution as presented did not provide sufficient checks and balances to effectively protect the citizens from the government. (The original Constitution did not include a Bill of Rights—the Bill of Rights, which includes the Second Amendment, was added to the Constitution after its adoption expressly to better protect individual rights from government encroachment.)
- No. 82: Discusses why a Bill of Rights is necessary to protect the rights of individuals against government overreach, and specifically discusses the need to preserve the right of the citizens to have militias, as opposed to a standing army under the control of a central government that does not answer directly to the People.

Anti-Federalist No. 7

Adoption of the Constitution Will Lead to Civil War

by Philanthropos (an anonymous Virginia Antifederalist)

The Virginia Journal and Alexandria Advertiser, December 6, 1787

The time in which the constitution or government of a nation undergoes any particular change, is always interesting and critical. Enemies are vigilant, allies are in suspense, friends hesitating between hope and fear; and all men are in eager expectation to see what such a change may produce. But the state of our affairs at present, is of such moment, as even to arouse the dead ...

[A certain defender of the Constitution has stated that objections to it] are more calculated to alarm the fears of the people than to answer any valuable end. Was that the case, as it is not, will any man in his sober senses say, that the least infringement or appearance of infringement on our liberty—that liberty which has lately cost so much blood and treasure, together with anxious days and sleepless nights—ought not both to rouse our fears and awaken our jealousy? ... The new constitution in its present form is calculated to produce despotism, thralldom and confusion, and if the United States do swallow it, they will find it a bolus, that will create convulsions to their utmost extremities. Were they mine enemies, the worst imprecation I could devise would be, may they adopt it. For tyranny, where it has been chained (as for a few years past) is always more cursed, and sticks its teeth in deeper than before. Were Col. [George] Mason's objections obviated, the improvement would be very considerable, though even then, not so complete as might be. The Congress's having power without control—to borrow money on the credit of the United States; their having power to appoint their own salaries, and their being paid out of the treasury of the United States, thereby, in some measure, rendering them independent of the individual states; their being judges of the qualification and election of their own members, by which means they can get men to suit any purpose; together with Col. Mason's wise and judicious objections—are grievances, the very idea of which is enough to make every honest citizen exclaim in the language of Cato, O Liberty, O my country! Our present constitution, with a few additional powers to Congress, seems better calculated to preserve the rights and defend the liberties of our citizens, than the one proposed, without proper amendments. Let us therefore, for once, show our judgment and solidity by continuing it, and prove the opinion to be erroneous, that levity and fickleness are not only the foibles of our tempers, but the reigning principles in these states. There are men amongst us, of such dissatisfied tempers, that place them in Heaven, they would find something to blame; and so restless and self-sufficient, that they must be eternally reforming the state. But the misfortune is, they always leave affairs worse than they find them. A change of government is at all times dangerous, but at present may be fatal, without the utmost caution, just after emerging out of a tedious and expensive war. Feeble in our nature, and complicated in our form, we are little able to bear the rough Posting of civil dissensions which are likely to ensue. Even now, discontent and opposition distract our councils. Division and despondency affect our people. Is it then a time to alter our government, that government which even now totters on its foundation, and will, without tender care, produce ruin by its fall?

Beware my countrymen! Our enemies —uncontrolled as they are in their ambitious schemes, fretted with losses, and perplexed with disappointments— will exert their whole power and policy to increase and continue our confusion. And while we are destroying one another, they will be repairing their losses, and ruining our trade.

Of all the plagues that infest a nation, a civil war is the worst. Famine is severe, pestilence is dreadful; but in these, though men die, they die in peace. The father expires without the guilt of the son; and the son, if he survives, enjoys the inheritance of his father. Cities may be thinned, but they neither plundered nor burnt. But when a civil war is kindled, there is then forth no security of property nor protection from any law. Life and fortune become precarious. And all that is dear to men is at the discretion of profligate soldiery, doubly licentious on such an occasion. Cities are exhausted by heavy contributions, or sacked because they cannot answer exorbitant demand. Countries are eaten up by the parties they favor, and ravaged by the one they oppose. Fathers and sons, sheath their swords in anothers bowels in the field, and their wives and daughters are exposed to rudeness and lust of ruffians at home. And when the sword has decided quarrel, the scene is closed with banishments, forfeitures, and barbarous executions that entail distress on children then unborn. May Heaven avert the dreadful catastrophe! In the most limited governments, what wranglings, animosities, factions, partiality, and all other evils that tend to embroil a nation and weaken a state, are constantly practised by legislators. What then may we expect if the new constitution be adopted as it now stands? The great will struggle for power, honor and wealth; the poor become a prey to avarice, insolence and oppression. And while some are studying to supplant their neighbors, and others striving to keep their stations, one villain will wink at the oppression of another, the people be fleeced, and the public business neglected. From despotism and tyranny good Lord deliver us.

Anti-Federalist No. 8

The Power Vested in Congress of Sending Troops for Suppressing Insurrections Will Always Enable Them to Stifle the First Struggles of Freedom

by A Federal Republican (an anonymous Virginia Antifederalist)

The Norfolk and Portsmouth Register, March 5, 1788

.... By the Articles of Confederation, the congress of the United State was vested with powers for conducting the common concerns of the continent. They had the sole and exclusive right and power of determining on peace and war; of sending and receiving ambassadors; of entering into treaties and alliances; and of pointing out the respective quotas of men and men which each state should furnish. But it was expressly provided that the money to be supplied by each state should be raised by the authority and direction of the legislature thereof– thus reserving to the states the important privilege of levying taxes upon their citizens in such manner as might be most conformable to their peculiar circumstances and form of government. With powers thus constituted was congress enabled to unite the general exertions of the continent in the cause of liberty and to carry us triumphantly through a long and bloody war. It was not until sometime after peace and a glorious independence had been established that defects were discovered in that system of federal government which had procured to us those blessings. It was then perceived that the Articles of Confederation were inadequate to the purposes of the union; and it was particularly suggested as necessary to vest in congress the further power of exclusively regulating the commerce of the United States, as well to enable us, by a system more uniform, to counteract the policy of foreign nations, as for other important reasons. Upon this principle, a general convention of the United States was proposed to be held, and deputies were accordingly appointed by twelve of the states charged with power to revise, alter, and amend the Articles of Confederation. When these deputies met, instead of confining themselves to the powers with which they were entrusted, they pronounced all amendments to the Articles of Confederation wholly impracticable; and with a spirit of amity and concession truly remarkable proceeded to form a government entirely new, and totally different in its principles and its organization. Instead of a congress whose members could serve but three years out of six-and then to return to a level with their fellow citizens; and who were liable at all times, whenever the states might deem it necessary, to be recalled– Congress, by this new constitution, will be composed of a body whose members during the time they are appointed to serve, can receive no check from their constituents. Instead of the powers formerly granted to congress of ascertaining each state's quota of men and money-to be raised by the legislatures of the different states in such a mode as they might think proper-- congress, by this new government, will be invested with the formidable powers of raising armies, and lending money, totally independent of the different states. They will moreover, have the power of leading troops among you in order to suppress those struggles which may sometimes happen among a free people, and which tyranny will impiously brand with the name of sedition. On one day the state collector will call on you for your proportion of those taxes which have been laid on you by the general assembly, where you are fully and adequately represented; on the next will come the Continental collector to demand from you those taxes which shall be levied by the continental congress, where the whole state of Virginia will be represented by only ten men! Thus shall we imprudently confer on so small a number the very important power of taking our money out of our pockets, and of levying taxes without control-a right which the wisdom of our state constitution will, in vain, have confided to the most numerous branch of the legislature. Should the sheriff or state collector in any manner aggrieve you either in person or property, these sacred rights are amply secured by the most solemn compact. Beside, the arm of government is always at hand to shield you from his injustice and oppression. But if a Continental collector, in the execution of his office, should invade your freedom (according to this new government, which has expressly declared itself paramount to all state laws and constitutions) the state of which you are a citizen will have no authority to afford you relief. A continental court may, indeed, be established in the state, and it may be urged that you will find a remedy here; but, my fellow citizens, let me ask, what protection this will afford you against the insults or rapacity of a continental officer, when he will have it in his power to appeal to the seat of congress perhaps at several hundred miles distance, and by this means oblige you to expend hundreds of pounds in obtaining redress for twenty shillings unjustly extorted? Thus will you be necessarily compelled either to make a bold effort to extricate yourselves from these grievous and oppressive extortions, or you will be fatigued by fruitless attempts into the quiet and peaceable surrender of those rights, for which the blood of your fellow citizens has been shed in vain. But the latter will, no doubt, be the melancholy fate of a people once inspired with the love of liberty, as the power vested in congress of sending troops for suppressing insurrections will always enable them to stifle the first struggles of freedom.

A FEDERAL REPUBLICAN

Anti-Federalist No. 9

A Consolidated Government Is a Tyranny

by "Montezuma," (regarded as a Pennsylvanian)

The Independent Gazeteer, October 17, 1787

We the Aristocratic party of the United States, lamenting the many inconveniences to which the late confederation subjected the well-born, the better kind of people, bringing them down to the level of the rabble – and holding in utter detestation that frontispiece to every bill of rights, "that all men are born equal" – beg leave (for the purpose of drawing a line between such as we think were ordained to govern, and such as were made to bear the weight of government without having any share in its administration) to submit to our Friends in the first class for their inspection, the following defense of our monarchical, aristocratical democracy.

1st. As a majority of all societies consist of men who (though totally incapable of thinking or acting in governmental matters) are more readily led than driven, we have thought meet to indulge them in something like a democracy in the new constitution, which part we have designated by the popular name of the House of Representatives. But to guard against every possible danger from this lower house, we have subjected every bill they bring forward, to the double negative of our upper house and president. Nor have we allowed the populace the right to elect their representatives annually . . . lest this body should be too much under the influence and control of their constituents, and thereby prove the "weatherboard of our grand edifice, to show the shiftings of every fashionable gale," – for we have not yet to learn that little else is wanting to aristocratize the most democratical representative than to make him somewhat independent of his political creators. We have taken away that rotation of appointment which has so long perplexed us – that grand engine of popular influence. Every man is eligible into our government from time to time for life. This will have a two-fold good effect. First, it prevents the representatives from mixing with the lower class, and imbibing their foolish sentiments, with which they would have come charged on re-election.

2d. They will from the perpetuality of office be under our eye, and in a short time will think and act like us, independently of popular whims and prejudices. For the assertion "that evil communications corrupt good manners," is not more true than its reverse. We have allowed this house the power to impeach, but we have tenaciously reserved the right to try. We hope gentlemen, you will see the policy of this clause – for what matters it who accuses, if the accused is tried by his friends. In fine, this plebeian house will have little power, and that little be rightly shaped by our house of gentlemen, who will have a very extensive influence – from their being chosen out of the genteeler class ... It is true, every third senatorial seat is to be vacated duennually, but two-thirds of this influential body will remain in office, and be ready to direct or (if necessary) bring over to the good old way, the young members, if the old ones should not be returned. And whereas many of our brethren, from a laudable desire to support their rank in life above the commonalty, have not only deranged their finances, but subjected their persons to indecent treatment (as being arrested for debt, etc.) we have framed a privilege clause, by which they may laugh at the fools who trusted them. But we have given out, that this clause was provided, only that the members might be able without interruption, to deliberate on the important business of their country.

We have frequently endeavored to effect in our respective states, the happy discrimination which pervades this system; but finding we could not bring the states into it individually, we have determined ... and have taken pains to leave the legislature of each free and independent state, as they now call themselves, in such a situation that they will eventually be absorbed by our grand continental vortex, or dwindle into petty corporations, and have power over little else than yoking hogs or determining the width of cart wheels. But (aware that an intention to annihilate state legislatures, would be objected to our favorite scheme) we have made their existence (as a board of electors) necessary to ours. This furnishes us and our advocates with a fine answer to any clamors that may be raised on this subject. We have so interwoven continental and state legislatures that they cannot exist separately; whereas we in truth only leave them the power of electing us, for what can a provincial legislature do when we possess the exclusive regulation of external and internal commerce, excise, duties, imposts, post-offices and roads; when we and we alone, have the power to wage war, make peace, coin money (if we can get bullion) if not, borrow money, organize the militia and call them forth to execute our decrees, and crush insurrections assisted by a noble body of veterans subject to our nod, which we have the power of raising and keeping even in the time of peace. What have we to fear from state legislatures or even from states, when we are armed with such powers, with a president at our head? (A name we thought proper to adopt in conformity to the prejudices of a silly people who are so foolishly fond of a Republican government, that we were obliged to accommodate in names and forms to them, in order more effectually to secure the substance of our proposed plan; but we all know that Cromwell was a King, with the title of Protector). I repeat it, what have we to fear armed with such powers, with a president at our head who is captain – general of the army, navy and militia of the United States, who can make and unmake treaties, appoint and commission ambassadors and other ministers, who can grant or refuse reprieves or pardons, who can make judges of the supreme and other continental courts – in short, who will be the source, the fountain of honor, profit and power, whose influence like the rays of the sun, will diffuse itself far and wide, will exhale all democratical vapors and break the clouds of popular insurrection? But again gentlemen, our judicial power is a strong work, a masked battery, few people see the guns we can and will ere long play off from it. For the judicial power embraces every question which can arise in law or equity, under this constitution and under the laws of "the United States" (which laws will be, you know, the supreme laws of the land). This power extends to all cases, affecting ambassadors or other public ministers, "and consuls; to all cases of admiralty and maritime jurisdiction; to controversies to which the United States shall be a party; to controversies between two or more States; between a State and citizens of another State; between citizens of different States; between citizens of the same State, claiming lands under grants of different States; and between a State or the citizens thereof, and foreign States, citizens or subjects."

Now, can a question arise in the colonial courts, which the ingenuity or sophistry of an able lawyer may not bring within one or other of the above cases? Certainly not. Then our court will have original or appellate jurisdiction in all cases – and if so, how fallen are state judicatures – and must not every provincial law yield to our supreme flat? Our constitution answers yes. . . . And finally we shall entrench ourselves so as to laugh at the cabals of the commonalty. A few regiments will do at first; it must be spread abroad that they are absolutely necessary to defend the frontiers. Now a regiment and then a legion must be added quietly; by and by a frigate or two must be built, still taking care to intimate that they are essential to the support of our revenue laws and to prevent smuggling. We have said nothing about a bill of rights, for we viewed it as an eternal clog upon our designs, as a lock chain to the wheels of government – though, by the way, as we have not insisted on rotation in our offices, the simile of a wheel is ill. We have for some time considered the freedom of the press as a great evil – it spreads information, and begets a licentiousness in the people which needs the rein more than the spur; besides, a daring printer may expose the plans of government and lessen the consequence of our president and senate – for these and many other reasons we have said nothing with respect to the "right of the people to speak and publish their sentiments" or about their "palladiums of liberty" and such stuff. We do not much like that sturdy privilege of the people – the right to demand the writ of habeas corpus. We have therefore reserved the power of refusing it in cases of rebellion, and you know we are the judges of what is rebellion.... Our friends we find have been assiduous in representing our federal calamities, until at length the people at large – frightened by the gloomy picture on one side, and allured by the prophecies of some of our fanciful and visionary adherents on the other – are ready to accept and confirm our proposed government without the delay or forms of examination – which was the more to be wished, as they are wholly unfit to investigate the principles or pronounce on the merit of so exquisite a system. Impressed with a conviction that this constitution is calculated to restrain the influence and power of the LOWER CLASS – to draw that discrimination we have so long sought after; to secure to our friends privileges and offices, which were not to be ... [obtained] under the former government, because they were in common; to take the burden of legislation and attendance on public business off the commonalty, who will be much better able thereby to prosecute with effect their private business; to destroy that political thirteen headed monster, the state sovereignties; to check the licentiousness of the people by making it dangerous to speak or publish daring or tumultuary sentiments; to enforce obedience to laws by a strong executive, aided by military pensioners; and finally to promote the public and private interests of the better kind of people – we submit it to your judgment to take such measures for its adoption as you in your wisdom may think fit.

Signed by unanimous order of the lords spiritual and temporal.

MONTEZUMA

Anti-Federalist No. 10

On The Preservation of Parties, Public Liberty Depends

by John Francis Mercer (a Maryland Farmer)

The Maryland Gazette and *Baltimore Advertiser*, March 18, 1788

The opposite qualities of the first confederation were rather caused by than the cause of two parties, which from its first existence began and have continued their operations, I believe, unknown to their country and almost unknown to themselves – as really but few men have the capacity or resolution to develop the secret causes which influence their daily conduct. The old Congress was a national government and an union of States, both brought into one political body, as these opposite powers – I do not mean parties were so exactly blended and very nearly balanced, like every artificial, operative machine where action is equal to reaction. It stood perfectly still. It would not move at all. Those who were merely confederal in their views, were for dividing the public debt. Those who were for national government, were for increasing of it. Those who thought any national government would be destructive to the liberties of America . . . assisted those who thought it our only safety – to put everything as wrong as possible. Requisitions were made, which everybody knew it was impossible to comply with. Either in 82 or 83, ten millions of hard dollars, if not thirteen, were called into the continental treasury, when there could not be half that sum in the whole tract of territory between Nova-Scotia and Florida. The States neglected them in despair. The public honor was tarnished, and our governments abused by their servants and best friends. In fine, it became a cant word things are not yet bad enough to mend. However, as [a] great part of the important objects of society were entrusted to this mongrel species of general government, the sentiment of pushing it forward became general throughout America, and the late Convention met at Philadelphia under the uniform impression, that such was the desire of their constituents. But even then the advantages and disadvantages of national government operated so strongly, although silently, on each individual, that the conflict was nearly equal. A third or middle opinion, which always arises in such cases, broke off and took the lead – the national party [thus] assisted, pursued steadily their object – the federal party dropped off, one by one, and finally, when the middle party came to view the offspring which they had given birth to, and in a great measure reared, several of them immediately disowned the child. Such has been hitherto the progress of party; or rather of the human mind dispassionately contemplating our separate and relative situation, and aiming at that perfect completion of social happiness and grandeur, which perhaps can be combined only in ideas. Every description of men entertain the same wishes (excepting perhaps a few very bad men of each) – they forever will differ about the mode of accomplishment – and some must be permitted to doubt the practicability.

As our citizens are now apprized of the progress of parties or political opinions on the continent, it is fit they should also be informed of the present state, force and designs of each, in order that they may form their decisions with safety to the public and themselves – this shall be given with all the precision and impartiality the author is capable of.

America is at present divided into three classes or descriptions of men, and in a few years there will be but two.

[First]. The first class comprehends all those men of fortune and reputation who stepped forward in the late revolution, from opposition to the administration, rather than the government of Great Britain. All those aristocrats whose pride disdains equal law. Many men of very large fortune, who entertain real or imaginary fears for the security of property. Those young men, who have sacrificed their time and their talents to public service, without any prospect of an adequate pecuniary or honorary reward. All your people of fashion and pleasure who are corrupted by the dissipation of the French, English and American armies; and a love of European manners and luxury. The public creditors of the continent, whose interest has been heretofore sacrificed by their friends, in order to retain their services on this occasion. A large majority of the mercantile people, which is at present a very unformed and consequently dangerous interest. Our old native merchants have been almost universally ruined by the receipt of their debts in paper during the war, and the payment in hard money of what they owed their British correspondents since peace. Those who are not bankrupts, have generally retired and given place to a set of young men, who conducting themselves as rashly as ignorantly, have embarrassed their affairs and lay the blame on the government, and who are really unacquainted with the true mercantile interest of the country – which is perplexed from circumstances rather temporary than permanent. The foreign merchants are generally not to be trusted with influence in our government – they are most of them birds of passage. Some, perhaps British emissaries increasing and rejoicing in our political mistakes, and even those who have settled among us with an intention to fix themselves and their posterity in our soil, have brought with them more foreign prejudices than wealth. Time must elapse before the mercantile interest will be so organized as to govern themselves, much less others, with propriety. And lastly, to this class I suppose we may ultimately add the Tory interest, with the exception of very many respectable characters, who reflect with a gratification mixed with disdain, that those principles are now become fashionable for which they have been persecuted and hunted down – which, although by no means so formidable as is generally imagined, is still considerable. They are at present wavering. They are generally, though with very many exceptions, openly for the proposed, but secretly against any American government. A burnt child dreads the fire. But should they see any fair prospect of confusion arise, these gentry will be off at any moment for these five and twenty years to come. Ultimately, should the administration promise stability to the new government, they may be counted on as the Janizaries of power, ready to efface all suspicion by the violence of their zeal.

In general, all these various people would prefer a government, as nearly copied after that of Great Britain, as our circumstances will permit. Some would strain these circumstances. Others still retain a deep rooted jealousy of the executive branch and strong republican prejudices as they are called. Finally, this class contains more aggregate wisdom and moral virtue than both the other two together. It commands nearly two thirds of the property and almost one half the numbers of America, and has at present, become almost irresistible from the name of the truly great and amiable man who it has been said, is disposed to patronize it, and from the influence which it has over the second class. This [first] class is nearly at the height of their power; they must decline or moderate, or another revolution will ensue, for the opinion of America is becoming daily more unfavorable to those radical changes which high – toned government requires. A conflict would terminate in the destruction of this class, or the liberties of their country May the Guardian Angel of America prevent both!

[Second]. The second class is composed of those descriptions of men who are certainly more numerous with us than in any other part of the globe. First, those men who are so wise as to discover that their ancestors and indeed all the rest of mankind were and are fools. We have a vast over-proportion of these great men, who, when you tell them that from the earliest period at which mankind devoted their attention to social happiness, it has been their uniform judgment, that a government over governments cannot exist – that is two governments operating on the same individual – assume the smile of confidence, and tell you of two people traveling the same road – of a perfect and precise division of the duties of the individual. Still, however, the political apothegm is as old as the proverb – That no man can serve two masters – and whoever will run their noddles against old proverbs will be sure to break them, however hard they may be. And if they broke only their own, all would be right; but it is very horrible to reflect that all our numskulls must be cracked in concert. Second. The trimmers, who from sympathetic indecision are always united with, and when not regularly employed, always fight under the banners of these great men, These people are forever at market, and when parties are nearly equally divided, they get very well paid for their services. Thirdly. The indolent, that is almost every second man of independent fortune you meet with in America – these are quite easy, and can live under any government. If men can be said to live, who scarcely breathe; and if breathing was attended with any bodily exertion, would give up their small portion of life in despair. These men do not swim with the stream as the trimmers do, but are dragged like mud at the bottom. As they have no other weight than their tat flesh, they are hardly worth mentioning when we speak of the sentiments and opinions of America. As this second class never can include any of the yeomanry of the union, who never affect superior wisdom, and can have no interests but the public good, it can be only said to exist at the birth of government, and as soon as the first and third classes become more decided in their views, this will divide with each and dissipate like a mist, or sink down into what are called moderate men, and become the tools and instruments of others. These people are prevented by a cloud from having any view; and if they are not virtuous, they at least preserve the appearance, which in this world amounts to the same thing.

[Third]. At the head of the third class appear the old rigid republicans, who although few in number, are still formidable. Reverence will follow these men in spite of detraction, as long as wisdom and virtue are esteemed among mankind. They are joined by the true democrats, who are in general fanatics and enthusiasts, and some few sensible, charming madmen. A decided majority of the yeomanry of America will, for a length of years, be ready to support these two descriptions of men. But as this last class is forced to act as a residuary legatee, and receive all the trash and filth, it is in some measure disgraced and its influence weakened. 3dly. The freebooters and plunderers, who infest all countries and ours perhaps as little as any other whatever. These men have that natural antipathy to any kind or sort of government, that a rogue has to a halter. In number they are few indeed such characters are the offspring of dissipation and want, and there is not that country in the world where so much real property is shared so equally among so few citizens, for where property is as easily acquired by fair means, very few indeed will resort to foul. Lastly, by the poor mob, infoelix pecus! The property of whoever will feed them and take care of them – let them be spared. Let the burden of taxation sit lightly on their shoulders. But alas! This is not their fate. It is here that government forever falls with all its weight. It is here that the proposed government will press where it should scarcely be felt. . . .

In this [third] class may be counted men of the greatest mental powers and of as sublime virtue as any in America. They at present command nearly one-third of the property and above half the numbers of the United States, and in either event they must continue to increase in influence by great desertions from both the other classes. ... If the [proposed] government is not adopted, theirs will be the prevalent opinion. The object of this class either is or will be purely federal – an union of independent States, not a government of individuals. And should the proposed federal plan fail, from the obstinacy of those who will listen to no conditional amendments, although such as they cannot disapprove; or should it ultimately in its execution upon a fair trial, disappoint the wishes and expectations of our country – [then] an union purely federal is what the reasonable and dispassionate patriots of America must bend their views to. My countrymen, preserve your jealousy – reject suspicion, it is the fiend that destroys public and private happiness. I know some weak, but very few if any wicked men in public confidence. And learn this most difficult and necessary lesson: That on the preservation of parties, public liberty depends. Whenever men are unanimous on great public questions, whenever there is but one party, freedom ceases and despotism commences. The object of a free and wise people should be so to balance parties, that from the weakness of all you may be governed by the moderation of the combined judgments of the whole, not tyrannized over by the blind passions of a few individuals.

A FARMER

Anti-Federalist No. 29 (Part 1)

Objections to National Control of the Militia

by "A Democratic Federalist"

The Pennsylvania Packet, October 23, 1787

Hume, an aristocratical writer, has candidly confessed that an army is a moral distemper in a government, of which it must at last inevitably perish (2d Burgh, 349); and the Earl of Oxford (Oxford the friend of France and the Pretender, the attainted Oxford), said in the British parliament, in a speech on the mutiny bill, that, "While he had breath he would speak for the liberties of his country, and against courts martial and a standing army in peace, as dangerous to the Constitution." (Ibid., page 455.) Such were the speeches even of the enemies of liberty when Britain had yet a right to be called free. But, says Mr. [James] Wilson, "It is necessary to maintain the appearance of strength even in times of the most profound tranquillity." And what is this more than a threadbare hackneyed argument, which has been answered over and over in different ages, and does not deserve even the smallest consideration? Had we a standing army when the British invaded our peaceful shores? Was it a standing army that gained the battles of Lexington and Bunker Hill, and took the ill-fated Burgoyne? Is not a well-regulated militia sufficient for every purpose of internal defense? And which of you, my fellow citizens, is afraid of any invasion from foreign powers that our brave militia would not be able immediately to repel?

Mr. Wilson says, that he does not know of any nation in the world which has not found it necessary to maintain the appearance of strength in a season of the most profound tranquillity. If by this equivocal assertion he has meant to say that there is no nation in the world without a standing army in time of peace, he has been mistaken. I need only adduce the example of Switzerland, which, like us, is a republic, whose thirteen cantons, like our thirteen States, are under a federal government, and which besides is surrounded by the most powerful nations in Europe, all jealous of its liberty and prosperity. And yet that nation has preserved its freedom for many ages, with the sole help of a militia, and has never been known to have a standing army, except when in actual war. Why should we not follow so glorious an example; and are we less able to defend our liberty without an army, than that brave but small nation which, with its militia alone has hitherto defied all Europe?

A DEMOCRATIC FEDERALIST

Anti-Federalist No. 29 (Part 2)

Objections to National Control of the Militia

Melancton Smith

The Address And Reasons of Dissent of The Minority of
The Convention of The State of Pennsylvania to Their Constituents,
December 12, 1787

The framers of this constitution appear to have been . . . sensible that no dependence could be placed on the people for their support; but on the contrary, that the government must be executed by force. They have therefore made a provision for this purpose in a permanent standing army and a militia that may be objected to as strict discipline and government.

A standing army in the hands of a government placed so independent of the people, may be made a fatal instrument to overturn the public liberties; it may be employed to enforce the collection of the most oppressive taxes; and to carry into execution the most arbitrary measures. An ambitious man who may have the army at his devotion, may step up into the throne, and seize upon absolute power.

The absolute unqualified command that Congress have over the militia may be made instrumental to the destruction of all liberty both public and private; whether of a personal, civil or religious nature.

First, the personal liberty of every man, probably from sixteen to sixty years of age, may be destroyed by the power Congress have in organizing and governing of the militia. As militia they may be subjected to fines to any amount, levied in a military manner; they may be subjected to corporal punishments of the most disgraceful and humiliating kind; and to death itself, by the sentence of a court martial. To this our young men will be more immediately subjected, as a select militia, composed of them, will best answer the purposes of government.

Secondly, the rights of conscience may be violated, as there is no exemption of those persons who are conscientiously scrupulous of hearing arms. These compose a respectable proportion of the community in the State [Pennsylvania]. This is the more remarkable, because even when the distresses of the late war and the evident disaffection of many citizens of that description inflamed our passions, and when every person who was obliged to risk his own life must have been exasperated against such as on any account kept back from the common danger, yet even then, when outrage and violence might have been expected, the rights of conscience were held sacred.

At this momentous crisis, the framers of our State Constitution made the most express and decided declaration and stipulations in favor of the rights of conscience; but now, when no necessity exists, those dearest rights of men are left insecure.

Thirdly, the absolute command of Congress over the militia may be destructive of public liberty; for under the guidance of an arbitrary government, they may be made the unwilling instruments of tyranny. The militia of Pennsylvania may be marched to New England or Virginia to quell an insurrection occasioned by the most galling oppression, and aided by the standing army, they will no doubt be successful in subduing their liberty and independency. But in so doing, although the magnanimity of their minds will be extinguished, yet the meaner passions of resentment and revenge will be increased, and these in turn will be the ready and obedient instruments of despotism to enslave the others; and that with an irritated vengeance. Thus may the militia be made the instruments of crushing the last efforts of expiring liberty, of riveting the chains of despotism on their fellow-citizens, and on one another. This power can be exercised not only without violating the Constitution, but in strict conformity with it; it is calculated for this express purpose, and will doubtless be executed accordingly.

As this government will not enjoy the confidence of the people, but be executed by force, it will be a very expensive and burdensome government. The standing army must be numerous, and as a further support, it wilt be the policy of this government to multiply officers in every department; judges, collectors, tax-gatherers, excisemen and the whole host of revenue officers, will swarm over the land, devouring the hard earnings of the industrious like the locusts of old, impoverishing and desolating all before them. . . .

Anti-Federalist No. 51

Do Checks and Balances Really Secure the Rights of the People?

Aristocrotis

This satire is from a pamphlet of "ARISTOCROTIS": *The Government of Nature Delineated; Or An Exact Picture of the New Federal Constitution* (Carlisle, PA, 1788)

The present is an active period. Europe is in a ferment breaking their constitutions; America is in a similar state, making a constitution. For this valuable purpose a convention was appointed, consisting of such as excelled in wisdom and knowledge, who met in Philadelphia last May. For my own part, I was so smitten with the character of the members, that I had assented to their production, while it was yet in embryo. And I make no doubt but every good republican did so too. But how great was my surprise, when it appeared with such a venerable train of names annexed to its tail, to find some of the people under different signatures-such as Centinel, Old Whig, Brutus, etc. - daring to oppose it, and that too with barefaced arguments, obstinate reason and stubborn truth. This is certainly a piece of the most extravagant impudence to presume to contradict the collected wisdom of the United States; or to suppose a body, who engrossed the whole wisdom of the continent, was capable of erring. I expected the superior character of the convention would have secured it from profane sallies of a plebeian's pen; and its inherent infallibility debarred the interference of impertinent reason or truth. It was too great an act of condescension to permit the people, by their state conventions, "to assent and ratify," what the grand convention prescribed to them; but to inquire into its principles, or investigate its properties, was a presumption too daring to escape resentment. Such licentious conduct practised by the people, is a striking proof of our feeble governments, and calls aloud for the pruning knife, i.e., the establishment of some proper plan of discipline. This the convention, in the depth of their united wisdom hath prescribed, which when established, will certainly put a stop to the growing evil. A consciousness of this, is, no doubt, the cause which stimulates the people to oppose it with so much vehemence. They deprecate the idea of being confined within their proper sphere; they cannot endure the thought of being obliged to mind their own business, and leave the affairs of government to those whom nature hath destined to rule. I say nature, for it is a fundamental principle, as clear as an axiom, that nature hath placed proper degrees and subordinations amongst mankind and ordained a few(1) to rule, and many to obey. I am not obliged to prove this principle because it would be madness in the extreme to attempt to prove a self- evident truth.

(1) If any person is so stupidly dull as not to discern who these few are, I would refer such to nature herself for information. Let them observe her ways and be wise. Let them mark those men whom she hath endued with the necessary qualifications of authority; such as the dictatorial air, the magisterial voice, the imperious tone, the haughty countenance, the lofty look, the majestic mien. Let them consider those whom she hath taught to command with authority, but comply with disgust; to be fond of sway, but impatient of control; to consider themselves as Gods, and all the rest of mankind as two legged brutes. Now it is evident that the possessors of these divine qualities must have been ordained by nature to dominion and empire; for it would be blasphemy against her supreme highness to suppose that she confers her gifts in vain. Fortune hath also distinguished those upon whom nature hath imprinted the lineaments of authority. She hath heaped her favors and lavished her gifts upon those very persons whom nature delighteth to honor. Indeed, instinct hath taught those men that authority is their natural right, and therefore they grasp at it with an eagerness bordering on rapacity.

But with all due submission to the infallible wisdom of the grand convention, let me presume to examine whether they have not, in the new plan of government, inviolably adhered to this supreme principle. . . .

In article first, section first, of the new plan, it is declared that "all legislative powers herein granted shall be vested in a Congress of the United States which shall consist of a Senate"-very right, quite agreeable to nature and House of Representatives"-not quite so right. This is a palpable compliance with the humors and corrupt practices of the times. But what follows in section 2 is still worse: "The House of Representatives shall be composed of members chosen every second year by the people of the several states." This is a most dangerous power, and must soon produce fatal and pernicious consequences, were it not circumscribed and poised by proper checks and balances. But in this is displayed the unparalleled sagacity of the august convention: that when such bulwarks of prejudice surrounded the evil, so as to render it both difficult and dangerous to attack it by assault and storm, they have invested and barricaded it so closely as will certainly deprive it of its baneful influence and prevent its usual encroachments. They have likewise stationed their miners and sappers so judiciously, that they will certainly, in process of time, entirely reduce and demolish this obnoxious practice of popular election. There is a small thrust given to it in the body of the conveyance itself. The term of holding elections is every two years; this is much better than the detestable mode of annual elections, so fatal to energy. However, if nothing more than this were done, it would still remain an insupportable inconvenience. But in section 4 it is provided that congress by law may alter and make such regulations with respect to the times, places, and manner of holding elections, as to them seemeth fit and proper. This is certainly a very salutary provision, most excellently adapted to counterbalance the great and apparently dangerous concessions made to the plebeians in the first and second sections. With such a prudent restriction as this they are quite harmless: no evil can arise from them if congress have only the sagacity and fortitude to avail themselves of the power they possess by this section. For when the stated term (for which the primary members was elected) is nigh expired, congress may appoint [the] next election to be held in one place in each state; and so as not to give the rabble needless disgust, they may appoint the most central place for that purpose. They can never be at a loss for an ostensible reason to vary and shift from place to place until they may fix it at any extremity of the state it suits. This will be the business of the senate, to observe the particular places in each state, where their influence is most extensive, and where the inhabitants are most obsequious to the will of their superiors, and there appoint the elections to be held. By this means, such members will be returned to the house of representatives (as it is called) as the president and senate shall be pleased to recommend; and they no doubt will recommend such gentlemen only as are distinguished by some peculiar federal feature-so that unanimity and concord will shine conspicuous through every branch of government. This section is ingeniously calculated, and must have been intended by the convention, to exterminate electioneering entirely. For by putting the time of election in the hands of congress they have thereby given them a power to perpetuate themselves when they shall find it safe and convenient to make the experiment. For though a preceding clause says,

"that representatives shall be chosen for two years, and senators for six years," yet this clause being subsequent annuls the former, and puts it in the power of congress, (when some favorable juncture intervenes) to alter the time to four and twelve years. This cannot be deemed an unconstitutional stretch of power, for the constitution in express terms puts the time of holding elections in their power, and certainly they are the proper judges when to exert that power. Thus by doubling the period from time to time, its extent will soon be rendered coeval with the life of man. And it is but a very short and easy transition from this to hereditary succession, which is most agreeable to the institutions of nature, who in all her works, hath ordained the descendant of every species of beings to succeed its immediate progenitor, in the same actions, ends and order.

The indefatigable laborious ass never aspires to the honors, nor assumes the employment of the sprightly warlike steed, nor does he ever pretend that it is his right to succeed him in all his offices and dignities, because he bears some resemblance to the defunct in his figure and nature. The llama, though useful enough for the purposes for which he was intended by nature, is every way incompetent to perform the offices of the elephant; nor does he ever pretend to usurp his elevated station. Every species of beings, animate and inanimate, seem fully satisfied with the station assigned them by nature. But perverse, obstinate man, he alone spurns at her institutions, and inverts her order.' He alone repines at his situation, and endeavors to usurp the station of his superiors. But this digression has led me from the subject in hand. . . .

(2) This is only to be understood of the inferior class of mankind. The superior order have aspiring feelings given them by nature, such as ambition, emulation, etc., which makes it their duty to persevere in the pursuit of gratifying these refined passions.

The next object that presents itself is the power which the new constitution gives to congress to regulate the manner of elections. The common practice of voting at present is by ballot. By this mode it is impossible for a gentleman to know how he is served by his dependent, who may be possessed of a vote. Therefore this mode must be speedily altered for that viva voce, which will secure to a rich man all the votes of his numerous dependents and friends and their dependents. By this means he may command any office in the gift of the people, which he pleases to set up for. This will answer a good end while electioneering exists; and will likewise contribute something towards its destruction. A government founded agreeable to nature must be entirely independent; that is, it must be beyond the reach of annoyance or control from every power on earth, Now in order to render it thus, several things are necessary.

The next object that presents itself is the power which the new constitution gives to congress to regulate the manner of elections. The common practice of voting at present is by ballot. By this mode it is impossible for a gentleman to know how he is served by his dependent, who may be possessed of a vote. Therefore this mode must be speedily altered for that viva voce, which will secure to a rich man all the votes of his numerous dependents and friends and their dependents. By this means he may command any office in the gift of the people, which he pleases to set up for. This will answer a good end while electioneering exists; and will likewise contribute something towards its destruction. A government founded agreeable to nature must be entirely independent; that is, it must be beyond the reach of annoyance or control from every power on earth, Now in order to render it thus, several things are necessary.

2dly. It will create and diffuse a spirit of industry among the people. They will then be obliged to labor for money to pay their taxes. There will be no trifling from time to time, as is done now. The new government will have energy sufficient to compel immediate payment.

3dly. This will make the people attend to their own business, and not be dabbling in politics - things they are entirely ignorant of; nor is it proper they should understand. But it is very probable that the exercise of this power may be opposed by the refractory plebeians, who (such is the perverseness of their natures) often refuse to comply with what is manifestly for their advantage. But to prevent all inconvenience from this quarter the congress have power to raise and support armies. This is the second thing necessary to render government independent. The creatures who compose these armies are a species of animals, wholly at the disposal of government; what others call their natural rights they resign into the hands of their superiors- even the right of self-preservation (so precious to all other beings) they entirely surrender, and put their very lives in the power of their masters. Having no rights of their own to care for, they become naturally jealous and envious of those possessed by others. They are therefore proper instruments in the hands of government to divest the people of their usurped rights. But the capital business of these armies will be to assist the collectors of taxes, imposts, and excise, in raising the revenue; and this they will perform with the greatest alacrity, as it is by this they are supported; but for this they would be in a great measure useless; and without this they could not exist. ...

From these remarks, I think it is evident, that the grand convention hath dexterously provided for the removal of everything that hath ever operated as a restraint upon government in any place or age of the world. But perhaps some weak heads may think that the constitution itself will be a check upon the new congress. But this I deny, for the convention has so happily worded themselves, that every part of this constitution either bears double meaning, or no meaning at all; and if any concessions are made to the people in one place, it is effectually cancelled in another- so that in fact this constitution is much better and gives more scope to the rulers than they durst safely take if there was no constitution at all. For then the people might contend that the power was inherent in them, and that they had made some implied reserves in the original grant. But now they cannot, for everything is expressly given away to government in this plan. Perhaps some people may think that power which the house of representatives possesses, of impeaching the officers of government, will be a restraint upon them. But this entirely vanishes, when it is considered that the senate hath the principal say in appointing these officers, and that they are the sole judges of all impeachments. Now it would be absurd to suppose that they would remove their own servants for performing their secret orders. ... For the interest of rulers and the ruled will then be two distinct things. The mode of electing the president is another excellent regulation, most wisely calculated to render him the obsequious machine of congress. He is to be chosen by electors appointed in such manner as the state legislators shall direct. But then the highest in votes cannot be president, without he has the majority of all the electors; and if none have this majority, then the congress is to choose the president out of the five highest on the return. By this means the congress will always have the making of the president after the first election. So that if the reigning president pleases his masters, he need be under no apprehensions of being turned out for any severities used to the people, for though the congress may not have influence enough to procure him the majority of the votes of the electoral college, yet they will always be able to prevent any other from having such a majority; and to have him returned among the five highest, so that they may have the appointing of him themselves. All these wise regulations, prove to a demonstration, that the grand convention was infallible. The congress having thus disentangled themselves from all popular checks and choices, and being supported by a well disciplined army and active militia, will certainly command dread and respect abroad, obedience and submission at home. They will then look down with awful dignity and tremendous majesty from the pinnacle of glory to which fortune has raised them upon the insignificant creatures, their subjects, whom they have reduced to that state of vassalage and servile submission, for which they were primarily destined by nature. America will then be great amongst the nations(3) and princess amongst the provinces. Her fleets will cover the deserts of the ocean and convert it into a popular city; and her invincible armies overturn the thrones of princes. The glory of Britain (4) shall fall like lightning before her puissant arm; when she ariseth to shake the nations, and take vengeance on all who dare oppose her. O! thou most venerable and august congress! with what astonishing ideas my mind is ravished! when I contemplate thy rising grandeur, and anticipate thy future glory! Happy thy servants! happy thy vassals! and happy thy slaves, which fit under the shade of thy omnipotent authority, and behold the glory of thy majesty! for such a state who would not part with ideal blessings of liberty? who would not cheerfully resign the nominal advantages of freedom? the dazzling splendor of Assyrian, Persian, Macedonian and Roman greatness will then be totally eclipsed by the radiant blaze of this glorious western luminary! These beautiful expressions, aristocracy, and oligarchy, upon which the popular odium hath fixed derision and contempt, will then resume their natural emphasis; their genuine signification will be perfectly understood, and no more perverted or abused.

(3) That is, if we may credit the prognostications with which our federal newspapers and pamphlets daily teem.

(4) Britain once the supreme ruler of this country, but her authority was rejected. Not, as a great many believe, because her claims were tyrannical and oppressive, but because her dominion excluded those from monopolizing the government into their own hands, whom nature had qualified to rule. It is certainly no more than the natural right of rulers "to bind their subjects, in all cases whatsoever." This power is perfectly synonymous with that clause in the constitution which invests congress with power to make all laws which shall be "necessary and proper for carrying into execution the foregoing powers and all other powers," etc., and that which says "the constitution, laws, and treaties of congress shall be the supreme law of the land; anything in the constitutions or laws of any of the states to the contrary notwithstanding." But nothing less would satisfy Britain, than a power to bind the natural rulers as well as subjects.

ARISTOCROTIS

Anti-Federalist No. 84

On the Lack of a Bill of Rights

By "BRUTUS"

When a building is to be erected which is intended to stand for ages, the foundation should be firmly laid. The Constitution proposed to your acceptance is designed, not for yourselves alone, but for generations yet unborn. The principles, therefore, upon which the social compact is founded, ought to have been clearly and precisely stated, and the most express and full declaration of rights to have been made. But on this subject there is almost an entire silence.

If we may collect the sentiments of the people of America, from their own most solemn declarations, they hold this truth as self-evident, that all men are by nature free. No one man, therefore, or any class of men, have a right, by the law of nature, or of God, to assume or exercise authority over their fellows. The origin of society, then, is to be sought, not in any natural right which one man has to exercise authority over another, but in the united consent of those who associate. The mutual wants of men at first dictated the propriety of forming societies: and when they were established, protection and defense pointed out the necessity of instituting government. In a state of nature every individual pursues his own interest; in this pursuit it frequently happened, that the possessions or enjoyments of one were sacrificed to the views and designs of another; thus the weak were a prey to the strong, the simple and unwary were subject to impositions from those who were more crafty and designing. In this state of things, every individual was insecure; common interest, therefore, directed that government should be established, in which the force of the whole community should be collected, and under such directions, as to protect and defend everyone who composed it. The common good, therefore, is the end of civil government, and common consent, the foundation on which it is established. To effect this end, it was necessary that a certain portion of natural liberty should be surrendered, in order that what remained should be preserved. How great a proportion of natural freedom is necessary to be yielded by individuals, when they submit to government, I shall not inquire. So much, however, must be given, as will be sufficient to enable those to whom the administration of the government is committed, to establish laws for the promoting the happiness of the community, and to carry those laws into effect. But it is not necessary, for this purpose, that individuals should relinquish all their natural rights. Some are of such a nature that they cannot be surrendered. Of this kind are the rights of conscience, the right of enjoying and defending life, etc. Others are not necessary to be resigned in order to attain the end for which government is instituted; these therefore ought not to be given up. To surrender them, would counteract the very end of government, to wit, the common good. From these observations it appears, that in forming a government on its true principles, the foundation should be laid in the manner I before stated, by expressly reserving to the people such of their essential rights as are not necessary to be parted with. The same reasons which at first induced mankind to associate and institute government, will operate to influence them to observe this precaution. If they had been disposed to conform themselves to the rule of immutable righteousness, government would not have been requisite. It was because one part exercised fraud, oppression and violence, on the other, that men came together, and agreed that certain rules should be formed to regulate the conduct of all, and the power of the whole community lodged in the hands of rulers to enforce an obedience to them. But rulers have the same propensities as other men; they are as likely to use the power with which they are vested, for private purposes, and to the injury and oppression of those over whom they are placed, as individuals in a state of nature are to injure and oppress one another. It is therefore as proper that bounds should be set to their authority, as that government should have at first been instituted to restrain private injuries.

This principle, which seems so evidently founded in the reason and nature of things, is confirmed by universal experience. Those who have governed, have been found in all ages ever active to enlarge their powers and abridge the public liberty. This has induced the people in all countries, where any sense of freedom remained, to fix barriers against the encroachments of their rulers. The country from which we have derived our origin, is an eminent example of this. Their magna carta and bill of rights have long been the boast, as well as the security of that nation. I need say no more, I presume, to an American, than that this principle is a fundamental one, in all the Constitutions of our own States; there is not one of them but what is either founded on a declaration or bill of rights, or has certain express reservation of rights interwoven in the body of them. From this it appears, that at a time when the pulse of liberty beat high, and when an appeal was made to the people to form Constitutions for the government of themselves, it was their universal sense, that such declarations should make a part of their frames of government. It is, therefore, the more astonishing, that this grand security to the rights of the people is not to be found in this Constitution.

It has been said, in answer to this objection, that such declarations of rights, however requisite they might be in the Constitutions of the States, are not necessary in the general Constitution, because, "in the former case, everything which is not reserved is given; but in the latter, the reverse of the proposition prevails, and everything which is not given is reserved." It requires but little attention to discover, that this mode of reasoning is rather specious than solid. The powers, rights and authority, granted to the general government by this Constitution, are as complete, with respect to every object to which they extend, as that of any State government-it reaches to everything which concerns human happiness-life, liberty, and property are under its control. There is the same reason, therefore, that the exercise of power, in this case, should be restrained within proper limits, as in that of the State governments. To set this matter in a clear light, permit me to instance some of the articles of the bills of rights of the individual States, and apply them to the case in question.

For the security of life, in criminal prosecutions, the bills of rights of most of the States have declared, that no man shall be held to answer for a crime until he is made fully acquainted with the charge brought against him; he shall not be compelled to accuse, or furnish evidence against himself-the witnesses against him shall be brought face to face, and he shall be fully heard by himself or counsel. That it is essential to the security of life and liberty, that trial of facts be in the vicinity where they happen. Are not provisions of this kind as necessary in the general government, as in that of a particular State? The powers vested in the new Congress extend in many cases to life; they are authorized to provide for the punishment of a variety of capital crimes, and no restraint is laid upon them in its exercise, save only, that "the trial of all crimes, except in cases of impeachment, shall be by jury; and such trial shall be in the State where the said crimes shall have been committed." No man is secure of a trial in the county where he is charged to have committed a crime; he may be brought from Niagara to New York, or carried from Kentucky to Richmond for trial for an offense supposed to be committed. What security is there, that a man shall be furnished with a full and plain description of the charges against him? That he shall be allowed to produce all proof he can in his favor? That he shall see the witnesses against him face to face, or that he shall be fully heard in his own defense by himself or counsel?

For the security of liberty it has been declared, "that excessive bail should not be required, nor excessive fines imposed, nor cruel or unusual punishments inflicted. That all warrants, without oath or affirmation, to search suspected places, or seize any person, his papers or property, are grievous and oppressive."

These provisions are as necessary under the general government as under that of the individual States; for the power of the former is as complete to the purpose of requiring bail, imposing fines, inflicting punishments, granting search warrants, and seizing persons, papers, or property, in certain cases, as the other.

For the purpose of securing the property of the citizens, it is declared by all the States, "that in all controversies at law, respecting property, the ancient mode of trial by jury is one of the best securities of the rights of the people, and ought to remain sacred and inviolable."

Does not the same necessity exist of reserving this right under their national compact, as in that of the States? Y et nothing is said respecting it. In the bills of rights of the States it is declared, that a well regulated militia is the proper and natural defense of a free government; that as standing armies in time of peace are dangerous, they are not to be kept up, and that the military should be kept under strict subordination to, and controlled by, the civil power.

The same security is as necessary in this Constitution, and much more so; for the general government will have the sole power to raise and to pay armies, and are under no control in the exercise of it; yet nothing of this is to be found in this new system.

I might proceed to instance a number of other rights, which were as necessary to be reserved, such as, that elections should be free, that the liberty of the press should be held sacred; but the instances adduced are sufficient to prove that this argument is without foundation. Besides, it is evident that the reason here assigned was not the true one, why the framers of this Constitution omitted a bill of rights; if it had been, they would not have made certain reservations, while they totally omitted others of more importance. We find they have, in the ninth section of the first article declared, that the writ of habeas corpus shall not be suspended, unless in cases of rebellion, -that no bill of attainder, or ex post facto law, shall be passed, -that no title of nobility shall be granted by the United States, etc. If everything which is not given is reserved, what propriety is there in these exceptions? Does this Constitution any where grant the power of suspending the habeas corpus, to make ex post facto laws, pass bills of attainder, or grant titles of nobility? It certainly does not in express terms. The only answer that can be given is, that these are implied in the general powers granted. With equal truth it may be said, that all the powers which the bills of rights guard against the abuse of, are contained or implied in the general ones granted by this Constitution.

So far is it from being true, that a bill of rights is less necessary in the general Constitution than in those of the States, the contrary is evidently the fact. This system, if it is possible for the people of America to accede to it, will be an original compact; and being the last wilt, in the nature of things, vacate every former agreement inconsistent with it. For it being a plan of government received and ratified by the whole people, all other forms which are in existence at the time of its adoption, must yield to it. This is expressed in positive and unequivocal terms in the sixth article: "That this Constitution, and the laws of the United States which shall be made in pursuance thereof, and all treaties made, or which shall be made, under the authority of the United States, shall be the supreme law of the land; and the judges in every State shall be bound thereby, anything in the Constitution, or laws of any State, to the contrary notwithstanding."

"The senators and representatives before-mentioned, and the members of the several State legislatures, and all executive and judicial officers, both of the United States, and of the several States, shall be bound, by oath or affirmation, to support this Constitution."

It is therefore not only necessarily implied thereby, but positively expressed, that the different State Constitutions are repealed and entirely done away, so far as they are inconsistent with this, with the laws which shall be made in pursuance thereof, or with treaties made, or which shall be made, under the authority of the United States. Of what avail will the Constitutions of the respective States be to preserve the rights of its citizens? Should they be pled, the answer would be, the Constitution of the United States, and the laws made in pursuance thereof, is the supreme law, and all legislatures and judicial officers, whether of the General or State governments, are bound by oath to support it. No privilege, reserved by the bills of rights, or secured by the State governments, can limit the power granted by this, or restrain any laws made in pursuance of it. It stands, therefore, on its own bottom, and must receive a construction by itself, without any reference to any other. And hence it was of the highest importance, that the most precise and express declarations and reservations of rights should have been made.

This will appear the more necessary, when it is considered, that not only the Constitution and laws made in pursuance thereof, but alt treaties made, under the authority of the United States, are the supreme law of the land, and supersede the Constitutions of all the States. The power to make treaties, is vested in the president, by and with the advice and consent of two-thirds of the senate. I do not find any limitation or restriction to the exercise of this power. The most important article in any Constitution may therefore be repealed, even without a legislative act. Ought not a government, vested with such extensive and indefinite authority, to have been restricted by a declaration of rights? It certainly ought.

So clear a point is this, that I cannot help suspecting that persons who attempt to persuade people that such reservations were less necessary under this Constitution than under those of the States, are wilfully endeavoring to deceive, and to lead you into an absolute state of vassalage.

BRUTUS

The Federalist Papers
(1787–1788)

After the proposed new constitution had been finalized and submitted to the states for ratification, both those who supported it and those who didn't like it lobbied heavily for or against its adoption. The pro-constitution side was better organized than the anti-constitution side. The various essays that have come to be known as the Anti-Federalist Papers were produced by individuals, writing for themselves and with little or no coordination with other anti-federalists.

On the pro-constitution side, on the other hand, active proponents coordinated their efforts. In particular, three strong advocates for the new constitution joined together to produce the series of essays now called The Federalist Papers. These three men were Alexander Hamilton (51 essays), James Madison (29 essays), and John Jay (5 essays). As was the case with the authors of The Anti-Federalist Papers, the Federalist authors wrote their essays anonymously, all publishing under the name "Publius."

Of the 85 essays, two stand out as being of special interest in discussing the Second Amendment and the Bill of Rights:

- No. 46: Argues that the strong central government contemplated by the proposed new constitution would be limited and constrained in the exercise of its powers by the states and by the people themselves. The eighth paragraph discusses a standing army, and proposes that no matter how strong a standing army might be, "This proportion would not yield, in the United States, an army of more than twenty-five or thirty thousand men. To these would be opposed a militia amounting to near half a million of citizens with arms in their hands, officered by men chosen from among themselves, fighting for their common liberties, and united and conducted by governments possessing their affections and confidence. It may well be doubted, whether a militia thus circumstanced could ever be conquered by such a proportion of regular troops. Those who are best acquainted with the last successful resistance of this country against the British arms, will be most inclined to deny the possibility of it. Besides the advantage of being armed, which the Americans possess over the people of almost every other nation, the existence of subordinate governments, to which the people are attached, and by which the militia officers are appointed, forms a barrier against the enterprises of ambition, more insurmountable than any which a simple government of any form can admit of." Clearly, in this essay Madison is accepting it as a precondition of the ratification of the new constitution that the People would be armed and that armed citizens would and should outnumber any standing army and be equally or more heavily armed than any standing army.

- No. 84: Argues that a specific Bill of Rights is not needed because the proposed constitution as drafted includes adequate provisions to safeguard individual rights and liberties.

Federalist No. 46

The Influence of the State and Federal Governments Compared

James Madison (writing as "Publius")
From the *New York Packet*
Tuesday, January 29, 1788.

To the People of the State of New York:

RESUMING the subject of the last paper, I proceed to inquire whether the federal government or the State governments will have the advantage with regard to the predilection and support of the people. Notwithstanding the different modes in which they are appointed, we must consider both of them as substantially dependent on the great body of the citizens of the United States.

I assume this position here as it respects the first, reserving the proofs for another place. The federal and State governments are in fact but different agents and trustees of the people, constituted with different powers, and designed for different purposes. The adversaries of the Constitution seem to have lost sight of the people altogether in their reasonings on this subject; and to have viewed these different establishments, not only as mutual rivals and enemies, but as uncontrolled by any common superior in their efforts to usurp the authorities of each other. These gentlemen must here be reminded of their error. They must be told that the ultimate authority, wherever the derivative may be found, resides in the people alone, and that it will not depend merely on the comparative ambition or address of the different governments, whether either, or which of them, will be able to enlarge its sphere of jurisdiction at the expense of the other. Truth, no less than decency, requires that the event in every case should be supposed to depend on the sentiments and sanction of their common constituents. Many considerations, besides those suggested on a former occasion, seem to place it beyond doubt that the first and most natural attachment of the people will be to the governments of their respective States.

Into the administration of these a greater number of individuals will expect to rise. From the gift of these a greater number of offices and emoluments will flow. By the superintending care of these, all the more domestic and personal interests of the people will be regulated and provided for. With the affairs of these, the people will be more familiarly and minutely conversant. And with the members of these, will a greater proportion of the people have the ties of personal acquaintance and friendship, and of family and party attachments; on the side of these, therefore, the popular bias may well be expected most strongly to incline.

Experience speaks the same language in this case. The federal administration, though hitherto very defective in comparison with what may be hoped under a better system, had, during the war, and particularly whilst the independent fund of paper emissions was in credit, an activity and importance as great as it can well have in any future circumstances whatever.

It was engaged, too, in a course of measures which had for their object the protection of everything that was dear, and the acquisition of everything that could be desirable to the people at large. It was, nevertheless, invariably found, after the transient enthusiasm for the early Congresses was over, that the attention and attachment of the people were turned anew to their own particular governments; that the federal council was at no time the idol of popular favor; and that opposition to proposed enlargements of its powers and importance was the side usually taken by the men who wished to build their political consequence on the prepossessions of their fellow-citizens. If, therefore, as has been elsewhere remarked, the people should in future become more partial to the federal than to the State governments, the change can only result from such manifest and irresistible proofs of a better administration, as will overcome all their antecedent propensities. And in that case, the people ought not surely to be precluded from giving most of their confidence where they may discover it to be most due; but even in that case the State governments could have little to apprehend, because it is only within a certain sphere that the federal power can, in the nature of things, be advantageously administered. The remaining points on which I propose to compare the federal and State governments, are the disposition and the faculty they may respectively possess, to resist and frustrate the measures of each other. It has been already proved that the members of the federal will be more dependent on the members of the State governments, than the latter will be on the former. It has appeared also, that the prepossessions of the people, on whom both will depend, will be more on the side of the State governments, than of the federal government. So far as the disposition of each towards the other may be influenced by these causes, the State governments must clearly have the advantage.

But in a distinct and very important point of view, the advantage will lie on the same side. The prepossessions, which the members themselves will carry into the federal government, will generally be favorable to the States; whilst it will rarely happen, that the members of the State governments will carry into the public councils a bias in favor of the general government. A local spirit will infallibly prevail much more in the members of Congress, than a national spirit will prevail in the legislatures of the particular States. Every one knows that a great proportion of the errors committed by the State legislatures proceeds from the disposition of the members to sacrifice the comprehensive and permanent interest of the State, to the particular and separate views of the counties or districts in which they reside. And if they do not sufficiently enlarge their policy to embrace the collective welfare of their particular State, how can it be imagined that they will make the aggregate prosperity of the Union, and the dignity and respectability of its government, the objects of their affections and consultations? For the same reason that the members of the State legislatures will be unlikely to attach themselves sufficiently to national objects, the members of the federal legislature will be likely to attach themselves too much to local objects. The States will be to the latter what counties and towns are to the former. Measures will too often be decided according to their probable effect, not on the national prosperity and happiness, but on the prejudices, interests, and pursuits of the governments and people of the individual States. What is the spirit that has in general characterized the proceedings of Congress? A perusal of their journals, as well as the candid acknowledgments of such as have had a seat in that assembly, will inform us, that the members have but too frequently displayed the character, rather of partisans of their respective States, than of impartial guardians of a common interest; that where on one occasion improper sacrifices have been made of local considerations, to the aggrandizement of the federal government, the great interests of the nation have suffered on a hundred, from an undue attention to the local prejudices, interests, and views of the particular States. I mean not by these reflections to insinuate, that the new federal government will not embrace a more enlarged plan of policy than the existing government may have pursued; much less, that its views will be as confined as those of the State legislatures; but only that it will partake sufficiently of the spirit of both, to be disinclined to invade the rights of the individual States, or the prerogatives of their governments. The motives on the part of the State governments, to augment their prerogatives by defalcations from the federal government, will be overruled by no reciprocal predispositions in the members. Were it admitted, however, that the Federal government may feel an equal disposition with the State governments to extend its power beyond the due limits, the latter would still have the advantage in the means of defeating such encroachments. If an act of a particular State, though unfriendly to the national government, be generally popular in that State and should not too grossly violate the oaths of the State officers, it is executed immediately and, of course, by means on the spot and depending on the State alone. The opposition of the federal government, or the interposition of federal officers, would but inflame the zeal of all parties on the side of the State, and the evil could not be prevented or repaired, if at all, without the employment of means which must always be resorted to with reluctance and difficulty.

On the other hand, should an unwarrantable measure of the federal government be unpopular in particular States, which would seldom fail to be the case, or even a warrantable measure be so, which may sometimes be the case, the means of opposition to it are powerful and at hand. The disquietude of the people; their repugnance and, perhaps, refusal to co-operate with the officers of the Union; the frowns of the executive magistracy of the State; the embarrassments created by legislative devices, which would often be added on such occasions, would oppose, in any State, difficulties not to be despised; would form, in a large State, very serious impediments; and where the sentiments of several adjoining States happened to be in unison, would present obstructions which the federal government would hardly be willing to encounter. But ambitious encroachments of the federal government, on the authority of the State governments, would not excite the opposition of a single State, or of a few States only. They would be signals of general alarm. Every government would espouse the common cause. A correspondence would be opened. Plans of resistance would be concerted. One spirit would animate and conduct the whole. The same combinations, in short, would result from an apprehension of the federal, as was produced by the dread of a foreign, yoke; and unless the projected innovations should be voluntarily renounced, the same appeal to a trial of force would be made in the one case as was made in the other. But what degree of madness could ever drive the federal government to such an extremity. In the contest with Great Britain, one part of the empire was employed against the other.

The more numerous part invaded the rights of the less numerous part. The attempt was unjust and unwise; but it was not in speculation absolutely chimerical. But what would be the contest in the case we are supposing? Who would be the parties? A few representatives of the people would be opposed to the people themselves; or rather one set of representatives would be contending against thirteen sets of representatives, with the whole body of their common constituents on the side of the latter. The only refuge left for those who prophesy the downfall of the State governments is the visionary supposition that the federal government may previously accumulate a military force for the projects of ambition. The reasonings contained in these papers must have been employed to little purpose indeed, if it could be necessary now to disprove the reality of this danger. That the people and the States should, for a sufficient period of time, elect an uninterupted succession of men ready to betray both; that the traitors should, throughout this period, uniformly and systematically pursue some fixed plan for the extension of the military establishment; that the governments and the people of the States should silently and patiently behold the gathering storm, and continue to supply the materials, until it should be prepared to burst on their own heads, must appear to every one more like the incoherent dreams of a delirious jealousy, or the misjudged exaggerations of a counterfeit zeal, than like the sober apprehensions of genuine patriotism.

Extravagant as the supposition is, let it however be made. Let a regular army, fully equal to the resources of the country, be formed; and let it be entirely at the devotion of the federal government; still it would not be going too far to say, that the State governments, with the people on their side, would be able to repel the danger. The highest number to which, according to the best computation, a standing army can be carried in any country, does not exceed one hundredth part of the whole number of souls; or one twenty-fifth part of the number able to bear arms. This proportion would not yield, in the United States, an army of more than twenty-five or thirty thousand men. To these would be opposed a militia amounting to near half a million of citizens with arms in their hands, officered by men chosen from among themselves, fighting for their common liberties, and united and conducted by governments possessing their affections and confidence. It may well be doubted, whether a militia thus circumstanced could ever be conquered by such a proportion of regular troops. Those who are best acquainted with the last successful resistance of this country against the British arms, will be most inclined to deny the possibility of it. Besides the advantage of being armed, which the Americans possess over the people of almost every other nation, the existence of subordinate governments, to which the people are attached, and by which the militia officers are appointed, forms a barrier against the enterprises of ambition, more insurmountable than any which a simple government of any form can admit of. Notwithstanding the military establishments in the several kingdoms of Europe, which are carried as far as the public resources will bear, the governments are afraid to trust the people with arms. And it is not certain, that with this aid alone they would not be able to shake off their yokes. But were the people to possess the additional advantages of local governments chosen by themselves, who could collect the national will and direct the national force, and of officers appointed out of the militia, by these governments, and attached both to them and to the militia, it may be affirmed with the greatest assurance, that the throne of every tyranny in Europe would be speedily overturned in spite of the legions which surround it. Let us not insult the free and gallant citizens of America with the suspicion, that they would be less able to defend the rights of which they would be in actual possession, than the debased subjects of arbitrary power would be to rescue theirs from the hands of their oppressors. Let us rather no longer insult them with the supposition that they can ever reduce themselves to the necessity of making the experiment, by a blind and tame submission to the long train of insidious measures which must precede and produce it. The argument under the present head may be put into a very concise form, which appears altogether conclusive. Either the mode in which the federal government is to be constructed will render it sufficiently dependent on the people, or it will not. On the first supposition, it will be restrained by that dependence from forming schemes obnoxious to their constituents. On the other supposition, it will not possess the confidence of the people, and its schemes of usurpation will be easily defeated by the State governments, who will be supported by the people. On summing up the considerations stated in this and the last paper, they seem to amount to the most convincing evidence, that the powers proposed to be lodged in the federal government are as little formidable to those reserved to the individual States, as they are indispensably necessary to accomplish the purposes of the Union; and that all those alarms which have been sounded, of a meditated and consequential annihilation of the State governments, must, on the most favorable interpretation, be ascribed to the chimerical fears of the authors of them.

PUBLIUS

Federalist No. 84

Certain General and Miscellaneous Objections to the Constitution Considered and Answered

Alexander Hamilton (writing as "Publius")
From *McLEAN'S Edition*, New York.

To the People of the State of New York:

IN THE course of the foregoing review of the Constitution, I have taken notice of, and endeavored to answer most of the objections which have appeared against it. There, however, remain a few which either did not fall naturally under any particular head or were forgotten in their proper places. These shall now be discussed; but as the subject has been drawn into great length, I shall so far consult brevity as to comprise all my observations on these miscellaneous points in a single paper.

The most considerable of the remaining objections is that the plan of the convention contains no bill of rights. Among other answers given to this, it has been upon different occasions remarked that the constitutions of several of the States are in a similar predicament. I add that New York is of the number. And yet the opposers of the new system, in this State, who profess an unlimited admiration for its constitution, are among the most intemperate partisans of a bill of rights. To justify their zeal in this matter, they allege two things: one is that, though the constitution of New York has no bill of rights prefixed to it, yet it contains, in the body of it, various provisions in favor of particular privileges and rights, which, in substance amount to the same thing; the other is, that the Constitution adopts, in their full extent, the common and statute law of Great Britain, by which many other rights, not expressed in it, are equally secured.

To the first I answer, that the Constitution proposed by the convention contains, as well as the constitution of this State, a number of such provisions.

Independent of those which relate to the structure of the government, we find the following: Article 1, section 3, clause 7 "Judgment in cases of impeachment shall not extend further than to removal from office, and disqualification to hold and enjoy any office of honor, trust, or profit under the United States; but the party convicted shall, nevertheless, be liable and subject to indictment, trial, judgment, and punishment according to law." Section 9, of the same article, clause 2 "The privilege of the writ of habeas corpus shall not be suspended, unless when in cases of rebellion or invasion the public safety may require it." Clause 3 "No bill of attainder or ex-post-facto law shall be passed." Clause 7 "No title of nobility shall be granted by the United States; and no person holding any office of profit or trust under them, shall, without the consent of the Congress, accept of any present, emolument, office, or title of any kind whatever, from any king, prince, or foreign state." Article 3, section 2, clause 3 "The trial of all crimes, except in cases of impeachment, shall be by jury; and such trial shall be held in the State where the said crimes shall have been committed; but when not committed within any State, the trial shall be at such place or places as the Congress may by law have directed." Section 3, of the same article "Treason against the United States shall consist only in levying war against them, or in adhering to their enemies, giving them aid and comfort. No person shall be convicted of treason, unless on the testimony of two witnesses to the same overt act, or on confession in open court." And clause 3, of the same section "The Congress shall have power to declare the punishment of treason; but no attainder of treason shall work corruption of blood, or forfeiture, except during the life of the person attainted." It may well be a question, whether these are not, upon the whole, of equal importance with any which are to be found in the constitution of this State. The establishment of the writ of habeas corpus, the prohibition of ex-post-facto laws, and of titles of nobility, to which we have no corresponding provision in our constitution, are perhaps greater securities to liberty and republicanism than any it contains. The creation of crimes after the commission of the fact, or, in other words, the subjecting of men to punishment for things which, when they were done, were breaches of no law, and the practice of arbitrary imprisonments, have been, in all ages, the favorite and most formidable instruments of tyranny. The observations of the judicious Blackstone, in reference to the latter, are well worthy of recital: "To bereave a man of life," says he, "or by violence to confiscate his estate, without accusation or trial, would be so gross and notorious an act of despotism, as must at once convey the alarm of tyranny throughout the whole nation; but confinement of the person, by secretly hurrying him to jail, where his sufferings are unknown or forgotten, is a less public, a less striking, and therefore a more dangerous engine of arbitrary government." And as a remedy for this fatal evil he is everywhere peculiarly emphatical in his encomiums on the habeas-corpus act, which in one place he calls "the bulwark of the British Constitution."[2]

Nothing need be said to illustrate the importance of the prohibition of titles of nobility. This may truly be denominated the corner-stone of republican government; for so long as they are excluded, there can never be serious danger that the government will be any other than that of the people.

To the second that is, to the pretended establishment of the common and state law by the Constitution, I answer, that they are expressly made subject "to such alterations and provisions as the legislature shall from time to time make concerning the same." They are therefore at any moment liable to repeal by the ordinary legislative power, and of course have no constitutional sanction. The only use of the declaration was to recognize the ancient law and to remove doubts which might have been occasioned by the Revolution. This consequently can be considered as no part of a declaration of rights, which under our constitutions must be intended as limitations of the power of the government itself.

It has been several times truly remarked that bills of rights are, in their origin, stipulations between kings and their subjects, abridgements of prerogative in favor of privilege, reservations of rights not surrendered to the prince. Such was MAGNA CARTA, obtained by the barons, sword in hand, from King John. Such were the subsequent confirmations of that charter by succeeding princes. Such was the PETITION OF RIGHT assented to by Charles I., in the beginning of his reign. Such, also, was the Declaration of Right presented by the Lords and Commons to the Prince of Orange in 1688, and afterwards thrown into the form of an act of parliament called the Bill of Rights. It is evident, therefore, that, according to their primitive signification, they have no application to constitutions professedly founded upon the power of the people, and executed by their immediate representatives and servants. Here, in strictness, the people surrender nothing; and as they retain everything they have no need of particular reservations. "WE, THE PEOPLE of the United States, to secure the blessings of liberty to ourselves and our posterity, do ORDAIN and ESTABLISH this Constitution for the United States of America." Here is a better recognition of popular rights, than volumes of those aphorisms which make the principal figure in several of our State bills of rights, and which would sound much better in a treatise of ethics than in a constitution of government.

But a minute detail of particular rights is certainly far less applicable to a Constitution like that under consideration, which is merely intended to regulate the general political interests of the nation, than to a constitution which has the regulation of every species of personal and private concerns. If, therefore, the loud clamors against the plan of the convention, on this score, are well founded, no epithets of reprobation will be too strong for the constitution of this State. But the truth is, that both of them contain all which, in relation to their objects, is reasonably to be desired.

I go further, and affirm that bills of rights, in the sense and to the extent in which they are contended for, are not only unnecessary in the proposed Constitution, but would even be dangerous. They would contain various exceptions to powers not granted; and, on this very account, would afford a colorable pretext to claim more than were granted. For why declare that things shall not be done which there is no power to do? Why, for instance, should it be said that the liberty of the press shall not be restrained, when no power is given by which restrictions may be imposed? I will not contend that such a provision would confer a regulating power; but it is evident that it would furnish, to men disposed to usurp, a plausible pretense for claiming that power. They might urge with a semblance of reason, that the Constitution ought not to be charged with the absurdity of providing against the abuse of an authority which was not given, and that the provision against restraining the liberty of the press afforded a clear implication, that a power to prescribe proper regulations concerning it was intended to be vested in the national government. This may serve as a specimen of the numerous handles which would be given to the doctrine of constructive powers, by the indulgence of an injudicious zeal for bills of rights.

On the subject of the liberty of the press, as much as has been said, I cannot forbear adding a remark or two: in the first place, I observe, that there is not a syllable concerning it in the constitution of this State; in the next, I contend, that whatever has been said about it in that of any other State, amounts to nothing. What signifies a declaration, that "the liberty of the press shall be inviolably preserved"? What is the liberty of the press? Who can give it any definition which would not leave the utmost latitude for evasion? I hold it to be impracticable; and from this I infer, that its security, whatever fine declarations may be inserted in any constitution respecting it, must altogether depend on public opinion, and on the general spirit of the people and of the government.[3] And here, after all, as is intimated upon another occasion, must we seek for the only solid basis of all our rights.

There remains but one other view of this matter to conclude the point. The truth is, after all the declamations we have heard, that the Constitution is itself, in every rational sense, and to every useful purpose, A BILL OF RIGHTS. The several bills of rights in Great Britain form its Constitution, and conversely the constitution of each State is its bill of rights. And the proposed Constitution, if adopted, will be the bill of rights of the Union. Is it one object of a bill of rights to declare and specify the political privileges of the citizens in the structure and administration of the government? This is done in the most ample and precise manner in the plan of the convention; comprehending various precautions for the public security, which are not to be found in any of the State constitutions. Is another object of a bill of rights to define certain immunities and modes of proceeding, which are relative to personal and private concerns? This we have seen has also been attended to, in a variety of cases, in the same plan. Adverting therefore to the substantial meaning of a bill of rights, it is absurd to allege that it is not to be found in the work of the convention. It may be said that it does not go far enough, though it will not be easy to make this appear; but it can with no propriety be contended that there is no such thing. It certainly must be immaterial what mode is observed as to the order of declaring the rights of the citizens, if they are to be found in any part of the instrument which establishes the government. And hence it must be apparent, that much of what has been said on this subject rests merely on verbal and nominal distinctions, entirely foreign from the substance of the thing.

Another objection which has been made, and which, from the frequency of its repetition, it is to be presumed is relied on, is of this nature: "It is improper" say the objectors, "to confer such large powers, as are proposed, upon the national government, because the seat of that government must of necessity be too remote from many of the States to admit of a proper knowledge on the part of the constituent, of the conduct of the representative body." This argument, if it proves anything, proves that there ought to be no general government whatever. For the powers which, it seems to be agreed on all hands, ought to be vested in the Union, cannot be safely intrusted to a body which is not under every requisite control. But there are satisfactory reasons to show that the objection is in reality not well founded. There is in most of the arguments which relate to distance a palpable illusion of the imagination. What are the sources of information by which the people in Montgomery County must regulate their judgment of the conduct of their representatives in the State legislature? Of personal observation they can have no benefit. This is confined to the citizens on the spot. They must therefore depend on the information of intelligent men, in whom they confide; and how must these men obtain their information? Evidently from the complexion of public measures, from the public prints, from correspondences with their representatives, and with other persons who reside at the place of their deliberations. This does not apply to Montgomery County only, but to all the counties at any considerable distance from the seat of government.

It is equally evident that the same sources of information would be open to the people in relation to the conduct of their representatives in the general government, and the impediments to a prompt communication which distance may be supposed to create, will be overbalanced by the effects of the vigilance of the State governments. The executive and legislative bodies of each State will be so many sentinels over the persons employed in every department of the national administration; and as it will be in their power to adopt and pursue a regular and effectual system of intelligence, they can never be at a loss to know the behavior of those who represent their constituents in the national councils, and can readily communicate the same knowledge to the people. Their disposition to apprise the community of whatever may prejudice its interests from another quarter, may be relied upon, if it were only from the rivalship of power. And we may conclude with the fullest assurance that the people, through that channel, will be better informed of the conduct of their national representatives, than they can be by any means they now possess of that of their State representatives.

It ought also to be remembered that the citizens who inhabit the country at and near the seat of government will, in all questions that affect the general liberty and prosperity, have the same interest with those who are at a distance, and that they will stand ready to sound the alarm when necessary, and to point out the actors in any pernicious project. The public papers will be expeditious messengers of intelligence to the most remote inhabitants of the Union.

Among the many curious objections which have appeared against the proposed Constitution, the most extraordinary and the least colorable is derived from the want of some provision respecting the debts due TO the United States. This has been represented as a tacit relinquishment of those debts, and as a wicked contrivance to screen public defaulters. The newspapers have teemed with the most inflammatory railings on this head; yet there is nothing clearer than that the suggestion is entirely void of foundation, the offspring of extreme ignorance or extreme dishonesty. In addition to the remarks I have made upon the subject in another place, I shall only observe that as it is a plain dictate of common-sense, so it is also an established doctrine of political law, that "states neither lose any of their rights, nor are discharged from any of their obligations, by a change in the form of their civil government." The last objection of any consequence, which I at present recollect, turns upon the article of expense. If it were even true, that the adoption of the proposed government would occasion a considerable increase of expense, it would be an objection that ought to have no weight against the plan.

The great bulk of the citizens of America are with reason convinced, that Union is the basis of their political happiness. Men of sense of all parties now, with few exceptions, agree that it cannot be preserved under the present system, nor without radical alterations; that new and extensive powers ought to be granted to the national head, and that these require a different organization of the federal government a single body being an unsafe depositary of such ample authorities. In conceding all this, the question of expense must be given up; for it is impossible, with any degree of safety, to narrow the foundation upon which the system is to stand. The two branches of the legislature are, in the first instance, to consist of only sixty-five persons, which is the same number of which Congress, under the existing Confederation, may be composed. It is true that this number is intended to be increased; but this is to keep pace with the progress of the population and resources of the country. It is evident that a less number would, even in the first instance, have been unsafe, and that a continuance of the present number would, in a more advanced stage of population, be a very inadequate representation of the people.

Whence is the dreaded augmentation of expense to spring? One source indicated, is the multiplication of offices under the new government. Let us examine this a little.

It is evident that the principal departments of the administration under the present government, are the same which will be required under the new. There are now a Secretary of War, a Secretary of Foreign Affairs, a Secretary for Domestic Affairs, a Board of Treasury, consisting of three persons, a Treasurer, assistants, clerks, etc. These officers are indispensable under any system, and will suffice under the new as well as the old. As to ambassadors and other ministers and agents in foreign countries, the proposed Constitution can make no other difference than to render their characters, where they reside, more respectable, and their services more useful. As to persons to be employed in the collection of the revenues, it is unquestionably true that these will form a very considerable addition to the number of federal officers; but it will not follow that this will occasion an increase of public expense. It will be in most cases nothing more than an exchange of State for national officers. In the collection of all duties, for instance, the persons employed will be wholly of the latter description. The States individually will stand in no need of any for this purpose. What difference can it make in point of expense to pay officers of the customs appointed by the State or by the United States? There is no good reason to suppose that either the number or the salaries of the latter will be greater than those of the former.

Where then are we to seek for those additional articles of expense which are to swell the account to the enormous size that has been represented to us? The chief item which occurs to me respects the support of the judges of the United States. I do not add the President, because there is now a president of Congress, whose expenses may not be far, if anything, short of those which will be incurred on account of the President of the United States. The support of the judges will clearly be an extra expense, but to what extent will depend on the particular plan which may be adopted in regard to this matter. But upon no reasonable plan can it amount to a sum which will be an object of material consequence.

Let us now see what there is to counterbalance any extra expense that may attend the establishment of the proposed government. The first thing which presents itself is that a great part of the business which now keeps Congress sitting through the year will be transacted by the President. Even the management of foreign negotiations will naturally devolve upon him, according to general principles concerted with the Senate, and subject to their final concurrence. Hence it is evident that a portion of the year will suffice for the session of both the Senate and the House of Representatives; we may suppose about a fourth for the latter and a third, or perhaps half, for the former. The extra business of treaties and appointments may give this extra occupation to the Senate. From this circumstance we may infer that, until the House of Representatives shall be increased greatly beyond its present number, there will be a considerable saving of expense from the difference between the constant session of the present and the temporary session of the future Congress.

But there is another circumstance of great importance in the view of economy. The business of the United States has hitherto occupied the State legislatures, as well as Congress. The latter has made requisitions which the former have had to provide for. Hence it has happened that the sessions of the State legislatures have been protracted greatly beyond what was necessary for the execution of the mere local business of the States. More than half their time has been frequently employed in matters which related to the United States. Now the members who compose the legislatures of the several States amount to two thousand and upwards, which number has hitherto performed what under the new system will be done in the first instance by sixty-five persons, and probably at no future period by above a fourth or fifth of that number. The Congress under the proposed government will do all the business of the United States themselves, without the intervention of the State legislatures, who thenceforth will have only to attend to the affairs of their particular States, and will not have to sit in any proportion as long as they have heretofore done. This difference in the time of the sessions of the State legislatures will be clear gain, and will alone form an article of saving, which may be regarded as an equivalent for any additional objects of expense that may be occasioned by the adoption of the new system.

The result from these observations is that the sources of additional expense from the establishment of the proposed Constitution are much fewer than may have been imagined; that they are counterbalanced by considerable objects of saving; and that while it is questionable on which side the scale will preponderate, it is certain that a government less expensive would be incompetent to the purposes of the Union.

PUBLIUS.

Contemporary Quotations Relevant to the Right to Keep and Bear Arms

In the course of the debate over adoption of the new constitution, aside from the Federalist Papers and the Anti-Federalist Papers, many other influential members of society (including a number of prominent Revolutionary personalities and members of the Congress) made statements or promulgated essays addressing their views of the proposed constitution and the right to keep and bear arms. Some of those statements are reproduced here, for the purpose of providing additional context in support of the view that the full intent of the Constitution of the United States was that the People have both a right, and a duty and responsibility to be armed.

* * * * *

"No free man shall ever be debarred the use of arms. The strongest reason for the people to retain the right to keep and bear arms is, as a last resort, to protect themselves against tyranny in government"

– Thomas Jefferson, 1 Thomas Jefferson Papers, 334

"The very atmosphere of firearms anywhere and everywhere restrains evil interference – they deserve a place of honor with all that's good"

– George Washington

"The best we can hope for concerning the people at large is that they be properly armed."

– Alexander Hamilton, *The Federalist Papers*

"They that can give up essential liberty to obtain a little temporary safety deserve neither liberty nor safety."

– Benjamin Franklin, *Historical Review of Pennsylvania*, 1759.

"I hold it, that a little rebellion, now and then, is a good thing, and as necessary in the political world as storms in the physical."

– Thomas Jefferson, Letter to James Madison, January 30, 1787

Men trained in arms from their infancy, and animated by the love of liberty, will afford neither a cheap or easy conquest.

– From the Declaration of the Continental Congress, July 1775.

"As to the species of exercise, I advise the gun. While this gives [only] moderate exercise to the body, it gives boldness, enterprise, and independence to the mind. Games played with the ball and others of that nature, are too violent for the body and stamp no character on the mind. Let your gun, therefore, be the constant companion to your walks."

– Thomas Jefferson, writing to his teenaged nephew.

"Government is not reason, it is not eloquence, it is force; like fire, a troublesome servant and a fearful master. Never for a moment should it be left to irresponsible action."

– George Washington, in a speech of January 7, 1790

"A militia, when properly formed, are in fact the people themselves ... and include all men capable of bearing arms."

— Richard Henry Lee, 1788,

The spirit of resistance to government is so valuable on certain occasions, that I wish it always to be kept alive. It will often be exercised when wrong, but better so than not to be exercised at all. I like a little rebellion now and then. It is like a storm in the Atmosphere.

– Thomas Jefferson, letter to Abigail Adams, 1787

& what country can preserve its liberties, if its rulers are not warned from time to time that his people preserve the spirit of resistance? Let them take arms.

– Thomas Jefferson, letter to Col. William S. Smith, 1787

"Guard with jealous attention the public liberty. Suspect everyone who approaches that jewel. Unfortunately, nothing will preserve it but downright force. Whenever you give up that force, you are inevitably ruined."

– Patrick Henry, speech of June 5 1788

Are we at last brought to such a humiliating and debasing degradation, that we cannot be trusted with arms for our own defence? Where is the difference between having our arms in our own possession and under our own direction, and having them under the management of Congress? If our defence be the *real* object of having those arms, in whose hands can they be trusted with more propriety, or equal safety to us, as in our own hands?

– Patrick Henry, speech of June 9 1788

"To disarm the people ... was the best and most effectual way to enslave them."

– George Mason, speech of June 14, 1788

"The great object is, that every man be armed. [...] Everyone who is able may have a gun."

– Patrick Henry, speech of June 14 1788

Such are a well regulated militia, composed of the freeholders, citizen and husbandman, who take up arms to preserve their property, as individuals, and their rights as freemen.

– "M.T. Cicero", in a newspaper letter of 1788 touching the "militia"

That the said Constitution shall never be construed to authorize Congress to infringe the just liberty of the press or the rights of conscience; or to prevent the people of the United states who are peaceable citizens from keeping their own arms...

– Samuel Adams, in *Phila. Independent Gazetteer*, August 20, 1789

"The Constitution shall never be construed... to prevent the people of the United States who are peaceable citizens from keeping their own arms."

– Samuel Adams

"The supreme power in America cannot enforce unjust laws by the sword; because the whole body of the people are armed, and constitute a force superior to any band of regular troops that can be, on any pretense, raised in the United States."

– Noah Webster

"A free people ought not only to be armed, but disciplined; to which end a uniform and well-digested plan is requisite; and their safety and interest require that they should promote such manufactories as tend to render them independent of others for essential, particularly military, supplies."

– George Washington

"What country can preserve its liberties if their rulers are not warned from time to time that their people preserve the spirit of resistance? Let them take arms."

– Thomas Jefferson

"The laws that forbid the carrying of arms are laws of such a nature. They disarm only those who are neither inclined nor determined to commit crimes.... Such laws make things worse for the assaulted and better for the assailants; they serve rather to encourage than to prevent homicides, for an unarmed man may be attacked with greater confidence than an armed man."

– Thomas Jefferson

"I ask who are the militia? They consist now of the whole people, except a few public officers."

– George Mason

"The militia of these free commonwealths, entitled and accustomed to their arms, when compared with any possible army, must be tremendous and irresistible. Who are the militia? Are they not ourselves? Is it feared, then, that we shall turn our arms each man against his own bosom. Congress have no power to disarm the militia. Their swords, and every other terrible implement of the soldier, are the birth-right of an American ... the unlimited power of the sword is not in the hands of either the federal or state governments, but, where I trust in God it will ever remain, in the hands of the people."

— Tench Coxe, *Pennsylvania Gazette*, February 20, 1788

"The people are not to be disarmed of their weapons. They are left in full possession of them."

— Zachariah Johnson

The Constitution of the United States (1788)

The draft of the prosed constitution of the United States was completed on September 17, 1787, and was formally submitted to the Congress of the Confederation (the legal governing body under the Articles of Confederation) on September 28, 1787. That body approved submitting the proposed new constitution to the states for ratification by a vote taken the next day, September 29, 1787.

With the debate over the new constitution now shifted from the convention to the individual states, discussion was intense. Leading advocates on both sides published numerous essays expounding their views. These documents have come to be known as *The Federalist Papers* and *The Anti-Federalist Papers*. [Some of each are found in this collection, immediately preceding this chapter.]

The proposed constitution required ratification of a minimum of two-thirds of the states (nine) for acceptance. By January of 1788, only five states had ratified the document: Connecticut, Delaware, Georgia, New Jersey, and Pennsylvania. One of the primary objections in several of the states was the absence of a Bill of Rights (which Alexander Hamilton had advocated against strongly in *The Federalist papers* number 84).

Proponents of federalism reluctantly recognized that a Bill of Rights would have to be conceded if there was to be any hope of ratifying the new constitution. With the promise of immediate amendments to accomplish this upon ratification, Massachusetts voted to ratify on February 6, 1788.

Opposition to the new constitution was so strong in New Hampshire that the Federalists adjourned their convention in order to avoid a defeat. Rhode Island voted against the new constitution by a tally of 10–to–1 on March 24, 1788. However, on April 28, 1788, Maryland voted overwhelmingly (63–to–11) in favor of ratification. South Carolina voted in favor of ratification in May, after which New Hampshire reconvened its convention and voted in favor at the end of June.

With the minimum number of favorable votes secured, the new Constitution was approved. In the months that followed, proponents of the new Constitution succeeded in obtaining favorable votes in New York and Virginia.

With ratification secured, the now-lame duck Congress of the Confederation appointed a committee to organize an orderly transition to the new Constitution.

The changes were significant. The government assumed new powers to regulate interstate and international commerce. The form of government changed from a single, unicameral (one chamber) Congress that acted as the legislative branch, the judicial branch, and the executive branch, to a new government with separate branches for the executive function, the judicial function, and the legislative function. The legislature itself changed from a unicameral chamber to a bi-cameral legislature, with the members of the House of Representatives chosen by popular election in the respective states, and the members of the Senate to be chosen by the state legislatures in the respective states.

As initially ratified, however, the new Constitution did not include the Bill of Rights.

Full Text of the Constitution of the United States

As originally ratified, without the Bill of Rights

We the People of the United States, in Order to form a more perfect Union, establish Justice, insure domestic Tranquility, provide for the common defence, promote the general Welfare, and secure the Blessings of Liberty to ourselves and our Posterity, do ordain and establish this Constitution for the United States of America.

Article. I.

Section. 1.

All legislative Powers herein granted shall be vested in a Congress of the United States, which shall consist of a Senate and House of Representatives.

Section. 2.

The House of Representatives shall be composed of Members chosen every second Year by the People of the several States, and the Electors in each State shall have the Qualifications requisite for Electors of the most numerous Branch of the State Legislature.

No Person shall be a Representative who shall not have attained to the Age of twenty five Years, and been seven Years a Citizen of the United States, and who shall not, when elected, be an Inhabitant of that State in which he shall be chosen.

Representatives and direct Taxes shall be apportioned among the several States which may be included within this Union, according to their respective Numbers, which shall be determined by adding to the whole Number of free Persons, including those bound to Service for a Term of Years, and excluding Indians not taxed, three fifths of all other Persons. The actual Enumeration shall be made within three Years after the first Meeting of the Congress of the United States, and within every subsequent Term of ten Years, in such Manner as they shall by Law direct. The Number of Representatives shall not exceed one for every thirty Thousand, but each State shall have at Least one Representative; and until such enumeration shall be made, the State of New Hampshire shall be entitled to chuse three, Massachusetts eight, Rhode-Island and Providence Plantations one, Connecticut five, New-York six, New Jersey four, Pennsylvania eight, Delaware one, Maryland six, Virginia ten, North Carolina five, South Carolina five, and Georgia three.

When vacancies happen in the Representation from any State, the Executive Authority thereof shall issue Writs of Election to fill such Vacancies.

The House of Representatives shall chuse their Speaker and other Officers; and shall have the sole Power of Impeachment.

Section. 3.

The Senate of the United States shall be composed of two Senators from each State, chosen by the Legislature thereof, for six Years; and each Senator shall have one Vote.

Immediately after they shall be assembled in Consequence of the first Election, they shall be divided as equally as may be into three Classes. The Seats of the Senators of the first Class shall be vacated at the Expiration of the second Year, of the second Class at the Expiration of the fourth Year, and of the third Class at the Expiration of the sixth Year, so that one third may be chosen every second Year; and if Vacancies happen by Resignation, or otherwise, during the Recess of the Legislature of any State, the Executive thereof may make temporary Appointments until the next Meeting of the Legislature, which shall then fill such Vacancies.

No Person shall be a Senator who shall not have attained to the Age of thirty Years, and been nine Years a Citizen of the United States, and who shall not, when elected, be an Inhabitant of that State for which he shall be chosen.

The Vice President of the United States shall be President of the Senate, but shall have no Vote, unless they be equally divided.

The Senate shall chuse their other Officers, and also a President pro tempore, in the Absence of the Vice President, or when he shall exercise the Office of President of the United States.

The Senate shall have the sole Power to try all Impeachments. When sitting for that Purpose, they shall be on Oath or Affirmation. When the President of the United States is tried, the Chief Justice shall preside: And no Person shall be convicted without the Concurrence of two thirds of the Members present.

Judgment in Cases of Impeachment shall not extend further than to removal from Office, and disqualification to hold and enjoy any Office of honor, Trust or Profit under the United States: but the Party convicted shall nevertheless be liable and subject to Indictment, Trial, Judgment and Punishment, according to Law.

Section. 4.

The Times, Places and Manner of holding Elections for Senators and Representatives, shall be prescribed in each State by the Legislature thereof; but the Congress may at any time by Law make or alter such Regulations, except as to the Places of chusing Senators.

The Congress shall assemble at least once in every Year, and such Meeting shall be on the first Monday in December, unless they shall by Law appoint a different Day.

Section. 5.

Each House shall be the Judge of the Elections, Returns and Qualifications of its own Members, and a Majority of each shall constitute a Quorum to do Business; but a smaller Number may adjourn from day to day, and may be authorized to compel the Attendance of absent Members, in such Manner, and under such Penalties as each House may provide.

Each House may determine the Rules of its Proceedings, punish its Members for disorderly Behaviour, and, with the Concurrence of two thirds, expel a Member.

Each House shall keep a Journal of its Proceedings, and from time to time publish the same, excepting such Parts as may in their Judgment require Secrecy; and the Yeas and Nays of the Members of either House on any question shall, at the Desire of one fifth of those Present, be entered on the Journal.

Neither House, during the Session of Congress, shall, without the Consent of the other, adjourn for more than three days, nor to any other Place than that in which the two Houses shall be sitting.

Section. 6.

The Senators and Representatives shall receive a Compensation for their Services, to be ascertained by Law, and paid out of the Treasury of the United States. They shall in all Cases, except Treason, Felony and Breach of the Peace, be privileged from Arrest during their Attendance at the Session of their respective Houses, and in going to and returning from the same; and for any Speech or Debate in either House, they shall not be questioned in any other Place.

No Senator or Representative shall, during the Time for which he was elected, be appointed to any civil Office under the Authority of the United States, which shall have been created, or the Emoluments whereof shall have been encreased during such time; and no Person holding any Office under the United States, shall be a Member of either House during his Continuance in Office.

Section. 7.

All Bills for raising Revenue shall originate in the House of Representatives; but the Senate may propose or concur with Amendments as on other Bills.

Every Bill which shall have passed the House of Representatives and the Senate, shall, before it become a Law, be presented to the President of the United States; If he approve he shall sign it, but if not he shall return it, with his Objections to that House in which it shall have originated, who shall enter the Objections at large on their Journal, and proceed to reconsider it. If after such Reconsideration two thirds of that House shall agree to pass the Bill, it shall be sent, together with the Objections, to the other House, by which it shall likewise be reconsidered, and if approved by two thirds of that House, it shall become a Law. But in all such Cases the Votes of both Houses shall be determined by yeas and Nays, and the Names of the Persons voting for and against the Bill shall be entered on the Journal of each House respectively. If any Bill shall not be returned by the President within ten Days (Sundays excepted) after it shall have been presented to him, the Same shall be a Law, in like Manner as if he had signed it, unless the Congress by their Adjournment prevent its Return, in which Case it shall not be a Law.

Every Order, Resolution, or Vote to which the Concurrence of the Senate and House of Representatives may be necessary (except on a question of Adjournment) shall be presented to the President of the United States; and before the Same shall take Effect, shall be approved by him, or being disapproved by him, shall be repassed by two thirds of the Senate and House of Representatives, according to the Rules and Limitations prescribed in the Case of a Bill.

Section. 8.

The Congress shall have Power To lay and collect Taxes, Duties, Imposts and Excises, to pay the Debts and provide for the common Defence and general Welfare of the United States; but all Duties, Imposts and Excises shall be uniform throughout the United States;

To borrow Money on the credit of the United States;

To regulate Commerce with foreign Nations, and among the several States, and with the Indian Tribes;

To establish an uniform Rule of Naturalization, and uniform Laws on the subject of Bankruptcies throughout the United States;

To coin Money, regulate the Value thereof, and of foreign Coin, and fix the Standard of Weights and Measures;

To provide for the Punishment of counterfeiting the Securities and current Coin of the United States;

To establish Post Offices and post Roads;

To promote the Progress of Science and useful Arts, by securing for limited Times to Authors and Inventors the exclusive Right to their respective Writings and Discoveries;

To constitute Tribunals inferior to the supreme Court;

To define and punish Piracies and Felonies committed on the high Seas, and Offences against the Law of Nations;

To declare War, grant Letters of Marque and Reprisal, and make Rules concerning Captures on Land and Water;

To raise and support Armies, but no Appropriation of Money to that Use shall be for a longer Term than two Years;

To provide and maintain a Navy;

To make Rules for the Government and Regulation of the land and naval Forces;

To provide for calling forth the Militia to execute the Laws of the Union, suppress Insurrections and repel Invasions;

To provide for organizing, arming, and disciplining, the Militia, and for governing such Part of them as may be employed in the Service of the United States, reserving to the States respectively, the Appointment of the Officers, and the Authority of training the Militia according to the discipline prescribed by Congress;

To exercise exclusive Legislation in all Cases whatsoever, over such District (not exceeding ten Miles square) as may, by Cession of particular States, and the Acceptance of Congress, become the Seat of the Government of the United States, and to exercise like Authority over all Places purchased by the Consent of the Legislature of the State in which the Same shall be, for the Erection of Forts, Magazines, Arsenals, dock-Yards, and other needful Buildings;—And

To make all Laws which shall be necessary and proper for carrying into Execution the foregoing Powers, and all other Powers vested by this Constitution in the Government of the United States, or in any Department or Officer thereof.

Section. 9.

The Migration or Importation of such Persons as any of the States now existing shall think proper to admit, shall not be prohibited by the Congress prior to the Year one thousand eight hundred and eight, but a Tax or duty may be imposed on such Importation, not exceeding ten dollars for each Person.

The Privilege of the Writ of Habeas Corpus shall not be suspended, unless when in Cases of Rebellion or Invasion the public Safety may require it.

No Bill of Attainder or ex post facto Law shall be passed.

No Capitation, or other direct, Tax shall be laid, unless in Proportion to the Census or enumeration herein before directed to be taken.

No Tax or Duty shall be laid on Articles exported from any State.

No Preference shall be given by any Regulation of Commerce or Revenue to the Ports of one State over those of another: nor shall Vessels bound to, or from, one State, be obliged to enter, clear, or pay Duties in another.

No Money shall be drawn from the Treasury, but in Consequence of Appropriations made by Law; and a regular Statement and Account of the Receipts and Expenditures of all public Money shall be published from time to time.

No Title of Nobility shall be granted by the United States: And no Person holding any Office of Profit or Trust under them, shall, without the Consent of the Congress, accept of any present, Emolument, Office, or Title, of any kind whatever, from any King, Prince, or foreign State.

Section. 10.

No State shall enter into any Treaty, Alliance, or Confederation; grant Letters of Marque and Reprisal; coin Money; emit Bills of Credit; make any Thing but gold and silver Coin a Tender in Payment of Debts; pass any Bill of Attainder, ex post facto Law, or Law impairing the Obligation of Contracts, or grant any Title of Nobility.

No State shall, without the Consent of the Congress, lay any Imposts or Duties on Imports or Exports, except what may be absolutely necessary for executing it's inspection Laws: and the net Produce of all Duties and Imposts, laid by any State on Imports or Exports, shall be for the Use of the Treasury of the United States; and all such Laws shall be subject to the Revision and Controul of the Congress.

No State shall, without the Consent of Congress, lay any Duty of Tonnage, keep Troops, or Ships of War in time of Peace, enter into any Agreement or Compact with another State, or with a foreign Power, or engage in War, unless actually invaded, or in such imminent Danger as will not admit of delay.

Article. II.

Section. 1.

The executive Power shall be vested in a President of the United States of America. He shall hold his Office during the Term of four Years, and, together with the Vice President, chosen for the same Term, be elected, as follows

Each State shall appoint, in such Manner as the Legislature thereof may direct, a Number of Electors, equal to the whole Number of Senators and Representatives to which the State may be entitled in the Congress: but no Senator or Representative, or Person holding an Office of Trust or Profit under the United States, shall be appointed an Elector.

The Electors shall meet in their respective States, and vote by Ballot for two Persons, of whom one at least shall not be an Inhabitant of the same State with themselves. And they shall make a List of all the Persons voted for, and of the Number of Votes for each; which List they shall sign and certify, and transmit sealed to the Seat of the Government of the United States, directed to the President of the Senate. The President of the Senate shall, in the Presence of the Senate and House of Representatives, open all the Certificates, and the Votes shall then be counted. The Person having the greatest Number of Votes shall be the President, if such Number be a Majority of the whole Number of Electors appointed; and if there be more than one who have such Majority, and have an equal Number of Votes, then the House of Representatives shall immediately chuse by Ballot one of them for President; and if no Person have a Majority, then from the five highest on the List the said House shall in like Manner chuse the President. But in chusing the President, the Votes shall be taken by States, the Representation from each State having one Vote; A quorum for this Purpose shall consist of a Member or Members from two thirds of the States, and a Majority of all the States shall be necessary to a Choice. In every Case, after the Choice of the President, the Person having the greatest Number of Votes of the Electors shall be the Vice President. But if there should remain two or more who have equal Votes, the Senate shall chuse from them by Ballot the Vice President.

The Congress may determine the Time of chusing the Electors, and the Day on which they shall give their Votes; which Day shall be the same throughout the United States.

No Person except a natural born Citizen, or a Citizen of the United States, at the time of the Adoption of this Constitution, shall be eligible to the Office of President; neither shall any Person be eligible to that Office who shall not have attained to the Age of thirty five Years, and been fourteen Years a Resident within the United States.

In Case of the Removal of the President from Office, or of his Death, Resignation, or Inability to discharge the Powers and Duties of the said Office, the Same shall devolve on the Vice President, and the Congress may by Law provide for the Case of Removal, Death, Resignation or Inability, both of the President and Vice President, declaring what Officer shall then act as President, and such Officer shall act accordingly, until the Disability be removed, or a President shall be elected.

The President shall, at stated Times, receive for his Services, a Compensation, which shall neither be encreased nor diminished during the Period for which he shall have been elected, and he shall not receive within that Period any other Emolument from the United States, or any of them.

Before he enter on the Execution of his Office, he shall take the following Oath or Affirmation:—"I do solemnly swear (or affirm) that I will faithfully execute the Office of President of the United States, and will to the best of my Ability, preserve, protect and defend the Constitution of the United States."

Section. 2.

The President shall be Commander in Chief of the Army and Navy of the United States, and of the Militia of the several States, when called into the actual Service of the United States; he may require the Opinion, in writing, of the principal Officer in each of the executive Departments, upon any Subject relating to the Duties of their respective Offices, and he shall have Power to grant Reprieves and Pardons for Offences against the United States, except in Cases of Impeachment.

He shall have Power, by and with the Advice and Consent of the Senate, to make Treaties, provided two thirds of the Senators present concur; and he shall nominate, and by and with the Advice and Consent of the Senate, shall appoint Ambassadors, other public Ministers and Consuls, Judges of the supreme Court, and all other Officers of the United States, whose Appointments are not herein otherwise provided for, and which shall be established by Law: but the Congress may by Law vest the Appointment of such inferior Officers, as they think proper, in the President alone, in the Courts of Law, or in the Heads of Departments.

The President shall have Power to fill up all Vacancies that may happen during the Recess of the Senate, by granting Commissions which shall expire at the End of their next Session.

Section. 3.

He shall from time to time give to the Congress Information of the State of the Union, and recommend to their Consideration such Measures as he shall judge necessary and expedient; he may, on extraordinary Occasions, convene both Houses, or either of them, and in Case of Disagreement between them, with Respect to the Time of Adjournment, he may adjourn them to such Time as he shall think proper; he shall receive Ambassadors and other public Ministers; he shall take Care that the Laws be faithfully executed, and shall Commission all the Officers of the United States.

Section. 4.

The President, Vice President and all civil Officers of the United States, shall be removed from Office on Impeachment for, and Conviction of, Treason, Bribery, or other high Crimes and Misdemeanors.

Article III.

Section. 1.

The judicial Power of the United States, shall be vested in one supreme Court, and in such inferior Courts as the Congress may from time to time ordain and establish. The Judges, both of the supreme and inferior Courts, shall hold their Offices during good Behaviour, and shall, at stated Times, receive for their Services, a Compensation, which shall not be diminished during their Continuance in Office.

Section. 2.

The judicial Power shall extend to all Cases, in Law and Equity, arising under this Constitution, the Laws of the United States, and Treaties made, or which shall be made, under their Authority;—to all Cases affecting Ambassadors, other public Ministers and Consuls;—to all Cases of admiralty and maritime Jurisdiction;—to Controversies to which the United States shall be a Party;—to Controversies between two or more States;— between a State and Citizens of another State,—between Citizens of different States,—between Citizens of the same State claiming Lands under Grants of different States, and between a State, or the Citizens thereof, and foreign States, Citizens or Subjects.

In all Cases affecting Ambassadors, other public Ministers and Consuls, and those in which a State shall be Party, the supreme Court shall have original

Jurisdiction. In all the other Cases before mentioned, the supreme Court shall have appellate Jurisdiction, both as to Law and Fact, with such Exceptions, and under such Regulations as the Congress shall make.

The Trial of all Crimes, except in Cases of Impeachment, shall be by Jury; and such Trial shall be held in the State where the said Crimes shall have been committed; but when not committed within any State, the Trial shall be at such Place or Places as the Congress may by Law have directed.

Section. 3.

Treason against the United States, shall consist only in levying War against them, or in adhering to their Enemies, giving them Aid and Comfort. No Person shall be convicted of Treason unless on the Testimony of two Witnesses to the same overt Act, or on Confession in open Court.

The Congress shall have Power to declare the Punishment of Treason, but no Attainder of Treason shall work Corruption of Blood, or Forfeiture except during the Life of the Person attainted.

Article. IV.

Section. 1.

Full Faith and Credit shall be given in each State to the public Acts, Records, and judicial Proceedings of every other State. And the Congress may by general Laws prescribe the Manner in which such Acts, Records and Proceedings shall be proved, and the Effect thereof.

Section. 2.

The Citizens of each State shall be entitled to all Privileges and Immunities of Citizens in the several States.

A Person charged in any State with Treason, Felony, or other Crime, who shall flee from Justice, and be found in another State, shall on Demand of the executive Authority of the State from which he fled, be delivered up, to be removed to the State having Jurisdiction of the Crime.

No Person held to Service or Labour in one State, under the Laws thereof, escaping into another, shall, in Consequence of any Law or Regulation therein, be discharged from such Service or Labour, but shall be delivered up on Claim of the Party to whom such Service or Labour may be due.

Section. 3.

New States may be admitted by the Congress into this Union; but no new State shall be formed or erected within the Jurisdiction of any other State; nor any

State be formed by the Junction of two or more States, or Parts of States, without the Consent of the Legislatures of the States concerned as well as of the Congress.

The Congress shall have Power to dispose of and make all needful Rules and Regulations respecting the Territory or other Property belonging to the United States; and nothing in this Constitution shall be so construed as to Prejudice any Claims of the United States, or of any particular State.

Section. 4.

The United States shall guarantee to every State in this Union a Republican Form of Government, and shall protect each of them against Invasion; and on Application of the Legislature, or of the Executive (when the Legislature cannot be convened) against domestic Violence.

Article. V.

The Congress, whenever two thirds of both Houses shall deem it necessary, shall propose Amendments to this Constitution, or, on the Application of the Legislatures of two thirds of the several States, shall call a Convention for proposing Amendments, which, in either Case, shall be valid to all Intents and Purposes, as Part of this Constitution, when ratified by the Legislatures of three fourths of the several States, or by Conventions in three fourths thereof, as the one or the other Mode of Ratification may be proposed by the Congress; Provided that no Amendment which may be made prior to the Year One thousand eight hundred and eight shall in any Manner affect the first and fourth Clauses in the Ninth Section of the first Article; and that no State, without its Consent, shall be deprived of its equal Suffrage in the Senate.

Article. VI.

All Debts contracted and Engagements entered into, before the Adoption of this Constitution, shall be as valid against the United States under this Constitution, as under the Confederation.

This Constitution, and the Laws of the United States which shall be made in Pursuance thereof; and all Treaties made, or which shall be made, under the Authority of the United States, shall be the supreme Law of the Land; and the Judges in every State shall be bound thereby, any Thing in the Constitution or Laws of any State to the Contrary notwithstanding.

The Senators and Representatives before mentioned, and the Members of the several State Legislatures, and all executive and judicial Officers, both of the United States and of the several States, shall be bound by Oath or Affirmation, to support this Constitution; but no religious Test shall ever be required as a Qualification to any Office or public Trust under the United States.

Article. VII.

The Ratification of the Conventions of nine States, shall be sufficient for the Establishment of this Constitution between the States so ratifying the Same.

The Word, "the," being interlined between the seventh and eighth Lines of the first Page, The Word "Thirty" being partly written on an Erazure in the fifteenth Line of the first Page, The Words "is tried" being interlined between the thirty second and thirty third Lines of the first Page and the Word "the" being interlined between the forty third and forty fourth Lines of the second Page.

Attest William Jackson Secretary

done in Convention by the Unanimous Consent of the States present the Seventeenth Day of September in the Year of our Lord one thousand seven hundred and Eighty seven and of the Independance of the United States of America the Twelfth In witness whereof We have hereunto subscribed our Names,

G°. Washington
Presidt and deputy from Virginia

Delaware

Geo: Read
Gunning Bedford jun
John Dickinson
Richard Bassett
Jaco: Broom

Maryland

James McHenry
Dan of St Thos. Jenifer
Danl. Carroll

Virginia

John Blair
James Madison Jr.

North Carolina

Wm. Blount
Richd. Dobbs Spaight
Hu Williamson

South Carolina

J. Rutledge
Charles Cotesworth Pinckney
Charles Pinckney
Pierce Butler

Georgia

William Few
Abr Baldwin

New Hampshire

John Langdon
Nicholas Gilman

Massachusetts

Nathaniel Gorham
Rufus King

Connecticut

Wm. Saml. Johnson
Roger Sherman

New York

Alexander Hamilton

New Jersey

Wil: Livingston
David Brearley
Wm. Paterson
Jona: Dayton

Pennsylvania

B Franklin
Thomas Mifflin
Robt. Morris
Geo. Clymer
Thos. FitzSimons
Jared Ingersoll
James Wilson
Gouv Morris

The Bill of Rights
(1791)

After the proposed new constitution was presented to the states for ratification, the process quickly encountered strong opposition from many of the states. As a major concession in order to move the ratification process forward, the pro-Federalist side eventually agreed to the demand of the Anti-Federalist side that, upon ratification, the new constitution would immediately be amended to include a Bill of Rights to safeguard individual rights and freedoms from abuse by the government.

The original draft of the Bill of Rights included twelve proposed amendments. Of those twelve, ten were ratified by the states and incorporated into the Constitution as the first ten amendments. The originally-proposed first and second amendments were not ratified by the states and thus did not (at the time) become part of the Constitution.

Accordingly, the original third article became the First Amendment, the original fourth article became the Second Amendment, and so forth in sequence. The ten amendments that constitute the Bill of Rights as we know it today were ratified by the states on December 15, 1791. The second proposed article was finally ratified in 1992, becoming part of the Constitution 203 years after it was first proposed.

The text of the first two proposed amendment that were not ratified was as follows:

Article the first... After the first enumeration required by the first article of the Constitution, there shall be one Representative for every thirty thousand, until the number shall amount to one hundred, after which the proportion shall be so regulated by Congress, that there shall be not less than one hundred Representatives, nor less than one Representative for every forty thousand persons, until the number of Representatives shall amount to two hundred; after which the proportion shall be so regulated by Congress, that there shall not be less than two hundred Representatives, nor more than one Representative for every fifty thousand persons.

Article the second... No law, varying the compensation for the services of the Senators and Representatives, shall take effect, until an election of Representatives shall have intervened. [*Adopted as the 27th Amendment to the Constitution in 1992.*]

Text of the Bill of Rights
(1791)

(The Ten Rights Ratified By the States)

Congress of the United States
begun and held at the City of New-York, on
Wednesday the fourth of March, one thousand seven hundred and
eighty nine.

THE Conventions of a number of the States, having at the time of their adopting the Constitution, expressed a desire, in order to prevent misconstruction or abuse of its powers, that further declaratory and restrictive clauses should be added: And as extending the ground of public confidence in the Government, will best ensure the beneficent ends of its institution.

RESOLVED by the Senate and House of Representatives of the United States of America, in Congress assembled, two thirds of both Houses concurring, that the following Articles be proposed to the Legislatures of the several States, as amendments to the Constitution of the United States, all, or any of which Articles, when ratified by three fourths of the said Legislatures, to be valid to all intents and purposes, as part of the said Constitution; viz.

ARTICLES in addition to, and Amendment of the Constitution of the United States of America, proposed by Congress, and ratified by the Legislatures of the several States, pursuant to the fifth Article of the original Constitution.

Amendment I

Congress shall make no law respecting an establishment of religion, or prohibiting the free exercise thereof; or abridging the freedom of speech, or of the press; or the right of the people peaceably to assemble, and to petition the Government for a redress of grievances.

Amendment II

A well regulated Militia, being necessary to the security of a free State, the right of the people to keep and bear Arms shall not be infringed.

Amendment III

No Soldier shall, in time of peace be quartered in any house, without the consent of the Owner, nor in time of war, but in a manner to be prescribed by law.

Amendment IV

The right of the people to be secure in their persons, houses, papers, and effects, against unreasonable searches and seizures, shall not be violated, and no Warrants shall issue, but upon probable cause, supported by Oath or affirmation, and particularly describing the place to be searched, and the persons or things to be seized.

Amendment V

No person shall be held to answer for a capital, or otherwise infamous crime, unless on a presentment or indictment of a Grand Jury, except in cases arising in the land or naval forces, or in the Militia, when in actual service in time of War or public danger; nor shall any person be subject for the same offence to be twice put in jeopardy of life or limb; nor shall be compelled in any criminal case to be a witness against himself, nor be deprived of life, liberty, or property, without due process of law; nor shall private property be taken for public use, without just compensation.

Amendment VI

In all criminal prosecutions, the accused shall enjoy the right to a speedy and public trial, by an impartial jury of the State and district wherein the crime shall have been committed, which district shall have been previously ascertained by law, and to be informed of the nature and cause of the accusation; to be confronted with the witnesses against him; to have compulsory process for obtaining witnesses in his favor, and to have the Assistance of Counsel for his defence.

Amendment VII

In Suits at common law, where the value in controversy shall exceed twenty dollars, the right of trial by jury shall be preserved, and no fact tried by a jury, shall be otherwise re-examined in any Court of the United States, than according to the rules of the common law.

Amendment VIII

Excessive bail shall not be required, nor excessive fines imposed, nor cruel and unusual punishments inflicted.

Amendment IX

The enumeration in the Constitution, of certain rights, shall not be construed to deny or disparage others retained by the people.

Amendment X

The powers not delegated to the United States by the Constitution, nor prohibited by it to the States, are reserved to the States respectively, or to the people.

The Militia Acts
of 1792, 1795, 1808, 1903, and 1908

Most people who are involved to even a small degree in shooting sports and matters pertaining to the Second Amendment know the language of the Second Amendment almost by heart: "A well regulated Militia, being necessary to the security of a free State, the right of the people to keep and bear Arms, shall not be infringed." The question of whether or not the Second Amendment right to keep and bear arms (RKBA) is dependent on being a member of the militia has become a point of contention between anti-gun forces and pro-right to keep and bear arms defenders.

There was never a question about this for the first one hundred-plus years of the United States' existence. It was simply understood and accepted that "the People" had a right to keep and bear arms, and numerous writings by several prominent people around the time of the creation of the United States and its Constitution demonstrate this. And yet, in the twentieth century, anti-gun activists succeeded in sowing the seeds of doubt, and those seeds took root and sprouted.

Just a few short years after the enactment of the Gun Control Act of 1934, the case of *United States v. Miller* reached the Supreme Court. In that case, the Supreme Court ruled that the Second Amendment right to keep and bear arms applied only to firearms which had or could have a purpose in the military. The decision discussed at some length the history of the militia in the early United States, and obviously were in favor of the argument that the right to keep and bear arms, if not based directly on service in the militia, certainly applied only to firearms that the military might have a use for.

The firearm in question was a sawed-off shotgun, which was regulated by the then-new National Firearms Act of 1934 (NFA). Miller was a criminal who was in possession of a sawed-off shotgun that was not registered under the NFA. While the case was making its way through the lower courts on its way to the Supreme Court, Miller was killed in an execution-style slaying. Consequently, when his appeal reached the Supreme Court, the government showed up to defend the law but Miller was not represented. For this reason alone, as well as because of the lack of scholarship underlying the Court's decision, *Miller* has always been regarded by pro-Second Amendment scholars as a flawed decision. Indeed, the well-researched and well-documented decision in the 2008 case of *District of Columbia et al v. Heller* (*Heller*) reached the opposite conclusion, stating outright that "The Second Amendment is naturally divided into two parts: its prefatory clause and its operative clause. The former does not limit the latter grammatically, but rather announces a purpose," and "Putting all of these textual elements together, we find that they guarantee the individual right to possess and carry weapons in case of confrontation," and, finally, "As we said in *United States* v. *Cruikshank*, 92 U. S. 542, 553 (1876), "[t]his is not a right granted by the Constitution. Neither is it in any manner dependent upon that instrument for its existence. The Second amendment declares that it shall not be infringed . . . ."

Although the *Heller* decision effectively skewered the underlying link between the right to keep and bear arms and service in the militia, *Heller* stopped short of completely reversing *Miller*—most likely because doing so would have invalidated the NFA, which the Supreme Court was unwilling to do. Despite *Heller*, anti-gun activists still maintain that the right to keep and bear arms only guarantees a right to serve in the National Guard. This is reason enough why it is important to be aware of the Militia Act, and to fully understand that the militia is not limited to the National Guard.

Some pro-RKBA advocates and some anti-gun activists know, but many do not, the United States law still includes a Militia Act, which defines who is in the militia—and the militia is not limited to the National Guard. What is even less well-known is that United States law has included a version of a Militia Act since 1792. The original was two separate acts, enacted a few days apart. The original Militia Act was for a duration of only two years—until the expiration of that session of the Congress. The Militia Act was renewed in 1795, at which time it was made permanent. It was subsequently revised in 1808, and again in 1903 (known as the Dick Act).

The United States law that currently defines the militia is taken from the first section of the 1903 Militia Act. The current law is found at 10 U.S. Code § 246 – Militia: composition and classes. While militias have existed in the United States since 1636, and even the web site of the National Guard itself claims that the National Guard dates to 1636, in fact the militias of the individual towns and colonies far pre-dated the National Guard. The term "National Guard" was not applied to state defense forces until Connecticut used the term in 1861, with other states following this practice after the Civil War. The tern "National Guard" was not universally applied to state defense forces until they were reorganized in a way that made them more closely integrated into the federal military structure as part of the National Defense Act of 1908. Even after the NDA of 1908, the National Guard represented only the organized militia, and the body of able-bodied males between the ages of 18 and 45 years remained (and continue to remain to this day) as the unorganized militia.

The Militia Act of 1903 superceded earlier militia acts, and established two classes of militia: The organized militia, which consists of the National Guard and the Naval Militia; and the unorganized militia, which is basically all other males between the ages of 18 and 45 years of age who are not members of the National Guard or the Naval Militia. Thus, there are a great many people in the United

States today who vehemently oppose firearms and the Second Amendment, who are members of the militia and don't know it.

The Militia Act of 1903 is codified in federal law at 10 U.S. Code § 246 - Militia: composition and classes

The next several pages will present the various editions of the Militia Act, in their order of adoption.

Full Text of the First Militia Act of 1792

CHAP. XXVIII—*An Act to provide for calling forth the Militia to execute the laws of the Union, suppress insurrections and repel invasions.*

SECTION 1. *Be it enacted by the Senate and House of Representatives of the United States of America in Congress assembled,* That whenever the United States shall be invaded, or be in imminent danger of invasion from any foreign nation or Indian tribe, it shall be lawful for the President of the United States, to call forth such number of the militia of the state or states most convenient to the place of danger or scene of action, as he may judge necessary to repel such invasion, and to issue his orders for that purpose, to such officer or officers of the militia as he shall think proper; and in case of an insurrection in any state, against the government thereof, it shall be lawful for the President of the United States, on application of the legislature of such state, or of the executive (when the legislature cannot be convened) to call forth such number of the militia of any other state or states, as may be applied for, or as he may judge sufficient to suppress such insurrection.

SEC. 2. *And be it further enacted,* That whenever the laws of the United States shall be opposed, or the execution thereof obstructed, in any state, by combinations too powerful to be suppressed by the ordinary course of judicial proceedings, or by the powers vested in the marshals by this act, the same being notified to the President of the United States, by an associate justice or the district judge, it shall be lawful for the President of the United States to call forth the militia of such state to suppress such combinations, and to cause the laws to be duly executed. And if the militia of a state, where such combinations may happen, shall refuse, or be insufficient to suppress the same, it shall be lawful for the President, if the legislature of the United States be not in session, to call forth and employ such numbers of the militia of any other state or states most convenient thereto, as may be necessary, and the use of militia, so to be called forth, may be continued, if necessary, until the expiration of thirty days after the commencement of the ensuing session.

SEC. 3. *Provided always, and be it further enacted,* That whenever it may be necessary, in the judgment of the President, to use the military force hereby directed to be called forth, the President shall forthwith, and previous thereto, by proclamation, command such insurgents to disperse, and retire peaceably to their respective abodes, within a limited time.

SEC. 4. *And be it further enacted,* That the militia employed in the service of the United States, shall receive the same pay and allowances, as the troops of the United States, who may be in service at the same time, or who were last in service, and shall be subject to the same rules and articles of war: And that no officer, non-commissioned officer or private of the militia shall be compelled to serve more than three months in any one year, nor more than in due rotation with every other able-bodied man of the same rank in the battalion to which he belongs.

SEC. 5. *And be it further enacted,* That every officer, non-commissioned officer or private of the militia, who shall fail to obey the orders of the President of the United States in any of the cases before recited, shall forfeit a sum not exceeding one year's pay, and not less than one month's pay, to be determined and adjudged by a court martial; and such officer shall, moreover, be liable to be cashiered by sentence of a court martial: and such non-commissioned officers and privates shall be liable to be imprisoned by a like sentence, on failure of payment of the fines adjudged against them, for the space of one calendar month for every five dollars of such fine.

SEC. 6. *And be it further enacted,* That courts martial for the trial of militia shall be composed of militia officers only.

SEC. 7. *And be it further enacted,* That all fines to be assessed, as aforesaid, shall be certified by the presiding officer of the court martial before whom the same shall be assessed, to the marshal of the district, in which the delinquent shall reside, or to one of his deputies; and also to the supervisor of the revenue of the same district, who shall record the said certificate in a book to be kept for that purpose. The said marshal or his deputy shall forthwith proceed to levy the said fines with costs, by distress and sale of the goods and chattels of the delinquent, which costs and the manner of proceeding, with respect to the sale of the goods distrained, shall be agreeable to the laws of the state, in which the same shall be, in other cases of distress; and where any non-commissioned officer or private shall be adjudged to suffer imprisonment, there being no goods or chattels to be found, whereof to levy the said fines, the marshal of the district or his deputy may commit such delinquent to gaol, during the term, for which he shall be so adjudged to imprisonment, or until the fine shall be paid, in the same manner as other persons condemned to fine and imprisonment at the suit of the United States, may be committed.

SEC. 8. *And be it further enacted,* That the marshals and their deputies shall pay all such fines by them levied to the supervisor of the revenue, in the district in which they are collected, within two months after they shall have received the same, deducting therefrom five per centum, as a compensation for their trouble; and in case of failure, the same shall be recoverable by action of debt or information in any court of the United States, of the district, in which such fines shall be levied, having cognizance thereof, to be sued for, prosecuted and recovered, in the name of the supervisor of the district, with interest and costs.

SEC. 9. *And be it further enacted,* That the marshals of the several districts and their deputies, shall have the same powers in executing the laws of the United

States, as sheriffs and their deputies in the several states have by law, in executing the laws of their respective states.

SEC. 10. *And be it further enacted,* That this act shall continue and be in force, for and during the term of two years, and from thence to the end of the next session of Congress thereafter, and no longer.

APPROVED, May 2, 1792.

Full Text of the Second Militia Act of 1792

CHAP. XXXIII—*An Act more effectually to provide for the National Defence by establishing an Uniform Militia throughout the United States.*

SECTION 1. *Be it enacted by the Senate and House of Representatives of the United States of America in Congress assembled,* That each and every free able-bodied white male citizen of the respective states, resident therein, who is or shall be of the age of eighteen years, and under the age of forty-five years (except as is herein after excepted) shall severally and respectively be enrolled in the militia by the captain or commanding officer of the company, within whose bounds such citizen shall reside, and that within twelve months after the passing of this act. And it shall at all times hereafter be the duty of every such captain or commanding officer of a company to enrol every such citizen, as aforesaid, and also those who shall, from time to time, arrive at the age of eighteen years, or being of the age of eighteen years and under the age of forty-five years (except as before excepted) shall come to reside within his bounds; and shall without delay notify such citizen of the said enrolment, by a proper non-commissioned officer of the company, by whom such notice may be proved. That every citizen so enrolled and notified, shall, within six months thereafter, provide himself with a good musket or firelock, a sufficient bayonet and belt, two spare flints, and a knapsack, a pouch with a box therein to contain not less than twenty-four cartridges, suited to the bore of his musket or firelock, each cartridge to contain a proper quantity of powder and ball: or with a good rifle, knapsack, shot-pouch and powder-horn, twenty balls suited to the bore of his rifle, and a quarter of a pound of powder; and shall appear, so armed, accoutred and provided, when called out to exercise, or into service, except, that when called out on company days to exercise only, he may appear without a knapsack. That the commissioned officers shall severally be armed with a sword or hanger and espontoon, and that from and after five years from the passing of this act, all muskets for arming the militia as herein required, shall be of bores sufficient for balls of the eighteenth part of a pound. And every citizen so enrolled, and providing himself with the arms, ammunition and accoutrements required as aforesaid, shall hold the same exempted from all suits, distresses, executions or sales, for debt or for the payment of taxes.

SEC. 2. *And be it further enacted,* That the Vice President of the United States; the officers judicial and executive of the government of the United States; the members of both Houses of Congress, and their respective officers; all custom-house officers with their clerks; all post-officers, and stage drivers, who are employed in the care and conveyance of the mail of the post-office of the United States; all ferrymen employed at any ferry on the post road; all inspectors of exports; all pilots; all mariners actually employed in the sea service of any citizen or merchant within the United States; and all persons who now are or may hereafter be exempted by the laws of the respective states, shall be, and are hereby exempted from militia duty, notwithstanding their being above the age of eighteen, and under the age of forty-five years.

SEC. 3. *And be it further enacted,* That within one year after the passing of this act, the militia of the respective states shall be arranged into divisions, brigades, regiments, battalions and companies, as the legislature of each state shall direct; and each division, brigade and regiment, shall be numbered at the formation thereof; and a record made of such numbers in the adjutant-general's office in the state; and when in the field, or in service in the state, each division, brigade and regiment shall respectively take rank according to their numbers, reckoning the first or lowest number highest in rank. That if the same be convenient, each brigade shall consist of four regiments; each regiment of two battalions; each battalion of five companies; each company of sixty-four privates. That the said militia shall be officered by the respective states, as follows: To each division, one major-general and two aids-de-camp, with the rank of major; to each brigade, one brigadier-general, with one brigade inspector, to serve also as brigade-major, with the rank of a major; to each regiment, one lieutenant-colonel commandant; and to each battalion one major; to each company one captain, one lieutenant, one ensign, four sergeants, four corporals, one drummer and one fifer or bugler. That there shall be a regimental staff, to consist of one adjutant and one quartermaster, to rank as lieutenants; one paymaster; one surgeon, and one surgeon's mate; one sergeant-major; one drum-major, and one fife-major.

SEC. 4. *And be it further enacted,* That out of the militia enrolled, as is herein directed, there shall be formed for each battalion at least one company of grenadiers, light infantry or riflemen; and that to each division there shall be at least one company of artillery, and one troop of horse: there shall be to each company of artillery, one captain, two lieutenants, four sergeants, four corporals, six gunners, six bombadiers, one drummer, and one fifer. The officers to be armed with a sword or hanger, a fusee, bayonet and belt, with a cartridge-box to contain twelve cartridges; and each private or matross shall furnish himself with all the equipments of a private in the infantry, until proper ordnance and field artillery is provided. There shall be to each troop of horse, one captain, two lieutenants, one cornet, four sergeants, four corporals, one saddler, one farrier, and one trumpeter. The commissioned officers to furnish themselves with good horses of at least fourteen hands and an half high, and to be armed with a sword and pair of pistols, the holsters of which to be covered with bearskin caps. Each dragoon to furnish himself with a serviceable horse, at least fourteen hands and an half high, a good saddle, bridle, mailpillion and valise, holsters, and a breast-plate and crupper, a pair of boots and spurs, a pair of pistols, a sabre, and a cartouch-box, to contain twelve cartridges for pistols. That each company of artillery and troop of horse shall be formed of volunteers from the brigade, at the discretion of the commander-in-chief of the state, not exceeding one company of each to a regiment, nor more in number than one eleventh part of the infantry, and shall be uniformly clothed in regimentals, to be furnished at their own expense; the colour and fashion to be determined by the brigadier commanding the brigade to which they belong.

SEC. 5. *And be it further enacted,* That each battalion and regiment shall be provided with the state and regimental colours by the field officers, and each company with a drum and fife, or bugle-horn, by the commissioned officers of the company, in such manner as the legislature of the respective states shall direct.

SEC. 6. *And be it further enacted,* That there shall be an adjutant-general appointed in each state, whose duty it shall be to distribute all orders from the commander-in-chief of the state to the several corps; to attend all public reviews when the commander-in-chief of the state shall review the militia, or any part thereof; to obey all orders from him relative to carrying into execution and perfecting the system of military discipline established by this act; to furnish blank forms of different returns that may be required, and to explain the principles on which they should be made; to receive from the several officers of the different corps throughout the state, returns of the militia under their command, reporting the actual situation of their arms, accoutrements, and ammunition, their delinquencies, and every other thing which relates to the general advancement of good order and discipline: all which the several officers of the divisions, brigades, regiments, and battalions, are hereby required to make in the usual manner, so that the said adjutant-general may be duly furnished therewith: from all which returns he shall make proper abstracts, and lay the same annually before the commander-in-chief of the state.

SEC. 7. *And be it further enacted,* That the rules of discipline, approved and established by Congress in their resolution of the twenty-ninth of March, one thousand seven hundred and seventy-nine, shall be the rules of discipline to be observed by the militia throughout the United States, except such deviations from the said rules as may be rendered necessary by the requisitions of this act, or by some other unavoidable circumstances. It shall be the duty of the commanding officer at every muster, whether by battalion, regiment, or single company, to cause the militia to be exercised and trained agreeably to the said rules of discipline.

SEC. 8. *And be it further enacted,* That all commissioned officers shall take rank according to the date of their commissions; and when two of the same grade bear an equal date, then their rank to be determined by lot, to be drawn by them before the commanding officer of the brigade, regiment, battalion, company, or detachment.

9. *And be it further enacted,* That if any person, whether officer or soldier, belonging to the militia of any state, and called out into the service of the United

States, be wounded or disabled while in actual service, he shall be taken care of and provided for at the public expense.

SEC. 10. *And be it further enacted,* That it shall be the duty of the brigade-inspector to attend the regimental and battalion meetings of the militia composing their several brigades, during the time of their being under arms, to inspect their arms, ammunition, and accoutrements; superintend their exercise and manœuvres, and introduce the system of military discipline before described throughout the brigade, agreeable to law, and such orders as they shall from time to time receive from the commander-in-chief of the state; to make returns to the adjutant-general of the state, at least once in every year, of the militia of the brigade to which he belongs, reporting therein the actual situation of the arms, accoutrements, and ammunition of the several corps, and every other thing which, in his judgment, may relate to their government and the general advancement of good order and military discipline; and the adjutant-general shall make a return of all the militia of the state to the commander-in-chief of the said state, and a duplicate of the same to the President of the United States.

And whereas sundry corps of artillery, cavalry, and infantry now exist in several of the said states, which by the laws, customs, or usages thereof have not been incorporated with, or subject to the general regulations of the militia:

SEC. 11. *Be it further enacted,* That such corps retain their accustomed privileges, subject, nevertheless, to all other duties required by this act, in like manner with the other militia.

APPROVED, May 8, 1792.

Full Text of the Militia Act of 1795

THIRD CONGRESS
OF THE
UNITED STATES:
AT THE SECOND SESSION,
Begun and held at the city of Philadelphia, in the state of Pennsylvania,
on Monday, the third of November, one thousand seven hundred and ninety-four.

An ACT *to provide for calling forth the militia to execute the laws of the Union, suppress insurrections, and repel invasions; and to repeal the act now in force for those purposes, 28 February 1795.*

SEC. 1. BE *it enacted by the Senate and House of Representatives of the United States of America, in Congress assembled*, That whenever the United States shall be invaded, or be in imminent danger of invasion, from any foreign nation or Indian tribe, it shall be lawful for the President of the United States to call forth such number of the militia of the state or states, most convenient to the place of danger, or scene of action, as he may judge necessary to repel such invasion, and to issue his orders, for that purpose, to such officer or officers of the militia as he shall think proper. And in case of an insurrection in any state, against the government thereof, it shall be lawful for the President of the United States, on application of the legislature of such state, or of the Executive, (when the legislature cannot be convened,) to call forth such number of the militia of any other state or states, as may be applied for, as he may judge sufficient to suppress such insurrection.

SEC. 2. That whenever the laws of the United States shall be opposed, or the execution thereof obstructed, in any state, by combinations too powerful to be suppressed by the ordinary course of judicial proceedings, or by the powers vested in the marshals by this act, it shall be lawful for the President of the United States to call forth the militia of such state, or of any other state or states, as may be necessary to suppress such combinations, and to cause the laws to be duly executed; and the use of militia so to be called forth may be continued, if necessary, until the expiration of thirty days after the commencement of the then next session of Congress.

SEC. 3. That whenever it may be necessary, in the judgment of the President, to use the military force hereby directed to be called forth, the President shall forthwith, by proclamation, command such insurgents to disperse, and retire peaceably to their respective abode, within a limited time.

SEC. 4. That the militia employed in the service of the United States shall be subject to the same rules and articles of war as the troops of the United States: and that no officer, non-commissioned officer, or private, of the militia, shall be compelled to serve more than three months after his arrival at the place of rendezvous, in any one year, nor more than in due rotation with every other able-bodied man of the same rank in the battalion to which he belongs.

SEC. 5. That every officer, non-commissioned officer, or private, of the militia, who shall fail to obey the orders of the President of the United States, in any of the cases before recited, shall forfeit a sum not exceeding one year's pay, and not less than one month's pay, to be determined and adjudged by a court-martial; and such officer shall, moreover, be liable to be cashiered by sentence of a court-martial, and be incapacitated from holding a commission in the militia, for a term not exceeding twelve months, at the discretion of the said court: and such non-commissioned officers and privates shall be liable to be imprisoned, by a like sentence, on failure of the payment of fines adjudged against them, for one calendar month, for every five dollars of such fine.

SEC. 6. That courts-martial for the trial of militia, shall be composed of militia officers only.

SEC. 7. That all fines to be assessed, as aforesaid, shall be certified by the presiding officer of the court-martial before whom the same shall be assessed, to the marshal of the district in which the delinquent shall reside, or to one of his deputies and also to the supervisor of the revenue of the same district, who shall record the said certificate in a book to be kept for that purpose. The said marshal, or his deputy, shall forthwith proceed to levy the said fines, with costs, by distress and sale of the goods and chattels of the delinquent; which costs, and the manner of proceeding, with respect to the sale of the goods distrained, shall be agreeable to the laws of the state in which the same shall be, in other cases of distress. And where any non-commissioned officer or private shall be adjudged to suffer imprisonment, there being no goods or chattels to be found whereof to levy the said fines, the marshal of the district, or his deputy, may commit such delinquent to jail, during the term for which he shall be so adjudged to imprisonment, or until the fine shall be paid, in the same manner as other persons condemned to fine and imprisonment at the suit of the United States may be committed.

SEC. 8. That the marshals and their deputies shall pay all such fines by them levied, to the supervisor of the revenue in the district in which they are collected, within two months after they shall have received the same, deducting therefrom five per centum as a compensation for their trouble; and in case of failure, the same shall be recoverable by action of debt or information, in any court of the United States, of the district in which such fines shall be levied, having cognizance thereof, to be sued for, prosecuted, and recovered, in the name of the supervisor of the district, with interest and costs.

SEC. 9. That the marshals of the several districts, and their deputies, shall have the same powers, in executing the laws of the United States, as sheriffs, and their deputies, in the several states, have by law in executing the laws of the respective states.

SEC. 10. That the act entitled "An act to provide for calling forth the militia to execute the laws of the Union, suppress insurrections, and repel invasions;" passed the 2d day of May, 1792, shall be, and the same is hereby, repealed.

[Approved, February 28, 1795.]

Full Text of the Militia Act of 1808

CHAP. LV.—*An act making provision for arming and equipping the whole body of the Militia of the United States.*

Be it enacted by the Senate and House of Representatives of the United States of America in Congress assembled, That the annual sum of two hundred thousand dollars be, and the same hereby is appropriated, for the purpose of providing arms and military equipments for the whole body of the militia of the United States, either by purchase or manufacture, by and on account of the United States.

SEC. 2. And be it further enacted, That the President of the United States be, and be hereby is authorized, to purchase sites for, and erect such additional arsenals and manufactories of arms, as he may deem expedient, under the limitations and restrictions now provided by law: Provided also, that so much of any law as restricts the number of workmen in the armories of the United States to one hundred men, be, and the same hereby is repealed.

SEC. 3. And be it further enacted, That all the arms procured in virtue of this act, shall be transmitted to the several states composing this Union, and territories thereof, to each state and territory respectively, in proportion to the number of the effective militia in each state and territory, and by each state and territory to be distributed, to the militia in such state and territory, under such rules and regulations as shall be by law prescribed by the legislature of each state and territory.

Approved, April 23, 1808

Full Text of the Militia Act of 1903
(The Dick Act)

CHAP. 196.-An Act To promote the efficiency of the militia, and for other purposes.

Be it enacted by the Senate and House of Representatives of the United States of America in Congress assembled, That the militia shall consist of every able-bodied male citizen of the respective States, Territories, and the District of Columbia, and every able-bodied male of foreign birth who has declared his intention to become a citizen, who is more than eighteen and less than forty-five years of age, and shall be divided into two classes-the organized militia, to be known as the National Guard of the State, Territory, or District of Columbia, or by such other designations as may be given them by the laws of the respective States or Territories, and the remainder to be known as the Reserve Militia.

SEC. 2. That the Vice-President of the United States, the officers, judicial and executive, of the Government of the United States, the members and officers of each House of Congress, persons in the military or naval service of the United States, all custom-house officers with their clerks, postmasters and persons employed by the United States in the transmission of the mail, ferrymen employed at any ferry on a post road, artificers and workmen employed in the armories and arsenals of the United States, pilots, mariners actually employed in the sea service of any citizen or merchant within the United States, and all persons who are exempted by the laws of the respective States or Territories shall be exempted from militia duty, without regard to age: Provided, That nothing in this Act shall be construed to require or compel any member of any well-recognized religious sect or organization at present organized and existing whose creed forbids its members to participate in war in any form, and whose religious convictions are against war or participation therein, in accordance with the creed of said religious organization, to serve in the militia or any other armed or volunteer force under the jurisdiction and authority of the United States.

SEC. 3. That the regularly enlisted, organized, and uniformed active Organized militia in the several States and Territories and the District of Columbia who have heretofore participated or shall hereafter participate in the apportionment of the annual appropriation provided by section sixteen hundred and sixty-one of the Revised Statutes of the United States, as amended, whether known and designated as National Guard, militia, or otherwise, shall constitute the organized militia. The organization, armament, and discipline of the organized militia in the several States and Territories and in the District of Columbia shall be the same as that which is now or may hereafter be prescribed for the Regular and Volunteer Armies of the United States, within five years from the date of the approval of this Act: *Provided*, That the President of the United States, in time of peace, may by order fix the minimum number of enlisted men in each company, troop, battery, signal corps, engineer corps, and hospital corps: *And provided further*, That any corps of artillery, cavalry and infantry existing in any of the States at the passage of the Act of May eighth, seventeen hundred and ninety-two, which, by the laws, customs or usages of the said States have been in continuous existence since the passage of said Act under its provisions and under the provisions of Section two hundred and thirty-two and Sections sixteen hundred and twenty-five to sixteen hundred and sixty, both inclusive, of Title sixteen of the Revised Statutes of the United States relating to the Militia, shall be allowed to retain their accustomed privileges, subject, nevertheless, to all other duties required by law in like manner as the other Militia.

SEC. 4. That whenever the United States is invaded, or in danger of invasion from any foreign nation, or of rebellion against the authority of the Government of the United States, or the President is unable, with the other forces at his command, to execute the laws of the Union in any part thereof, it shall be lawful for the President to call forth, for a period not exceeding nine months, such number of the militia of the State or of the States or Territories or of the District of Columbia as he may deem necessary to repel such invasion, suppress such rebellion, or to enable him to execute such laws, and to issue his orders for that purpose to such officers of the militia as he may think proper.

SEC. 5. That whenever the President calls forth the militia of any State or Territory or of the District of Columbia to be employed in the service of the United States, he may specify in his call the period for which such service is required, not exceeding nine months, and the militia so called shall continue to serve during the term so specified, unless sooner discharged by order of the President.

SEC. 6. That when the militia of more than one State is called into the actual service of the United States by the President he may, in his discretion, apportion them among such States or Territories or to the District of Columbia according to representative population.

SEC. 7. That every officer and enlisted man of the militia who shall be called forth in the manner hereinbefore prescribed and shall be found fit for military service shall be mustered or accepted into the United States service by a duly authorized mustering officer of the United States: *Provided, however*, That any officer or enlisted man of the militia who shall refuse or neglect to present himself to such mustering officer upon being called forth as herein prescribed shall be subject to trial by court-martial, and shall be punished as such court-martial may direct.

SEC. 8. That courts-martial for the trial of officers or men of the militia, when in the service of the United States, shall be composed of militia officers only.

SEC. 9. That the militia, when called into the actual service of the United States, shall be subject to the same Rules and Articles of War as the regular troops of the United States.

SEC. 10. That the militia, when called into the actual service of the United States, shall, during their time of service, be entitled to the same pay and allowances as are or may be provided by law for the Regular Army.

SEC. 11. That when the militia is called into the actual service of the United States, or any portion of the militia is accepted under the provisions of this Act, their pay shall commence from the day of their appearing at the place of company rendezvous. But this provision shall not be construed to authorize any species of expenditure previous to arriving at such places of rendezvous which is not provided by existing laws to be paid after their arrival at such places of rendezvous.

SEC. 12. That there shall be appointed in each State, Territory and District of Columbia, an Adjutant-General, who shall perform such duties as may be prescribed by the laws of such State, Territory, and District, respectively, and make returns to the Secretary of War, at such times and in such form as he shall from time to time prescribe, of the strength of the organized militia, and also make such reports as may from time to time be required by the Secretary of War. That the Secretary of War shall, with his annual report of each year, transmit to Congress an abstract of the returns and reports of the adjutants-general of the States, Territories, and the District of Columbia, with such observations thereon as he may deem necessary for the information of Congress.

SEC. 13. That the Secretary of War is hereby authorized to issue, on the requisitions of the governors of the several States and Territories, or of the commanding general of the militia of the District of Columbia, such number of the United States standard service magazine arms, with bayonets, bayonet scabbards, gun slings, belts, and such other necessary accouterments and equipments as are required for the Army of the United States, for arming all of the organized militia in said States and Territories and District of Columbia, without charging the cost or value thereof, or any which have been issued since December first, nineteen hundred and one, or any expense connected therewith, against the allotment to said State, Territory, or District of Columbia, out of the annual appropriation provided by section sixteen hundred and sixty-one of the Revised Statutes, as amended, or requiring payment therefor, and to exchange, without receiving any money credit therefor, ammunition, or parts thereof, suitable to the new arms, round for round, for corresponding ammunition suitable to the old arms theretofore issued to said State, Territory, or District by the United States: *Provided*, That said rifles and carbines and other property shall be receipted for and shall remain the property of the United States and be annually accounted for by the governors of the States and Territories as now required by law, and that each State, Territory, and District shall, on receipt of the new arms, turn in to the Ordnance Department of the United States Army, without receiving any money credit therefor, and without expense for transportation, all United States rifles and carbines now in its possession.

To provide means to carry into effect the provisions of this section, the necessary money to cover the cost of exchanging or issuing the new arms, accouterments, equipments, and ammunition to be exchanged or issued hereunder is hereby appropriated out of any moneys in the Treasury not otherwise appropriated.

SEC. 14. That whenever it shall appear by the report of inspections, which it shall be the duty of the Secretary of War to cause to be made at least once in each year by officers detailed by him for that purpose, that the organized militia of a State or Territory or of the District of Columbia is sufficiently armed, uniformed, and equipped for active duty in the field, the Secretary of War is authorized, on the requisition of the governor of such State or Territory, to pay to the quartermaster-general thereof, or to such other officer of the militia of said State as the said governor may designate and appoint for the purpose, so much of its allotment out of the said annual appropriation under section sixteen hundred and sixty-one of the Revised Statutes as amended as shall be necessary for the payment, subsistence, and transportation of such portion of said organized militia as shall engage in actual field or camp service for instruction, and the officers and enlisted men of such militia while so engaged shall be entitled to the same pay, subsistence, and transportation or travel allowances as officers and enlisted men of corresponding grades of the Regular Army are or may hereafter be entitled by law, and the officer so designated and appointed shall be regarded as a disbursing officer of the United States, and shall render his accounts through the War Department to the proper accounting officers of the Treasury for settlement, and he shall be required to give good and sufficient bonds to the United States, in such sums as the Secretary of War may direct, faithfully to account for the safe-keeping and payment of the public moneys so intrusted to him for disbursement.

SEC. 15. That the Secretary of War is hereby authorized to provide for participation by any part of the organized militia, of any State or Territory on the request of the governor thereof in the encampment, maneuvers, and field instruction of any part of the Regular Army at or near any military post or camp or lake or seacoast defenses of the United States. In such case the organized militia so participating shall receive the same pay, subsistence, and transportation as is provided by law for the officers and men of the Regular Army, to be paid out of the appropriation for the pay, subsistence, and transportation of the Army: Provided, That the command of such military post or camp and of the officers and troops of the United States there stationed shall remain with the regular commander of the post without regard to the rank of the commanding or other officers of the militia temporarily so encamped within its limits or in its vicinity.

SEC. 16. That whenever any officer of the organized militia shall, upon recommendation of the governor of any State, Territory, or general commanding the District of Columbia, and when authorized by the President, attend and pursue a regular course of study at any military school or college of the United States such officer shall receive from the annual appropriation for the support of the Army the same travel allowances, and quarters, or commutation of quarters, to which an officer of the Regular Army would be entitled if attending such school or college under orders from proper military authority, and shall also receive commutation of subsistence at the rate of one dollar per day while in actual attendance upon the course of instruction.

SEC. 17. That the annual appropriation made by section sixteen hundred and sixty-one, Revised Statutes, as amended, shall be available for the purpose of providing for issue to the organized militia any stores and supplies or publications which are supplied to the Army by any department. Any State, Territory, or the District of Columbia may, with the approval of the Secretary of War, purchase for cash from the War Department, for the use of its militia, stores, supplies, material of war, or military publications, such as are furnished to the Army, in addition to those issued under the provisions of this Act, at the price at which they are listed for issue to the Army, with the cost of transportation added, and funds received from such sales shall be credited to the appropriations to which they belong and shall not be covered into the Treasury, but shall be available until expended to replace therewith the supplies sold to the States and Territories and to the District of Columbia in the manner herein provided.

SEC. 18. That each State or Territory furnished with material of war under the provisions of this or former Acts of Congress shall, during the year next preceding each annual allotment of funds, in accordance with section sixteen hundred and sixty-one of the Revised Statutes as amended, have required every company, troop, and battery in its organized militia not excused by the governor of such State or Territory to participate in practice marches or go into camp of instruction at least five consecutive days, and to assemble for drill and instruction at company, battalion, or regimental armories or rendezvous or for target practice not less than twenty-four times, and shall also have required during such year an inspection of each such company, troop. and battery to be made by an officer of such militia or an officer of the Regular Army.

SEC. 19. That upon the application of the governor of any State or Territory furnished with material of war under the provisions of this Act or former laws of Congress, the Secretary of War may detail one or more officers of the Army to attend any encampment of the organized militia, and to give such instruction and information to the officers and men assembled in such camp as may be requested by the governor. Such officer or officers shall immediately make a report of such encampment to the Secretary of War, who shall furnish a copy thereof to the governor of the State or Territory.

SEC. 20. That upon application of the governor of any State or Territory furnished with material of war under the provisions of this Act or former laws of Congress, the Secretary of War may, in his discretion, detail one or more officers of the Army to report to the governor of such State or Territory for duty in connection with the organized militia. All such assignments may be revoked at the request of the governor of such State or Territory or at the pleasure of the Secretary of War.

SEC. 21. That the troops of the militia encamped at any military post or camp of the United States may be furnished such amounts of ammunition for instruction in firing and target practice as may be prescribed by the Secretary of War, and such instruction in firing shall be carried on under the direction of an officer selected for that purpose by the proper military commander.

SEC. 22. That when any officer, noncommissioned officer, or private of the militia is disabled by reason of wounds or disabilities received or incurred in the service of the United States he shall be entitled to all the benefits of the pension laws existing at the time of his service, and in case such officer, noncommissioned officer, or private dies in the service of the United States or in returning to his place of residence after being mustered out of such service, or at any time, in consequence of wounds or disabilities received in such service, his widow and children, if any, shall be entitled to all the benefits of such pension laws.

SEC. 23. That for the purpose of securing a list of persons specially qualified to hold commissions in any volunteer force which may here-after be called for and organized under the authority of Congress, other than a force composed of organized militia, the Secretary of War is authorized from time to time to convene boards of officers at suitable and convenient army posts in different parts of the United States, who shall examine as to their qualifications for the command of troops or for the performance of staff duties all applicants who shall have served in the Regular Army of the United States, in any of the volunteer forces of the United States, or in the organized militia of any State or Territory or District of Columbia, or who, being a citizen of the United States, shall have attended or pursued a regular course of instruction in any military school or college of the United States Army, or shall have graduated from any educational institution to which an officer of the Army or Navy has been detailed as superintendent or professor pursuant to law after having creditably pursued the course of military instruction therein provided. Such examinations shall be under rules and regulations prescribed by the Secretary of War, and shall be especially directed to ascertain the practical capacity of the applicant. The record of previous service of the applicant shall be considered as a part of the examination. Upon the conclusion of each examination the board shall certify to the War Department its judgment as to the fitness of the applicant, stating the office, if any, which it deems him qualified to fill, and, upon approval by the President, the names of the persons certified to be qualified shall be inscribed in a register to be kept in the War Department for that purpose. The persons so certified and registered shall, subject to a physical examination at the time, constitute an eligible class for commissions pursuant to such certificates in any volunteer force hereafter called for and organized under the authority of

Congress, other than a force composed of organized militia, and the President may authorize persons from this class, to attend and pursue a regular course of study at any military school or college of the United States other than the Military Academy at West Point and to receive from the annual appropriation for the support of the Army the same allowances and commutations as provided in this Act for officers of the organized militia: *Provided*, That no person shall be entitled to receive a commission as a second lieutenant after he shall have passed the age of thirty; as first lieutenant after he shall have passed the age of thirty-five; as captain after he shall have passed the age of forty; as major after he shall have passed the age of forty-five; as lieutenant-colonel after he shall have passed the age of fifty, or as colonel after he shall have passed the age of fifty-five: *And provided further*, That such appointments shall be distributed proportionately, as near as may be, among the various States contributing such volunteer force: *And provided*, That the appointments in this section provided for shall not be deemed to include appointments to any office in any company, troop, battery, battalion, or regiment of the organized militia which volunteers as a body or the officers of which are appointed by the governor of a State or Territory.

SEC. 24. That all the volunteer forces of the United States called for by authority of Congress shall, except as hereinbefore provided, be organized in the manner provided by the Act entitled "An Act to provide for temporarily increasing the military establishment of the United States in time of war, and for other purposes," approved April twenty-second, eighteen hundred and ninety-eight.

SEC. 25. That sections sixteen hundred and twenty-five to sixteen hundred and sixty, both included, of title sixteen of the Revised Statutes, and section two hundred and thirty-two thereof, relating to the militia, are hereby repealed.

SEC. 26. That this Act shall take effect upon the date of its approval.

Approved, January 21, 1903.

The National Defense Act of 1916

The Militia Act of 1903 (The Dick Act) created the National Guard as an entity, establish the distinction between the organized militia and the unorganized militia, and transferred the primary responsibility for arming and equipping the state militia units comprising the National Guard from the individual states to the federal government. Left unchanged by the Act was the fact that all able-bodied men between the ages of 18 and 45 were members of the militia—the unorganized militia, unless they were enrolled in the National Guard or the Naval Militia[2].

An act of Congress passed on May 27, 1908[3], made a number of technical revisions to the Militia Act of 1903 that continued the transition of the National Guard from a home defense militia to a component of the federal Army of the United States. This Act occupies only four pages in the Congressional Record.

The National Defense Act of 1916 was, another adjustment of, and amendment to, the Militia Act of 1903 (as previously amended). This Act increased the number of days National Guard of training that the federal government would pay for from five days to fifteen days for annual encampments, and added that the federal government would also pay for up to 48 individual days of drill (for weekend training sessions throughout the year).

The Act also revised the President's authority for calling out the National Guard for federal service. Prior to the Act, the President could call up the National Guard only for federal service within the United States, and only for a period not to exceed nine months. The Act also made it possible for the President to transfer members of the National Guard to the Regular Army for service outside of the United States, and for unlimited periods of time.

The Act formalized the distinction among the Regular Army, the Volunteer Army, The Officers' Reserve Corps (ROTC), and the National Guard (while in the service of the United States).

The National Defense Act of 1916 takes up 52 pages of the Federal Register. The Act goes into considerable detail regarding the organization of the Regular

---

[2] The Naval Militia still exists under federal law as a component of the Organized Militia. However, as of the date of this publication only six states (Alaska, California, New York, Ohio, South Carolina, and Texas) have active Naval Militia units.

[3] The full text of the 1908 amendments to the Militia Act of 1903 can be found on-line at: https://www.loc.gov/law/help/statutes-at-large/60th-congress/session-1/c60s1ch204.pdf

Army. Discussion of the National Guard doesn't begin until Section 58 of the Act, which is found mid-way on the 32nd page, and ends at Section 119, on the 48th page. In the interest of brevity and conciseness, only those sections of the Act addressing the National Guard and the Militia are reproduced on the following pages.[4]

As a result of the National Defense Act of 1916, the National Guard for the first time became substantially the military organization we know it as today, rather than a collection of individual groups of self-armed civilians enrolled for the sole purpose of defending their own respective states.

The importance of this change with respect to the Second Amendment right to keep and bear arms cannot be overstated. The traditional answer to suggestions that the Second Amendment gives every American a right to keep and bear arms is that "The right to keep and bear arms only applies to the militia [a position that was repudiated in the Supreme Court decision in *District of Columbia v. Heller*, 2008], and the National Guard is the militia."

The latter statement is only partially true, and only since 1916. Since the National Guard was not created and the term was not even used until the early part of the 20th century, it should be obvious that the Founders did not intend for the Second Amendment to apply only to the National Guard. Further, the National Guard is only a part of the Militia—the organized militia portion. The balance of the Militia as currently established under federal law is all able-bodied males between the ages of 18 and 45 who are not in the military or who do not hold certain specifically exempted jobs—the unorganized militia. This means that there are literally millions of American males who are members of the unorganized militia; to suggest that the Second Amendment does not and was not intended to allow them to keep and bear arms is nothing more than intellectual dishonesty.

A detailed reading of the National Defense Act of 1916 will reveal that, although the National Guard is deemed to comprise a part of the militia (the organized militia), the Act established such total control over the funding, organization, manning, and operation of the National Guard that it functions primarily as an arm of the federal armed forces, rather than as the citizens' home defense forces that were in existence and which were contemplated by the Founders at the time the Constitution and the Bill or Rights were drafted and adopted.

---

[4] The full text of the National Defense Act of 1916 can be found on-line at: https://www.loc.gov/law/help/statutes-at-large/64th-congress/session-1/c64s1ch134.pdf

Selected Text of the National Defense Act of 1916

SEC. 57. COMPOSITION OF THE MILITIA.—The militia of the United States shall consist of all able-bodied male citizens of the United States and all other able-bodied males who have or shall have declared their intention to become citizens of the United States, who shall be more than eighteen years of age and, except as hereinafter provided, not more than forty-five years of age, and said militia shall be divided into three classes, the National Guard, the Naval Militia, and the Unorganized Militia.

SEC. 58. COMPOSITION OF THE NATIONAL GUARD.—The National Guard shall consist of the regularly enlisted militia between the ages of eighteen and forty-five years organized, armed, and equipped as hereinafter provided, and of commissioned officers between the ages of twenty-one and sixty-four years.

SEC. 59. EXEMPTIONS FROM MILITIA DUTY.-The Vice President of the United States; the officers, judicial and executive, of the Government of the United States and of the several States and Territories; persons in the military or naval service of the United States; customhouse clerks; persons employed by the United States in the transmission of the mail; artificers and workmen employed in the armories, arsenals, and navy yards of the United States; pilots; mariners actually employed in the sea service of any citizen or merchant within the United States, shall be exempt from militia duty without regard to age, and all persons who because of religious belief shall claim exemption from military service, if the conscientious holding of such belief by such person shall be established under such regulations as the President shall prescribe, shall be exempted from militia service in a combatant capacity; but no person so exempted shall be exempt from militia service in any capacity that the President shall declare to be noncombatant.

SEC. 60. ORGANIZATION OF NATIONAL GUARD UNITS.—Except as otherwise specifically provided herein, the organization of the National Guard, including the composition of all units thereof, shall be the same as that which is or may hereafter be prescribed for the Regular Army, subject in time of peace to such general exceptions as may be authorized by the Secretary of War. And the President may prescribe the particular unit or units, as to branch or arm of service, to be maintained in each State, Territory, or the District of Columbia in order to secure a force which, when combined, shall form complete higher tactical units.

SEC. 61. MAINTENANCE OF OTHER TROOPS BY THE STATES.—No State shall maintain troops in time of peace other than as authorized in accordance with the organization prescribed under this Act: *Provided*, That nothing contained in this

Act shall be construed as limiting the rights of the States and Territories in the use of the state National Guard within their respective borders in time of peace: *Provided further*, That nothing contained in this Act shall prevent the organization and maintenance of State police or constabulary.

SEC. 62. NUMBER OF THE NATIONAL GUARD.—The number of enlisted men of the National Guard to be organized under this Act within one year from its passage shall be for each State in the proportion of two hundred such men for each Senator and Representative in Congress from such State, and a number to be determined by the President for each Territory and the District of Columbia, and shall be increased each year thereafter in the proportion of not less than fifty per centum until a total peace strength of not less than eight hundred enlisted men for each Senator and Representative in Congress shall have been reached: *Provided*, That in States which have but one Representative in Congress such increase shall be at the discretion of the President: *Provided further*, That this shall not be construed to prevent any State, Territory, or the District of Columbia from organizing the full number of troops required under this section in less time than is specified in this section, or from maintaining existing organizations if they shall conform to such rules and regulations regarding organization, strength, and armament as the President may prescribe: *And provided further*, That nothing in this Act shall be construed to prevent any State with but one Representative in Congress from organizing one or more regiments of troops, with such auxiliary troops as the President may prescribe; such organizations and members of such organizations to receive all the benefits accruing under this Act under the conditions set forth herein: *Provided further*, That the word Territory as used in this Act and in all laws relating to the land militia and National Guard shall include and apply to Hawaii, Alaska, Porto [*sic*]Rico, and the Canal Zone, and the militia of the Canal Zone shall be organized under such rules and regulations, not in conflict with the provisions of this Act, as the President may prescribe.

SEC. 63. Any corps of Artillery, Cavalry, or Infantry existing in any of the States on the passage of the Act of May eighth, seventeen hundred and ninety-two, which by the laws, customs, or usages of said States has been in continuous existence since the passage of said Act, under its provisions and under the provisions of section two hundred and thirty-two and sections sixteen hundred and twenty-five to sixteen hundred and sixty, both inclusive, of title sixteen of the Revised Statutes of eighteen hundred and seventy-three, and the Act of January twenty-first, nineteen hundred and three, relating to the militia, shall be allowed to retain its ancient privileges, subject, nevertheless, to all duties required by law of militia: *Provided*, That said organizations may be a part of the National Guard and entitled to all the privileges of this Act, and shall conform in all respects to the organization, discipline, and training of the National Guard in time of war: *Provided further*, That for purposes of training and when on active duty in the service of the United States they may be assigned to higher units, as the President may direct, and shall be subject to the orders of officers under whom they shall be serving.

SEC. 64. ASSIGNMENT OF NATIONAL GUARD TO BRIGADES AND DIVISIONS.—For the purpose of maintaining appropriate organization and to assist in instruction and training, the President may assign the National Guard of the several States and Territories and the District of Columbia to divisions, brigades, and other tactical units, and may detail officers either from the National Guard or the Regular Army to command such units: *Provided*, That where complete units are organized within a State, Territory, or the District of Columbia the commanding officers thereof shall not be displaced under the provisions of this section.

SEC. 65. CHIEFS OF STAFF OF NATIONAL GUARD DIVISIONS.—The President may detail one officer of the Regular Army as chief of staff and one officer of the Regular Army or the National Guard as assistant to the chief of staff of any division of the National Guard in the service of the United States as a National Guard organization: *Provided*, That in order to insure the prompt mobilization of the National Guard in time of war or other emergency, the President may, in time of peace, detail an officer of the Regular Army to perform the duties of chief of staff for each fully organized tactical division of the National Guard.

SEC. 66. ADJUTANTS GENERAL OF STATES, AND SO FORTH.—The adjutants general of the States, Territories, and the District of Columbia and the officers of the National Guard shall make such returns and reports to the Secretary of War, or to such officers as he may designate, at such times and in such form as the Secretary of War may from time to time prescribe: *Provided* That the adjutants general of the Territories and of the District of Columbia shall be appointed by the President with such rank and qualifications as he may prescribe, and each adjutant general for a Territory shall be a citizen of the Territory for which he is appointed.

SEC. 67. APPROPRIATION, APPORTIONMENT, AND DISBURSEMENT OF FUNDS FOR THE NATIONAL GUARD.—A sum of money shall hereafter be appropriated annually, to be paid out of any money in the Treasury not otherwise appropriated, for the support of the National Guard, including the expense of providing arms, ordnance stores, quartermaster stores, and camp equipage, and all other military supplies for issue to the National Guard, and such other expenses pertaining to said guard as are now or may hereafter be authorized by law.

The appropriation provided for in this section shall be apportioned among the several States and Territories under just and equitable procedure to be prescribed by the Secretary of War and in direct ratio to the number of enlisted men in active service in the National Guard existing in such States and Territories at the date of apportionment of said appropriation, and to the District of Columbia, under such regulations as the President may prescribe: *Provided*, That the sum so apportioned among the several States, Territories, and the District of Columbia, shall be available under such rules as may be prescribed by the Secretary of War for the actual and necessary expenses incurred by officers and enlisted men of the Regular Army when traveling on duty in connection with the National Guard; for the transportation of supplies furnished to the National Guard for the permanent equipment thereof; for office rent and necessary office expenses of officers of the Regular Army on duty with the National Guard; for the expenses of the Militia Bureau, including clerical services, now authorized for the Division of Militia Affairs; for expenses of enlisted men of the Regular Army on duty with the National Guard, including quarters, fuel, light, medicines, and medical attendance; and such expenses shall constitute a charge against the whole sum annually appropriated for the support of the National Guard, and shall be paid therefrom and not from the allotment duly apportioned to any particular State, Territory, or the District of Columbia; for the promotion of rifle practice, including the acquisition, construction, maintenance, and equipment of shooting galleries and suitable target ranges; for the hiring of horses and draft animals for the use of mounted troops, batteries, and wagons; for forage for the same; and for such other incidental expenses in connection with lawfully authorized encampments, maneuvers, and field instruction as the Secretary of War may deem necessary, and for such other expenses pertaining to the National Guard as are now or may hereafter be authorized by law.

The governor of each State and Territory and the commanding general of the National Guard of the District of Columbia shall appoint, designate, or detail, subject to the approval of the Secretary of War, an officer of the National Guard of the State, Territory, or District of Columbia who shall be regarded as property and disbursing officer for the United States. He shall receipt and account for all funds and property belonging to the United States in possession of the National Guard of his State, Territory, or District, and shall make such returns and reports concerning the same as may be required by the Secretary of War. The Secretary of War is authorized, on the requisition of the governor of a State or Territory or the commanding general of the National Guard of the District of Columbia, to pay to the property and disbursing officer thereof so much of its allotment out of the annual appropriation for the support of the National Guard as shall, in the judgment of the Secretary of War, be necessary for the purposes enumerated therein. He shall render, through the War Department, such accounts of Federal funds intrusted to him for disbursement as may be required by the Treasury Department. Before entering upon the performance of his duties as property and disbursing officer he shall be required to give good and sufficient bond to the United States, the amount thereof to be determined by the Secretary of War, for the faithful performance of his duties and for the safe-keeping and proper disposition of the Federal property and funds intrusted to his care. He shall, after having qualified as property and disbursing officer, receive pay for his services at a rate to be fixed by the Secretary of War, and such compensation shall be a charge against the whole sum annually appropriated for the support of the National Guard: *Provided*, That when traveling in the performance of his official duties under orders issued by the proper authorities he shall be reimbursed for his actual necessary traveling expenses, the sum to be made a charge against the allotment of the State, Territory, or District of Columbia: *Provided further*, That the Secretary of War shall cause an inspection of the accounts and records of the property and disbursing officer to be made by an inspector general of the Army at least once each year: *And provided further*, That the Secretary of War is empowered to make all rules and regulations necessary to carry into effect the provisions of this section.

SEC. 68. LOCATION OF UNIT.—The States and Territories shall have the right to determine and fix the location of the units and headquarters of the National Guard within their respective borders: *Provided*, That no organization of the National Guard, members of which shall be entitled to and shall have received compensation under the provisions of this Act, shall be disbanded without the consent of the President, nor, without such consent, shall the commissioned or enlisted strength of any such organization be reduced below the minimum that shall be prescribed therefor by the President.

SEC. 69. ENLISTMENTS IN THE NATIONAL GUARD.—Hereafter the period of enlistment in the National Guard shall be for six years, the first three years of which shall be in an active organization and the remaining three years in the National Guard Reserve, hereinafter provided for, and the qualifications for enlistment shall be the same as those prescribed for admission to the Regular Army: *Provided*, That in the National Guard the privilege of continuing in active service during the whole of an enlistment period and of reenlisting in said service shall not be denied by reason of anything contained in this Act.

SEC. 70. FEDERAL ENLISTMENT CONTRACT.—Enlisted men in the National Guard of the several States, Territories, and the District of Columbia now serving under enlistment contracts which contain an obligation to defend the Constitution of the United States and to obey the orders of the President of the United States shall be recognized as members of the National Guard under the provisions of this Act for the unexpired portion of their present enlistment contracts. When any such enlistment contract does not contain such obligation, the enlisted man shall not be recognized as a member of the National Guard until he shall have signed an enlistment contract and taken and subscribed to the following oath of enlistment, upon signing which credit shall be given for the period already served under the old enlistment contract: "I do hereby acknowledge to have voluntarily enlisted this — day of ——, 19—, as a soldier in the National Guard of the United States and of the State of -, for the period of three years in service and three years in the reserve, under the conditions prescribed by law, unless sooner discharged by proper authority. And I do solemnly swear that I will bear true faith and allegiance to the United States of America and to the State of ——, and that I will serve them honestly and faithfully against all their enemies whomsoever, and that I will obey the orders of the President of the United States and of the governor of the State of ——, and of the officers appointed over me according to law and the rules and articles of war."

SEC. 71. Hereafter all men enlisting for service in the National Guard shall sign an enlistment contract and take and subscribe to the oath prescribed in the preceding section of this Act.

SEC. 72. DISCHARGE OF ENLISTED MEN FROM THE NATIONAL GUARD.—An enlisted man discharged from service in the National Guard shall receive a discharge in writing in such form and with such classification as is or shall be prescribed for the Regular Army, and in time of peace discharges may be given prior to the expiration of terms of enlistment under such regulations as the President may prescribe.

SEC. 73. FEDERAL OATH FOR NATIONAL GUARD OFFICERS.—Commissioned officers of the National Guard of the several States, Territories, and the District of Columbia now serving under commissions regularly issued shall continue in office, as officers of the National Guard without the issuance of new commissions: *Provided*, That said officers have taken, or shall take and subscribe to the following oath of office: "I, ——, do solemnly swear that I will support and defend the Constitution of the United States and the constitution of the State of ——, against all enemies, foreign and domestic that I will bear true faith and allegiance to the same; that I will obey the orders of the President of the United States and of the governor of the State of ——; that I make this obligation freely, without any mental reservation or purpose of evasion, and that I will well and faithfully discharge the duties of the office of —— in the National Guard of the United States and of the State of —— upon which I am about to enter, so help me God."

SEC. 74. QUALIFICATIONS FOR NATIONAL GUARD OFFICERS.—Persons hereafter commissioned as officers of the National Guard shall hereafter. not be recognized as such under any of the provisions of this Act unless they shall have been selected from the following classes and shall have taken and subscribed to the oath of office prescribed in the preceding section of this Act: Officers or enlisted men of the National Guard; officers on the reserve or unassigned list of the National Guard; officers active or retired, and former officers of the United States Army, Navy, and Marine Corps; graduates of the United States Military and Naval Academies and graduates of schools, colleges, and universities where military science is taught under the supervision of an officer of the Regular Army, and, for the technical branches and staff corps or departments, such other civilians as may be especially qualified for duty therein.

SEC. 75. The provisions of this Act shall not apply to any person hereafter appointed an officer of the National Guard unless he first shall have successfully passed such tests as to his physical, moral, and professional fitness as the President shall prescribe. The examination to determine such qualifications for commission shall be conducted by a board of three commissioned officers appointed by the Secretary of War from the Regular Army or the National Guard, or both.

SEC. 76. FILLING OF VACANCIES WHEN DRAFTED INTO FEDERAL SERVICE.—All vacancies occurring in any grade of commissioned officers in any organization in the military service of the United States and composed of persons drafted from the National Guard under the provisions of this Act shall be filled by the President, as far as practicable, by the appointment of persons similarly taken from said guard, and in the manner prescribed by law for filling similar vacancies occurring in the volunteer forces.

SEC. 77. ELIMINATION AND DISPOSITION OF OFFICERS.—At any time the moral character, capacity, and general fitness for the service of any National Guard officer may be determined by an efficiency board of three commissioned officers, senior in rank to the officer whose fitness for service shall be under investigation, and if the findings of such board be unfavorable to such officer and be approved by the official authorized to appoint such an officer, he shall be discharged. Commissions of officers of the National Guard may be vacated upon resignation, absence without leave for three months, upon the recommendation of an efficiency board, or pursuant to sentence of a court-martial. Officers of said guard rendered surplus by the disbandment of their organizations shall be placed in the National Guard Reserve. Officers may, upon their own application, be placed in the said reserve.

SEC. 78. THE NATIONAL GUARD RESERVE.–Subject to such rules and regulations as the President may prescribe, a National Guard Reserve shall be organized in each State, Territory, and the District of Columbia, and shall consist of such organizations, officers, and enlisted men as the President may prescribe, or members thereof may be assigned as reserves to an active organization of the National Guard: *Provided* That members of said reserve, when engaged in training, field or coast-defense training with the active National Guard, shall receive the same Federal pay and allowances as enlisted men of like grade on the active list of said guard when likewise engaged: *Provided further*, That, except as otherwise specifically provided in this Act, no commissioned or enlisted reservist shall receive any pay or allowances out of any appropriation made by Congress for National Guard purposes.

SEC. 79. RESERVE BATTALIONS FOR RECRUIT TRAINING.—When members of the National Guard and the enlisted reserve thereof of any State, Territory, or the District of Columbia shall have been brought into the service of the United States in time of war, there shall be immediately organized, either from such enlisted reserve or from the unorganized militia, in such State, Territory, or District, one reserve battalion for each regiment of Infantry or Cavalry, or each nine batteries of Field Artillery, or each twelve companies of Coast Artillery, brought into the service of the United States and such reserve battalion shall constitute the fourth battalion of any such regiment or twelve companies of Coast Artillery. Reserve battalions shall consist of four companies of such strength as may be prescribed by the President of the United States. When the members of three or more regiments of the National Guard of any State, Territory, or District shall have been brought into the service of the United States, the reserve battalions of such regiments may be organized into provisional regiments and higher units. If for any reason there shall not be enough voluntary enlistments ,to keep the reserve battalions at the prescribed strength, a sufficient number of the unorganized militia shall be drafted into the service of the United States to maintain each of such battalions at the proper strength. As vacancies occur from death or other causes any organization in the service of the United States and composed of men taken from the National Guard, men shall be transferred from the reserve battalions to the organizations in the field so that such organizations may be maintained at war strength. Officers for the reserve battalions provided for herein shall be drafted from the National Guard Reserve or Coast Artillery companies of the National Guard or the Officers' Reserve Corps, such officers to be taken, if practicable, from the States, respectively, in which the battalions shall be organized. Officers and noncommissioned officers returned to their home stations because of their inability to perform active field service may be assigned to reserve battalions for duty, and all soldiers invalided home shall be assigned to and carried on the rolls of reserve battalions until returned to duty or until discharged.

SEC. 80. LEAVES OF ABSENCE FOR CERTAIN GOVERNMENT EMPLOYEES.—All officers and employees of the United States and of the District of Columbia who shall be members of the National Guard shall be entitled to leave of absence from their respective duties, without loss of pay, time, or efficiency rating on all days during which they shall be engaged in field or coast-defense training ordered or authorized under the provisions of this Act.

SEC. 81. MILITIA BUREAU OF THE WAR DEPARTMENT.—The National Militia Board created by section eleven of the Act of May twenty-seventh, nineteen hundred and eight, amending section twenty of the Act of January twenty-first, nineteen hundred and three, shall, from the date of the approval of this Act, be abolished. The Militia Division now existing in the War Department shall hereafter be known as the Militia Bureau of said department, shall, like other bureaus of said department, be under the immediate supervision of the Secretary of War, and shall not form a part of any other bureau, office, or other organization, but the Chief of the Militia Bureau shall be ex officio a member of the General Staff Corps: *Provided*, That the President may, in his discretion, assign to duty in the Militia Bureau as assistants to the chief thereof not to exceed one colonel and one lieutenant colonel of the National Guard, for terms of four years, and any such officer while so assigned shall, subject to such regulations as the President may prescribe, receive out of the whole fund appropriated for the support of the militia the pay and allowances of a Regular Army officer having the same rank and length of service as said National Guard officer, whose prior service in the Organized Militia shall be counted in ascertaining his rights under this proviso.

SEC. 82. ARMAMENT EQUIPMENT, AND UNIFORM OF THE NATIONAL GUARD.—The National Guard of the United States shall, as far as practicable, be uniformed, armed, and equipped with the same type of uniforms, arms, and equipments as are or shall be provided for the Regular Army.

SEC. 83. The Secretary of War is hereby authorized to procure, under such regulations as the President may prescribe, by purchase or manufacture, within the limits of available appropriations made by Congress, and to issue from time to time to the National Guard, upon requisition of the governors of the several States and Territories or the commanding general of the National Guard of the District of Columbia, such number of United States service arms, with all accessories, field-artillery materiel, engineer, coast artillery, signal, and sanitary materiel, accouterments, field uniforms, clothing, equipage, publications, and military stores of all kinds, including public animals, as are necessary to arm, uniform, and equip for field service the National Guard in the several States, Territories, and the District of Columbia: *Provided*, That as a condition precedent to the issue of any property as provided for by this Act, the State, Territory, or the District of Columbia desiring such issue shall make adequate provision, to the satisfaction of the Secretary of War, for the protection and care of such property: Provided further, That, whenever it shall be shown to the satisfaction of the Secretary of War that the National Guard of any State Territory, or the District of Columbia, is properly organized, armed, and equipped for field service, funds allotted to that State, Territory, or District for the support of its National Guard may be used for the purchase, from the War Department, of any article issued by any of the supply departments of the Army.

SEC. 84. Under such regulations as the President may prescribe, whenever a new type of equipment, small arm, or field gun shall have been issued to the National Guard of the several States, Territories, and the District of Columbia, such equipment, small arms, and field guns, including all accessories, shall be furnished without charging the cost or value thereof or any expense connected therewith against the appropriations provided for the support of the National Guard.

SEC. 85. Each State, Territory, and the District of Columbia shall, on the receipt of new property issued to replace obsolete or condemned prior issues, turn in to the War Department or otherwise dispose of, in accordance with the directions of the Secretary of War, all property so replaced or condemned, and shall not receive any money credit therefor.

SEC. 86. Any State, Territory, or the District of Columbia may, with the approval of the Secretary of War, purchase for cash from the War Department for the use of the National Guard, including the officers thereof, any stores, supplies, material of war, and military publications furnished to the Army, in addition to those issued under the provisions of this Act, at the price at which they shall be listed to the Army, with cost of transportation added. The funds received from such sale shall be credited to the appropriation to which they shall belong, shall not be covered into the Treasury, and shall be available until expended to replace therewith the supplies sold to the States in the manner herein authorized: *Provided*, That stores, supplies, and materiel of war so purchased by a State, Territory, or the District of Columbia may, in time of actual or threatened war, be requisitioned by the United States for use in the military service thereof, and when so requisitioned by the United States and delivered credit for the ultimate return of such property in kind shall be allowed to such State, Territory, or the District of Columbia.

SEC. 87. DISPOSITION AND REPLACEMENT OF DAMAGED PROPERTY AND SO FORTH.—All military property issued to the National Guard as herein provided shall remain the property of the United States. Whenever any such property issued to the National Guard in any State or Territory or the District of Columbia shall have been lost, damaged, or destroyed, or become unserviceable or unsuitable by use in service or from any other cause, it shall be examined by a disinterested surveying officer of the Regular Army or the National Guard, detailed by the Secretary of War, and the report of such surveying officer shall be forwarded to the Secretary of War, or to such officer as he shall designate to receive such reports; and if it shall appear to the Secretary of War from the record of survey that the property was lost, damaged, or destroyed through unavoidable causes, he is hereby authorized to relieve the State or Territory or the District of Columbia from further accountability therefor. If it shall appear that the loss, damage, or destruction of property was due to carelessness or neglect, or that its loss, damage, or destruction could have been avoided by the exercise of reasonable care, the money value of such property shall be charged to the accountable State, Territory, or District of Columbia, to be paid from State, Territory, or District funds, or any funds other than Federal. If the articles so surveyed are found to be unserviceable or unsuitable, the Secretary of War shall direct what disposition, by sale or otherwise, shall be made of them; and if sold, the proceeds of such sale, as well as stoppages against officers and enlisted men, and the net proceeds of collections made from any person or from any State, Territory, or District to reimburse the Government for the loss, damage, or destruction of any property, shall be deposited in the Treasury of the United States as a credit to said State, Territory, or the District of Columbia, accountable for said property, and as a part of and in addition to that portion of its allotment set aside for the purchase of similar supplies, stores, or material of war: *Provided further*, That if any State, Territory, or the District of Columbia shall neglect or refuse to pay, or to cause to be paid, the money equivalent of any loss, damage, or destruction of property charged against such State, Territory, or the District of Columbia by the Secretary of War after survey by a disinterested officer appointed as hereinbefore provided, the Secretary of War is hereby authorized to debar such State, Territory, or the District of Columbia from further participation in any and all appropriations for the National Guard until such payment shall have been made.

SEC. 88. The net proceeds of the sale of condemned stores issued to the National Guard and not charged to State allotments shall be covered into the Treasury of the United States, as shall also stoppages against officers and enlisted men, and the net proceeds of collections made from any person to reimburse the Government for the loss, damage, or destruction of said property not charged against the State allotment issued for the use of the National Guard.

SEC. 89. HORSES FOR CAVALRY AND FIELD ARTILLERY OF NATIONAL GUARD.—Funds allotted by the Secretary of War for the support of the National Guard shall be available for the purchase, under such regulations as the Secretary of War may prescribe, of horses conforming to the Regular Army standards for the use of Field Artillery and Cavalry of the National Guard, said horses to remain the property of the United States and to be used solely for military purposes.

Horses so purchased may be issued not to exceed thirty-two to any one battery or troop, under such regulations as the Secretary of War may prescribe; and the Secretary of War is further authorized to issue, in lieu of purchase, for the use of such organizations, condemned Army horses which are no longer fit for service, but which may be suitable for the purposes of instruction, such horses to be sold as now provided by law when said purposes shall have been served.

SEC. 90. Funds allotted by the Secretary of War for the support of the National Guard shall be available for the purchase and issue of forage, bedding, shoeing, and veterinary services, and supplies for the Government horses issued to any battery or troop, and for the compensation of competent help for the care of the material, animals, and equipment thereof, under such regulations as the Secretary of War may prescribe: *Provided*, That the men to be compensated, not to exceed five for each battery or troop, shall be duly enlisted therein and shall be detailed by the battery or troop commander, under such regulations as the Secretary of War may prescribe, and shall be paid by the United States disbursing officer in each State, Territory, and the District of Columbia.

SEC. 91. DISCIPLINE TO CONFORM TO THAT OF REGULAR ARMY.—The discipline (which includes training) of the National Guard shall conform to the system which is now or may hereafter be prescribed for the Regular Army, and the training shall be carried out by the several States, Territories, and the District of Columbia so as to conform to the provisions of this Act.

SEC. 92. TRAINING OF THE NATIONAL GUARD.—Each company, troop, battery, and detachment in the National Guard shall assemble for drill and instruction, including indoor target practice, not less than forty-eight times each year, and shall, in addition thereto, participate in encampments, maneuvers, or other exercises, including outdoor target practice, at least fifteen days in training each year, including target practice, unless such company, troop, battery, or detachment shall have been excused from participation in any part by the Secretary of War: *Provided*, That credit for an assembly for drill or for indoor target practice shall not be given unless the number of officers and enlisted men present for duty at such assembly shall equal or exceed a minimum to be prescribed by the President, nor unless the period of actual military duty and instruction participated in by each officer and enlisted man at each such assembly at which he shall be credited as having been present shall be of at least one and one-half hours' duration and the character of training such as may be prescribed by the Secretary of War.

SEC. 93. INSPECTIONS OF THE NATIONAL GUARD.—The Secretary of War shall cause an inspection to be made at least once each year by inspectors general, and if necessary by other officers, of the Regular Army, detailed by him for that purpose, to determine whether the amount and condition of the property in the hands of the National Guard is satisfactory; whether the National Guard is organized as hereinbefore prescribed; whether the officers and enlisted men possess the physical and other qualifications prescribed; whether the organization and the officers and enlisted men thereof are sufficiently armed, uniformed, equipped, and being trained and instructed for active duty in the field or coast defense, and whether the records are being in accordance with the requirements of this Act. The reports of such inspections shall serve as the basis for deciding as to the issue to and retention by the National Guard of the military property provided for by this Act, and for determining what organizations and individuals shall be considered as constituting parts of the National Guard within the meaning of this Act.

SEC. 94. ENCAMPMENTS AND MANEUVERS.—Under such regulations as the President may prescribe the Secretary of War is authorized to provide for the participation of the whole or any part of the National Guard in encampments, maneuvers, or other exercises, including outdoor target practice, for field or coast-defense instruction, either independently or in conjunction with any part of the Regular Army, and there may be set aside from the funds appropriated for that purpose and allotted to any State, Territory, or the District of Columbia, such portion of said funds as may be necessary for the payment, subsistence transportation, and other proper expenses of such portion of the National Guard of such State, Territory, or the District of Columbia as shall participate in such encampments, maneuvers, or other exercises, including outdoor target practice, for field and coast-defense instruction; and the officers and enlisted men of such National Guard while so engaged shall be entitled to the same pay, subsistence, and transportation as officers and enlisted men of corresponding grades of the Regular Army are or hereafter may be entitled by law.

SEC. 95. When any part of the National Guard participates in encampments, maneuvers, or other exercises, including outdoor target practice, for field or coast-defense instruction at a United States military post, or reservation, or elsewhere, if in conjunction with troops of the United States, the command of such military post or reservation and of the officers and troops of the United States on duty there or elsewhere shall remain with the commander of the United States troops without regard to the rank of the commanding or other officer of the National Guard temporarily engaged in the encampments, maneuvers, or other exercises.

SEC. 96. USE OF REGULAR ARMY PERSONNEL.-The Secretary of War may detail one or more officers and enlisted men of the Regular Army to attend any encampment, maneuver, or other exercise for field or coast-defense instruction of the National Guard, who shall give such instruction and information to the officers and men assembled for such encampment, maneuver, or other exercise as may be directed by the Secretary of War or requested by the governor or by the commanding officer of the National Guard there on duty.

SEC. 97. Under such regulations as the President may prescribe the Secretary of War may provide camps for the instruction of officers and enlisted men of the National Guard. Such camps shall be conducted by officers of the Regular Army detailed by the Secretary of War for that purpose, and may be located either within or without the State, Territory, or District of Columbia to which the members of the National Guard designated to attend said camps shall belong. Officers and enlisted men attending such camps shall be entitled to pay and transportation, and enlisted men to subsistence in addition, at the same rates as for encampments or maneuvers for field or coast-defense instruction.

SEC. 98. When any portion of the National Guard shall participate in encampments, maneuvers, or other exercises, including outdoor target practice, for field or coast-defense instruction. under the provisions of this Act, it may, after being duly mustered, be paid at any time after such muster for the period from. the date of leaving the home rendezvous to date of return thereto as determined in advance, both dates inclusive; and such payment, if otherwise correct, shall pass to the credit of the disbursing officer making the same.

SEC. 99. NATIONAL GUARD OFFICERS AND MEN AT SERVICE SCHOOLS, AND SO FORTH.—Under such regulations as the President may prescribe, the Secretary of War may, upon the recommendation of the governor of any State or Territory or the commanding general of the National Guard of the District of Columbia, authorize a limited number of selected officers or enlisted men of the National Guard to attend and pursue a regular course of study at any military service school of the United States, except the United States Military Academy; or to be attached to an organization of the same arm, corps, or department to which such officer or enlisted man shall belong, for routine practical instruction at or near an Army post during a period of field training or other outdoor exercises; and such officer or enlisted man shall receive, out of any National Guard allotment of funds available for the purpose, the same travel allowances and quarters, or commutation of quarters, and the same pay, allowances, and subsistence to which an officer or enlisted man of the Regular Army would be entitled for attending such school, college, or practical course of instruction under orders from proper military authority, while in actual attendance at such school, college, or practical course of instruction: *Provided*, That in no case shall the pay and allowances authorized by this section exceed those of a captain.

SEC. 100. DETAIL OF OFFICERS OF REGULAR ARMY TO DUTY WITH THE NATIONAL GUARD.-The Secretary of War shall detail officers of the active list of the Army to duty with the National Guard in each State, Territory, or District of Columbia, and officers so detailed may accept commissions in the National Guard, with the permission of the President and terminable in his discretion, without vacating their commissions in the Regular Army or being prejudiced in their relative or lineal standing therein. The Secretary of War may, upon like application, detail one or more enlisted men of the Regular Army with each State, Territory, or District of Columbia for duty in connection with the National Guard. But nothing in this section shall be so construed as to prevent the detail of retired officers as now provided by law.

SEC. 101. NATIONAL GUARD, WHEN SUBJECT TO LAWS GOVERNING REGULAR ARMY.—The National Guard when called as such into the service of the United States shall, from the time they are required by the terms of the call to respond thereto, be subject to the laws and regulations governing the Regular Army, so far as such laws and regulations are applicable to officers and enlisted men whose permanent retention in the military service, either on the active list or on the retired list, is not contemplated by existing law.

SEC. 102. System of courts-martial for National Guard.—Except in organizations in the service of the United States, court-martial in the National Guard shall be of three kinds, namely, general courts-martial, special courts-martial, and summary courts-martial. They shall be constituted like, and have cognizance of the same subjects, and possess like powers, except as to punishments, as similar courts provided for by the laws and regulations governing the Army of the United States, and the proceedings of courts-martial of the National Guard shall follow the forms and modes of procedure prescribed for said similar courts.

SEC. 103. General courts-martial of the National Guard not in the service of the United States may be convened by orders of the President, or of the governors of the respective States and Territories, or by the commanding general of the National Guard of the District of Columbia, and such courts shall have the power to impose fines not exceeding $200; to sentence to forfeiture of pay and allowances; to a reprimand; to dismissal or dishonorable discharge from the service; to reduction of noncommissioned officers to the ranks; or any two or more of such punishments may be combined in the sentences imposed by such courts.

SEC. 104. In the National Guard, not in the service of the United States, the commanding officer of each garrison, fort, post, camp, or other place, brigade, regiment, detached battalion, or other detached command, may appoint special courts-martial for his command; but such special courts-martial may in any case be appointed by superior authority when by the latter deemed desirable. Special courts-martial shall have power to try any person subject to military law, except a commissioned officer, for any crime or offense made punishable by the military laws of the United States, and such special courts-martial shall have the same powers of punishment as do general courts-martial, except that fines imposed by such courts shall not exceed $100.

SEC. 105. In the National Guard, not in the service of the United States, the commanding officer of each garrison, fort, post, or other place, regiment or corps, detached battalion, company, or other detachment of the National Guard may appoint for such place or command a summary court to consist of one officer, who shall have power to administer oaths and to try the enlisted men of such place or command for breaches of discipline and violations of laws governing such organizations; and said court, when satisfied of the guilt of such soldier, may impose fines not exceeding $25 for any single offense; may sentence noncommissioned officer to reduction to the ranks; may sentence to forfeiture of pay and allowances. The proceedings of such court shall be informal, and the minutes thereof shall be the same as prescribed for summary courts of the Army of the United States.

SEC. 106. All courts-martial of the National Guard, not in the service of the United States, including summary courts, shall have power to sentence to confinement in lieu of fines authorized to be imposed: *Provided*, That such sentences of confinement shall not exceed one day for each dollar of fine authorized.

SEC. 107. No sentence of dismissal from the service or dishonorable discharge, imposed by a National Guard court-martial, not in the service of the United States, shall be executed until approved by the governor of the State or Territory concerned, or by the commanding general of the National Guard of the District of Columbia.

SEC. 108. In the National Guard, not in the service of the United States, presidents of courts-martial and summary court officers shall have power to issue warrants to arrest accused persons and to bring them before the court for trial whenever such persons shall have disobeyed an order in writing from the convening authority to appear before such court, a copy of the charge or charges having been delivered to the accused with such order, and to issue subpoenas and subpoenas duces tecum and to enforce by attachment attendance of witnesses and the production of books and papers, and to sentence for a refusal to be sworn or to answer as provided in actions before civil courts.

All processes and sentences of said courts shall be executed by such civil officers as may be prescribed by the laws of the several States and Territories, and in any State where no provision shall have been made for such action, and in the Territories and the District of Columbia, such processes and sentences shall be executed by a United States marshal or his duly appointed deputy, and it shall be the duty of any United States marshal to execute all such processes and sentences and make return thereof to the officer issuing or imposing the same.

SEC. 109. PAY FOR NATIONAL GUARD OFFICERS.—Certain commissioned officers on the active list belonging to organizations of the National Guard of each State, Territory, and the District of Columbia participating in the apportionment of the annual appropriation for the support of the National Guard shall receive compensation for their services, except during periods of service for which they may become lawfully entitled to the same pay as officers of corresponding grades of the Regular Army, as follows, not to include longevity pay: A captain $500 per year and the same pay shall be paid to every officer of higher rank than that of captain, a first lieutenant $240 per year, and a second lieutenant $200 per year. Regulations to be prescribed by the Secretary of War shall determine the amount and character of service that must be rendered by officers to entitle them to the whole or specific parts of the maximum pay hereinbefore authorized: *Provided*, That all staff officers, aids-de-camp, and chaplains shall receive not to exceed one-half of the pay of a captain, except that regimental adjutants, and majors and captains in command of machine-gun companies, ambulance companies, field hospital companies, or sanitary troops shall receive the pay hereinbefore authorized for a captain.

SEC. 110. PAY FOR NATIONAL GUARD ENLISTED MEN.—Each enlisted man on the active list belonging to an organization of the National Guard of a State, Territory, or the District of Columbia, participating in the apportionment of the annual appropriation for the support of the National Guard, shall receive compensation for his services, except during periods of service for which he may become lawfully entitled to the same pay as an enlisted man of corresponding grade in the Regular Army, at a rate equal to twenty-five per centum of the initial pay now provided by law for enlisted men of corresponding grades of the Regular Army: *Provided*, That such enlisted man shall receive the compensation herein provided if he shall have attended not less than forty-eight regular drills during any one year, and a proportionate amount for attendance upon a lesser number of such drills, not less than twenty-four; and no such enlisted man shall receive any part of said compensation except as authorized by this proviso and the three provisos next following: *Provided further*, That the compensation provided herein shall be computed for semiannual periods, beginning the first day of January and the first day of July of each year, in proportion to the number of drills attended; and no compensation shall be paid to any enlisted man for the first semiannual period of any year unless he shall have attended during said period at least twenty-four drills, but any lesser number of drills attended during said period shall be reckoned with the drills attended during the second semiannual period in computing for the compensation, if any, due him for that year: Provided further, That when any man enters into an enlistment other than an immediate reenlistment he shall be entitled to proportional compensation for that year if during the remainder of the year he shall attend a number of drills whose ratio to twenty-four is not less than the ratio of the part of the year so served to the whole year; and when any man's enlistment shall expire the compensation, if any, to which he may be entitled shall be determined in like manner: *Provided further*, That periods of any actual military duty equivalent to the drills herein prescribed (except those periods of service for which members of the National Guard may become lawfully entitled to the same pay as officers and enlisted men of the corresponding grades in the Regular Army) may be accepted as service in lieu of such drills when so provided by the Secretary of War.

All amounts appropriated for the purpose of this and the last preceding section shall be disbursed and accounted for by the officers and agents of the Quartermaster Corps of the Army, and all disbursements under the foregoing provisions of this section shall be made as soon as practicable after the thirty-first day of December and the thirtieth day of June of each year upon pay rolls prepared and authenticated in the manner to be prescribed by the Secretary of War: *Provided*, That stoppages may be made against the compensation payable to any officer or enlisted man hereunder to cover the cost of public property lost or destroyed by and chargeable to such officer or enlisted man.

Except as otherwise specifically provided herein, no money appropriated under the provisions of this or the last preceding section shall be paid to any person not on the active list, nor to any person over sixty-four years of age, nor to any person who shall fail to qualify as to fitness for military service under such regulations as the Secretary of War shall prescribe, nor to any State, Territory, or District, or officer or enlisted man in the National Guard thereof, unless and until such State, Territory, or District provides by law that staff officers, including officers of the Pay, Inspection, Subsistence, and Medical Departments, hereafter appointed shall have had previous military experience and shall hold their positions until they shall have reached the age of sixty-four years, unless retired prior to that time by reason of resignation, disability, or for cause to be determined by a court-martial legally convened for that purpose, and that vacancies among said officers shall be filled by appointment from the officers of the militia of such State, Territory, or District: *Provided further*, That the preceding proviso shall not apply to any State, Territory, or District until sixty days next after the adjournment of the next session of its legislature held after the approval of this Act.

SEC. 111. NATIONAL GUARD WHEN DRAFTED INTO FEDERAL SERVICE.—When Congress shall have authorized the use of the armed land forces of the United States, for any purpose requiring the use of troops in excess of those of the Regular Army, the President may, under such regulations, including such physical examination, as he may prescribe, draft into the military service of the United States, to serve therein for the period of the war unless sooner discharged, any or all members of the National Guard and of the National Guard Reserve. All persons so drafted shall, from the date of their draft, stand discharged from the militia, and shall from said date be subject to such laws and regulations for the government of the Army of the United States as may be applicable to members of the Volunteer Army, and shall be embodied in organizations corresponding as far as practicable to those of the Regular Army or shall be otherwise assigned as the President may direct. The commissioned officers of said organizations shall be appointed from among the members thereof, officers with rank not above that of colonel to be appointed by the President alone, and all other officers to be appointed by the President by and with the advice and consent of the Senate. Officers and enlisted men in the service of the United States under the terms of this section shall have the same pay and allowances as officers and enlisted men of the Regular Army of the same grades and the same prior service.

SEC. 112. RIGHTS TO PENSIONS.—When any officer or enlisted man of the National Guard drafted into the service of the United States in time of war is disabled by reason of wounds or disability received or incurred while in the active service of the United States in time of war, he shall be entitled to all the benefits of the pension laws existing at the time of his service, and in case such officer or enlisted man dies in the active service of the United States in time of war or in returning to his place of residence after being mustered out of such service, or at any other time in consequence of wounds or disabilities received in such active service, his widow and children, if any, shall be entitled to all the benefits of such pension laws.

SEC. 113. ENCOURAGEMENT OF RIFLE PRACTICE.-The Secretary of War shall annually submit to Congress recommendations and estimates for the establishment and maintenance of indoor and outdoor rifle ranges, under such a comprehensive plan as will ultimately result in providing adequate facilities for rifle practice in all sections of the country. And that all ranges so established and all ranges which may have already been constructed, in whole or in part, with funds provided by Congress shall be open for use by those in any branch of the military or naval service of the United States and by all able-bodied males capable of bearing arms, under reasonable regulations to be prescribed by the controlling authorities and approved by the Secretary of War. That the President may detail capable officers and noncommissioned officers of the Regular Army and National Guard to duty at such ranges as instructors for the purpose of training the citizenry in the use of the military arm. Where rifle ranges shall have been so established and instructors assigned to duty thereat, the Secretary of War shall be authorized to provide for the issue of a reasonable number of standard military rifles and such quantities of ammunition as may be available for use in conducting such rifle practice.

SEC. 114. TEMPORARY VACANCIES IN REGULAR ARMY DUE TO DETAILS TO THE NATIONAL GUARD.—In time of war the temporary vacancies created in any grade not above that of colonel among the commissioned personnel of any arm, staff corps, or department of the Regular Army, through appointments of officers thereof to higher rank in organizations composed of members taken from the National Guard, shall be filled by temporary promotions according to seniority in rank from officers holding commissions in the next lower grade in said arm, staff corps, or department, and all vacancies created in any grade by such temporary promotions shall be in like manner filled from, and thus create temporary vacancies in, the next lower grade, and the vacancies that shall remain thereafter in said arm, staff corps, or department and that can not be filled by temporary promotions, as prescribed in this section, may be filled by the temporary appointment of officers of such number and grade or grades as shall maintain said arm, corps, or department at the full commissioned strength authorized by law: *Provided*, That in the staff corps and departments subject to the provisions of sections twenty-six and twenty-seven of the Act of February second, nineteen hundred and one, and Acts amendatory thereof, temporary vacancies that can not [*sic*] be filled by temporary promotions as hereinbefore prescribed shall be filled by temporary details in the manner prescribed in said sections twenty-six and twenty-seven, and Acts amendatory thereof, and the resulting temporary vacancies in the branches of the Army from which the details shall be so made shall be filled as hereinbefore in this section prescribed: *Provided further*, That officers temporarily promoted or appointed under the terms of this section shall be promoted or appointed by the President, by and with the advice and consent of the Senate, for terms that shall not extend beyond the war or the passing of the emergency for which additional forces were brought into the military service of the United States, and at the termination of the war or the passing of the emergency said officers shall be discharged from the positions held by them under their temporary commissions or appointments, and officers detailed as herein authorized shall be relieved from their temporary details: *And provided further*, That officers temporarily promoted under the provisions of this section shall not vacate their permanent commissions nor be prejudiced in their relative or lineal standing in the Regular Army.

SEC. 115. PHYSICAL EXAMINATION.—Every officer and enlisted man of the National Guard who shall be called into the service of the United States as such shall be examined as to his physical fitness under such regulations as the President may prescribe without further commission or enlistment: *Provided*, That immediately preceding the muster out of an officer or enlisted man called into the active service of the United States he shall be physically examined under rules prescribed by the President of the United States, and the record thereof shall be filed and kept in the War Department.

SEC. 116. NONCOMPLIANCE WITH FEDERAL ACT.—Whenever any State shall, within a limit of time to be fixed by the President, have failed or refused to comply with or enforce any requirement of this Act, or any regulation promulgated thereunder and in aid thereof by the President or the Secretary of War, the National Guard of such State shall be debarred, wholly or in part, as the President may direct, from receiving from the United States any pecuniary or other aid, benefit, or privilege authorized or provided by this Act or any other law.

SEC. 117. APPLICABLE TO LAND FORCES ONLY.—The provisions of this Act in respect to the militia shall be applicable only to militia organized as a land force and not to the Naval Militia, which shall consist of such part of the militia as may be prescribed by the President for each State, Territory, or District: *Provided*, That each State, Territory, or District maintaining a Naval Militia as herein prescribed may be credited to the extent of the number thereof in the quota that would otherwise be required by section sixty-two of this Act.

SEC. 118. NECESSARY RULES AND REGULATIONS.—The President shall make all necessary rules and regulations and issue such orders as may be necessary for the thorough organization, discipline, and government of the militia provided for in this Act.

SEC. 119. ANNUAL ESTIMATES REQUIRED.—The Secretary of War shall .cause to be estimated annually the amount necessary for carrying out the provisions of so much of this Act as relates to the militia, and no money shall be expended under said provisions except as shall from time to time be appropriated for carrying them out.

The National Defense Act of 1920

Although World War 1 was in progress when the National Defense Act of 1916 was drafted and enacted and the act must have contemplated the role of the National Guard in a wartime setting, the United States did not enter the war until April 6, 1917, when the United States declared war on Germany. Germany signed an armistice on the morning of November 11, 1918, and fighting ended later that day. Thus, a year after the National Defense Act of 1916 transformed and reorganized the land forces of the United States, the country entered into a two-year period of world war in which the new organizational structure was immediately put to the ultimate test.

In the aftermath of "The Great War," various changes and improvements were proposed. The best of these proposals were incorporated into the National Defense Act of 1920, which again reorganized the land forces of the United States, and further integrated the role of the National Guard into the overall structure of the Army of the United States.

In addition for making it possible for National Guard officers to serve on the General Staff, in order to improve communication and coordination between the National Guard and the Regular Army. The Act also provided for the National Guard to greatly outnumber the Regular Army, with authorized troop strengths of 430,000 for the National Guard compared to 280,000 for the Regular Army. The Act also required that decisions affecting the National Guard be made by committees on which the National Guard had representatives.

With the passage of the National Defense Act of 1920, any lingering vestiges of the National Guard as the local, indigenous, home defense force militias of the pre-Revolutionary colonies were eradicated. The National Guard was officially transformed into a major component of the federal standing army; its role as state defense forces became secondary. The traditional role of the militia was left to the unorganized militia—those able-bodied males between the ages of 18 and 45 who were not members of the Regular Army, the National Guard, or the Naval Militia.

The National Defense Act of 1920 occupies 54 pages in the *Federal Register*; in the interest of conserving space and sparing readers time perusing page after page of information unrelated to the National Guard or the Second Amendment, the following pages will reproduce those sections the editor feels are most important in documenting the shift of the National Guard away from being a number of local militias to becoming an integral part of the Army of the United States.

* * * * *

Readers who wish to research the entire Act can find it on-line at: https://www.loc.gov/law/help/statutes-at-large/66th-congress/session-2/c66s2ch227.pdf

Selected Text from the National Defense Act of 1920

SIXTY-SIXTH CONGRESS. SESS. II. CH. 227. 1920.

CHAP. 227.—An Act To amend an Act entitled "An Act for making further and more effectual provision for the national defense, and for other purposes," approved June 3, 1916, and to establish military justice.

Be it enacted by the Senate and House of Representatives of the United States of America in Congress assembled,

CHAPTER I.

That the Act entitled "An Act for making further and more effectual provision for the national defense, and for other purposes," approved June 3, 1916, be amended as follows:

That section 1 of said Act be, and the same is hereby, amended by striking out the same and inserting the following in lieu thereof:

"That the Army of the United States shall consist of the Regular Army, the National Guard while in the service of the United States, and the Organized Reserves, including the Officers' Reserve Corps and the Enlisted Reserve Corps."

SEC. 2. That section 2 of said Act be, and the same is hereby, amended by striking out the same and inserting the following in lieu thereof:

"SEC. 2. COMPOSITION OF THE REGULAR ARMY.—The Regular Army of the United States shall consist of the Infantry, the Cavalry, the Field Artillery, the Coast Artillery Corps, the Air Service, the Corps of Engineers, the Signal Corps, which shall be designated as the combatant arms or the line of the Army; the General Staff Corps; the Adjutant General's Department; the Inspector General's Department; the Judge Advocate General's Department; the Quartermaster Corps; the Finance Department; the Medical Department; the Ordnance Department; the Chemical Warfare Service; the officers of the Bureau of Insular Affairs; the officers and enlisted men under the jurisdiction of the Militia Bureau; the chaplains; the professors and cadets of the United States Military Academy; the present military store-keeper; detached officers; detached enlisted men; unassigned recruits; the Indian Scouts; the officers and enlisted men of the retired list; and such other officers and enlisted men as are now or may hereafter be provided for. Except in time of war or similar emergency when the public safety demands it, the number of enlisted men of the Regular Army shall not exceed two hundred and eighty thousand, including the Philippine Scouts."

SEC. 3. That section 3 of said Act be, and the same is hereby, amended by striking out the same and inserting the following in lieu thereof:

"SEC. 3. ORGANIZATION OF THE ARMY.-The Organized peace establishment, including the Regular Army, the National Guard and the Organized Reserves, shall include all of those divisions and other military organizations necessary to form the basis for a complete and immediate mobilization for the national defense in the event of a national emergency declared by Congress. The Army shall at all times be organized so far as practicable into brigades, divisions and army corp, and whenever the President may deem it expedient, into armies. For purposes of administration, training and tactical control, the continental area of the United States shall be divided on a basis of military population into corps areas. Each corps area shall contain at least one division of the National Guard or Organized Reserves, and such other troops as the President may direct. The President is authorized to group any or all corps areas into army areas or departments."

"SEC. 3a. THE INITIAL ORGANIZATION OF THE NATIONAL GUARD AND THE ORGANIZED RESERVES.–In the reorganization of the National Guard and in the initial organization of the Organized Reserves, the names, numbers and other designations, flags, and records of the divisions and subordinate units thereof that served in the World War between April 6, 1917, and November 11, 1918, shall be preserved as such as far as practicable. Subject to revision and approval by the Secretary of War, the plans and regulations under which the initial organization and territorial distribution of the National Guard and the Organized Reserves shall be made, shall be prepared by a committee of the branch or division of the War Department General Staff hereinafter provided for, which is charged with the preparation of plans for the national defense and for the mobilization of the land forces of the United States. For the purpose of this task said committee shall be composed of members of said branch or division of the General Staff and an equal number of reserve officers, including reserve officers who hold or have held commissions in the National Guard. Subject to general regulations approved by the Secretary of War, the location and designation of units of the National Guard and of the Organized Reserves entirely comprised within the limits of any State or Territory shall be determined by a board, a majority of whom shall be reserve officers including reserve officers who hold or have held commissions in the National Guard and recommended for this duty by the governor of the State or Territory concerned."

* * * * *

SEC. 36. That section 60 of said Act be, and the same is hereby, amended by adding the following at the end thereof: "Until July 1, 1921, companies and corresponding units of the National Guard may be recognized at a minimum enlisted strength of fifty: *Provided*, That the National Guard of any State, Territory, and the District of Columbia may include such detachments or parts of units as may be necessary in order to form complete tactical units when combined with troops of other States."

SEC. 37. That section 69 of said Act be, and the same is hereby, amended by striking out the same and inserting the following in lieu thereof:

"SEC. 69. Original enlistments in the National Guard shall be for a period of three years and subsequent enlistments for periods of one year each: *Provided*, That persons who have served in the Army for not less than six months, and have been honorably discharged therefrom, may, within two years after the passage of this Act, enlist in the National Guard for a period of one year and reenlist for like periods."

SEC. 38. That section 70 of said Act be, and the same is hereby amended by striking out the same and inserting the following in lieu thereof:

"SEC. 70. Men enlisting in the National Guard of the several States, Territories, and the District of Columbia, shall sign an enlistment contract and subscribe to the following oath of enlistment: 'I do hereby acknowledge to have voluntarily enlisted this —— day of ——, 19––, as a soldier in the National Guard of the United States and of the State of ——, for the period of three (or one) year ––, under the conditions prescribed by law, unless sooner discharged by proper authority. And I do solemnly swear that I will bear true faith and allegiance to the United States of America and to the State of ——, and that I will serve them honestly and faithfully against all their enemies whomsoever, and that I will obey the orders of the President of the United States and of the governor of the State of ——, and of the officers appointed over me according to law and the rules and Articles of War."

SEC. 40. That section 72 of said Act be, and the same is hereby amended, by striking out the same, and inserting the following in lieu thereof:

"SEC. 72. DISCHARGE OF ENLISTED MEN FROM THE NATIONAL GUARD.—An enlisted man discharged from service in the National Guard, except when drafted into the military service of the United States under the provisions of section 111 of this Act, shall receive a discharge in writing in such form and with such classification as is or shall be prescribed for the Regular Army, and in time of peace discharges may be given prior to the expiration of terms of enlistment under such regulations as the President may prescribe."

SEC. 41. That section 74 of said Act be, and the same is hereby, amended by striking out the same and inserting the following in lieu thereof:

"SEC. 74. QUALIFICATIONS FOR NATIONAL GUARD OFFICERS.— Persons hereafter commissioned as officers of the National Guard shall not be recognized as such under any of the provisions of this Act unless they shall have been selected from the following classes, and shall have taken and subscribed to the oath of office prescribed in the preceding section of this Act; officers or enlisted men of the National Guard; officers, active or retired, reserve officers, and former officers of the Army, Navy or Marine Corps, enlisted men and former enlisted men of the

Army, Navy, or Marine Corps who have received an honorable discharge therefrom; graduates of the United States Military and Naval Academies; and graduates of schools, colleges, universities, and officers' training camps, where they have received military instruction under the supervision of an officer of the Regular Army who certified their fitness for appointment as commissioned officers; and for the technical branches or Staff Corps and departments, such other civilians as may be specially qualified for duty therein."

* * * * *

SEC. 49. That section 111 of said Act be, and the same is hereby, amended by striking out the same and inserting the following in lieu thereof:

"SEC. 111. NATIONAL GUARD WHEN DRAFTED INTO FEDERAL SERVICE.—When Congress shall have authorized the use of the armed land forces of the United States for any purpose requiring the use of troops in excess of those of the Regular Army, the President may, under such regulations, including such physical examination as he may prescribe, draft into the military service of the United States, to serve therein for the period of the war or emergency, unless sooner discharged, any or all members of the National Guard and of the National Guard Reserve. All persons so drafted shall, from the date of their draft, stand discharged from the militia, and shall be subject to such laws and regulations for the government of the Army of the United States as may be applicable to members of the Army, whose permanent retention in the military service is not contemplated by law, and shall be organized into units corresponding as far as practicable to those of the Regular Army or shall be otherwise assigned as the President may direct. The commissioned officers of said organizations shall be appointed from among the members thereof; officers with rank not above that of colonel to be appointed by the President alone, and all other officers to be appointed by the President by and with the advice and consent of the Senate. Officers and enlisted men while in the service of the United States under the terms of this section shall have the same pay and allowances as officers and enlisted men of the Regular Army of the same grades and the same prior service. On the termination of the emergency all persons so drafted shall be discharged from the Army, shall resume their membership in the militia, and, if the State so provide, shall continue to serve in the National Guard until the dates upon which their enlistments entered into prior to their draft, would have expired if uninterrupted."

The National Defense Act Amendments of 1933

Enacted on June 15, 1933, the National Defense Act Amendments of 1933 made additional revisions to the National Defense Act of 1916, further consolidating the incorporation of the National Guard into the overall structure of the federal Army of the United States. The act made (among others) the following changes to provisions affecting the National Guard:

- All policies and organizational decisions pertaining to the National Guard would ne made by the General Staff of the War Department;
- All persons appointed officers in the National Guard of the United States would thereafter also be reserve officers commissioned in the Army of the United States. Such appointments in grades below that of brigadier general would be made by the President alone, and general officers by and with the advice and consent of the Senate. Thus, the governors of the respective states would not exercise control over the appointment of the officers in their respective state units of the National Guard.
- The Act established federal control over the terms of enlistment in the National Guard, and gave the President the authority to extend terms of enlistment in the event of an emergency declared by the Congress.
- The name of the agency with the War Department formerly known as the Militia Bureau was changed to the National Guard Bureau.
- The Act revised the terms under which members of the National Guard could be called up for federal duty as part of the Army of the United States.

The National Defense Act Amendments of 1933 continued and consolidated the shift of the National Guard from being primarily or exclusively a local/state militia to being primarily an extension of the Regular Army, with most decisions affecting staffing, manning, organizing and training of the National Guard being removed from state control and exercised by the federal War Department. With the removal of the name "Militia Bureau" from the office within the War Department that exercised control over the National Guard, all pretense that the National Guard was in any way the militia referred to and envisioned by the Framers was completely canceled.

Full Text of National Defense Act Amendments of 1933

AN ACT

To amend the National Defense Act of June 3, 1916, as amended.

Be it enacted by the Senate and House of Representatives of the United States of America in Congress assembled, That section 1 of the National Defense Act of June 3, 1916, as amended, be, and the same is hereby, amended by striking out the same and inserting the following in lieu thereof:

"SECTION 1. That the Army of the United States shall consist of the Regular Army, the National Guard of the United States, the National Guard while in the service of the United States, the Officers' Reserve Corps, the Organized Reserves, and the Enlisted Reserve Corps."

SEC. 2. That the fourth paragraph of section 5 of said Act be, and the same is hereby, amended by striking out the same and inserting the following in lieu thereof:

"All policies and regulations affecting the organization and distribution of the National Guard of the United States, and all policies and regulations affecting the organization, distribution, and training of the National Guard, shall be prepared by committees of appropriate branches or divisions of the War Department General Staff, to which shall be added an equal number of officers from the National Guard of the United States, whose names are borne on lists of officers suitable for such duty, submitted by the governors of their respective States and Territories, and for the District of Columbia by the Commanding General, District of Columbia National Guard.

"All policies and regulations affecting the organization, distribution, training, appointment, assignment, promotion, and discharge of members of the Officers' Reserve Corps, the Organized Reserves, and the Enlisted Reserve Corps shall be prepared by committees of appropriate branches or divisions of the War Department General Staff to which shall be added an equal number of officers from the Officers' Reserve Corps: *Provided*, That when the subject to be studied affects the National Guard of the United States or the National Guard and the Officers' Reserve Corps, the Organized Reserves or the Enlisted Reserve Corps, such committees shall consist of an equal representation from the Regular Army, the National Guard of the United States, and the Officers' Reserve Corps. There shall be not less than ten officers on duty in the War Department General Staff, one half of whom shall be from the National Guard of the United States and one half from the Officers' Reserve Corps. For the purpose specified herein such officers shall be regarded as additional members of the General Staff while so serving: *Provided further*, That the Chief of Staff shall transmit to the Secretary of War the policies and regulations prepared as hereinbefore prescribed in this paragraph and advise him in regard thereto. After action by the Secretary of War thereon the Chief of Staff shall act as the agent of the Secretary of War in carrying the same into effect.

The Chief of Staff shall exercise the same supervision and control of the reserve components of the Army of the United States as he does over the Regular Army.

SEC. 3. That section 37 of said Act be, and the same is hereby, amended by striking out the same and inserting the following in lieu thereof:

"SEC. 37. OFFICERS RESERVE CORPS.—For the purpose of providing a reserve of officers available for military service when needed there shall be organized an Officers' Reserve Corps consisting of general officers and officers assigned to sections corresponding to the various branches of the Regular Army and such additional sections as the President may direct. The grades in each section and the number in each grade shall be as the President may prescribe. All persons appointed in the Officers' Reserve Corps are reserve officers and shall be commissioned in the Army of the United States. Such appointments in grades below that of brigadier general shall be made by the President alone, and general officers by and with the advice and consent of the Senate. Appointment in every case in the Officers' Reserve Corps shall be for a period of five years, but an appointment in force at the outbreak of war shall continue in force until six months after its termination: *Provided*, That an officer of the Officers' Reserve Corps shall be entitled to be relieved from active Federal service within six months after its termination if he makes application therefor. Any officer of the Officers' Reserve Corps may be discharged at any time in the discretion of the President. In time of peace an officer of the Officers' Reserve Corps must at the time of his appointment be a citizen of the United States between the ages of twenty-one and sixty years. Any person who has been an officer of the Army of the United States at any time between April 6, 1917, and June 30, 1919, or who has been an officer of the Regular Army at any time, if qualified, may be appointed in the Officers' Reserve Corps in the highest grade which he held or any lower grade. No other person except as herein provided shall in time of peace be originally appointed as a reserve officer of Infantry, Cavalry, Field Artillery, Coast Artillery, or Air Corps in a grade above that of second lieutenant. In time of peace appointments in the Infantry, Cavalry, Field Artillery, Coast Artillery, and Air Corps shall be limited to former officers of the Army, former officers of the National Guard of the United States, graduates of the Reserve Officers' Training Corps, as provided in section 47b hereof; warrant officers, and enlisted men of the Regular Army, National Guard of the United States, and Enlisted Reserve Corps and persons who served in the Army at some time between April 6, 1917, and November 11, 1918. Promotions in all grades of officers who have established, or may hereafter establish, their qualifications for such promotion, and transfer, shall be made under such regulations as may be prescribed by the

Secretary of War, and shall be based so far as practicable upon recommendations made in the established chain of command. So far as practicable, in time of peace, officers of the Officers' Reserve Corps shall be assigned to units in the locality of their places of residence. Nothing in this Act shall operate to deprive an officer of the reserve appointment he now holds: *Provided*, That this shall not apply to the discretionary-discharge power of the President previously mentioned. Members of the Officers' Reserve Corps, while not on active duty, shall not, by reason solely of their appointments, oaths, commissions, or status as such, or any duties or functions performed or pay or allowances received as such, be held or deemed to be officers or employees of the United States, or persons holding any office of trust or profit or dis charging any official function under or in connection with any department of the Government of the United States."

SEC. 4. That section 38 of said Act be, and the same is hereby, amended by striking out the same and inserting the following in lieu thereof:

"SEC. 38. OFFICERS, NATIONAL GUARD OF THE UNITED STATES.—All persons appointed officers in the National Guard of the United States are reserve officers and shall be commissioned in the Army of the United States. Such appointments in grades below that of brigadier general shall be made by the President alone, and general officers by and with the advice and consent of the Senate.

"Officers in the National Guard of the United States shall be appointed for the period during which they are federally recognized in the same grade and branch in the National Guard: *Provided*, That an appointment in force at the outbreak of war shall continue in force until six months after its termination: *And provided further*, That such officer shall be entitled to be relieved from active Federal service within six months after its termination if he makes application therefor.

"In time of peace the President may order to active duty, with their consent, officers of the National Guard of the United States for the purposes set forth in sections 5 and 81 of this Act. When on such active duty an officer of the National Guard of the United States shall receive the same pay and allowances as an officer of the Regular Army of the same grade and length of active service and mileage from his home to his first station and from his last station to his home, but shall not be entitled to retirement or retired pay: *Provided*, That such officers ordered to such active duty shall be paid out of the funds appropriated for the pay of the National Guard.

"Officers of the National Guard of the United States, while not on active duty, shall not, by reason solely of their appointments, oaths, commissions, or status as such, or any duties or functions performed or pay or allowances received as such, be held or deemed to be officers or employees of the United States, or persons holding any office of trust or profit or discharging any official function under or in connection with any department of the Government of the United States."

SEC.5. That section 58 of said Act be, and the same is hereby, amended by striking out the same and inserting the following in lieu thereof:

"SEC. 58. COMPOSITION OF THE NATIONAL GUARD AND THE NATIONAL GUARD OF THE UNITED STATES.—The National Guard of each State, Territory, and the District of Columbia shall consist of members of the militia voluntarily enlisted therein, who upon original enlistment shall be not less than eighteen nor more than forty-five years of age, or who in subsequent enlistment shall be not more than sixty-four years of age, organized, armed, equipped, and federally recognized as hereinafter provided, and of commissioned officers and warrant officers who are citizens of the United States between the ages of twenty-one and sixty-four years: *Provided*, That former members of the Regular Army, Navy, or Marine Corps under sixty-four years of age may enlist in said National Guard."

"The National Guard of the United States is hereby established. It shall be a reserve component of the Army of the United States and shall consist of those federally recognized National Guard units, and organizations and of the officers, warrant officers, and enlisted members of the National Guard of the several States, Territories, and the District of Columbia, who shall have been appointed, enlisted and appointed, or enlisted, as the case may be, in the National Guard of the United States, as hereinafter provided, and of such other officers and warrant officers as may be appointed therein as provided in section 111 hereof: *Provided*, That the members of the National Guard of the United States shall not be in the active service of the United States except when ordered thereto in accordance with law, and, in time of peace, they shall be administered, armed, uniformed, equipped, and trained in their status as the National Guard of the several States, Territories, and the District of Columbia, as provided in this Act: *And provided further*, That under such regulations as the Secretary of War shall prescribe, noncommissioned officers, first-class privates, and enlisted specialists of the National Guard may be appointed in corresponding grades, ratings, and branches of the National Guard of the United States, without vacating their respective grades and ratings in the National Guard."

SEC. 6. That section 60 of said Act be, and the same is hereby, amended by striking out the same and inserting the following in lieu thereof:

"SEC. 60. ORGANIZATION OF NATIONAL GUARD UNITS.—Except as otherwise specifically provided herein, the organization of the National Guard, including the composition of all units thereof, shall be the same as that which is or may hereafter be prescribed for the Regular Army, subject in time of peace to such general exceptions as may be authorized by the Secretary of War. And the President may prescribe the particular unit or units, as to branch or arm of service, to be maintained in each State, Territory, or the District of Columbia in order to secure a force which, when combined, shall form complete higher tactical units: *Provided*, That no change in allotment, branch, or arm of units or organizations wholly within a single State will be made without the approval of the governor of the State concerned."

SEC. 7. That section 69 of said Act be, and the same is hereby, amended by striking out the same and inserting the following in lieu thereof:

"SEC. 69. ENLISTMENTS IN THE NATIONAL GUARD AND IN THE NATIONAL GUARD OF THE UNITED STATES.—Original enlistments in the National Guard and in the National Guard of the United States shall be for a period of three years, and subsequent enlistments for periods of one or three years each: *Provided*, That all enlisted men of the National Guard on the date of approval of this Act may, under such regulations as may be prescribed by the Secretary of War, be enlisted in grade, rating, and branch in the National Guard of the United States for the remaining unexpired portions of their enlistments in the National Guard: *And Provided further*, That in the event of an emergency declared by Congress the period of any enlistment which otherwise would expire may by Presidential proclamation be extended for a period of six months after the termination of the emergency."

SEC. 8 That section 70 of said Act be, and the same is hereby amended by striking out the same and inserting the following in lieu thereof:

"SEC. 70. Men enlisting in the National Guard of the several States, Territories, and the District of Columbia, and in the National Guard of the United States, shall sign an enlistment contract and subscribe to the following oath or affirmation:

"I do hereby acknowledge to have voluntarily enlisted this _ _ _ _ _ day of _ _ _ _ _ _, 19_ _, as a soldier in the National Guard of the United States and the State of _ _ _ _ _ _, for the period of three (or one) year _ _, under the conditions prescribed by law, unless sooner discharged by proper authority. And I do solemnly swear that I will bear true faith and allegiance to the United States of America and to the State of _ _ _ _ _ _, and that I will serve them honestly and faithfully against all their enemies whomsoever, and that I will obey the orders of the President of the United States and of the Governor of the State of _ _ _ _ _ _, and of the officers appointed over me according to law and the rules and Articles of War."

SEC. 9. That said Act be amended by adding section 71 thereto, as follows:

"SEC. 71. DEFINITIONS.—In this Act, unless the context or subject matter otherwise requires—

" (a) 'National Guard' or 'National Guard of the several States, Territories, and the District of Columbia' means that portion of the Organized Militia of the several States, Territories, and the District of Columbia, active and inactive, federally recognized as provided in this Act and organized, armed, and equipped in whole or in part at Federal expense and officered and trained under paragraph 16, section 8, article I of the Constitution.

" (b) 'National Guard of the United States' means a reserve component of the Army of the United States composed of those federally recognized units and organizations and persons duly appointed and commissioned in the active and inactive National Guard of the several States, Territories, and the District of

Columbia, who have taken and subscribed to the oath of office prescribed in section 73 of this Act, and who have been duly appointed by the President in the National Guard of the United States, as provided in this Act, and of those officers and warrant officers appointed as prescribed in sections 75 and 111 of this Act, and of those persons duly enlisted in the National Guard of the United States and of the several States, Territories, and the District of Columbia who have taken and subscribed to the oath of enlistment prescribed in section 70 of this Act."

SEC. 10. That section 72 of said Act be, and the same is hereby, amended by striking out the same and inserting the following in lieu thereof:

"SEC. 72. An enlisted man discharged from service in the National Guard and the National Guard of the United States shall receive a discharge in writing in such form and with such classification as is or shall be prescribed for the Regular Army, and in time of peace discharges may be given prior to the expiration of terms of enlistment under such regulations as the Secretary of War may prescribe."

SEC. 11. That section 73 of said Act be, and the same is hereby, amended by striking out the same and inserting the following in lieu thereof:

"SEC. 73. OATHS OF NATIONAL GUARD OFFICERS—APPOINTMENT IN THE NATIONAL GUARD OF THE UNITED STATES.—Commissioned officers and warrant officers of the National Guard of the several States, Territories, and the District of Columbia and in the National Guard of the United States shall take and subscribe to the following oath of office:

"I, ______, do solemnly swear that I will support and defend the Constitution of the United States and the constitution of the State of ______ against all enemies, foreign and domestic; that I will bear true faith and allegiance to the same; that I will obey the orders of the President of the United States and of the Governor of the State of ______; that I make this obligation freely, without any mental reservation or purpose of evasion, and that I will well and faithfully discharge the duties of the office of ______ in the National Guard of the United States and of the State of ______ upon which I am about to enter, so help me God.

"The President is authorized to appoint in the same grade and branch in the National Guard of the United States any person who is an officer or warrant officer in the National Guard of any State, Territory, or the District of Columbia and who is federally recognized in that grade and branch: *Provided*, That acceptance of appointment in the same grade and branch in the National Guard of the United States, by an officer of the National Guard of a State, Territory, or the District of Columbia, shall not operate to vacate his State, Territory, or District of Columbia National Guard office.

"Officers or warrant officers of the National Guard who are in a federally recognized status on the date of the approval of this Act shall take the oath of office herein prescribed and shall be appointed in the National Guard of the United States in the same grade and branch without further examination, other than physical, within a time limit to be fixed by the President, and shall in the meantime continue to enjoy all the rights, benefits, and privileges conferred by this Act."

SEC. 12. That section 75 of said Act be, and the same is hereby, amended by striking out the same and inserting the following in lieu thereof:

"SEC. 75. The provisions of this Act shall not apply to any person hereafter appointed as an officer of the National Guard unless he first shall have successfully passed such tests as to his physical, moral, and professional fitness as the President shall prescribe. The examination to determine such qualifications for appointment shall be conducted by a board of three commissioned officers appointed by the Secretary of War from the Regular Army or the National Guard of the United States, or both. The examination herein provided for may be held prior to the original appointment or promotion of any individual as an officer or warrant officer and if the applicant has been found qualified, he may be issued a certificate of eligibility by the Chief of the National Guard Bureau, which certificate, in the event of appointment or promotion within two years to the office for which he was found qualified, shall entitle the holder to Federal recognition without further examination, except as to his physical condition.

"Upon being federally recognized such officers and warrant officers may be appointed in the National Guard of the United States."

SEC. 13. That section 76 of said Act be, and the same is hereby, amended by striking out the same and inserting the following in lieu thereof:

"SEC. 76. WITHDRAWAL OF FEDERAL RECOGNITION.—Under such regulations as the President shall prescribe the capacity and general fitness of any officer or warrant officer of the National Guard of the several States, Territories, and the District of Columbia for continued Federal recognition may at any time be investigated by an efficiency board of officers senior in rank to the officer under investigation, appointed by the Secretary of War from the Regular Army or the National Guard of the United States, or both. If the findings of said board be unfavorable to the officer under investigation and be approved by the President, Federal recognition shall be withdrawn and he shall be discharged from the National Guard of the United States. Federal recognition may be withdrawn by the Secretary of War and his appointment in the National Guard of the United States may be terminated when an officer or warrant officer of the National Guard of any State, Territory, or the District of Columbia has been absent without leave for three months."

SEC. 14. That section 77 of said Act be, and the same is hereby, amended by striking out the same and inserting the following in lieu thereof:

"SEC. 77. ELIMINATION AND DISPOSITION OF OFFICERS OF THE NATIONAL GUARD OF THE UNITED STATES.—The appointments of officers therefor. and warrant officers of the National Guard may be terminated or vacated in such manner as the several States, Territories, or the District of Columbia shall provide by law.

Whenever the appointment of an officer or warrant officer of the National Guard of a State, Territory, or the District of Columbia has been vacated or terminated, or upon reaching the age of sixty-four, the Federal recognition of such officer shall be withdrawn and he shall be discharged from the National Guard of the United States: *Provided*, That under such regulations as the Secretary of War may prescribe upon termination of service in the active National Guard an officer of the National Guard of the United States may, if he makes application therefor, remain in the National Guard of the United States in the same grade and branch of service. When Federal recognition is withdrawn from any officer or warrant officer of the National Guard of any State, Territory, or the District of Columbia, as provided in section 76 of this Act, or upon reaching the age of sixty-four years, he shall thereupon cease to be a member thereof and shall begiven a discharge certificate therefrom by the official authorized to appoint such officer."

SEC. 15. That section 78 of said Act be, and the same is hereby, amended by striking out the same and inserting the following in lieu thereof:

"SEC. 78. Men duly qualified for enlistment in the active National Guard may enlist for one term only in the inactive National Guard and in the National Guard of the United States for a period of one or three years, under such regulations as the Secretary of War shall prescribe, and on so enlisting they shall sign an enlistment contract and subscribe to the oath or affirmation in section 70 of this Act.

"Under such regulations as the Secretary of War may prescribe, enlisted men of the active National Guard, not formerly enlisted in the inactive National Guard or the National Guard of the United States, may be transferred to the inactive National Guard; likewise enlisted men hereafter enlisted in or transferred to the inactive National Guard may be transferred to the active National Guard: *Provided*, That in time of peace no enlisted man shall be required to serve under any enlistment for a longer time than the period for which he enlisted in the active or inactive National Guard, as the case may be. Members of said inactive National Guard, when engaged in field or coast-defense training with the active National Guard, shall receive the same Federal pay and allowances as those occupying like grades on the active list of said National Guard when likewise engaged."

SEC. 16. That section 81 of said Act be, and the same is hereby, amended by striking out the same and inserting the following in lieu thereof:

"SEC. 81. THE NATIONAL GUARD BUREAU.—The Militia Bureau of the War Department shall hereafter be known as the National Guard Bureau. The Chief of the National Guard Bureau shall be appointed by the President, by and with the advice and consent of the Senate, by selection from lists of officers of the National Guard of the United States recommended as suitable for such appointment by their respective governors, and who have had ten or more years' commissioned service in the active National Guard, at least five of which have been in the line, and who have attained at least the grade of colonel. The Chief of the National Guard Bureau shall hold office for four years unless sooner removed for cause, and shall not be eligible to succeed himself, and when sixty-four years of age shall cease to hold such office. Upon accepting his office, the Chief of the National Guard Bureau shall be appointed a major general in the National Guard of the United States, and commissioned in the Army of the United States, and while so serving he shall have the rank, pay, and allowances of a major general, provided by law, but shall not be entitled to retirement or retired pay.

"For duty in the National Guard Bureau and for instruction of the National Guard the President shall assign such number of officers of the Regular Army as he may deem necessary; also, such number of enlisted men of the Regular Army for duty in the instruction of the National Guard. The President may also order, with their consent, to active duty in the National Guard Bureau, not more than four officers who at the time of their initial assignments hold appointments in the National Guard of the United States, and any such officers while so assigned shall receive the pay and allowances provided by law.

"In case the office of the Chief of the National Guard Bureau becomes vacant or the incumbent because of disability is unable to discharge the powers and duties of the office, the senior officer on duty in the National Guard Bureau, appointed from the National Guard of the United States, shall act as chief of said bureau until the incumbent is able to resume his duties or the vacancy in the office is regularly filled. The pay and allowances provided in this section for the Chief of the National Guard Bureau and for the officers ordered to active duty from the National Guard of the United States shall be paid out of the funds appropriated for the pay of the National Guard."

SEC. 17. That section 82 of said Act be, and the same is hereby, amended by striking out the same and inserting the following in lieu thereof:

"SEC. 82. ARMAMENT, EQUIPMENT, AND UNIFORM OF THE NATIONAL GUARD.—The National Guard shall, as far as practicable, be uniformed, armed, and equipped with the same type of uniforms, arms, and equipments as are or shall be provided for the Regular Army."

SEC. 18. That section 111 of said Act be, and the same is hereby, amended by striking out the same and inserting the following in lieu thereof:

"SEC. 111. When Congress shall have declared a national emergency and shall have authorized the use of armed land forces of the United States for any purpose requiring the use of troops in excess of those of the Regular Army, the President may, under such regulations, including such physical examination as he may prescribe, order into the active military service of the United States, to serve therein for the period of the war or emergency, unless sooner relieved, any or all units and the members thereof of National Guard of the United States. All persons so ordered into the active military service of the United States shall from the date of such order stand relieved from duty in the National Guard of their respective States, Territories, and the District of Columbia so long as they shall remain in the active military service of the United States, and during such time shall be subject to such laws and regulations for the government of the Army of the United States as may be applicable to members of the Army whose permanent retention in active military service is not contemplated by law. The organization of said units existing at the date of the order into active Federal service shall be maintained intact insofar as practicable.

"Commissioned officers and warrant officers appointed in the National Guard of the United States and commissioned or holding duty warrants in the Army of the United States, ordered into Federal service as herein provided, shall be ordered to active duty under such appointments and commissions or warrants: *Provided*, That those officers and warrant officers of the National Guard who do not hold appointments in the National Guard of the United States and commissions or warrants in the Army of the United States may be appointed and commissioned or tendered warrants therein by the President, in the same grade and branch they hold in the National Guard.

"Officers and enlisted men while in the service of the United States under the terms of this section shall receive the pay and allowances provided by law for officers and enlisted men of the reserve forces when ordered to active duty, except brigadier generals and major generals, who shall receive the same pay and allowances as provided by law for brigadier generals and major generals of the Regular Army, respectively. Upon being relieved from active duty in the military service of the United States all individuals and units shall thereupon revert to their National Guard status.

"In the initial mobilization of the National Guard of the United States, war-strength officer personnel shall be taken from the National Guard as far as practicable, and for the purpose of this expansion warrant officers and enlisted men of the National Guard may, in time of peace, be appointed officers in the National Guard of the United States and commissioned in the Army of the United States."

SEC. 19. That section 112 of said Act be, and the same is hereby, amended by striking out the same and inserting the following in lieu thereof:

"SEC. 112. RIGHTS TO PENSIONS.—When any officer, warrant officer, or enlisted man of the National Guard or the National Guard of the United States called or ordered into the active service of the United States, or when any officer of the Officers' Reserve Corps or any person in the Enlisted Reserve Corps ordered into active service except for training, is disabled by reason of wounds or disability received or incurred while in the active service of the United States, he shall be entitled to all the benefits of the pension laws existing at the time of his active service; and in case such officer or enlisted man dies in the active service of the United States or in returning to his place of residence after being mustered out of active service, or at any other time in consequence of wounds or disabilities received in such active service, his widow and children, if any, shall be entitled to all the benefits of such pension laws."

SEC. 20. That the seventh paragraph of section 127a of said Act be, and the same is hereby, amended by striking out the same and inserting the following in lieu thereof:

"In time of war any officer of the Regular Army may be appointed to higher temporary grade without vacating his permanent appointment. In time of war any officer of the Regular Army appointed to higher temporary grade, and all other persons appointed, as officers, shall be appointed and commissioned in the Army of the United States. Such appointments in grades below that of brigadier general shall be made by the President alone, and general officers by and with the advice and consent of the Senate: *Provided*, That an appointment, other than that of a member of the Regular Army made in time of war, shall continue until six months after its termination, and an officer appointed in time of war shall be entitled to be relieved from active Federal service within six months after its termination if he makes application therefor."

Approved, June 15, 1933.

The Militia Act Today

Most Americans today do not know that the residual portions of the various iterations of the Militia Acts the National Defense Act and its subsequent amendments still exist in federal law, codified as Sections 246 and 247 of Article 10 the United States Code.

Opponents of the Second Amendment and the right to keep and bear arms might be surprised to learn that many of them are, in fact, members of the unorganized militia—the same militia that they proclaim does not exist because it was replaced by the National Guard.

A small number of states today maintain organizations generally referred to as "State Guard" (or some variation on that) that are regarded as official state militias. Where they exist, state guards more or less fulfill the role that was originally assigned to the National Guard before the federal laws that integrated the National Guard into the overall Army of the United States. State Guards are not National Guard, although they may train with their respective states' National Guard, and they cannot be federalized.

States that currently maintain State Guard units include Alaska, California, Connecticut, Georgia, Indiana, Louisiana, Maryland, Michigan, Mississippi, New Mexico, New York, Ohio, South Carolina, Tennessee, Texas, Vermont, Virginia, and Washington. In my home state of Connecticut, the State's web site specifically says that the State Guard is the organized militia for this state:

> "The Connecticut State Guard is the organized militia portion of the state military. As a State Defense Force it is a military entity authorized by both Connecticut General Statutes and Executive Order. The Connecticut State Guard is the state's authorized militia and assumes the state mission of the Connecticut National Guard in the event the Guard is mobilized. The Connecticut State Guard comprises retired active and reserve military personnel and selected professional persons who volunteer their time and talents in further service to the state."[5]

The sections of the federal United States Code on the following page reproduce the current federal law establishing that "the militia" consists not only of the National Guard and the Naval Militia, but also of the unorganized militia.

---

[5] https://portal.ct.gov/MIL/Organization/State-Guard/Connecticut-State-Guard

10 U.S. Code § 246 – Militia: composition and classes

(a) The militia of the United States consists of all able-bodied males at least 17 years of age and, except as provided in section 313 of title 32, under 45 years of age who are, or who have made a declaration of intention to become, citizens of the United States and of female citizens of the United States who are members of the National Guard.

(b) The classes of the militia are—

(1) the organized militia, which consists of the National Guard and the Naval Militia; and

(2) the unorganized militia, which consists of the members of the militia who are not members of the National Guard or the Naval Militia.

10 U.S. Code § 247 – Militia duty: exemptions

(a) The following persons are exempt from militia duty:

(1) The Vice President.

(2) The judicial and executive officers of the United States, the several States, the Commonwealth of Puerto Rico, Guam, and the Virgin Islands.

(3) Members of the armed forces, except members who are not on active duty.

(4) Customhouse clerks.

(5) Persons employed by the United States in the transmission of mail.

(6) Workmen employed in armories, arsenals, and naval shipyards of the United States.

(7) Pilots on navigable waters.

(8) Mariners in the sea service of a citizen of, or a merchant in, the United States.

(b) A person who claims exemption because of religious belief is exempt from militia duty in a combatant capacity, if the conscientious holding of that belief is established under such regulations as the President may prescribe. However, such a person is not exempt from militia duty that the President determines to be noncombatant.

National Firearms Act of 1934

The National Firearms Act of 1934 is, technically, not a gun control law but a tax act. That fact notwithstanding, the fundamental purpose of the Act was as much to regulate firearms as it was to raise revenue for the federal government.

The NFA was enacted during the time of Prohibition, famous (or "notorious") gangsters, and speakeasies. This was the era of Elliott Ness and The Untouchables. As exemplified in the Saint Valentine's Day Massacre, the big mobs of that era didn't hesitate to resort to violence in exerting their influence and enforcing their claims on territory. Submachine guns such as the Thompson (the "Chicago Typewriter") were often used in gangland gun battles and assassinations. The National Firearms Act of 1934 was the government's attempt to curtail the availability of such weaponry to the general public in order to curtail availability to the mobs.

In summary, the Act required owners of machine guns, certain firearms with short barrels, and suppressors ("silencers") to register them with the Secretary of the Treasury. In order to register a firearm or a suppressor, the applicant had to pay a $200 tax. Although this doesn't sound like a lot of money today, $200 in 1934 is equivalent to $$3,925.58 in 2021 dollars. Failure to pay the tax and register an "NFA firearm" was a federal crime. It was a way for the federal government to arrest and convict gangsters for paperwork crimes if they couldn't find witnesses to testify against them for more serious crimes.

It was in innovative strategy. As a shining example of a similar approach to putting mobsters in prison, the famous Chicago gangster, Al Capone, was finally convicted and imprisoned not for murder, not for extortion, not for kidnapping, but for tax evasion.

The $200 NFA registration fee is exclusive of the cost of the firearm; the $200 is only the cost of the tax stamp to register the firearm. The $200 cost for the registration tax has not been changed since 1934, and it remains at $200 today.

Full Text of National Firearms Act of 1934

AN ACT

To provide for the taxation of manufacturers, importers, and dealers in certain firearms and machine guns, to tax the sale or other disposal of such weapons, and to restrict importation and regulate interstate transportation thereof.

Be it enacted by the Senate and House of Representatives of the United States of America in Congress assembled, That for the purposes of this Act—

(a) The term "firearm" means a shotgun or rifle having a barrel of less than eighteen inches in length, or any other weapon, except a pistol or revolver, from which a shot is discharged by an explosive if such weapon is capable of being concealed on the person, or a machine gun, and includes a muffler or silencer for any firearm whether or not such firearm is included within the foregoing definition.

(b) The term "machine gun" means any weapon which shoots, or is designed to shoot, automatically or semiautomatically, more than one shot, without manual reloading, by a single function of the trigger.

(c) The term "person" includes a partnership, company, association, or corporation, as well as a natural person.

(d) The term "continental United States" means the States of the United States and the District of Columbia.

(e) The term "importer" means any person who imports or brings firearms into the continental United States for sale.

(f) The term "manufacturer" means any person who is engaged within the continental United States in the manufacture of firearms, or who otherwise produces therein any firearm for sale or disposition.

(g) The term "dealer" means any person not a manufacturer or importer engaged -within the continental United States in the business of selling firearms. The term "dealer" shall include wholesalers, pawnbrokers, and dealers in used firearms.

(h) The term "interstate commerce" means transportation from any State or Territory or District, or any insular possession of the United States ([including the Philippine Islands), to any other State or to the District of Columbia.

(i) The term "Commissioner" means the Commissioner of Internal Revenue.

(i) The term "Secretary" means the Secretary of the Treasury.

(k) The term "to transfer" or "transferred" shall include to sell, assign, pledge, lease, loan, give away, or otherwise dispose of.

SEC. 2. (a) Within fifteen days after the effective date of this Act, or upon first engaging in business, and thereafter on or before the 1st day of July of each year, every importer, manufacturer, and dealer in firearms shall register with the collector of internal revenue for each district in which such business is to be carried on his name or style, principal place of business, and places of business in such district, and pay a special tax at the following rates: Importers or manufacturers, $500 a year; dealers, other than pawnbrokers, $200 a year; pawnbrokers, $300 a year. Where the tax is payable on the 1st day of July in any year it shall be computed for one year; where the tax is payable on any other day it shall be computed proportionately from the 1st day of the month in which the liability to the tax accrued to the 1st day of July following.

(b) It shall be unlawful for any person required to register under the provisions of this section to import, manufacture, or deal in firearms without having registered and paid the tax imposed by this section.

SEC. 3. (a) There shall be levied, collected, and paid upon firearms transferred in the continental United States a tax at the rate of $200 for each firearm, such tax to be paid by the transferor, and to be represented by appropriate stamps to be provided by the Commissioner, with the approval of the Secretary; and the stamps herein provided shall be affixed to the order for such firearm, hereinafter provided for. The tax imposed by this section shall be in addition to any import duty imposed on such firearm.

(b) All provisions of law (including those relating to special taxes, to the assessment, collection, remission, and refund of internal revenue taxes, to the engraving, issuance, sale, accountability, cancelation, and distribution of tax-paid stamps provided for in the internal revenue laws, and to penalties) applicable with respect to the taxes imposed by section 1 of the Act of December 17, 1914, as amended (U.S.C., Supp. VII, title 26, secs. 1040 and 1383), and all other provisions of the internal-revenue laws shall, insofar as not inconsistent with the provisions of this Act, be applicable with respect to the taxes imposed by this Act.

(c) Under such rules and regulations as the Commissioner, with the approval of the Secretary, may prescribe, and upon proof of the exportation of any firearm to any foreign country (whether exported as part of another article or not) with respect to which the transfer tax under this section has been paid by the manufacturer, the Commissioner shall refund to the manufacturer the amount of the tax so paid, or, if the manufacturer waives all claim for the amount to be refunded, the refund shall be made to the exporter.

SEC. 4. (a) It shall be unlawful' for any person to transfer a firearm except in pursuance of a written order from the person seeking to obtain such article, on an application form issued in blank in duplicate for that purpose by the Commissioner. Such order shall identify the applicant by such means of identification as may be prescribed by regulations under this Act: *Provided*, That, if the applicant is an individual, such identification shall include fingerprints and a photograph thereof.

(b) The Commissioner, with the approval of the Secretary, shall cause suitable forms to be prepared for the purposes above mentioned, and shall cause the same to be distributed to collectors of internal revenue.

(c) Every person so transferring a firearm shall set forth in each copy of such order the manufacturer's number or other mark identifying such firearm, and shall forward a copy of such order to the Commissioner. The original thereof with stamps affixed, shall be returned to the applicant.

(d) No person shall transfer a firearm which has previously been transferred on or after the effective date of this Act, unless such person, in addition to complying with subsection (c), transfers therewith the stamp-affixed order provided for in this section for each such prior transfer, in compliance with such regulations as may be prescribed under this Act for proof of payment of all taxes on such firearms.

(e) If the transfer of a firearm is exempted from the provisions of this Act as provided in section 13 hereof, the person transferring such firearm shall notify the Commissioner of the name and address of the applicant, the number or other mark identifying such firearm, and the date of its transfer, and shall file with the Commissioner such documents in proof thereof as the Commissioner may by regulations prescribe.

(f) Importers, manufacturers, and dealers who have registered and paid the tax as provided for in section 2(a) of this Act shall not be required to conform to the provisions of this section with respect to transactions in firearms with dealers or manufacturers if such dealers or manufacturers have registered and have paid such tax, but shall keep such records and make such reports regarding such transactions as may be prescribed by regulations under this Act.

SEC. 5. (a) Within sixty days after the effective date of this Act every person possessing a firearm shall register, with the collector of the district in which he resides, the number or other mark identifying such firearm, together with his name, address, place where such firearm is usually kept, and place of business or employment and, if such person is other than a natural person, the name and home address of an executive officer thereof: *Provided*, That no person shall be required to register under this section with respect to any firearm acquired after the effective date of, and in conformity with the provisions of, this Act.

(b) Whenever on trial for a violation of section 6 hereof the defendant is shown to have or to have had possession of such firearm at any time after such period of sixty days without having registered as required by this section, such possession shall create a presumption that such firearm came into the possession of the defendant subsequent to the effective date of this Act, but this presumption shall not be conclusive.

SEC. 6. It shall be unlawful for any person to receive or possess any firearm which has at any time been transferred in violation of section 3 or 4 of this Act.

SEC. 7. Any firearm which has at any time been transferred in violation of the provisions of this Act shall be subject to seizure and forfeiture, and (except as provided in subsection (b)) all the provisions of internal-revenue laws relating to searches, seizures, and forfeiture of unstamped articles are extended to and made to apply to the articles taxed under this Act, and the persons to whom this Act applies.

(b) In the case of the forfeiture of any firearm by reason of a violation of this Act: No notice of public sale shall be required; no such firearm shall be sold at public sale; if such firearm is in the possession of any officer of the United States except the Secretary, such officer shall deliver the firearm to the Secretary; and the Secretary may order such firearm destroyed or may sell such firearm to any State, Territory, or possession (including the Philippine Islands), or political subdivision thereof, or the District of Columbia, or retain it for the use of the Treasury Department or transfer it without charge to any Executive department or independent establishment of the Government for use by it.

SEC. 8. (a) Each manufacturer and importer of a firearm shall identify it with a number or other identification mark approved by the Commissioner, such number or mark to be stamped or otherwise placed thereon in a manner approved by the Commissioner.

(b) It shall be unlawful for anyone to obliterate, remove, change, or alter such number or other identification mark. Whenever on trial for a violation of this subsection the defendant is shown to have or to have had possession of any firearm upon which such number or mark shall have been obliterated, removed, changed, or altered, such conviction, possession shall be deemed sufficient evidence to authorize conviction, unless the defendant explains such possession to the satisfaction of the jury.

SEC. 9. Importers, manufacturers, and dealers shall keep such books and records and render such returns in relation to the transactions in firearms specified in this Act as the Commissioner, with the approval of the Secretary, may by regulations require.

Sec. 10. (a) No firearm shall be imported or brought into the United States or any territory under its control or jurisdiction under control of United (including the Philippine Islands), except that, under regulations prescribed by the Secretary, any firearm may be so imported or brought in when (1) the purpose thereof is shown to be lawful and (2) such firearm is unique or of a type which cannot be obtained within the United States or such territory.

(b) It shall be unlawful (1) fraudulently or knowingly to import or bring any firearm into the United States or any territory under its control or jurisdiction (including the Philippine Islands), in violation of the provisions of this Act; or (2) knowingly to assist in so doing; or (3) to receive, conceal, buy, sell, or in any manner facilitate the transportation, concealment, or sale of any such firearm after being imported or brought in, knowing the same to have been imported or brought in contrary to law. Whenever on trial for a violation of this section the defendant is shown to have or to have had possession of such firearm, such possession shall be deemed sufficient evidence to authorize conviction unless the defendant explains such possession to the satisfaction of the jury.

SEC. 11. It shall be unlawful for any person who is required to register as provided in section 5 hereof and who shall not have so registered, or any other person who has not in his possession a stamp-affixed order as provided in section 4 hereof, to ship, carry, or deliver any firearm in interstate commerce.

SEC. 12. The Commissioner, with the approval of the Secretary, shall prescribe such rules and regulations as may be necessary for carrying the provisions of this Act into effect.

SEC. 13. This Act shall not apply to the transfer of firearms (1) to the United States Government, any State, Territory, or possession of the United States, or to any political subdivision thereof, or to the District of Columbia; (2) to any peace officer or any Federal officer designated by regulations of the Commissioner; (3)

to the transfer of any firearm which is unserviceable and which is transferred as a curiosity or ornament.

SEC. 14. Any person who violates or fails to comply with any of the requirements of this Act shall, upon conviction, be fined not more than $2,000 or be imprisoned for not more than five years, or both, in the discretion of the court.

SEC. 15. The taxes imposed by paragraph (a) of section 600 of the Revenue Act of 1926 (U.S.C., Supp. VII, title 26, sec. 1120) and by section 610 of the Revenue Act of 1932 (47 Stat. 169, 264), shall not apply to any firearm on which the tax provided by section 3 of this Act has been paid.

SEC. 16. If any provision of this Act, or the application thereof to any person or circumstance, is held invalid, the remainder of the Act, and the application of such provision to other persons or circumstances, shall not be affected thereby.

SEC. 17. This Act shall take effect on the thirtieth day after the date of its enactment.

SEC. 18. This Act may be cited as the "National Firearms Act."

Approved, June 26, 1934

United States *v* Miller et al.
1939

Between 1791, when the Second Amendment was ratified, and the early part of the 20th century, the Supreme Court heard very few cases involving the second Amendment. In 1938, almost 150 years after the ratification of the Second Amendment, a case involving the Second Amendment was accepted by the Supreme Court. Because of the linguistic construction of the Second Amendment, the case of *United States v. Miller et al* had, and continues to have, a profound impact on the evolution of Second Amendment jurisprudence.

The National Firearms Act of 1934 provided that shotguns with barrels under 18 inches in length had to be registered under the NFA. Two career criminals, Jack Miller and Frank Layton, were indicted under federal law for transporting an unregistered shotgun with a barrel length less than 18 inches across state lines. At the trial, the defendants argued that the NFA was unconstitutional because it unlawfully infringed the Second Amendment. The district court judge quashed the indictment, freeing the defendants. The government appealed directly to the Supreme Court.

Jack Miller was the lead defendant, but he was also a bank robber who had recently testified in court against members of his own former gang. He was a marked man so, when he was released on the NFA charge, he immediately went into hiding. He didn't may his attorney to appear at the Supreme Court hearing on his case, which meant that the government presented its arguments unopposed.

The Supreme Court ruled that the short-barreled shotgun that was the focus of the case was not protected by the Second Amendment because the court was not presented any evidence that there was a use for such a firearm in militia service. In reality, shotguns had been widely used in the trench warfare of World War 1, but with no attorney for the defendants to present that argument, the Supreme Court was able to advance the claim that

> "The Court cannot take judicial notice that a shotgun having a barrel less than 18 inches long has today any reasonable relation to the preservation or efficiency of a well regulated militia, and therefore cannot say that the Second Amendment guarantees to the citizen the right to keep and bear such a weapon.
>
> "In the absence of any evidence tending to show that possession or use of a 'shotgun having a barrel of less than eighteen inches in length' at this time has some reasonable relationship to the preservation or

> efficiency of a well regulated militia, we cannot say that the Second Amendment guarantees the right to keep and bear such an instrument. Certainly it is not within judicial notice that this weapon is any part of the ordinary military equipment, or that its use could contribute to the common defense."

In the years following the *Miller* decision, lower courts have cited *Miller* as authority for ruling that the Second Amendment protects only a right to keep and bear arms in connection with militia service. That held sway until the case of *District of Columbia v Heller* in 2008. Although the majority decision in *Heller* effectively reversed *Miller*, gun control advocates continue to insist that the Second Amendment protects only a right to keep and bear arms in militia service. (And, since their argument is that the National Guard is the militia, they contend that the second Amendment today does not apply outside of service in the National Guard.)

The *Heller* decision will be presented later in this book.

United States v. Miller et al.

UNITED STATES *v.* MILLER ET AL.

APPEAL FROM THE DISTRICT COURT OF THE UNITED STATES FOR THE WESTERN DISTRICT OF ARKANSAS.

No. 696. Argued March 30, 1939.—Decided May 15, 1939.

The National Firearms Act, as applied to one indicted for transporting in interstate commerce a 12-gauge shotgun with a barrel less than 18 inches long, without having registered it and without having in his possession a stamp-affixed written order for it, as required by the Act, *held:*

1. Not unconstitutional as an invasion of the reserved powers of the States. Citing *Sonzinsky* v. *United States*, 300 U. S. 506, and Narcotic Act cases. P. 177.

2. Not violative of the Second Amendment of the Federal Constitution. P. 178.

The Court can not take judicial notice that a shotgun having a barrel less than 18 inches long has today any reasonable relation to the preservation or efficiency of a well regulated militia; and therefore can not say that the Second Amendment guarantees to the citizen the right to keep and bear such a weapon.

26 F. Supp. 1002, reversed.

APPEAL under the Criminal Appeals Act from a judgment sustaining a demurrer to an indictment for violation of the National Firearms Act.

Mr. Gordon Dean argued the cause, and *Solicitor General Jackson, Assistant Attorney General McMahon,* and *Messrs. William W. Barron, Fred E. Strine, George F. Kneip, W. Marvin Smith,* and *Clinton R. Barry* were on a brief, for the United States.

No appearance for appellees.

MR. JUSTICE MCREYNOLDS delivered the opinion of the Court.

An indictment in the District Court Western District Arkansas, charged that Jack Miller and Frank Layton

"did unlawfully, knowingly, wilfully, and feloniously transport in interstate commerce from the town of Claremore in the State of Oklahoma to the town of Siloam Springs in the State of Arkansas a certain firearm, to-wit, a double barrel 12-gauge Stevens shotgun having a barrel less than 18 inches in length, bearing identification number 76230, said defendants, at the time of so transporting said firearm in interstate commerce as aforesaid, not having registered said firearm as required by Section 1132d of Title 26, United States Code (Act of June 26, 1934, c. 737, Sec. 4 [§ 5], 48 Stat. 1237), and not having in their possession a stamp-affixed written order for said firearm as provided by Section 1132c, Title 26, United States Code (June 26, 1934, c. 737, Sec. 4, 48 Stat. 1237) and the regulations issued under authority of the said Act of Congress known as the 'National Firearms Act' approved June 26, 1934, contrary to the form of the statute in such case made and provided, and against the peace and dignity of the United States." [1]

---

[1] Act of June 26, 1934, c. 757, 48 Stat. 1236–1240, 26 U. S. C. § 1132.

That for the purposes of this Act—

"(a) The term 'firearm' means a shotgun or rifle having a barrel of less than eighteen inches in length, or any other weapon, except

A duly interposed demurrer alleged: The National Firearms Act is not a revenue measure but an attempt to usurp police power reserved to the States, and is therefore unconstitutional. Also, it offends the inhibition of the Second Amendment to the Constitution—"A well regulated Militia, being necessary to the security of a free State, the right of people to keep and bear Arms, shall not be infringed."

---

a pistol or revolver, from which a shot is discharged by an explosive if such weapon is capable of being concealed on the person, or a machine gun, and includes a muffler or silencer for any firearm whether or not such firearm is included within the foregoing definition, [The Act of April 10, 1936, c. 169, 49 Stat. 1192 added the words] but does not include any rifle which is within the foregoing provisions solely by reason of the length of its barrel if the caliber of such rifle is .22 or smaller and if its barrel is sixteen inches or more in length.

"Sec. 3. (a) There shall be levied, collected, and paid upon firearms transferred in the continental United States a tax at the rate of $200 for each firearm, such tax to be paid by the transferor, and to be represented by appropriate stamps to be provided by the Commissioner, with the approval of the Secretary; and the stamps herein provided shall be affixed to the order for such firearm, hereinafter provided for. The tax imposed by this section shall be in addition to any import duty imposed on such firearm.

"Sec. 4. (a) It shall be unlawful for any person to transfer a firearm except in pursuance of a written order from the person seeking to obtain such article, on an application form issued in blank in duplicate for that purpose by the Commissioner. Such order shall identify the applicant by such means of identification as may be prescribed by regulations under this Act: *Provided*, That, if the applicant is an individual, such identification shall include fingerprints and a photograph thereof.

"(c) Every person so transferring a firearm shall set forth in each copy of such order the manufacturer's number or other mark identifying such firearm, and shall forward a copy of such order to the Commissioner. The original thereof with stamps affixed, shall be returned to the applicant.

"(d) No person shall transfer a firearm which has previously been transferred on or after the effective date of this Act, unless such

The District Court held that section eleven of the Act violates the Second Amendment. It accordingly sustained the demurrer and quashed the indictment.

The cause is here by direct appeal.

Considering *Sonzinsky* v. *United States* (1937), 300 U. S. 506, 513, and what was ruled in sundry causes aris-

---

person, in addition to complying with subsection (c), transfers therewith the stamp-affixed order provided for in this section for each such prior transfer, in compliance with such regulations as may be prescribed under this Act for proof of payment of all taxes on such firearms.

"Sec. 5. (a) Within sixty days after the effective date of this Act every person possessing a firearm shall register, with the collector of the district in which he resides, the number or other mark identifying such firearm, together with his name, address, place where such firearm is usually kept, and place of business or employment, and, if such person is other than a natural person, the name and home address of an executive officer thereof: *Provided*, That no person shall be required to register under this section with respect to any firearm acquired after the effective date of, and in conformity with the provisions of, this Act.

"Sec. 6. It shall be unlawful for any person to receive or possess any firearm which has at any time been transferred in violation of section 3 or 4 of this Act.

"Sec. 11. It shall be unlawful for any person who is required to register as provided in section 5 hereof and who shall not have so registered, or any other person who has not in his possession a stamp-affixed order as provided in section 4 hereof, to ship, carry, or deliver any firearm in interstate commerce.

"Sec. 12. The Commissioner, with the approval of the Secretary, shall prescribe such rules and regulations as may be necessary for carrying the provisions of this Act into effect.

"Sec. 14. Any person who violates or fails to comply with any of the requirements of this Act shall, upon conviction, be fined not more than $2,000 or be imprisoned for not more than five years, or both, in the discretion of the court.

"Sec. 16. If any provision of this Act, or the application thereof to any person or circumstance, is held invalid, the remainder of the Act, and the application of such provision to other persons or circumstances, shall not be affected thereby.

"Sec. 18. This Act may be cited as the 'National Firearms Act.'"

161299°—39——12

ing under the Harrison Narcotic Act[2]—*United States* v. *Jin Fuey Moy* (1916), 241 U. S. 394; *United States* v. *Doremus* (1919), 249 U. S. 86, 94; *Linder* v. *United States* (1925), 268 U. S. 5; *Alston* v. *United States* (1927), 274 U. S. 289; *Nigro* v. *United States* (1928), 276 U. S. 332—the objection that the Act usurps police power reserved to the States is plainly untenable.

In the absence of any evidence tending to show that possession or use of a "shotgun having a barrel of less than eighteen inches in length" at this time has some reasonable relationship to the preservation or efficiency of a well regulated militia, we cannot say that the Second Amendment guarantees the right to keep and bear such an instrument. Certainly it is not within judicial notice that this weapon is any part of the ordinary military equipment or that its use could contribute to the common defense. *Aymette* v. *State,* 2 Humphreys (Tenn.) 154, 158.

The Constitution as originally adopted granted to the Congress power—"To provide for calling forth the Militia to execute the Laws of the Union, suppress Insurrections and repel Invasions; To provide for organizing, arming, and disciplining, the Militia, and for governing such Part of them as may be employed in the Service of the United States, reserving to the States respectively, the Appointment of the Officers, and the Authority of training the Militia according to the discipline prescribed by Congress." With obvious purpose to assure the continuation and render possible the effectiveness of such forces the declaration and guarantee of the Second Amendment were made. It must be interpreted and applied with that end in view.

The Militia which the States were expected to maintain and train is set in contrast with Troops which they

---

[2]Act December 17, 1914, c. 1, 38 Stat. 785; February 24, 1919, c. 18, 40 Stat. 1057.

were forbidden to keep without the consent of Congress. The sentiment of the time strongly disfavored standing armies; the common view was that adequate defense of country and laws could be secured through the Militia—civilians primarily, soldiers on occasion.

The signification attributed to the term Militia appears from the debates in the Convention, the history and legislation of Colonies and States, and the writings of approved commentators. These show plainly enough that the Militia comprised all males physically capable of acting in concert for the common defense. "A body of citizens enrolled for military discipline." And further, that ordinarily when called for service these men were expected to appear bearing arms supplied by themselves and of the kind in common use at the time.

Blackstone's Commentaries, Vol. 2, Ch. 13, p. 409 points out "that king Alfred first settled a national militia in this kingdom," and traces the subsequent development and use of such forces.

Adam Smith's Wealth of Nations, Book V, Ch. 1, contains an extended account of the Militia. It is there said: "Men of republican principles have been jealous of a standing army as dangerous to liberty." "In a militia, the character of the labourer, artificer, or tradesman, predominates over that of the soldier: in a standing army, that of the soldier predominates over every other character; and in this distinction seems to consist the essential difference between those two different species of military force."

"The American Colonies In The 17th Century," Osgood, Vol. 1, ch. XIII, affirms in reference to the early system of defense in New England—

"In all the colonies, as in England, the militia system was based on the principle of the assize of arms. This implied the general obligation of all adult male inhabitants to possess arms, and, with certain exceptions, to cooperate in the work of defence." "The possession of arms also implied the possession of ammunition, and the authorities paid quite as much attention to the latter as to the former." "A year later [1632] it was ordered that any single man who had not furnished himself with arms might be put out to service, and this became a permanent part of the legislation of the colony [Massachusetts]."

Also "Clauses intended to insure the possession of arms and ammunition by all who were subject to military service appear in all the important enactments concerning military affairs. Fines were the penalty for delinquency, whether of towns or individuals. According to the usage of the times, the infantry of Massachusetts consisted of pikemen and musketeers. The law, as enacted in 1649 and thereafter, provided that each of the former should be armed with a pike, corselet, head-piece, sword, and knapsack. The musketeer should carry a 'good fixed musket,' not under bastard musket bore, not less than three feet, nine inches, nor more than four feet three inches in length, a priming wire, scourer, and mould, a sword, rest, bandoleers, one pound of powder, twenty bullets, and two fathoms of match. The law also required that two-thirds of each company should be musketeers."

The General Court of Massachusetts, January Session 1784, provided for the organization and government of the Militia. It directed that the Train Band should "contain all able bodied men, from sixteen to forty years of age, and the Alarm List, all other men under sixty years of age, . . ." Also, "That every non-commissioned officer and private soldier of the said militia not under the controul of parents, masters or guardians, and being of sufficient ability therefor in the judgment of the Selectmen of the town in which he shall dwell, shall equip himself, and be constantly provided with a good fire arm," &c.

By an Act passed April 4, 1786 the New York Legislature directed: "That every able-bodied Male Person, being a Citizen of this State, or of any of the United States, and residing in this State, (except such Persons as are hereinafter excepted) and who are of the Age of Sixteen, and under the Age of Forty-five Years, shall, by the Captain or commanding Officer of the Beat in which such Citizens shall reside, within four Months after the passing of this Act, be enrolled in the Company of such Beat. . . . That every Citizen so enrolled and notified, shall, within three Months thereafter, provide himself, at his own Expense, with a good Musket or Firelock, a sufficient Bayonet and Belt, a Pouch with a Box therein to contain not less than Twenty-four Cartridges suited to the Bore of his Musket or Firelock, each Cartridge containing a proper Quantity of Powder and Ball, two spare Flints, a Blanket and Knapsack; . . ."

The General Assembly of Virginia, October, 1785, (12 Hening's Statutes) declared, "The defense and safety of the commonwealth depend upon having its citizens properly armed and taught the knowledge of military duty."

It further provided for organization and control of the Militia and directed that "All free male persons between the ages of eighteen and fifty years," with certain exceptions, "shall be inrolled or formed into companies." "There shall be a private muster of every company once in two months."

Also that "Every officer and soldier shall appear at his respective muster-field on the day appointed, by eleven o'clock in the forenoon, armed, equipped, and accoutred, as follows: . . . every non-commissioned officer and private with a good, clean musket carrying an ounce ball, and three feet eight inches long in the barrel, with a good bayonet and iron ramrod well fitted thereto, a cartridge box properly made, to contain and secure twenty cartridges fitted to his musket, a good knapsack and canteen, and moreover, each non-commissioned officer and private shall have at every muster one pound of good powder, and four pounds of lead, including twenty blind cartridges; and each serjeant shall have a pair of moulds fit to cast balls for their respective companies, to be purchased by the commanding officer out of the monies arising on delinquencies. *Provided,* That the militia of the counties westward of the Blue Ridge, and the counties below adjoining thereto, shall not be obliged to be armed with muskets, but may have good rifles with proper accoutrements, in lieu thereof. And every of the said officers, non-commissioned officers, and privates, shall constantly keep the aforesaid arms, accoutrements, and ammunition, ready to be produced whenever called for by his commanding officer. If any private shall make it appear to the satisfaction of the court hereafter to be appointed for trying delinquencies under this act that he is so poor that he cannot purchase the arms herein required, such court shall cause them to be purchased out of the money arising from delinquents."

Most if not all of the States have adopted provisions touching the right to keep and bear arms. Differences in the language employed in these have naturally led to somewhat variant conclusions concerning the scope of the right guaranteed. But none of them seem to afford any material support for the challenged ruling of the court below.

In the margin some of the more important opinions and comments by writers are cited.[3]

[3] Concerning The Militia—*Presser* v. *Illinois,* 116 U. S. 252; *Robertson* v. *Baldwin,* 165 U. S. 275; *Fife* v. *State,* 31 Ark. 455; *Jeffers* v. *Fair,* 33 Ga. 347; *Salina* v. *Blaksley,* 72 Kan. 230; 83 P. 619; *People* v. *Brown,* 253 Mich. 537; 235 N. W. 245; *Aymette* v. *State,* 2 Humphr. (Tenn.) 154; *State* v. *Duke,* 42 Texas 455; *State* v. *Workman,* 35 W. Va. 367; 14 S. E. 9; Cooley's Constitutional Limitations, Vol. 1, p. 729; Story on The Constitution, 5th Ed., Vol. 2, p. 646; Encyclopaedia of the Social Sciences, Vol. X, p. 471, 474.

We are unable to accept the conclusion of the court below and the challenged judgment must be reversed. The cause will be remanded for further proceedings.

Mr. Justice Douglas took no part in the consideration or decision of this cause.

The Gun Control Act of 1968

Congressional discussions and proposals that eventually coalesced into the Gun Control Act of 1968 began in the wake of the assassination of President John F. Kennedy in 1963. Although a number of proposals were advanced, nothing came of them until 1968. In 1968, the country witnessed the assassination of Martin Luther King, Jr., on April 4, 1968, followed soon thereafter by the assassination of Robert F. Kennedy on June 5, 1968.

The assassination of two such prominent political figures with such a short time span galvanized the Congress into taking action. Legislation that had been proposed in previous years but rejected was brought back, edited and amended, and introduced as new legislation.

Initially, a vote in the House Judiciary Committee on June 11, 1968, resulted in a tie. This prevented the proposed bill from advancing to the floor of the House for discussion and a vote. Just nine days later, the bill was reconsidered by the House Judiciary Committee and, this time, it passed and was advanced to the full House for consideration. A companion bill followed a similar path through the Senate.

The bill was passed by both the House and the Senate, and President Lyndon B. Johnson signed it into law on October 22, 1968.

Impact

- Because the rifle used to shoot President Kennedy had been purchased by mail, a key component of the Gun Control Act of 1968 was the creation of a federal license for selling forearms. As a result of the Act, firearms could not be purchased by mail and delivered directly to the buyer's home; once the law took effect, transfers of firearms had to go through a federally-licensed firearms dealer (FFL).
- New restrictions were imposed on imported firearms. Imported firearms had to be suitable for "sporting purposes," as defined in the law.
- The law required for the first time that all new commercially-manufactured firearms must be marked with the name of the manufacturer and a unique serial number. Although most manufacturers in the United States already applied serial numbers even before the adoption of the law, the Act made it mandatory.

Full Text of The Gun Control Act of 1968

Public Law 90-618

AN ACT

To amend title 18, United States Code, to provide for better control of the interstate traffic in firearms.

Be it enacted by the Senate and House of Representatives of the United States of America in Congress assembled, That this Act may be cited as the 'Gun Control Act of 1968".

TITLE I—STATE FIREARMS CONTROL ASSISTANCE

PURPOSE

SEC. 101. The Congress hereby declares that the purpose of this title is to provide support to Federal, State, and local law enforcement officials in their fight against crime and violence, and it is not the purpose of this title to place any undue or unnecessary Federal restrictions or burdens in law-abiding citizens with respect to the acquisition, possession, or use of firearms appropriate to the purpose of hunting, trapshooting, target shooting, personal protection, or any other lawful activity, and that this title is not intended to discourage or eliminate the private ownership or use of firearms by law-abiding citizens for lawful purposes, or provide for the imposition by Federal regulations of any procedures or requirements other than those reasonably necessary to implement and effectuate the provisions of this title.

SEC. 102. Chapter 44 of title 18, United States Code, is amended to read as follows:

"Chapter 44.—FIREARMS

"Sec.

"921. Definitions.

"922. Unlawful acts.

"923. Licensing.

"924. Penalties.

"925. Exceptions: Relief from disabilities.

"926. Rules and regulations.

"§ 921. Definitions

"(a) As used in this chapter—

"(1) The term 'person' and the term 'whoever' include any individual, corporation, company, association, firm, partnership, society, or joint stock company.

"(2) The term 'interstate or foreign commerce' includes commerce between any place in a State and any place outside of that State, or within any possession of the United States (not including the Canal Zone) or the District of Columbia, but such term does not include commerce between places within the same State but through any place outside of that State. The term 'State' includes the District of Columbia, the Commonwealth of Puerto Rico, and the possessions of the United States (not including the Canal Zone).

"(3) The term 'firearm' means (A) any weapon (including a starter gun) which will or is designed to or may readily be converted to expel a projectile by the action of an explosive; (B) the frame or receiver of any such weapon; (C) any firearm muffler or firearm silencer; or (D) any destructive device. Such term does not include an antique firearm.

"(4) The term 'destructive device' means—

"(A) any explosive, incendiary, or poison gas—

"(i) bomb,

"(ii) grenade,

"(iii) rocket having a propellant charge of more than four ounces,

"(iv) missile having an explosive or incendiary charge of more than one -quart er ounce,

"(v) mine, or

"(vi) device similar to any of the devices described in the preceding clauses;

"(B) any type of weapon (other than a shotgun or a shotgun shell which the Secretary finds is generally recognized as particularly suitable for sporting purposes) by whatever name known which will, or which may be readily converted to, expel a projectile by the action of an explosive or other propellant, and which has any barrel with a bore of more than one - half inch in diameter; and

"(C) any combination of parts either designed or intended for use in converting any device into any destructive device described in subparagraph (A) or (B) and from which a destructive device may be readily assembled.

The term 'destructive device' shall not include any device which is neither designed nor redesigned for use as a weapon; any device, although originally designed for use as a weapon, which is redesigned for use as a signaling, pyrotechnic, line throwing, safety, or similar device; surplus ordnance sold, loaned, or given by the Secretary of the Army pursuant to the provisions of section 4684(2), 4685, or 4686 of title 10; or any other device which the Secretary of the Treasury finds is not likely to be used as a weapon, is an antique, or is a rifle which the owner intends to use solely for sporting, recreational or cultural purposes.

"(5) The term 'shotgun' means a weapon designed or redesigned, made or remade, and intended to be fired from the shoulder and designed or redesigned and made or remade to use the energy of an explosive to fire through a smooth bore either a number of ball shot or a single projectile for each single pull of the trigger.

"(6) The term 'short -barreled shotgun' means a shotgun having one or more barrels less than eighteen inches in length and any weapon made from a shotgun (whether by alteration, modification, or otherwise) if such weapon as modified has an overall length of less than twenty-six inches.

"(7) The term 'rifle' means a weapon designed or redesigned, made or remade, and intended to be fired from the shoulder and designed or redesigned and made or remade to use the energy of an explosive to fire only a single projectile through a rifled bore for each single pull of the trigger.

"(8) The term 'short-barreled rifle' means a rifle having one or more barrels less than sixteen inches in length and any weapon made from a rifle (whether by alteration, modification, or otherwise) if such weapon, as modified, has an overall length of less than twenty-six inches.

"(9) The term 'importer' means any person engaged in the business of importing or bringing firearms or ammunition into the United States for purposes of sale or distribution; and the term "licensed importer" means any such person licensed under the provisions of this chapter.

"(10) The term 'manufacturer' means any person engaged in the business of manufacturing firearms or ammunition for purposes of sale or distribution ; and the term 'licensed manufacturer' means any such person licensed under the provisions of this chapter.

"(11) The term 'dealer' means (A) any person engaged in the business of selling firearms at wholesale or retail, (B) any person engaged in the business of repairing firearms or of making or fitting special barrels, stocks, or trigger mechanisms to firearms, or (C) any person who is a pawnbroker. The term 'licensed dealer' means any dealer who is licensed under the provisions of this chapter.

"(12) The term 'pawnbroker' means any person whose business or occupation includes the taking or receiving, by way of pledge or pawn, of any firearm as security for the payment or repayment of money.

"(13) The term 'collector' means any person who acquires, holds, or disposes of firearms as curios or relics, as the Secretary shall by regulation define, and the term 'licensed collector' means any such person licensed under the provisions of this chapter.

"(14) The term 'indictment' includes an indictment or information in any court under which a crime punishable by imprisonment for a term exceeding one year may be prosecuted.

"(15) The term 'fugitive from justice' means any person who has fled from any State to avoid prosecution for a crime or to avoid giving testimony in any criminal proceeding.

"(16) The term 'antique firearm' means—

"(A) any firearm (including any firearm with a matchlock, flintlock, percussion cap, or similar type of ignition system) manufactured in or before 1898; or

"(B) any replica of any firearm described in subparagraph (A) if such replica—

"(i) is not designed or redesigned for using rimfire or conventional centerfire fixed ammunition, or

"(ii) uses rimfire or conventional centerfire fixed ammunition which is no longer manufactured in the United States and which is not readily available in the ordinary channels of commercial trade.

"(C) any muzzle loading rifle, muzzle loading shotgun, or muzzle loading pistol, which is designed to use black powder, or a black powder substitute, and which cannot use fixed ammunition. For purposes of this subparagraph, the term 'antique firearm' shall not include any weapon which incorporates a firearm frame or receiver, any firearm which is converted into a muzzle loading weapon, or any muzzle loading weapon which can be readily converted to fire fixed ammunition by replacing the barrel, bolt, breechblock, or any combination thereof.

"(17) The term 'ammunition' means ammunition or cartridge cases, primers, bullets, or propellent powder designed for use in any firearm.

"(18) The term 'Secretary' or 'Secretary of the Treasury' means the Secretary of the Treasury or his delegate.

"(19) The term 'published ordinance' means a published law of any political subdivision of a State which the Secretary determines to be relevant to the enforcement of this chapter and which is contained on a list compiled by the Secretary, which list shall be published in the Federal Register, revised annually, and furnished to each licensee under this chapter.

"(20) The term 'crime punishable by imprisonment for a term exceeding one year' does not include (A) any Federal or State offenses pertaining to antitrust violations, unfair trade practices, restraints of trade, or other similar offenses relating to the regulation of business practices, or (B) any State offense classified by the laws of the State as a misdemeanor and punishable by a term of imprisonment of two years or less.

"(b) For the purposes of this chapter, a member of the Armed Forces on active duty is a resident of the State in which his permanent duty station is located.

"§ 922. Unlawful acts

"(a) It shall be unlawful—

"(1) for any person, except a licensed importer, licensed manufacturer, or licensed dealer, to engage in the business of importing, manufacturing, or dealing in firearms or ammunition, or in the course of such business to ship, transport, or receive any firearm or ammunition in interstate or foreign commerce.

"(2) for any importer, manufacturer, dealer, or collector licensed under the provisions of this chapter to ship or transport in interstate or foreign commerce any firearm to any person other than a licensed importer, licensed manufacturer, licensed dealer, or licensed collector, except that—

"(A) this paragraph and subsection (b) (3) shall not be held to preclude a licensed importer, licensed manufacturer, licensed dealer, or licensed collector from returning a firearm or replacement firearm of the same kind and type to a person from whom it was received; and this paragraph shall not be held to preclude an individual from mailing a firearm owned in compliance with Federal, State, and local law to a licensed importer, licensed manufacturer, or licensed dealer for the sole purpose of repair or customizing;

"(B) this paragraph shall not be held to preclude a licensed importer, licensed manufacturer, or licensed dealer from depositing a firearm for conveyance in the mails to any officer, employee, agent, or watchman who, pursuant to the provisions of section 1715 of this title, is eligible to receive through the mails pistols, revolvers, and other firearms capable of being concealed on the person, for use in connection with his official duty; and

"(C) nothing in this paragraph shall be construed as applying in any manner in the District of Columbia, the Commonwealth of Puerto Rico, or any possession of the United States differently than it would apply if the District of Columbia, the Commonwealth of Puerto Rico, or the possession were in fact a State of the United States;

"(3) for any person, other than a licensed importer, licensed manufacturer, licensed dealer, or licensed collector to transport into or receive in the State where he resides (or if the person is a corporation or other business entity, the State where it maintains a place of business) any firearm purchased or otherwise obtained by such person outside that State, except that this paragraph (A) shall not preclude any person who lawfully acquires a firearm by bequest or intestate succession in a State other than his State of residence from transporting the firearm into or receiving it in that State, if it is lawful for such person to purchase or possess such firearm in that State, (B) shall not apply to the transportation or receipt of a rifle or shotgun obtained in conformity with subsection (b)(3) of this section, and (C) shall not apply to the transportation of any firearm acquired in any State prior to the effective date of this chapter;

"(4) for any person, other than a licensed importer, licensed manufacturer, licensed dealer, or licensed collector, to transport in interstate or foreign commerce any destructive device, machinegun (as defined in section 5845 of the Internal Revenue Code of 1954), short-barreled shotgun, or short -barreled rifle, except as specifically authorized by the Secretary consistent with public safety and necessity;

"(5) for any person (other than a licensed importer, licensed manufacturer, licensed dealer, or licensed collector) to transfer, sell, trade, give, transport, or deliver any firearm to any person (other than a licensed importer, licensed manufacturer, licensed dealer, or licensed collector) who the transferor knows or has reasonable cause to believe resides in any State other than that in which the transferor resides (or other than that in which its place of business is located if the transferor is a corporation or other business entity); except that this paragraph shall not apply to (A) the transfer, transportation, or delivery of a firearm made to carry out a bequest of a firearm to, or an acquisition by intestate succession of a firearm by, a person who is permitted to acquire or possess a firearm under the laws of the State of his residence, and (B) the loan or rental of a firearm to any person for temporary use for lawful sporting purposes; and

"(6) for any person in connection with the acquisition or attempted acquisition of any firearm or ammunition from a licensed importer, licensed manufacturer, licensed dealer, or licensed collector, knowingly to make any false or fictitious oral or written statement or to furnish or exhibit any false, fictitious, or misrepresented identification, intended or likely to deceive such importer, manufacturer, dealer, or collector with respect to any fact material to the lawfulness of the sale or other disposition of such firearm or ammunition under the provisions of this chapter.

"(b) It shall be unlawful for any licensed importer, licensed manufacturer, licensed dealer, or licensed collector to sell or deliver—

"(1) any firearm or ammunition to any individual who the licensee knows or has reasonable cause to believe is less than eighteen years of age, and, if the firearm or ammunition is other than a shotgun or rifle, or ammunition for a shotgun or rifle, to any individual who the licensee knows or has reasonable cause to believe is less than twenty-one years of age.

"(2) any firearm or ammunition to any person in any State where the purchase or possession by such person of such firearm or ammunition would be in violation of any State law or any published ordinance applicable at the place of sale, delivery or other disposition, unless the licensee knows or has reasonable cause to believe that the purchase or possession would not be in violation of such State law or such published ordinance;

"(3) any firearm to any person who the licensee knows or has reasonable cause to believe does not reside in (or if the person is a corporation or other business entity, does not maintain a place of business in) the State in which the licensee's place of business is located, except that this paragraph (A) shall not apply to the sale or delivery of a rifle or shotgun to a resident of a State contiguous to the State in which the licensee's place of business is located if the purchaser's State of residence permits such sale or delivery by law, the sale fully complies with the legal conditions of sale in both such contiguous States, and the purchaser and the licensee have, prior to the sale, or delivery for sale, of the rifle or shotgun, complied with all of the requirements of section 922(c) applicable to intrastate transactions other than at the licensee's business premises, (B) shall not apply to the loan or rental of a firearm to any person for temporary use for lawful sporting purposes, and (C) shall not preclude any person who is participating in any organized rifle or shotgun match or contest, or is engaged in hunting, in a State other than his State of residence and whose rifle or shotgun has been lost or stolen or has become inoperative in such other State, from purchasing a rifle or shotgun in such other State from a licensed dealer if such person presents to such dealer a sworn statement (i) that his rifle or shotgun was lost or stolen or became inoperative while participating in such a match or contest, or while engaged in hunting, in such other State, and (ii) identifying the chief law enforcement officer of the locality in which such person resides, to whom such licensed dealer shall forward such statement by registered mail;

"(4) to any person any destructive device, machinegun (as defined in section 5845 of the Internal Revenue Code of 1954), short-barreled shotgun, or short-barreled rifle, except as specifically authorized by the Secretary consistent with public safety and necessity; and

"(5) any firearm or ammunition to any person unless the licensee notes in his records, required to be kept pursuant to section 923 of this chapter, the name, age, and place of residence of such person if the person is an individual, or the identity and principal and local places of business of such person if the person is a corporation or other business entity.

Paragraphs (1), (2), (3), and (4) of this subsection shall not apply to transactions between licensed importers, licensed manufacturers, licensed dealers, and licensed collectors. Paragraph (4) of this subsection shall not apply to a sale or delivery to any research organization designated by the Secretary.

"(c) In any case not otherwise prohibited by this chapter, a licensed importer, licensed manufacturer, or licensed dealer may sell a firearm to a person who does not appear in person at the licensee's business premises (other than another licensed importer, manufacturer, or dealer) only if—

"(1) the transferee submits to the transferor a sworn statement in the following form:

"'Subject to penalties provided by law, I swear that, in the case of any firearm other than a shotgun or a rifle, I am twenty-one years or more of age, or that, in the case of a shotgun or a rifle, I am eighteen years or more of age; that I am not prohibited by the provisions of chapter 44 of title 18, United States Code, from receiving a firearm in interstate or foreign commerce; and that my receipt of this firearm will not be in violation of any statute of the State and published ordinance applicable to the locality in which I reside. Further, the true title, name, and address of the principal law enforcement officer of the locality to which the firearm will be delivered are

----

Signature _________________________ Date _____.'

and containing blank spaces for the attachment of a true copy of any permit or other information required pursuant to such statute or published ordinance;

"(2) the transferor has, prior to the shipment or delivery of the firearm, forwarded by registered or certified mail (return receipt requested) a copy of the sworn statement, together with a description of the firearm, in a form prescribed by the Secretary, to the chief law enforcement officer of the transferee's place of residence, and has received a return receipt evidencing delivery of the statement or has had the statement returned due to the refusal of the named addressee to accept such letter in accordance with United States Post Office Department regulations; and

"(3) the transferor has delayed shipment or delivery for a period of at least seven days following receipt of the notification of the acceptance or refusal of delivery of the statement.

A copy of the sworn statement and a copy of the notification to the local law enforcement officer, together with evidence of receipt or rejection of that notification shall be retained by the licensee as a part of the records required to be kept under section 923(g).

"(d) It shall be unlawful for any person to sell or otherwise dispose of any firearm or ammunition to any person knowing or having reasonable cause to believe that such person—

"(1) is under indictment for, or has been convicted in any court of, a crime punishable by imprisonment for a term exceeding one year;

"(2) is a fugitive from justice;

"(3) is an unlawful user of or addicted to marihuana or any depressant or stimulant drug (as defined in section 201 (v) of the Federal Food, Drug, and Cosmetic Act) or narcotic drug (as defined in section 4731 (a) of the Internal Revenue Code of 1954; or

"(4) has been adjudicated as a mental defective or has been committed to any mental institution;

This subsection shall not apply with respect to the sale or disposition of a firearm or ammunition to a licensed importer, licensed manufacturer, licensed dealer, or licensed collector who pursuant to subsection (b) of section 925 of this chapter is not precluded from dealing in firearms or ammunition, or to a person who has been granted relief from disabilities pursuant to subsection (c) of section 925 of this chapter.

"(e) It shall be unlawful for any person knowingly to deliver or cause to be delivered to any common or contract carrier for transportation or shipment in interstate or foreign commerce, to persons other than licensed importers, licensed manufacturers, licensed dealers, or licensed collectors, any package or other container in which there is any firearm or ammunition without written notice to the carrier that such firearm or ammunition is being transported or shipped; except that any passenger who owns or legally possesses a firearm or ammunition being transported aboard any common or contract carrier for movement with the passenger in interstate or foreign commerce may deliver said firearm or ammunition into the custody of the pilot, captain, conductor or operator of such common or contract carrier for the duration of the trip without violating any of the provisions of this chapter.

"(f) It shall be unlawful for any common or contract carrier to transport or deliver in interstate or foreign commerce any firearm or ammunition with knowledge or reasonable cause to believe that the shipment, transportation, or receipt thereof would be in violation of the provisions of this chapter.

"(g) It shall be unlawful for any person—

"(1) who is under indictment for, or who has been convicted in any court of, a crime punishable by imprisonment for a term exceeding one year;

"(2) who is a fugitive from justice;

"(3) who is an unlawful user of or addicted to marihuana or any depressant or stimulant drug (as defined in section 201 (v) of the Federal Food, Drug, and Cosmetic Act) or narcotic drug (as defined in section 4731 of the Internal Revenue Code of 1954); or

"(4) who has been adjudicated as a mental defective or who has been committed to a mental institution;

to ship or transport any firearm or ammunition in interstate or foreign commerce.

"(h) It shall be unlawful for any person—

"(1) who is under indictment for, or who has been convicted in any court of, a crime punishable by imprisonment for a term exceeding one year;

"(2) who is a fugitive from justice;

"(3) who is an unlawful user of or addicted to marihuana or any depressant or stimulant drug (as defined in section 201 (v) of the Federal Food, Drug, and Cosmetic Act) or narcotic drug (as defined in section 4731 of the Internal Revenue Code of 1954); or

"(4) who has been adjudicated as a mental defective or who has been committed to a mental institution;

to receive any firearm or ammunition which has been shipped or transported in interstate or foreign commerce.

"(i) It shall be unlawful for any person to transport or ship in interstate or foreign commerce, any stolen firearm or stolen ammunition, knowing or having reasonable cause to believe that the firearm or ammunition was stolen.

"(j) It shall be unlawful for any person to receive, conceal, store, barter, sell, or dispose of any stolen firearm or stolen ammunition, or pledge or accept as security for a loan any stolen firearm or stolen ammunition, which is moving as, which is a part of, or which constitutes, interstate or foreign commerce, knowing or having reasonable cause to believe that the firearm or ammunition was stolen.

"(k) It shall be unlawful for any person knowingly to transport, ship, or receive, in interstate or foreign commerce, any firearm which has had the importer's or manufacturer's serial number removed, obliterated, or altered.

"(l) Except as provided in section 925(d) of this chapter, it shall be unlawful for any person knowingly to import or bring into the United States or any possession thereof any firearm or ammunition; and it shall be unlawful for any person knowingly to receive any firearm or ammunition which has been imported or brought into the United States or any possession thereof in violation of the provisions of this chapter.

"(m) It shall be unlawful for any licensed importer, licensed manufacturer, licensed dealer, or licensed collector knowingly to make any false entry in, to fail to make appropriate entry in, or to fail to properly maintain, any record which he is required to keep pursuant to section 923 of this chapter or regulations promulgated thereunder.

"§ 923. Licensing

"(a) No person shall engage in business as a firearms or ammunition importer, manufacturer, or dealer until he has filed an application with, and received a license to do so from, the Secretary. The application shall be in such form and contain such information as the Secretary shall by regulation prescribe. Each applicant shall pay a fee for obtaining such a license, a separate fee being required for each place in which the applicant is to do business, as follows:

"(1) If the applicant is a manufacturer—

"(A) of destructive devices or ammunition for destructive devices, a fee of $1,000 per year;

"(B) of firearms other than destructive devices, a fee of $50 per year; or

"(C) of ammunition for firearms other than destructive devices, a fee of $10 per year.

"(2) If the applicant is an importer—

(A) of destructive devices or ammunition for destructive devices, a fee of $1,000 per year; or

"(B) of firearms other than destructive devices or ammunition for firearms other than destructive devices, a fee of $50 per year.

"(3) If the applicant is a dealer—

"(A) in destructive devices or ammunition for destructive devices, a fee of $1,000 per year;

"(B) who is a pawnbroker dealing in firearms other than destructive devices or ammunition for firearms other than destructive devices, a fee of $25 per year; or

"(C) who is not a dealer in destructive devices or a pawn- broker, a fee of $10 per year,

"(b) Any person desiring to be licensed as a collector shall file an application for such license with the Secretary. The application shall be in such form and contain such information as the Secretary shall by regulation prescribe. The fee for such license shall be $10 per year. Any license granted under this subsection shall only apply to transactions in curios and relics.

"(c) Upon the filing of a proper application and payment of the prescribed fee, the Secretary shall issue to a qualified applicant the appropriate license which, subject to the provisions of this chapter and other applicable provisions of law, shall entitle the licensee to transport, ship, and receive firearms and ammunition covered by such license in interstate or foreign commerce during the period stated in the license.

"(d) (1) Any application submitted under subsection (a) or (b) of this section shall be approved if —

"(A) the applicant is twenty-one years of age or over;

"(B) the applicant (including, in the case of a corporation, partnership, or association, any individual possessing, directly or indirectly, the power to direct or cause the direction of the management and policies of the corporation, partnership, or association) is not prohibited from transporting, shipping, or receiving firearms or ammunition in interstate or foreign commerce under section 922(g) and (n) of this chapter;

"(C) the applicant has not willfully violated any of the provisions of this chapter or regulations issued thereunder;

"(D) the applicant has not willfully failed to disclose any material information required, or has not made any false statement as to any material fact, in connection with his application; and

"(E) the applicant has in a State (i) premises from which he conducts business subject to license under this chapter or from which he intends to conduct such business within a reasonable period of time, or (ii) in the case of a collector, premises from which he conducts his collecting subject to license under this chapter or from which he intends to conduct such collecting within a reasonable period of time;

"(2) The Secretary must approve or deny an application for a license within the forty-five day period beginning on the date it is received. If the Secretary fails to act within such period, the applicant may file an action under section 1361 of title 28 to compel the Secretary to act. If the Secretary approves an applicant's application, such applicant shall be issued a license upon the payment of the prescribed fee.

"(e) The Secretary may, after notice and opportunity for hearing, revoke any license issued under this section if the holder of such license has violated any provision of this chapter or anv rule or regu- lation prescribed by the Secretary under this chapter, he Secretary's action under this subsection may be reviewed only as provided in sub- section (f) of this section.

"(f) (1) Any person whose application for a license is denied and any holder of a license which is revoked shall receive a written notice from the Secretary stating specifically the grounds upon which the application was denied or upon which the license was revoked. Any notice of a revocation of a license shall be given to the holder of such license before the effective date of the revocation.

"(2) If the Secretary denies an application for, or revokes, a license, he shall, upon request by the aggrieved party, promptly hold a hearing to review his denial or revocation, In the case of a revocation of a license, the Secretary shall upon the request of the holder of the license stay the effective date of the revocation. A hearing held under this paragraph shall be held at a location convenient to the aggrieved party

"(3) If after a hearing held under paragraph (2) the Secretary decides not to reverse his decision to deny an application or revoke a license, the Secretary shall give notice of his decision to the aggrieved party. The aggrieved party may at any time within sixty days after the date notice was given under this paragraph file a petition with the United States district court for the district in which he resides or has his principal place of business for a judicial review of such denial or revocation. In a proceeding conducted under this subsection, the court may consider any evidence submitted by the parties to the proceeding). If the court decides that the Secretary was not authorized to deny the application or to revoke the license, the court shall order the Secretary to take such action as may be necessary to comply with the judgment of the court.

"(g) Each licensed importer, licensed manufacturer, licensed dealer, and licensed collector shall maintain such records of importation, production, shipment, receipt, sale, or other disposition of firearms and ammunition at such place, for such period, and in such form, as the Secretary may by regulations prescribe. Such importers, manufacturers, dealers, and collectors shall make records available for inspection at all reasonable times, and shall submit to the Secretary such reports and information with respect to such records and the contents thereof as he shall by regulations prescribe. The Secretary may enter during business hours the premises (including places of storage) of any firearms or ammunition importer, manufacturer, dealer, or col- lector for the purpose of inspecting or examining (1) any records or documents required to be kept by such importer, manufacturer, dealer, or collector under the provisions of this chapter or regulations issued under this chapter, and (2) any firearms or ammunition kept or stored by such importer, manufacturer, dealer, or collector at such premises. Upon the request of any State or any political subdivision thereof, the Secretary may make available to such State or any political subdivision thereof, any information which he may obtain by reason of the provisions of this chapter with respect to the identification of persons within such State or political subdivision thereof, who have purchased or received firearms or ammunition, together with a description of such firearms or ammunition.

"(2) If the Secretary denies an application for, or revokes, a license, he shail, upon request by the aggrieved party, promptly hold a hearing to review his denial or revocation, In the case of a revocation of a license, the Secretary shall upon the request of the holder of the license stay the effective date of the revocation. A hearing held under this paragraph shall be held at a location convenient to the aggrieved party.

"(3) If after a hearing held under paragraph (2) the Secretary decides not to reverse his decision to deny an application or revoke a license, the Secretary shall give notice of his decision to the aggrieved party. The aggrieved party may at any time within sixty days after the date notice was given under this paragraph file a petition with the United States district court for the district in which he resides or has his principal place of business for a judicial review of such denial or revocation. In a proceeding conducted under this subsection, the court may consider any evidence submitted by the parties to the proceeding. If the court decides that the Secretary was not authorized to deny the application or to revoke the license, the court shall order the Secretary to take such action as may be necessary to comply with the judgment of the court

"(g) Each 1icensed importer , licensed manufacturer , licensed dealer, and licensed collector shall maintain such records of importation, production, shipment,, receipt, sale, or other disposition, of firearms and ammunition at such place, for such period, and in such form as the Secretary may by regulations prescribe. Such importers, manufacturers, dealers, and collectors shall make such records available for inspection at all reasonable times, and shall submit to the Secretary such reports and information with respect to such records and the contents thereof as he shall by regulations prescribe. The Secretary may enter during business hours the premises (including places of storage) of any firearms or ammunition importer, manufacturer, dealer, or collector for the purpose of inspecting or examining (1) any records or documents required to be kept by such importer, manufacturer, dealer, or collector under the provisions of this chapter or regulations issued under this chapter, and (2) any firearms or ammunition kept or stored by such importer, manufacturer, dealer, or collector at such premises. Upon the request of any State or any political subdivision thereof, the Secretary may make available to such State or any political subdivision thereof, any information which he may obtain by reason of the provisions of this chapter with respect to the identification of persons within such State or political subdivision thereof, who have purchased or received firearms or ammunition, together with a description of such firearms or ammunition.

"(h) Licenses issued under the provisions of subsection (c) of this section shall be kept posted and kept available for inspection on the premises covered by the license.

"(i) Licensed importers and licensed manufacturers shall identify, by means of a serial number engraved or cast on the receiver or frame of the weapon, in such manner as the Secretary shall by regulations prescribe, each firearm imported or manufactured by such importer or manufacturer.

"(j) This section shall not apply to anyone who engages only in hand loading, reloading, or custom loading ammunition for his own firearm, and who does not hand load, reload, or custom load ammunition for others.

"§ 924. Penalties

"(a) Whoever violates any provision of this chapter or knowingly makes any false statement or representation with respect to the information required hj the provisions of this chapter to be kept in the records of a person licensed under this chapter, or in applying for any license or exemption or relief from disability under the provisions of this chapter, shall be fined not more than $5,000, or imprisoned not more than five years, or both, and shall become eligible for parole as the Board of Parole shall determine*

"(b) Whoever, with intent to commit therewith an offense punish- able by imprisonment for a term exceeding one year, or with knowledge or reasonable cause to believe that an offense punishable by imprisonment for a term exceeding one year is to be committed therewith, ships, transports, or receives a firearm or any ammunition in interstate or foreign commerce shall be fined not more than $10,000, or imprisoned not more than ten years, or both.

"(c) Whoever—

"(1) uses a firearm to commit any felony which may be prosecuted in a court of the United States, or

"(2) carries a firearm unlawfully during the commission of any felony which may be prosecuted in a court of the United States,

shall be sentenced to a term of imprisonment for not less than one year nor more than 10 years. In the case of his second or subsequent conviction under this subsection, such person shall be sentenced to a term of imprisonment for not less than five years nor more than 25 years, and, notwithstanding any other provision of law, the court shall not suspend the sentence of such person or give him a probationary sentence,

"(d) Any firearm or ammunition involved in or used or intended to be used in, any violation of the provisions of this chapter or any rule or regulation promulgated thereunder, or any violation of any other criminal law of the United States, shall be subject to seizure and forfeiture and all provisions of the Internal Revenue Code of 1954 relating to the seizure, forfeiture, and disposition of firearms, as defined in section 5845(a) of that Code, shall, so far as applicable, extend to seizures and forfeitures under the provisions of this chapter.

"§ 925. Exceptions: Relief from disabilities

"(a) (1) The provisions of this chapter shall not apply with respect to the transportation, shipment, receipt, or importation of any fire- arm or ammunition imported for, sold or shipped to, or issued for the use of, the United States or any department or agency thereof or any State or any department, agency, or political subdivision thereof.

"(2) The provisions of this chapter shall not apply with respect to (A) the shipment or receipt of firearms or ammunition when sold or issued by the Secretary of the Army pursuant to section 4808 of title 10, and (B) the transportation of any such firearm or ammunition carried out to enable a person, who lawfully received such firearm or ammunition from the Secretary of the Army, to engage in military training or in competitions.

"(3) Unless otherwise prohibited by this chapter or any other Federal law, a licensed importer, licensed manufacturer, or licensed dealer may ship to a member of the United States Armed Forces on active duty outside the United States or to clubs, recognized by the Department of Defense, whose entire membership is composed of such members, and such members or clubs may receive a firearm or ammunition determined by the Secretary of the Treasury to be generally recognized as particularly suitable for sporting purposes and intended for the personal use oi such member or club.

"(4) When established to the satisfaction of the Secretary to be consistent with the provisions of this chapter and other applicable Federal and State laws and published ordinances, the Secretary may

authorize the transportation, shipment, receipt, or importation into the United States to the place of residence of any member of the United States Armed Forces who is on active duty outside the United States (or who has been on active duty outside the United States within the sixty day period immediately preceding the transportation, shipment, receipt, or importation), of any firearm or ammunition which is (A) determined by the Secretary to be generally recognized as particularly suitable for sporting purposes, or determined By the Department of Defense to be a type of firearm normally classified as a war souvenir, and (B) intended for the personal use of such member.

"(5) For the purpose, of paragraphs (3) and (4) of this subsection, the term 'United States* means each of the several States and the District of Columbia.

"(b) A licensed importer, licensed manufacturer, 1icensed dealer, or licensed collector who is indicted for a crime punishable by imprisonment for a term exceeding one year, may, notwithstanding any other provision of this chapter, continue operation pursuant to his existing license (if prior to the expiration of the term of the existing license timely application is made for a new license) during the term of such indictment and until any conviction pursuant to the indictment becomes final.

"(c) A person who has been convicted of a crime punishable by imprisonment for a term exceeding one year (other than a crime involving the use of a firearm or other weapon or a violation of this chapter or of the National Firearms Act) may make application to the Secretary for relief from the disabilities imposed by Federal laws with respect to the acquisition, receipt, transfer, shipment, or possession of firearms and incurred by reason of such conviction, and the Secretary may grant such relief if it is established to his satisfaction that the circumstances regarding the conviction, and the applicant's record and reputation, are such that the applicant will not be likely to act in a manner dangerous to public safety and that the granting of the relief would not be contrary to the public interest. A licensed importer, licensed manufacturer, licensed dealer, or li (reused collector conducting operations under this chapter, who makes application for 'relief from the disabilities incurred under this chapter by reason of such a conviction, shall not be barred by such conviction from further operations under his license pending final action on an application for relief filed pursuant to this section. Whenever the Secretary grants relief to any person pursuant to this section he shall promptly publish in the Federal Register notice of such action, together with the reasons therefor.

"(d) The Secretary may authorize a firearm or ammunition to be imported or brought into the United States or any possession thereof if the person importing or bringing in the firearm or ammunition establishes to the satisfaction of the Secretary that the firearm or ammunition—

"(1} is being imported or brought in for scientific or research purposes, or is for use in connection with competition or training pursuant to chapter 401 of title 10;

"(2) is an unserviceable firearm, other than a machinegun as defined in section 5845(b) of the Internal Revenue Code of 1954 (not readily restorable to firing condition), imported or brought in as a curio or museum piece;

"(3) is of a type that does not fall within the definition of a firearm as defined in section 5845 (a) of the Internal Revenue Code of 1954 and is generally recognized as particularly suitable for or readily adaptable to sporting purposes, excluding surplus military firearms; or

"(4) was previously taken out of the United States or a possession by the person who is bringing in the firearm or ammunition.

The Secretary may permit the conditional importation or bringing in of a firearm or ammunition for examination and testing in connection with the making of a determination as to whether the importation or bringing in of such firearm or ammunition will be allowed under this subsection.

"§ 926. Rules and regulations

"The Secretary may prescribe such rules and regulations as he deems reasonably necessary to carry out the provisions of this chapter, including—

"(1) regulations providing that a person licensed under this chapter, when dealing with another person so licensed, shall pro- vide such other licensed person a certified copy of this license; and

"(2) regu1ations providing for the issuance , at a reasonable cost, to a person licensed under this chapter, of certified copies of his license for use as provided under regulations issued under para- graph (1) of this subsection.

The Secretary shall give reasonable public notice, and afford to interested parties opportunity for hearing, prior to prescribing such rules and regulations.

"§ 927. Effect on State law

"No provision of this chapter shall be construed as indicating an intent on the part of the Congress to occupy the field in which provision operates to the exclusion of the law of any State on the subject matter, unless there is a direct and positive conflict between such provision and the law of the State so that the two cannot be reconciled or consistently stand together.

"§ 928. Separability

"If any (provision of this chapter or the application thereof to any person or circumstance is held invalid, the remainder of the chapter and the application of such provision to other persons not similarly situated or to other circumstances shall not be affected thereby."

SEC. 103. The administration and enforcement of the amendment made by this title shall lie vested in the Secretary of the Treasury,

SEC. 104. Nothing in this title or the amendment made thereby shall be construed as modifying or affecting any provision of—

(a) the National Firearms Act (chapter 53 of the Internal Revenue Code of 1954);

(b) section 414 of the Mutual Security Act of 1954 (22 U.S.C. 1934), as amended, relating to munitions control; or

(c) section 1715 of title 18, United States Code, relating to non-mailable firearms.

SEC. 105. (a) Except as provided in subsection (b), the provisions of chapter 44 of title 18, United States Code, as amended by section 102 of this title, shall take effect on December 16, 1968.

(b) The following sections of chapter 44 of title 18, United States Code, as amended by section 102 of this title shall take effect on the date of the enactment of this title: Sections 921, 922(1), 925(a) (1), and 925(d).

TITLE II—MACHINE GUNS, DESTRUCTIVE DEVICES, AND CERTAIN OTHER FIREARMS

SEC. 201. Chapter 53 of the Internal Revenue Code of 1954 is amended to read as follows:

"Chapter 53.—MACHINE GUNS, DESTRUCTIVE DEVICES, AND CERTAIN OTHER FIREARMS

"Subchapter A. Taxes.
"Subchapter B. General provisions and exemptions.
"Subchapter C. Prohibited acts.
"Subchapter D. Penalties and forfeitures.

"Subchapter A—Taxes

"Part I. Special (occupational) taxes
"Part II. Tax on transferring firearms.
"Part III. Tax on making firearms.

"PART I—SPECIAL (OCCUPATIONAL) TAXES

"Sec. 5801. Tax
"Sec. 5802. Registration of importers, manufacturers, and dealers.

"SEC 5801. TAX.

"On first engaging in business and thereafter on or before the first day of July of each year, every importer, manufacturer, and dealer in firearms snail pay a special (occupational) tax for each place of business at the following rates :

"(1) Importers.— $500 r year or fraction thereof;

"(2) Manufacturers. — $500 a year or fraction thereof;

"(3) Dealers.— $200 a year or fraction thereof.

Except an importer, manufacturer, or dealer who imports, manufactures, or deals in only weapons classified as 'any other weapon' under section 5845(e), shall pay a special (occupational) tax for each place of business at the following rates: Importers, $25 a year or fraction thereof; manufacturers, $25 a year or fraction thereof; dealers, $10 a year or fraction thereof.

"SEC. 5802. REGISTRATION OF IMPORTERS, MANUFACTURERS, AND DEALERS.

"On first engaging in business and thereafter on or before the first day of July of each year, each importer, manufacturer, and dealer in firearms shall register with the Secretary or his delegate in each internal revenue district in which such business is to be carried on, his name, including any trade name, and the address of each location in the district where he will conduct such business. Where there is a change during the taxable year in the location of, or the trade name used in, such business, the importer, manufacturer, or dealer shall file an application with the Secretary or his delegate to amend his registration. Firearms operations of an importer, manufacturer, or dealer may not be commenced at the new location or under a new trade name prior to approval by the Secretary or his delegate of the application.

"PART II— TAX ON TRANSFERRING FIREARMS

"Sec. 5811. Transfer tax.
"Sec. 5812. Transfers,

"SEC 5811. TRANSFER TAX.

"(a) Rate.—There shall be levied, collected, and paid on firearms transferred a tax at the rate of $200 for each firearm transferred, except, the transfer tax on any firearm classified as any other weapon under section 5S45{e) shall be at the rate of $5 for each such firearm transferred.

"(b) By Whom Paid,—The tax imposed by subsection (a) of this section shall be paid by the transferor.

"(c) Payment.—The tax imposed by subsection {a) of this section shall be payable by the appropriate stamps prescribed for payment by the Secretary or his delegate.

"SEC 5812. TRANSFERS.

"(a) Application.—A firearm shall not be transferred unless (1) the transferor of the firearm has filed with the Secretary or his dele- gate a written application, in duplicate, for the transfer and registration of the firearm to the transferee on the application form prescribed by the Secretary or his delegate; (2) any tax payable on the transfer is paid as evidenced by the proper stamp affixed to the original application form; (3) the transferee is identified in the application form in such manner as the Secretary or his delegate may by regulations prescribe, except that, if such person is an individual, the identification must include his fingerprints and his photograph; (4) the transferor of the firearm is identified in the application form in such manner as the Secretary or his delegate may by regulations prescribe; (5) the firearm is identified in the application form in such manner as the Secretary or his delegate may by regulations prescribe; and (6) the application form shows that the Secretary or his delegate has approved the transfer and the registration of the firearm to the transferee. Ap- plications shall be denied if the transfer, receipt, or possession of the firearm would place the transferee in violation of law.

" (b) Transfer of Possession. — The transferee of a firearm shall not take possession of the firearm unless the Secretary or his delegate has approved the transfer and registration of the firearm to the transferee as required by subsection (a) of this section.

"PART III—TAX ON MAKING FIREARMS

"SEC. 5821. MAKING TAX.

"(a) RATE.—There shall be levied, collected, and paid upon the making of a firearm a tax at the rate of $*200 for each firearm made,

"(b) BY WHOM PAID.—The tax imposed by subsection (a) of this section shall be paid by the person making the firearm.

"(c) PAYMENT.—The tax imposed by subsection (a) of this section shall be payable by the stamp prescribed for payment by the Secretary or his delegate.

"SEC. 5822. MAKING.

"No person shall make a firearm unless he has (a) filed with the Secretary or his delegate a written application, in duplicate, to make and register the firearm on the form prescribed by the Secretary or his delegate; (b) paid any tax payable on the making and such payment is evidenced by the proper stamp affixed to the original application form; (c) identified the firearm to be made in the application form in such manner as the Secretary or his delegate may by regulations prescribe; (d) identified himself in the application form in such manner as the Secretary or his delegate may by regulations prescribe, except that, if such person is an individual, the identification must include his fingerprints and his photograph; and (e) obtained the approval of the Secretary or his delegate to make and register the firearm and the application form shows such approval. Applications shall be denied if the making or possession of the firearm would place the person making the firearm in violation of law.

"Subchapter B — General Provisions and Exemptions

"PART I — GENERAL PROVISIONS

"Sec. 5848. Restrictive use of information,
"Sec. 084&. Citation of chapter.

"SEC. 5841. REGISTRATION OF FIREARMS.

"(a) CENTRAL REGISTRY. The Secretary or his delegate shall maintain a central registry of all firearms in the United States which are not in the possession or under the control of the United States, This registry shall be known as the National Firearms Registration and Transfer Record. The registry shall include—

"(1) identification of the firearm;

"(2) date of registration; and

"(3) identification and address of person entitled to possession of the firearm.

"(b) BY WHOM REGISTERED.—Each manufacturer, importer, and maker shall register each firearm he manufactures, imports, or makes. Each firearm transferred shall be registered to the transferee by the transferor.

"(c) HOW REGISTERED.—Each manufacturer shall notify the Secretary or his delegate of the manufacture of a firearm in such manner as may by regulations be prescribed and such notification shall effect the registration of the firearm required by this section. Each importer, maker, and transferor of a firearm shall, prior to importing, making, or transferring a firearm, obtain authorization in such manner as re- quired by this chapter or regulations issued thereunder to import, make, or transfer the firearm, and such authorization shall effect the registration of the firearm required by this section,

"(d) FIREARMS REGISTERED ON EFFECTIVE DATE OF THIS ACT.—A person shown as possessing a firearm by the records maintained by the Secretary or his delegate pursuant to the National Firearms Act in force on the day immediately prior to the effective date of the National Firearms Act of 1968 shall be considered to have registered under this section the firearms in his possession which are disclosed by that record as being in his possession.

"(e) PROOF OF REGISTRATION.—A person possessing a firearm registered as required by this section .shall retain proof of registration which shall be made available to the Secretary or his delegate upon request.

"SEC 5842, IDENTIFICATION OF FIREARMS.

"(a) IDENTIFICATION OF FIREARMS OTHER THAN DESTRUCTIVE DEVICES.—Each manufacturer and importer and anyone making a firearm shall identify each firearm, other than a destructive device, manufactured, imported, or made by a serial number which may not he readily removed, obliterated, or altered, the name of the manufacturer, importer, or maker, and such other identification as the Secretary or his delegate may by regulations prescribe.

"(b) FIREARMS WITHOUT SERIAL NUMBER.—Any person who possesses a firearm, other than a destructive device, which does not bear the serial number and other information required by subsection (a) of this section shall identify the firearm with a serial number assigned by the Secretary or his delegate and any other information the Secretary or his delegate may by regulations prescribe.

"(c) IDENTIFICATION OF DESTRUCTIVE DEVICE.—Any firearm classified as a destructive device shall be identified in such manner as the Secretary or his delegate may by regulations prescribe.

"SEC. 5843, RECORDS AND RETURNS*

"Importers, manufacturers, and dealers shall keen such records of, and render such returns in relation to, the importation, manufacture, making, receipt, and sale, or other disposition, of firearms as the Secretary or his delegate may by regulations prescribe.

"SEC, 5844. IMPORTATION.

"No firearm shall be imported or brought into the Ignited States or any territory under its control or jurisdiction unless the importer establishes, under regulations as maybe prescribed by the Secretary or his delegate, that the firearm to be imported or brought in is—

"(1) being imported or brought in for the use of the United States or any department, independent establishment, or agency thereof or any State or possession or any political subdivision thereof; or

"(2) being imported or brought in for scientific or research purposes; or

"(3) being imported or brought in solely for testing or use as a model by a registered manufacturer or solely for use as a sample by a registered importer or registered dealer;

except that, the Secretary or his delegate may permit the conditional importation or bringing in of a firearm for examination and testing in connection with classifying the firearm.

"SEC. 5845. DEFINITIONS.

"For the purpose of this chapter—

"(a) FIREARM.—The term 'firearm 3 means (1) a shotgun having a barrel or barrels of less than 18 inches in length; (2) a weapon made from a shotgun if such weapon as modified has an overall length of less than 26 inches or a barrel or barrels of less than 18 inches in length ; (8) a rifle having a barrel or barrels of less than 16 inches in length; (4) a weapon made from a rifle if such weapon as modified has an overall length of less than 26 inches or a barrel or barrels of less than 16 inches in length; (5) any other weapon, as defined in subsection (e) ; (6) a machinegun; (7) a muffler or a silencer for any firearm whether or not such firearm is included within this definition ; and (8) a destructive device. The term 'firearm 1 shall not include an antique firearm or any device (other than a machinegun or destructive device) which, although designed as a weapon, the Secretary or his delegate finds by reason of the date of its manufacture, value, design, and other characteristics is primarily a collector's item and is not likely to be used as a weapon.

"(b) MACHINEGUN.—The term 'machinegun' means any weapon which shoots, is designed to shoot, or can be readily restored to shoot, automatically more than one shot, without manual reloading, by a single function of the trigger. The term shall also include the frame or receiver of any such weapon, any combination of parts designed and intended for use in converting a weapon into a machinegun, and any combination of parts from which a machinegun can be assembled if such parts are in the possession or under the control of a person,

"(c) RIFLE.—The term 'rifle' means a weapon designed or rede- signed, made or remade, and intended to be fired from the shoulder and designed or redesigned and made or remade to use the energy of the explosive in a fixed cartridge to fire only a single projectile through a rifled bore for each single pull of the trigger, and shall include any such weapon which may be readily restored to fire a fixed cartridge.

"(d) SHOTGUN.—The term Shotgun' means a weapon designed or redesigned, made or remade, and intended to be fired from the shoulder and designed or redesigned and made or remade to use the energy of the explosive in a fixed shotgun shell to fire through a smooth bore either a number of projectiles {ball shot) or a single projectile for each pull of the trigger, and shall include any such weapon which may be readily restored to fire a fixed shotgun shell.

"(e) ANY OTHER WEAPON.—The term 'any other weapon' means any weapon or device capable of being concealed on the person from which a shot can be discharged through the energy of an explosive, a pistol or revolver having a barrel with a smooth bore designed or redesigned to fire a fixed shotgun shell, weapons with combination shotgun and rifle barrels 12 inches or more, less than 18 inches in length, from which only a single discharge can be made from either barrel without manual reloading, and shall include any such weapon which may be readily restored to fire. Such term shall not include a pistol or a revolver having a rifled bore, or rifled bores, or weapons designed, made, or intended to be fired from the shoulder and not capable of firing fixed ammunition.

"(f) DESTRUCTIVE DEVICE.—The term 'destructive device' means (1) any explosive, incendiary, or poison gas (A) bomb, (B) grenade, (C) rocket having a propellent charge of more than four ounces, (D) missile having an explosive or incendiary charge of more than one- quarter ounce, (E) mine, or (F) similar device; (2) any type of weapon by whatever name known which will, or which may be readily converted to, expel a projectile by the action of an explosive or other propellant, the barrel or barrels of which have a bore of more than one-half inch in diameter, except a shotgun or shotgun shell which the Secretary or his delegate finds is generally recognized as particularly suitable for sporting purposes; and (3) any combination of parts either designed or intended for use in converting any device into a destructive device as defined in subparagraphs (1) and (2) and from which a destructive device may be readily assembled. The term 'destructive device' shall not include any device which is neither designed nor redesigned for use as a weapon; any device, although originally designed for use as a weapon, which is redesigned for use as a signaling, pyrotechnic, line throwing, safety, or similar device; surplus ordnance sold, loaned, or given by the Secretary of the Army pursuant to the provisions of section 4684(2), 4685, or 4686 of title 10 of the United States Code; or any other device which the Secretary of the Treasury or his delegate finds is not likely to be used as a weapon, or is an antique or is a rifle which the owner intends to use solely for sporting purposes.

"(g) ANTIQUE FIREARM.—The term 'antique firearm' means any firearm not designed or redesigned for using rimfire or conventional center fire ignition with fixed ammunition and manufactured in or before- 1898 (including any matchlock, flintlock, percussion cap, or similar type of ignition system or replica thereof, whether actually manufactured before or after the year 1808) and also any firearm using fixed ammunition manufactured in or before 1898, for which ammunition is no longer manufactured in the United States and is not readily available in the ordinary channels of commercial trade.

"(h) UNSERVICEABLE FIREARM.—The term 'unserviceable firearm' means a firearm which is incapable of discharging a shot by means of an explosive and incapable of being readily restored to a firing condition.

"(i) MAKE.—The term 'make', and the various derivatives of such word, shall include manufacturing (other than by one qualified to engage in such business under this chapter), putting together, altering, any combination of these, or otherwise producing a firearm.

"(j) TRANSFER—The term 'transfer' and the various derivatives of such word, shall include selling, assigning, pledging, leasing, loaning, giving away, or otherwise disposing of.

"(k) DEALER—The term 'dealer' means any person, not a manufacturer or importer, engaged in the business of selling, renting, leasing, or loaning firearms and shall include pawnbrokers who accept firearms as collateral for loans.

"(l) IMPORTER.—The term 'importer' means any person who is engaged in the business of importing or bringing firearms into the United States.

"(m) MANUFACTURER.—The term 'manufacturer' means any person who is engaged in the business of manufacturing firearms.

"SEC. 5846. OTHER LAWS APPLICABLE.

"All provisions of law relating to special taxes imposed by chapter 51 and to engraving, issuance, sale, accountability, cancellation, and 5692, distribution of stamps for tax payment shall, insofar as not inconsistent with the provisions of this chapter, be applicable with respect to the taxes imposed by sections 5801, 5811, and 5821.

"SEC. 5847. EFFECT ON OTHER LAWS.

"Nothing in this chapter shall be construed as modifying or affecting the requirements of section 414 of the Mutual Security Act of 1954, as amended, with respect to the manufacture, exportation, and importation of arms, ammunition, and implements of war.

"SEC. 5848. RESTRICTIVE USE OF INFORMATION.

"(a) General Rule.—No information or evidence obtained from an application, registration, or records required to be submitted or retained by a natural person in order to comply with any provision of this chapter or regulations issued thereunder, shall, except as pro- vided in subsection (b) of this section, be used, directly or indirectly, as evidence against that person in a criminal proceeding with respect to a violation of law occurring prior to or concurrently with the filing of the application or registration, or the compiling of the records containing the information or evidence.

"(b) Furnishing False Information,—Subsection (a) of this section shall not preclude the use of any such information or evidence in a prosecution or other action under any applicable provision of law with respect to the furnishing of false information.

"SEC 5849. CITATION OF CHAPTER.

"This chapter may be cited as the 'National Firearms Act' and any reference in any other provision of law to the 'National Firearms Act' shall be held to refer to the provisions of this chapter.

"PART II — EXEMPTIONS

"Sec. 5831. Special (occupational) tax exemption,
"Sec. 5852, General transfer and making exemption.
"See. 5853. Exemption from transfer and making tax available to certain governmental entities and officials.
"Sec. 5854. Exportation of firearms exempt from transfer tax.

"SEC. 5851. SPECIAL (OCCUPATIONAL) TAX EXEMPTION.

"(a) Business With United States.—Any person required to pay special (occupational) tax under section 5801 shall be relieved from payment, of that tax if he establishes to the satisfaction of the Secretary or his delegate that his business is conducted exclusively with, or on behalf of, the United States or any department, independent establishment, or agency thereof. The Secretary or his delegate may relieve any person manufacturing firearms for, or on behalf of, the United States from compliance with any provision of this chapter in the con- duct of such business.

"(b) Application.—The exemption provided for in subsection (a) of this section may be obtained by 'filing with the Secretary or his dele- gate an application on such form and containing such information as may by regulations be prescribed. The exemptions must thereafter be renewed on or before July 1 of each year. Approval of the application by the Secretary or his delegate shall entitle the applicant to the exemptions stated on the approved application.

"SEC 5852, GENERAL TRANSFER AND MAKING TAX EXEMPTION.

"(a) TRANSFER.—Any firearm may be transferred to the United States or any department, independent establishment, or agency thereof, without payment of the transfer tax imposed by section 5811.

"(b) MAKING BY A PERSON OTHER THAN A QUALIFIED MANU-FACTURER.—Any firearm may be made by, or on behalf of, the United States, or any department, independent establishment, or agency thereof, without payment of the making tax imposed by section 5821.

"(c) MAKING BY A QUALIFIED MANUFACTURER,—A manufacturer qualified under this chapter to engage in such business may make the type of firearm which he is qualified to manufacture without payment of the making tax imposed by section 5821.

"(d) TRANSFERS BETWEEN SPECIAL {OCCUPATIONAL) TAXPAYERS.—A firearm registered to a person qualified under this chapter to engage in business as an importer, manufacturer, or dealer may be transferred by that person without payment of the transfer tax imposed by section 5811 to any other person qualified under this chapter to manufacture, import, or deal in that type of firearm.

"(e) UNSERVICEABLE FIREARM—An unserviceable firearm may be transferred as a curio or ornament without payment of the transfer tax imposed by section 5811, under such requirements as the Secretary or his delegate may by regulations prescribe.

"(f) RIGHT TO EXEMPTION.—No firearm may be transferred or made exempt from tax under the provisions of this section unless the trans- fer or making is performed pursuant to an application in such form and manner as the Secretary or his delegate may by regulations prescribe,

"SEC. 5853. TRANSFER AND MAKING TAX EXEMPTION AVAIL-ABLE TO CERTAIN GOVERNMENTAL ENTITIES,

"(a) TRANSFER—A firearm may be transferred without the payment of the transfer tax imposed by section 5811 to any State, possession of the United States, any political subdivision thereof, or any official police organization of such a government entity engaged in criminal investigations.

"(b) MAKING.—A firearm may be made without payment of the making tax imposed by section 5821 by, or on behalf of, any State, or possession of the United States, any political subdivision thereof, or any official police organization of such a government entity engaged in criminal investigations.

"(c) RIGHT TO EXEMPTION.—No firearm may be transferred or made exempt from tax under this section unless the transfer or making is performed pursuant to an application in such form and manner as the Secretary or his delegate may by regulations prescribe.

"SEC 5854. EXPORTATION OF FIREARMS EXEMPT FROM TRANSFER TAX.

"A firearm may be exported without payment of the transfer tax imposed under section 5811 provided that proof of the exportation is furnished in such form and manner as the Secretary or his delegate may by regulations prescribe.

"Subchapter C— Prohibited Acts

"SEC. 5861. PROHIBITED ACTS.

"It shall be unlawful for any person —

"(a) to engage in business as a manufacturer or importer of, or dealer in, firearms without having paid the special (occupational) tax required by section 5801 for his business or having registered as required oy section 5802; or

"(b) to receive or possess a firearm transferred to him in viola- t ion of the provisions of this chapter; or

"(c) to receive or possess a firearm made in violation of the provisions of this chapter; or

"(d) to receive or possess a firearm which is not registered to him in the National Firearms Registration and Transfer Record; or

"(e) to transfer a firearm in violation of the provisions of this chapter; or

"(f) to make a firearm in violation of the provisions of this chapter; or

"(g) to obliterate, remove, change, or alter the serial number or other identification of a firearm required by this chapter; or

"(h) to receive or possess a firearm having the. serial number or other identification required by this chapter obliterated, removed, changed, or altered; or

"(i) to receive or possess a firearm which is not identified by a serial number as required by this chapter; or

"(j) to transport, deliver, or receive any firearm in interstate commerce which has not been registered as required by this chapter; or

"(k) to receive or possess a firearm which has been imported or brought into the United States in violation of section 5844; or

"(l) to make, or cause the making of, a false entry on any application, return, or record require! by' this chapter, knowing such entry to be false.

"Subchapter D—Penalties and Forfeitures

"SEC. 5871. PENALTIES.

"Any person who violates or fails to comply with any provision of this chapter shall, upon conviction, be fined not more than $10,000, or be imprisoned not more than ten years, or both, and shall become eligible for parole as the Board of Parole shall determine.

"SEC 5872. FORFEITURES.

"(a) LAWS APPLICABLE.—Any firearm involved in any violation of the provisions of this chapter shall lie subject to seizure and forfeiture, and (except as provided in subsection (b)) all the provisions of internal revenue laws relating to searches, seizures, and forfeitures of unstamped articles are extended to and made to apply to the articles taxed under this chapter, and the persona to whom this chapter applies.

"(b) DISPOSAL.—In the case of the forfeiture of any firearm by reason of a violation of this chapter, no notice of public sale shall be required ; no such firearm shall be sold at public sale ; if such firearm is forfeited for a violation of this chapter and there is no remission or mitigation of forfeiture thereof, it shall be delivered by the Secretary or his delegate to the Administrator of General Services, General Services Administration, who may order such firearm destroyed or may sell it to any State, or possession, or political subdivision thereof, or at the request of the Secretary or his delegate, may authorize its retention for official use of the Treasury Department, or may transfer ir without charge to any executive department or independent establishment of the Government for use by it."

SEC. 202. The amendments made by section 201 of this title shall be cited as the "National Firearms Act Amendments of 1968".

SEC. 203. (a) Section 6107 of the Internal Revenue Code of 1954 is repealed.

(b) The table of sections for subchapter B of chapter 61 of the Internal Revenue Code of 1054 is amended by striking out:

"SEC. 6107. List of special taxpayers for public inspection."

SEC. 204. Section 6806 of the Internal Revenue Code of 1954 is amended to read as follows:

"SEC. 6806. OCCUPATIONAL TAX STAMPS.

"Every person engaged in any business, avocation, or employment, who is thereby made liable to a special tax (other than a special tax under subchapter B of chapter 35, under subchapter B of chapter 36, or under subtitle E) shall place and keep conspicuously in his establishment or place of business all stamps denoting payment of such special tax."

SEC. 205. Section 7273 of the Internal Revenue Code of 1954 is amended to read as follows;

"SEC. 7273. PENALTIES FOR OFFENSES RELATING TO SPECIAL TAXES.

"Any person who shall fail to place and keep stamps denoting the payment of the special tax as provided in section 6806 shall be liable to a penalty (not less than $10) equal to the special tax for which his business rendered him liable, unless such failure is shown to be due to reasonable cause. If such failure to comply with section 6806 is through willful neglect or refusal, then the penalty shall be double the amount above prescribed."

SEC. 206. (a) Section 5692 of the Internal Revenue Code of 1954 is repealed.

(b) The table of sections for part V of subchapter J of chapter 51 of the Internal Revenue Code of 1954 is amended by striking out:

"Sec. 5692. Penalties relating to porting of special tax stamps."

Sec. 207. (a) Section 201 of this title shall take effect on the first day of the first month following the month in which it is enacted.

(b) Notwithstanding the provisions of subsection (a) or any other provision of law, any person possessing a firearm as defined in section 5845(a) of the Internal Revenue Code of 1954 (as amended by this title) which is not registered to him in the National Firearms Registration and Transfer Record shall register each firearm so possessed with. the Secretary of the Treasury or his delegate in such form and manner as the Secretary or his delegate may require within the thirty days immediately following the effective date of section 201 of this Act. Such registrations shall become a part of the National Firearms Registration and Transfer Record required to be maintained by section 5841 of the Internal Revenue Code of 1954 (as amended by this title), No information or evidence required to be submitted or retained by a natural person to register a firearm under this section shall be used, directly or indirectly, as evidence against such person in any criminal proceeding with respect to a prior or concurrent violation of law.

(c) The amendments made by sections 202 through 206 of this title shall take effect on the date of enactment,

(d) The Secretary of the Treasury, after publication in the Federal Register of his intention to do so, is authorized to establish such periods of amnesty, not to exceed ninety days in the case of any single period, and immunity from liability during any such period, as the Secretary determines will contribute to the purposes of this title.

TITLE III—AMENDMENTS TO TITLE VII OF THE OMNIBUS CRIME CONTROL AND SAFE STREETS ACT OF 1968

SEC. 301. (a) Title VII of the Omnibus Crime Control and Safe Streets Act of 1968 (Public Law 90-351) is amended—

(1) by striking out "other than honorably discharged" in section 1201, and substituting therefor "discharged under dishonorable conditions"; and

(2) by striking out "other than honorable conditions" in sub- sections (a) (2) and (b) (2) of section 1202 and substituting there- for in each instance "dishonorable conditions".

(b) Section 1202(c) (2) of such title is amended to read as follows:

"(2) 'felony' means any offense punishable by imprisonment, for a term exceeding one year, but does not include any offense (other than one involving a firearm or explosive) classified as a misdemeanor under the laws of a State and punishable by a term of imprisonment of two years or less;"

SEC. 302. The amendments made by paragraphs (1) and (2) of subsection (a) of section 301 shall take effect as of June 19, 1968.

Approved October 22, 1968.

Congressional Report on the Right to Keep and Bear Arms (1982)

In 1982, a joint subcommittee of the House of Representatives and the Senate convened to research and to document the history and the true intent of the Right to Keep and Bear Arms as set forth in the Second Amendment to the Constitution of the United States. The subcommittee produced a lengthy (151 pages), thorough, and extensively footnoted report that includes one of the most complete discussions of the history of the Right to Keep and Bear Arms and the Second Amendment to that date.

In fact, the report includes two summary histories of the Right to Keep and Bear Arms. One occupies pages 1 through 9 of the body of the report (pages ___ through ___ of this book). Further along, the report incorporates by reference a longer history of the Right to Keep and Bear Arms written by David T. Hardy, Esq. This history is found at pages 34 through 48 of the document (pages ___ through __ of this book).

At the conclusion of his preface to the report, Senator Orrin Hatch, the Chairman of the subcommittee, wrote:

> "When our ancestors forged a land "conceived in liberty", they did so with musket and rifle. When they reacted to attempts to dissolve their free institutions, and established their identity as a free nation, they did so as a nation of armed freemen. When the sought to record forever a guarantee of their rights, they devoted one full amendment out of ten to nothing but the protection of their right to keep and bear arms against government interference."

The body of the report was highly critical of the Bureau of Alcohol, Tobacco and Firearms (BATF—currently the Bureau of Alcohol, Tobacco, Firearms and Explosives, or BATFE) for exceeding its statutory authority and for "... trampl[ing] upon the second amendment by chilling exercise of the right to keep and bear arms by law-abiding citizens." The report concludes that the Gun Control Act of 1968 should be amended to correct and prevent government abuses of citizens who had no intention or motive to violate highly technical (and sometimes unpublished) laws and regulations.

Today, in this writer's opinion, the primary value of this report lies in the excellent historical context it provides as background to the Second Amendment and the Right to Keep and Bear Arms. That said, the body of the report (that is, the official opinion of a bi-partisan, bi-cameral subcommittee of the 97th Congress of the United States, included the following conclusions:

> "The Second Amendment right to keep and bear arms therefore, is a right of the individual citizen to privately posses and carry in a peaceful manner firearms and similar arms. Such an "individual rights" interpretation is in full accord with the history of the right to keep and bear arms, as previously discussed. It is moreover in accord with contemporaneous statements and formulations of the right by such founders of this nation as Thomas Jefferson and Samuel Adams, and accurately reflects the majority of the proposals which led up to the Bill of Rights itself."

> "Finally, the individual rights interpretation gives full meaning to the words chosen by the first Congress to reflect the right to keep and bear arms. The framers of the Bill of Rights consistently used the words "right of the people" to reflect individual rights—as when these words were used to recognize the "right of the people" to peaceably assemble, and the "right of the people" against unreasonable searches and seizures. They distinguished between the rights of the people and of the state in the Tenth Amendment."

> "That the National Guard is not the "Militia" referred to in the second amendment is even clearer today. Congress has organized the National Guard under its power to "raise and support armies" and not its power to "Provide for organizing, arming and disciplining the Militia"."

> "The conclusion is thus inescapable that the history, concept, and wording of the second amendment to the Constitution of the United States, as well as its interpretation by every major commentator and court in the first half-century after its ratification, indicates that what is protected is an individual right of a private citizen to own and carry firearms in a peaceful manner."

Note: Although this report is an official government document, produced by a subcommittee of the United States Congress, it is difficult or impossible to find it on any United States government web site. The full report can be found on-line at:
https://constitution.org/1-Activism/mil/rkba82.pdf

Note: Because of mechanical issues affecting the production of paperback books, I learned that the size of this book as planned exceeded the maximum page count by more than 200 pages. Along with dissenting opinions in the Supreme Court decisions for the Heller and McDonald cases, I also reluctantly made the decision to omit the several essays regarding the right to keep and bear arms that form a lengthy appendix to the Congressional subcommittee report. These outside opinions are of considerable potential interest to legal scholars, but they are not part of the body of the report and thus do not represent the final conclusions of the report. Readers who wish to peruse the supplementary opinions attached to the report can find them in the on-line version of the report at the Internet address provided above.

THE RIGHT TO KEEP AND BEAR ARMS

Report of the Subcommittee on the Constitution

United States Senate
Ninety-Seventh Congress

Second Session

97th Congress
2d Session

COMMITTEE PRINT

THE RIGHT TO KEEP AND BEAR ARMS

REPORT

OF THE

SUBCOMMITTEE ON THE CONSTITUTION

OF THE

COMMITTEE ON THE JUDICIARY

UNITED STATES SENATE

NINETY-SEVENTH CONGRESS

SECOND SESSION

FEBRUARY 1982

Printed for the use of the Committee on the Judiciary

U.S. GOVERNMENT PRINTING OFFICE
88-618 O WASHINGTON : 1982

For sale by the Superintendent of Documents, U. S. Government Printing Office
Washington, D.C. 20402

COMMITTEE ON THE JUDICIARY

STROM THURMOND, South Carolina, *Chairman*

CHARLES McC. MATHIAS, JR., Maryland
PAUL LAXALT, Nevada
ORRIN G. HATCH, Utah
ROBERT DOLE, Kansas
ALAN K. SIMPSON, Wyoming
JOHN P. EAST, North Carolina
CHARLES E. GRASSLEY, Iowa
JEREMIAH DENTON, Alabama
ARLEN SPECTER, Pennsylvania

JOSEPH R. BIDEN, Delaware
EDWARD M. KENNEDY, Massachusetts
ROBERT C. BYRD, West Virginia
HOWARD M. METZENBAUM, Ohio
DENNIS DECONCINI, Arizona
PATRICK J. LEAHY, Vermont
MAX BAUCUS, Montana
HOWELL HEPLIN, Alabama

VINTON DE VANE LIDE, *Chief Counsel*
QUENTIN CROMMELIN, *Jr.*, *Staff Director*

SUBCOMMITTEE ON THE CONSTITUTION

ORIN G. HATCH, Utah, *Chairman*

STROM THURMOND, South Carolina
CHARLES E. GRASSLEY, Iowa

DENNIS DECONCINI, Arizona
PATRICK J. LEAHY, Vermont

Stephen J. Markman, *Chief Counsel and Staff Director*
Randall Rader, *General Counsel*
Peter E. Ornsby, *Counsel*
Robert Feidler, *Minority Counsel*

CONTENTS

PREFACE

"To preserve liberty, it is essential that the whole body of the people always possess arms, and be taught alike, especially when young, how to use them." (Richard Henry Lee, Virginia delegate to the Continental Congress, initiator of the Declaration of Independence, and member of the first Senate, which passed the Bill of Rights.)

"The great object is that every man be armed . . . Everyone who is able may have a gun." (Patrick Henry, in the Virginia Convention on the ratification of the Constitution.)

"The advantage of being armed . . . the Americans possess over the people of all other nations . . . Notwithstanding the military establishments in the several Kingdoms of Europe, which are carried as far as the public resources will bear, the governments are afraid to trust the people with arms." (James Madison, author of the Bill of Rights, in his Federalist Paper No. 26.)

"A well regulated Militia, being necessary to the security of a free State, the right of the people to keep and bear Arms, shall not be infringed." (Second Amendment to the Constitution.)

In my studies as an attorney and as a United States Senator, I have constantly been amazed by the indifference or even hostility shown the Second Amendment by courts, legislatures, and commentators. James Madison would be startled to hear that his recognition of a right to keep and bear arms, which passed the House by a voice vote without objection and hardly a debate, has since been construed in but a single, and most ambiguous, Supreme Court decision, whereas his proposals for freedom of religion, which he made reluctantly out of fear that they would be rejected or narrowed beyond use, and those for freedom of assembly, which passed only after a lengthy and bitter debate, are the subject of scores of detailed and favorable decisions. Thomas Jefferson, who kept a veritable armory of pistols, rifles and shotguns at Monticello, and advised his nephew to forsake other sports in favor of hunting, would be astounded to hear supposed civil libertarians claim firearm ownership should be restricted. Samuel Adams, a handgun owner who pressed for an amendment stating that the "Constitution shall never be construed . . . to prevent the people of the United States who are peaceable citizens from keeping their own arms," would be shocked to hear that his native state today imposes a year's sentence, without probation or parole, for carrying a firearm without a police permit.

This is not to imply that courts have totally ignored the impact of the Second Amendment in the Bill of Rights. No fewer than twenty-one decisions by the courts of our states have recognized an individual right to keep and bear arms, and a majority of these have not only recognized the right but invalidated laws or regulations which abridged it. Yet in all too many instances, courts or commentators have sought, for reasons only tangentially related to constitutional history, to construe this right out of existence. They argue that the Second Amendment's words "right of the people" mean "a right of the state"—apparently overlooking the impact of those same words when used in the First and Fourth Amendments. The "right of the people" to assemble or to be free from unreasonable searches and seizures is not contested as an individual guarantee. Still they ignore consistency and claim that the right to "bear arms" relates only to military uses. This not only violates a consistent constitutional reading of "right of the people" but also ignores that the second amendment protects a right to "keep" arms. These commentators contend instead that the amendment's preamble regarding the necessity of a "well regulated militia . . . to a free state" means that the right to keep and bear arms applies only to a National Guard. Such a reading fails to note that the Framers used the term "militia" to relate to every citizen capable of bearing arms, and that Congress has established the present National Guard under its power to raise armies, expressly stating that it was not doing so under its power to organize and arm the militia.

When the first Congress convened for the purpose of drafting a Bill of Rights, it delegated the task to James Madison. Madison did not write upon a blank tablet. Instead, he obtained a pamphlet listing the State proposals for a bill of rights and sought to produce a briefer version incorporating all the vital proposals of these. His purpose was to incorporate, not distinguish by technical changes, proposals such as that of the Pennsylvania minority, Sam Adams, or the New Hampshire delegates. Madison proposed among other rights that "That right of the people to keep and bear arms shall not be infringed; a well armed and well regulated militia being the best security of a free country; but no person religiously scrupulous of bearing arms shall be compelled to render military service in person." In the House, this was initially modified so that the militia clause came before the proposal recognizing the right. The proposals for the Bill of Rights were then trimmed in the interests of brevity. The conscientious objector clause was removed following objections by Elbridge Gerry, who complained that future Congresses might abuse the exemption to excuse everyone from military service.

The proposal finally passed the House in its present form: "A well regulated militia, being necessary to the security of a free state, the right of the people to keep and bear arms, shall not be infringed.:" In this form it was submitted into the Senate, which passed it the following day. The Senate in the process indicated its intent that the right be an individual one, for private purposes, by rejecting an amendment which would have limited the keeping and bearing of arms to bearing "For the common defense".

The earliest American constitutional commentators concurred in giving this broad reading to the amendment. When St. George Tucker, later Chief Justice of the Virginia Supreme Court, in 1803 published an edition of Blackstone annotated to American law, he followed Blackstone's citation of the right of the subject "of having arms suitable to their condition and degree, and such as are allowed by law" with a citation to the Second Amendment, "And this without any qualification as to their condition or degree, as is the case in the British government." William Rawle's "View of the Constitution" published in Philadelphia in 1825 noted that under the Second Amendment: "The prohibition is general. No clause in the Constitution could by a rule of construction be conceived to give to Congress a power to disarm the people. Such a flagitious attempt could only be made under some general pretense by a state legislature. But if in blind pursuit of inordinate power, either should attempt it, this amendment may be appealed to as a restraint on both." The Jefferson papers in the Library of Congress show that both Tucker and Rawle were friends of, and corresponded with, Thomas Jefferson. Their views are those of contemporaries of Jefferson, Madison and others, and are entitled to special weight. A few years later, Joseph Story in his "Commentaries on the Constitution" considered the right to keep and bear arms as "the palladium of the liberties of the republic", which deterred tyranny and enabled the citizenry at large to overthrow it should it come to pass.

Subsequent legislation in the second Congress likewise supports the interpretation of the Second Amendment that creates an individual right. In the Militia Act of 1792, the second Congress defined "militia of the United States" to include almost every free adult male in the United States. These persons were obligated by law to possess a firearm and a minimum supply of ammunition and military equipment. This statute, incidentally, remained in effect into the early years of the present century as a legal requirement of gun ownership for most of the population of the United States. There can be little doubt from this that when the Congress and the people spoke of a "militia", they had reference to the traditional concept of the entire populace capable of bearing arms, and not to any formal group such as what is today called the National Guard. The purpose was to create an armed citizenry, which the political theorists at the time considered essential to ward off tyranny. From this militia, appropriate measures might create a "well regulated militia" of individuals trained in their duties and responsibilities as citizens and owners of firearms.

If gun laws in fact worked, the sponsors of this type of legislation should have no difficulty drawing upon long lists of examples of crime rates reduced by such legislation. That they cannot do so after a century and a half of trying—that they must sweep under the rug the southern attempts at gun control in the 1870-1910 period, the northeastern attempts in the 1920-1939 period, the attempts at both Federal and State levels in 1965-1976—establishes the repeated, complete and inevitable failure of gun laws to control serious crime.

Immediately upon assuming chairmanship of the Subcommittee on the Constitution, I sponsored the report which follows as an effort to study, rather than ignore, the history of the controversy over the right to keep and bear arms. Utilizing the research capabilities of the Subcommittee on the Constitution, the resources of the Library of Congress, and the assistance of constitutional scholars such as Mary Kaaren Jolly, Steven Halbrook, and David T. Hardy, the subcommittee has managed to uncover information on the right to keep and bear arms which documents quite clearly its status as a major individual right of American citizens. We did not guess at the purpose of the British 1689 Declaration of Rights; we located the Journals of the House of Commons and private notes of the Declaration's sponsors, now dead for two centuries. We did not make suppositions as to colonial interpretations of that Declaration's right to keep arms; we examined colonial newspapers which discussed it. We did not speculate as to the intent of the framers of the second amendment; we examined James Madison's drafts for it, his handwritten outlines of speeches upon the Bill of Rights, and discussions of the second amendment by early scholars who were personal friends of Madison, Jefferson, and Washington and wrote while these still lived. What the Subcommittee on the Constitution uncovered was clear—and long-lost—proof that the second amendment to our Constitution was intended as an individual right of the American citizen to keep and carry arms in a peaceful manner, for protection of himself, his family, and his freedoms. The summary of our research and findings forms the first portion of this report.

In the interest of fairness and the presentation of a complete picture, we also invited groups which were likely to oppose this recognition of freedoms to submit their views. The statements of two associations who replied are reproduced here following the report of the Subcommittee. The Subcommittee also invited statements by Messrs. Halbrook and Hardy, and by the National Rifle Association, whose statements likewise follow our report.

When I became chairman of the Subcommittee on the Constitution, I hoped that I would be able to assist in the protection of the constitutional rights of American citizens, rights which have too often been eroded in the belief that government could be relied upon for quick solutions to difficult problems.

Both as an American citizen and as a United States Senator I repudiate this view. I likewise repudiate the approach of those who believe to solve American problems you simply become something other than American. To my mind, the uniqueness of our free institutions, the fact that an American citizen can boast freedoms unknown in any other land, is all the more reason to resist any erosion of our individual rights. When our ancestors forged a land "conceived in liberty", they did so with musket and rifle. When they reacted to attempts to dissolve their free institutions, and established their identity as a free nation, they did so as a nation of armed freemen. When they sought to record forever a guarantee of their rights, they devoted one full amendment out of ten to nothing but the protection of their right to keep and bear arms against government interference. Under my chairmanship the Subcommittee on the Constitution will concern itself with a proper recognition of, and respect for, this right most valued by free men.

ORRIN G. HATCH,
Chairman,
Subcommittee on the Constitution.

JANUARY 20, 1982.

The right to bear arms is a tradition with deep roots in American society. Thomas Jefferson proposed that "no free man shall ever be debarred the use of arms," and Samuel Adams called for an amendment banning any law "to prevent the people of the United States who are peaceable citizens from keeping their own arms." The Constitution of the State of Arizona, for example, recognizes the "right of an individual citizen to bear arms in defense of himself or the State."

Even though the tradition has deep roots, its application to modern America is the subject of intense controversy. Indeed, it is a controversy into which the Congress is beginning, once again, to immerse itself. I have personally been disappointed that so important an issue should have generally been so thinly researched and so minimally debated both in Congress and the courts. Our Supreme Court has but once touched on its meaning at the Federal level and that decision, now nearly a half-century old, is so ambiguous that any school of thought can find some support in it. All Supreme Court decisions on the second amendment's application to the States came in the last century, when constitutional law was far different than it is today. As ranking minority member of the Subcommittee on the Constitution, I, therefore, welcome the effort which led to this report—a report based not only upon the independent research of the subcommittee staff, but also upon full and fair presentation of the cases by all interested groups and individual scholars.

I personally believe that it is necessary for the Congress to amend the Gun Control Act of 1968. I welcome the opportunity to introduce this discussion of how best these amendments might be made.

The Constitution subcommittee staff has prepared this monograph bringing together proponents of both sides of the debate over the 1968 Act. I believe that the statements contained herein present the arguments fairly and thoroughly. I commend Senator Hatch, chairman of the subcommittee, for having this excellent reference work prepared. I am sure that it will be of great assistance to the Congress as it debates the second amendment and considers legislation to amend the Gun Control Act.

DENNIS DECONCINI,
Ranking Minority Member,
Subcommittee On the Constitution.

JANUARY 20, 1982.

The right to keep and bear arms as a part of English and American law antedates not only the Constitution, but also the discovery of firearms. Under the laws of Alfred the Great, whose reign began in 872 A. D., all English citizens from the nobility to the peasants were obliged to privately purchase weapons and be available for military duty.[1] This was in sharp contrast to the feudal system as it evolved in Europe, under which armament and military duties were concentrated in the nobility. The body of armed citizens were known as the "fyrd".

While a great many of the Saxon rights were abridged following the Norman conquest, the right and duty of arms possession was retained. Under the Assize of Arms of 1181, "the whole community of freemen" between the ages of 15 and 40 were required by law to possess certain arms, which were arranged in proportion to their possessions.[2] They were required twice a year to demonstrate to Royal Officials that they were appropriately armed. In 1253, another Assize of Arms expanded the duty of armament to include not only freeman, but also villeins, who were the English equivalent of serfs. Now all "citizens, burgesses, free tenants, villeins and others from 15 to 60 years of age" were obliged to be armed.[3] While on the Continent the villeins were regarded as little more than animals hungering for rebellion, the English legal system not only permitted, but affirmatively required them, to be armed.

The thirteenth century saw further definitions of this right as the long bow, a formidable armor-piercing weapon, became increasingly the mainstay of British national policy. In 1285, Edward I commanded that all persons comply with the earlier Assizes and added that "anyone else who can afford them shall keep bows and arrows".[4] The right of armament was subject only to narrow limitations. In 1279, it was ordered that those appearing in Parliament or other public assemblies "shall come without all force and armor, well and peaceably".[5] In 1328, the statute of Northampton ordered that no one use their arms in "affray of the peace, nor to go nor ride armed by day or by night in fairs, markets, nor in the presence of the justices or other ministers".[6] English courts construed this ban consistently with the general right of private armament as applying only to wearing of arms "accompanied with such circumstances as are apt to terrify the people".[7] In 1369, the King ordered that the sheriffs of London require all citizens "at leisure time on holidays" to "use in their recreation bowes and arrows" and to stop all other games which might distract them from this practice.[8]

The Tudor kings experimented with limits upon specialized weapons—mainly crossbows and the then-new firearms. These measures were not intended to disarm the citizenry, but on the contrary, to prevent their being diverted from longbow practice by (pg 2) sport with other weapons which were considered less effective. Even these narrow measures were shortlived. In 1503, Henry VII limited shooting (but not possession) of crossbows to those with land worth 200 marks annual rental, but provided an exception for those who "shote owt of a howse for the lawefull defens of the same".[9] In 1511, Henry VIII increased the property requirement to 300 marks. He also expanded the requirement of longbow ownership, requiring all citizens to "use and exercyse shootyng in longbowes, and also have a bowe and arrowes contynually" in the house.[10] Fathers were required by law to purchase bows and arrows for their sons between the age of 7 and 14 and to train them in longbow use.

In 1514 the ban on crossbows was extended to include firearms.[11] But in 1533, Henry reduced the property qualification to 100 pounds per year; in 1541 he limited it to possession of small firearms ("of the length of one hole yard" for some firearms and "thre quarters of a yarde" for others)[12] and eventually he repealed the entire statute by proclamation.[13] The later Tudor monarchs continued the system and Elizabeth added to it by creating what came to be known as "train bands", selected portions of the citizenry chosen for special training. These trained bands were distinguished from the "militia", which term was first used during the Spanish Armada crisis to designate the entire of the armed citizenry.[14]

The militia continued to be a pivotal force in the English political system. The British historian Charles Oman considers the existence of the armed citizenry to be a major reason for the moderation of monarchical rule in Great Britain; "More than once he [Henry VIII] had to restrain himself, when he discovered that the general feeling of his subjects was against him.... His 'gentlemen pensioners' and his yeomen of the guard were but a handful, and bills or bows were in every farm and cottage".[15]

When civil war broke out in 1642, the critical issue was whether the King or Parliament had the right to control the militia.[16] The aftermath of the civil war saw England in temporary control of a military government, which repeatedly dissolved Parliament and authorized its officers to "search for, and seize all arms" owned by Catholics, opponents of the government, "or any other person whom the commissioners had judged dangerous to the peace of this Commonwealth".[17] The military government ended with the restoration of Charles II. Charles in turn opened his reign with a variety of repressive legislation, expanding the definition of treason, establishing press censorship and ordering his supporters to form their own troops, "the officers to be numerous, disaffected persons watched and not allowed to assemble, and their arms seized".[18] In 1662, a Militia Act was enacted empowering officials "to search for and seize all arms in the custody or possession of any person or persons whom the said lieutenants or any two or more of their deputies shall judge dangerous to the peace of the kingdom".[19] Gunsmiths were ordered to deliver to the government lists of all purchasers.[20] These confiscations were continued under James II, who directed them particularly against the Irish populations: "Although the country was infested by predatory bands, a Protestant gentleman could scarcely obtain permission to keep a brace of pistols."[21]

In 1668, the government of James was overturned in a peaceful uprising which came to be known as "The Glorious Revolution". Parliament resolved that James had abdicated and promulgated a Declaration of Rights, later enacted as the Bill of Rights. Before coronation, his successor William of Orange, was required to swear to respect these rights. The debates in the House of Commons over this Declaration of Rights focused largely upon the disarmament under the 1662 Militia Act. One member complained that "an act of Parliament was made to disarm all Englishmen, who the lieutenant should suspect, by day or night, by force or otherwise—this was done in Ireland for the sake of putting arms into Irish hands." The speech of another is summarized as "militia bill—power to disarm all England—now done in Ireland." A third complained "Arbitrary power exercised by the ministry.... Militia .... imprisoning without reason; disarming—himself disarmed." Yet another summarized his complaints "Militia Act—an abominable thing to disarm the nation. ..."[22]

The Bill of Rights, as drafted in the House of Commons, simply provided that "the acts concerning the militia are grievous to the subject" and that "it is necessary for the public Safety that the Subjects, which are Protestants, should provide and keep arms for the common defense; And that the Arms which have been seized, and taken from them, be restored."[23] The House of Lords changed this to make it a more positive declaration of an individual right under English law: "That the subjects which are Protestant may have arms for their defense suitable to their conditions and as allowed by law."[24] The only limitation was on ownership by Catholics, who at that time composed only a few percent of the British population and were subject to a wide variety of punitive legislation. The Parliament subsequently made clear what it meant by "suitable to their conditions and as allowed by law". The poorer citizens had been restricted from owning firearms, as well as traps and other commodities useful for hunting, by the 1671 Game Act. Following the Bill of Rights, Parliament reenacted that statute, leaving its operative parts unchanged with one exception—which removed the word "guns" from the list of items forbidden to the poorer citizens.[25] The right to keep and bear arms would henceforth belong to all English subjects, rich and poor alike.

In the colonies, availability of hunting and need for defense led to armament statues comparable to those of the early Saxon times. In 1623, Virginia forbade its colonists to travel unless they were "well armed"; in 1631 it required colonists to engage in target practice on Sunday and to "bring their peeces to church."[26] In 1658 it required every householder to have a functioning firearm within his house and in 1673 its laws provided that a citizen who claimed he was too poor to purchase a firearm would have one purchased for him by the government, which would then require him to pay a reasonable price when able to do so.[27] In Massachusetts, the first session of the legislature ordered that not only freemen, but also indentured servants own firearms and in 1644 it imposed a stern 6 shilling fine upon any citizen who was not armed.[28]

When the British government began to increase its military presence in the colonies in the mid-eighteenth century, Massachusetts responded by calling upon its citizens to arm themselves in defense. One colonial newspaper argued that it was impossible to complain that this act was illegal since they were "British subjects, to whom the privilege of possessing arms is expressly recognized by the Bill of Rights" while another argued that this "is a natural right which the people have reserved to themselves, confirmed by the Bill of Rights, to keep arms for their own defense".[29] The newspaper cited Blackstone's commentaries on the laws of England, which had listed the "having and using arms for self preservation and defense" among the "absolute rights of individuals." The colonists felt they had an absolute right at common law to own firearms.

Together with freedom of the press, the right to keep and bear arms became one of the individual rights most prized by the colonists. When British troops seized a militia arsenal in September, 1774, and incorrect rumors that colonists had been killed spread through Massachusetts, 60,000 citizens took up arms.[30] A few months later, when Patrick Henry delivered his famed "Give me liberty or give me death" speech, he spoke in support of a proposition "that a well regulated militia, composed of gentlemen and freemen, is the natural strength and only security of a free government...." Throughout the following revolution, formal and informal units of armed citizens obstructed British communication, cut off foraging parties, and harassed the thinly stretched regular forces. When seven states adopted state "bills of rights" following the Declaration of Independence, each of those bills of rights provided either for protection of the concept of a militia or for an express right to keep and bear arms.[31]

Following the revolution but previous to the adoption of the Constitution, debates over militia proposals occupied a large part of the political scene. A variety of plans were put forth by figures ranging from George Washington to Baron von Steuben.[32] All of the proposals called for a general duty of all citizens to be armed, although some proposals (most notably von Steuben's) also emphasized a "select militia" which would be paid for its services and given special training. In this respect, this "select militia" was the successor of the "trained bands" and the predecessor of what is today the "national guard". In the debates over the Constitution, von Steubon's proposals were criticized as undemocratic. In Connecticut one writer complained of a proposal that "this looks too much like Baron von Steubon's militia, by which a standing army was meant and intended."[33] In Pennsylvania, a delegate argued "Congress may give us a select militia which will, in fact, be a standing army—or Congress, afraid of a general militia, may say there will be no militia at all. When a select militia is formed, the people in general may be disarmed."[34] Richard Henry Lee, in his widely read pamphlet "Letters from the Federal Farmer to the Republican" worried that the people might be disarmed "by modelling the militia. Should one fifth or one eighth part of the people capable of bearing arms be made into a select militia, as has been proposed, and those the young and ardent parts of the community, possessed of little or no property, the former will answer all the purposes of an army, while the latter will be defenseless." He proposed that "the Constitution ought to secure a genuine, and guard against a select militia," adding that "to preserve liberty, it is essential that the whole body of the people always possess arms and be taught alike, especially when young, how to use them."[35]

The suspicion of select militia units expressed in these passages is a clear indication that the framers of the Constitution did not seek to guarantee a State right to maintain formed groups similar to the National Guard, but rather to protect the right of individual citizens to keep and bear arms. Lee, in particular, sat in the Senate which approved the Bill of Rights. He would hardly have meant the second amendment to apply only to the select militias he so feared and disliked.

Other figures of the period were of like mind. In the Virginia convention, George Mason, drafter of the Virginia Bill of Rights, accused the British of having plotted "to disarm the people—that was the best and most effective way to enslave them", while Patrick Henry observed that "The great object is that every man be armed" and "everyone who is able may have a gun".[36]

Nor were the antifederalist, to whom we owe credit for a Bill of Rights, alone on this account. Federalist arguments also provide a source of support for an individual rights view. Their arguments in favor of the proposed Constitution also relied heavily upon universal armament. The proposed Constitution had been heavily criticized for its failure to ban or even limit standing armies. Unable to deny this omission, the Constitution's supporters frequently argued to the people that the universal armament of Americans made such limitations unnecessary. A pamphlet written by Noah Webster, aimed at swaying Pennsylvania toward ratification, observed

> Before a standing army can rule, the people must be disarmed; as they are in almost every kingdom in Europe. The supreme power in America cannot enforce unjust laws by the sword, because the whole body of the people are armed, and constitute a force superior to any band of regular troops that can be, on any pretense, raised in the United States.[37]

In the Massachusetts convention, Sedgwick echoed the same thought, rhetorically asking if an oppressive army could be formed or "if raised, whether they could subdue a Nation of freemen, who know how to prize liberty, and who have arms in their hands?"[38] In Federalist Paper 46, Madison, later author of the Second Amendment, mentioned "The advantage of being armed, which the Americans possess over the people of all other countries" and that "notwithstanding the military establishments in the several kingdoms of Europe, which are carried as far as the public resources will bear, the governments are afraid to trust the people with arms."

A third and even more compelling case for an individual rights perspective on the Second Amendment comes from the State demands for a bill of rights. Numerous state ratifications called for adoption of a Bill of Rights as a part of the Constitution. The first such call came from a group of Pennsylvania delegates. Their proposals, which were not adopted but had a critical effect on future debates, proposed among other rights that "the people have a right to bear arms for the defense of themselves and their own state, or the United States, or for the purpose of killing game; and no law shall be passed for disarming the people or any of them, unless for crimes committed, or a real danger of public injury from individuals."[39] In Massachusetts, Sam Adams unsuccessfully pushed for a ratification conditioned on adoption of a Bill of Rights, beginning with a guarantee "That the said Constitution shall never be construed to authorize Congress to infringe the just liberty of the press or the rights of conscience; or to prevent the people of the United States who are peaceable citizens from keeping their own arms...."[40] When New Hampshire gave the Constitution the ninth vote needed for its passing into effect, it called for adoption of a Bill of Rights which included the provision that "Congress shall never disarm any citizen unless such as are or have been in actual rebellion".[41] Virginia and North Carolina thereafter called for a provision "that the people have the right to keep and bear arms; that a well regulated militia composed of the body of the people trained to arms is the proper, natural and safe defense of a free state."[42]

When the first Congress convened for the purpose of drafting a Bill of Rights, it delegated the task to James Madison. Madison did not write upon a blank tablet. Instead, he obtained a pamphlet listing the State proposals for a Bill of Rights and sought to produce a briefer version incorporating all the vital proposals of these. His purpose was to incorporate, not distinguish by technical changes, proposals such as that of the Pennsylvania minority, Sam Adams, and the New Hampshire delegates. Madison proposed among other rights that:

> "The right of the people to keep and bear arms shall not be infringed; a well armed and well regulated militia being the best security of a free country; but no person religiously scrupulous of bearing arms shall be compelled to render military service in person."[43]

In the House, this was initially modified so that the militia clause came before the proposal recognizing the right. The proposals for the Bill of Rights were then trimmed in the interests of brevity. The conscientious objector clause was removed following objections by Elbridge Gerry, who complained that future Congresses might abuse the exemption for the scrupulous to excuse everyone from militia service. The proposal finally passed the House in its present form: "A well regulated militia, being necessary to the security of a free state, the right of the people to keep and bear arms, shall not be infringed." In this form it was submitted into the Senate, which passed it the following day. The Senate in the process indicated its intent that the right be an individual one, for private purposes, by rejecting an amendment which would have limited the keeping and bearing of arms to bearing "for the common defense".

The earliest American constitutional commentators concurred in giving this broad reading to the amendment. When St. George Tucker, later Chief Justice of the Virginia Supreme Court, in 1803 published an edition of Blackstone annotated to American law, he followed Blackstone's citation of the right of the subject "of having arms suitable to their condition and degree, and such as are allowed by law" with a citation to the Second Amendment, "And this without any qualification as to their condition or degree, as is the case in the British government".[44] William Rawle's "View of the Constitution" published in Philadelphia in 1825 noted that under the Second Amendment

> The prohibition is general. No clause in the Constitution could by a rule of construction be conceived to give to Congress a power to disarm the people. Such a flagitious attempt could only be made under some general pretense by a state

legislature. But if in blind pursuit of inordinate power, either should attempt it, this amendment may be appealed to as a restraint on both."[45]

The Jefferson papers in the Library of Congress show that both Tucker and Rawle were friends of, and corresponded with Thomas Jefferson. This suggests that their assessment, as contemporaries of the Constitution's drafters, should be afforded special consideration.

Later commentators agreed with Tucker and Rawle. For instance, Joseph Story in his "Commentaries on the Constitution" considered the right to keep and bear arms as "the palladium of the liberties of the republic", which deterred tyranny and enabled the citizenry at large to overthrow it should it come to pass.[46]

Subsequent legislation in the Second Congress likewise supports the interpretation of the second amendment that creates an individual right. In the Militia Act of 1792, the second Congress defined "militia of the United States" to include almost every free adult male in the United States. These persons were obliged by law to possess a firearm and a minimum supply of ammunition and military equipment.[47] This statute, incidentally remained in effect into the early years of the present century as a legal requirement of gun ownership for most of the population of the United States. There can be little doubt from this that when the Congress and the people spoke of a "militia", they had reference to the traditional concept of the entire populace capable of bearing arms, and not to any formal group such as what is today called the National Guard. The purpose was to create an armed citizenry, such as the political theorists at the time considered essential to ward off tyranny.From this militia, appropriate measures might create a "well regulated militia" of individuals trained in their duties and responsibilities as citizens and owners of firearms.

The Second Amendment as such was rarely litigated prior to the passage of the Fourteenth Amendment. Prior to that time, most courts accepted that the commands of the federal Bill of Rights did not apply to the states. Since there was no federal firearms legislation at this time, there was no legislation which was directly subject to the Second Amendment, if the accepted interpretations were followed. However, a broad variety of state legislation was struck down under state guarantees of the right to keep and bear arms and even in a few cases, under the Second Amendment, when it came before courts which considered the federal protections applicable to the states. Kentucky in 1813 enacted the first carrying concealed weapon statute in the United States; in 1822 the Kentucky Court of Appeals struck down the law as a violation of the state constitutional protection of the right to keep and bear arms: "And can there be entertained a reasonable doubt but the provisions of that act import a restraint on the right of the citizen to bear arms? The court apprehends it not. The right existed at the adoption of the Constitution; it then had no limit short of the moral power of the citizens to exercise it, and in fact consisted of nothing else but the liberty of the citizen to bear arms."[48] On the other hand, a similar measure was sustained in Indiana, not upon the grounds that a right to keep and bear arms did not apply, but rather upon the notion that a statute banning only concealed carrying still permitted the carrying of arms and merely regulated one possible way of carrying them.[49] A few years later, the Supreme Court of Alabama upheld a similar statute but added "We do not desire to be understood as maintaining, that in regulating the manner of wearing arms, the legislature has no other limit than its own discretion. A statute which, under the pretense of regulation, amounts to a destruction of that right, or which requires arms to be so borne as to render them wholly useless for the purpose of defense, would be clearly unconstitutional."[50] When the Arkansas Supreme Court in 1842 upheld a carrying concealed weapons statute, the chief justice explained that the statute would not "detract anything from the power of the people to defend their free state and the established institutions of the country. It prohibits only the wearing of certain arms concealed. This is simply a regulation as to the manner of bearing such arms as are specified", while the dissenting justice proclaimed "I deny that any just or free government upon earth has the power to disarm its citizens.[51]

Sometimes courts went farther. When in 1837, Georgia totally banned the sale of pistols (excepting the larger pistols "known and used as horsemen's pistols") and other weapons, the Georgia Supreme Court in *Nunn v. State* held the statute unconstitutional under the Second Amendment to the federal Constitution. The court held that the Bill of Rights protected natural rights which were fully as capable of infringement by states as by the federal government and that the Second Amendment provided "the right of the whole people, old and young, men, women and boys, and not militia only, to keep and bear arms of every description, and not merely such as are used by the militia, shall not be infringed, curtailed, or broken in on, in the slightest degree; and all this for the important end to be attained: the rearing up and qualifying of a well regulated militia, so vitally necessary to the security of a free state."[52] Prior to the Civil War, the Supreme Court of the United States likewise indicated that the privileges of citizenship included the individual right to own and carry firearms. In the notorious *Dred Scott* case, the court held that black Americans were not citizens and could not be made such by any state. This decision, which by striking down the Missouri Compromise did so much to bring on the Civil War, listed what the Supreme Court considered the rights of American citizens by way of illustrating what rights would have to be given to black Americans if the Court were to recognize them as full fledged citizens:

> It would give to persons of the negro race, who are recognized as citizens in any one state of the Union, the right to enter every other state, whenever they pleased.... and it would give them full liberty of speech in public and in private upon all subjects upon which its own citizens might meet; to hold public meetings upon political affairs, and to keep and cany arms wherever they went.[53]

Following the Civil War, the legislative efforts which gave us three amendments to the Constitution and our earliest civil rights acts likewise recognized the right to keep and bear arms as an existing constitutional right of the individual citizen and as a right specifically singled out as one protected by the civil rights acts and by the Fourteenth Amendment to the Constitution, against infringement by state authorities. Much of the reconstruction effort in the South had been hinged upon the creation of "black militias" composed of the armed and newly freed blacks, officered largely by black veterans of the Union Army. In the months after the Civil War, the existing southern governments struck at these units with the enactment of "black codes" which either outlawed gun ownership by blacks entirely, or imposed permit systems for them, and permitted the confiscation of firearms owned by blacks. When the Civil Rights Act of 1866 was debated members both of the Senate and the House referred to the disarmament of blacks as a major consideration.[54] Senator Trumbull cited provisions outlawing ownership of arms by blacks as among those which the Civil Rights Act would prevent;[55] Senator Sulsbury complained on the other hand that if the act were to be passed it would prevent his own state from enforcing a law banning gun ownership by individual free blacks.[56] Similar arguments were advanced during the debates over the "anti-KKK act"; its sponsor at one point explained that a section making it a federal crime to deprive a person of "arms or weapons he may have in his house or possession for the defense of his person, family or property" was "intended to enforce the well-known constitutional provisions guaranteeing the right in the citizen to 'keep and bear arms'."[57] Likewise, the debates over the Fourteenth Amendment

Congress frequently referred to the Second Amendment as one of the rights which it intended to guarantee against state action.[58]

Following adoption of the Fourteenth Amendment, however, the Supreme Court held that that Amendment's prohibition against states depriving any persons of their federal "privileges and immunities" was to be given a narrow construction. In particular, the "privileges and immunities" under the Constitution would refer only to those rights which were not felt to exist as a process of natural right, but which were created solely by the Constitution. These might refer to rights such as voting in federal elections and of interstate travel, which would clearly not exist except by virtue of the existence of a federal government and which could not be said to be "natural rights".[59] This paradoxically meant that the rights which most persons would accept as the most important—those flowing from concepts of natural justice—were devalued at the expense of more technical rights. Thus when individuals were charged with having deprived black citizens of their right to freedom of assembly and to keep and bear arms, by violently breaking up a peaceable assembly of black citizens, the Supreme Court in *United States v. Cruikshank*[60] held that no indictment could be properly brought since the right "of bearing arms for a lawful purpose" is "not a right granted by the Constitution. Neither is it in any manner dependent upon that instrument for its existence." Nor, in the view of the Court, was the right to peacefully assemble a right protected by the Fourteenth Amendment: "The right of the people peaceably to assemble for lawful purposes existed long before the adoption of the Constitution of the United States. In fact, it is and has always been one of the attributes of citizenship under a free government.... It was not, therefore, a right granted to the people by the Constitution." Thus the very importance of the rights protected by the First and Second Amendment was used as the basis for the argument that they did not apply to the states . under the Fourteenth Amendment. In later opinions, chiefly *Presser v. Illinois*[61] and *Miller v. Texas,*[62] the Supreme Court adhered to the view. *Cruikshank* has clearly been superseded by twentieth century opinions which hold that portions of the Bill of Rights—and in particular the right to assembly with which *Cruikshank* dealt in addition to the Second Amendment—are binding upon the state governments. Given the legislative history of the Civil Rights Acts and the Fourteenth Amendment, and the more expanded views of incorporation which have become accepted in our own century, it is clear that the right to keep and bear arms was meant to be and should be protected under the civil rights statutes and the Fourteenth Amendment against infringement by officials acting under color of state law.

Within our own century, the only occasion upon which the Second Amendment has reached the Supreme Court came in *United States v. Miller.*[63] There, a prosecution for carrying a sawed off shotgun was dismissed before trial on Second Amendment grounds. In doing so, the court took no evidence as to the nature of the firearm or indeed any other factual matter. The Supreme Court reversed on procedural grounds, holding that the trial court could not take judicial notice of the relationship between a firearm and the Second Amendment, but must receive some manner of evidence. It did not formulate a test nor state precisely what relationship might be required. The court's statement that the amendment was adopted "to assure the continuation and render possible the effectiveness of such [militia] forces" and "must be interpreted and applied with that end in view", when combined with the court's statement that all constitutional sources "show plainly enough that the militia comprised all males physically capable of acting in concert for the common defense.... these men were expected to appear bearing arms supplied by themselves and of the kind in common use at the time,"[64] suggests that at the very least private ownership by a person capable of self defense and using an ordinary privately owned firearm must be protected by the Second Amendment. What the Court did not do in *Miller* is even more striking: It did not suggest that the lower court take evidence on whether Miller belonged to the National Guard or a similar group. The hearing was to be on the nature of the firearm, not on the nature of its use; nor is there a single suggestion that National Guard status is relevant to the case.

The Second Amendment right to keep and bear arms therefore, is a right of the individual citizen to privately posses and carry in a peaceful manner firearms and similar arms. Such an "individual rights" interpretation is in full accord with the history of the right to keep and bear arms, as previously discussed. It is moreover in accord with contemporaneous statements and formulations of the right by such founders of this nation as Thomas Jefferson and Samuel Adams, and accurately reflects the majority of the proposals which led up to the Bill of Rights itself. A number of state constitutions, adopted prior to or contemporaneously with the federal Constitution and Bill of Rights, similarly provided for a right of the people to keep and bear arms. If in fact this language creates a right protecting the states only, there might be a reason for it to be inserted in the federal Constitution but no reason for it to be inserted in state constitutions. State bills of rights necessarily protect only against action by the state, and by definition a state cannot infringe its own rights; to attempt to protect a right belonging to the state by inserting it in a limitation of the state's own powers would create an absurdity. The fact that the contemporaries of the framers did insert these words into several state constitutions would indicate clearly that they viewed the right as belonging to the individual citizen, thereby making it a right which could be infringed either by state or federal government and which must be protected against infringement by both.

Finally, the individual rights interpretation gives full meaning to the words chosen by the first Congress to reflect the right to keep and bear arms. The framers of the Bill of Rights consistently used the words "right of the people" to reflect individual rights—as when these words were used to recognize the "right of the people" to peaceably assemble, and the "right of the people" against unreasonable searches and seizures. They distinguished between the rights of the people and of the state in the Tenth Amendment. As discussed earlier, the "militia" itself referred to a concept of a universally armed people, not to any specifically organized unit. When the framers referred to the equivalent of our National Guard, they uniformly used the term "select militia" and distinguished this from "militia". Indeed, the debates over the Constitution constantly referred to organized militia units as a threat to freedom comparable to that of a standing army, and stressed that such organized units did not constitute, and indeed were philosophically opposed to, the concept of a militia.

That the National Guard is not the "Militia" referred to in the second amendment is even clearer today. Congress has organized the National Guard under its power to "raise and support armies" and not its power to "Provide for organizing, arming and disciplining the Militia".[65] This Congress chose to do in the interests of organizing reserve military units which were not limited in deployment by the strictures of our power over the constitutional militia, which can be called forth only "to execute the laws of the Union, suppress insurrections and repel invasions." The modern National Guard was specifically intended to avoid status as the constitutional militia, a distinction recognized by 10 U.S.C. Sec 31 l(a).

The conclusion is thus inescapable that the history, concept, and wording of the second amendment to the Constitution of the United States, as well as its interpretation by every major commentator and court in the first half-century after its ratification, indicates that what is protected is an individual right of a private citizen to own and carry firearms in a peaceful manner.

REFERENCES

[1] Charles Hollister, Anglo-Saxon Military Institutions 11-42 (Oxford University Press 1962); Francis Grose, Military Antiquities Respecting a History of the British Army, Vol. I at 1-2 (London, 1812).

[2] Grose, supra, at 9-11; Bruce Lyon, A Constitutional and Legal History of Medieval England 273 (2d. ed. New York 1980).

[3] J. J. Bagley and P. B. Rowley, A Documentary History of England 1066-1540, Vol. 1 at 155-56 (New York 1965).

[4] Statute of Winchester (13 Edw. I c. 6). See also Bagley and Rowley, supra at 158.

[5] 7 Ed. I c. 2 (1279).

[6] Statute of Northampton (2 Edw. III c. 3).

[7] Rex v. Knight, 90 Eng. Rep. 330; 87 Eng. Rep. 75 (King's Bench, 1686).

[8] E. G. Heath, The Grey Goose Wing 109 (London, 1971).

[9] 19 Hen. VII c. 4 (1503).

[10] 3 Hen. VIII c. 13 (1511).

[11] 64 Hen. VIII c. 13 (1514).

[12] 33 Hen. VIII c. 6 (1514).

[13] Noel Perrin, Giving Up the Gun 59-60 (Boston, 1979).

[14] Jim Hill, The Minuteman in War and Peace 26-27 (Harrisburg, 1968).

[15] Charles Oman. A History of the Art of War in the Sixteenth Century 288 (New York. 1937).

[16] William Blackstone, Commentaries, Vol. 2 at 412 (St. George Tucker, ed., Philadelphia 1803).

[17] "An Act for Settling the Militia," Ordinances and Acts of the Interregnum, Vol. 2 1320 (London, HMSO 1911).

[18] 8 Calendar of State Papers (Domestic), Charles II, No. 188, p. 150.

[19] 14 Car. II c. 3 (1662).

[20] Joyce Malcolm, Disarmed: The Loss of the Right to Bear Arms in Restoration England, at 11 (Mary Ingraham Bunting Institute, Radcliffe College 1980).

[21] Thomas Macaulay, The History of England from the Accession of Charles II, Vol. II at 137 (London, 1856).

[22] Phillip, Earl of Hardwicke, Miscellaneous State Papers from 1501-1726, vol. 2 at 407-17 (London, 1778).

[23] J. R. Western, Monarchy and Revolution: The English State in the 1680's, at 339 (Totowa, N.J., 1972).

[24] Journal of the House of Commons from December 26, 1688, to October 26, 1693, at 29. (London, 1742). The Bill of Rights was ultimately enacted in this form. 1 Gul. and Mar., Sess. 2, c. 2 (1689).

[25] Joyce Malcolm, supra, at 16.

[26] William Hening, The Statutes at Large: Being a Collection of All the Laws of Virginia from the First Session of the Legislature in 1619, at pp. 127, 173-74 (New York, 1823).

[27] Id.

[28] William Brigham, The Compact with the Charter and Laws of the Colony of New Plymouth, 31, 76 (Boston, 1836).

[29] Oliver Dickerson, ed., Boston Under Military Rule, 61, 79, (Boston, 1936).

[30] Steven Patterson. Political Parties in Revolutionary Massachusetts, at 103 (Univ. of Wisconsin Press, 1973).

[31] See Sprecher, The Lost Amendment, 51 A.B.A.J. 554, 665 (1965).

[32] The most extensive studies of these militia proposals are John McAuley Palmer, Washington, Lincoln, Wilson: Three War Statesmen (New York, 1930); Frederick Stern,

Citizen Army (New York, 1957); John Mahon, The American Militia: Decade of Decision 1789-1800 (Univ of Florida, 1960).

33. Merrill Jensen, ed., The Documentary of History of the Ratification of the Constitution, vol. 3 at 378 (Madison, Wisc.).

34. Id., vol. 2 at 508.

35. Walter Bennett, eu., Letters from the Federal Farmer to the Republican, at 21, 22, 124 (Univ. of Alabama Press, 1975).

36. Debates and other Proceedings of the Convention of Virginia, . . . taken in shorthand by David Robertson of Petersburg, at 271, 275 (2d ed. Richmond, 1805).

37. Noah Webster, "An Examination into the Leading Principles of the Federal Constitution . . .", in Paul Ford, ed., Pamphlets on the Constitution of the United States, at 56 (New York, 1888).

38. Johnathan Elliott, ed., Debates in the Several State Conventions on the Adoption of the Federal Constitution, vol. 2 at 97 (2d ed., 1888).

39. Merrill Jensen, supra, vol. 2 at 597-98.

40. Debates and Proceedings in the Convention of the Commonwealth of Massachusetts, at 86-87 (Peirce & Hale, eds., Boston, 1850); 2 B. Schwartz, the Bill of Rights 675 (1971).

41. Documents Illustrative of the Formation of the Union of the American States, at 1026 (Washington, D.C.: GPO, 1927).

42. Id. at 1030.

43. Annals of Congress 434 (1789).

44. St. George Tucker, ed., Blackstone's Commentaries, Volume 1 at 143 n. 40, 41 (Philadelphia, 1803).

45. William Rawle, A View of the Constitution 125-6 (2d ed., Philadelphia. 1803).

46. Joseph Story, Commentaries on the Constitution, vol. 2 at 746 (1833).

47. Act of May 8, 1792; Second Cong., First Session, ch. 33.

48. Bliss v. Commonwealth, 12 Ken. (2 Litt.) 90, 92 (1822).

49. State v. Mitchell, (3 Black.) 229.

50. State v. Reid, 1 Ala. 612, 35 Am. Dec. 44 (1840).

51. State v. Buzzard, 4 Ark. 18, 27, 36 (1842). The Arkansas Constitutional provision at issue was narrower than the second amendment, as it protected keeping and bearing arms "for the common defense." Id. at 34.

52. Nunn v. State, 1 Ga. 243, 251 (1846).

53. Dred Scott v. Sandford, 60 U.S. 691,705.

54. The most comprehensive work in this field of constitutional law is Steven Halbrook, the Jurisprudence of the Second and Fourteenth Amendments (Institute for Humane Studies, Menlo Park, California, 1979), reprinted in 4 George Mason L. Rev. 1 (1981).

55. Cong. Globe, 39th Congress, 1st Sess., pt. 1, p. 474 (Jan. 29, 1866).

56. Id. at 478.

57. H.R. Rep. No. 37, 41st Cong., 3d sess., p. 3 (1871).

58. See generally Halbrook, supra, at 42-62.

59. Slaughterhouse Cases, 83 U.S. 36 (1873).

60. United States v. Cruikshank, 92 U.S. 542 (1876).

61. Presser v. Illinois, 116 U.S. 252 (1886).

62. Miller v. Texas, 153 U.S. 535 (1894).

63. United States v. Miller, 307 U.S. 175 (1939).

64. Id. at 178, 179.

65. H.R. Report No. 141, 73d Cong., 1st sess. at 2-5 (1933).

APPENDIX

CASE LAW

The United States Supreme Court has only three times commented upon the meaning of the second amendment to our constitution. The first comment, in *Dred Scott,* indicated strongly that the right to keep and bear arms was an individual right; the Court noted that, were it to hold free blacks to be entitled to equality of citizenship, they would be entitled to keep and carry arms wherever they went. The second, in *Miller,* indicated that a court cannot take judicial notice that a short-barrelled shotgun is covered by the second amendment — but the Court did not indicate that National Guard status is in any way required for protection by that amendment, and indeed defined "militia" to include all citizens able to bear arms. The third, a footnote in *Lewis v. United States,* indicated only that "these legislative restrictions on the use of firearms" — a ban on possession by felons — were permissable. But since felons may constitutionally be deprived of many of the rights of citizens, including that of voting, this dicta reveals little. These three comments constitute all significant explanations of the scope of the second amendment advanced by our Supreme Court. The case of *Adam v. Williams* has been cited as contrary to the principle that the second amendment is an individual right. In fact, that reading of the opinion comes only in Justice Douglas's dissent from the majority ruling of the Court.

The appendix which follows represents a listing of twenty-one American decisions, spanning the period from 1822 to 1981, which have analysed right to keep and bear arms provisions in the light of statutes ranging from complete bans on handgun sales to bans on carrying of weapons to regulation of carrying by permit systems. Those decisions not only explained the nature of such a right, but also struck down legislative restrictions as violative of it, are designated by asterisks.

20th century cases

1. * *State v. Blacker*, 291 Or. 255, ——— P.2d ——— (1981).

"The statute is written as a total proscription of the mere possession of certain weapons, and that mere possession, insofar as a billy is concerned, is constitutionally protected."

"In these circumstances, we conclude that it is proper for us to consider defendant's 'overbreadth' attack to mean that the statute swept so broadly as to infringe rights that it could notreach, which in this setting means the right to possess arms guaranteed by sec 27."

2. * *State v. Kessler*, 289 Or. 359, 614 P.2d 94, at 95, at 98 (1980).

"We are not unmindful that there is current controversy over the wisdom of a right to bear arms, and that the original motivations for such a provision might not seem compelling if debated as a new issue. Our task, however, in construing a constitutional provision is to respect the principles given the status of constitutional guarantees and limitations by the drafters; it is not to abandon these principles when this fits the needs of the moment."

"Therefore, the term 'arms' as used by the drafters of the constitutions probably was intended to include those weapons used by settlers for both personal and military defense. The term 'arms' was not limited to firearms, but included several handcarried weapons commonly used for defense. The term 'arms' would not have included cannon or other heavy ordnance not kept by militia-men or private citizens."

3. *Motley v. Kellogg,* 409 N.E.2d 1207, at 1210 (Ind. App. 1980) (motion to transfer denied 1-27-1981).

"[N]ot making applications available at the chiefs office effectively denied members of the community the opportunity to obtain a gun permit and bear arms for their self-defense."

4. *Schubert v. DeBard,* 398 N.E.2d 1339, at 1341 (Ind. App. 1980) (motion to transfer denied 8-28-1980).

"We think it clear that our constitution provides our citizenry the right to bear arms for their self-defense."

5. *Taylor v. McNeal,* 523 S.W.2d 148, at 150 (Mo. App. 1975).

"The pistols in question are not contraband. * * * Under Art. I, sec 23, Mo. Const. 1945, V.A.M.S., every citizen has the right to keep and bear arms in defense of his home, person and property, with the limitation that this section shall not justify the wearing of concealed arms."

6. * *City of Lakewood v. Pillow,* 180 Colo. 20, 501 P.2d 744, at 745 (en banc 1972).

"As an example, we note that this ordinance would prohibit gunsmiths, pawnbrokers and sporting goods stores from carrying on a substantial part of their business. Also, the ordinance appears to prohibit individuals from transporting guns to and from such places of business. Furthermore, it makes it unlawful for a person to possess a firearm in a vehicle or in a place of business for the purpose of self-defense. Several of these activities are constitutionally protected. Colo. Const. art. II, sec 13."

7. * *City of Las Vegas v. Moberg,* 82 N.M. 626, 485 P.2d 737, at 738 (N.M. App. 1971).

"It is our opinion that an ordinance may not deny the people the constitutionally guaranteed right to bear arms, and to that extent the ordinance under consideration is void."

8. *State v. Nickerson,* 126 Mt. 157, 247 P.2d 188, at 192 (1952).

"The law of this jurisdiction accords to the defendant the right to keep and bear arms and to use same in defense of his own home, his person and property."

9. *People v. Liss,* 406 Ill. 419, 94 N.E. 2d 320, at 323 (1950).

"The second amendment to the constitution of the United States provides the right of the people to keep and bear arms shall not be infringed. This of course does not prevent the enactment of a law against carrying concealed weapons, but it does indicate it should be kept in mind, in the construction of a statute of such character, that it is aimed at persons of criminal instincts, and for the prevention of crime, and not against use in the protection of person or property."

10. * *People v. Nakamura,* 99 Colo. 262, at 264, 62 P.2d 246 (en banc 1936).

"It is equally clear that the act wholly disarms aliens for all purposes. The state ... cannot disarm any class of persons or deprive them of the right guaranteed under section 13, article II of the Constitution, to bear arms in defense of home, person and property. The guaranty thus extended is meaningless if any person is denied the right to posses arms for such protection."

11.* *Glasscock v. City of Chattanooga,* 157 Tenn. 518, at 520, 11 S.W. 2d 678 (1928).

"There is no qualifications of the prohibition against the carrying of a pistol in the city ordinance before us but it is made unlawful 'to carry on or about the person any pistol,' that is, any sort of pistol in any sort of manner. *** [W]e must accordingly hold the provision of this ordinance as to the carrying of a pistol invalid."

12. * *People v. Zerillo,* 219 Mich. 635, 189 N.W. 927, at 928 (1922).

"The provision in the Constitution granting the right to all persons to bear arms is a limitation upon the power of the Legislature to enact any law to the contrary. The exercise of a right guaranteed by the Constitution cannot be made subject to the will of the sheriff."

13 * *State v. Kerner,* 181 N.C. 574, 107 S.E. 222, at 224 (1921).

"We are of the opinion, however, that 'pistol' ex vi termini is properly included within the word 'arms,' and that the right to bear such arms cannot be infringed. The historical use of pistols as 'arms' of offense and defense is beyond controversy."

"The maintenance of the right to bear arms is a most essential one to every free people and should not be whittled down by technical constructions."

14. * *State v. Rosenthal,* 75 VT. 295, 55 A. 610, at 611 (1903).

"The people of the state have a right to bear arms for the defense of themselves and the state. *** The result is that Ordinance No. 10, so far as it relates to the carrying of a pistol, is inconsistent with and repugnant to the Constitution and the laws of the state, and it is therefore to that extent, void."

15. * In re *Brickey,* 8 Ida. 597, at 598-99, 70 p. 609 (1902).

"The second amendment to the federal constitution is in the following language: 'A well-regulated militia, being necessary to the security of a free state, the right of the people to keep and bear arms, shall not be infringed.' The language of section 11, article I of the constitution of Idaho, is as follows: The people have the right to bear arms for their security and defense, but the legislature shall regulate the exercise of this right by law.' Under these constitutional provisions, the legislature has no power to prohibit a citizen from bearing arms in any portion of the state of Idaho, whether within or without the corporate limits of cities, towns, and villages."

19th century cases

16. * *Wilson* v. *State,* 33 Ark. 557, at 560, 34 Am. Rep. 52, at 54 (1878).

"If cowardly and dishonorable men sometimes shoot unarmed men with army pistols or guns, the evil must be prevented by the . penitentiary and gallows, and not by a general deprivation of constitutional privilege."

17. * *Jennings v. State,* 5 Tex. Crim. App. 298, at 300-01 (1878).

"We believe that portion of the act which provides that, in case of conviction, the defendant shall forfeit to the county the weapon or weapons so found on or about his person is not within the scope of legislative authority. * * * One of his most sacred rights is that of having arms for his own defence and that of the State. This right is one of the surest safeguards of liberty and self-preservation."

18. * *Andrews v. State,* 50 Tenn. 165, 8 Am. Rep. 8, at 17 (1871).

"The passage from Story shows clearly that this right was intended, as we have maintained in this opinion, and was guaranteed to and to be exercised and enjoyed by the citizen as such, and not by him as a soldier, or in defense solely of his political rights."

19. * *Nunn v. State,* 1 Ga. (1 Kel.) 243, at 251 (1846).

"The right of the people to bear arms shall not be infringed.' The right of the whole people, old and young, men, women and boys, and not militia only, to keep and bear arms of every description, and not such merely as are used by the militia, shall not be infringed, curtailed, or broken in upon, in the smallest degree; and all this for the important end to be attained: the rearing up and qualifying a well-regulated militia, so vitally necessary to the security of a free State."

20. *Simpson v. State,* 13 Tenn. 356, at 359-60 (1833).

"But suppose it to be assumed on any ground, that our ancestors adopted and brought over with them this English statute, [the statute of Northampton,] or portion of the common law, our constitution has completely abrogated it; it says, 'that the freemen of this State have a right to keep and bear arms for their common defence.' Article II, sec. 26. * * * By this clause of the constitution, an express power is given and secured to all the free citizens of the State to keep and bear arms for their defence, without any qualification whatever as to their kind or nature; and it is conceived, that it would be going much too far, to impair by construction or abridgement a constitutional privilege, which is so declared; neither, after so solumn an instrument hath said the people may carry arms, can we be permitted to impute to the acts thus licensed, such a necessarily consequent operation as terror to the people to be incurred thereby; we must attribute to the framers of it, the absence of such a view."

21. *Bliss v. Commonwealth,* 12 Ky. (2 Litt.) 90, at 92, and 93, 13 Am. Dec. 251 (1822).

"For, in principle, there is no difference between a law prohibiting the wearing concealed arms, and a law forbidding the wearing such as are exposed; and if the former be unconstitutional, the latter must be so likewise."

"But it should not be forgotten, that it is not only a part of the right that is secured by the constitution; it is the right entire and complete, as it existed at the adoption of the constitution; and if any portion of that right be impaired, immaterial how small the part may be, and immaterial the order of time at which it be done, it is equally forbidden by the constitution."

The following represents a list of twelve scholarly articles which have dealt with the subject of the right to keep and bear arms as reflected in the second amendment to the Constitution of the United States. The scholars who have undertaken this research range from professors of law, history and philosophy to a United States Senator. All have concluded that the second amendment is an individual right protecting American citizens in their peaceful use of firearms.

BIBLIOGRAPHY

Hays, THE RIGHT TO BEAR ARMS, A STUDY IN JUDICIAL MISINTERPRETATION, 2 Wm. & Mary L.R. 381 (1960)

Sprecher, THE LOST AMENDMENT, 51 Am. Bar Assn. J. 554 & 665 (2 parts) (1965)

Comment, THE RIGHT TO KEEP AND BEAR ARMS; A NECESSARY CONSTITUTIONAL GUARANTEE OR AN OUTMODED PROVISION OF THE BILL OF RIGHTS? 31 Albany L.R. 74 (1967)

Levine & Saxe, THE SECOND AMENDMENT: THE RIGHT TO BEAR ARMS, 7 Houston L. R. 1 (1969)

McClure, FIREARMS AND FEDERALISM, 7 Idaho L. R. 197 (1970)

Hardy & Stompoly, OF ARMS AND THE LAW, 51 Chi.-Kent L. R. 62 (1974)

Weiss, A REPLY TO ADVOCATES OF GUN CONTROL LAW, 52 Jour. Urban Law 577 (1974)

Whisker, HISTORICAL DEVELOPMENT AND SUBSEQUENT EROSION OF THE RIGHT TO KEEP AND BEAR ARMS, 78 W. Va. L. R. 171 (1976)

Caplan, RESTORING THE BALANCE: THE SECOND AMENDMENT REVISITED, 5 Fordham Urban L.J. 31 (1976)

Caplan, HANDGUN CONTROL: CONSTITUTIONAL OR UNCONSTITUTIONAL?, 10 N.C. Central L.J. 53 (1979)

Cantrell, THE RIGHT TO BEAR ARMS, 53 Wis. Bar Bull. 21 (Oct. 1980)

Halbrook, THE JURISPRUDENCE OF THE SECOND AND FOURTEENTH AMENDMENTS, 4 Geo. Mason L. Rev. 1 (1981)

Enforcement of Federal Firearms Laws From the Perspective of the Second Amendment

Federal involvement in firearms possession and transfer was not significant prior to 1934, when the National Firearms Act was adopted. The National Firearms Act as adopted covered only fully automatic weapons (machine guns and submachine guns) and rifles and shotguns whose barrel length or overall length fell below certain limits. Since the Act was adopted under the revenue power, sale of these firearms was not made subject to a ban or permit system. Instead, each transfer was made subject to a $200 excise tax, which must be paid prior to transfer; the identification of the parties to the transfer indirectly accomplished a registration purpose.

The 1934 Act was followed by the Federal Firearms Act of 1938, which placed some limitations upon sale of ordinary firearms. Persons engaged in the business of selling those firearms in interstate commerce were required to obtain a Federal Firearms License, at an annual cost of $1, and to maintain records of the name and address of persons to whom they sold firearms. Sales to persons convicted of violent felonies were prohibited, as were interstate shipments to persons who lacked the permits required by the law of their state.

Thirty years after adoption of the Federal Firearms Act, the Gun Control Act of 1968 worked a major revision of federal law. The Gun Control Act was actually a composite of two statutes. The first of these, adopted as portions of the Omnibus Crime and Safe Streets Act, imposed limitations upon imported firearms, expanded the requirement of dealer licensing to cover anyone "engaged in the business of dealing" in firearms, whether in interstate or local commerce, and expanded the recordkeeping obligations for dealers. It also imposed a variety of direct limitations upon sales of handguns. No transfers were to be permitted between residents of different states (unless the recipient was a federally licensed dealer), even where the transfer was by gift rather than sale and even where the recipient was subject to no state law which could have been evaded. The category of persons to whom dealers could not sell was expanded to cover persons convicted of any felony (other than certain business-related felonies such as antitrust violations), persons subject to a mental commitment order or finding of mental incompetence, persons who were users of marijuana and other drugs, and a number of other categories. Another title of the Act defined persons who were banned from possessing firearms. Paradoxically, these classes were not identical with the list of classes prohibited from purchasing or receiving firearms.

The Omnibus Crime and Safe Streets Act was passed on June 5, 1968, and set to take effect in December of that year. Barely two weeks after its passage, Senator Robert F. Kennedy was assassinated while campaigning for the presidency. Less than a week after his death, the second bill which would form part of the Gun Control Act of 1968 was introduced in the House. It was reported out of Judiciary ten days later, out of Rules Committee two weeks after that, and was on the floor barely a month after its introduction. the second bill worked a variety of changes upon the original Gun Control Act. Most significantly, it extended to rifles and shotguns the controls which had been imposed solely on handguns, extended the class of persons prohibited from possessing firearms to include those who were users of marijuana and certain other drugs, expanded judicial review of dealer license revocations by mandating a de novo hearing once an appeal was taken, and permitted interstate sales of rifles and shotguns only where the parties resided in contiguous states, both of which had enacted legislation permitting such sales. Similar legislation was passed by the Senate and a conference of the Houses produced a bill which was essentially a modification of the

House statute. This became law before the Omnibus Crime Control and Safe Streets Act, and was therefore set for the same effective date.

Enforcement of the 1968 Act was delegated to the Department of the Treasury, which had been responsible for enforcing the earlier gun legislation. This responsibility was in turn given to the Alcohol and Tobacco Tax Division of the Internal Revenu Service. This division had traditionally devoted itself to the pursuit of illegal producers of alcohol; at the time of enactment of the Gun Control Act, only 8.3 percent of its arrests were for firearms violations. Following enactment of the Gun Control Act the Alcohol and Tobacco Tax Division was retitled the Alcohol, Tobacco and Firearms Division of the IRS. By July, 1972 it had nearly doubled in size and became a complete Treasury bureau under the name of Bureau of Alcohol, Tobacco and Firearms.

The mid-1970's saw rapid increases in sugar prices, and these in turn drove the bulk of the "moonshiners" out of business. Over 15,000 illegal distilleries had been raided in 1956; but by 1976 this had fallen to a mere 609. The BATF thus began to devote the bulk of its efforts to the area of firearms law enforcement.

Complaints regarding the techniques used by the Bureau in an effort to generate firearms cases led to hearings before the Subcommittee on Treasury, Post Office, and General Appropriations of the Senate Appropriations Committee in July 1979 and April 1980, and before the Subcommittee on the Constitution of the Senate Judiciary Committee in October 1980. At these hearings evidence was received from various citizens who had been charged by BATF, from experts who had studied the BATF, and from officials of the Bureau itself.

Based upon these hearings, it is apparent that enforcement tactics made possible by current federal firearms laws are constitutionally, legally, and practically reprehensible. Although Congress adopted the Gun Control Act with the primary object of limiting access of felons and high-risk groups to firearms, the overbreadth of the law has led to neglect of precisely this area of enforcement. For example the Subcommittee on the Constitution received correspondence from two members of the Illinois Judiciary, dated in 1980, indicating that they had been totally unable to persuade BATF to accept cases against felons who were in possession of firearms including sawed-off shotguns. The Bureau's own figures demonstrate that in recent years the percentage of its arrests devoted to felons in possession and persons knowingly selling to them have dropped from 14 percent down to 10 percent of their firearms cases. To be sure, genuine criminals are sometimes prosecuted under other sections of the law. Yet, subsequent to these hearings, BATF stated that 55 percent of its gun law prosecutions overall involve persons with no record of a felony conviction, and a third involve citizens with no prior police contact at all.

The Subcommittee received evidence that BATF has primarily devoted its firearms enforcement efforts to the apprehension, upon technical malum prohibitum charges, of individuals who lack all criminal intent and knowledge. Agents anxious to generate an impressive arrest and gun confiscation quota have repeatedly enticed gun collectors into making a small number of sales—often as few as four—from their personal collections. Although each of the sales was completely legal under state and federal law, the agents then charged the collector with having "engaged in the business" of dealing in guns without the required license. Since existing law permits a felony conviction upon these charges even where the individual has no criminal knowledge or intent numerous collectors have been ruined by a felony record carrying a potential sentence of five years in federal prison. Even in cases where the collectors secured acquittal, or grand juries failed to indict, or prosecutors refused to file criminal charges, agents of the Bureau have generally confiscated the entire collection of the potential defendant upon the ground that he intended to use it in that violation of the law. In several cases, the agents have refused to return the collection even after acquittal by jury.

The defendant, under existing law is not entitled to an award of attorney's fees, therefore, should he secure return of his collection, an individual who has already spent thousands of dollars establishing his innocence of the criminal charges is required to spend thousands more to civilly prove his innocence of the same acts, without hope of securing any redress. This, of course, has given the enforcing agency enormous bargaining power in refusing to return confiscated firearms. Evidence received by the Subcommittee on the Constitution demonstrated that Bureau agents have tended to concentrate upon collector's items rather than "criminal street guns". One witness appearing before the Subcommittee related the confiscation of a shotgun valued at $7,000. Even the Bureau's own valuations indicate that the value of firearms confiscated by their agents is over twice the value which the Bureau has claimed is typical of "street guns" used in crime. In recent months, the average value has increased rather than decreased, indicating that the reforms announced by the Bureau have not in fact redirected their agents away from collector's items and toward guns used in crime.

The Subcommittee on the Constitution has also obtained evidence of a variety of other misdirected conduct by agents and supervisors of the Bureau. In several cases, the Bureau has sought conviction for supposed technical violations based upon policies and interpretations of law which the Bureau had not published in the Federal Register, as required by 5 U.S.C. § 552. For instance, beginning in 1975, Bureau officials apparently reached a judgment that a dealer who sells to a legitimate purchaser may nonetheless be subject to prosecution or license revocation if he knows that that individual intends to transfer the firearm to a nonresident or other unqualified purchaser. This position was never published in the Federal Register and is indeed contrary to indications which Bureau officials had given Congress, that such sales were not in violation of existing law. Moreover, BATF had informed dealers that an adult purchaser could legally buy for a minor, barred by his age from purchasing a gun on his own. BATF made no effort to suggest that this was applicable only where the barrier was one of age. Rather than informing the dealers of this distinction, Bureau agents set out to produce mass arrests upon these "straw man" sale charges, sending out undercover agents to entice dealers into transfers of this type. The first major use of these charges, in South Carolina in 1975, led to 37 dealers being driven from business, many convicted on felony charges. When one of the judges informed Bureau officials that he felt dealers had not been fairly treated and given information of the policies they were expected to follow, and refused to permit further prosecutions until they were informed, Bureau officials were careful to inform only the dealers in that one state and even then complained in internal memoranda that this was interfering with the creation of the cases. When BATF was later requested to place a warning to dealers on the front of the Form 4473, which each dealer executes when a sale is made, it instead chose to place the warning in fine print upon the back of the form, thus further concealing it from the dealer's sight.

The Constitution Subcommittee also received evidence that the Bureau has formulated a requirement, of which dealers were not informed that requires a dealer to keep official records of sales even from his private collection. BATF has gone farther than merely failing to publish this requirement. At one point, even as it was prosecuting a dealer on this charge (admitting that he had no criminal intent), the Director of the Bureau wrote Senator S. I. Hayakawa to indicate that there was no such legal requirement and it was completely lawful for a dealer to sell from his collection without recording it. Since that date, the Director of the Bureau has stated that that is not the Bureau's position and that such sales are completely illegal; after making that statement, however, he was quoted in an interview for a magazine read primarily by licensed firearms dealers as stating that such sales were in fact legal and permitted by the Bureau. In these and similar areas, the Bureau has violated not only the dictates of common sense, but of 5 U.S.C. Sec 552, which was intended to prevent "secret lawmaking" by administrative bodies.

These practices, amply documented in hearings before this Subcommittee, leave little doubt that the Bureau has disregarded rights guaranteed by the constitution and laws of the United States.

It has trampled upon the second amendment by chilling exercise of the right to keep and bear arms by law-abiding citizens.

It has offended the fourth amendment by unreasonably searching and seizing private property.

It has ignored the Fifth Amendment by taking private property without just compensation and by entrapping honest citizens without regard for their right to due process of law.

The rebuttal presented to the Subcommittee by the Bureau was utterly unconvincing. Richard Davis, speaking on behalf of the Treasury Department, asserted vaguely that the Bureau's priorities were aimed at prosecuting willful violators, particularly felons illegally in possession, and at confiscating only guns actually likely to be used in crime. He also asserted that the Bureau has recently made great strides toward achieving these priorities. No documentation was offered for either of these assertions. In hearings before BATF's Appropriations Subcommittee, however, expert evidence was submitted establishing that approximately 75 percent of BATF gun prosecutions were aimed at ordinary citizens who had neither criminal intent nor knowledge, but were enticed by agents into unknowing technical violations. (In one case, in fact, the individual was being prosecuted for an act which the Bureau's acting director had stated was perfectly lawful.) In those hearings, moreover, BATF conceded that in fact (1) only 9.8 percent of their firearm arrests were brought on felons in illicit possession charges; (2) the average value of guns seized was $116, whereas BATF had claimed that "crime guns" were priced at less than half that figure; (3) in the months following the announcement of their new "priorities", the percentage of gun prosecutions aimed at felons had in fact fallen by a third, and the value of confiscated guns had risen. All this indicates that the Bureau's vague claims, both of focus upon gun-using criminals and of recent reforms, are empty words.

In light of this evidence, reform of federal firearm laws is necessary to protect the most vital rights of American citizens. Such legislation is embodied in S. 1030. That legislation would require proof of a willful violation as an element of a federal gun prosecution, forcing enforcing agencies to ignore the easier technical cases and aim solely at the intentional breaches. It would restrict confiscation of firearms to those actually used in an offense, and require their return should the owner be acquitted of the charges. By providing for award of attorney's fees in confiscation cases, or in other cases if the judge finds charges were brought without just basis or from improper motives, this proposal would be largely self-enforcing. S. 1030 would enhance vital protection of constitutional and civil liberties of those Americans who choose to exercise their Second Amendment right to keep and bear arms.

The Firearm Owners Protection Act of 1986

Part of the reason for the 1982 Congressional subcommittee report was to study the effects of the Gun Control Act of 968, and its implications with regard to constitutionality. Indeed, one of the opinions expressed in the report was that the Gun Control Act of 1968 should be amended. One of the factors leading up to this was a proliferation of reports of Bureau of Alcohol, Tobacco and Firearms (BATF) abusing their authority to harass law-abiding citizens.

The Congress responded to the complaints by enacting the Firearms Owners Protection Act of 1986. Although the Act made some small steps to protect law-abiding firearms owners from governmental harassment, the Act also imposed some new restrictions on firearms ownership.

- The act made provision for "safe passage" of people traveling from one state to another with firearms. Unfortunately, as recent cases have demonstrated, the language used was primarily based on an apparent assumption of travel by automobile, with the result that in recent years there have been several prosecutions (some high profile) of people being arrested and charged for attempting to travel by commercial airline from one state to another. In addition, the language leaves a gray area pertaining to long trips by automobile: If a driver has to stop for the night, is he/she allowed to remove the firearm(s) from the vehicle and keep them in a hotel room overnight, or must the firearm(s) remain locked in the vehicle? This question has not been resolved by the courts.
- The Act made it illegal for civilians to purchase machine guns manufactured after the effective date of the legislation. The National Firearms Act of 1934 had made machine guns subject to payment of a $200 tax any time a machine gun was transferred. The prohibition of civilian purchase of new machine guns meant that the pool of machine guns available for purchase and possession by civilians was instantly fixed. The result was a stratospheric increase in the asking price of legal, pre-1986 machine guns.
- The act also provided that BATF agents could only inspect licensed firearms dealers (FFLs) once in each calendar year, unless the dealer had a history of violations.

Full Text of the Firearm Owners' Protection Act of 1986

Public Law 99-308
99th Congress

An Act

To amend chapter 44 (relating to firearms) of title 18, United States Code, and for other purposes.

Be it enacted by the Senate and House of Representatives of the United States of America in Congress assembled,

SECTION 1. SHORT TITLE AND CONGRESSIONAL FINDINGS.

(a) SHORT TITLE.—This Act may be cited as the "Firearms Owners' Protection Act".

(b) CONGRESSIONAL FINDINGS.—The Congress finds that—

(1) the rights of citizens—

(A) to keep and bear arms under the second amendment to the United States Constitution;

(B) to security against illegal and unreasonable searches and seizures under the fourth amendment;

(C) against uncompensated taking of property, double jeopardy, and assurance of due process of law under the fifth amendment; and

(D) against unconstitutional exercise of authority under the ninth and tenth amendments; require additional legislation to correct existing firearms statutes and enforcement policies; and

(2) additional legislation is required to reaffirm the intent of the Congress, as expressed in section 101 of the Gun Control Act of 1968, that "it is not the purpose of this title to place any undue or unnecessary Federal restrictions or burdens on law-abiding citizens with respect to the acquisition, possession, or use of firearms appropriate to the purpose of hunting, trap-shooting, target shooting, personal protection, or any other lawful activity, and that this title is not intended to discourage or eliminate the private ownership or use of firearms by law-abiding citizens for lawful purposes.".

SEC. 101. AMENDMENTS TO SECTION 921.

Section 921 of title 18, United States Code, is amended—

(1) in subsection (a)(10), by striking out "manufacture o f and inserting in lieu thereof "business of manufacturing";

(2) in subsection (a)(11)(A), by striking out "or ammunition";

(3) in subsection (a)(12), by striking out "or ammunition";

(4) in subsection (a)(13), by striking out "or ammunition";

(5) by amending paragraph (20) of subsection (a) to read as follows:

"(20) The term 'crime punishable by imprisonment for a term exceeding one year' does not include—

"(A) any Federal or State offenses pertaining to antitrust and crime, violations, unfair trade practices, restraints of trade, or other similar offenses relating to the regulation of business practices, or

"(B) any State offense classified by the laws of the State as a misdemeanor and punishable by a term of imprisonment of two years or less.

What constitutes a conviction of such a crime shall be determined in accordance with the law of the jurisdiction in which the proceedings were held. Any conviction which has been expunged, or set aside or for which a person has been pardoned or has had civil rights restored shall not be considered a conviction for purposes of this chapter, unless such pardon, expungement, or restoration of civil rights expressly provides that the person may not ship, transport, possess, or receive firearms."; and

(6) in subsection (a), by inserting after paragraph (20) the following new paragraphs:

"(21) The term 'engaged in the business' means—

"(A) as applied to a manufacturer of firearms, a person who devotes time, attention, and labor to manufacturing firearms as a regular course of trade or business with the principal objective of livelihood and profit through the sale or distribution of the firearms manufactured;

"(B) as applied to a manufacturer of ammunition, a person who devotes time, attention, and labor to manufacturing ammunition as a regular course of trade or business with the principal objective of livelihood and profit through the sale or distribution of the ammunition manufactured;

"(C) as applied to a dealer in firearms, as defined in section 921(a)(11)(A), a person who devotes time, attention, and labor to dealing in firearms as a regular course of trade or business with the principal objective of livelihood and profit through the repetitive purchase and resale of firearms, but such term shall not include a person who makes occasional sales, exchanges, or purchases of firearms for the enhancement of a personal collection or for a hobby, or who sells all or part of his personal collection of firearms;

"(D) as applied to a dealer in firearms, as defined in section 921(a)(11)(B), a person who devotes time, attention, and labor to engaging in such activity as a regular course of trade or business with the principal objective of livelihood and profit, but such term shall not include a person who makes occasional repairs of firearms, or who occasionally fits special barrels, stocks, or trigger mechanisms to firearms;

"(E) as applied to an importer of firearms, a person who devotes time, attention, and labor to importing firearms as a regular course of trade or business with the principal objective of livelihood and profit through the sale or distribution of the firearms imported; and

"(F) as applied to an importer of ammunition, a person who devotes time, attention, and labor to importing ammunition as a regular course of trade or business with the principal objective of livelihood and profit through the sale or distribution of the ammunition imported.

"(22) The term 'with the principal objective of livelihood and profit' means that the intent underlying the sale or disposition of firearms is predominantly one of obtaining livelihood and pecuniary gain, as opposed to other intents, such as improving or liquidating a personal firearms collection.

"(23) The term 'machinegun' has the meaning given such term in section 58450)) of the National Firearms Act (26 U.S.C. 5845(b)).

"(24) The terms 'firearm silencer' and 'firearm muffler' mean any device for silencing, muffling, or diminishing the report of a portable firearm, including any combination of parts, designed or redesigned, and intended for use in assembling or fabricating a firearm silencer or firearm muffler, and any part intended only for use in such assembly or fabrication.".

SEC. 102. AMENDMENTS TO SECTION 922.

Section 922 of title 18, United States Code, is amended—

(1) so that paragraph (1) of subsection (a) reads as follows:

"(1) for any person—

"(A) except a licensed importer, licensed manufacturer, or licensed dealer, to engage in the business of importing, manufacturing, or dealing in firearms, or in the course of such business to ship, transport, or receive any firearm in interstate or foreign commerce; or

"(B) except a licensed importer or licensed manufacturer, to engage in the business of importing or manufacturing ammunition, or in the course of such business, to ship, transport, or receive any ammunition in interstate or foreign commerce;";

(2) in subsection (a)(2)—

(A) by striking out "or ammunition"; and

(B) by striking out "or licensed dealer for the sole purpose of repair or customizing;" and inserting in lieu thereof "licensed dealer, or licensed collector;";

(3) in subsection (a)(3), by striking out "(B)" and all that follows through "(b)(3) of this section," and inserting in lieu thereof the following: "(B) shall not apply to the transportation or receipt of a firearm obtained in conformity with subsection (b)(3) of this section,";

(4) in subsection (b)—

(A) in paragraph (2), by striking out "or ammunition" each place it appears;

(B) in paragraph (3), by striking out "(A)" and all that follows through "intrastate transactions other than at the licensee's business premises," and inserting in lieu thereof "(A) shall not apply to the sale or delivery of any rifle or shotgun to a resident of a State other than a State in which the licensee's place of business is located if the transferee meets in person with the transferor to accomplish the transfer, and the sale, delivery, and receipt fully comply with the legal conditions of sale in both such States (and any licensed manufacturer, importer or dealer shall be presumed, for purposes of this subparagraph, in the absence of evidence to the contrary, to have had actual knowledge of the State laws and published ordinances of both States),";

(C) in paragraph (3), by inserting "and" before "(B)";

(D) in paragraph (3), by striking out ", and (C)" and all that follows through the end of such paragraph and inserting in lieu thereof a semicolon; and

(E) in paragraph (5), by striking out "or ammunition except .22 caliber rimfire ammunition" and inserting "or armor-piercing ammunition" in lieu thereof;

(5) in subsection (d)—

(A) by striking out "licensed importer, licensed manufacturer, licensed dealer, or licensed collector" the first place it appears and inserting in lieu thereof "person";

(B) by amending paragraph (3) to read as follows:

"(3) is an unlawful user of or addicted to any controlled substance (as defined in section 102 of the Controlled Substances Act (21 U.S.C. 802));";

(C) in paragraph (4), by striking out the period and inserting in lieu thereof a semicolon; and

(D) by inserting after paragraph (4) the following:

"(5) who, being an alien, is illegally or unlawfully in the United States;

"(6) who has been discharged from the Armed Forces under dishonorable conditions; or

"(7) who, having been a citizen of the United States, has renounced his citizenship.";

(6) in subsection (g)—

(A) in paragraph (1), by striking out "is under indictment for, or who";

(B) by amending paragraph (3) to read as follows:

"(3) is an unlawful user of or addicted to any controlled substance (as defined in section 102 of the Controlled Substances Act (21 U.S.C. 802));";

(C) by inserting after paragraph (4) the following new paragraphs:

"(5) who, being an alien, is illegally or unlawfully in the United States;

"(6) who has been discharged from the Armed Forces under dishonorable conditions; or

"(7) who, having been a citizen of the United States, has renounced his citizenship;"; and

(D) by striking out "to ship or transport any firearm or ammunition in interstate or foreign commerce." and inserting in lieu thereof "to ship or transport in interstate or foreign commerce, or possess in or affecting commerce, any firearm or ammunition; or to receive any firearm or ammunition which has been shipped or transported in interstate or foreign commerce.";

(7) so that subsection (h) reads as follows:

"(h) It shall be unlawful for any individual, who to that individual's knowledge and while being employed for any person described in any paragraph of subsection (g) of this section, in the course of such employment—

"(1) to receive, possess, or transport any firearm or ammunition in or affecting interstate or foreign commerce; or

"(2) to receive any firearm or ammunition which has been shipped or transported in interstate or foreign commerce.";

(8) by inserting after subsection (m) the following:

"(n) It shall be unlawful for any person who is under indictment for a crime punishable by imprisonment for a term exceeding one year to ship or transport in interstate or foreign commerce any firearm or ammunition or receive any firearm or ammunition which has been shipped or transported in interstate or foreign commerce."; and

(9) by inserting after the subsection added by paragraph (8) of this section the following:

"(o)(1) Except as provided in paragraph (2), it shall be unlawful for any person to transfer or possess a machinegun.

"(2) This subsection does not apply with respect to—

"(A) a transfer to or by, or possession by or under the authority of, the United States or any department or agency thereof or a State, or a department, agency, or political subdivision thereof; or

"(B) any lawful transfer or lawful possession of a machinegun that was lawfully possessed before the date this subsection takes effect.".

SEC. 103. AMENDMENTS TO SECTION 923.

Section 923 of title 18, United States Code, is amended—

(1) in subsection (a)—

(A) by striking out the first sentence and inserting in lieu thereof "No person shall engage in the business of importing, manufacturing, or dealing in firearms, or importing or manufacturing ammunition, until he has filed an application with and received a license to do so from the Secretary."; and

(B) by striking out "and contain such information", and inserting in lieu thereof "and contain only that information necessary to determine eligibility for licensing.";

(2) in subsection (a)(3)(B), by striking out "or ammunition for firearms other than destructive devices,";

(3) in subsection (b), by striking out "and contain such information" and inserting in lieu thereof "and contain only that information necessary to determine eligibility";

(4) in subsection (c), by adding at the end "Nothing in this chapter shall be construed to prohibit a licensed manufacturer, importer, or dealer from maintaining and disposing of a personal collection of firearms, subject only to such restrictions as apply in this chapter to dispositions by a person other than a licensed manufacturer, importer, or dealer. If any firearm is so disposed of by a licensee within one year after its transfer from his business inventory into such licensee's personal collection or if such disposition or any other acquisition is made for the purpose of willfully evading the restrictions placed upon licensees by this chapter, then such firearm shall be deemed part of such licensee's business inventory.";

(5) in subsection (e), by inserting "willfully" before "violated";

(6) in subsection (f)—

(A) in paragraph (3)—

(i) by inserting "de novo" before "judicial"; and

(ii) by inserting "whether or not such evidence was considered at the hearing held under paragraph (2)." after "to the proceeding"; and

(B) by adding at the end the following new paragraph:

"(4) If criminal proceedings are instituted against a licensee alleging any violation of this chapter or of rules or regulations prescribed under this chapter, and the licensee is acquitted of such charges, or such proceedings are terminated, other than upon motion of the Government before trial upon such charges, the Secretary shall be absolutely barred from denying or revoking any license granted under this chapter where such denial or revocation is based in whole or in part on the facts which form the basis of such criminal charges. No proceedings for the revocation of a license shall be instituted by the Secretary more than one year after the filing of the indictment or information.";

(7) so that subsection (g) reads as follows:

"(g)(1)(A) Each licensed importer, licensed manufacturer, and licensed dealer shall maintain such records of importation, production, shipment, receipt, sale, or other disposition of firearms at his place of business for such period, and in such form, as the Secretary may by regulations prescribe. Such importers, manufacturers, and dealers shall not be required to submit to the Secretary reports and information with respect to such records and the contents thereof, except as expressly required by this section. The Secretary, when he has reasonable cause to believe a violation of this chapter has occurred and that evidence thereof may be found on such premises, may, upon demonstrating such cause before a Federal magistrate and securing from such magistrate a warrant authorizing entry, enter during business hours the premises (including places of storage) of any licensed firearms importer, licensed manufacturer, licensed dealer, licensed collector, or any licensed importer or manufacturer of ammunition, for the purpose of inspecting or examining—

"(i) any records or documents required to be kept by such licensed importer, licensed manufacturer, licensed dealer, or licensed collector under this chapter or rules or regulations under this chapter, and

"(ii) any firearms or ammunition kept or stored by such licensed importer, licensed manufacturer, licensed dealer, or licensed collector, at such premises.

"(B) The Secretary may inspect or examine the inventory and records of a licensed importer, licensed manufacturer, or licensed dealer without such reasonable cause or warrant—

"(i) in the course of a reasonable inquiry during the course of a criminal investigation of a person or persons other than the licensee;

"(ii) for ensuring compliance with the record keeping requirements of this chapter not more than once during any twelve-month period; or

"(iii) when such inspection or examination may be required for determining the disposition of one or more particular firearms in the course of a bona fide criminal investigation.

"(C) The Secretary may inspect the inventory and records of a licensed collector without such reasonable cause or warrant—

"(i) for ensuring compliance with the record keeping requirements of this chapter not more than once during any twelve-month period; or

"(ii) when such inspection or examination may be required for determining the disposition of one or more particular firearms in the course of a bona fide criminal investigation.

"(D) At the election of a licensed collector, the annual inspection of records and inventory permitted under this paragraph shall be performed at the office of the Secretary designated for such inspections which is located in closest proximity to the premises where the inventory and records of such licensed collector are maintained. The inspection and examination authorized by this paragraph shall not be construed as authorizing the Secretary to seize any records or other documents other than those records or documents constituting material evidence of a violation of law. If the Secretary seizes such records or documents, copies shall be provided the licensee within a reasonable time. The Secretary may make available to any Federal, State and local State, or local law enforcement agency any information which he governments, may obtain by reason of this chapter with respect to the identification of persons prohibited from purchasing or receiving firearms or ammunition who have purchased or received firearms or ammunition, together with a description of such firearms or ammunition, and he may provide information to the extent such information may be contained in the records required to be maintained by this chapter, when so requested by any Federal, State, or local law enforcement agency.

"(2) Each licensed collector shall maintain in a bound volume the nature of which the Secretary may by regulations prescribe, records of the receipt, sale, or other disposition of firearms. Such records shall include the name and address of any person to whom the collector sells or otherwise disposes of a firearm. Such collector shall not be required to submit to the Secretary reports and information with respect to such records and the contents thereof, except as expressly required by this section.

"(3) Each licensee shall prepare a report of multiple sales or other Reports, dispositions whenever the licensee sells or otherwise disposes of, at one time or during any five consecutive business days, two or more pistols, or revolvers, or any combination of pistols and revolvers totalling two or more, to an unlicensed person. The report shall be prepared on a form specified by the Secretary and forwarded to the office specified thereon not later than the close of business on the day that the multiple sale or other disposition occurs.

"(4) Where a firearms or ammunition business is discontinued and succeeded by a new licensee, the records required to be kept by this chapter shall appropriately reflect such facts and shall be delivered to the successor. Where discontinuance of the business is absolute, such records shall be delivered within thirty days after the business discontinuance to the Secretary. However, where State law or local ordinance requires the delivery of records to other responsible authority, the Secretary may arrange for the delivery of such records to such other responsible authority.

"(5)(A) Each licensee shall, when required by letter issued by the Secretary, and until notified to the contrary in writing by the Secretary, submit on a form specified by the Secretary, for periods and at the times specified in such letter, all record information required to be kept by this chapter or such lesser record information as the Secretary in such letter may specify.

"(B) The Secretary may authorize such record information to be submitted in a manner other than that prescribed in subparagraph (A) of this paragraph when it is shown by a licensee that an alternate method of reporting is reasonably necessary and will not unduly hinder the effective administration of this chapter. A licensee may use an alternate method of reporting if the licensee describes the proposed alternate method of reporting and the need therefor in a letter application submitted to the Secretary, and the Secretary approves such alternate method of reporting."; and

(8) so that subsection (j) reads as follows:

"(j) A licensed importer, licensed manufacturer, or licensed dealer may, under rules or regulations prescribed by the Secretary, conduct business temporarily at a location other than the location specified on the license if such temporary location is the location for a gun show or event sponsored by any national, State, or local organization, or any affiliate of any such organization devoted to the collection, competitive use, or other sporting use of firearms in the community, and such location is in the State which is specified on the license. Records of receipt and disposition of firearms transactions conducted at such temporary location shall include the location of the sale or other disposition and shall be entered in the permanent records of the licensee and retained on the location specified on the license. Nothing in this subsection shall authorize any licensee to conduct business in or from any motorized or towed vehicle. Notwithstanding the provisions of subsection (a) of this section, a separate fee shall not be required of a licensee with respect to business conducted under this subsection. Any inspection or examination of inventory or records under this chapter by the Secretary at such temporary location shall be limited to inventory consisting of, or records relating to, firearms held or disposed at such temporary location. Nothing in this subsection shall be construed to authorize the Secretary to inspect or examine the inventory or records of a licensed importer, licensed manufacturer, or licensed dealer at any location other than the location specified on the license. Nothing in this subsection shall be construed to diminish in any manner any right to display, sell, or otherwise dispose of firearms or ammunition, which is in effect before the date of the enactment of the Firearms Owners' Protection Act.".

SEC. 104. AMENDMENTS TO SECTION 924.

(a) IN GENERAL.—Section 924 of title 18, United States Code, is amended—

(1) so that subsection (a) reads as follows:

"(a)(1) Except as otherwise provided in paragraph (2) of this subsection, subsection (b) or (c) of this section, or in section 929, whoever—

"(A) knowingly makes any false statement or representation with respect to the information required by this chapter to be kept in the records of a person licensed under this chapter or in applying for any license or exemption or relief from disability under the provisions of this chapter;

"(B) knowingly violates subsection (a)(4), (a)(6), (f), (g), (i), (j), or (k) of section 922;

"(C) knowingly imports or brings into the United States or any possession thereof any firearm or ammunition in violation of section 922(1); or

"(D) willfully violates any other provision of this chapter, shall be fined not more than $5,000, imprisoned not more than five years, or both, and shall become eligible for parole as the Parole Commission shall determine.

"(2) Any licensed dealer, licensed importer, licensed manufacturer, or licensed collector who knowingly—

"(A) makes any false statement or representation with respect to the information required by the provisions of this chapter to be kept in the records of a person licensed under this chapter, or

"(B) violates subsection (m) of section 922,

shall be fined not more than $1,000, imprisoned not more than one year, or both, and shall become eligible for parole as the Parole Commission shall determine.";

(2) in subsection (c)—

(A) by inserting "(1)" before "Whoever,";

(B) by striking out "violence" each place it appears and inserting in lieu thereof "violence or drug trafficking crime,";

(C) by inserting "or drug trafficking crime" before "in which the firearm was used or carried.";

(D) in the first sentence, by striking out the period at the end and inserting in lieu thereof ", and if the firearm is a machinegun, or is equipped with a firearm silencer or firearm muffler, to imprisonment for ten years.";

(E) in the second sentence, by striking out the period at the end and inserting in lieu thereof ", and if the firearm is a machinegun, or is equipped with a firearm silencer or firearm muffler, to imprisonment for twenty years."; and

(F) by adding at the end the following:

"(2) For purposes of this subsection, the term 'drug trafficking crime' means any felony violation of Federal law involving the distribution, manufacture, or importation of any controlled substance (as defined in section 102 of the Controlled Substances Act (21 U.S.C. 802)).

"(3) For purposes of this subsection the term 'crime of violence' means an offense that is a felony and—

"(A) has as an element the use, attempted use, or threatened use of physical force against the person or property of another, or

"(B) that by its nature, involves a substantial risk that physical force against the person or property of another may be used in the course of committing the offense.";

(3) by amending subsection (d) to read as follows:

"(d)(1) Any firearm or ammunition involved in or used in any imports, knowing violation of subsection (a)(4), (a)(6), (f), (g), (h), (i), (j), or (k) of section 922, or knowing importation or bringing into the United States or any possession thereof any firearm or ammunition in violation of section 922(1), or knowing violation of section 924, or willful violation of any other provision of this chapter or any rule or regulation promulgated thereunder, or any violation of any other criminal law of the United States, or any firearm or ammunition intended to be used in any offense referred to in paragraph (3) of this subsection, where such intent is demonstrated by clear and convincing evidence, shall be subject to seizure and forfeiture, and all provisions of the Internal Revenue Code of 1954 relating to the seizure, forfeiture, and disposition of firearms, as defined in section 5845(a) of that Code, shall, so far as applicable, extend to seizures and forfeitures under the provisions of this chapter: *Provided*, That upon acquittal of the owner or possessor, or dismissal of the charges against him other than upon motion of the Government prior to trial, the seized firearms or ammunition shall be returned forthwith to the owner or possessor or to a person delegated by the owner or possessor unless the return of the firearms or ammunition would place the owner or possessor or his delegate in violation of law. Any action or proceeding for the forfeiture of firearms or ammunition shall be commenced within one hundred and twenty days of such seizure.

"(2)(A) In any action or proceeding for the return of firearms or ammunition seized under the provisions of this chapter, the court shall allow the prevailing party, other than the United States, a reasonable attorney's fee, and the United States shall be liable therefor.

"(B) In any other action or proceeding under the provisions of this chapter, the court, when it finds that such action was without foundation, or was initiated vexatiously, frivolously, or in bad faith, shall allow the prevailing party, other than the United States, a reasonable attorney's fee, and the United States shall be liable therefor.

"(C) Only those firearms or quantities of ammunition particularly named and individually identified as involved in or used in any violation of the provisions of this chapter or any rule or regulation issued thereunder, or any other criminal law of the United States or as intended to be used in any offense referred to in paragraph (3) of this subsection, where such intent is demonstrated by clear and convincing evidence, shall be subject to seizure, forfeiture, and disposition.

"(D) The United States shall be liable for attorneys' fees under this paragraph only to the extent provided in advance by appropriation Acts.

"(3) The offenses referred to in paragraphs (1) and (2)(C) of this subsection are—

"(A) any crime of violence, as that term is defined in section 924(c)(3) of this title;

"(B) any offense punishable under the Controlled Substances Act (21 U.S.C. 801 et seq.) or the Controlled Substances Import and Export Act (21 U.S.C. 951 et seq.);

"(C) any offense described in section 922(a)(1), 922(a)(3), 922(a)(5), or 922(b)(3) of this title, where the firearm or ammunition intended to be used in any such offense is involved in a pattern of activities which includes a violation of any offense described in section 922(a)(1), 922(a)(3), 922(a)(5), or 922(b)(3) of this title;

"(D) any offense described in section 922(d) of this title where the firearm or ammunition is intended to be used in such offense by the transferor of such firearm or ammunition;

"(E) any offense described in section 922(i), 9220"), 922(1), 922(n), or 924(b) of this title; and

"(F) any offense which may be prosecuted in a court of the United States which involves the exportation of firearms or ammunition."; and

(4) by adding at the end the following new subsection:

"(e)(1) In the case of a person who violates section 922(g) of this title and has three previous convictions by any court referred to in section 922(g)(1) of this title for robbery or burglary, or both, such person shall be fined not more than $25,000 and imprisoned not less than fifteen years, and, notwithstanding any other provision of law, the court shall not suspend the sentence of, or grant a probationary sentence to, such person with respect to the conviction under section 922(g), and such person shall not be eligible for parole with respect to the sentence imposed under this subsection.

"(2) As used in this subsection—

"(A) the term 'robbery' means any crime punishable by a term of imprisonment exceeding one year and consisting of the taking of the property of another from the person or presence of another by force or violence, or by threatening or placing another person in fear that any person will imminently be subjected to bodily harm; and

"(B) the term 'burglary' means any crime punishable by a term of imprisonment exceeding one year and consisting of entering or remaining surreptitiously within a building that is the property of another with intent to engage in conduct constituting a Federal or State offense.".

(b) CONFORMING REPEAL.—Title VII of the Omnibus Crime Control and Safe Streets Act of 1968 (18 U.S.C. App. 1201 et seq.) is repealed.

SEC. 105. AMENDMENTS TO SECTION 925.

Section 925 of title 18, United States Code, is amended—

(1) in subsection (c)—

(A) by striking out "has been convicted of a crime punishable by imprisonment for a term exceeding one year (other than a crime involving the use of a firearm or other weapon or a violation of this chapter or of the National Firearms Act)" and inserting in lieu thereof "is prohibited from possessing, shipping, transporting, or receiving firearms or ammunition";

(B) by inserting "transportation," after "shipment,";

(C) by striking out "and incurred by reason of such conviction"; and

(D) by inserting "Any person whose application for relief from disabilities is denied by the Secretary may file a petition with the United States district court for the district in which he resides for a judicial review of such denial. The court may in its discretion admit additional evidence where failure to do so would result in a miscarriage of justice." after "the public interest."; and

(2) in subsection (d)—

(A) by striking out "may authorize" and inserting in lieu thereof "shall authorize";

(B) by striking out "the person importing or bringing in the firearm or ammunition establishes to the satisfaction of the Secretary that";

(C) in paragraph (3), by inserting before the semicolon ", except in any case where the Secretary has not authorized the importation of the firearm pursuant to this paragraph, it shall be unlawful to import any frame, receiver, or barrel of such firearm which would be prohibited if assembled"; and

(D) by striking out "may permit" and inserting in lieu thereof "shall permit".

SEC. 106. AMENDMENTS TO SECTION 926.

Section 926 of title 18 of the United States Code is amended—

(1) by inserting "(a)" before "The Secretary" the first place it occurs;

(2) by inserting "only" after "prescribe";

(3) by striking out "as he deems reasonably" and inserting in lieu thereof "as are";

(4) by striking out the last sentence and inserting in lieu thereof "No such rule or regulation prescribed after the date of the enactment of the Firearms Owners' Protection Act may require that records required to be maintained under this chapter or any portion of the contents of such records, be recorded at or transferred to a facility owned, managed, or controlled by the United States or any State or any political subdivision thereof, nor that any system of registration of firearms, firearms owners, or firearms transactions or dispositions be established. Nothing in this section expands or restricts the Secretary's authority to inquire into the disposition of any firearm in the course of a criminal investigation."; and

(5) by adding at the end the following:

"(b) The Secretary shall give not less than ninety days public notice, and shall afford interested parties opportunity for hearing, before prescribing such rules and regulations.

"(c) The Secretary shall not prescribe rules or regulations that require purchasers of black powder under the exemption provided in section 845(a)(5) of this title to complete affidavits or forms attesting to that exemption.".

SEC. 107. TRANSPORTATION OF FIREARMS.

(a) IN GENERAL.—Chapter 44 of title 18, United States Code, is amended by inserting between section 926 and section 927 the flowing new section:

"§ 926a. Interstate transportation of firearms.

"Any person not prohibited by this chapter from transporting, shipping, or receiving a firearm shall be entitled to transport an unloaded, not readily accessible firearm in interstate commerce notwithstanding any provision of any legislation enacted, or any rule or regulation prescribed by any State or political subdivision thereof.".

(b) CLERICAL AMENDMENT.—The table of sections for chapter 44 of title 18, United States Code, is amended by inserting between the item relating to section 926 and the item relating to section 927 the following new item:

"926A. Interstate transportation of firearms.".

SEC. 108. AMENDMENTS TO SECTION 929.

Section 929(a) of title 18, United States Code, is amended—

(1) by inserting "(1)" before "Whoever,";

(2) by striking out "violence" each place it appears and inserting in lieu thereof "violence or drug trafficking crime,"; and

(3) by adding at the end the following:

"(2) For purposes of this subsection, the term 'drug trafficking crime' means any felony violation of Federal law involving the distribution, manufacture, or importation of any controlled substance (as defined in section 102 of the Controlled Substances Act (21 U.S.C. 802)).".

SEC. 109. AMENDMENT OF NATIONAL FIREARMS ACT.

(a) Section 5845(b) of the National Firearms Act (26 U.S.C. 5845(b)) is amended by striking out "any combination of parts designed and intended for use in converting a weapon into a machinegun," and inserting in lieu thereof "any part designed and intended solely and exclusively, or combination of parts designed and intended, for use in converting a weapon into a machinegun.".

(b) CONFORMING AMENDMENT.—Section 5845(a)(7) of the National Firearms Act (26 U.S.C. 5845(a)(7) is amended to read "(7) any silencer (as defined in section 921 of title 18, United States Code);".

SEC. 110. EFFECTIVE DATE.

(a) IN GENERAL.—The amendments made by this Act shall become effective one hundred and eighty days after the date of the enactment of this Act. Upon their becoming effective, the Secretary shall publish and provide to all licensees a compilation of the State laws and published ordinances of which licensees are presumed to have knowledge pursuant to chapter 44 of title 18, United States Code, as amended by this Act. All amendments to such State laws and published ordinances as contained in the aforementioned compilation shall be published in the Federal Register, revised annually, and furnished to each person licensed under chapter 44 of title 18, United States Code, as amended by this Act.

(b) PENDING ACTIONS, PETITIONS, AND APPELLATE PROCEEDINGS.—The amendments made by sections 103(6)(B), 105, and 107 of this Act shall be applicable to any action, petition, or appellate proceeding pending on the date of the enactment of this Act.

(c) MACHINEGUN PROHIBITION.—Section 102(9) shall take effect on the date of the enactment of this Act.

Approved May 19, 1986

1994 Assault Weapons Ban

The 1994 Assault Weapons Ban was formally entitled the Public Safety and Recreational Firearms Use Protection Act. It was enacted as part of a larger legislative initiative, the Violent Crime Control and Law Enforcement Act of 1994. The Act created an entirely new class of firearms that it called "assault weapons" defined by characteristics that do not pertain to how the firearm operates. What constituted an "assault weapon" under the Act was any of a lengthy list of specifically-named firearms, as well as any other firearms that were characterized by certain features.

The Act was at least in part a reaction to several highly publicized mass shootings that had involved firearms capable of firing a large number of rounds fairly rapidly. These incidents included the 1989 Cleveland Elementary School shooting in Stockton, California, in which five children were killed and 32 more were injured; and the 1991 Luby's Cafeteria shooting in Killeen, Texas, in which 23 people were killed and another 27 were wounded.

The assault weapons ban was advanced by proponents as a measure to reduce crime, or at least fatalities resulting from crimes committed with firearms. However, it was never disputed that that the percentage of crimes committed using the types of firearms addressed by the ban was extremely small, or that many of the traits that defined an arm as an "assault weapon" weren't pertinent to whether they were used in crimes or their lethality. After ten years the data could not support a showing that the Act had had any effect on reducing crime or on reducing fatalities. In the decade since passage of the Act, the composition of Congress had changed, and any effort to renew or expand the terms of the Act faced the possibility of a veto rather than executive support.

In general, the Act defined as an "assault weapon" any semi-automatic rifle that had a detachable magazine plus any two or more of the following features:

- A folding or telescoping stock;
- A pistol grip that protrudes conspicuously beneath the action of the firearm;
- A bayonet mount;
- A flash suppressor or threaded barrel designed to accommodate a flash suppressor;
- A grenade launcher.

The Act also named and defined some semi-automatic shotguns and handguns, but the most widely affected class of firearms was semi-automatic rifles. In addition, the Act classified all detachable magazines with a capacity greater than ten rounds as "large capacity ammunition feeding devices" and prohibited the sale of such magazines if they were manufactured after the effective date of the law.

The Act included a "grandfather" clause, under which any "assault weapons" legally owned prior to the effective date of the legislation were allowed to remain in the owners' possession, and remained legal to buy or sell. Likewise, any magazines with a capacity of more than ten rounds that were manufactured before the effective date of the legislation were also legal to possess and to sell.

Lastly, the Act included an unusual "sunset" provision, which established that it would terminate after ten years unless renewed or extended by the Congress. The sunset provision was included in the face of bipartisan resistance to inclusion of the AWB itself.

* * * * *

A number of states also enacted assault weapons bans at around the same time that the federal government adopted the Public Safety and Recreational Firearms Use Protection Act. Some were adopted prior to enactment of the federal law and some shortly after and, although most generally adhered to the definition of "assault weapon" as it appeared in the federal law, some differed. One major difference between the federal law and the state bans is that the state bans did not have a sunset clause. Thus, they remained in effect after the federal assault weapons ban expired. States that had or have their own assault weapons bans in force in addition to the federal ban include:

- California
- Connecticut
- Hawaii
- Maryland
- Massachusetts
- New Jersey
- New York

It should also be noted that the state assault weapons bans have been amended from time to time in the years since their enactment, usually to make them more restrictive.

Full Text of 1994 Assault Weapons Ban

H.R. 3355

TITLE XI—FIREARMS

Subtitle A—Assault Weapons

SEC. 110101. SHORT TITLE.

This subtitle may be cited as the "Public Safety and Recreational Firearms Use Protection Act".

SEC. 110102. RESTRICTION ON MANUFACTURE, TRANSFER, AND POSSESSION OF CERTAIN SEMIAUTOMATIC ASSAULT WEAPONS.

(a) RESTRICTION.—Section 922 of title 18, United States Code, is amended by adding at the end the following new subsection:

"(v)(1) It shall be unlawful for a person to manufacture, transfer, or possess a semiautomatic assault weapon.

"(2) Paragraph (1) shall not apply to the possession or transfer of any semiautomatic assault weapon otherwise lawfully possessed under Federal law on the date of the enactment of this subsection.

"(3) Paragraph (1) shall not apply to—

"(A) any of the firearms, or replicas or duplicates of the firearms, specified in Appendix A to this section, as such firearms were manufactured on October 1, 1993;

"(B) any firearm that—

"(i) is manually operated by bolt, pump, lever, or slide action;

"(ii) has been rendered permanently inoperable; or

"(iii) is an antique firearm;

"(C) any semiautomatic rifle that cannot accept a detachable magazine that holds more than 5 rounds of ammunition; or

"(D) any semiautomatic shotgun that cannot hold more than 5 rounds of ammunition in a fixed or detachable magazine.

The fact that a firearm is not listed in Appendix A shall not be construed to mean that paragraph (1) applies to such firearm. No firearm exempted by this subsection may be deleted from Appendix A so long as this subsection is in effect.

"(4) Paragraph (1) shall not apply to—

"(A) the manufacture for, transfer to, or possession by the United States or a department or agency of the United States or a State or a department, agency, or political subdivision of a State, or a transfer to or possession by a law enforcement officer employed by such an entity for purposes of law enforcement (whether on or off duty);

"(B) the transfer to a licensee under title I of the Atomic Energy Act of 1954 for purposes of establishing and maintaining an on-site physical protection system and security organization required by Federal law, or possession by an employee or contractor of such licensee on-site for such purposes or off-site for purposes of licensee-authorized training or transportation of nuclear materials;

"(C) the possession, by an individual who is retired from service with a law enforcement agency and is not otherwise prohibited from receiving a firearm, of a semiautomatic assault weapon transferred to the individual by the agency upon such retirement; or

"(D) the manufacture, transfer, or possession of a semiautomatic assault weapon by a licensed manufacturer or licensed importer for the purposes of testing or experimentation authorized by the Secretary.".

(b) DEFINITION OF SEMIAUTOMATIC ASSAULT WEAPON.—Section 921(a) of title 18, United States Code, is amended by adding at the end the following new paragraph:

"(30) The term 'semiautomatic assault weapon' means—

"(A) any of the firearms, or copies or duplicates of the firearms in any caliber, known as—

"(i) Norinco, Mitchell, and Poly Technologies Avtomat Kalashnikovs (all models);

"(ii) Action Arms Israeli Military Industries UZI and Galil;

"(iii) Beretta Ar70 (SC–70);

"(iv) Colt AR–15;

"(v) Fabrique National FN/FAL, FN/LAR, and FNC; H. R. 3355—203

"(vi) SWD M–10, M–11, M–11/9, and M–12;

"(vii) Steyr AUG;

"(viii) INTRATEC TEC–9, TEC–DC9 and TEC–22; and

"(ix) revolving cylinder shotguns, such as (or similar to) the Street Sweeper and Striker 12;

(B) a semiautomatic rifle that has an ability to accept a detachable magazine and has at least 2 of—

"(i) a folding or telescoping stock;

"(ii) a pistol grip that protrudes conspicuously beneath the action of the weapon;

"(iii) a bayonet mount;

"(iv) a flash suppressor or threaded barrel designed to accommodate a flash suppressor; and

"(v) a grenade launcher;

"(C) a semiautomatic pistol that has an ability to accept a detachable magazine and has at least 2 of—

"(i) an ammunition magazine that attaches to the pistol outside of the pistol grip;

"(ii) a threaded barrel capable of accepting a barrel extender, flash suppressor, forward handgrip, or silencer;

"(iii) a shroud that is attached to, or partially or completely encircles, the barrel and that permits the shooter to hold the firearm with the nontrigger hand without being burned;

"(iv) a manufactured weight of 50 ounces or more when the pistol is unloaded; and

"(v) a semiautomatic version of an automatic firearm; and

"(D) a semiautomatic shotgun that has at least 2 of—

"(i) a folding or telescoping stock;

"(ii) a pistol grip that protrudes conspicuously beneath the action of the weapon;

"(iii) a fixed magazine capacity in excess of 5 rounds; and "(iv) an ability to accept a detachable magazine.".

(c) PENALTIES.—

(1) VIOLATION OF SECTION 922(V).—Section 924(a)(1)(B) of such title is amended by striking "or (q) of section 922" and inserting "(r), or (v) of section 922".

(2) USE OR POSSESSION DURING CRIME OF VIOLENCE OR DRUG TRAFFICKING CRIME.—Section 924(c)(1) of such title is amended in the first sentence by inserting ", or semiautomatic assault weapon," after "short-barreled shotgun,".

(d) IDENTIFICATION MARKINGS FOR SEMIAUTOMATIC ASSAULT WEAPONS.—Section 923(i) of such title is amended by adding at the end the following: "The serial number of any semiautomatic assault weapon manufactured after the date of the enactment of this sentence shall clearly show the date on which the weapon was manufactured.".

SEC. 110103. BAN OF LARGE CAPACITY AMMUNITION FEEDING DEVICES.

(a) PROHIBITION.—Section 922 of title 18, United States Code, as amended by section 110102(a), is amended by adding at the end the following new subsection:

"(w)(1) Except as provided in paragraph (2), it shall be unlawful for a person to transfer or possess a large capacity ammunition feeding device.

"(2) Paragraph (1) shall not apply to the possession or transfer of any large capacity ammunition feeding device otherwise lawfully possessed on or before the date of the enactment of this subsection.

"(3) This subsection shall not apply to—

"(A) the manufacture for, transfer to, or possession by the United States or a department or agency of the United States or a State or a department, agency, or political subdivision of a State, or a transfer to or possession by a law enforcement officer employed by such an entity for purposes of law enforcement (whether on or off duty);

"(B) the transfer to a licensee under title I of the Atomic Energy Act of 1954 for purposes of establishing and maintaining an on-site physical protection system and security organization required by Federal law, or possession by an employee or contractor of such licensee on-site for such purposes or off-site for purposes of licensee-authorized training or transportation of nuclear materials;

"(C) the possession, by an individual who is retired from service with a law enforcement agency and is not otherwise prohibited from receiving ammunition, of a large capacity ammunition feeding device transferred to the individual by the agency upon such retirement; or

"(D) the manufacture, transfer, or possession of any large capacity ammunition feeding device by a licensed manufacturer or licensed importer for the purposes of testing or experimentation authorized by the Secretary.".

"(4) If a person charged with violating paragraph (1) asserts that paragraph (1) does not apply to such person because of paragraph (2) or (3), the Government shall have the burden of proof to show that such paragraph (1) applies to such person. The lack of a serial number as described in section 923(i) of title 18, United States Code, shall be a presumption that the large capacity ammunition feeding device is not subject to the prohibition of possession in paragraph (1).".

(b) Definition of Large Capacity Ammunition Feeding Device.—Section 921(a) of title 18, United States Code, as amended by section 110102(b), is amended by adding at the end the following new paragraph:

"(31) The term 'large capacity ammunition feeding device'—

"(A) means a magazine, belt, drum, feed strip, or similar device manufactured after the date of enactment of the Violent Crime Control and Law Enforcement Act of 1994 that has a capacity of, or that can be readily restored or converted to accept, more than 10 rounds of ammunition; but

"(B) does not include an attached tubular device designed to accept, and capable of operating only with, .22 caliber rimfire ammunition.".

(c) Penalty.—Section 924(a)(1)(B) of title 18, United States Code, as amended by section 110102(c)(1), is amended by striking "or (v)" and inserting "(v), or (w)".

(d) Identification Markings for Large Capacity Ammunition Feeding Devices.—Section 923(i) of title 18, United States Code, as amended by section 110102(d) of this Act, is amended by adding at the end the following: "A large capacity ammunition feeding device manufactured after the date of the enactment of this sentence shall be identified by a serial number that clearly shows that the device was manufactured or imported after the effective date of this subsection, and such other identification as the Secretary may by regulation prescribe.".

SEC. 110104. STUDY BY ATTORNEY GENERAL.

(a) Study.—The Attorney General shall investigate and study the effect of this subtitle and the amendments made by this subtitle, and in particular shall determine their impact, if any, on violent and drug trafficking crime. The study shall be conducted over a period of 18 months, commencing 12 months after the date of enactment of this Act.

(b) Report.—Not later than 30 months after the date of enactment of this Act, the Attorney General shall prepare and submit to the Congress a report setting forth in detail the findings and determinations made in the study under subsection (a).

SEC. 110105. EFFECTIVE DATE.

This subtitle and the amendments made by this subtitle—

(1) shall take effect on the date of the enactment of this Act; and

(2) are repealed effective as of the date that is 10 years after that date.

SEC. 110106. APPENDIX A TO SECTION 922 OF TITLE 18.

Section 922 of title 18, United States Code, is amended by adding at the end the following appendix:

"APPENDIX A

Centerfire Rifles—Autoloaders

Browning BAR Mark II Safari Semi-Auto Rifle
Browning BAR Mark II Safari Magnum Rifle
Browning High-Power Rifle
Heckler & Koch Model 300 Rifle
Iver Johnson M–1 Carbine
Iver Johnson 50th Anniversary M–1 Carbine
Marlin Model 9 Camp Carbine
Marlin Model 45 Carbine
Remington Nylon 66 Auto-Loading Rifle
Remington Model 7400 Auto Rifle
Remington Model 7400 Rifle
Remington Model 7400 Special Purpose Auto Rifle
Ruger Mini-14 Autoloading Rifle (w/o folding stock)
Ruger Mini Thirty Rifle

Centerfire Rifles—Lever & Slide

Browning Model 81 BLR Lever-Action Rifle
Browning Model 81 Long Action BLR

Browning Model 1886 Lever-Action Carbine
Browning Model 1886 High Grade Carbine
Cimarron 1860 Henry Replica
Cimarron 1866 Winchester Replicas
Cimarron 1873 Short Rifle
Cimarron 1873 Sporting Rifle
Cimarron 1873 30" Express Rifle
Dixie Engraved 1873 Rifle
E.M.F. 1866 Yellowboy Lever Actions
E.M.F. 1860 Henry Rifle
E.M.F. Model 73 Lever-Action Rifle
Marlin Model 336CS Lever-Action Carbine
Marlin Model 30AS Lever-Action Carbine
Marlin Model 444SS Lever-Action Sporter
Marlin Model 1894S Lever-Action Carbine
Marlin Model 1894CS Carbine
Marlin Model 1894CL Classic
Marlin Model 1895SS Lever-Action Rifle
Mitchell 1858 Henry Replica
Mitchell 1866 Winchester Replica
Mitchell 1873 Winchester Replica
Navy Arms Military Henry Rifle
Navy Arms Henry Trapper
Navy Arms Iron Frame Henry
Navy Arms Henry Carbine
Navy Arms 1866 Yellowboy Rifle
Navy Arms 1873 Winchester-Style Rifle
Navy Arms 1873 Sporting Rifle
Remington 7600 Slide Action
Remington Model 7600 Special Purpose Slide Action
Rossi M92 SRC Saddle-Ring Carbine
Rossi M92 SRS Short Carbine
Savage 99C Lever-Action Rifle
Uberti Henry Rifle
Uberti 1866 Sporting Rifle
Uberti 1873 Sporting Rifle
Winchester Model 94 Side Eject Lever-Action Rifle
Winchester Model 94 Trapper Side Eject
Winchester Model 94 Big Bore Side Eject
Winchester Model 94 Ranger Side Eject Lever-Action Rifle
Winchester Model 94 Wrangler Side Eject

Centerfire Rifles—Bolt Action

Alpine Bolt-Action Rifle
A-Square Caesar Bolt-Action Rifle
A-Square Hannibal Bolt-Action Rifle
Anschutz 1700D Classic Rifles
Anschutz 1700D Custom Rifles
Anschutz 1700D Bavarian Bolt-Action Rifle
Anschutz 1733D Mannlicher Rifle
Barret Model 90 Bolt-Action Rifle
Beeman/HW 60J Bolt-Action Rifle
Blaser R84 Bolt-Action Rifle
BRNO 537 Sporter Bolt-Action Rifle
BRNO ZKB 527 Fox Bolt-Action Rifle
BRNO ZKK 600, 601, 602 Bolt-Action Rifles
Browning A-Bolt Rifle
Browning A-Bolt Stainless Stalker
Browning A-Bolt Left Hand
Browning A-Bolt Short Action
Browning Euro-Bolt Rifle
Browning A-Bolt Gold Medallion
Browning A-Bolt Micro Medallion
Century Centurion 14 Sporter
Century Enfield Sporter #4
Century Swedish Sporter #38
Century Mauser 98 Sporter
Cooper Model 38 Centerfire Sporter
Dakota 22 Sporter Bolt-Action Rifle
Dakota 76 Classic Bolt-Action Rifle
Dakota 76 Short Action Rifles
Dakota 76 Safari Bolt-Action Rifle
Dakota 416 Rigby African
E.A.A./Sabatti Rover 870 Bolt-Action Rifle
Auguste Francotte Bolt-Action Rifles
Carl Gustaf 2000 Bolt-Action Rifle
Heym Magnum Express Series Rifle
Howa Lightning Bolt-Action Rifle
Howa Realtree Camo Rifle
Interarms Mark X Viscount Bolt-Action Rifle
Interarms Mini-Mark X Rifle
Interarms Mark X Whitworth Bolt-Action Rifle
Interarms Whitworth Express Rifle
Iver Johnson Model 5100A1 Long-Range Rifle
KDF K15 American Bolt-Action Rifle
Krico Model 600 Bolt-Action Rifle

Krico Model 700 Bolt-Action Rifles
Mauser Model 66 Bolt-Action Rifle
Mauser Model 99 Bolt-Action Rifle
McMillan Signature Classic Sporter
McMillan Signature Super Varminter
McMillan Signature Alaskan
McMillan Signature Titanium Mountain Rifle
McMillan Classic Stainless Sporter
McMillan Talon Safari Rifle
McMillan Talon Sporter Rifle
Midland 1500S Survivor Rifle
Navy Arms TU–33/40 Carbine
Parker-Hale Model 81 Classic Rifle
Parker-Hale Model 81 Classic African Rifle
Parker-Hale Model 1000 Rifle
Parker-Hale Model 1100M African Magnum
Parker-Hale Model 1100 Lightweight Rifle
Parker-Hale Model 1200 Super Rifle Parker
Hale Model 1200 Super Clip Rifle
Parker-Hale Model 1300C Scout Rifle
Parker-Hale Model 2100 Midland Rifle
Parker-Hale Model 2700 Lightweight Rifle
Parker-Hale Model 2800 Midland Rifle
Remington Model Seven Bolt-Action Rifle
Remington Model Seven Youth Rifle
Remington Model Seven Custom KS
Remington Model Seven Custom MS Rifle
Remington 700 ADL Bolt-Action Rifle
Remington 700 BDL Bolt-Action Rifle
Remington 700 BDL Varmint Special
Remington 700 BDL European Bolt-Action Rifle
Remington 700 Varmint Synthetic Rifle
Remington 700 BDL SS Rifle
Remington 700 Stainless Synthetic Rifle
Remington 700 MTRSS Rifle
Remington 700 BDL Left Hand
Remington 700 Camo Synthetic Rifle
Remington 700 Safari
Remington 700 Mountain Rifle
Remington 700 Custom KS Mountain Rifle
Remington 700 Classic Rifle
Ruger M77 Mark II Rifle
Ruger M77 Mark II Magnum Rifle
Ruger M77RL Ultra Light

Ruger M77 Mark II All-Weather Stainless Rifle
Ruger M77 RSI International Carbine
Ruger M77 Mark II Express Rifle
Ruger M77VT Target Rifle
Sako Hunter Rifle
Sako Fiberclass Sporter
Sako Safari Grade Bolt Action
Sako Hunter Left-Hand Rifle
Sako Classic Bolt Action
Sako Hunter LS Rifle
Sako Deluxe Lightweight
Sako Super Deluxe Sporter
Sako Mannlicher-Style Carbine
Sako Varmint Heavy Barrel
Sako TRG–S Bolt-Action Rifle
Sauer 90 Bolt-Action Rifle
Savage 110G Bolt-Action Rifle
Savage 110CY Youth/Ladies Rifle
Savage 110WLE One of One Thousand Limited Edition Rifle
Savage 110GXP3 Bolt-Action Rifle
Savage 110F Bolt-Action Rifle
Savage 110FXP3 Bolt-Action Rifle
Savage 110GV Varmint Rifle
Savage 112FV Varmint Rifle
Savage Model 112FVS Varmint Rifle
Savage Model 112BV Heavy Barrel Varmint Rifle
Savage 116FSS Bolt-Action Rifle
Savage Model 116FSK Kodiak Rifle
Savage 110FP Police Rifle
Steyr-Mannlicher Sporter Models SL, L, M, S, S/T
Steyr-Mannlicher Luxus Model L, M, S
Steyr-Mannlicher Model M Professional Rifle
Tikka Bolt-Action Rifle
Tikka Premium Grade Rifles
Tikka Varmint/Continental Rifle
Tikka Whitetail/Battue Rifle
Ultra Light Arms Model 20 Rifle
Ultra Light Arms Model 28, Model 40 Rifles
Voere VEC 91 Lightning Bolt-Action Rifle
Voere Model 2165 Bolt-Action Rifle
Voere Model 2155, 2150 Bolt-Action Rifles
Weatherby Mark V Deluxe Bolt-Action Rifle
Weatherby Lasermark V Rifle
Weatherby Mark V Crown Custom Rifles

Weatherby Mark V Sporter Rifle
Weatherby Mark V Safari Grade Custom Rifles
Weatherby Weathermark Rifle
Weatherby Weathermark Alaskan Rifle
Weatherby Classicmark No. 1 Rifle
Weatherby Weatherguard Alaskan Rifle
Weatherby Vanguard VGX Deluxe Rifle
Weatherby Vanguard Classic Rifle
Weatherby Vanguard Classic No. 1 Rifle
Weatherby Vanguard Weatherguard Rifle
Wichita Classic Rifle
Wichita Varmint Rifle
Winchester Model 70 Sporter
Winchester Model 70 Sporter WinTuff
Winchester Model 70 SM Sporter
Winchester Model 70 Stainless Rifle
Winchester Model 70 Varmint
Winchester Model 70 Synthetic Heavy Varmint Rifle
Winchester Model 70 DBM Rifle
Winchester Model 70 DBM–S Rifle
Winchester Model 70 Featherweight
Winchester Model 70 Featherweight WinTuff
Winchester Model 70 Featherweight Classic
Winchester Model 70 Lightweight Rifle
Winchester Ranger Rifle
Winchester Model 70 Super Express Magnum
Winchester Model 70 Super Grade
Winchester Model 70 Custom Sharpshooter
Winchester Model 70 Custom Sporting Sharpshooter Rifle

Centerfire Rifles—Single Shot

Armsport 1866 Sharps Rifle, Carbine
Brown Model One Single Shot Rifle
Browning Model 1885 Single Shot Rifle
Dakota Single Shot Rifle
Desert Industries G–90 Single Shot Rifle
Harrington & Richardson Ultra Varmint Rifle
Model 1885 High Wall Rifle
Navy Arms Rolling Block Buffalo Rifle
Navy Arms #2 Creedmoor Rifle
Navy Arms Sharps Cavalry Carbine
Navy Arms Sharps Plains Rifle
New England Firearms Handi-Rifle
Red Willow Armory Ballard No. 5 Pacific

Red Willow Armory Ballard No. 1.5 Hunting Rifle
Red Willow Armory Ballard No. 8 Union Hill Rifle
Red Willow Armory Ballard No. 4.5 Target Rifle
Remington-Style Rolling Block Carbine
Ruger No. 1B Single Shot
Ruger No. 1A Light Sporter
Ruger No. 1H Tropical Rifle
Ruger No. 1S Medium Sporter
Ruger No. 1 RSI International
Ruger No. 1V Special Varminter
C. Sharps Arms New Model 1874 Old Reliable
C. Sharps Arms New Model 1875 Rifle
C. Sharps Arms 1875 Classic Sharps
C. Sharps Arms New Model 1875 Target & Long Range
Shiloh Sharps 1874 Long Range Express
Shiloh Sharps 1874 Montana Roughrider
Shiloh Sharps 1874 Military Carbine
Shiloh Sharps 1874 Business Rifle
Shiloh Sharps 1874 Military Rifle
Sharps 1874 Old Reliable
Thompson/Center Contender Carbine
Thompson/Center Stainless Contender Carbine
Thompson/Center Contender Carbine Survival System
Thompson/Center Contender Carbine Youth Model
Thompson/Center TCR '87 Single Shot Rifle
Uberti Rolling Block Baby Carbine

Drillings, Combination Guns, Double Rifles

Beretta Express SSO O/U Double Rifles
Beretta Model 455 SxS Express Rifle
Chapuis RGExpress Double Rifle
Auguste Francotte Sidelock Double Rifles
Auguste Francotte Boxlock Double Rifle
Heym Model 55B O/U Double Rifle
Heym Model 55FW O/U Combo Gun
Heym Model 88b Side-by-Side Double Rifle
Kodiak Mk. IV Double Rifle
Kreighoff Teck O/U Combination Gun
Kreighoff Trumpf Drilling
Merkel Over/Under Combination Guns
Merkel Drillings
Merkel Model 160 Side-by-Side Double Rifles
Merkel Over/Under Double Rifles
Savage 24F O/U Combination Gun

Savage 24F–12T Turkey Gun
Springfield Inc. M6 Scout Rifle/Shotgun
Tikka Model 412s Combination Gun
Tikka Model 412S Double Fire
A. Zoli Rifle-Shotgun O/U Combo

Rimfire Rifles—Autoloaders

AMT Lightning 25/22 Rifle
AMT Lightning Small-Game Hunting Rifle II
AMT Magnum Hunter Auto Rifle
Anschutz 525 Deluxe Auto
Armscor Model 20P Auto Rifle
Browning Auto-22 Rifle
Browning Auto-22 Grade VI
Krico Model 260 Auto Rifle
Lakefield Arms Model 64B Auto Rifle
Marlin Model 60 Self-Loading Rifle
Marlin Model 60ss Self-Loading Rifle
Marlin Model 70 HC Auto
Marlin Model 990l Self-Loading Rifle
Marlin Model 70P Papoose
Marlin Model 922 Magnum Self-Loading Rifle
Marlin Model 995 Self-Loading Rifle
Norinco Model 22 ATD Rifle
Remington Model 522 Viper Autoloading Rifle
Remington 552BDL Speedmaster Rifle
Ruger 10/22 Autoloading Carbine (w/o folding stock)
Survival Arms AR–7 Explorer Rifle
Texas Remington Revolving Carbine
Voere Model 2115 Auto Rifle

Rimfire Rifles—Lever & Slide Action

Browning BL–22 Lever-Action Rifle
Marlin 39TDS Carbine
Marlin Model 39AS Golden Lever-Action Rifle
Remington 572BDL Fieldmaster Pump Rifle
Norinco EM–321 Pump Rifle
Rossi Model 62 SA Pump Rifle
Rossi Model 62 SAC Carbine
Winchester Model 9422 Lever-Action Rifle
Winchester Model 9422 Magnum Lever-Action Rifle

Rimfire Rifles—Bolt Actions & Single Shots

Anschutz Achiever Bolt-Action Rifle
Anschutz 1416D/1516D Classic Rifles
Anschutz 1418D/1518D Mannlicher Rifles
Anschutz 1700D Classic Rifles
Anschutz 1700D Custom Rifles
Anschutz 1700 FWT Bolt-Action Rifle
Anschutz 1700D Graphite Custom Rifle
Anschutz 1700D Bavarian Bolt-Action Rifle
Armscor Model 14P Bolt-Action Rifle
Armscor Model 1500 Rifle
BRNO ZKM–452 Deluxe Bolt-Action Rifle
BRNO ZKM 452 Deluxe
Beeman/HW 60–J–ST Bolt-Action Rifle
Browning A-Bolt 22 Bolt-Action Rifle
Browning A-Bolt Gold Medallion
Cabanas Phaser Rifle
Cabanas Master Bolt-Action Rifle
Cabanas Espronceda IV Bolt-Action Rifle
Cabanas Leyre Bolt-Action Rifle
Chipmunk Single Shot Rifle
Cooper Arms Model 36S Sporter Rifle
Dakota 22 Sporter Bolt-Action Rifle
Krico Model 300 Bolt-Action Rifles
Lakefield Arms Mark II Bolt-Action Rifle
Lakefield Arms Mark I Bolt-Action Rifle
Magtech Model MT–22C Bolt-Action Rifle
Marlin Model 880 Bolt-Action Rifle
Marlin Model 881 Bolt-Action Rifle
Marlin Model 882 Bolt-Action Rifle
Marlin Model 883 Bolt-Action Rifle
Marlin Model 883SS Bolt-Action Rifle
Marlin Model 25MN Bolt-Action Rifle
Marlin Model 25N Bolt-Action Repeater
Marlin Model 15YN "Little Buckaroo"
Mauser Model 107 Bolt-Action Rifle
Mauser Model 201 Bolt-Action Rifle
Navy Arms TU–KKW Training Rifle
Navy Arms TU–33/40 Carbine
Navy Arms TU–KKW Sniper Trainer
Norinco JW–27 Bolt-Action Rifle
Norinco JW–15 Bolt-Action Rifle
Remington 541–T
Remington 40–XR Rimfire Custom Sporter

Remington 541–T HB Bolt-Action Rifle
Remington 581–S Sportsman Rifle
Ruger 77/22 Rimfire Bolt-Action Rifle
Ruger K77/22 Varmint Rifle
Ultra Light Arms Model 20 RF Bolt-Action Rifle
Winchester Model 52B Sporting Rifle

Competition Rifles—Centerfire & Rimfire

Anschutz 64–MS Left Silhouette
Anschutz 1808D RT Super Match 54 Target
Anschutz 1827B Biathlon Rifle
Anschutz 1903D Match Rifle
Anschutz 1803D Intermediate Match
Anschutz 1911 Match Rifle
Anschutz 54.18MS REP Deluxe Silhouette Rifle
Anschutz 1913 Super Match Rifle
Anschutz 1907 Match Rifle
Anschutz 1910 Super Match II
Anschutz 54.18MS Silhouette Rifle
Anschutz Super Match 54 Target Model 2013
Anschutz Super Match 54 Target Model 2007
Beeman/Feinwerkbau 2600 Target Rifle
Cooper Arms Model TRP–1 ISU Standard Rifle
E.A.A./Weihrauch HW 60 Target Rifle
E.A.A./HW 660 Match Rifle
Finnish Lion Standard Target Rifle
Krico Model 360 S2 Biathlon Rifle
Krico Model 400 Match Rifle
Krico Model 360S Biathlon Rifle
Krico Model 500 Kricotronic Match Rifle
Krico Model 600 Sniper Rifle
Krico Model 600 Match Rifle
Lakefield Arms Model 90B Target Rifle
Lakefield Arms Model 91T Target Rifle
Lakefield Arms Model 92S Silhouette Rifle
Marlin Model 2000 Target Rifle
Mauser Model 86–SR Specialty Rifle
McMillan M–86 Sniper Rifle
McMillan Combo M–87/M–88 50-Caliber Rifle
McMillan 300 Phoenix Long Range Rifle
McMillan M–89 Sniper Rifle
McMillan National Match Rifle
McMillan Long Range Rifle
Parker-Hale M–87 Target Rifle

Parker-Hale M–85 Sniper Rifle
Remington 40–XB Rangemaster Target Centerfire
Remington 40–XR KS Rimfire Position Rifle
Remington 40–XBBR KS
Remington 40–XC KS National Match Course Rifle
Sako TRG–21 Bolt-Action Rifle
Steyr-Mannlicher Match SPG–UIT Rifle
Steyr-Mannlicher SSG P–I Rifle
Steyr-Mannlicher SSG P–III Rifle
Steyr-Mannlicher SSG P–IV Rifle
Tanner Standard UIT Rifle
Tanner 50 Meter Free Rifle
Tanner 300 Meter Free Rifle
Wichita Silhouette Rifle

Shotguns—Autoloaders

American Arms/Franchi Black Magic 48/AL
Benelli Super Black Eagle Shotgun
Benelli Super Black Eagle Slug Gun
Benelli M1 Super 90 Field Auto Shotgun
Benelli Montefeltro Super 90 20-Gauge Shotgun
Benelli Montefeltro Super 90 Shotgun
Benelli M1 Sporting Special Auto Shotgun
Benelli Black Eagle Competition Auto Shotgun
Beretta A–303 Auto Shotgun
Beretta 390 Field Auto Shotgun
Beretta 390 Super Trap, Super Skeet Shotguns
Beretta Vittoria Auto Shotgun
Beretta Model 1201F Auto Shotgun
Browning BSA 10 Auto Shotgun
Browning BSA 10 Stalker Auto Shotgun
Browning A–500R Auto Shotgun
Browning A–500G Auto Shotgun
Browning A–500G Sporting Clays
Browning Auto-5 Light 12 and 20
Browning Auto-5 Stalker
Browning Auto-5 Magnum 20
Browning Auto-5 Magnum 12
Churchill Turkey Automatic Shotgun
Cosmi Automatic Shotgun
Maverick Model 60 Auto Shotgun
Mossberg Model 5500 Shotgun
Mossberg Model 9200 Regal Semi-Auto Shotgun
Mossberg Model 9200 USST Auto Shotgun

Mossberg Model 9200 Camo Shotgun
Mossberg Model 6000 Auto Shotgun
Remington Model 1100 Shotgun
Remington 11–87 Premier Shotgun
Remington 11–87 Sporting Clays
Remington 11–87 Premier Skeet
Remington 11–87 Premier Trap
Remington 11–87 Special Purpose Magnum
Remington 11–87 SPS–T Camo Auto Shotgun
Remington 11–87 Special Purpose Deer Gun
Remington 11–87 SPS–BG-Camo Deer/Turkey Shotgun
Remington 11–87 SPS-Deer Shotgun
Remington 11–87 Special Purpose Synthetic Camo
Remington SP–10 Magnum-Camo Auto Shotgun
Remington SP–10 Magnum Auto Shotgun
Remington SP–10 Magnum Turkey Combo
Remington 1100 LT–20 Auto
Remington 1100 Special Field
Remington 1100 20-Gauge Deer Gun
Remington 1100 LT–20 Tournament Skeet
Winchester Model 1400 Semi-Auto Shotgun

Shotguns—Slide Actions

Browning Model 42 Pump Shotgun
Browning BPS Pump Shotgun
Browning BPS Stalker Pump Shotgun
Browning BPS Pigeon Grade Pump Shotgun
Browning BPS Pump Shotgun (Ladies and Youth Model)
Browning BPS Game Gun Turkey Special
Browning BPS Game Gun Deer Special
Ithaca Model 87 Supreme Pump Shotgun
Ithaca Model 87 Deerslayer Shotgun
Ithaca Deerslayer II Rifled Shotgun
Ithaca Model 87 Turkey Gun
Ithaca Model 87 Deluxe Pump Shotgun
Magtech Model 586–VR Pump Shotgun
Maverick Models 88, 91 Pump Shotguns
Mossberg Model 500 Sporting Pump
Mossberg Model 500 Camo Pump
Mossberg Model 500 Muzzleloader Combo
Mossberg Model 500 Trophy Slugster
Mossberg Turkey Model 500 Pump
Mossberg Model 500 Bantam Pump
Mossberg Field Grade Model 835 Pump Shotgun

Mossberg Model 835 Regal Ulti-Mag Pump
Remington 870 Wingmaster
Remington 870 Special Purpose Deer Gun
Remington 870 SPS–BG-Camo Deer/Turkey Shotgun
Remington 870 SPS-Deer Shotgun
Remington 870 Marine Magnum
Remington 870 TC Trap
Remington 870 Special Purpose Synthetic Camo
Remington 870 Wingmaster Small Gauges
Remington 870 Express Rifle Sighted Deer Gun
Remington 879 SPS Special Purpose Magnum
Remington 870 SPS–T Camo Pump Shotgun
Remington 870 Special Field
Remington 870 Express Turkey
Remington 870 High Grades
Remington 870 Express
Remington Model 870 Express Youth Gun
Winchester Model 12 Pump Shotgun
Winchester Model 42 High Grade Shotgun
Winchester Model 1300 Walnut Pump
Winchester Model 1300 Slug Hunter Deer Gun
Winchester Model 1300 Ranger Pump Gun Combo & Deer Gun
Winchester Model 1300 Turkey Gun
Winchester Model 1300 Ranger Pump Gun

Shotguns—Over/Unders

American Arms/Franchi Falconet 2000 O/U
American Arms Silver I O/U
American Arms Silver II Shotgun
American Arms Silver Skeet O/U
American Arms/Franchi Sporting 2000 O/U
American Arms Silver Sporting O/U
American Arms Silver Trap O/U
American Arms WS/OU 12, TS/OU 12 Shotguns
American Arms WT/OU 10 Shotgun
Armsport 2700 O/U Goose Gun
Armsport 2700 Series O/U
Armsport 2900 Tri-Barrel Shotgun
Baby Bretton Over/Under Shotgun
Beretta Model 686 Ultralight O/U
Beretta ASE 90 Competition O/U Shotgun
Beretta Over/Under Field Shotguns
Beretta Onyx Hunter Sport O/U Shotgun
Beretta Model SO5, SO6, SO9 Shotguns

Beretta Sporting Clay Shotguns
Beretta 687EL Sporting O/U
Beretta 682 Super Sporting O/U
Beretta Series 682 Competition Over/Unders
Browning Citori O/U Shotgun
Browning Superlight Citori Over/Under
Browning Lightning Sporting Clays
Browning Micro Citori Lightning
Browning Citori Plus Trap Combo
Browning Citori Plus Trap Gun
Browning Citori O/U Skeet Models
Browning Citori O/U Trap Models
Browning Special Sporting Clays
Browning Citori GTI Sporting Clays
Browning 325 Sporting Clays
Centurion Over/Under Shotgun
Chapuis Over/Under Shotgun
Connecticut Valley Classics Classic Sporter O/U
Connecticut Valley Classics Classic Field Waterfowler
Charles Daly Field Grade O/U
Charles Daly Lux Over/Under
E.A.A./Sabatti Sporting Clays Pro-Gold O/U
E.A.A/Sabatti Falcon-Mon Over/Under
Kassnar Grade I O/U Shotgun
Krieghoff K–80 Sporting Clays O/U
Krieghoff K–80 Skeet Shotgun
Krieghoff K–80 International Skeet
Krieghoff K–80 Four-Barrel Skeet Set
Krieghoff K–80/RT Shotguns
Krieghoff K–80 O/U Trap Shotgun
Laurona Silhouette 300 Sporting Clays
Laurona Silhouette 300 Trap
Laurona Super Model Over/Unders
Ljutic LM–6 Deluxe O/U Shotgun
Marocchi Conquista Over/Under Shotgun
Marocchi Avanza O/U Shotgun
Merkel Model 200E O/U Shotgun
Merkel Model 200E Skeet, Trap Over/Unders
Merkel Model 203E, 303E Over/Under Shotguns
Perazzi Mirage Special Sporting O/U
Perazzi Mirage Special Four-Gauge Skeet
Perazzi Sporting Classic O/U
Perazzi MX7 Over/Under Shotguns
Perazzi Mirage Special Skeet Over/Under

Perazzi MX8/MX8 Special Trap, Skeet
Perazzi MX8/20 Over/Under Shotgun
Perazzi MX9 Single Over/Under Shotguns
Perazzi MX12 Hunting Over/Under
Perazzi MX28, MX410 Game O/U Shotguns
Perazzi MX20 Hunting Over/Under
Piotti Boss Over/Under Shotgun
Remington Peerless Over/Under Shotgun
Ruger Red Label O/U Shotgun
Ruger Sporting Clays O/U Shotgun
San Marco 12-Ga. Wildflower Shotgun
San Marco Field Special O/U Shotgun
San Marco 10-Ga. O/U Shotgun
SKB Model 505 Deluxe Over/Under Shotgun
SKB Model 685 Over/Under Shotgun
SKB Model 885 Over/Under Trap, Skeet, Sporting Clays
Stoeger/IGA Condor I O/U Shotgun
Stoeger/IGA ERA 2000 Over/Under Shotgun
Techni-Mec Model 610 Over/Under
Tikka Model 412S Field Grade Over/Under
Weatherby Athena Grade IV O/U Shotguns
Weatherby Athena Grade V Classic Field O/U
Weatherby Orion O/U Shotguns
Weatherby II, III Classic Field O/Us
Weatherby Orion II Classic Sporting Clays O/U
Weatherby Orion II Sporting Clays O/U
Winchester Model 1001 O/U Shotgun
Winchester Model 1001 Sporting Clays O/U
Pietro Zanoletti Model 2000 Field O/U

Shotguns—Side by Sides

American Arms Brittany Shotgun
American Arms Gentry Double Shotgun
American Arms Derby Side-by-Side
American Arms Grulla #2 Double Shotgun
American Arms WS/SS 10
American Arms TS/SS 10 Double Shotgun
American Arms TS/SS 12 Side-by-Side
Arrieta Sidelock Double Shotguns
Armsport 1050 Series Double Shotguns
Arizaga Model 31 Double Shotgun
AYA Boxlock Shotguns
AYA Sidelock Double Shotguns
Beretta Model 452 Sidelock Shotgun

Beretta Side-by-Side Field Shotguns
Crucelegui Hermanos Model 150 Double
Chapuis Side-by-Side Shotgun
E.A.A./Sabatti Saba-Mon Double Shotgun
Charles Daly Model Dss Double
Ferlib Model F VII Double Shotgun
Auguste Francotte Boxlock Shotgun
Auguste Francotte Sidelock Shotgun
Garbi Model 100 Double
Garbi Model 101 Side-by-Side
Garbi Model 103A, B Side-by-Side
Garbi Model 200 Side-by-Side
Bill Hanus Birdgun Doubles
Hatfield Uplander Shotgun
Merkel Model 8, 47E Side-by-Side Shotguns
Merkel Model 47LSC Sporting Clays Double
Merkel Model 47S, 147S Side-by-Sides
Parker Reproductions Side-by-Side
Piotti King No. 1 Side-by-Side
Piotti Lunik Side-by-Side
Piotti King Extra Side-by-Side
Piotti Piuma Side-by-Side
Precision Sports Model 600 Series Doubles
Rizzini Boxlock Side-by-Side
Rizzini Sidelock Side-by-Side
Stoeger/IGA Uplander Side-by-Side Shotgun
Ugartechea 10-Ga. Magnum Shotgun

Shotguns—Bolt Actions & Single Shots

Armsport Single Barrel Shotgun
Browning BT–99 Competition Trap Special
Browning BT–99 Plus Trap Gun
Browning BT–99 Plus Micro
Browning Recoilless Trap Shotgun
Browning Micro Recoilless Trap Shotgun
Desert Industries Big Twenty Shotgun
Harrington & Richardson Topper Model 098
Harrington & Richardson Topper Classic Youth Shotgun
Harrington & Richardson N.W.T.F. Turkey Mag
Harrington & Richardson Topper Deluxe Model 098
Krieghoff KS–5 Trap Gun
Krieghoff KS–5 Special
Krieghoff K–80 Single Barrel Trap Gun
Ljutic Mono Gun Single Barrel

Ljutic LTX Super Deluxe Mono Gun
Ljutic Recoilless Space Gun Shotgun
Marlin Model 55 Goose Gun Bolt Action
New England Firearms Turkey and Goose Gun
New England Firearms N.W.T.F. Shotgun
New England Firearms Tracker Slug Gun
New England Firearms Standard Pardner
New England Firearms Survival Gun
Perazzi TM1 Special Single Trap
Remington 90–T Super Single Shotgun
Snake Charmer II Shotgun
Stoeger/IGA Reuna Single Barrel Shotgun
Thompson/Center TCR '87 Hunter Shotgun.".

Subtitle B—Youth Handgun Safety

SEC. 110201. PROHIBITION OF THE POSSESSION OF A HANDGUN OR AMMUNITION BY, OR THE PRIVATE TRANSFER OF A HANDGUN OR AMMUNITION TO, A JUVENILE.

(a) OFFENSE.—Section 922 of title 18, United States Code, as amended by section 110103(a), is amended by adding at the end the following new subsection:

"(x)(1) It shall be unlawful for a person to sell, deliver, or otherwise transfer to a person who the transferor knows or has reasonable cause to believe is a juvenile—

"(A) a handgun; or

"(B) ammunition that is suitable for use only in a handgun.

"(2) It shall be unlawful for any person who is a juvenile to knowingly possess—

"(A) a handgun; or

"(B) ammunition that is suitable for use only in a handgun.

"(3) This subsection does not apply to—

"(A) a temporary transfer of a handgun or ammunition to a juvenile or to the possession or use of a handgun or ammunition by a juvenile if the handgun and ammunition are possessed and used by the juvenile—

"(i) in the course of employment, in the course of ranching or farming related to activities at the residence of the juvenile (or on property used for ranching or farming at which the juvenile, with the permission of the property owner or lessee, is performing activities related to the operation of the farm or ranch), target practice, hunting, or a course of instruction in the safe and lawful use of a handgun;

"(ii) with the prior written consent of the juvenile's parent or guardian who is not prohibited by Federal, State, or local law from possessing a firearm, except—

"(I) during transportation by the juvenile of an unloaded handgun in a locked container directly from the place of transfer to a place at which an activity described in clause (i) is to take place and transportation by the juvenile of that handgun, unloaded and in a locked container, directly from the place at which such an activity took place to the transferor; or

"(II) with respect to ranching or farming activities as described in clause (i), a juvenile may possess and use a handgun or ammunition with the prior written approval of the juvenile's parent or legal guardian and at the direction of an adult who is not prohibited by Federal, State or local law from possessing a firearm;

"(iii) the juvenile has the prior written consent in the juvenile's possession at all times when a handgun is in the possession of the juvenile; and

"(iv) in accordance with State and local law;

"(B) a juvenile who is a member of the Armed Forces of the United States or the National Guard who possesses or is armed with a handgun in the line of duty;

"(C) a transfer by inheritance of title (but not possession) of a handgun or ammunition to a juvenile; or

"(D) the possession of a handgun or ammunition by a juvenile taken in defense of the juvenile or other persons against an intruder into the residence of the juvenile or a residence in which the juvenile is an invited guest.

"(4) A handgun or ammunition, the possession of which is transferred to a juvenile in circumstances in which the transferor is not in violation of this subsection shall not be subject to permanent confiscation by the Government if its possession by the juvenile subsequently becomes unlawful because of the conduct of the juvenile, but shall be returned to the lawful owner when such handgun or ammunition is no longer required by the Government for the purposes of investigation or prosecution.

"(5) For purposes of this subsection, the term 'juvenile' means a person who is less than 18 years of age.

"(6)(A) In a prosecution of a violation of this subsection, the court shall require the presence of a juvenile defendant's parent or legal guardian at all proceedings.

"(B) The court may use the contempt power to enforce subparagraph (A).

"(C) The court may excuse attendance of a parent or legal guardian of a juvenile defendant at a proceeding in a prosecution of a violation of this subsection for good cause shown.".

(b) PENALTIES.—Section 924(a) of title 18, United States Code, is amended—

(1) in paragraph (1) by striking "paragraph (2) or (3) of"; and

(2) by adding at the end the following new paragraph:

"(5)(A)(i) A juvenile who violates section 922(x) shall be fined under this title, imprisoned not more than 1 year, or both, except that a juvenile described in clause (ii) shall be sentenced to probation on appropriate conditions and shall not be incarcerated unless the juvenile fails to comply with a condition of probation.

"(ii) A juvenile is described in this clause if—

"(I) the offense of which the juvenile is charged is possession of a handgun or ammunition in violation of section 922(x)(2); and

"(II) the juvenile has not been convicted in any court of an offense (including an offense under section 922(x) or a similar State law, but not including any other offense consisting of conduct that if engaged in by an adult would not constitute an offense) or adjudicated as a juvenile delinquent for conduct that if engaged in by an adult would constitute an offense.

"(B) A person other than a juvenile who knowingly violates section 922(x)—

"(i) shall be fined under this title, imprisoned not more than 1 year, or both; and

"(ii) if the person sold, delivered, or otherwise transferred a handgun or ammunition to a juvenile knowing or having reasonable cause to know that the juvenile intended to carry or otherwise possess or discharge or otherwise use the handgun or ammunition in the commission of a crime of violence, shall be fined under this title, imprisoned not more than 10 years, or both.".

(c) TECHNICAL AMENDMENT OF JUVENILE DELINQUENCY PROVISIONS IN TITLE 18, UNITED STATES CODE.—

(1) SECTION 5031.—Section 5031 of title 18, United States Code, is amended by inserting "or a violation by such a person of section 922(x)" before the period at the end.

(2) SECTION 5032.—Section 5032 of title 18, United States Code, is amended—

(A) in the first undesignated paragraph by inserting "or (x)" after "922(p)"; and

(B) in the fourth undesignated paragraph by inserting "or section 922(x) of this title," before "criminal prosecution on the basis".

(d) TECHNICAL AMENDMENT OF THE JUVENILE JUSTICE AND DELINQUENCY PREVENTION ACT OF 1974.—Section 223(a)(12)(A) of the Juvenile Justice and Delinquency Prevention Act of 1974 (42 U.S.C. 5633(a)(12)(A)) is amended by striking "which do not constitute violations of valid court orders" and inserting "(other than an offense that constitutes a violation of a valid court order or a violation of section 922(x) of title 18, United States Code, or a similar State law)."

(e) MODEL LAW.—The Attorney General, acting through the Director of the National Institute for Juvenile Justice and Delinquency Prevention, shall—

(1) evaluate existing and proposed juvenile handgun legislation in each

State;

(2) develop model juvenile handgun legislation that is constitutional and enforceable;

(3) prepare and disseminate to State authorities the findings made as the result of the evaluation; and

(4) report to Congress by December 31, 1995, findings and recommendations concerning the need or appropriateness of further action by the Federal Government.

Subtitle C—Licensure

SEC. 110301. FIREARMS LICENSURE AND REGISTRATION TO REQUIRE A PHOTOGRAPH AND FINGERPRINTS.

(a) FIREARMS LICENSURE.—Section 923(a) of title 18, United States Code, is amended in the second sentence by inserting "and shall include a photograph and fingerprints of the applicant" before the period.

(b) REGISTRATION.—Section 5802 of the Internal Revenue Code of 1986 is amended by inserting after the first sentence the following: "An individual required to register under this section shall include a photograph and fingerprints of the individual with the initial application.".

SEC. 110302. COMPLIANCE WITH STATE AND LOCAL LAW AS A CONDITION TO LICENSE.

Section 923(d)(1) of title 18, United States Code, is amended—

(1) by striking "and" at the end of subparagraph (D);

(2) by striking the period at the end of subparagraph (E) and inserting "; and"; and

(3) by adding at the end the following new subparagraph: "(F) the applicant certifies that—

"(i) the business to be conducted under the license is not prohibited by State or local law in the place where the licensed premise is located;

"(ii)(I) within 30 days after the application is approved the business will comply with the requirements of State and local law applicable to the conduct of the business; and

"(II) the business will not be conducted under the license until the requirements of State and local law applicable to the business have been met; and

"(iii) that the applicant has sent or delivered a form to be prescribed by the Secretary, to the chief law enforcement officer of the locality in which the premises are located, which indicates that the applicant intends to apply for a Federal firearms license.".

SEC. 110303. ACTION ON FIREARMS LICENSE APPLICATION.

Section 923(d)(2) of title 18, United States Code, is amended by striking "forty-five-day" and inserting "60-day".

SEC. 110304. INSPECTION OF FIREARMS LICENSEES' INVENTORY AND RECORDS.

Section 923(g)(1)(B)(ii) of title 18, United States Code, is amended to read as follows:

"(ii) for ensuring compliance with the record keeping requirements of this chapter—

"(I) not more than once during any 12-month period; or

"(II) at any time with respect to records relating to a firearm involved in a criminal investigation that is traced to the licensee.".

SEC. 110305. REPORTS OF THEFT OR LOSS OF FIREARMS.

Section 923(g) of title 18, United States Code, is amended by adding at the end the following new paragraph:

"(6) Each licensee shall report the theft or loss of a firearm from the licensee's inventory or collection, within 48 hours after the theft or loss is discovered, to the Secretary and to the appropriate local authorities.".

SEC. 110306. RESPONSES TO REQUESTS FOR INFORMATION.

Section 923(g) of title 18, United States Code, as amended by section 110405, is amended by adding at the end the following new paragraph:

"(7) Each licensee shall respond immediately to, and in no event later than 24 hours after the receipt of, a request by the Secretary for information contained in the records required to be kept by this chapter as may be required for determining the disposition of 1 or more firearms in the course of a bona fide criminal investigation. The requested information shall be provided orally or in writing, as the Secretary may require. The Secretary shall implement a system whereby the licensee can positively identify and establish that an individual requesting information via telephone is employed by and authorized by the agency to request such information.".

SEC. 110307. NOTIFICATION OF NAMES AND ADDRESSES OF FIREARMS LICENSEES.

Section 923 of title 18, United States Code, is amended by adding at the end the following new subsection:

"(1) The Secretary of the Treasury shall notify the chief law enforcement officer in the appropriate State and local jurisdictions of the names and addresses of all persons in the State to whom a firearms license is issued.".

Subtitle D—Domestic Violence

SEC. 110401. PROHIBITION AGAINST DISPOSAL OF FIREARMS TO, OR RECEIPT OF FIREARMS BY, PERSONS WHO HAVE COMMITTED DOMESTIC ABUSE.

(a) INTIMATE PARTNER DEFINED.—Section 921(a) of title 18, United States Code, as amended by section 110103(b), is amended by inserting at the end the following new paragraph:

"(32) The term 'intimate partner' means, with respect to a person, the spouse of the person, a former spouse of the person, an individual who is a parent of a child of the person, and an individual who cohabitates or has cohabited with the person.".

(b) PROHIBITION AGAINST DISPOSAL OF FIREARMS.—Section 922(d) of title 18, United States Code, is amended—

(1) by striking "or" at the end of paragraph (6);

(2) by striking the period at the end of paragraph (7) and inserting "; or"; and

(3) by inserting after paragraph (7) the following new paragraph:

"(8) is subject to a court order that restrains such person from harassing, stalking, or threatening an intimate partner of such person or child of such intimate partner or person, or engaging in other conduct that would place an intimate partner in reasonable fear of bodily injury to the partner or child, except that this paragraph shall only apply to a court order that—

"(A) was issued after a hearing of which such person received actual notice, and at which such person had the opportunity to participate; and

"(B)(i) includes a finding that such person represents a credible threat to the physical safety of such intimate partner or child; or

"(ii) by its terms explicitly prohibits the use, attempted use, or threatened use of physical force against such intimate partner or child that would reasonably be expected to cause bodily injury.".

(c) PROHIBITION AGAINST RECEIPT OF FIREARMS.—Section 922(g) of title 18, United States Code, is amended—

(1) by striking "or" at the end of paragraph (6);

(2) by inserting "or" at the end of paragraph (7); and

(3) by inserting after paragraph (7) the following:

"(8) who is subject to a court order that—

"(A) was issued after a hearing of which such person received actual notice, and at which such person had an opportunity to participate;

"(B) restrains such person from harassing, stalking, or threatening an intimate partner of such person or child of such intimate partner or person, or engaging in other conduct that would place an intimate partner in reasonable fear of bodily injury to the partner or child; and

"(C)(i) includes a finding that such person represents a credible threat to the physical safety of such intimate partner or child; or

"(ii) by its terms explicitly prohibits the use, attempted use, or threatened use of physical force against such intimate partner or child that would reasonably be expected to cause bodily injury,".

(d) STORAGE OF FIREARMS.—Section 926(a) of title 18, United States Code, is amended—

(1) by striking "and" at the end of paragraph (1);

(2) by striking the period at the end of paragraph (2) and inserting "; and"; and

(3) by inserting after paragraph (2) the following:

"(3) regulations providing for effective receipt and secure storage of firearms relinquished by or seized from persons described in subsection (d)(8) or (g)(8) of section 922.".

(e) RETURN OF FIREARMS.—Section 924(d)(1) of title 18, United States Code, is amended by striking "the seized" and inserting "or lapse of or court termination of the restraining order to which he is subject, the seized or relinquished".

Subtitle E—Gun Crime Penalties

SEC. 110501. ENHANCED PENALTY FOR USE OF A SEMIAUTOMATIC FIREARM DURING A CRIME OF VIOLENCE OR A DRUG TRAFFICKING CRIME.

(a) AMENDMENT TO SENTENCING GUIDELINES.—Pursuant to its authority under section 994 of title 28, United States Code, the United States Sentencing Commission shall amend its sentencing guidelines to provide an appropriate enhancement of the punishment for a crime of violence (as defined in section 924(c)(3) of title 18, United States Code) or a drug trafficking crime (as defined in section 924(c)(2) of title 18, United States Code) if a semiautomatic firearm is involved.

(b) SEMIAUTOMATIC FIREARM.—In subsection (a), "semiautomatic firearm" means any repeating firearm that utilizes a portion of the energy of a firing cartridge to extract the fired cartridge case and chamber the next round and that requires a separate pull of the trigger to fire each cartridge.

SEC. 110502. ENHANCED PENALTY FOR SECOND OFFENSE OF USING AN EXPLOSIVE TO COMMIT A FELONY.

Pursuant to its authority under section 994 of title 28, United States Code, the United States Sentencing Commission shall promulgate amendments to the sentencing guidelines to appropriately enhance penalties in a case in which a defendant convicted under section 844(h) of title 18, United States Code, has previously been convicted under that section.

SEC. 110503. SMUGGLING FIREARMS IN AID OF DRUG TRAFFICKING.

Section 924 of title 18, United States Code, as amended by section 60013, is amended by adding at the end the following new subsection:

"(j) A person who, with intent to engage in or to promote conduct that—

"(1) is punishable under the Controlled Substances Act (21 U.S.C. 801 et seq.), the Controlled Substances Import and Export Act (21 U.S.C. 951 et seq.), or the Maritime Drug Law Enforcement Act (46 U.S.C. App. 1901 et seq.);

"(2) violates any law of a State relating to any controlled substance (as defined in section 102 of the Controlled Substances Act, 21 U.S.C. 802); or

"(3) constitutes a crime of violence (as defined in subsection (c)(3), smuggles or knowingly brings into the United States a firearm, or attempts to do so, shall be imprisoned not more than 10 years, fined under this title, or both.".

SEC. 110504. THEFT OF FIREARMS AND EXPLOSIVES.

(a) FIREARMS.—Section 924 of title 18, United States Code, as amended by section 110203(a), is amended by adding at the end the following new subsection: "(k) A person who steals any firearm which is moving as, or is a part of, or which has moved in, interstate or foreign commerce shall be imprisoned for not more than 10 years, fined under this title, or both.".

(b) EXPLOSIVES.—Section 844 of title 18, United States Code, is amended by adding at the end the following new subsection:

"(k) A person who steals any explosives materials which are moving as, or are a part of, or which have moved in, interstate or foreign commerce shall be imprisoned for not more than 10 years, fined under this title, or both.".

SEC. 110505. REVOCATION OF SUPERVISED RELEASE AFTER IMPRISONMENT.

Section 3583 of title 18, United States Code, is amended—

(1) in subsection (d) by striking "possess illegal controlled substances" and inserting "unlawfully possess a controlled substance";

(2) in subsection (e)—

(A) by striking "person" each place such term appears in such subsection and inserting "defendant"; and

(B) by amending paragraph (3) to read as follows:

"(3) revoke a term of supervised release, and require the defendant to serve in prison all or part of the term of supervised release authorized by statute for the offense that resulted in such term of supervised release without credit for time previously served on postrelease supervision, if the

court, pursuant to the Federal Rules of Criminal Procedure applicable to revocation of probation or supervised release, finds by a preponderance of the evidence that the defendant violated a condition of supervised release, except that a defendant whose term is revoked under this paragraph may not be required to serve more than 5 years in prison if the offense that resulted in
the term of supervised release is a class A felony, more than 3 years in prison if such offense is a class B felony, more than 2 years in prison if such offense is a class C or D felony, or more than one year in any other case; or"; and

(3) by striking subsection (g) and inserting the following:

"(g) MANDATORY REVOCATION FOR POSSESSION OF CONTROLLED SUBSTANCE OR FIREARM OR FOR REFUSAL TO COMPLY WITH DRUG TESTING.—If the defendant—

"(1) possesses a controlled substance in violation of the condition set forth in subsection (d);

"(2) possesses a firearm, as such term is defined in section 921 of this title, in violation of Federal law, or otherwise violates a condition of supervised release prohibiting the defendant from possessing a firearm; or

"(3) refuses to comply with drug testing imposed as a condition of supervised release; the court shall revoke the term of supervised release and require the defendant to serve a term of imprisonment not to exceed the maximum term of imprisonment authorized under subsection (e)(3).

"(h) SUPERVISED RELEASE FOLLOWING REVOCATION.—When a term of supervised release is revoked and the defendant is required to serve a term of imprisonment that is less than the maximum term of imprisonment authorized under subsection (e)(3), the court may include a requirement that the defendant be placed on a term of supervised release after imprisonment. The length of such a term of supervised release shall not exceed the term of supervised release authorized by statute for the offense that resulted in the original term of supervised release, less any term of imprisonment that was imposed upon revocation of supervised release.

"(i) DELAYED REVOCATION.—The power of the court to revoke a term of supervised release for violation of a condition of supervised release, and to order the defendant to serve a term of imprisonment and, subject to the limitations in subsection (h), a further term of supervised release, extends beyond the expiration of the term of supervised release for any period reasonably necessary for the adjudication of matters arising before its expiration if, before its expiration, a warrant or summons has been issued on the basis of an allegation of such a violation.".

SEC. 110506. REVOCATION OF PROBATION.

(a) IN GENERAL.—Section 3565(a) of title 18, United States Code, is amended—

(1) in paragraph (2) by striking "impose any other sentence that was

available under subchapter A at the time of the initial sentencing" and inserting "resentence the defendant under subchapter A"; and

(2) by striking the last sentence.

(b) MANDATORY REVOCATION.—Section 3565(b) of title 18, United States Code, is amended to read as follows:

"(b) MANDATORY REVOCATION FOR POSSESSION OF CONTROLLED SUBSTANCE OR FIREARM OR REFUSAL TO COMPLY WITH DRUG TESTING.—If the defendant—

"(1) possesses a controlled substance in violation of the condition set forth in section 3563(a)(3);

"(2) possesses a firearm, as such term is defined in section 921 of this title, in violation of Federal law, or otherwise violates a condition of probation prohibiting the defendant from possessing a firearm; or

"(3) refuses to comply with drug testing, thereby violating the condition imposed by section 3563(a)(4),

the court shall revoke the sentence of probation and resentence the defendant under subchapter A to a sentence that includes a term of imprisonment.".

SEC. 110507. INCREASED PENALTY FOR KNOWINGLY MAKING FALSE, MATERIAL STATEMENT IN CONNECTION WITH THE ACQUISITION OF A FIREARM FROM A LICENSED DEALER.

Section 924(a) of title 18, United States Code, is amended—

(1) in subsection (a)(1)(B) by striking "(a)(6),"; and

(2) in subsection (a)(2) by inserting "(a)(6)," after "subsections".

SEC. 110508. POSSESSION OF EXPLOSIVES BY FELONS AND OTHERS.

Section 842(i) of title 18, United States Code, is amended by inserting "or possess" after "to receive".

SEC. 110509. SUMMARY DESTRUCTION OF EXPLOSIVES SUBJECT TO FORFEITURE.

Section 844(c) of title 18, United States Code, is amended—

(1) by inserting "(1)" after "(c)"; and

(2) by adding at the end the following new paragraphs:

"(2) Notwithstanding paragraph (1), in the case of the seizure of any explosive materials for any offense for which the materials would be subject to forfeiture in which it would be impracticable or unsafe to remove the materials to a place of storage or would be unsafe to store them, the seizing officer may destroy the explosive materials forthwith. Any destruction under this paragraph shall be in the presence of at least 1 credible witness. The seizing officer shall make a report of the seizure and take samples as the Secretary may by regulation prescribe.

"(3) Within 60 days after any destruction made pursuant to paragraph (2), the owner of (including any person having an interest in) the property so destroyed may make application to the Secretary for reimbursement of the value of the property. If the claimant establishes to the satisfaction of the Secretary that—

"(A) the property has not been used or involved in a violation of law; or

"(B) any unlawful involvement or use of the property was without the claimant's knowledge, consent, or willful blindness, the Secretary shall make an allowance to the claimant not exceeding the value of the property destroyed.".

SEC. 110510. ELIMINATION OF OUTMODED LANGUAGE RELATING TO PAROLE.

(a) SECTION 924(e)(1) OF TITLE 18.—Section 924(e)(1) of title 18, United States Code, is amended by striking ", and such person shall not be eligible for parole with respect to the sentence imposed under this subsection".

(b) SECTION 924(c)(1) OF TITLE 18.—Section 924(c)(1) of title 18, United States Code, is amended by striking "No person sentenced under this subsection shall be eligible for parole during the term of imprisonment imposed under this subsection.".

SEC. 110511. PROHIBITION AGAINST TRANSACTIONS INVOLVING STOLEN FIREARMS WHICH HAVE MOVED IN INTERSTATE OR FOREIGN COMMERCE.

Section 922(j) of title 18, United States Code, is amended to read as follows:

"(j) It shall be unlawful for any person to receive, possess, conceal, store, barter, sell, or dispose of any stolen firearm or stolen ammunition, or pledge or accept as security for a loan any stolen firearm or stolen ammunition, which is moving as, which is a part of, which constitutes, or which has been shipped or transported in, interstate or foreign commerce, either before or after it was stolen, knowing or having reasonable cause to believe that the firearm or ammunition was stolen.".

SEC. 110512. USING A FIREARM IN THE COMMISSION OF COUNTERFEITING OR FORGERY.

Pursuant to its authority under section 994 of title 28, United States Code, the United States Sentencing Commission shall amend its sentencing guidelines to provide an appropriate enhancement of the punishment for a defendant convicted of a felony under chapter 25 of title 18, United States Code, if the defendant used or carried a firearm (as defined in section 921(a)(3) of title 18, United States Code) during and in relation to the felony.

SEC. 110513. ENHANCED PENALTIES FOR FIREARMS POSSESSION BY VIOLENT FELONS AND SERIOUS DRUG OFFENDERS.

Pursuant to its authority under section 994 of title 28, United States Code, the United States Sentencing Commission shall amend its sentencing guidelines to—

(1) appropriately enhance penalties in cases in which a defendant convicted under section 922(g) of title 18, United States Code, has 1 prior conviction by any court referred to in section 922(g)(1) of title 18 for a violent felony (as defined in section 924(e)(2)(B) of that title) or a serious drug offense (as defined in section 924(e)(2)(A) of that title); and

(2) appropriately enhance penalties in cases in which such a defendant has 2 prior convictions for a violent felony (as so defined) or a serious drug offense (as so defined).

SEC. 110514. RECEIPT OF FIREARMS BY NONRESIDENT.

Section 922(a) of title 18, United States Code, is amended—

(1) by striking "and" at the end of paragraph (7);

(2) by striking the period at the end of paragraph (8) and inserting "; and"; and

(3) by adding at the end the following new paragraph:

"(9) for any person, other than a licensed importer, licensed manufacturer, licensed dealer, or licensed collector, who does not reside in any State to receive any firearms unless such receipt is for lawful sporting purposes.".

SEC. 110515. THEFT OF FIREARMS OR EXPLOSIVES FROM LICENSEE.

(a) FIREARMS.—Section 924 of title 18, United States Code, as amended by section 110504(a), is amended by adding at the end the following new subsection:

"(l) A person who steals any firearm from a licensed importer, licensed manufacturer, licensed dealer, or licensed collector shall be fined under this title, imprisoned not more than 10 years, or both.".

(b) EXPLOSIVES.—Section 844 of title 18, United States Code, as amended by section 110204(b), is amended by adding at the end the following new subsection:

"(l) A person who steals any explosive material from a licensed importer, licensed manufacturer, or licensed dealer, or from any permittee shall be fined under this title, imprisoned not more than 10 years, or both.".

SEC. 110516. DISPOSING OF EXPLOSIVES TO PROHIBITED PERSONS.

Section 842(d) of title 18, United States Code, is amended by striking "licensee" and inserting "person".

SEC. 110517. INCREASED PENALTY FOR INTERSTATE GUN TRAFFICKING.

Section 924 of title 18, United States Code, as amended by section 110515(a), is amended by adding at the end the following new subsection:

"(m) A person who, with the intent to engage in conduct that constitutes a violation of section 922(a)(1)(A), travels from any State or foreign country into any other State and acquires, or attempts to acquire, a firearm in such other State in furtherance of such purpose shall be imprisoned for not more than 10 years.".

SEC. 110518. FIREARMS AND EXPLOSIVES CONSPIRACY.

(a) FIREARMS.—Section 924 of title 18, United States Code, as amended by section 110517(a), is amended by adding at the end the following new subsection:

"(n) A person who conspires to commit an offense under subsection (c) shall be imprisoned for not more than 20 years, fined under this title, or both; and if the firearm is a machinegun or destructive device, or is equipped with a firearm silencer or muffler, shall be imprisoned for any term of years or life.".

(b) EXPLOSIVES.—Section 844 of title 18, United States Code, as amended by section 110515(b), is amended by adding at the end the following new subsection:

"(m) A person who conspires to commit an offense under subsection (h) shall be imprisoned for any term of years not exceeding 20, fined under this title, or both.

SEC. 110519. DEFINITION OF ARMOR PIERCING AMMUNITION.

Section 921(a)(17) of title 18, United States Code, is amended by revising subparagraph (B) and adding a new subparagraph (C) to read as follows:

"(B) The term 'armor piercing ammunition' means—

"(i) a projectile or projectile core which may be used in a handgun and which is constructed entirely (excluding the presence of traces of other substances) from one or a combination of tungsten alloys, steel, iron, brass, bronze, beryllium copper, or depleted uranium; or

"(ii) a full jacketed projectile larger than .22 caliber designed and intended for use in a handgun and whose jacket has a weight of more than 25 percent of the total weight of the projectile.

"(C) The term 'armor piercing ammunition' does not include shotgun shot required by Federal or State environmental or game regulations for hunting purposes, a frangible projectile designed for target shooting, a projectile which the Secretary finds is primarily intended to be used for sporting purposes, or any other projectile or projectile core which the Secretary finds is intended to be used for industrial purposes, including a charge used in an oil and gas well perforating device.".

Federal Gun Free Zone Laws

Despite the Constitution stating that "the right of people to keep and bear arms shall not be infringed," a number of federal laws do infringe that right by establishing places under federal control where carrying or even possessing firearms is illegal. The most widespread in effect of these laws is 18 U.S. Code Section 930 – Possession of firearms and dangerous weapons in Federal facilities. This law prohibits the possession of firearms and dangerous weapons *in* buildings owned or leased by the federal government where federal employees are normally present in the performance of their work. In addition, there are individual laws applying to the U.S. Postal Service and to the Veterans Administration which go beyond 18 U.S.C. 930 by prohibiting possession of firearms anywhere on the property rather than limiting the application of the law to inside the buildings.

In addition to 18 U.S.C. 930, federal law also includes the Gun Free School Zone Act, 18 U.S.C. 922 – Unlawful acts, which prohibits carrying firearms anywhere within 1,000 feet of any public, private, or parochial school unless the bearer has a permit or license to carry that was issued by the state in which the school zone is located. Seldom enforced, the Gun Free School Zone Act is a hidden legalistic land mine for people who rely on interstate reciprocity laws to carry firearms for self defense in states other than their own, home state. As more states adopt permitless (sometimes referred to as "Constitutional") carry, the Gun Free School Zone Act will also become a potential problem for those who choose to carry in their home states without obtaining or maintain a carry permit.

The pages that follow reproduce the text of 18 U.S. Code Sections 922 and 930, as well as Code of Federal Regulations 39 C.F.R. 232.1 – Conduct on postal property, and 38 C.F.R. 1.218 – Security and law enforcement at VA facilities.

Gun Free School Zones Act
18 U.S.C. § 922(q)
(1996)

(q)(1) The Congress finds and declares that—

(A) crime, particularly crime involving drugs and guns, is a pervasive, nationwide problem;

(B) crime at the local level is exacerbated by the interstate movement of drugs, guns, and criminal gangs;

(C) firearms and ammunition move easily in interstate commerce and have been found in increasing numbers in and around schools, as documented in numerous hearings in both the Committee on the Judiciary of the House of Representatives and the Committee on the Judiciary of the Senate;

(D) in fact, even before the sale of a firearm, the gun, its component parts, ammunition, and the raw materials from which they are made have considerably moved in interstate commerce;

(E) while criminals freely move from State to State, ordinary citizens and foreign visitors may fear to travel to or through certain parts of the country due to concern about violent crime and gun violence, and parents may decline to send their children to school for the same reason;

(F) the occurrence of violent crime in school zones has resulted in a decline in the quality of education in our country;

(G) this decline in the quality of education has an adverse impact on interstate commerce and the foreign commerce of the United States;

(H) States, localities, and school systems find it almost impossible to handle gun-related crime by themselves—even States, localities, and school systems that have made strong efforts to prevent, detect, and punish gun-related crime find their efforts unavailing due in part to the failure or inability of other States or localities to take strong measures; and

(I) the Congress has the power, under the interstate commerce clause and other provisions of the Constitution, to enact measures to ensure the integrity and safety of the Nation's schools by enactment of this subsection.

(2)(A) It shall be unlawful for any individual knowingly to possess a firearm that has moved in or that otherwise affects interstate or foreign commerce at a place that the individual knows, or has reasonable cause to believe, is a school zone.

(B) Subparagraph (A) does not apply to the possession of a firearm—

(i) on private property not part of school grounds;

(ii) if the individual possessing the firearm is licensed to do so by the State in which the school zone is located or a political subdivision of the State, and the law of the State or political subdivision requires that, before an individual obtains such a license, the law enforcement authorities of the State or political subdivision verify that the individual is qualified under law to receive the license;

(iii) that is—

(I) not loaded; and

(II) in a locked container, or a locked firearms rack that is on a motor vehicle;

(iv) by an individual for use in a program approved by a school in the school zone;

(v) by an individual in accordance with a contract entered into between a school in the school zone and the individual or an employer of the individual;

(vi) by a law enforcement officer acting in his or her official capacity; or

(vii) that is unloaded and is possessed by an individual while traversing school premises for the purpose of gaining access to public or private lands open to hunting, if the entry on school premises is authorized by school authorities.

(3)(A) Except as provided in subparagraph (B), it shall be unlawful for any person, knowingly or with reckless disregard for the safety of another, to discharge or attempt to discharge a firearm that has moved in or that otherwise affects interstate or foreign commerce at a place that the person knows is a school zone.

(B) Subparagraph (A) does not apply to the discharge of a firearm—

(i) on private property not part of school grounds;

(ii) as part of a program approved by a school in the school zone, by an individual who is participating in the program;

(iii) by an individual in accordance with a contract entered into between a school in a school zone and the individual or an employer of the individual; or

(iv) by a law enforcement officer acting in his or her official capacity.

(4) Nothing in this subsection shall be construed as preempting or preventing a State or local government from enacting a statute establishing gun-free g un free school zones as provided in this subsection.

18 USC § 921 Definitions

(a) As used in this chapter—

(25) The term "school zone" means—

(A) in, or on the grounds of, a public, parochial or private school; or

(B) within a distance of 1,000 feet from the grounds of a public, parochial or private school.

(26) The term "school" means a school which provides elementary or secondary education, as determined under State law.

18 U.S. Code Section 930 – Possession of firearms and dangerous weapons in Federal facilities

(a) Except as provided in subsection (d), whoever knowingly possesses or causes to be present a firearm or other dangerous weapon in a Federal facility (other than a Federal court facility), or attempts to do so, shall be fined under this title or imprisoned not more than 1 year, or both.

(b) Whoever, with intent that a firearm or other dangerous weapon be used in the commission of a crime, knowingly possesses or causes to be present such firearm or dangerous weapon in a Federal facility, or attempts to do so, shall be fined under this title or imprisoned not more than 5 years, or both.

(c) A person who kills any person in the course of a violation of subsection (a) or (b), or in the course of an attack on a Federal facility involving the use of a firearm or other dangerous weapon, or attempts or conspires to do such an act, shall be punished as provided in sections 1111, 1112, 1113, and 1117.

(d) Subsection (a) shall not apply to—

(1) the lawful performance of official duties by an officer, agent, or employee of the United States, a State, or a political subdivision thereof, who is authorized by law to engage in or supervise the prevention, detection, investigation, or prosecution of any violation of law;

(2) the possession of a firearm or other dangerous weapon by a Federal official or a member of the Armed Forces if such possession is authorized by law; or

(3) the lawful carrying of firearms or other dangerous weapons in a Federal facility incident to hunting or other lawful purposes.

(e) (1) Except as provided in paragraph (2), whoever knowingly possesses or causes to be present a firearm or other dangerous weapon in a Federal court facility, or attempts to do so, shall be fined under this title, imprisoned not more than 2 years, or both.

(2) Paragraph (1) shall not apply to conduct which is described in paragraph (1) or (2) of subsection (d).

(f) Nothing in this section limits the power of a court of the United States to punish for contempt or to promulgate rules or orders regulating, restricting, or prohibiting the possession of weapons within any building housing such court or any of its proceedings, or upon any grounds appurtenant to such building.

(g) As used in this section:

(1) The term "Federal facility" means a building or part thereof owned or leased by the Federal Government, where Federal employees are regularly present for the purpose of performing their official duties.

(2) The term "dangerous weapon" means a weapon, device, instrument, material, or substance, animate or inanimate, that is used for, or is readily capable of, causing death or serious bodily injury, except that such term does not include a pocket knife with a blade of less than 2½ inches in length.

(3) The term "Federal court facility" means the courtroom, judges' chambers, witness rooms, jury deliberation rooms, attorney conference rooms, prisoner holding cells, offices of the court clerks, the United States attorney, and the United States marshal, probation and parole offices, and adjoining corridors of any court of the United States.

(h) Notice of the provisions of subsections (a) and (b) shall be posted conspicuously at each public entrance to each Federal facility, and notice of subsection (e) shall be posted conspicuously at each public entrance to each Federal court facility, and no person shall be convicted of an offense under subsection (a) or (e) with respect to a Federal facility if such notice is not so posted at such facility, unless such person had actual notice of subsection (a) or (e), as the case may be.

38 C.F.R § 1.218 – Security and law enforcement at VA facilities

(a) Authority and rules of conduct. Pursuant to 38 U.S.C. 901, the following rules and regulations apply at all property under the charge and control of VA (and not under the charge and control of the General Services Administration) and to all persons entering in or on such property. The head of the facility is charged with the responsibility for the enforcement of these rules and regulations and shall cause these rules and regulations to be posted in a conspicuous place on the property.

(1) Closing property to public. The head of the facility, or designee, shall establish visiting hours for the convenience of the public and shall establish specific hours for the transaction of business with the public. The property shall be closed to the public during other than the hours so established. In emergency situations, the property shall be closed to the public when reasonably necessary to ensure the orderly conduct of Government business. The decision to close a property during an emergency shall be made by the head of the facility or designee. The head of the facility or designee shall have authority to designate areas within a facility as closed to the public.

(2) Recording presence. Admission to property during periods when such property is closed to the public will be limited to persons authorized by the head of the facility or designee. Such persons may be required to sign a register and/or display identification documents when requested to do so by VA police, or other authorized individual. No person, without authorization, shall enter upon or remain on such property while the property is closed. Failure to leave such premises by unauthorized persons shall constitute an offense under this paragraph.

(3) Preservation of property. The improper disposal of rubbish on property; the spitting on the property; the creation of any hazard on property to persons or things; the throwing of articles of any kind from a building; the climbing upon the roof or any part of the building, without permission; or the willful destruction, damage, or removal of Government property or any part thereof, without authorization, is prohibited. The destruction, mutilation, defacement, injury, or removal of any monument, gravestone, or other structure within the limits of any national cemetery is prohibited.

(4) Conformity with signs and emergency conditions. The head of the facility, or designee, shall have authority to post signs of a prohibitory and directory nature. Persons, in and on property, shall comply with such signs of a prohibitory or directory nature, and during emergencies, with the direction of police authorities and other authorized officials. Tampering with, destruction, marring, or removal of such posted signs is prohibited.

(5) Disturbances. Conduct on property which creates loud or unusual noise; which unreasonably obstructs the usual use of entrances, foyers, lobbies, corridors, offices, elevators, stairways, or parking lots; which otherwise impedes or disrupts the performance of official duties by Government employees; which prevents one from obtaining medical or other services provided on the property in a timely manner; or the use of loud, abusive, or otherwise improper language; or unwarranted loitering, sleeping, or assembly is prohibited. In addition to measures designed to secure voluntary terminations of violations of this paragraph the head of the facility or designee may cause the issuance of orders for persons who are creating a disturbance to depart the property. Failure to leave the premises when so ordered constitutes a further disturbance within the meaning of this rule, and the offender is subject to arrest and removal from the premises.

(6) Gambling. Participating in games for money or for tangible or intangible things, or the operating of gambling devices, the conduct of a lottery or pool, or the selling or purchasing of numbers tickets, in or on property is prohibited.

(7) Alcoholic beverages and narcotics. Operating a motor vehicle on property by a person under the influence of alcoholic beverages, narcotic drugs, hallucinogens, marijuana, barbiturates, or amphetamines is prohibited. Entering property under the influence of any narcotic drug, hallucinogen, marijuana, barbiturate, amphetamine, or alcoholic beverage (unless prescribed by a physician) is prohibited. The use on property of any narcotic drug, hallucinogen, marijuana, barbiturate, or amphetamine (unless prescribed by a physician) is prohibited. The introduction or possession of alcoholic beverages or any narcotic drug, hallucinogen, marijuana, barbiturate, and amphetamine on property is prohibited, except for liquor or drugs prescribed for use by medical authority for medical purposes. Provided such possession is consistent with the laws of the State in which the facility is located, liquor may be used and maintained in quarters assigned to employees as their normal abode, and away from the abode with the written consent of the head of the facility which specifies a special occasion for use and limits the area and period for the authorized use.

(8) Soliciting, vending, and debt collection. Soliciting alms and contributions, commercial soliciting and vending of all kinds, displaying or distributing commercial advertising, or collecting private debts in or on property is prohibited. This rule does not apply to (i) national or local drives for funds for welfare, health, or other purposes as authorized under Executive Order 12353, Charitable Fund Raising (March 23, 1982), as amended by Executive Order 12404 (February 10, 1983), and regulations issued by the Office of Personnel Management implementing these Executive Orders; (ii) concessions or personal notices posted by employees on authorized bulletin boards; and (iii) solicitation of labor organization membership or dues under 5 U.S.C. chapter 71.

(9) Distribution of handbills. The distributing of materials such as pamphlets, handbills, and/or flyers, and the displaying of placards or posting of materials

on bulletin boards or elsewhere on property is prohibited, except as authorized by the head of the facility or designee or when such distributions or displays are conducted as part of authorized Government activities.

(10) Photographs for news, advertising, or commercial purposes. Photographs for advertising or commercial purposes may be taken only with the written consent of the head of the facility or designee. Photographs for news purposes may be taken at entrances, lobbies, foyers, or in other places designated by the head of the facility or designee.

(11) Animals.

(i) Service animals, as defined in paragraph (a)(11)(viii) of this section, are permitted on VA property when those animals accompany individuals with disabilities and are trained for that purpose. A service animal shall be under the control of the person with the disability or an alternate handler at all times while on VA property. A service animal shall have a harness, leash, or other tether, unless either the handler is unable because of a disability to use a harness, leash, or other tether, or the use of a harness, leash, or other tether would interfere with the service animal's safe, effective performance of work or tasks, in which case the service animal must be otherwise under the handler's control (e.g., voice control, signals, or other effective means). VA is not responsible for the care or supervision of a service animal. Service animal presence on VA property is subject to the same terms, conditions, and regulations as generally govern admission of the public to the property.

(ii) A service animal will be denied access to VA property or removed from VA property if:

(A) The animal is not under the control of the individual with a disability or an alternate handler;

(B) The animal is not housebroken. The animal must be trained to eliminate its waste in an outdoor area; or

(C) The animal otherwise poses a risk to the health or safety of people or other service animals. In determining whether an animal poses a risk to the health or safety of people or other service animals, VA will make an individualized assessment based on objective indications to ascertain the severity of the risk. Such indications include but are not limited to:

(1) External signs of aggression from the service animal, such as growling, biting or snapping, baring its teeth, lunging; or

(2) External signs of parasites on the service animal (e.g. fleas, ticks), or other external signs of disease or bad health (e.g. diarrhea or vomiting).

(iii) Service animals will be restricted from accessing certain areas of VA property under the control of the Veterans Health Administration (VHA properties) to ensure patient care, patient safety, or infection control standards are not compromised. Such areas include but are not limited to:

(A) Operating rooms and surgical suites;

(B) Areas where invasive procedures are being performed;

(C) Acute inpatient hospital settings when the presence of the service animal is not part of a documented treatment plan;

(D) Decontamination, sterile processing, and sterile storage areas;

(E) Food preparation areas (not to include public food service areas); and

(F) Any areas where personal protective clothing must be worn or barrier protective measures must be taken to enter.

(iv) Service animals will be restricted from accessing certain areas of VA property under the control of the National Cemetery Administration (NCA properties) to ensure that public safety, facilities and grounds care, and maintenance control are not compromised. Such areas include but are not limited to:

(A) Open interment areas, except as approved to observe an individual interment or inurnment.

(B) Construction or maintenance sites; and

(C) Grounds keeping and storage facilities.

(v) If a service animal is denied access to VA property or removed from VA property in accordance with (a)(11)(ii) of this section, or restricted from accessing certain VA property in accordance with paragraphs (a)(11)(iii) and (iv) of this section, then VA will give the individual with a disability the opportunity to obtain services without having the service animal on VA property.

(vi) Unless paragraph (a)(11)(vii) of this section applies, an individual with a disability must not be required to provide documentation, such as proof that an animal has been certified, trained, or licensed as a service animal, to gain access to VA property accompanied by the service animal. However, an individual may be asked if the animal is required because of a disability, and what work or task the animal has been trained to perform.

(vii) An individual with a disability, if such individual will be accompanied by the service animal while receiving treatment in a VHA residential program, must provide VA with documentation that confirms the service animal has had a current rabies vaccine as determined by state and local public health requirements, and current core canine vaccines as dictated by local veterinary practice standards (e.g. distemper, parvovirus, and adenovirus-2).

(viii) A service animal means any dog that is individually trained to do work or perform tasks for the benefit of an individual with a disability, including a physical, sensory, psychiatric, intellectual, or other mental disability. Other species of animals, whether wild or domestic, trained or untrained, are not service animals for the purposes of this definition. The work or tasks performed by a service animal must be directly related to the individual's disability. The crime deterrent effects of an animal's presence and the provision of emotional support, well-being, comfort, or companionship do not constitute work or tasks for the purposes of this definition. Service dogs in training are not considered service animals. This definition applies regardless of whether VA is providing benefits to support a service dog under 38 CFR 17.148.

(ix) Generally, animals other than service animals ("non-service animals") are not permitted to be present on VA property, and any individual with a non-service animal must remove it. However, a VA facility head or designee may permit certain non-service animals to be present on VA property for the following reasons:

(A) Animals may be permitted to be present on VA property for law enforcement purposes;

(B) Animals under the control of the VA Office of Research and Development may be permitted to be present on VA property;

(C) Animal-assisted therapy (AAT) animals may be permitted to be present on VHA property when the presence of such animals would not compromise patient care, patient safety, or infection control standards. AAT is a goal-directed clinical intervention, as provided or facilitated by a VA therapist or VA clinician, that incorporates the use of an animal into the treatment regimen of a patient. Any AAT animal present on VHA property must facilitate achievement of patient-specific treatment goals, as documented in the patient's treatment plan. AAT animals must be up to date with all core vaccinations or immunizations, prophylactic parasite control medications, and regular health screenings as determined necessary by a licensed veterinarian consistent with local veterinary practice standards. Proof of compliance with these requirements must be documented and accessible in the area(s) where patients receive AAT.

(D) Animal-assisted activity (AAA) animals may be permitted to be present on VHA property when the presence of such animals would not compromise patient care, patient safety, or infection control standards. AAA involves animals in activities to provide patients with casual opportunities for motivational, educational, recreational, and/or therapeutic benefits. AAA is not a goal-directed clinical intervention that must be provided or facilitated by a VA therapist or clinician, and therefore is not necessarily incorporated into the treatment regimen of a patient or documented in the patient's medical record as treatment. AAA animals must be up to date with all core vaccinations or immunizations, prophylactic parasite control medications, and regular health screenings as determined necessary by a licensed veterinarian consistent with local veterinary practice standards. Proof of compliance with these requirements must be documented and accessible in the area(s) where patients may participate in AAA.

(E) Animals participating in a VA Community Living Center (CLC) residential animal program or a Mental Health Residential Rehabilitation Treatment Program (MHRRTP) may be permitted to be present on VHA property, when the presence of such animals would not compromise patient care, patient safety, or infection control standards. A residential animal program in a VA CLC or a MHRRTP is a program that uses the presence of animals to create a more homelike environment to foster comfort for veterans, while also stimulating a sense of purpose, familiarity, and belonging. Any VA CLC or MHRRTP residential animal present on VHA property must facilitate achievement of therapeutic outcomes (such as described above), as documented in patient treatment plans. Residential animals in a VA CLC or MHRRTP must be up to date with all core vaccinations and immunizations, prophylactic parasite control medications, and regular health screenings as determined necessary by a licensed veterinarian consistent with local veterinary practice standards. Proof of compliance with these requirements must be documented and accessible in the VA CLC or MHRRTP.

(F) Animals may be present on NCA property for ceremonial purposes during committal services, interments, and other memorials, if the presence of such animals would not compromise public safety, facilities and grounds care, and maintenance control standards.

(x) For purposes of this section, a disability means, with respect to an individual, a physical or mental impairment that substantially limits one or more major life activities of the individual; a record of such an impairment; or being regarded as having such an impairment.

(12) Vehicular and pedestrian traffic. Drivers of all vehicles in or on property shall drive in a careful and safe manner at all times and shall comply with the signals and directions of police and all posted traffic signs. The blocking of entrances, driveways, walks, loading platforms, or fire hydrants in or on property is prohibited; parking in unauthorized locations or in locations reserved for other persons or contrary to the direction of posted signs is prohibited. Creating excessive noise on hospital or cemetery premises by muffler cut out, the excessive use of a horn, or other means is prohibited. Operation of a vehicle in a reckless or unsafe manner, drag racing, bumping, overriding curbs, or leaving the roadway is prohibited.

(13) Weapons and explosives. No person while on property shall carry firearms, other dangerous or deadly weapons, or explosives, either openly or concealed, except for official purposes.

(14) Demonstrations.

(i) All visitors are expected to observe proper standards of decorum and decency while on VA property. Toward this end, any service, ceremony, or demonstration, except as authorized by the head of the facility or designee, is prohibited. Jogging, bicycling, sledding and other forms of physical recreation on cemetery grounds is prohibited.

(ii) For the purpose of the prohibition expressed in this paragraph, unauthorized demonstrations or services shall be defined as, but not limited to, picketing, or similar conduct on VA property; any oration or similar conduct to assembled groups of people, unless the oration is part of an authorized service; the display of any placards, banners, or foreign flags on VA property unless approved by the head of the facility or designee; disorderly conduct such as fighting, threatening, violent, or tumultuous behavior, unreasonable noise or coarse utterance, gesture or display or the use of abusive language to any person present; and partisan activities, i.e., those involving commentary or actions in support of, or in opposition to, or attempting to influence, any current policy of the Government of the United States, or any private group, association, or enterprise.

(15) Key security. The head of the facility of designee, will determine which employees, by virtue of their duties, shall have access to keys or barrier-card keys which operate locks to rooms or areas on the property. The unauthorized possession, manufacture, and/or use of such keys or barrier cards is prohibited. The surreptitious opening or attempted opening of locks or card-operated barrier mechanisms is prohibited.

(16) Sexual misconduct. Any act of sexual gratification on VA property involving two or more persons, who do not reside in quarters on the property, is prohibited. Acts of prostitution or solicitation for acts of prostitution on VA property is prohibited. For the purposes of this paragraph, an act of prostitution is defined as the performance or the offer or agreement to perform any sexual act for money or payment.

(b) Schedule of offenses and penalties. Conduct in violation of the rules and regulations set forth in paragraph (a) of this section subjects an offender to arrest and removal from the premises. Whomever shall be found guilty of violating these rules and regulations while on any property under the charge and control of VA is subject to a fine as stated in the schedule set forth herein or, if appropriate, the payment of fixed sum in lieu of appearance (forfeiture of collateral) as may be provided for in rules of the United States District Court. Violations included in the schedule of offenses and penalties may also subject an offender to a term of imprisonment of not more than six months, as may be determined appropriate by a magistrate or judge of the United States District Court:

(1) Improper disposal of rubbish on property, $200.

(2) Spitting on property, $25.

(3) Throwing of articles from a building or the unauthorized climbing upon any part of a building, $50.

(4) Willful destruction, damage, or removal of Government property without authorization, $500.

(5) Defacement, destruction, mutilation or injury to, or removal, or disturbance of, grave marker or headstone, $500.

(6) Failure to comply with signs of a directive and restrictive nature posted for safety purposes, $50.

(7) Tampering with, removal, marring, or destruction of posted signs, $150.

(8) Entry into areas posted as closed to the public or others (trespass), $50.

(9) Unauthorized demonstration or service in a national cemetery or on other VA property, $250.

(10) Creating a disturbance during a burial ceremony, $250.

(11) Disorderly conduct which creates loud, boisterous, and unusual noise, or which obstructs the normal use of entrances, exits, foyers, offices, corridors, elevators, and stairways or which tends to impede or prevent the normal operation of a service or operation of the facility, $250.

(12) Failure to depart premises by unauthorized persons, $50.

(13) Unauthorized loitering, sleeping or assembly on property, $50.

(14) Gambling-participating in games of chance for monetary gain or personal property; the operation of gambling devices, a pool or lottery; or the taking or giving of bets, $200.

(15) Operation of a vehicle under the influence of alcoholic beverages or nonprescribed narcotic drugs, hallucinogens, marijuana, barbiturates, or amphetamines, $500.

(16) Entering premises under the influence of alcoholic beverages or narcotic drugs, hallucinogens, marijuana, barbiturates or amphetamines, $200.

(17) Unauthorized use on property of alcoholic beverages or narcotic drugs, hallucinogens, marijuana, barbiturates, or amphetamines, $300.

(18) Unauthorized introduction on VA controlled property of alcoholic beverages or narcotic drugs, hallucinogens, marijuana, barbiturates, or amphetamines or the unauthorized giving of same to a patient or beneficiary, $500.

(19) Unauthorized solicitation of alms and contributions on premises, $50.

(20) Commercial soliciting or vending, or the collection of private debts on property, $50.

(21) Distribution of pamphlets, handbills, and flyers, $25.

(22) Display of placards or posting of material on property, $25.

(23) Unauthorized photography on premises, $50.

(24) Failure to comply with traffic directions of VA police, $25.

(25) Parking in spaces posted as reserved for physically disabled persons, $50.

(26) Parking in no-parking areas, lanes, or crosswalks so posted or marked by yellow borders or yellow stripes, $25.

(27) Parking in emergency vehicle spaces, areas and lanes bordered in red or posted as EMERGENCY VEHICLES ONLY or FIRE LANE, or parking within 15 feet of a fire hydrant, $50.

(28) Parking within an intersection or blocking a posted vehicle entrance or posted exit lane, $25.

(29) Parking in spaces posted as reserved or in excess of a posted time limit, $15.

(30) Failing to come to a complete stop at a STOP sign, $25.

(31) Failing to yield to a pedestrian in a marked and posted crosswalk, $25.

(32) Driving in the wrong direction on a posted one-way street, $25.

(33) Operation of a vehicle in a reckless or unsafe manner, too fast for conditions, drag racing, overriding curbs, or leaving the roadway, $100.

(34) Exceeding posted speed limits:

(i) By up to 10 mph, $25.

(ii) By up to 20 mph, $50.

(iii) By over 20 mph, $100.

(35) Creating excessive noise in a hospital or cemetery zone by muffler cut out, excessive use of a horn, or other means, $50.

(36) Failure to yield right of way to other vehicles, $50.

(37) Possession of firearms, carried either openly or concealed, whether loaded or unloaded (except by Federal or State law enforcement officers on official business, $500.

(38) Introduction or possession of explosives, or explosive devices which fire a projectile, ammunition, or combustibles, $500.

(39) Possession of knives which exceed a blade length of 3 inches; switchblade knives; any of the variety of hatchets, clubs and hand-held weapons; or brass knuckles, $300.

(40) The unauthorized possession of any of the variety of incapacitating liquid or gas-emitting weapons, $200.

(41) Unauthorized possession, manufacture, or use of keys or barrier card-type keys to rooms or areas on the property, $200.

(42) The surreptitious opening, or attempted opening, of locks or card-operated barrier mechanisms on property, $500.

(43) Soliciting for, or the act of, prostitution, $250.

(44) Any unlawful sexual activity, $250.

(45) Jogging, bicycling, sledding or any recreational physical activity conducted on cemetery grounds, $50.

(c) Enforcement procedures.

(1) VA administration directors will issue policies and operating procedures governing the proper exercise of arrest and other law enforcement actions, and limiting the carrying and use of weapons by VA police officers. VA police officers found qualified under respective VA administration directives and duly appointed heads of facilities for the purposes of 38 U.S.C. 902(b)(1), will enforce these rules and regulations and other Federal laws on VA property in accordance with the policies and operating procedures issued by respective VA administration directors and under the direction of the head of the facility.

(2) VA administration directors will prescribe training for VA police officers of the scope and duration necessary to assure the proper exercise of the law enforcement and arrest authority vested in them and to assure their abilities in the safe handling of situations involving patients and the public in general. VA police officers will successfully complete prescribed training in law enforcement procedures and the safe handling of patients as a condition of their retention of statutory law enforcement and arrest authority.

(3) Nothing contained in the rules and regulations set forth in paragraph (a) of this section shall be construed to abrogate any other Federal laws or regulations, including assimilated offenses under 18 U.S.C. 13, or any State or local laws and regulations applicable to the area in which the property is situated.

39 C.F.R. § 232.1 — Conduct on postal property

(a) Applicability. This section applies to all real property under the charge and control of the Postal Service, to all tenant agencies, and to all persons entering in or on such property. This section shall be posted and kept posted at a conspicuous place on all such property. This section shall not apply to -

(i) Any portions of real property, owned or leased by the Postal Service, that are leased or subleased by the Postal Service to private tenants for their exclusive use;

(ii) With respect to sections 232.1(h)(1) and 232.1(o), sidewalks along the street frontage of postal property falling within the property lines of the Postal Service that are not physically distinguishable from adjacent municipal or other public sidewalks, and any paved areas adjacent to such sidewalks that are not physically distinguishable from such sidewalks.

(b) Inspection, recording presence.

(1) Purses, briefcases, and other containers brought into, while on, or being removed from the property are subject to inspection. However, items brought directly to a postal facility's customer mailing acceptance area and deposited in the mail are not subject to inspection, except as provided by section 274 of the Administrative Support Manual. A person arrested for violation of this section may be searched incident to that arrest.

(2) Vehicles and their contents brought into, while on, or being removed from restricted nonpublic areas are subject to inspection. A prominently displayed sign shall advise in advance that vehicles and their contents are subject to inspection when entering the restricted nonpublic area, while in the confines of the area, or when leaving the area. Persons entering these areas who object and refuse to consent to the inspection of the vehicle, its contents, or both, may be denied entry; after entering the area without objection, consent shall be implied. A full search of a person and any vehicle driven or occupied by the person may accompany an arrest.

(3) Except as otherwise ordered, properties must be closed to the public after normal business hours. Properties also may be closed to the public in emergency situations and at such other times as may be necessary for the orderly conduct of business. Admission to properties during periods when such properties are closed to the public may be limited to authorized

individuals who may be required to sign the register and display identification documents when requested by security force personnel or other authorized individuals.

(c) Preservation of property. Improperly disposing of rubbish, spitting, creating any hazard to persons or things, throwing articles of any kind from a building, climbing upon the roof or any part of a building, or willfully destroying, damaging, or removing any property or any part thereof, is prohibited.

(d) Conformity with signs and directions. All persons in and on property shall comply with official signs of a prohibitory or directory nature, and with the directions of security force personnel or other authorized individuals.

(e) Disturbances. Disorderly conduct, or conduct which creates loud and unusual noise, or which impedes ingress to or egress from post offices, or otherwise obstructs the usual use of entrances, foyers, corridors, offices, elevators, stairways, and parking lots, or which otherwise tends to impede or disturb the public employees in the performance of their duties, or which otherwise impedes or disturbs the general public in transacting business or obtaining the services provided on property, is prohibited.

(f) Gambling. Participating in games for money or other personal property, the operation of gambling devices, the conduct of a lottery or pool, or the selling or purchasing of lottery tickets, is prohibited on postal premises. In accordance with 20 U.S.C. 107a(a)(5), this prohibition does not apply to the vending or exchange of State Lottery tickets at vending facilities operated by licensed blind persons where such lotteries are authorized by state law.

(g) Alcoholic beverages, drugs, and smoking.

(1) A person under the influence of an alcoholic beverage or any drug that has been defined as a "controlled substance" may not enter postal property or operate a motor vehicle on postal property. The possession, sale, or use of any "controlled substance" (except when permitted by law) or the sale or use of any alcoholic beverage (except as authorized by the Postmaster General or designee) on postal premises is prohibited. The term "controlled substance" is defined in section 802 of title 21 U.S.C.

(2) Smoking (defined as having a lighted cigar, cigarette, pipe, or other smoking material) is prohibited in all postal buildings and office space, including public lobbies.

(h) Soliciting, electioneering, collecting debts, vending, and advertising.

(1) Soliciting alms and contributions, campaigning for election to any public office, collecting private debts, soliciting and vending for commercial purposes (including, but not limited to, the vending of newspapers and other publications), displaying or distributing commercial advertising, collecting signatures on petitions, polls, or surveys (except as otherwise authorized by Postal Service regulations), are prohibited. These prohibitions do not apply to:

(i) Commercial or nonprofit activities performed under contract with the Postal Service or pursuant to the provisions of the Randolph-Sheppard Act;

(ii) Posting notices on bulletin boards as authorized in § 243.2(a) of this chapter;

(iii) The solicitation of Postal Service and other Federal military and civilian personnel for contributions by recognized agencies as authorized under Executive Order 12353, of March 23, 1982.

(2) Solicitations and other actions which are prohibited by paragraph (h)(1) of this section when conducted on Postal Service property should not be directed by mail or telephone to postal employees on Postal Service property. The Postal Service will not accept or distribute mail or accept telephone calls directed to its employees which are believed to be contrary to paragraph (h)(1) of this section.

(3) Leafleting, distributing literature, picketing, and demonstrating by members of the public are prohibited in lobbies and other interior areas of postal buildings open to the public. Public assembly and public address, except when conducted or sponsored by the Postal Service, are also prohibited in lobbies and other interior areas of postal building open to the public.

(4) Voter registration. Voter registration may be conducted on postal premises only with the approval of the postmaster or installation head provided that all of the following conditions are met:

(i) The registration must be conducted by government agencies or nonprofit civic leagues or organizations that operate for the promotion of social welfare but do not participate or intervene in any political campaign on behalf of any candidate or political party for any public office.

(ii) Absolutely no partisan or political literature may be available, displayed, or distributed. This includes photographs, cartoons, and other likenesses of elected officials and candidates for public office.

(iii) The registration is permitted only in those areas of the postal premises regularly open to the public.

(iv) The registration must not interfere with the conduct of postal business, postal customers, or postal operations.

(v) The organization conducting the voter registration must provide and be responsible for any equipment and supplies.

(vi) Contributions may not be solicited.

(vii) Access to the workroom floor is prohibited.

(viii) The registration activities are limited to an appropriate period before an election.

(5) Except as part of postal activities or activities associated with those permitted under paragraph (h)(4) of this section, no tables, chairs, freestanding signs or posters, structures, or furniture of any type may be placed in postal lobbies or on postal walkways, steps, plazas, lawns or landscaped areas, driveways, parking lots, or other exterior spaces.

(i) Photographs for news, advertising, or commercial purposes. Except as prohibited by official signs or the directions of security force personnel or other authorized personnel, or a Federal court order or rule, photographs for news purposes may be taken in entrances, lobbies, foyers, corridors, or auditoriums when used for public meetings. Other photographs may be taken only with the permission of the local postmaster or installation head.

(j) Dogs and other animals. Dogs and other animals, except those used to assist persons with disabilities, must not be brought upon postal property for other than official purposes.

(k) Vehicular and pedestrian traffic.

(1) Drivers of all vehicles in or on property shall be in possession of a current and valid state or territory issued driver's license and vehicle registration, and the vehicle shall display all current and valid tags and licenses required by the jurisdiction in which it is registered.

(2) Drivers who have had their privilege or license to drive suspended or revoked by any state or territory shall not drive any vehicle in or on property during such period of suspension or revocation.

(3) Drivers of all vehicles in or on property shall drive in a careful and safe manner at all times and shall comply with the signals and directions of security force personnel, other authorized individuals, and all posted traffic signs.

(4) The blocking of entrances, driveways, walks, loading platforms, or fire hydrants in or on property is prohibited.

(5) Parking without authority, parking in unauthorized locations or in locations reserved for other persons, or continuously in excess of 18 hours without permission, or contrary to the direction of posted signs is prohibited. This section may be supplemented by the postmaster or installation head from time to time by the issuance and posting of specific traffic directives as may be required. When so issued and posted such directives shall have the same force and effect as if made a part hereof.

(l) Weapons and explosives. Notwithstanding the provisions of any other law, rule or regulation, no person while on postal property may carry firearms, other dangerous or deadly weapons, or explosives, either openly or concealed, or store the same on postal property, except for official purposes.

(m) Nondiscrimination. There must be no discrimination by segregation or otherwise against any person or persons because of race, color, religion, national origin, sex, or disability, in furnishing, or by refusing to furnish to such person or persons the use of any facility of a public nature, including all services, privileges, accommodations, and activities provided on postal property.

(n) Conduct with regard to meetings of the Board of Governors.

(1) Without the permission of the chairman no person may participate in, film, televise, or broadcast any portion of any meeting of the Board or any subdivision or committee of the Board. Any person may electronically record or photograph a meeting, as long as that action does not tend to impede or disturb the members of the Board in the performance of their duties, or members of the public while attempting to attend or observe a meeting.

(2) Disorderly conduct, or conduct which creates loud or unusual noise, obstructs the ordinary use of entrances, foyers, corridors, offices, meeting rooms, elevators, stairways, or parking lots, or otherwise tends to impede or disturb the members of the Board in the performance of their duties, or members of the public while attempting to attend or observe a meeting of the Board or of any subdivision, or committee of the Board, is prohibited.

(3) Any person who violates paragraph (n) (1) or (2) of this section may, in addition to being subject to the penalties prescribed in paragraph (p) of this section, be removed from and barred from reentering postal property during the meeting with respect to which the violation occurred.

(4) A copy of the rules of this section governing conduct on postal property, including the rules of this paragraph appropriately highlighted, shall be posted in prominent locations at the public entrances to postal property and outside the meeting room at any meeting of the Board of Governors or of any subdivision or committee of the Board.

(o) Depositing literature. Depositing or posting handbills, flyers, pamphlets, signs, poster, placards, or other literature, except official postal and other Governmental notices and announcements, on the grounds, walks, driveways, parking and maneuvering areas, exteriors of buildings and other structures, or on the floors, walls, stairs, racks, counters, desks, writing tables, window-ledges, or furnishings in interior public areas on postal premises, is prohibited. This prohibition does not apply to:

(1) Posting notices on bulletin boards as authorized in § 243.2(a) of this chapter;

(2) Interior space assigned to tenants for their exclusive use;

(3) Posting of notices by U.S. Government-related organizations, such as the Inaugural Committee as defined in 36 U.S.C. 501.

(p) Penalties and other law.

(1) Alleged violations of these rules and regulations are heard, and the penalties prescribed herein are imposed, either in a Federal district court or by a Federal magistrate in accordance with applicable court rules. Questions regarding such rules should be directed to the regional counsel for the region involved.

(2) Whoever shall be found guilty of violating the rules and regulations in this section while on property under the charge and control of the Postal Service is subject to a fine as provided in 18 U.S.C. 3571 or imprisonment of not more than 30 days, or both. Nothing contained in these rules and regulations shall be construed to abrogate any other Federal laws or regulations or any State and local laws and regulations applicable to any area in which the property is situated.

(q) Enforcement.

(1) Members of the U.S. Postal Service security force shall exercise the powers provided by 18 U.S.C. 3061(c)(2) and shall be responsible for enforcing the regulations in this section in a manner that will protect Postal Service property and persons thereon.

(2) Local postmasters and installation heads may, pursuant to 40 U.S.C. 1315(d)(3) and with the approval of the chief postal inspector or his designee, enter into agreements with State and local enforcement agencies to insure that these rules and regulations are enforced in a manner that will protect Postal Service property.

(3) Postal Inspectors, Office of Inspector General Criminal Investigators, and other persons designated by the Chief Postal Inspector may likewise enforce regulations in this section.

Whether the Second Amendment Secures an Individual Right

MEMORANDUM OPINION FOR THE ATTORNEY GENERAL (2004)

In 2004, the Attorney General of the United States, John Ashcroft, assigned his staff to research the question of whether the Second Amendment to the Constitution guaranteed an individual right to keep and bear arms, or only a collective right, tied to service in the militia. This was the last year of George W. Bush's first term as President, and the last year of Ashcroft's tenure as Attorney General. (He left office in February of 2995).

The principal staff heading up the project included Assistant Attorneys General Steven G. Bradbury, C. Kevin Marshall, and Howard C. Nielson, Jr. On December 17, 2004, as the year drew to a close, the team submitted their final report in the form of a Memorandum Opinion for the Attorney General. The report filled 151 pages and was meticulously researched and documented. It discussed much of the history leading up to the drafting of the Constitution of the United States, with mention being made of many of the documents compiled in this book.

The summery conclusion of the report appears on the top of the Table of Contents page:

> The Second Amendment secures a right of individuals generally, not a right of states or a right restricted to persons serving in militias.

The report covers not only the historical backdrop for the Second Amendment, it also reviews the grammatical construction of the amendment, the meaning and importance of the prefatory militia clause, and a "structural analysis" of the Second Amendment that discusses the meaning of "the people" in the ten amendments constituting the Bill of Rights and, especially, the first four amendments. The report concludes:

> For the foregoing reasons, we conclude that the Second Amendment secures an individual right to keep and to bear arms. Current case law leaves open and unsettled the question of whose right is secured by the Amendment. Although we do not address the scope of the right, our

examination of the original meaning of the Amendment provides extensive reasons to conclude that the Second Amendment secures an individual right, and no persuasive basis for either the collective right or quasi-collective right views.

* * * * *

NOTE: The copy of the report on the following pages is presented exactly as taken from a United States government web site. Because the report contains a table of contents that refers to numbered pages, the original page numbering has been retained in addition to the sequential number of pages for this volume.

Whether the Second Amendment Secures an Individual Right

The Second Amendment secures a right of individuals generally, not a right of states or a right restricted to persons serving in militias.

August 24, 2004

MEMORANDUM OPINION FOR THE ATTORNEY GENERAL

Whether the Second Amendment Secures an Individual Right

The Second Amendment of the Constitution provides: "A well regulated Militia, being necessary to the security of a free State, the right of the people to keep and bear Arms, shall not be infringed." You have asked for the opinion of this Office on one aspect of the right secured by this Amendment. Specifically, you have asked us to address the question whether the right secured by the Second Amendment belongs only to the states, only to persons serving in state-organized militia units like the National Guard, or to individuals generally. This memorandum memorializes and expands upon advice that this Office provided to you on this question in 2001.

As relevant to the question addressed herein, courts and commentators have relied on three different interpretations of the Second Amendment. Under the "individual right" view, the Second Amendment secures to individuals a personal right to keep and to bear arms, whether or not they are members of any militia or engaged in military service or training. According to this view, individuals may bring claims or raise challenges based on a violation of their rights under the Second Amendment just as they do to vindicate individual rights secured by other provisions of the Bill of Rights.[1] Under the "collective right" view, the Second Amendment is a federalism provision that provides to states a prerogative to establish and maintain armed and organized militia units akin to the National Guard, and only states may assert this prerogative.[2] Finally, there is a range of intermediate views according to which the Amendment secures a right only to select persons to keep and bear arms in connection with their service in an organized state militia such as the National Guard. Under one typical formulation, individuals may keep arms only if they are "members of a functioning, organized state militia" and the state has not provided the necessary arms, and they may bear arms only "while and as a part of actively participating in" that militia's activities.[3] In essence, such a view would allow a private cause of action (or defense) to some persons to vindicate a state's power to establish and maintain an armed and organized militia such as the National Guard.[4] We therefore label this group of intermediate positions the "quasi-collective right" view.

The Supreme Court has not decided among these three potential interpretations, and the federal circuits are split. The Executive Branch has taken different views over the years. Most recently, in a 2001 memorandum to U.S. Attorneys, you endorsed the view that the Second Amendment protects a "'right of individuals, including those not then actually a member of any militia or engaged in active military service or training, to privately possess and bear their own firearms'" but allows for "reasonable restrictions" designed "to prevent unfit persons from

[1] *See, e.g.*, *United States v. Emerson*, 270 F.3d 203, 220, 260 (5th Cir. 2001).

[2] *See, e.g.*, *Silveira v. Lockyer*, 312 F.3d 1052, 1060–61, 1086–87 (9th Cir. 2002).

[3] *Emerson*, 270 F.3d at 219 (describing intermediate view); *see also, e.g.*, *Cases v. United States*, 131 F.2d 916, 923 (1st Cir. 1942).

[4] *See, e.g.*, *United States v. Parker*, 362 F.3d 1279, 1283 (10th Cir. 2004).

possessing firearms or to restrict possession of firearms particularly suited to criminal misuse."[5]

As developed in the analysis below, we conclude that the Second Amendment secures a personal right of individuals, not a collective right that may only be invoked by a state or a quasi-collective right restricted to those persons who serve in organized militia units. Our conclusion is based on the Amendment's text, as commonly understood at the time of its adoption and interpreted in light of other provisions of the Constitution and the Amendment's historical antecedents. Our analysis is limited to determining whether the Amendment secures an individual, collective, or quasi-collective right. We do not consider the substance of that right, including its contours or the nature or type of governmental interests that would justify restrictions on its exercise, and nothing in this memorandum is intended to address or call into question the constitutionality, under the Second Amendment, of any particular limitations on owning, carrying, or using firearms.

This memorandum proceeds in four parts. Part I addresses the current unsettled state of the law in this area. Part II demonstrates that the text and structure of the Constitution support the individual right view of the Second Amendment. Part III shows why this view finds further support in the history that informed the understanding of the Second Amendment as it was written and ratified. Finally, Part IV examines the views of commentators and courts closest to the Second Amendment's adoption, which reflect an individual right view, and then concludes by describing how the modern alternative views of the Second Amendment took hold in the early twentieth century.

I. The Unsettled Legal Landscape

Recent interpretations of the Second Amendment have been characterized by disagreement and uncertainty. The Supreme Court has not decided the question that we address here, and at least three views prevail in the federal courts of appeals. The Executive Branch has taken varying positions, and the Amendment has been the subject of extensive academic debate for the past two decades.

The Supreme Court's most important decision on the meaning of the Second Amendment, *United States v. Miller*,[6] grew out of the enactment of the National Firearms Act of 1934.[7] That Act was the first federal regulation of private

---

[5] Memorandum for United States Attorneys from the Attorney General, *Re: United States v. Emerson* (Nov. 9, 2001) (quoting *Emerson*, 270 F.3d at 260), *reprinted in* Brief for the United States in Opposition, App., *Emerson v. United States*, 536 U.S. 907 (2002) (No. 01-8780) (denying certiorari). You added that the Department of Justice "can and will continue to defend vigorously the constitutionality, under the Second Amendment, of all existing federal firearms laws."

[6] 307 U.S. 174 (1939).

[7] Ch. 757, 48 Stat. 1236.

firearms.[8] It taxed (and thereby registered) transfers of sawed-off shotguns or rifles capable of being concealed, machine guns, and silencers. It also taxed dealers in such weapons and required anyone who possessed such a weapon acquired before 1934 to register it with federal tax authorities.

A Second Amendment challenge to this Act produced *Miller* in 1939, the closest that the Supreme Court has come to interpreting the substance of the Amendment. Miller and a co-defendant were indicted for transporting an unregistered sawed-off shotgun in interstate commerce from Oklahoma to Arkansas, and the district court sustained their Second Amendment challenge to the indictment. On appeal by the government, neither defendant appeared or filed a brief.[9] The Court, in reversing and remanding, held that the sawed-off shotgun was not among the "Arms" protected by the Second Amendment absent "evidence tending to show that" its use or possession "at this time has some reasonable relationship to the preservation or efficiency of a well regulated militia." Citing an 1840 decision of the Tennessee Supreme Court, *Aymette v. State*, the Court concluded that it was not "within judicial notice" that a sawed-off shotgun was a weapon that was "any part of the ordinary military equipment" or whose use "could contribute to the common defence." Absent evidence, therefore, the Court could not "say that the Second Amendment guarantees the right to keep and bear such an instrument."[10]

After this one-paragraph discussion, the Court quoted the powers that Article I, Section 8, Clauses 15 and 16 of the Constitution grant to Congress to provide for calling forth, organizing, arming, and disciplining "the Militia," and stated that the Second Amendment's "declaration and guarantee" were made "[w]ith obvious purpose to assure the continuation and render possible the effectiveness of" the militia, and that the Amendment "must be interpreted and applied with that end in view."[11] The Court then added a historical discussion demonstrating that "the term Militia" as used in various provisions of the Constitution, including the Second Amendment, referred to a body that "comprised all males physically capable of acting in concert for the common defense," who "were expected to appear" for occasional training "bearing arms supplied by themselves and of the kind in common use at the time," which in the 1700s usually meant a "good" musket of proper length.[12]

Miller did not resolve the question addressed in this memorandum. Although the meaning of the decision is much debated, three points appear evident. First, the

---

[8] *See National Firearms Act: Hearings on H.R. 9066 Before the House Comm. on Ways and Means*, 73d Cong. 90 (1934) (statement of Ass't Att'y Gen. Keenan); *United States v. Lopez*, 2 F.3d 1342, 1348 (5th Cir. 1993), *aff'd*, 514 U.S. 549 (1995).

[9] 307 U.S. at 175–77.

[10] *Id.* at 178 (citing *Aymette v. State*, 21 Tenn. (2 Hum.) 154, 158 (1840)). We discuss *Aymette* below in Part IV.B.2.

[11] *Id.*

[12] *Id.* at 179; *see id.* at 179–82 (describing militia regulations, including arms requirements).

holding was limited to the meaning of "Arms" in the Second Amendment and whether a sawed-off shotgun is among the arms protected. In determining that meaning, the Court also interpreted the term "Militia" as used in the Constitution. Second, the Court did not categorically reject Miller's Second Amendment challenge. The Court's decision to address the substance of this challenge to his indictment, as opposed to concluding that only states could bring such a challenge, appears to be inconsistent with a collective right view.

Finally, the Court did not clearly decide between the individual right and quasi-collective right views. Its holding regarding the meaning of "Arms" is consistent with either view: The Court's limitation of "Arms" to those weapons reasonably related to the preservation or efficiency of a well-regulated militia (such as those that are "part of the ordinary military equipment" or that "could contribute to the common defense") could be consistent with a right to "keep and bear" such arms that is restricted to service in an organized military unit such as the National Guard; but that holding is also consistent with an individual right to keep and bear whatever "Arms" the Amendment protects. Similarly, the Court's reference to the need to interpret the Second Amendment's "declaration and guarantee" with the "end in view" of furthering "the continuation and render[ing] possible the effectiveness of" the militia could be consistent with a quasi-collective right view; but it is also consistent with the understanding of the relationship between an individual right to keep and bear arms and the "Militia" that prevailed at the time of the Founding, an understanding confirmed by early authorities' discussions of the Second Amendment's preface.[13]

Even so, absent from the Court's opinion in *Miller* was any discussion of whether the defendants were members of the National Guard or any other organized military force, whether they were transporting the shotgun in the service of such a force, or whether they were "physically capable of" bearing arms in one and thus even eligible for service. The nature of the weapon at issue, not of the defendants or their activities, appeared to be the key fact, and this aspect of the opinion tends to point toward the individual right view rather than the quasi-collective right view. In addition, *Miller*'s broad reading of "Militia" is most consistent with the individual right view, as we explain below in Part II.C.2, and is in tension with the quasi-collective right view, under which the militia is understood to refer to select military units, akin to the modern National Guard, organized and armed by the states.[14]

---

[13] See below Parts II.C (discussing Second Amendment's preface), III.B–C (discussing Founders' recognition that the individual right to arms furthered the citizen militia), IV.A (discussing early commentators), IV.B.2 (discussing early cases), IV.D (discussing views of Thomas Cooley soon after Civil War).

[14] Later opinions of the Supreme Court appear to accept the individual right view, at least in dicta, although none is dispositive. In *Johnson v. Eisentrager*, 339 U.S. 763 (1950), the Court rejected a claim that the Fifth Amendment's criminal procedure protections applied to nonresident enemy aliens by pointing out, among other things, that a contrary view would require also applying the "companion

Three years after *Miller*, in *Cases v. United States*, the First Circuit read *Miller* to turn solely on the type of weapon at issue and to suggest an individual right view of the Second Amendment: "Apparently, then, under the Second Amendment [as interpreted in *Miller*], the federal government . . . cannot prohibit the possession or use of any weapon which has any reasonable relationship to the preservation or efficiency of a well regulated militia." But the court doubted that *Miller* "was attempting to formulate a general rule applicable to all cases," warned of the consequences of such a view, and asserted that it was "unlikely that the framers of the Amendment intended any such result."[15] The court, instead, adopted what amounted to a quasi-collective right view: A person has no right under the Second Amendment unless he is "a member of a[] military organization" or uses his weapon "in preparation for a military career," thus "contributing to the efficiency of the well regulated militia."[16] Neither in support of its assertion about the Framers' intent nor in its paragraph fashioning this rule did the court cite any text or other authority.

Also in 1942, the Third Circuit in *United States v. Tot* applied *Miller*'s definition of "Arms" to affirm the conviction of a defendant who received a pistol in interstate commerce after having been convicted of a felony involving violence.[17] Alternatively, the court rested its affirmance on the ground that the government may prohibit such a convict from possessing a firearm.[18] Although either of these

---

civil-rights Amendments" in the Bill of Rights, including the Second Amendment. *Id.* at 784 ("during military occupation irreconcilable enemy elements, guerrilla fighters, and 'werewolves' could require the American Judiciary to assure them freedoms of speech, press, and assembly as in the First Amendment, right to bear arms as in the Second, security against 'unreasonable' searches and seizures as in the Fourth, as well as rights to jury trial as in the Fifth and Sixth Amendments"). In *Konigsberg v. State Bar of Cal.*, 366 U.S. 36 (1961), the Court, citing *Miller*, again equated the Second Amendment right with the rights secured by the First Amendment. *Id.* at 49 n.10. More recent cases have assumed an individual right in dicta by listing the Second Amendment right among the personal rights composing the "liberty" that the Constitution's due process provisions protect. *See Planned Parenthood v. Casey*, 505 U.S. 833, 847 (1992); *Moore v. City of East Cleveland*, 431 U.S. 494, 502 (1977) (plurality opinion) (quoting *Poe v. Ullman*, 367 U.S. 497, 542–43 (1961) (Harlan, J., dissenting)); *id.* at 542 (White, J., dissenting) (same as plurality). *But see Adams v. Williams*, 407 U.S. 143, 150 (1972) (Douglas, J., dissenting) ("A powerful lobby dins into the ears of our citizenry that these gun purchases are constitutional rights protected by the Second Amendment," but "[t]here is no reason why all pistols should not be barred to everyone except the police."). The Court in *Lewis* v. *United States*, 445 U.S. 65 (1980), rejected an equal protection challenge to a prohibition against felons possessing firearms. In a one-sentence footnote explaining why it was applying rational basis review, the Court stated that such a prohibition is not "based upon constitutionally suspect criteria" and does not "trench upon any constitutionally protected liberties." *Id.* at 65 n.8. Although this language is consistent with the view that the Second Amendment does not secure a right of individuals, it is also consistent with the traditional understanding of the individual right view that the liberty protected by the Second Amendment does not extend to convicted felons. See notes 19 & 29 below, and the discussions referenced therein.

[15] 131 F.2d 916, 922 (1st Cir. 1942).

[16] *Id.* at 923.

[17] 131 F.2d 261, 266 (3d Cir. 1942), *rev'd on other grounds*, 319 U.S. 463 (1943).

[18] *Id.* The same ground appears to have been available in *Cases*. *See id.*, 131 F.2d at 919 n.1.

views is consistent with an individual right,[19] *Tot* added, in apparent dicta, a one-paragraph historical discussion in support of the view that the Amendment "was not adopted with individual rights in mind, but as a protection for the states in the maintenance of their militia organizations against possible encroachments by the federal power."[20] The court did not address the Amendment's text but instead chiefly relied on the *Aymette* case's account of the right that emerged from the English Revolution of 1688–1689.

Over the past few decades, the Executive Branch has taken differing views of the right secured by the Second Amendment.[21] In 1941, President Roosevelt signed legislation authorizing requisitions of private property for war use that prohibited requisitioning or new registration "of any firearms possessed by any individual for his personal protection or sport" and, moreover, any impairing or infringing of "the right of any individual to keep and bear arms."[22] In 1959, this Office reviewed a bill that would have secured the custody and disposition of missiles, rockets, and earth satellites. We questioned its definition of "missile," which included "projectile" and "seems to include conventional ammunition," and we commented that if the bill purported "to prohibit *private individuals* from acquiring, possessing, or receiving any standard ammunition for firearms . . . . serious constitutional problems would arise under the Second Amendment."[23] In commenting on similar bills in 1961 and 1962, this Office cited and reaffirmed its 1959 memorandum.[24] In

---

[19] Regarding violent felons, although the case involved possession, the court relied on authority for regulating the *bearing* of arms (banning carrying weapons concealed or to the terror of the people). For more on-point authority, see proposals made during the ratifying conventions, discussed below in Part III.C.1, and *Emerson*, 270 F.3d at 226 n.21; *cf. Lewis*, 445 U.S. at 65 n.8 (rejecting equal protection challenge to prohibition of felon possessing a firearm); *Richardson v. Ramirez*, 418 U.S. 24, 53–55 (1974) (holding constitutional the disenfranchisement of convicted felons who had completed their sentences and paroles).

[20] 131 F.2d at 266. The court cited some history from the Founding Era, which we address in Part III.C.1.

[21] We have not conducted a review of the government's litigating positions in the numerous firearms cases since *Miller*. In its brief in *Miller*, the government made two alternative arguments. The first was consistent with a quasi-collective right view. *See* Brief for United States at 9–18, *United States v. Miller*, 307 U.S. 174 (1939) (No. 696). The second (which the Court adopted) was consistent with either a quasi-collective or individual right view. *See id.* at 18–20. Its present litigating position appears to be consistent with your 2001 memorandum to U.S. Attorneys endorsing the individual right view. *See, e.g.*, *United States v. Lippman*, 369 F.3d 1039, 1045 (8th Cir. 2004) (Colloton, J., concurring in part and concurring in the judgment).

[22] Property Requisition Act, ch. 445, § 1, 55 Stat. 742, 742.

[23] Memorandum for Lawrence E. Walsh, Deputy Attorney General, from Paul A. Sweeney, Acting Assistant Attorney General, Office of Legal Counsel, *Re: H.R. 232, 86th Cong., 1st Sess., a bill "To provide for the securing of custody and disposition by the United States of missiles, rockets, earth satellites, and similar devices adaptable to military uses, and for other purposes"* at 1–2 (Apr. 9, 1959) (emphasis added).

[24] *See* Memorandum for Byron R. White, Deputy Attorney General, from Nicholas deB. Katzenbach, Assistant Attorney General, Office of Legal Counsel, *Re: H.R. 2057, a bill to provide for the securing of custody and disposition by the United States of missiles, rockets, earth satellites, and*

1965, however, the Justice Department expressly adopted the collective right interpretation in congressional testimony by Attorney General Katzenbach.[25]

Soon after, in 1968, Congress passed the first major federal gun regulation since 1938, the Omnibus Crime Control and Safe Streets Act.[26] This statute produced a flurry of decisions in the federal courts of appeals rejecting the individual right view. Following the Third Circuit's dicta in *Tot*, the Fourth, Sixth, Seventh, and Ninth Circuits eventually adopted the collective right view.[27] Following the First Circuit in *Cases*, the Eighth, Tenth, and Eleventh Circuits adopted quasi-collective right views.[28] As in *Tot* and *Cases*, many of these cases, particularly the initial ones, involved constitutional challenges by persons convicted of felonies or violent crimes,[29] and some involved challenges to restrictions

---

similar devices adaptable to military use (May 8, 1961); Memorandum for Byron R. White, Deputy Attorney General, from Nicholas deB. Katzenbach, Assistant Attorney General, Office of Legal Counsel, *Re: Proposed report of the Department of Defense on H.R. 2057 "To provide for the securing of custody and disposition by the United States of missiles, rockets, earth satellites and similar devices adaptable to Military uses, and for other purposes"* at 1 (Mar. 22, 1962).

[25] *See Federal Firearms Act: Hearings Before the Subcomm. to Investigative Juvenile Delinquency of the Senate Comm. on the Judiciary*, 89th Cong. 40–41 (1965) (statement of Attorney General Katzenbach). For subsequent treatment of the Second Amendment, *see, e.g.*, Memorandum for Richard G. Kleindienst, Deputy Attorney General, from William H. Rehnquist, Assistant Attorney General, Office of Legal Counsel, *Re: Proposed "Federal Gun Registration and Licensing Act of 1969"* (Feb. 19, 1969) (in one-sentence discussion, citing *Miller* and *Tot* to find no "serious legal obstacle" under Amendment to proposal for federal registration of firearms and limited federal licensing); Memorandum for D. Lowell Jensen, Assistant Attorney General, Criminal Division, from Theodore B. Olson, Assistant Attorney General, Office of Legal Counsel, *Re: Proposed Legislation Relating to Firearms and to Mandatory Sentencing*, at 2 (May 27, 1981) (citing *Miller* as basis for "perceiv[ing] no basis for suggesting that the [1968 Gun Control] Act so interferes with the powers of the States to raise militias as to transgress the Second Amendment"); Firearm Owners' Protection Act, Pub. L. No. 99-308, § 1(b)(1)(A), 100 Stat. 449, 449 (1986), *codified at* 18 U.S.C. § 921 note (2000) (law signed by President Reagan that recognized "the right[] of citizens . . . to keep and bear arms under the second amendment").

[26] Pub. L. No. 90-351, 82 Stat. 197.

[27] *See, e.g., Love v. Pepersack*, 47 F.3d 120, 122–24 (4th Cir. 1995); *United States v. Warin*, 530 F.2d 103, 105–07, 108 (6th Cir. 1976) (dismissing "the erroneous supposition that the Second Amendment is concerned with the rights of individuals rather than those of the States" and rejecting claim involving gun admittedly bearing reasonable relationship to preservation or efficiency of the army); *Gillespie v. City of Indianapolis*, 185 F.3d 693, 710–11 (7th Cir. 1999); *Hickman v. Block*, 81 F.3d 98, 99–102 (9th Cir. 1996). The Third Circuit's present position is at least the quasi-collective right view, if not the collective right view. *See United States v. Rybar*, 103 F.3d 273, 286 (3d Cir. 1996).

[28] *See, e.g., United States v. Hale*, 978 F.2d 1016, 1019–20 (8th Cir. 1992); *United States v. Oakes*, 564 F.2d 384, 387 (10th Cir. 1977); *United States v. Wright*, 117 F.3d 1265, 1272–74 (11th Cir. 1997), *vacated in part on other grounds*, 133 F.3d 1412 (1998). These courts make clear that the right under the quasi-collective right view protects only members of organized militia units such as the National Guard, not members of the "militia" defined more broadly. *Oakes*, for example, rejected a claim based on the defendant's membership in the Kansas militia, which consisted of all able-bodied men between twenty-one and forty-five. 564 F.2d at 387; *see also Wright*, 117 F.3d at 1271–74 (similar); *Hale*, 978 F.2d at 1020 (similar); *Warin*, 530 F.2d at 105, 106, 108 (similar).

[29] *See, e.g., United States v. Baer*, 235 F.3d 561, 564 (10th Cir. 2000); *Gillespie*, 185 F.3d at 710–11; *Marchese v. California*, 545 F.2d 645, 646 (9th Cir. 1976); *United States v. Johnson*, 497 F.2d 548,

on carrying concealed weapons.[30] These decisions did not analyze, at least not in depth, the Amendment's text or history. Rather, they relied on *Tot* or *Cases* (or their progeny), claimed support from *Miller*, or both. As the Ninth Circuit recently recognized in the course of adhering to its collective right position, these earlier decisions reached their conclusions "with comparatively little analysis," "largely on the basis of the rather cursory discussion in *Miller*, and touched only briefly on the merits of the debate."[31]

In contrast, the burgeoning scholarly literature on the Second Amendment in the past two decades has explored the meaning of the Second Amendment in great detail. The collective right and quasi-collective right positions have many adherents,[32] although the preponderance of modern scholarship appears to support the individual right view.[33]

---

550 (4th Cir. 1974) (per curiam); *Cody v. United States*, 460 F.2d 34, 35–37 (8th Cir. 1972); *Stevens v. United States*, 440 F.2d 144, 149 (6th Cir. 1971); *United States v. Synnes*, 438 F.2d 764, 766 (8th Cir. 1971), *vacated on other grounds*, 404 U.S. 1009 (1972). Courts have recognized that such holdings could be consistent with an individual right view. *See United States v. Price*, 328 F.3d 958, 961 (7th Cir. 2003); *supra* note 19 (discussing *Tot*); *cf. Emerson*, 270 F.3d at 261 (upholding prohibition on possession of firearm by person subject to domestic violence restraining order by concluding that Amendment protected an individual right but finding no violation); *Lippman*, 369 F.3d at 1044–45 (Colloton, J.) (similar).

[30] *See Hickman*, 81 F.3d at 99–103; *Thomas v. Members of City Council of Portland*, 730 F.2d 41, 42 (1st Cir. 1984) (per curiam). Courts have recognized that such holdings also could be consistent with an individual right view. *See Parker*, 362 F.3d at 1285–86 (Kelly, J., concurring) (arguing for upholding conviction on narrower ground that case involved reasonable restriction on concealed weapons, and criticizing circuit courts, in interpreting Second Amendment, for ignoring "the universal admonition to decide constitutional issues narrowly"); Part IV.B.2 (discussing cases recognizing individual right but rejecting right to carry concealed weapons).

[31] *Silveira*, 312 F.3d at 1063–64 & n.11.

[32] For a symposium of articles spanning the views, see *The Second Amendment Today: Historical and Contemporary Perspectives on the Constitutionality of Firearms Regulation*, 29 N. Ky. L. Rev. 643 (2002), and for articles critical of the individual right view, see *Symposium on the Second Amendment: Fresh Looks*, 76 Chi.-Kent L. Rev. 3 (2000). *See also, e.g.*, Garry Wills, *A Necessary Evil: A History of American Distrust of Government* 207–21, 256–60 (1999); Andrew D. Herz, *Gun Crazy: Constitutional False Consciousness and Dereliction of Dialogic Responsibility*, 75 B.U. L. Rev. 57 (1995); Richard M. Aborn, Essay, *The Battle Over the Brady Bill and the Future of Gun Control Advocacy*, 22 Fordham Urb. L.J. 417 (1995); Carl T. Bogus, Essay, *Race, Riots, and Guns*, 66 S. Cal. L. Rev. 1365 (1993); Dennis A. Henigan, *Arms, Anarchy and the Second Amendment*, 26 Val. U. L. Rev. 107 (1991); Wendy Brown, Comment, *Guns, Cowboys, Philadelphia Mayors, and Civic Republicanism: On Sanford Levinson's The Embarrassing Second Amendment*, 99 Yale L.J. 661 (1989); Keith A. Ehrman & Dennis A. Henigan, *The Second Amendment in the Twentieth Century: Have You Seen Your Militia Lately?*, 15 U. Dayton L. Rev. 5 (1989); Samuel Fields, *Guns, Crime and the Negligent Gun Ownerin*, 10 N. Ky. L. Rev. 141 (1982); Warren Spannaus, *State Firearms Regulation and the Second Amendment*, 6 Hamline L. Rev. 383 (1983); *cf.* David Yassky, *The Second Amendment: Structure, History, and Constitutional Change*, 99 Mich. L. Rev. 588 (2000); David C. Williams, *Civic Republicanism and the Citizen Militia: The Terrifying Second Amendment*, 101 Yale L.J. 551, 554–55 (1991).

[33] *See, e.g.*, 1 Laurence H. Tribe, *American Constitutional Law* 900 & 902 n.221 (3d ed. 2000); Nelson Lund, *The Ends of Second Amendment Jurisprudence: Firearms Disabilities and Domestic Violence Restraining Orders*, 4 Tex. Rev. L. & Pol. 157 (1999); Leonard W. Levy, *Origins of the Bill*

Whether the Second Amendment Secures an Individual Right

Recent decisions of the Fifth and Ninth Circuits have begun to remedy the relatively sparse judicial analysis of the meaning of the Second Amendment. In 2001, the Fifth Circuit in *United States v. Emerson* adopted the individual right view, based on an extensive analysis of the Amendment's text and history.[34] The following year, the Ninth Circuit in *Silveira v. Lockyer* rejected *Emerson* with an extended counter-analysis and reaffirmed its adherence to the collective right view.[35] Six members of the Ninth Circuit dissented from denial of rehearing en banc and endorsed an individual right view.[36]

In sum, the question of who possesses the right secured by the Second Amendment remains open and unsettled in the courts and among scholars. Accordingly, we turn to the Amendment's text, as commonly understood at the time of its adoption and interpreted in light of other provisions of the Constitution and the Amendment's historical antecedents, to discern its proper meaning.

---

of Rights 134 (1999); Ronald S. Resnick, *Private Arms as the Palladium of Liberty: The Meaning of the Second Amendment*, 77 U. Det. Mercy L. Rev. 1 (1999); Brannon P. Denning, *Gun Shy: The Second Amendment as an "Underenforced Constitutional Norm,"* 21 Harv. J.L. & Pub. Pol'y 719 (1998); L.A. Powe, Jr., *Guns, Words, and Constitutional Interpretation*, 38 Wm. & Mary L. Rev. 1311 (1997); Nelson Lund, *The Past and Future of the Individual's Right to Arms*, 31 Ga. L. Rev. 1 (1996); Randy E. Barnett & Don B. Kates, *Under Fire: The New Consensus on the Second Amendment*, 45 Emory L.J. 1139 (1996); Glenn Harlan Reynolds & Don B. Kates, *The Second Amendment and States' Rights: A Thought Experiment*, 36 Wm. & Mary L. Rev. 1737 (1995); David B. Kopel, *It Isn't About Duck Hunting: The British Origin of the Right to Arms*, 93 Mich. L. Rev. 1333, 1355 (1995); William Van Alstyne, Essay, *The Second Amendment and the Personal Right to Arms*, 43 Duke L.J. 1236; Joyce Lee Malcolm, *To Keep and Bear Arms: The Origins of an Anglo-American Right* (1994); Clayton E. Cramer, *For the Defense of Themselves and the State: The Original Intent and Judicial Interpretation of the Right to Keep and Bear Arms* (1994); Akhil Reed Amar, *The Bill of Rights as a Constitution*, 100 Yale L.J. 1131, 1162–68 (1991); Robert J. Cottrol & Raymond T. Diamond, *The Second Amendment: Toward an Afro-Americanist Reconsideration*, 80 Geo. L.J. 309 (1991); Sanford Levinson, Comment, *The Embarrassing Second Amendment*, 99 Yale L.J. 637 (1989); Nelson Lund, *The Second Amendment, Political Liberty, and the Right to Self-Preservation*, 39 Ala. L. Rev. 103 (1987); David T. Hardy, *Armed Citizens, Citizen Armies: Toward a Jurisprudence of the Second Amendment*, 9 Harv. J.L. & Pub. Pol'y 559 (1986); Don B. Kates, Jr., *The Second Amendment: A Dialogue*, 49 Law & Contemp. Probs. 143 (Winter 1986); Stephen P. Halbrook, *That Every Man Be Armed: The Evolution of a Constitutional Right* (1984); Don B. Kates, Jr., *Handgun Prohibition and the Original Meaning of the Second Amendment*, 82 Mich. L. Rev. 204 (1983); *see also Printz v. United States*, 521 U.S. 898, 938 n.2 (1997) (Thomas., J., concurring) (noting "growing body of scholarly commentary indicat[ing] that the [right]" is a personal one); *Emerson*, 270 F.3d at 220 (similar).

[34] 270 F.3d at 227–60.

[35] 312 F.3d at 1060–87.

[36] *Silveira v. Lockyer*, 328 F.3d 567, 570 (9th Cir. 2003) (Kleinfeld, J., joined by Kozinski, O'Scannlain, and T.G. Nelson, JJ., dissenting from denial of rehearing en banc); *see* 328 F.3d at 568 (Pregerson, J., same); *id.* at 568 (Kozinski, J., same); *id.* at 592 (Gould, J., joined by Kozinski, J., same). For other recent opinions of Ninth Circuit judges endorsing the individual right view and criticizing *Silveira*, see *Nordyke*, 319 F.3d at 1195 (Gould, J., concurring); *Nordyke v. King*, 364 F.3d 1025, 1025 (9th Cir. 2004) (Kleinfeld, J., dissenting from denial of rehearing en banc); *id.* at 1026 (Gould, J., joined by O'Scannlain, Kleinfeld, Tallman, and Bea, JJ., same).

II. Textual and Structural Analysis

The Second Amendment of the United States Constitution, part of the Bill of Rights, reads in full as follows:

> A well regulated Militia, being necessary to the security of a free State, the right of the people to keep and bear Arms, shall not be infringed.

The Amendment expressly protects a "right of the people," which is "to keep and bear Arms" and which has some relation to the prefatory declaration that a "well regulated Militia" is necessary for the ultimate end of "the security of a free State." We address each of these phrases in turn and then consider how the structure of the Constitution illuminates the Amendment's meaning.

As explained below, the text of the Second Amendment points to a personal right of individuals: A "right of the people" is ordinarily and most naturally a right of individuals, not of a state and not merely of those serving the state as militiamen. The phrase "keep arms" at the time of the Founding usually indicated the private ownership and retention of arms by individuals as individuals, not the stockpiling of arms by a government or its soldiers, and the phrase certainly had that meaning when used in connection with a "right of the people." While the phrase "bear arms" often referred to carrying of arms in military service, it also sometimes denoted carrying arms for private purposes. The Amendment's prefatory clause, considered under proper rules of interpretation, could not negate the individual right recognized in the clear language of the operative clause. In any event, the prefatory clause—particularly its reference to the "Militia," which was understood at the Founding to encompass all able-bodied male citizens, who were required to be enrolled for service—is fully consistent with an individual right reading of the operative language. Moreover, the Second Amendment appears in the Bill of Rights amid amendments securing numerous individual rights, a placement that makes it likely that the right of the people to keep and bear arms likewise belongs to individuals. Finally, a consideration of the powers that the original Constitution grants or allows over the militia makes it unlikely that the Second Amendment would secure a collective or quasi-collective right.

A. "The Right of the People"

The Second Amendment's recognition of a "right" that belongs to "the people" indicates a right of individuals. The word "right," standing by itself in the Constitution, is clear. Although in some contexts entities other than individuals are said to have "rights,"[37] the Constitution itself does not use the word "right" in this manner. Setting aside the Second Amendment, not once does the Constitution confer a "right" on any governmental entity, state or federal. Nor does it confer any "right" restricted to persons in governmental service, such as members of an organized military unit. In addition to its various references to a "right of the people" discussed below, the Constitution in the Sixth Amendment secures "right[s]" to an accused person, and in the Seventh secures a person's "right" to a jury trial in civil cases.[38] By contrast, governments, whether state or federal, have in the Constitution only "powers" or "authority."[39] It would be a marked anomaly if "right" in the Second Amendment departed from such uniform usage throughout the Constitution.

In any event, any possible doubt vanishes when "right" is conjoined with "the people," as it is in the Second Amendment. Such a right belongs to individuals: The "people" are not a "State," nor are they identical with the "Militia." Indeed, the Second Amendment distinctly uses all three of these terms, yet it secures a "right" only to the "people." The phrase "the right of the people" appears two other times in the Bill of Rights, and both times refers to a personal right, which belongs to individuals. The First Amendment secures "the right of the people peaceably to assemble, and to petition the Government for a redress of grievances," and the Fourth safeguards "[t]he right of the people to be secure in their persons, houses, papers, and effects, against unreasonable searches and seizures." In addition, the Ninth Amendment refers to "rights . . . retained by the people." We see no reason to read the phrase in the Second Amendment to mean something other than what it plainly means in these neighboring and contemporaneous amendments.

The Supreme Court, in interpreting the Fourth Amendment, likewise has recognized that the Constitution uses "the people," and especially "the right of the people," to refer to individuals:

> "[T]he people" seems to have been a term of art employed in select parts of the Constitution. The Preamble declares that the Constitution is ordained and established by "the People of the United States." The Second Amendment protects "the right of the people to keep and bear Arms," and the Ninth and Tenth Amendments provide that certain rights and powers are retained by and reserved to "the people." *See also* U.S. Const., Amdt. 1 ("Congress shall make no law . . .

---

[37] For example, Article II of the Articles of Confederation, drafted a decade before the Constitution, reserved to each state "every power, jurisdiction, and right" not expressly delegated to the federal government.

[38] In addition, the Copyright and Patent Clause authorizes Congress to grant an "exclusive Right" to authors and inventors for a limited time. U.S. Const. art. I, § 8, cl. 8.

[39] *See, e.g.*, U.S. Const. art. I, § 1; *id.* art. I, § 8; *id.* art. II, § 1; *id.* art. III, § 1; *id.* amend. X.

> abridging . . . *the right of the people* peaceably to assemble") (emphasis added); Art. I, § 2, cl. 1 ("The House of Representatives shall be composed of Members chosen every second Year *by the People of the several States*") (emphasis added). While this textual exegesis is by no means conclusive, it suggests that "the people" protected by the Fourth Amendment, and by the First and Second Amendments, and to whom rights and powers are reserved in the Ninth and Tenth Amendments, refers to a class of persons who are part of a national community or who have otherwise developed sufficient connection with this country to be considered part of that community.[40]

Thomas Cooley, the leading constitutional scholar after the Civil War, took the same view in explaining "the people" in the context of the First Amendment: "When the term 'the people' is made use of in constitutional law or discussions, it is often the case that those only are intended who have a share in the government through being clothed with the elective franchise. . . . But *in all the enumerations and guaranties of rights the whole people are intended*, because the rights of all are equal, and are meant to be equally protected."[41]

The Constitution confirms this meaning of "the people" as individuals by expressly distinguishing the "people" from the "States," using each word to refer to a distinct thing. Indeed, the Second Amendment itself refers separately to "the people" and the "State." And the difference is firmly established by the Tenth Amendment, which distinguishes between the powers reserved "to the States" and those reserved "to the people." The "people" are the individuals who compose the states, distinct from—and bearing their federal "rights" apart from—those entities.[42]

Similarly, the Constitution gives distinct meanings to "the people" and the "Militia." Again, the Second Amendment itself is a notable example, referring to

[40] *United States v. Verdugo-Urquidez*, 494 U.S. 259, 265 (1990); *see also id.* at 279 (Stevens, J., concurring in judgment) ("aliens who are lawfully present in the United States are among those 'people' who are entitled to the protection of the Bill of Rights, including the Fourth Amendment"); *id.* at 287–88 (Brennan, J., dissenting) (similar; contending that "'the people'" is broader than "'citizens,' 'freemen,' 'residents,' or 'the American people'"). The Ninth Circuit in *Silveira* did not discuss the "right of the people" in the Second Amendment, and it disregarded *Verdugo-Urquidez* except to cite its analysis of "the people" as an analogy in support of its own reading of "Militia." *See* 312 F.3d at 1069–70 & n.25, 1071 & n.27. While recognizing that "[t]he question . . . is not whether arms may be kept, but by whom and for what purpose," *id.* at 1074, the court in *Silveira* did not consider that the "who[]" might be "the people" to whom the Second Amendment's text—like that of the First, Fourth, and Ninth—expressly gives the right.

[41] Thomas M. Cooley, *The General Principles of Constitutional Law in the United States of America* 267–68 (1880; reprint 2000) (emphasis added).

[42] Of course the "people" might choose to exercise those individual rights in groups rather than alone, as in the First Amendment right to assemble and petition, but that does not make their rights "collective" or quasi-collective in the sense of depending on the will or actions of a state or on one's service to it.

the "well regulated Militia" but granting the "right" to "the people." The Constitution's other references to "rights" of "the people," noted above, cannot plausibly be construed as referring to the "Militia." In addition, when granting governmental power over the militia, the Constitution speaks of the militia expressly, without any reference to or suggestion of the broader "people."[43] And the Fifth Amendment's Grand Jury Clause, which distinguishes between all "person[s]" and those serving in the army, navy, or "the Militia, when in actual service," indicates that where the Constitution addresses rights that turn on service in the militia it does so expressly.

The only truly "collective" use of the "the people" at the time of the Founding was to refer to the people as they existed *apart from* government or any service to it. The Declaration of Independence refers to "one People" dissolving their political bonds with another and forming their own nation, and "We the people" created the Constitution in ratifying conventions chosen "by the People" of each state.[44] Thus, even in this context, the "people" are distinguished from "the government" or "the State"; nor can the term plausibly be limited to the "Militia." And when "the people" appears in the phrase "the *right* of the people" in the Constitution, we conclude that it indicates a personal right of individuals, whether that be a right to assemble and petition, to be secure in one's person and property, or to keep and bear arms.

B. "To Keep and Bear Arms"

The "right of the people" that the Second Amendment secures is a right "to keep and bear Arms." As the previous subpart showed, those who hold the right are, according to the text, "the people"—individuals—not the government or even the militia. The phrase "to keep and bear Arms" is consistent with this conclusion: The phrase "keep . . . Arms" reinforces it,[45] and the phrase "bear Arms" is not inconsistent with it.

---

[43] U.S. Const. art. I, § 8, cls. 15–16; *id.* art. II, § 2, cl. 1.

[44] The last quotation is from the Constitutional Convention's resolution transmitting the proposed Constitution to the Congress. 2 *The Records of the Federal Convention of 1787*, at 665 (Max Farrand ed., rev. ed. 1966). This distinction between the "people" and the government is why the Founders insisted that the Constitution be ratified by popularly elected special conventions rather than by the state governments, to ensure its supremacy over those governments. *See The Federalist No. 39*, at 253–54 (James Madison) (Jacob E. Cooke ed., 1961); James Madison, *Notes of Debates in the Federal Convention of 1787*, at 70 (1987) (remarks of Madison, June 5, 1787); *id.* at 348–49 (remarks of George Mason and Edmund Randolph, July 23, 1787); *id.* at 352–53 (remarks of Madison).

[45] Those who reject the individual right view tend to neglect "keep" or to treat it as redundant with "bear." In *Silveira*, the court found it "not clear" why the word "was included in the amendment" and concluded by summarizing the Amendment as merely protecting a right to "'bear arms'" in conjunction with militia service. 312 F.3d at 1074, 1086. *See also* Michael C. Dorf, *What Does the Second Amendment Mean Today?*, 76 Chi.-Kent L. Rev. 291, 317 (2000) (contending without citation that "keep and bear" is "a unitary phrase," with "keep" adding nothing to "bear," but admitting possibility that "the plain meaning of 'keep' would have been sufficient to connote an individual right"); H. Richard Uviller & William G.

1. "To Keep . . . Arms"

In eighteenth-century English, an individual could "keep arms," and keep them for private purposes, unrelated to militia duty, just as he could keep any other private property, and the phrase was commonly used in this sense. For example, in *Rex v. Gardner* (K.B. 1738), a defendant charged with "keeping a gun" in violation of a 1706 English statute (which prohibited commoners from keeping specified objects or "other engines" for the destruction of game) argued that "though there are many things for the bare keeping of which a man may be convicted; yet they are only such as can only be used for destruction of the game, whereas a gun is necessary for defence of a house, or for a farmer to shoot crows." The court agreed, reasoning that "a gun differs from nets and dogs, which can only be kept for an ill purpose."[46] The Court of Common Pleas six years later treated *Gardner* as having "settled and determined" that "a man may keep a gun for the defence of his house and family,"[47] and in 1752 the King's Bench reiterated that "a gun may be kept for the defence of a man's house, and for divers other lawful purposes."[48] The same usage appeared in an earlier prosecution of a man for "keeping of a gun" contrary to a statute that barred all but the wealthy from privately owning small handguns.[49]

William Blackstone, whose *Commentaries on the Laws of England*, first published in the decade before the American Revolution, was the leading legal authority in America at the Founding, wrote, without any reference to the militia, of "person[s]" who are "qualified to keep a gun" and are "shooting at a mark," apparently on their own property.[50] He also noted that certain persons could not

---

Merkel, *The Second Amendment in Context: The Case of the Vanishing Predicate*, 76 Chi.-Kent L. Rev. 403, 424–25, 508, 549–50, 593 (2000) (similar).

[46] 2 Strange Rep. 1098, 1098 (applying 5 Ann., c. 14 (1706)); *see Rex v. Gardner*, 87 Eng. Rep. 1240, 7 Mod. Rep. 279 (K.B. 1739) (apparently later case, but similar); *id.* at 1241 (defendant, arguing that "to charge only that he kept a gun is improper, for it includes every man that keeps a gun," and that guns are kept "for the defence of a man's house"); *id.* (Lee, C.J.) (words of statute "do not extend to prohibit a man from keeping a gun for his necessary defence"); *id.* (Probyn, J.) ("farmers are generally obliged to keep a gun, and are no more within the Act for doing so than they are for keeping a cabbage-net").

[47] *Mallock v. Eastly*, 87 Eng. Rep. 1370, 1374, 7 Mod. Rep. 482 (C.P. 1744).

[48] *Wingfield v. Stratford*, 96 Eng. Rep. 787, 787, Sayer Rep. 15 (K.B. 1752).

[49] *King v. Silcot*, 87 Eng. Rep. 186, 186, 3 Mod. Rep. 280 (K.B. 1690) (italics omitted) (interpreting 33 Hen. VIII, c. 6 (1541), and quashing indictment because it did not specifically allege that defendant's income was insufficient when he kept the gun).

[50] 4 William Blackstone, *Commentaries* *182. The qualification to which Blackstone refers is a wealth requirement tied to the game laws, *see id.* at *174–75, which we discuss in Part III.A and elsewhere. Regarding Blackstone's influence and authority, see, e.g., Madison, *Notes of Debates*, *supra* note 44, at 547 (remarks of Dickenson, Aug. 29, 1787); *The Federalist No. 69*, at 465 n.* (Alexander Hamilton); *The Federalist No. 84*, at 577 (Alexander Hamilton); Malcolm, *To Keep and Bear Arms*, *supra* note 33, at 130; *Schick v. United States*, 195 U.S. 65, 69 (1904). Edmund Burke informed Parliament that "they have sold nearly as many of Blackstone's Commentaries in America as in

"keep arms in their houses," pursuant to a statute that used "keep" to signify private ownership and control over arms, wherever located.[51] Colonial and early state statutes similarly used "keep" to "describe arms possession by individuals in all contexts," including requiring those exempt from militia service (such as the over-aged) to "keep" arms in their homes for both law enforcement and "the defense of their homes from criminals or foreign enemies."[52] At the Massachusetts Ratifying Convention in 1788, Samuel Adams proposed an amendment prohibiting Congress from "prevent[ing] the people of the United States, who are peaceable citizens, from keeping their own arms," indicating ownership by individuals of private arms.[53] And that state's Supreme Court, in a libel case soon after the Founding, likened the "right to keep fire arms" to the freedom of the press, both being individual but not unlimited rights—the former not protecting "him who uses them for annoyance or destruction."[54] The basic dictionary definition of "keep"—"[t]o retain" and "[t]o have in custody"—was consistent with this specific meaning.[55]

In short, the phrase "keep arms" was commonly understood to denote ownership of arms by private citizens for private purposes. When that phrase is read together with its subject—"the right of the people"—the evidence points strongly toward an individual right. Had the Constitution meant not to protect the right of the whole "people" to "keep" arms but instead to establish a "right" of the states or of only the members of their militias to store them, presumably it would have used different language.[56]

England." Speech Concerning Resolutions for Conciliation With the Colonies (Mar. 22, 1775), *in* Edmund Burke, *Pre-Revolutionary Writings* 206, 225 (Ian Harris ed., 1993).

[51] 4 William Blackstone, *Commentaries* *56; *see id.* (person barred from "keeping arms in his house"). *See also* 1 W. & M., 1st Sess., c. 15, § 3 (1688) ("no papist . . . shall or may have or keep in his house, or elsewhere, or in the possession of any other person to his use, or at his disposition, any arms, weapons, gunpowder, or ammunition").

[52] Kates, *supra* note 33, 82 Mich. L. Rev. at 215, 219.

[53] We discuss this proposal below in Part III.C.1.

[54] *Commonwealth v. Blanding*, 20 Mass. (3 Pick.) 304, 338 (1825).

[55] Samuel Johnson, *A Dictionary of the English Language* (1755) (unpaginated). *See* Noah Webster, *An American Dictionary of the English Language* (1828) (unpaginated) (defining "Keep" first as "To hold; to retain in one's power or possession").

[56] *See* Stephen P. Halbrook, *A Right to Bear Arms: State and Federal Bills of Rights and Constitutional Guarantees* 94 (1989) (contending that "common linguistic usage of the day . . . referr[ed] to the *depositing* of public arms in an arsenal, in contrast with the *keeping* of private arms by the people," and providing an example of the former usage in a 1789 state statute); *cf.* U.S. Const. art. I, § 10, cl. 3 ("No *State* shall . . . keep Troops" without Congress's consent) (emphasis added). When members of a militia, as opposed to the people in general, retained their own arms for militia service, common usage seems to have been to speak of them "providing" themselves with weapons, *see* Militia Act, ch. 33, § 1, 1 Stat. 271 (1792); Thomas Jefferson, *Notes on the State of Virginia* 88 (William Peden ed., 1955); 1 *The Papers of George Mason, 1725–1792*, at 212 (Robert A. Rutland ed., 1970), although we do not mean to claim that one could not speak of militiamen "keeping" arms for militia use.

2. "To . . . Bear Arms"

To "bear" was, at the Founding as now, a word with numerous definitions—used with great "latitude" and "in very different senses," as Samuel Johnson noted in his dictionary.[57] Its basic meaning was simply to "carry" or "wear" something, particularly carrying or wearing in a way that would be known to others, such as in bearing a message, bearing another person, or bearing something as a mark of authority or distinction.[58] As a result, "bear," when taking "arms" as its object, could refer to multiple contexts in which one might carry or wear arms in this way.[59] It is true that "bear arms" often did refer to carrying arms in military service.[60] But the phrase was not a term of art limited to this sense. Arms also could be "borne" for private, non-military purposes, principally tied to self-defense. For example, an early colonial statute in Massachusetts required every "freeman or other inhabitant" to provide arms for himself and anyone else in his household able to "beare armes," and one in Virginia required "all men that are fittinge to beare armes" to "bring their pieces" to church.[61]

There are also several examples closer to the Founding. In 1779, a committee of eminent Virginians including Thomas Jefferson and George Mason, charged with revising the new state's laws, authored a bill penalizing any person who, within a year of having violated a restriction on hunting deer, "shall bear a gun out of his inclosed ground, unless whilst performing military duty." This bill demonstrates that to "bear a gun" was not limited to "performing military duty." James Madison submitted this bill to the Virginia legislature in 1785.[62] Many early state

[57] Johnson, *Dictionary*, *supra* note 55 (unpaginated).

[58] *See id.* (defining "bear" as to "carry as a burden," "convey or carry," "carry as a mark of authority" (such as a sword), "carry as a mark of distinction" (such as to "*bear* arms in a coat"), and "carry as in show"); Webster, *American Dictionary*, *supra* note 55 (unpaginated) (defining "bear" as to "support," "sustain," "carry," "convey," "support and remove from place to place," "wear," and "bear as a mark of authority or distinction; as, to *bear* a sword, a badge, a name; to *bear* arms in a coat").

[59] In *Muscarello v. United States*, 524 U.S. 125 (1998), which involved a statute, the Court was unanimous in understanding "bear arms" to refer generally to a person carrying arms upon his person for the purpose of being armed and ready for offensive or defensive action, the dissent citing the Second Amendment in support of this view. The majority gave "carries a firearm" a broader meaning. *Id.* at 130; *id.* at 139–40, 143 (Ginsburg, J., dissenting).

[60] *See, e.g.*, Kates, *supra* note 33, 82 Mich. L. Rev. at 219 (explaining that, in early colonial statutes, "'bear' did generally refer to the carrying of arms by militiamen"); St. George Tucker, 2 *Blackstone's Commentaries* *408–09 n.1 (1803; reprint 1996) ("Tucker's Blackstone") (discussing Virginia law exempting from militia duty those "religiously scrupulous of bearing arms"); The Declaration of Independence para. 28 (1776) ("He has constrained our fellow Citizens taken Captive on the high Seas to bear Arms against their country."). Militia service was not, however, limited to "military" action. The Constitution speaks of using the militia "to execute the Laws of the Union," which is distinct from both "repel[ling] Invasions" and "suppress[ing] Insurrections." U.S. Const. art. I, § 8, cl. 15.

[61] *Quoted in* Malcolm, *To Keep and Bear Arms*, *supra* note 33, at 139.

[62] 2 *The Papers of Thomas Jefferson* 443–44 (Julian P. Boyd ed., 1950). Concerning the Committee of Revisors, see *id.* at 305; 1 Tucker's Blackstone, *supra* note 60, Note F, at 444–45.

constitutions, including some written before the Founding (Pennsylvania's and Vermont's) and one written a month after Secretary of State Jefferson declared the Bill of Rights ratified (Kentucky's), protected an individual's right to "bear arms" in "defense of himself and the State" or in "defense of themselves and the State," indicating that a person might be said to "bear arms" in self-defense.[63] A 1780 opinion of London's Recorder (the city's legal adviser and the primary judge in its criminal court) on the legality of a *private* self-defense association acknowledged "the rights of the people of this realm to bear arms, and to instruct themselves in the use of them, collectively," albeit within limits.[64] In a newspaper commentary published in major cities after Madison introduced the Bill of Rights in Congress, a friend of his wrote that the proposed Second Amendment would "confirm[]" the people's "right to keep and bear their private arms."[65] Supreme Court Justice Joseph Story, in his 1833 *Commentaries on the Constitution of the United States*, paraphrased as a "right to bear arms" the right of English "subjects . . . [to] have arms for their defence," an individual right not tied to service in the militia.[66] Finally, other examples of contemporaneous uses of "bear arms" to denote actions of individuals appear in cases from the early 1800s up to the Civil War, discussed below in Part IV.B.

The Minority Report issued by twenty-one delegates of the Pennsylvania Convention that ratified the Federal Constitution in late 1787 illustrates the various uses of the phrase at the time, including both the *right* of private "bearing" and the *duty* of "bearing" for the government in the militia. The Report recommended amending the Constitution to recognize "[t]hat the people have a right to bear arms for the defence of themselves and their own State or the United States, or for the purpose of killing game" and also urged exemption from militia service for those "conscientiously scrupulous of bearing arms." Although the Minority Report was a product of Anti-Federalists, who had lost at that convention and who lost the

---

[63] These are collected, through the Michigan Constitution of 1835, in *Emerson*, 270 F.3d at 230 n.29. We discuss the Pennsylvania and Vermont constitutions below in Part III.B.2. For an 1822 judicial interpretation confirming the plain meaning of the Kentucky provision as granting an individual right, see Part IV.B.1 below. Regarding ratification of the Bill of Rights, see Part III.C.2 below.

[64] Legality of the London Military Foot-Association (July 24, 1780), *reprinted in* William Blizard, *Desultory Reflections on Police: With an Essay on the Means of Preventing Crimes and Amending Criminals* 59, 59 (London 1785) (emphasis omitted). Regarding this opinion, which was "of wide interest," Leon Radzinowicz, 4 *A History of English Criminal Law* 107 (1968), *see id.* at 107–10; Malcolm, *To Keep and Bear Arms*, *supra* note 33, at 133–34; and our further discussion below in Part III.A. Regarding the Recorder, *see* 1 William Blackstone, *Commentaries* *76; 3 *id.* at *80–81 n.i; *id.* at *334; John H. Langbein, *Shaping the Eighteenth-Century Criminal Trial: A View From the Ryder Sources*, 50 U. Chi. L. Rev. 1, 8, 17–19, 34–36 (1983).

[65] This essay by Tench Coxe is discussed below in Part III.C.2.

[66] Joseph Story, *Commentaries on the Constitution of the United States* § 980, at 695 (Ronald D. Rotunda & John E. Nowak eds., 1833, reprint 1987) ("*Abridgement*"). The English right is discussed below in Part III.A.

battle over ratifying the Constitution, we are unaware of any contemporaneous criticisms that this widely circulated document misused language in giving such senses to the phrase "bear arms."[67]

In sum, although "bear arms" often referred to carrying or wearing arms in connection with military duty, it was not limited to such a meaning. When, as in the Second Amendment, those words are used in conjunction with "keep arms," which commonly did refer to private action, and the whole phrase "to keep and bear Arms" is used in the context of a "right of the people,"[68] we conclude that the core, operative text of the Amendment secures a personal right, which belongs to individuals. We next consider whether the Amendment's prefatory language requires a different conclusion.

C. "A Well Regulated Militia, Being Necessary to the Security of a Free State"

A feature of the Second Amendment that distinguishes it from the other rights that the Bill of Rights secures is its prefatory subordinate clause, declaring: "A well regulated Militia, being necessary to the security of a free State, ..." Advocates of the collective right and quasi-collective right interpretations rely on this declaration, particularly its reference to a well-regulated militia. On their interpretation, the "people" to which the Second Amendment refers is only the

---

[67] *See* 2 Bernard Schwartz, *The Bill of Rights: A Documentary History* 665, 672 (1971). We discuss the Pennsylvania Convention, including the Minority Report and its critics, in Part III.C.1 below. Regarding the Report's wide circulation, see *id.* at 628; 2 *The Documentary History of the Ratification of the Constitution* 617 (Merrill Jensen ed., 1976) (note); 15 *id.* at 7–10 (John P. Kaminski & Gaspare J. Saladino eds., 1984) (note).

[68] In addition, the Second Amendment's reference to "Arms" in the context of "keep" and "bear" reinforces our view that it protects an individual right. The mere word "Arms" could denote any weapon, including artillery. *See* Webster, *American Dictionary*, *supra* note 55 (unpaginated) (defining "arms" as "Weapons of offense, or armor for defense and protection of the body" and including explanation of "*Fire arms*" as "such as may be charged with powder, as cannon, muskets, mortars &c."; also defining the verb "arm" as including "[t]o furnish with means of defense; to prepare for resistance; to fortify"); Johnson, *Dictionary*, *supra* note 55 (unpaginated) (defining "arms" as "Weapons of offence, or armour of defence"). Certainly Congress's power in Article I, Section 8, Clause 16 to provide for "arming" the militia includes such weapons, particularly given that the Constitution contemplates that the states will use militias to defend themselves against surprise invasions. *See* U.S. Const. art. I, § 10, cl. 3 ("No State shall, without the Consent of Congress, . . . keep Troops, . . . or engage in War, unless actually invaded, or in such imminent Danger as will not admit of delay."); Militia Act § 4, 1 Stat. 271, 272 (1792) (requiring each division of state's militia to have a company of artillery and troop of horse). If the Second Amendment protected a state prerogative to have organized and effective militias, one would expect it to protect all of the arms essential for that purpose, including artillery. Yet its text suggests that the "Arms" that it protects do not include those that "the people" could not both "keep" and "bear"—those that an individual could not store and carry. This use of "Arms" points toward an individual right view rather than a right of states to have select "militias," and it also seems more consistent with an individual right than a quasi-collective right view, as the latter requires that the "militia" of which the claimant is a member be fully organized and equipped. *See, e.g.*, *United States v. Parker*, 362 F.3d 1279, 1283 (10th Cir. 2004).

"people" in a collective, organized capacity as the state governments, or a small subset of the "people" actively organized by those governments into military bodies. "People" becomes interchangeable with the "State" or its "organized militia."

This argument misunderstands the proper role of such prefatory declarations in interpreting the operative language of a provision. A preface can illuminate operative language but is ultimately subordinate to it and cannot restrict it.

Wholly apart from this interpretive principle, this argument also rests on an incomplete understanding of the preface's language. Although the Amendment's prefatory clause, standing alone, might suggest a collective or possibly quasi-collective right to a modern reader, when its words are read as they were understood at the Founding, the preface is fully consistent with the individual right that the Amendment's operative language sets out. The "Militia" as understood at the Founding was not a select group such as the National Guard of today. It consisted of all able-bodied male citizens. The Second Amendment's preface identifies as a justification for the individual right that a necessary condition for an effective citizen militia, and for the "free State" that it helps to secure, is a citizenry that is privately armed and able to use its private arms.

1. The Limits of Prefatory Language

In the eighteenth century, the proper approach to interpreting a substantive or "operative" legal provision to which a lawmaker had joined a declaration (whether a "Whereas" clause or analogous language) was (1) to seek to interpret the operative provision on its own, and (2) then to look to the declaration only to clarify any ambiguity remaining in the operative provision.[69] It was desirable, if consistent with the operative text, to interpret the operative provision so that it generally fulfilled the justification that the preface declared, but a narrow declaration provided no warrant for restricting the operative text, and the preface could not itself create an ambiguity. This rule applied equally to declarations located in any part of a law, not simply at the beginning of it, and to both statutes and constitutions. We therefore consider this rule applicable to the Second Amendment.

---

[69] This rule assumes that the legislature incorporated the declaration during the ordinary legislative process, not adopting it separately (with little consideration) or leaving it to others to insert. 2A Norman J. Singer, *Sutherland on Statutory Construction* § 47.04, at 220 & 223 (6th ed. 2000); *see* 1 James Kent, *Commentaries on American Law* 516 (9th ed. 1858) (noting that titles and preambles "generally . . . are loosely and carelessly inserted, and are not safe expositors of the law"); *see also King v. Williams*, 96 Eng. Rep. 51, 52, 1 Blackst. Rep. 93 (K.B. 1758) ("The conciseness of the title shall not control the body of the Act. The title is no part of the law; it does not pass with the same solemnity as the law itself. One reading is often sufficient for it."); Thomas Jefferson, *A Manual of Parliamentary Practice for the Use of the Senate of the United States* 41 (1801; reprint 1993) (noting desirability that preamble "be consistent with" a bill but possibility that it may not be, because of legislative procedures).

Opinions of the Office of Legal Counsel in Volume 28

English Parliaments of the 1700s and late 1600s regularly included prefaces throughout statutes—not only at the beginning (constituting the first section) but also in particular sections.[70] The same rule of interpretation applied to both uses of prefaces. As an example of the latter, a section of a bankruptcy statute recited the problem of persons who "convey *their* goods to other men upon good consideration" before becoming bankrupt, yet continue to act as owners of the goods; the immediately following clause of the statute provided that if a bankrupt debtor possessed "*any* goods or chattels" with "the consent and permission of the true owner," was their reputed owner, and disposed of them as an owner, such property should repay the debtor's debts rather than return to the true owner. The difficulty arose when the bankrupt debtor possessed property that never had been his, such as property in trust. A leading case in 1716 read the enacting language to apply even in such cases and rejected the argument "that the preamble shall restrain the operation of the enacting clause; and that, because the preamble is too narrow or defective, therefore the enacting clause, which has general words, shall be restrained from its full latitude, and from doing that good which the words would otherwise, and of themselves, import."[71] The King's Bench reiterated the rule in 1723, rejecting in a criminal case an argument based on declaratory language introducing part of a statute: "Now those general words in the enacting part, shall never be restrained by any words introducing that part; for it is no rule in the exposition of statutes to confine the general words of the enacting part to any particular words either introducing it, or to any such words even in the preamble itself." The court acknowledged that "a construction which agrees with the preamble" was desirable, "but not such as may confine the enacting part to it."[72]

---

[70] Examples of both include the statutes discussed or cited below in Part III.A. *See, e.g.*, the Militia Act of 1662, 13 & 14 Car. II, c. 3, §§ 1, 3, 14, 20; the Game Act of 1671, 32 & 33 Car. II, c. 25, §§ 1, 2, 4, 5, 6, 7; the Act to Disarm Papists, 1 W. & M., 1st Sess., c. 15, §§ 1, 3 (1688); the Bill of Rights, 1 W. & M., 2d Sess., c. 2, §§ 1, 9 (1689); the Game Act of 1692, 4 & 5 W. & M., c. 23, §§ 1, 3, 4, 5, 7, 10; the act repealing the ban on hail-shot, 6 & 7 Will. III, c. 13, §§ 1, 3 (1695); and the Game Act of 1706, 5 Ann., c. 14, §§ 1, 3, 5.

[71] *Copeman v. Gallant*, 24 Eng. Rep. 404, 407, 1 P. Wms. Rep. 314 (Ch. 1716); *id.* at 405 (quoting statute) (emphases added); *see* 2A *Sutherland, supra* note 69, § 47.04, at 220 ("Copeman . . . established the rule that the preamble could not be used to restrict the effect of the words used in the purview."). In *Ryall v. Rolle*, 26 Eng. Rep. 107, 1 Atkyns Rep. 165 (Ch. 1749), although the question was not at issue, *see id.* at 116 (Lee, C.J.); *id.* at 118 (Hardwicke, Ch.), some judges voiced disagreement with *Copeman*'s interpretation of that statute because of the great "inconvenience" it would cause to commercial arrangements such as trusts, agency, and bailment, but they still recognized the general rule, *see id.* at 113 (Parker, C.B.) (recognizing another case holding "[t]hat the preamble shall not restrain the enacting clause" and recognizing that *Copeman* "exploded the notion of the preamble's governing the enacting clause," but adding that "if the not restraining the generality of the enacting clause will be attended with an inconvenience, the preamble shall restrain it"); *id.* at 118 (Hardwicke, Ch.) (agreeing with Parker).

[72] *King v. Athos*, 8 Mod. Rep. 136, 144 (K.B. 1723). *See id.* (Fortescue, J.) ("[I]t must be admitted, that a preamble may be a good expositor of a statute; but what was offered on the other side is not properly a preamble, but only introductive to an enacting part of a statute: besides . . . preambles are no more than recitals of inconveniences, which do not exclude any other to which a remedy is given by the

Blackstone summed up this understanding in explaining that, although the words of an enacting clause were "generally to be understood in their usual and most known signification," yet if its words, *after* due analysis, were "still dubious" or "ambiguous, equivocal, or intricate," one might look to the context, which included "the proeme, or preamble, [which] is often called in to help the construction of an act of parliament."[73] Chancellor Kent, a leading early American commentator, likewise reasoned that a preamble, although not technically part of the law, "may, at times, aid in the construction of" a statute or "be resorted to in order to ascertain the inducements to the making" of it, "but when the words of the enacting clause are clear and positive, recourse must not be had to the preamble."[74]

Prefatory language also was common in constitutions, and this rule of construction applied in the same way. Speaking of the preamble of the whole federal Constitution, Joseph Story in his *Commentaries* reiterated that statutory preambles are "properly resorted to, where doubts or ambiguities arise upon the words of the enacting part; for if they are clear and unambiguous, there seems little room for interpretation," and he could not see "any reason why, in a fundamental law or constitution of government," the same rule should not apply.[75] Similarly, the Supreme Court has held that the Constitution's preamble lacks any operative legal effect and that, even though it states the Constitution's "general purposes," it cannot be used to conjure a "spirit" of the document to confound clear operative language;[76] the Court has, however, also sought some guidance from the preamble when the operative text did not resolve a question.[77]

The same reasoning applied to declaratory phrases in the language of individual constitutional provisions, the closest analogies to the Second Amendment. The 1784 New Hampshire Constitution provided: "In criminal prosecutions, the trial of

---

enacting part."); *Kinaston v. Clark*, 26 Eng. Rep. 526, 527, 2 Atkyns Rep. 204 (Ch. 1741) ("There are many cases where the enacting part in a statute extends further than the preamble even in criminal matters . . . .").

[73] 1 William Blackstone, *Commentaries* *59–60. *See Crespigny v. Wittenoom*, 100 Eng. Rep. 1304, 1305, 4 Term Rep. 791 (K.B. 1792) (Buller, J.) ("I agree that the preamble cannot controul the enacting part of a statute, which is expressed in clear and unambiguous terms. But if any doubt arise on the words of the enacting part, the preamble may be resorted to, to explain it."); *id.* at 1306 (Grose, J.) ("Though the preamble cannot controul the enacting clause, we may compare it with the rest of the Act, in order to collect the intention of the Legislature.").

[74] 1 Kent, *Commentaries*, *supra* note 69, at 516. *See Mills v. Wilkins*, 87 Eng. Rep. 822, 822–23, 6 Mod. Rep. 62 (Q.B. 1703) ("[T]he title is not the law, but the name or description given to it by the makers: just as the preamble of a statute is no part thereof, but contains generally the motives or inducements thereof."); *see also* 2A *Sutherland*, *supra* note 69, § 47.04, at 221–22; *id.* at 224–25 ("The preamble can neither limit nor extend the meaning of a statute which is clear. Similarly, it cannot be used to create doubt or uncertainty.").

[75] 1 Joseph Story, *Commentaries on the Constitution of the United States* §§ 459–460, at 443–44 (1833; reprint 1991).

[76] *Jacobson v. Massachusetts*, 197 U.S. 11, 22 (1905).

[77] *See U.S. Term Limits, Inc. v. Thornton*, 514 U.S. 779, 821 n.31, 838 (1995); *id.* at 846 & n.1 (Thomas, J., dissenting); *see also Stenberg v. Carhart*, 530 U.S. 914, 953 (2000) (Scalia, J., dissenting).

facts in the vicinity where they happen, is so essential to the security of the life, liberty and estate of the citizen, that no crime or offence ought to be tried in any other county than that in which it is committed."[78] Even though in some cases a trial outside of the county where a crime was committed might bring it closer to the crime scene, or a judge might think a trial in the county where the crime occurred not "essential to" (or even in conflict with) "the security of the life, liberty and estate of the citizen," neither fact would justify disregarding the clear operative language of this constitutional provision.[79] Likewise, the pre-1787 constitutions of Massachusetts, New Hampshire, and Vermont declared that freedom of speech in the legislature was "so essential to the rights of the people" that words spoken there could not the basis of "any" suit.[80] One could not use this declaration to avoid the clear immunity conferred by the operative language, even where particular statements made in the legislature—such as an egregious slander unrelated to a pending bill—were not thought "essential to" the people's rights.[81] In addition, Madison's draft of what became the First Amendment's Free Press Clause read: "the freedom of the press, *as one of the great bulwarks of liberty*, shall be inviolable."[82] The emphasized declaratory language presumably could not have qualified or limited the freedom clearly conferred, such as by exempting from protection, as hostile to "liberty," publications advocating absolute monarchy.

A discussion at the Constitutional Convention demonstrates the same understanding, including that prefaces in a particular constitutional provision might merely state policy. What would become Article I, Section 8, Clause 16 of the Constitution, empowering Congress to "provide for organizing, arming, and disciplining the Militia," had reached its final form. But George Mason proposed "to preface" it with the phrase, "And that the liberties of the people may be better secured against the danger of standing armies in time of peace." He wished "to insert something pointing out and guarding against the danger of" standing armies. Madison spoke in favor, because the preface would "discountenance" a peacetime

---

[78] N.H. Const. art. I, § 17 (1784), *reprinted in* 4 *The Federal and State Constitutions, Colonial Charters, and Other Organic Laws* 2455 (Francis Newton Thorpe ed., 1909; reprint 1993).

[79] *See* Eugene Volokh, *The Commonplace Second Amendment*, 73 N.Y.U. L. Rev. 793, 798, 804–05, 808–09 (1998); *Emerson*, 270 F.3d at 234 n.32.

[80] Mass. Const. pt. I, art. 21 (1780), *reprinted in* 3 *Federal and State Constitutions*, *supra* note 78, at 1892; N.H. Const. art. I, § 30 (1784), *reprinted in* 4 *id.* at 2457; Vt. Const. ch. I, § 16 (1786), *reprinted in* 6 *id.* at 3753.

[81] *See* Volokh, *supra* note 79, 73 N.Y.U. L. Rev. at 794–95, 799–800. As with statutes, constitutional prefaces and operative language often do not match exactly, the latter sometimes being overinclusive compared to the declaration and sometimes underinclusive. *See id.* at 801–07 (providing examples).

[82] *Creating the Bill of Rights: The Documentary Record from the First Federal Congress* 12 (Helen E. Veit et. al. eds., 1991) (emphasis added).

standing army while "not restrain[ing] Congress from establishing" one.[83] No doubt an organized, armed, and disciplined militia *would* generally "better secure" liberties against peace-time standing armies (by reducing the need for such armies and the threat from any that were created), and thus the operative grant of power "agree[d] with" the declaratory preface;[84] but the preface did not restrain or confine the power.

We see no reason to except the Second Amendment from this broadly applicable interpretive rule.[85] Thus, the Amendment's declaratory preface could not overcome the unambiguously individual "right of the people to keep and bear Arms" conferred by the operative text—even if the collective right and quasi-collective right schools' understanding of the preface's meaning were correct, and even though the preface might help resolve any ambiguities concerning the scope of that individual right remaining after one has analyzed the operative text. At the same time, any interpretation of the right ought, if possible consistent with its text, to further the declared justification in general, as the Court in *Miller* recognized when it stated that interpretation of the Amendment should keep the "end in view" of assuring the continuation and rendering possible the effectiveness of the militia.[86] As we explain in the remainder of this subpart—considering in turn the meaning of "Militia," what a "well regulated Militia" was, and the ultimate end of "the security of a free State"—the individual right view does further the ends set forth in the prefatory language, and therefore the preface, properly understood, is fully consistent with the individual right interpretation of the operative text.

2. The "Militia"

A key claim of the collective right and quasi-collective right schools with regard to the Second Amendment's preface is that a "well regulated Militia" is a standing military organization or body of troops, of limited size, organized and governed by state governments, albeit concurrently with the federal government (akin to voluntary select forces such as the National Guard that were established over a hundred years after the Amendment was adopted). As a result, the argument goes, the Amendment merely protects the states against federal efforts to undermine such forces, either by protecting the states directly or by protecting only persons serving in those forces.[87]

---

[83] Madison, *Notes of Debates*, *supra* note 44, at 639 (Sept. 14, 1787). Mason's proposal was defeated, apparently on the ground that it improperly impugned soldiers. *Id.* at 639–40.

[84] *Athos*, 8 Mod. Rep. at 144.

[85] The Ninth Circuit in *Silveira* provided only one paragraph on the proper relationship between a preface and operative language, concluding that the latter must be read "to implement the policy" of the former. *See* 312 F.3d at 1075.

[86] *United States* v. *Miller*, 307 U.S. 174, 178 (1939).

[87] *See, e.g.*, *Silveira*, 312 F.3d at 1069–72.

This argument disregards the understanding of the "Militia" at the time of the Founding. As used in the Second Amendment, and elsewhere in the Constitution, "Militia" referred to a body consisting of all adult male citizens up to a certain age (anywhere from forty-five to sixty), the goal being to include all who were physically capable of service. It was not limited to a select force of persons in active military duty. This entire population of able-bodied male citizens was involuntarily "enrolled" by local militia officials, somewhat as men now register for the selective service (except that enrollment required no action by the citizen), and all enrolled citizens were required by law to join occasional "exercise"—to which they were expected to bring their own, private arms—but they otherwise remained in civilian life. The militia "rest[ed] upon the shoulders of the people,"[88] because, as then understood, it consisted of a large number of the "people" at any one time and of all of the able-bodied white men for a substantial portion of their lives. It was the people embodied as an armed force. Thus, a key aspect of the term "Militia" was the composition of the force to which it referred. As a result, the reference to the "Militia" in the Second Amendment's preface "agrees with" the individual right that the Amendment's operative text sets out,[89] because securing to "the people" a right to keep and to bear their own arms made such a broad-based, privately armed force more likely to exist and to be effective.[90]

The term "Militia" was used in contrast both to a regular, standing army and, more importantly, to a "select militia" or "corps."[91] The latter distinction is evident throughout contemporaneous usage, "select militia" denoting a significantly smaller body, consisting either of better trained military professionals who could remain active for extended periods, or of those chosen selectively, perhaps because of political or other discrimination.[92] For example, at the Constitutional Convention, George Mason mentioned the need for federal regulation of the

---

[88] *Nordyke v. King*, 364 F.3d 1025, 1031 (9th Cir. 2004) (Gould, J., joined by O'Scannlain, Kleinfeld, Tallman, and Bea, J.J., dissenting from denial of rehearing en banc).

[89] *Athos*, 8 Mod. Rep. at 144.

[90] *See* Kopel, *supra* note 33, 93 Mich. L. Rev. at 1355 ("[O]ne of the reasons Congress guaranteed the right of the people to keep and bear arms was so that a popular militia could be drawn from the body of the people.") (footnote omitted). Thus, the *Silveira* court's description of the militia as "the state-created and -organized military force," 312 F.3d at 1069, is technically true but critically incomplete, because it ignores the composition of the militia.

[91] On the former distinction, see U.S. Const. art. I, § 8, cls. 12–16; art. I, § 10, cl. 3; art. II, § 2, cl. 1; amend. V; Articles of Confed. art. VI (contrasting a "body of forces" with "a well regulated and disciplined militia, sufficiently armed and accoutered."); *Authority of President to Send Militia Into a Foreign Country*, 29 Op. Att'y Gen. 322, 322 (1912) (Wickersham, A.G.) ("[T]he militia has always been considered and treated as a military body quite distinct and different from the Regular or standing army.").

[92] *See* Malcolm, *To Keep and Bear Arms*, *supra* note 33, at 125 (discussing concerns of English Whigs after the English Revolution of 1688–1689 to maintain a citizens' militia as opposed to a select one); *id.* at 95–97, 103, 105 (discussing purges and selective disarmament of militia by Charles II and James II); *id.* at 63 (discussing Charles II's select militia).

militia to ensure that it was adequately trained. He suspected that the states would not relinquish "the power over the whole" but would "over a part as a select militia." He added that "a select militia" would be "as much as the Gen[eral] Gov[ernment] could advantageously be charged with," and thus suggested that it receive power only over "one tenth part" of the militia per year. Oliver Ellsworth, later to be a Senator and Chief Justice, objected because a "select militia" either would be impractical or would cause "a ruinous declension of the great body of the Militia."[93] Edmund Randolph, leader of the Virginia delegation, similarly equated the militia with "the whole mass" of the people.[94]

In the debate over ratification, both sides shared this broad understanding of "Militia." Among the Federalists, Madison in *The Federalist* predicted that a federal army bent on oppression would be opposed by "a militia amounting to near half a million of citizens with arms in their hands"—a group that he likened to the citizen bands that had fought in the Revolution and linked to "the advantage of being armed, which the Americans possess over the people of almost every other nation."[95] Alexander Hamilton described the militia as "the great body of the yeomanry and of the other classes of the citizens," "the great body of the people," and "the whole nation," which he contrasted with a "select corps."[96] A Connecticut Federalist writing as "The Republican" praised as "a capital circumstance in favour of our liberty" that "the people of this country have arms in their hands; they are not destitute of military knowledge; every citizen is required by Law to be a soldier; we are all martialed into companies, regiments, and brigades, for the defence of our country."[97] In a speech, later published, in response to South Carolina's vote to ratify, David Ramsay, a state legislator and delegate to the ratifying convention, praised the Constitution's militia powers and asked, "What European power will dare to attack us, when it is known that the yeomanry of the country uniformly armed and disciplined, may on any emergency be called out to our defence . . . ?"[98] Maryland's "Aristides," in a fairly widely circulated pamphlet, wrote simply that "the militia . . . is ourselves."[99]

Among the Anti-Federalists, Mason, in the Virginia Ratifying Convention, asked: "Who are the Militia? They consist now of the whole people," while

---

[93] Madison, *Notes of Debates, supra* note 44, at 478, 483–84 (Aug. 18, 1787).

[94] *Id.* at 515 (Aug. 23). John Adams also praised a militia of the whole people, as opposed to a select band, in works that he published in 1776 and 1787. See Part III.B.1 below.

[95] *The Federalist No. 46*, at 321 (James Madison). The population of all white males aged 16 and over in the 1790 census was 813,298, making Madison's number a fair approximation of the citizen militia. *See* U.S. Dept. of Commerce, Bureau of the Census, 1 *Historical Statistics of the United States* 16 (1975).

[96] *The Federalist No. 29*, at 183–85 (Alexander Hamilton).

[97] 1 *The Debate on the Constitution* 712 (Bernard Bailyn ed., 1993).

[98] 2 *id.* at 507. For Ramsey's biography, *see id.* at 1009.

[99] Aristides, *Remarks on the Proposed Plan of a Federal Government* (1788), *reprinted in* 15 *Ratification, supra* note 67, at 522, 533; *see id.* at 518–20 (note regarding circulation and responses).

warning that the new Congress might exempt the rich from service.[100] The Federal Farmer, a leading Anti-Federalist essayist, explained that the "militia, when properly formed, are in fact the people themselves," and counseled "that regular troops, and select corps, ought not to be kept up without evident necessity." If the federal government properly organized, armed, and disciplined the militia—including in it, "according to the past and general usage of the states, all men capable of bearing arms"—the country would have a "genuine" rather than "select militia." Under such wise regulation, "the militia are the people."[101]

This common sense of "Militia" also appeared in the House of Representatives' debates on the Second Amendment, discussed below in Part III.C.2, and the Second Congress applied it in the first Militia Act, enacted in 1792, two months after the Second Amendment was officially ratified. The Act required "each and every able-bodied white male citizen of the respective states, resident therein, who is or shall be of the age of eighteen years, and under the age of forty-five years," to be "enrolled in the militia" by the local commanding officer. Each enrolled citizen was required to provide his own arms—"a good musket or firelock" or "a good rifle"—plus ammunition and accouterments. These private arms were exempted from "all suits, distresses, executions or sales, for debt or for the payment of taxes." The enrollees were required to appear, armed, "when called out to exercise, or into service," although Congress left the details of exercise to each state.[102] (Since 1792, Congress has only expanded this definition, such as by eliminating the racial restriction and including some women.[103]) Finally, Noah Webster in his 1828 American dictionary defined "militia" in accord with this Act and the above understanding: "The militia of a country are *the able bodied men* organized into companies, regiments and brigades, with officers of all grades, and required by law to attend military exercises on certain days only, but at other times left to pursue their usual occupations." They were "enrolled for discipline, but not engaged in actual service except in emergencies."[104]

The analogy of the "Militia" to a select (and voluntary) corps such as the National Guard is further strained by the common law prohibition against the King's

---

[100] 10 *Ratification, supra* note 67, at 1312 (John P. Kaminski & Gaspare J. Saladino eds., 1993) (June 16, 1788).

[101] *Federal Farmer No. 18* (1788), *reprinted in* 2 *The Complete Anti-Federalist* 341–42 (Herbert J. Storing ed., 1981); *see also Federal Farmer No. 3* (1787), *reprinted in id.* at 242. Publius (Hamilton) recognized the *Federal Farmer* letters as among the best of the Anti-Federalists'. *See The Federalist No. 68*, at 457–58.

[102] Act of May 8, 1792, ch. 33, §§ 1–2, 1 Stat. at 271–72; *see* 2 Tucker's Blackstone, *supra* note 60, at *409 n.1.

[103] 10 U.S.C. § 311(a) (2000) (including in the militia "all able-bodied males at least 17 years of age and . . . under 45 years of age," both citizens and those "who have made a declaration of intention to become" citizens, certain men between 45 and 64, and "female citizens of the United States who are members of the National Guard").

[104] Webster, *American Dictionary, supra* note 55 (unpaginated) (emphasis added).

deploying the militia outside the country—a rule that Blackstone celebrated as part of the individual's "absolute right" of "personal liberty."[105] The Constitution appears to incorporate this rule, by specifying domestic reasons for the federal government to call out the militia: "to execute the Laws of the Union, suppress Insurrections and repel Invasions."[106] Implicit in the common law rule is that the militia was so composed that its members ought to be treated as ordinary citizens doing their duty, rather than as soldiers. President Taft's Attorney General reaffirmed this ancient rule in 1912 as Congress was developing the modern National Guard, which, partly to avoid this rule, was made a component of the regular military forces.[107]

The Supreme Court in *Miller*, relying on a brief historical survey, summarized as follows the definition of "Militia" that we have set out and explained above:

> The signification attributed to the term Militia appears from the debates in the Convention, the history and legislation of Colonies and States, and the writings of approved commentators. These show plainly enough that the Militia comprised *all males physically capable of acting in concert for the common defense*. "A body of citizens enrolled for military discipline." And further, that ordinarily when called for service these men were expected to *appear bearing arms supplied by themselves* and of the kind in common use at the time.[108]

If, as the Court recognized and historical usage confirms, the "Militia" was composed of the general population of able-bodied men, an individual right of the whole people to keep and bear arms would make eminent sense. A large portion of the "people" would be required to appear occasionally for service or simply training, and they were expected to bring their private arms. If the people could be disarmed, it would then, among other things, be impossible for militiamen to make the required provision of their privately provided arms when called up, and the citizen militia would be undermined.

---

[105] 1 William Blackstone, *Commentaries* *134, *138, *413.

[106] U.S. Const. art. I, § 8, cl. 15.

[107] *Authority of President to Send Militia Into a Foreign Country*, 29 Op. Att'y Gen. 322, 322 (1912) (Wickersham, A.G.); *see Perpich v. Dep't of Defense*, 496 U.S. 334, 341–44 (1990).

[108] 307 U.S. at 179 (emphases added); *see id.* at 179–82 (collecting historical support); *Presser v. Illinois*, 116 U.S. 252, 265 (1886) ("It is undoubtedly true that all citizens capable of bearing arms constitute the reserved military force or reserve militia of the United States as well as of the States."); *Maryland v. United States*, 381 U.S. 41, 46 (1965) (describing pre-World War I militia as "a citizen army").

Opinions of the Office of Legal Counsel in Volume 28

3. The "Well Regulated" Militia

Advocates of the collective right and quasi-collective right views argue that the Amendment's reference in its preface to a "well regulated" militia indicates that the preface refers to a select, organized body akin to today's National Guard. They claim additional support for this argument from usage of the term "Militia" elsewhere in the Constitution, in the context of governmental power over the Militia.[109] No doubt the "Militia" was, through enrollment, exercise, and command when activated by a governor or president, a creature of the government. But it does not follow that the meaning of "Militia" as used in the Second Amendment depended on congressional (or state) legislation organizing or regulating the Militia. The word's use elsewhere in the Constitution and the Amendment's prefatory reference to a "well regulated Militia," properly understood, in fact suggest the opposite.

The Constitution distinguishes not only between the "Militia" and the regular armed forces but also between different parts and conditions of the militia. The latter distinctions appear in (1) Article I, Section 8, Clause 15, authorizing Congress to "provide for *calling forth* the Militia"; (2) the immediately following clause authorizing Congress to "provide for *organizing*, arming, and disciplining the Militia, and for governing *such Part of them* as may be employed in the Service of the United States"; (3) Article II, Section 2, Clause 1, making the President Commander in Chief of "the Militia of the several States" when "called into the *actual Service* of the United States"; and (4) the Fifth Amendment, which withholds the protection of the Grand Jury Clause from persons whose cases arise in the militia, but only when "in *actual service* in time of War or public danger" (cases in the army and navy, by contrast, are always exempted).

These provisions indicate that the militia is of a size that will make complete mobilization usually unnecessary, that members of the militia will often not be in service (or that not all parts of the militia will always be in service), and that when any members are not employed in "actual service," they ought to be treated as ordinary citizens. The "Militia" is both large and largely latent. In addition, the reference to "organizing . . . the Militia" suggests an entity that in some sense exists and is definable apart from congressional regulation, in contrast to "Armies," which Congress must "raise," pursuant to another power in Article I, Section 8. Congress might not "organiz[e]" *all* of the "Militia"; it might organize some parts differently from others; and it would be expected to give necessary precision to the definition of the body's membership by laying down a specific age range for service (as Congress did in the first Militia Act). But the background meaning of the word would remain. As an Anti-Federalist writer recognized: "[T]he militia is divided into two classes, viz. active and inactive," the former, he

[109] *See, e.g.*, *Silveira*, 312 F.3d at 1069–72.

expected, likely to "consist of young men chiefly."[110] Thus, the use of "Militia" throughout the Constitution is consistent with the common understanding of the word at the Founding.

Nor does the preface's phrase "well regulated" alter this sense of "Militia"; rather, it presupposes it. Having an armed citizenry, which the operative text protects by establishing a right of individuals, becomes a necessary (albeit not sufficient) condition for a well-regulated militia once one properly defines "Militia." As one academic commentator has put it: "The Second Amendment simply forbids one form of inappropriate regulation," which would ensure a militia that was *not* well regulated, namely "disarming the people from whom the militia must necessarily be drawn. . . . [T]he one thing the government is forbidden to do is infringe the right of the people, who are the source of the militia's members, to keep and bear arms."[111] A militia composed of the whole body of able-bodied male citizens and only infrequently meeting for state-sponsored exercise is more likely to be "well regulated" in the bearing of arms, and can more readily be trained and disciplined, if its members possess their private arms and are accustomed to them from usage for private purposes between exercises.[112] And an individual right of the people to have arms has the indirect effect of securing the ability of states at least to have their militias armed.[113] As the Court stated in *Miller*, the Second Amendment seeks "to assure the continuation and *render possible* the effectiveness of" the militia of "all males physically capable of acting in concert for the common defense."[114] It protects the minimum for a well-regulated citizen militia.

In addition, the standard for a "well regulated *Militia*," as opposed to a well-regulated *select* militia, or well-regulated army, presupposes the background meaning of "Militia" by taking into account the body's large size and varied source. As the Militia Act of 1792 contemplated, it might be enough to have a county officer enroll persons and ensure that they possessed arms and knew how to use them through basic training once or twice a year. Similarly, the Virginia Declaration of Rights of 1776 defined "a well-regulated militia" as simply being "composed of the body of the people, trained to arms."[115] And the first New York Constitution declared that "the militia" should always "be armed and disciplined,

[110] Aristocrotis, *The Government of Nature Delineated, or An Exact Picture of the New Federal Constitution* (1788), *reprinted in* 3 *Complete Anti-Federalist*, *supra* note 101, at 202.

[111] Lund, *supra* note 33, 31 Ga. L. Rev. at 25, 26.

[112] *See Silveira*, 328 F.3d at 579 (Kleinfeld, J., joined by Kozinski, O'Scannlain, and T.G. Nelson, JJ., dissenting from denial of rehearing en banc) ("The panel seems to imagine that a well regulated militia is a people disarmed until the government puts guns in their hands after summoning them to service.").

[113] See Part IV.A below for St. George Tucker's discussion of a similar point.

[114] 307 U.S. at 178–79 (emphasis added).

[115] Va. Decl. of Rights § 13 (1776), *reprinted in 7 Federal and State Constitutions*, *supra* note 78, at 3814.

and in readiness for service" *because* "it is the duty of every man who enjoys the protection of society to be prepared and willing to defend it."[116]

Even those Founders skeptical of the benefits of the citizen militia, and who advocated a more highly regulated select corps, still recognized the distinction between the proper regulation of the two. Alexander Hamilton in *The Federalist* argued that it would be both "futile" and "injurious" for Congress to attempt to "disciplin[e] *all the militia* of the United States." Most enrolled citizens would need extensive "time and practice . . . under arms for the purpose of going through military exercises and evolutions as often as might be necessary to acquire the degree of perfection which would intitle them to the character of a well-regulated militia." But such a burden on so many citizens "would be a real grievance to the people and a serious public inconvenience and loss." Thus, as to "*the people at large*," he expected that "[l]ittle more can reasonably be aimed at . . . than to have them properly armed and equipped" and, for this purpose, "assemble them once or twice" a year. He therefore recommended that Congress use its constitutional power to provide for organizing the militia also to form a select militia—"*a select corps* of moderate size."[117] Hamilton was reiterating George Washington's well-known recommendations to Congress for a two-tiered militia, consisting of (1) "the Citizens of America . . . from 18 to 50 years of age," who would be put "on *the Militia Rolls*" and given minimal training, and (2) "a *Corps* in every State" consisting of those aged 18–25.[118] From the opposite political pole, the Federal Farmer likewise recognized that Congress might make just such distinctions in "modelling the militia" and warned that creation of a "*select corps* of militia" would lead to "inattention to *the general militia*."[119]

This understanding of the "well regulated Militia," and of the possibilities for congressional organization of it (or not), leads to a view of the preface that not only fits the meaning of "Militia" in common contemporaneous usage, including throughout the Constitution, but also most agrees with the meaning of the Second Amendment's operative text setting out a "right of the people." The "well regulated Militia" and the "people" were not identical, but because of their close relationship, a right of the latter—of individuals—to keep and bear arms would facilitate the former. By contrast, a view rejecting the individual right on the basis of the preface's reference to the "well regulated Militia" struggles to harmonize the operative language establishing a seemingly general and individual right with that prefatory language. As Justice Scalia has written, a narrow definition of "Militia" "produces a guarantee that goes far beyond its stated purpose—rather

---

[116] N.Y. Const. § 40 (1777), *reprinted in* 5 *id.* at 2637.

[117] *The Federalist No. 29*, at 183–84 (Alexander Hamilton) (emphases added).

[118] *Sentiments on a Peace Establishment* (1783), *reprinted in* 3 *The Founders' Constitution* 129 (Phillip B. Kurland and Ralph Lerner eds., 1987) (emphases added).

[119] *Federal Farmer No. 3*, *reprinted in* 2 *Complete Anti-Federalist*, *supra* note 101, at 242; *Federal Farmer No. 18*, *reprinted in id.* at 342 (emphases added).

like saying 'police officers being necessary to law and order, the right of the people to carry handguns shall not be infringed.'"[120] The "Militia" on this erroneous view consists only of those few citizens whom a state chooses to specially organize, arm, and train into professional units, which requires one to reject the normal, unambiguous meaning of the operative text as overbroad, rewriting "the people" to mean either "the select militia" or "the State." If that were the true meaning, the Amendment's authors chose singularly inartful language.

4. The "Security of a Free State"

The preface's express linking of the "well regulated Militia" to the ultimate necessity of "the security of a free State" is also fully consistent with the conclusion that the "right of the people to keep and bear Arms" is a personal one. The security of a free state at the Founding no doubt was understood to include those things necessary to the security of any state, such as "to execute the Laws . . . , suppress Insurrections and repel Invasions."[121] But the security of a *free* state was not just these things. It also was understood to include the security of freedom in a state. Thus, while Blackstone recognized the individual liberty of the press as "essential to the nature of a free state," pre-1787 state constitutions described the same right as "essential to the security of freedom in a state."[122] The Preamble of the Constitution states the goal of making "secure the Blessings of Liberty," and the Fourth Amendment highlights the importance of the individual "right of the people to be secure in their persons, houses, papers, and effects." A secure *free* state was one in which liberties and rights were secure.

This clause of the Second Amendment's preface reinforces the individual right to keep and bear arms in two related ways—by supporting the broad meaning of "Militia" set out above, and by identifying a benefit for individuals of the right that the operative text secures. First, to say at the time of the Founding that the militia was necessary to the security of a "free State" was to refer to the citizen militia, composed of the people, who retained the right to keep and use their private weapons. A select militia, particularly if it existed to the exclusion of the citizen militia, might undermine the free state, if citizens excluded from it were left defenseless, or if it disarmed the citizens and infringed their other rights (or both). As we show in Part III.A, that is what had happened in England during the

[120] Antonin Scalia, Response, *in A Matter of Interpretation: Federal Courts and the Law* 137 n.13 (1997).

[121] U.S. Const. art. I, § 8, cl. 15; *see id.* amend V (discussing militia service in "War or public danger").

[122] 4 William Blackstone, *Commentaries* *151; *e.g.*, Mass. Const. pt. I, art. 16 (1780), *reprinted in* 3 *Federal and State Constitutions*, *supra* note 78, at 1892. Similarly, the English Declaration of Rights, well known to the Founding Generation, see Part III.A below, charged King James II with having sought to "subvert and extirpate" the "liberties of this kingdom" by taking several actions "utterly and directly contrary to" the "freedom of this realm." 1 W. & M., 2d Sess., c. 2, § 1 (1689).

strife that produced in 1689 the express right of individual subjects to have and use arms for their defense, the ancestor of the right in the Second Amendment.[123] Thus the Virginia Declaration of Rights, the only state bill of rights before the adoption of the Second Amendment that expressly tied the militia to the security "of a free State," also emphasized that the "militia" was "composed of the body of the people."[124]

Contemporaneous writers across the political spectrum acknowledged the link between the citizen militia and securing the freedom of a state. "The Republican" praised "a militia of freemen" as among the "principal circumstances which render liberty secure," and singled out as "a capital circumstance in favour of our liberty" that "the people themselves are the military power of our country," having "arms in their hands" and "military knowledge."[125] The Federal Farmer listed among the "military forces of a free country" the "militia," by which he meant "the people themselves . . . when properly formed." A citizen militia was critical to "the duration of a free and mild government." Absent it, and in the face of an "anti-republican" select militia, "the substantial men, having families and property, will generally be without arms, without knowing the use of them, and defenceless; whereas, to preserve liberty, it is essential that the whole body of the people always possess arms, and be taught alike, especially when young, how to use them."[126] James Burgh, a Scotsman whose 1774 *Political Disquisitions* were well-known in America, including being cited in *The Federalist*, wrote that a "good militia" formed "the chief part of the constitution of every free government" and would "preserve the public liberty." He added that "[t]he possession of arms is the distinction between a freeman and a slave. . . . [H]e who thinks he is his own master, and has anything he may call his own, ought to have arms to defend himself and what he possesses, or else he lives precariously and at discretion."[127]

---

[123] *See also* Malcolm, *To Keep and Bear Arms*, *supra* note 33, at 50–53, 115–16, 123 (militia officers' use of discretionary power to disarm); *id.* at 45–46 (disarmament by Charles II prior to 1662); *id.* at 85 (disarmament by militia in 1678); *id.* at 103 (use of militia by James II to disarm suspicious persons); *id.* at 105 (attempted use of militia in 1686 to disarm by enforcing game act); *id.* at 31 (in Civil War); *see also id.* at 92–93, 95 (in response to 1683 Rye House plot; confiscated arms given to militia); *id.* at 100 (disarmament by Charles II in western England early in reign, and in response to Rye House plot later). Efforts to disarm and undermine the militia also included requiring its members to "store" their arms in government magazines. *See id.* at 38, 78–79, 96–97; *see also id.* at 3, 5, 10–11 (discussing private ownership and storage prior to English Civil War, and failed plans to require public storage). The actions of white militias toward freed blacks in the South after the American Civil War were similar. See Part IV.C below.

[124] Va. Decl. of Rights § 13 (1776), *reprinted in* 7 *Federal and State Constitutions*, *supra* note 78, at 3814; *see also* Md. Const., Decl. of Rights § 25 (1776), *reprinted in* 3 *id.* at 1688 ("That a well-regulated militia is the proper and natural defence of a free government.").

[125] 1 *Debate on the Constitution*, *supra* note 97, at 711–12.

[126] *Federal Farmer No. 18*, *reprinted in* 2 *Complete Anti-Federalist*, *supra* note 101, at 341–42.

[127] James Burgh, *Political Disquisitions*, *reprinted in part in* 3 *Founders' Constitution*, note 118, at 126, 125; *see The Federalist No. 56*, at 382 n.* (James Madison); *see also* 2 Tucker's Blackstone, *supra* note 60, at *245 n.7 (quoting Burgh's *Disquisitions*). In both passages, Burgh was loosely

Thus, "every male" should be trained in the use of arms, or at least "all men of property."[128]

Second, and related, the freedom of a state was understood at the time of the Founding to include a citizen's individual right of self-defense (that is, defense of his right to life and personal security) when the state cannot assist him. An individual right to arms such as that secured by the Second Amendment's operative text helps to preserve this basic right and thus a free state. As the preface indicates, the existence of a well-regulated citizen militia further secures the link between such an individual right and this aspect of a free state (by increasing the number of persons equipped and trained to exercise the right well), but, as the discussion of the militia in the previous paragraph suggests, this link was not understood to be confined to one's actions while participating in even such a broad-based entity.[129] Blackstone's summary of key English rights explains this point. With no mention of the militia, he described the "right of having and using arms for self-preservation and defence" as the last security of individual English subjects for keeping the state, including themselves, free:

> [T]he rights, or, as they are frequently termed, the liberties of Englishmen . . . consist primarily, in the free enjoyment of personal security, of personal liberty, and of private property. So long as these remain inviolate, the subject is perfectly free; for every species of compulsive tyranny and oppression must act in opposition to one or other of these rights, having no other object upon which it can possibly be employed. To preserve these from violation, it is necessary, that the constitution of parliament be supported in its full vigour; and limits, certainly known, be set to the royal prerogative. And lastly, to vindicate these rights, when actually violated or attacked, the subjects of England are entitled, in the first place, to the regular admin-

---

quoting Andrew Fletcher, a prominent member of the Scottish Parliament prior to union with England in 1707. *See A Discourse of Government With Relation to Militias* (1698), *reprinted in* Andrew Fletcher, *Political Works* 21–22 (John Robertson ed., 1997); *Speeches by a Member of the Parliament, No. 7* (1703), *reprinted in id.* at 149–50. Regarding Fletcher and Burgh, see David Thomas Konig, *The Second Amendment: A Missing Transatlantic Context for the Historical Meaning of "the Right of the People to Keep and Bear Arms,"* 22 L. & Hist. Rev. 119, 125–26, 136–39 (2004).

128 Burgh, *Political Disquisitions, reprinted in* 3 *Founders' Constitution*, note 118, at 124, 126. As Fletcher put it: "I cannot see, why arms should be denied to any man who is not a slave, since they are the only true badges of liberty . . . neither can I understand why any man that has arms, should not be taught the use of them." *A Discourse of Government, reprinted in* Fletcher, *Political Works, supra* note 127, at 23.

129 The duty to serve in the militia and the right to possess or carry weapons for self-defense were related but distinct in colonial America. One might have the latter without the former. *See* Cottrol & Diamond, *supra* note 33, 80 Geo. L.J. at 325–37 (surveying colonial laws and explaining the development of "the view that the security of the state was best achieved through the arming of all free citizens," regardless of eligibility for militia service); see also Part II.B.1 above (discussing right to "keep" arms for private purposes).

> istration and free course of justice in the courts of law; next, to the right of petitioning the king and parliament for redress of grievances; and, lastly, to the right of having and using arms for self-preservation and defence.

This right to arms, Blackstone added, facilitates self-defense "when the sanctions of society and laws are found insufficient to restrain the violence of oppression."[130] John Locke, although not explicitly discussing arms, similarly explained the individual right of self-defense that a free society allows. Discussing the right of self-defense against a robber, he wrote: "I have no reason to suppose that he who would *take away my liberty*, would not, when he had me in his power, take away everything else." Therefore "the law, which was made for my preservation, where it cannot interpose to secure my life from present force, which if lost, is capable of no reparation, permits me my own defence."[131]

It is therefore reasonable to conclude that the ability of a "right of the people to keep and bear Arms" to further the Second Amendment preface's ultimate end of the "security of a free State" consisted not merely in the existence of a trained band ready to act as soldiers should the state's *government* call upon them, but also in the ability of the citizens (many of them part of the privately armed citizen militia), by individually keeping and bearing arms, to help secure the freedoms of the state and its citizens.[132] Thus, the "people" in the Second Amendment were distinct from the "Militia" and a "State," but a right of the people to keep and bear arms was understood both to facilitate a well-regulated militia and to help maintain a state that was free. By contrast, the collective right and quasi-collective right views would sanction not only the creation of a select militia (to the exclusion of the citizen militia) but also the disarming of the rest of the citizenry, a

---

[130] 1 William Blackstone, *Commentaries* *144. Blackstone also described the fundamental "right of personal security" as including protection against "loss of limb," so as to guard a man's ability "to protect himself from external injuries in a state of nature," and condemned any destruction of limbs as "a manifest breach of civil liberty," *id.* at *129, *130; and he set out the basic common law rule of self-defense, "the primary law of nature," by which it is lawful for a person "forcibly attacked in his person or property . . . to repel force by force" without being liable for breach of the peace or a resulting homicide, 3 *id.* at *3–4. The importance of this right of self-defense was reinforced by the absence of any constitutional duty of government to defend citizens' lives, liberty, or property. *See DeShaney v. Winnebago Cnty. Soc. Servs. Dep't*, 489 U.S. 189, 195–97 (1989).

[131] John Locke, *Second Treatise of Government* §§ 18–19, at 12–13 (Richard H. Cox ed., 1982) (1689); *see also id.* §§ 204–10, at 126–29 (similar). Blackstone and Locke disagreed on the exact scope of the right of self-defense. 4 William Blackstone, *Commentaries* *181–82; *see also* 1 *id.* at *251. Locke was, after Blackstone and Montesquieu, the writer whom American political writers of the Founding cited most. Malcolm, *To Keep and Bear Arms*, *supra* note 33, at 142 & 214 n.44. His thinking is particularly evident in the Declaration of Independence. *See also* 2 Tucker's Blackstone, *supra* note 60, at *161 & n.25.

[132] *See* Van Alstyne, *supra* note 33, 43 Duke L.J. at 1243 (The Second Amendment "looks to an ultimate reliance on the common citizen who has a right to keep and bear arms . . . as an essential source of security [for] a free state."); *see also* Lund, *supra* note 33, 31 Ga. L. Rev. at 24.

result antithetical to the true "Militia" as understood at the Founding and to the "free State" that the Founding Generation understood it to secure.

D. Structural Considerations

Our conclusion that the text of the Second Amendment protects an individual right is further confirmed by the structure of the Constitution, in particular the Amendment's placement and its inter-relation with the powers that the Constitution grants over the militia.

1. The Bill of Rights

The Second Amendment is embedded within the Bill of Rights. Every one of the other rights and freedoms set forth in the first nine amendments of the Bill—whether or not phrased as a "right of the people"—protects individuals, not governments; none of its provisions protects persons only in connection with service to the government.[133] As Thomas Cooley summarized, writing of the Bill's first eight amendments, "[I]t is declared that certain enumerated liberties of the people shall not be taken away or abridged."[134] It is therefore reasonable to interpret the Second Amendment to protect individuals just as the rest of these nine amendments do.

More particularly, the Second Amendment is located within a subset of the Bill of Rights amendments, the First through Fourth, that relates most directly to personal freedoms (as opposed to judicial procedure regulating deprivation by the government of one's life, liberty, or property)—the amendments that, in Story's words in his *Commentaries*, "principally regard subjects properly belonging to a bill of rights."[135] These four amendments concern liberties that are tied to the right of individuals to possess and use certain property (the printing "press" in the First

---

[133] *Cf. Planned Parenthood v. Casey*, 505 U.S. 833, 847 (1992) (rejecting argument that the personal "liberty" that the Fourteenth Amendment protects "encompasses no more than those rights already guaranteed *to the individual* against federal interference by the express provisions *of the first eight Amendments*") (emphasis added) (citation omitted); *Moore v. City of East Cleveland*, 431 U.S. 494, 502 (1977) (plurality opinion) (similar, quoting *Poe v. Ullman*, 367 U.S. 497, 542–43 (1961) (Harlan, J., dissenting)); *Johnson v. Eisentrager*, 339 U.S. 763, 784 (1950) (describing First, Second, Fourth, Fifth, and Sixth Amendments as the "civil-rights Amendments"); *Robertson v. Baldwin*, 165 U.S. 275, 281 (1897) (describing Bill of Rights as embodying "certain guaranties and immunities which we had inherited from our English ancestors"). While some might argue that, as an original matter, the First Amendment's Establishment Clause (which makes no reference to any "right" or "freedom") was an exception to this rule, the Supreme Court has held that it too creates an individual right, applicable even against states. *See Zelman v. Simmons-Harris*, 536 U.S. 639, 678 (2002) (Thomas, J., concurring); *Everson v. Bd. of Educ.*, 330 U.S. 1, 8 (1947); David Currie, *The Constitution in the Supreme Court: The Second Century* 339–40 (1990).

[134] Cooley, *General Principles*, *supra* note 41, at 200.

[135] Story, *Abridgement*, *supra* note 66, § 984, at 698 (commencing discussion of First through Fourth, and Eighth through Tenth Amendments).

Amendment,[136] "house[s]" in the Third's restriction on quartering soldiers, and "houses, papers, and effects" in the Fourth's restriction on searches and seizures), or otherwise to act without undue governmental interference (worship, speech, assembly and petition). Again, it seems reasonable to interpret the Second Amendment, consistently with this context, to set out another personal liberty (keeping and bearing) and privileged form of individual property (arms), useful for protecting not only the citizen's person but also the "houses" that the Third and Fourth Amendments guard.[137]

Finally, the right in the Second Amendment immediately follows the right to assemble and petition, which concludes the First Amendment. The latter right is undeniably personal and individual, not depending on governmental organization, regulation, or service. And the two are aligned, not only in their placement but also in their origin, purpose, and limitations. Antecedents of both appeared in proximity in the English Bill of Rights of 1689.[138] Blackstone, in the passage block-quoted in the previous subpart, discussed in immediate succession their dual utility as guards of the great individual rights of life, liberty, and property,[139] and he did likewise in discussing the criminal law's limitations on abuses of those rights.[140] St. George Tucker, the first leading American commentator on Blackstone and the Constitution (discussed more in Part IV.A below), noted that both rights had been transplanted to the United States from England, both stripped of many English restrictions.[141] It follows that the former right—that secured by the Second Amendment—also would be individual.

---

[136] *See* 4 William Blackstone, *Commentaries* *152 n.a; John O. McGinnis, *The Once and Future Property-Based Vision of the First Amendment*, 63 U. Chi. L. Rev. 49, 92–94 (1996).

[137] *Compare* 1 William Blackstone, *Commentaries* *138 ("The third absolute right, inherent in every Englishman, is that of property: which consists in the free *use, enjoyment, and disposal* of all his acquisitions, without any control or diminution, save only by the laws of the land.") (emphasis added), *with id.* at *144 (recognizing "the right of *having and using* arms") (emphasis added); see Part II.B.1 above (discussing English cases in 1700s approving the "keeping" of arms for defense of one's self and home).

[138] 1 W. & M., 2d Sess., c. 2, § 1, paras. 5 & 7 of the list of rights.

[139] *See also* 1 William Blackstone, *Commentaries* *143–44 (similar); 2 Jean L. De Lolme, *The Rise and Progress of the English Constitution* 886–87 (A.J. Stephens ed., 1838) (1784) (noting that English Bill of Rights "expressly ensured to individuals the right of publicly preferring complaints against the abuses of the government, and, moreover, of being provided with arms for their own defence," and then quoting 1 William Blackstone, *Commentaries* *144 regarding these rights).

[140] *See* 4 *id.* at *145–49 (discussing the following misdemeanor breaches of the peace: affray, riot, rout, unlawful assembly, tumultuous petitioning, forcible entry or detainer, and going armed with dangerous or unusual weapons to the terror of the people). Among felonies against the public peace, Blackstone first listed violation of the Riot Act against "riotous assembling of twelve persons" and then described "unlawful hunting" in certain parks, which involved being disguised and "armed with offensive weapons." *Id.* at *142–44.

[141] 2 Tucker's Blackstone, *supra* note 60, at *143–44 nn. 38–41. *See also United States v. Cruikshank*, 92 U.S. 542, 551–53 (1876) (analyzing the two rights similarly); *Logan v. United States*, 144 U.S. 263, 286–87 (1892) (same).

2. The Militia Powers

Interpreting the Second Amendment in light of the militia powers granted to the federal government and the states in the original Constitution likewise suggests an individual right to keep and bear arms rather than a "right" of states, against the federal government, to maintain select militias or a quasi-collective right to be exercised only by persons who serve in such entities. Clauses 15 and 16 of Article I, Section 8, respectively grant power to Congress:

> To provide for calling forth the Militia to execute the Laws of the Union, suppress Insurrections and repel Invasions; [and]
>
> To provide for organizing, arming, and disciplining, the Militia, and for governing such Part of them as may be employed in the Service of the United States, reserving to the States respectively, the Appointment of the Officers, and the Authority of training the Militia according to the discipline prescribed by Congress.

In addition, Article II, Section 2, makes the President "Commander in Chief . . . of the Militia of the several States, when called into the actual Service of the United States."

These clauses, independently of the Second Amendment, presuppose the existence of functioning state militias and leave significant powers over them to the states. The states expressly retain the powers to appoint all officers and to train the militia according to federally specified rules. They implicitly retain the power of "governing" any parts of the militias not in actual service to the federal government, and of having those state-appointed officers govern the militias even when in such service, subject to the President's supreme authority. The provision regarding officers is why Hamilton could argue credibly in *The Federalist* that the states always would retain "a preponderating influence over the militia."[142] The Constitution, in elsewhere prohibiting states from "keep[ing] Troops, or Ships of War in time of peace," while still allowing them to "engage in War" if "actually invaded" or under an imminent threat, contemplates that the states will have, and have power to employ, usable militias to provide necessary defense and emergen-

---

[142] *The Federalist No. 29*, at 185 (Alexander Hamilton); *see also The Federalist No. 46*, at 321–22 (James Madison).

cy war-making ability.[143] More broadly, the states implicitly retain the power to call out the militia on their own for domestic purposes.[144]

The original Constitution also leaves to the states concurrent power to provide for organizing, arming, and disciplining their militias, so long as in so doing they do not interfere with the federal power. This interpretation has been recognized from the beginning: At the critical Virginia Ratifying Convention, Henry Lee (future Governor of Virginia and congressman), Edmund Randolph (a Framer who became the first Attorney General), Madison, and John Marshall all made this textual argument in response to attacks on the federal power to make such provision.[145] Story found the arguments for such a concurrent power "in their structure and reasoning satisfactory and conclusive."[146] The Supreme Court approved this reading in 1820 in *Houston v. Moore*,[147] and has recently reiterated it. Looking to the "general plan" of the Constitution, the Court noted in 1990 that, "Were it not for the Militia Clauses, it might be possible to argue," much as one could regarding federal power over foreign policy and the armed forces, "that the constitutional allocation of powers precluded the formation of organized state militia. The Militia Clauses, however, subordinate any such structural inferences to an express permission while also subjecting state militia to express federal limitations."[148] Even the Ninth Circuit in *Silveira* so interpreted Article I, Section 8, Clause 16: "The language indicates that the grant of power [to Congress] is permissive. . . . Nothing in the Article or elsewhere in the Constitution appears to bar the states from choosing to arm their respective militias as they wish."[149]

In at least two respects, the above militia powers in the Constitution suggest an individual right view of the Second Amendment. First, any constitutional amendment securing to the states power to maintain militias would have been largely redundant, whether the amendment protected the power through a "right" of states or a right restricted to persons serving in militia units that a state had organized. A provision should not be read to be redundant if another reasonable interpretation

---

[143] U.S. Const. art. I, § 10, cl. 3. *See Houston v. Moore*, 18 U.S. (5 Wheat.) 1, 52 (1820) (Story, J., dissenting); Va. Ratif. Conv., *in* 10 *Ratification*, *supra* note 67, at 1307 (remarks of John Marshall, June 16, 1788).

[144] *See* Story, *Abridgement*, *supra* note 66, § 593, at 425; Va. Ratif. Conv., *in* 10 *Ratification*, *supra* note 67, at 1304, 1311 (remarks of James Madison, June 16, 1788); *id.* at 1306–07 (remarks of John Marshall, same).

[145] *Compare* 9 *Ratification*, *supra* note 67, at 1074 (John P. Kaminski & Gaspare J. Saladino eds., 1990) (H. Lee, June 9, 1788), *id.* at 1102 (Randolph, June 10, 1788), 10 *id.* at 1273 (Madison, June 14, 1788), *id.* at 1306–08 (Marshall, June 14, 1788); *with* 9 *id.* at 957–58, 1066 (Patrick Henry, June 5 & 9, 1788), 10 *id.* at 1270–71 (George Mason, June 14, 1788), *id.* at 1305 (William Grayson, June 16, 1788). Henry Lee should not be confused with his Anti-Federalist cousin Richard Henry Lee.

[146] 3 Story, *Commentaries*, *supra* note 75, § 1202, at 85–86.

[147] 18 U.S. (5 Wheat.) 1 (1820). See Part IV.B.1 below.

[148] *Perpich*, 496 U.S. at 353–54 (footnotes omitted).

[149] 312 F.3d at 1081 n.43.

exists, and the individual right view of the Amendment is such an interpretation. Second, one also would expect a protection of the states' militia powers to use language analogous to that of Clause 16, which concludes by "*reserving to the States respectively*, the Appointment of the Officers, and *the Authority* of training the Militia according to the discipline prescribed by Congress."[150] Clause 16's parallel to the protection of state power in the Tenth Amendment, which provides that certain *powers* are "*reserved to the States respectively*" (while mentioning "the people" separately), is unmistakable, as is the contrast between such language and the Second Amendment's protection of a "right of the people." Given the ready availability of such language, it would be both surprising and inartful for a protection of state authority to create and maintain organized militias to be phrased as the Second Amendment is, whether one conceives of the protection as belonging to the states directly or to those serving it.

The Militia Clauses therefore suggest that the Second Amendment, to the extent that it furthers the states' authority to maintain organized militias, does so indirectly, as we discussed in Part II.C.2 & 3, by ensuring the minimum of a "well regulated Militia"—that the States' *people*, the pool for the citizen militia, would continue to be able to keep and to bear their private arms, having them ready and being familiar with them. Thus the Militia Clauses, along with the structure of the Bill of Rights and the preface of the Second Amendment, all support the personal, individual right to keep and bear arms that the Amendment's operative text sets out.

III. The Original Understanding of the Right to Keep and Bear Arms

In the previous part, we focused on the text and structure of the Constitution, considering the meaning of the Second Amendment's words and phrases when they were adopted and how the Amendment's meaning is informed by its interrelation with the rest of the Constitution. In this part, we take a broader view and consider the Anglo-American right to arms as it existed at the time of the Founding and informed the adoption of the Second Amendment. This history, like the text, indicates that the Amendment secures an individual right.

We first consider the historical context of the right to arms, both (A) in England beginning with the Revolution of 1688–1689 and (B) in America through the American Revolution and the first state constitutions. The right was consistently a personal one. Beginning with the right of individual English subjects to have arms for their defense, it was supplemented in revolutionary America with the notion that a citizen militia, comprising the armed citizenry, was a particularly important means of securing free government. As one judge recently put it, the Americans of the Founding Generation "were the heirs of two revolutions," both of which had

---

[150] As we explain below in Part III.C, several state ratifying conventions unsuccessfully proposed similar language in suggested amendments distinct from those securing the right to bear arms.

Opinions of the Office of Legal Counsel in Volume 28

impressed upon them the importance of an individual right to have and use arms.[151] This background understanding of the right is inconsistent with either the collective right or quasi-collective right views. Next, in Part III.C, we turn to (1) the framing and ratification of the Constitution and (2) the framing and ratification of the Second Amendment. This history demonstrates that the background understanding, far from being transformed or curtailed, was incorporated in that Amendment, just as the Bill of Rights incorporated many other traditional rights of individuals. By contrast, separate proposals to amend the Constitution to safeguard powers of the states to establish and maintain organized militias failed.

A. The Right Inherited From England

As the Supreme Court has recognized, "[t]he historical necessities and events of the English constitutional experience . . . were familiar to" the Framers and should "inform our understanding of the purpose and meaning of constitutional provisions."[152] This rule is particularly applicable to provisions such as the Second Amendment, because "[t]he law is perfectly well settled that the first ten amendments to the Constitution, commonly known as the Bill of Rights, were not intended to lay down any novel principles of government, but simply to embody certain guaranties and immunities which we had inherited from our English ancestors."[153]

The right to arms that colonial Americans inherited from England had been set out first in the English Declaration of Rights of 1689, and then had been expounded by William Blackstone in his authoritative *Commentaries on the Laws of England* in the decade before the American Revolution. Both the Declaration and Blackstone made clear that the English right was a personal, individual one, not a "right" belonging to any government or restricted to persons in governmental service. The English right could not have been a federalism provision, because England lacked a federal structure; and neither the Declaration nor the law as expounded by Blackstone conditioned the right on a subject's service in any militia.

The Declaration of Rights was a product of the English Revolution of 1688–1689 (commonly known as the Glorious Revolution). In 1660, a special "Convention" Parliament had restored the English monarchy by crowning Charles II,[154] and two statutes enacted under him provided background for the Declaration's provisions on arms. First was the Militia Act, enacted by the royalist Parliament in

151 *Silveira*, 328 F.3d at 580 (Kleinfeld, J., joined by Kozinski, O'Scannlain, and T.G. Nelson, JJ., dissenting from denial of rehearing en banc).

152 *Loving v. United States*, 517 U.S. 748, 766 (1996).

153 *Robertson v. Baldwin*, 165 U.S. 275, 281 (1897), discussed further below in Part IV.D.

154 *See* 1 William Blackstone, *Commentaries* *151.

1662.[155] It authorized militia officers on their own warrants "to search for and seize all arms" of anyone they judged "dangerous to the peace of the kingdom," including through entering houses by force if necessary, the arms to be handed over to the militia and no judicial recourse being available.[156] Charles II repeatedly used this power,[157] aided not only by the regular militia but also by a volunteer army that he had organized unilaterally,[158] and by a select militia of about 15,000 that he formed in 1666.[159] The second statute was the Game Act of 1671, which, in the name of protecting wildlife, was "the first law in English history that took from the majority of Englishmen the privilege of having firearms."[160] It outlawed possession of guns (not just their use in hunting) by anyone not among the few rich qualified to hunt game.[161]

Concerns escalated after the accession in 1685 of Charles's brother, King James II. He was openly Roman Catholic, at a time of sharp political distrust between England's Protestants and Catholics.[162] He disarmed the Protestant militia of Ireland by seizing their arms and placing them in government magazines, while returning the arms of Ireland's Roman Catholics. In England, he continued to use the militia to disarm persons of questioned loyalties, including through strictly

---

[155] The Founders were well aware of the events leading up to the Declaration. A delegate at the Massachusetts Ratifying Convention, warning against overreacting to the weakness of the Articles of Confederation, pointed to the Restoration, in which the people, "so vexed, harassed and worn down . . . [had] run mad with loyalty, and would have given Charles any thing he could have asked." 1 *Debate on the Constitution, supra* note 97, at 897 (remarks of Charles Turner, Jan. 17, 1788). A delegate at Virginia's convention drew the opposite lesson: The new Constitution would prevent the anarchy that had led England into the arms of Charles II. 2 *id.* at 756 (remarks of Zachariah Johnston, June 25, 1788).

[156] 13 & 14 Car. II, c. 3, § 14.

[157] Malcolm, *To Keep and Bear Arms, supra* note 33, at 36, 38, 43, 45–48, 50–53, 85, 100, 115–16, 123; *see also id.* at 92–93, 95; Lois G. Schwoerer, *The Declaration of Rights, 1689*, at 76 (1981) ("Charles II had made effective use of" the militia acts "to try to snuff out political and religious dissent," disarming individuals and towns and confiscating weapons). He had begun doing so as soon as he assumed the throne. An interim act in 1661 approved his actions and provided indemnity to militiamen. 12 Car. II, c. 6, § 3 (favorably recognizing that "divers arms have been seized and houses searched for arms"); *cf. The Federalist No. 69*, at 465 n. (Alexander Hamilton) (discussing 1661 act).

[158] Malcolm, *To Keep and Bear Arms, supra* note 33, at 36–39.

[159] *Id.* at 63. *See also* Schwoerer, *Declaration, supra* note 157, at 75–76 (describing Charles II's actions, including disarmament, and noting rise of complaints from Commons beginning in 1668).

[160] Malcolm, *To Keep and Bear Arms, supra* note 33, at 12; *see id.* at 69–76; Schwoerer, *Declaration, supra* note 157, at 78 (describing it as "the most stringent and comprehensive of the game laws") (internal quotation marks omitted).

[161] 22 & 23 Car. II, c. 25, § 3 (providing that all who did not have estate "of the clear yearly value of one hundred pounds" per year were "not allowed to have or keep for themselves, or any other person or persons, any guns, bows, greyhounds . . . or other engines").

[162] *See* 4 William Blackstone, *Commentaries* *55 (explaining various legal disabilities on certain Roman Catholics, including several dating from English Revolution or earlier, by stating that such persons "acknowledge a foreign power, superior to the sovereignty of the kingdom"); *id.* at *58 (hoping that "a time . . . should arrive" soon when it would be safe to "review and soften these rigorous edicts").

enforcing the Game Act, although he ultimately preferred to undermine the militia (whose loyalty he questioned), by restricting musters. He also accelerated and expanded his brother's policy of purging opponents, and Protestants in general, from the militia's and army's officer corps, and geometrically enlarged the standing army.[163]

James II fled soon after William of Orange landed in England in late 1688 at the invitation of leading Englishmen. A Convention Parliament in early 1689 adopted the Declaration of Rights, which William and his wife Mary (James's daughter) accepted before Parliament proclaimed them King and Queen, and which the ensuing regular Parliament enacted as the Bill of Rights.[164] A hundred years later, Alexander Hamilton in *The Federalist* celebrated "the revolution in 1688," when at last "English liberty was completely triumphant."[165]

The Declaration first listed twelve indictments of James II for having attempted to subvert "the laws and liberties of this kingdom," including:

> 5. By raising and keeping a standing army within this kingdom in time of peace, without consent of parliament, and quartering soldiers contrary to law.
>
> 6. By causing several good subjects, being protestants, to be disarmed, at the same time when papists were both armed and employed, contrary to law.

Then, in a roughly parallel list of thirteen "ancient rights and liberties," the Declaration stated:

> 6. That the raising or keeping a standing army within the kingdom in time of peace, unless it be with consent of parliament, is against law.
>
> 7. That the subjects which are protestants may have arms for their defence suitable to their conditions and as allowed by law.

---

[163] *See* Malcolm, *To Keep and Bear Arms, supra* note 33, at 95–106; Schwoerer, *Declaration, supra* note 157, at 71–73, 75–76; *see also The Federalist No. 26*, at 166 (Alexander Hamilton); *Marcus No. 4* (James Iredell) (1788), *reprinted in* 1 *Debate on the Constitution, supra* note 97, at 391; Mass. Ratif. Conv., *in id.* at 904 (remarks of Thomas Dawes, Jr., Jan. 24, 1788).

[164] The Bill of Rights is at 1 W. & M., 2d Sess., c. 2 (1689). Its first three sections, except for the initial preamble, consist of the Declaration, *see* Schwoerer, *Declaration, supra* note 157, at 295, App. 1 (reprinting Declaration), and it recounts the events of the Revolution. *See also* 1 W. & M., 1st Sess., c. 1, § 2 (1689) (noting presentation and acceptance of crown, and proclaiming Parliament to be regular from that date); *id.* c. 6 (establishing coronation oath); 1 William Blackstone, *Commentaries* *128, *152, *211–16, *245 (discussing events); *The Federalist No. 84*, at 578 (Alexander Hamilton) (similar).

[165] *The Federalist No. 26*, at 165–66. *See* Schwoerer, *Declaration, supra* note 157, at 289 (Americans greeted the revolution and Declaration "with enthusiasm").

Whether the Second Amendment Secures an Individual Right

This seventh article is most relevant here, and it set out a personal right. Neither this article nor the parallel sixth indictment ties possession of arms to service in the militia, which the Declaration never mentions. The sixth indictment instead indicates that being "armed" and being "employed" by the government are distinct—a distinction confirmed by the historical context, which, as we have explained, included subjects being disarmed *by* the militia. Furthermore, the right belonged to "subjects," not to any government, and these subjects were allowed arms "for *their* defence."[166]

Critics of the individual right view contend that the two concluding clauses of the seventh article—"suitable to their Conditions, and as allowed by Law"—so restricted the right that it was a dead letter. Among the restrictions to which these clauses referred was the Game Act, which literally, albeit likely not in practice, barred most subjects from owning firearms.[167] As Lois G. Schwoerer has argued: "English-men did not secure to 'ordinary citizens' the right to possess weapons. . . . Drafted by upper-class Protestants who had their own interests at heart, Article VII was a gun control measure."[168] The Declaration, therefore, the argument goes, could have had little relevance to the right in the Second Amendment.

But this argument regarding the *scope* of the right does not speak to the question that we consider here, which is whether the English right was a right of individuals, a right of government, or a right specifically connected with military service to the government. On that question, the answer is clear. Schwoerer herself recognizes that many articles of the Declaration "guaranteed rights to the individual," including the right "to bear arms (under certain restrictions)."[169] Class- and religion-based restrictions did not destroy the personal nature of the right, whatever its scope. The precedent for Americans was an individual right.

---

[166] Similarly, the same Parliament enacted a law providing that a "papist or reputed papist" could "have or keep . . . such necessary weapons, as shall be allowed to him by order of the justices of the peace . . . *for the defence of his house or person.*" 1 W. & M., 1st Sess., c. 15, § 3 (1688) (emphasis added).

[167] *See* Malcolm, *To Keep and Bear Arms*, *supra* note 33, at 86–89 (noting effect of wealth qualification but also dearth of prosecutions merely for possession). Blackstone complained that there was "fifty times the property required to enable a man to kill a partridge, as to vote for a knight of the shire." 4 William Blackstone, *Commentaries* *175. In addition, these clauses probably referred to two statutes from the 1540s restricting ownership and use of short handguns based on wealth, outlawing shot, and regulating the use of guns in cities or towns, *see* 33 Hen. VIII, c. 6 (1541); 2 & 3 Edw. VI, c. 14 (1548), and they may also have referred to the Militia Act, *see* Malcolm, *To Keep and Bear Arms*, *supra* note 33, at 120.

[168] Lois G. Schwoerer, *To Hold and Bear Arms: The English Perspective*, 76 Chi.-Kent L. Rev. 27, 59 (2000). She seems to misunderstand the individual right view as requiring an unlimited right. *See id.* at 56, 60.

[169] Schwoerer, *Declaration*, *supra* note 157, at 283; *see* Malcolm, *To Keep and Bear Arms*, *supra* note 33, at 119–20. *See also* 2 De Lolme, *English Constitution*, *supra* note 139, at 886 (Declaration "expressly ensured to individuals the right of [petition and] of being provided with arms for their own defence").

In addition, that Article 7 of the Declaration (and the Bill) only recognized a right to possess arms "as allowed by Law" does not mean that it did not secure a true right. In England's constitutional tradition, particularly evident in the events surrounding the Declaration of Rights described above, formal English rights restricted only the Crown's prerogative, not the legislature's power, which was unrestricted. Thus, although Blackstone was able to explain many years after the English Revolution that a royal proclamation "for disarming any protestant subjects, will not bind,"[170] the right to arms, like all other English rights, remained subject to revision or abolition by Parliament.[171] That characteristic of English rights hardly prevented Americans from borrowing and adapting them to a different constitutional structure.

Finally, whatever the actual ability of ordinary English subjects to have arms for their defense in 1689, by the Founding, a hundred years later, the right to do so extended to most of the country. As Judge Kleinfeld of the Ninth Circuit recently observed, "[t]he historical context of the Second Amendment is a long struggle by the English citizenry to enable common people to possess firearms."[172] In new game laws, particularly that of 1706, Parliament deleted guns from the list of implements that those not qualified to hunt game were prohibited from owning.[173] The courts determined that Parliament had made this deletion "purposely."[174] Thus, notwithstanding the list's catch-all prohibition of "any other engines," they interpreted the deletion—together with the existence of "divers . . . lawful purposes" for which one might keep a gun, such as "for the defence of his house and family"—as protecting the right of individuals to keep guns even if they were not qualified to hunt game, so long as they did not hunt with them.[175] This

[170] 1 William Blackstone, *Commentaries* *271.

[171] *See The Federalist No. 84*, at 578–79 (Alexander Hamilton) (arguing "that bills of rights are in their origin, stipulations between kings and their subjects, abridgments of prerogative in favor of privilege, reservations of rights not surrendered to the prince," and "[s]uch . . . was the declaration of rights presented by the lords and commons to the prince of Orange in 1688, and afterwards thrown into the form of an act of parliament called the bill of rights").

[172] *Silveira*, 328 F.3d at 582 (Kleinfeld, J., joined by Kozinski, O'Scannlain, and T.G. Nelson, JJ., dissenting from denial of rehearing en banc).

[173] 5 Ann., c. 14, § 3 (1706); *see* 4 & 5 W. & M., c. 23, § 3 (1693) (similar). Parliament also repealed the later of the two statutes of the 1540s mentioned in note 167, noting its desuetude. 6 & 7 Will. III, c. 13, § 3 (1695). Enforcement of the other was, at least in the 1600s, lax and selective. *See* Malcolm, *To Keep and Bear Arms*, *supra* note 33, at 80–81, 87. Efforts to revise the Militia Act failed, but the right in the Bill may have sufficed to restrain the King from disarming Protestants. *See id.* at 123–25; *see also* 1 William Blackstone, *Commentaries* *271; Schwoerer, *Declaration*, *supra* note 157, at 75–78, 267, 283.

[174] *Rex v. Gardner*, 87 Eng. Rep. 1240, 1241, 7 Mod. Rep. 279 (K.B. 1739).

[175] *Wingfield v. Stratford*, 96 Eng. Rep. 787, 787–88, Sayer Rep. 15 (K.B. 1752) (Lee, C.J., citing *Rex v. Gardner*, 2 Strange Rep. 1098 (K.B. 1738)); *Mallock v. Eastly*, 87 Eng. Rep. 1370, 1374, 7 Mod. Rep. 482 (C.P. 1744), respectively; *see also* Part II.B.1 (discussing use of "keep" in these and other cases); Malcolm, *To Keep and Bear Arms*, *supra* note 33, at 128 (quoting commentator of early 1800s reaffirming rule of these cases). In addition, it appears that courts strictly interpreted indictments

interpretation of the 1706 game act was considered "settled and determined" by 1744, and in 1752 the Chief Justice of the King's Bench reaffirmed that it was "not to be imagined" that Parliament in that act had intended "to disarm all the people of England."[176] By 1780, London's Recorder—the city's legal adviser and the primary judge of its criminal court—in an opinion supporting the legality of the city's private armed associations formed for self-defense against riots, could announce as "most clear and undeniable" the "right of his majesty's Protestant subjects, to have arms for their own defence, and to use them for lawful purposes," adding that "this right, which every Protestant most unquestionably possesses individually," also "may, and in many cases must, be exercised collectively," subject to certain restrictions.[177] Similarly, an English commentator in the early 1790s wrote that "every one is at liberty to keep or carry a gun, if he does not use it for the destruction of game."[178]

Blackstone's *Commentaries*, first published in 1765–1769, were for the colonists and the Founding Generation the leading exposition of England's laws and constitution. In them, he confirmed that the English right to arms was an individual one and explained that it had grounds broader and deeper than the right that had been declared in the Revolution of 1688–1689.

In the first chapter of the first book, Blackstone detailed the "absolute rights of individuals,"[179] that is, "such as appertain and belong to particular men, merely as individuals or single persons" and which "every man is entitled to enjoy, whether out of society or in it."[180] It was the purpose of law "to maintain and regulate"

under the game laws. *See King v. Silcot*, 87 Eng. Rep. 186, 186 n.(b), 3 Mod. Rep. 280 (K.B. 1690) (reporter's note from 1793).

[176] *Mallock*, 87 Eng. Rep. at 1374; *Wingfield*, 96 Eng. Rep. at 787 (Lee, C.J.).

[177] Legality of the London Military Foot-Association, *supra* note 64, at 59–60 (italics omitted). For background, see Part II.B.2 above. The Recorder found it "a matter of some difficulty to define the precise limits and extent of the rights of the people of this realm to bear arms, and to instruct themselves in the use of them, *collectively*." *Id.* at 59. At the very least, he opined, such a group needed to (1) have a "lawful" "professed purpose and object," (2) "demean themselves in a peaceable and orderly manner" consistent with that purpose, (3) not assemble in numbers that "manifestly and greatly exceed" that purpose; and (4) not "act without the authority of the civil magistrate" except to suppress "sudden, violent, and felonious breaches of the peace." *Id.* at 62 (italics omitted). *See also* 1 William Hawkins, *A Treatise on the Pleas of the Crown* ch. 63, § 10, at 136 (1724; reprint 1972) (noting legality of person "arm[ing] himself to suppress dangerous Rioters, Rebels, or Enemies" and "endeavour[ing] to suppress or resist such Disturbers of the Peace or Quiet of the Realm"); *id.* ch. 65, § 21, at 161 (noting right to do so when assisting Justice of Peace against riot).

[178] *See* William Blackstone, 2 *Commentaries on the Laws of England* *412 n.8 (William Draper Lewis ed., 1900) (reprinting annotation of Edward Christian). Christian's posthumous Blackstone was published in 1793–95, *see* Malcolm, *To Keep and Bear Arms*, *supra* note 33, at 134, 210, and available in America, *see* 1 Tucker's Blackstone, *supra* note 60, at *145 n.42. Although the law was clear, some questioned how much as a practical matter the revision of the game laws had benefited commoners, as we explain in the discussion of the Pennsylvania Constitution below in Part III.B.2.

[179] 1 William Blackstone, *Commentaries* *121; *id.* at *123, 124.

[180] *Id.* at *123. He contrasted "relative" individual rights, "which are incident to [persons] as members of society, and standing in various relations to each other." *Id.*

these rights in society, but "wanton and causeless restraint" was "a degree of tyranny."[181] He delineated three "principal or primary . . . rights of the people of England": "the right of personal security, the right of personal liberty, and the right of private property."[182]

But Blackstone recognized that declaring these three primary rights would be "in vain" and a "dead letter of the laws, if the constitution had provided no other method to secure their actual enjoyment." He therefore identified five "auxiliary subordinate rights of the subject"—"outworks or barriers to protect and maintain" the principal rights.[183] The first two were maintaining the constitution of Parliament and clear limits on the King's prerogative. Because these were more properly issues of governmental structure, he postponed their discussion to later chapters.[184] The other three, however, were plainly individual rights: (a) the "right of every Englishman . . . of applying to the courts of justice for redress of injuries"; (b) the "right, appertaining to every individual . . . of petitioning the king, or either house of parliament, for the redress of grievances," so long as no "riot or tumult" resulted; and (c) the "right of the subject . . . of having arms for their defence suitable to their condition and degree, and such as are allowed by law." He noted that the latter two rights both had been recognized in the 1689 Bill of Rights.[185]

Blackstone explained the subject's right of having arms as "a public allowance, under due restrictions, of the natural right of resistance and self-preservation, when the sanctions of society and laws are found insufficient to restrain the violence of oppression."[186] By tying the right to the natural—and thus individual and pre-political—right of self-defense, he recognized a deeper foundation than its declaration and enactment in 1689 and confirmed that the right existed independently of any bearing of arms in service to the militia, a subject that he did not mention in connection with the right.[187]

He returned to the right in concluding the first chapter. Again grouping together the last three auxiliary rights (suing, petitioning, and having arms), he explained that all were means for "the subjects of England" to "vindicate" the three primary rights "when actually violated or attacked." Thus, subjects were "entitled . . . to

---

181 *Id.* at *124–28.

182 *Id.* at *129. These reappear throughout the American Constitution, in general protections against deprivations of "life, liberty, or property, without due process of law" and in specific rights. See, for example, St. George Tucker's footnotes annotating Blackstone's exposition of the three principal rights with parallels in the Constitution, 2 Tucker's Blackstone, *supra* note 60, at *129, *133–40.

183 1 William Blackstone, *Commentaries* *140–41.

184 *See id.* at *141.

185 *Id.* at *141, *143–44.

186 *Id.* at *144.

187 *See also* 4 *id.* at *55–58 (elsewhere describing prohibitions against certain Roman Catholics keeping arms as hopefully temporary suspensions of rights). He summarized the militia in Chapter 13, 1 *id.* at *412–13.

the right of having and using arms for self-preservation and defence."[188] By his repeated reference to "self-preservation" and his description of the right as including both "having and *using*" arms, Blackstone reiterated that the right had a personal aspect and was linked to self-defense—to the right to use one's "limbs . . . to protect himself from external injuries," which was part of the individual right of personal security.[189]

Finally, Blackstone's view of the right as belonging to individuals re-appears in his repeated disparagement of game laws as a pretext to undermine commoners' ability to use or have arms. He traced them to "slavery" imposed after the fall of the Roman Empire by invading generals, who sought to "keep the *rustici* or natives . . . in as low a condition as possible, and especially to prohibit them the use of arms." Thus, "we find, in the feudal constitutions, one and the same law prohibiting the *rustici* in general from carrying arms, and also proscribing the use of nets, snares, or other engines for destroying the game."[190] He denounced those arising in England after the Norman Conquest of 1066 as a "tyranny to the commons,"[191] and thought their real rationale was an aristocratic desire to "disarm[] the bulk of the people."[192] He briefly described England's existing criminal game laws as confused and having a "questionable" nature, their "rational footing" being elusive.[193] But he approved hunting restrictions against trespassing[194] and did not criticize several other restrictions on the use and carrying of arms, involving breaches of the peace.[195]

---

[188] 1 *id.* at *144.

[189] *Id.* at *130. *See id.* at *134 (summarizing common law's special protection for "those limbs and members that may be necessary to a man in order to defend himself or annoy his enemy").

[190] 2 *id.* at *412, 413.

[191] 4 *id.* at *416; *see* 2 *id.* at *415–16 (forest laws produced "the most horrid tyrannies and oppressions").

[192] 2 *id.* at *412. As an example, he cited a popular book, by a bishop (and thus lord), that praised banning "Peasants and Mechanics" from hunting game: "It was not at all for the *public Good* to suffer [them] . . . to run up and down the Woods and Forests, armed; which . . . draws them on to Robbery and Brigandage: Nor to permit the populace, in Towns and Cities, to have, and carry *Arms* at their pleasure; which would give opportunity and encouragement to Sedition, and Commotions." 1 William Warburton, *The Alliance Between Church and State: Or, the Necessity and Equity of An Established Religion and a Test Law Demonstrated* 324 (London 4th ed. 1766).

[193] 4 William Blackstone, *Commentaries* *174–75.

[194] *See* 2 *id.* at *411–12 (approving as "natural" a ban on unauthorized hunting on private property); *see* 4 *id.* at *174 (being less critical of the "forest law," which simply prohibited hunting in the king's forests).

[195] *See* 4 *id.* at *144 (unlawful hunting—being disguised and "armed with offensive weapons" in breach of peace and to terror of public); *id.* at *145 (affray (public fighting), including attack with or drawing of weapon on church grounds); *id.* at *148 (forcible entry or detainer, "such as is carried on and maintained with force, with violence, and unusual weapons"); *id.* at *149 ("*riding* or *going armed*, with dangerous or unusual weapons . . . by terrifying" the people); *see also id.* at *146–47 (riots, routs, unlawful assemblies, and tumultuous petitioning); *id.* at *168 (quasi-nuisance of "making, keeping, or carriage, of too large a quantity of *gunpowder* at one time or in one place or vehicle"); *cf. id.* at *182 (excusable homicide by misadventure, such as "where a person qualified to keep a gun is shooting at a

Thus, the right to arms that America inherited from England was a right of individuals, and had deep roots by the time of the Framing. It did not depend on service in the government's militia, nor was it a federalism-related "right" of any government. It therefore provides no warrant for a quasi-collective right or collective right view of the Second Amendment. And, absent any evidence that Americans wished to abridge this individual right or transform it substantially, a question that we consider next, the English precedent supports an individual right view of that Amendment.

B. The Right in America Before the Framing

The English colonists in America recognized this right of individual subjects to have and use arms, and they retained it as they broke from the mother country. They also recognized that it furthered the citizen militia to which they looked as a security for their freedom. These related ideas of an individual right to arms and regard for the citizen militia formed the backdrop for the Second Amendment. We first consider the history of the American Revolution and then review the states' first constitutions, written during that war.

1. The Experience of the Revolution

As the Revolution approached and conflicts with royal authorities rose, colonial leaders both reaffirmed the individual right to arms inherited from England and praised the shared duty of being armed imposed by local law. The colonial militias were broad-based, composed of all able-bodied white men, who were expected to be armed with the private weapons that all households were required to keep (regardless of eligibility for militia duty), there being a "general obligation of all adult male inhabitants to possess arms, and, with certain exceptions, to cooperate in the work of defense."[196] Citizens sometimes were required not only to own

mark and undesignedly kills a man: for the act is lawful, and the effect is merely accidental"); 3 *id.* at *4 (noting limitation of self-defense to "resistance" that "does not exceed the bounds of mere defence and prevention").

[196] *United States v. Miller*, 307 U.S. 174, 179–80 (1939) (internal quotation marks omitted). *See* Kates, *supra* note 33, 82 Mich. L. Rev. at 215–16 ("With slight variations, the different colonies imposed a duty to keep arms and to muster occasionally for drill upon virtually every able-bodied white man between the age of majority and a designated cut-off age. Moreover, the duty to keep arms applied to *every* household, not just to those containing persons subject to militia service. Thus, the over-aged and seamen, who were exempt from militia service, were required to keep arms for law enforcement and for the defense of their homes from criminals or foreign enemies.") (footnotes omitted). In Virginia, "Every able-bodied freeman, between the ages of 16 and 50, is enrolled in the militia. . . . The law requires every militia-man to provide himself with the arms usual in the regular service." That requirement "was always indifferently complied with," and the militia's arms were "frequently called for to arm the regulars," so that "in the lower parts of the country they are entirely disarmed." But "[i]n the middle country a fourth or fifth part of them may have such firelocks as they had provided to destroy the noxious animals which infest their farms; and on the western side of the

weapons but also to carry them, and the class-based distinctions of England generally did not apply.[197] America had its own set of distinctions, based on race, but even free blacks were often allowed to possess arms as individuals, even though usually barred from militia service.[198]

Boston was the focus of early opposition to Britain, and its leaders invoked both the individual right to arms (as secured by the 1689 Bill of Rights and also as expounded by Blackstone) and the local duty of being armed. A 1768 town meeting led by Samuel Adams, John Hancock, and others resolved that the right enacted in the English Bill of Rights was "founded in Nature, Reason and sound Policy, and is well adapted for the necessary Defence of the Community," while also praising the colony's law requiring "every listed Soldier and other Householder" to be armed. The resolution thus requested that any Bostonian lacking arms "duly . . . observe the said Law."[199] Boston newspapers defended the meeting's actions:

> [I]t is certainly beyond human art and sophistry, to prove the British subjects, to whom the *privilege* of possessing arms is expressly recognized by the Bill of Rights, and, who live in a province where the law requires them to be equip'd with *arms*, &c. are guilty of an *illegal act*, in calling upon one another to be provided with them, as the *law directs*.[200]

Blue [R]idge they are generally armed with rifles." Jefferson, *Notes*, *supra* note 56, at 88. For more regarding the militia, see Part II.C.2–4 above.

[197] *See* Malcolm, *To Keep and Bear Arms*, *supra* note 33, at 139 (quoting colonial statutes from Rhode Island, Virginia, and Georgia); Kates, *supra* note 33, 82 Mich. L. Rev. at 216 (discussing Georgia law); *id.* at 240 ("the English Game Acts . . . had never been a part of the colonial law"); 5 Tucker's Blackstone, *supra* note 60, at *175 n.16 (describing game laws of Virginia, limited to prohibiting trespass and conversion and establishing hunting season for deer).

[198] *See* Cottrol & Diamond, *supra* note 33, 80 Geo. L.J. at 323–27 (noting that "the traditional English right" became "a much broader American one" as part of "a more general lessening of class, religious, and ethnic distinctions among whites in colonial America," but that "the law was much more ambivalent with respect to blacks"; surveying varying colonial laws regarding right of blacks to carry weapons or keep them in their homes, and noting usual exclusion from militia duty, except in "times of crisis"); Malcolm, *To Keep and Bear Arms*, *supra* note 33, at 140–41 ("The second group [after Indians] forbidden to possess weapons were black slaves, with restrictions sometimes extended to free blacks . . . . Northern colonies were ambivalent about blacks possessing firearms"; surveying colonial laws and drawing parallel to England's ambivalent treatment of right of Roman Catholics to have arms).

[199] Boston Chron., Sept. 19, 1768, at 363, col. 2, *quoted in* Halbrook, *Right to Bear Arms*, *supra* note 56, at 1–2. This resolution was republished in the *Maryland Gazette*. *See id.* at 61.

[200] Bos. Gazette, and Country J., Jan. 30, 1769, at 2, col. 1, *quoted in* Halbrook, *Right to Bear Arms*, *supra* note 56, at 6; *see Boston Under Military Rule, 1768–1769, as Revealed in a Journal of the Times* 61 (Oliver Morton Dickerson ed., 1936) (reprinting same passage from Boston Evening Post, Apr. 3, 1769).

A subsequent article by Adams recounted the English Revolution and then quoted both of Blackstone's primary discussions of the right to arms. Adams attacked critics of the "late vote of this town, calling upon the inhabitants to *provide themselves with arms for their defence*," as insufficiently "attend[ing] to the rights of the constitution."[201] The *New York Journal Supplement* reiterated this argument:

> It is a natural right which the people have reserved to themselves, confirmed by the Bill of Rights, to keep arms for their own defence; and as Mr. Blackstone observes, it is to be made use of when the sanctions of society and law are found insufficient to restrain the violence of oppression.[202]

The individual's right to have and use arms for self-defense was reaffirmed in the celebrated "Boston Massacre" murder trial, in 1770, of British soldiers for firing on a harassing crowd. (Soldiers had been garrisoned in Boston since late 1768.) John Adams, counsel for the soldiers, argued that they had acted in self-defense. In his closing argument, he quoted William Hawkins's *Treatise on the Pleas of the Crown* to establish that "'every private person seems to be authorized by the law, to arm himself'" to defend against dangerous rioters. Adams added: "Here every private person is authorized to arm himself, and on the strength of this authority, I do not deny the inhabitants had a right to arm themselves at that time, for their defence . . . ."[203] Adams reiterated that view in his 1787 *Defence of the Constitutions of Government of the United States of America*, recognizing the propriety of "arms in the hands of citizens, to be used . . . in private self-defence."[204]

British authorities, much like Charles II and James II a century before, moved to disarm the colonists as hostilities mounted in 1774. Britain banned the export of arms and ammunition to any of the colonies and ordered General Gage to consider how to disarm residents of rebellious areas. At least in Massachusetts, some disarmament occurred, and in the "Powder Alarm" of September 1, 1774, British

---

[201] Samuel Adams, Boston Gazette, Feb. 27, 1769, *reprinted in* 1 *Founders' Constitution*, note 118, at 90. Adams quoted 1 William Blackstone, *Commentaries* *143–44 & *144.

[202] *Boston, March 17*, N.Y.J. Supp., Apr. 13, 1769, at 1, col. 3, *reprinted in Boston Under Military Rule* at 79; *see* Halbrook, *Right to Bear Arms*, *supra* note 56, at 7 (quoting same passage).

[203] 3 *Legal Papers of John Adams* 248 (L. Kinvin Wroth & Hiller B. Zobel eds., 1965) (quoting "Hawkins p. 71, § 14"). For the facts, see *id.* at 1 (note). Adams secured several acquittals. *Id.* at 29.

[204] 3 John Adams, *A Defence of the Constitutions of Government of the United States of America* 475 (1787). The Ninth Circuit selectively quoted this sentence to claim that Adams "ridiculed . . . an individual right to personal arms" and asserted that "the general availability of arms" would "'demolish every constitution, and lay the laws prostrate, so that liberty can be enjoyed by no man—it is a dissolution of the government.'" *Silveira*, 312 F.3d at 1085. In these portions, Adams was merely arguing against command of the militia by private persons or localities, while also expressly reiterating the right of arming for private self-defense.

soldiers seized ammunition belonging to the colonial militia.[205] These actions stiffened resistance throughout the colonies[206] and led the colonists to form independent local militias with broad membership, the "Minutemen."[207] Gage's attempts in late 1774 and early 1775 to seize these groups' arms across Massachusetts provoked confrontations with large forces of armed colonists, and the Revolution was famously ignited by his efforts to do so at Concord and Lexington in April 1775.[208] Virginia Governor Dunmore's raid on an ammunitions store in Williamsburg soon thereafter prompted a similar response, as militiamen surrounded his home.[209] British authorities' continuing efforts to disarm colonists were among the actions that the Continental Congress cited when, in July 1775, it declared the colonies' reasons for taking up arms.[210]

As the colonists armed and organized themselves, their leaders continued to turn to their rights as British subjects and praised the citizen militias that these rights made possible. George Mason's actions in Virginia (in conjunction with George Washington and others) provide an example. In September 1774, he chaired a meeting of Fairfax County citizens to form a private militia association known as the Fairfax Independent Company. Being "threat'ned with the Destruction of our Civil-rights, & Liberty, and all that is dear to British Subjects & Freemen," members promised to keep themselves well armed and to train together under elected officers.[211] The following January, in a document attributed to Mason, the county's Committee of Safety recommended a tax to purchase ammunition, resolved that "a well regulated Militia, composed of gentlemen freeholders, and other freemen, is the natural strength and only stable security of a

---

[205] *See* Hardy, *supra* note 33, 9 Harv. J.L. & Pub. Pol'y at 590; Halbrook, *Right to Bear Arms, supra* note 56, at 9, 16, 72. Soldiers seized provincial armories in Cambridge and Charlestown. In response, "twenty thousand Yankees picked up their muskets and headed for Boston" to confront the British. Robert A. Gross, *The Minutemen and Their World* 55 (1976).

[206] *See* First Continental Congress, Appeal to the Inhabitants of Quebec (Oct. 1774), *reprinted in* 1 *American Political Writing During the Founding Era, 1760–1805*, at 237 (Charles S. Hyneman & Donald S. Lutz eds., 1983) ("The injuries of Boston have roused and associated every colony."); Halbrook, *Right to Bear Arms, supra* note 56, at 88–89 (quoting warning of South Carolina's governing body in 1774 against British "design of disarming the people of America" through the embargo).

[207] *See* Gross, *Minutemen, supra* note 205, at 59. In Concord, "Minutemen trained twice a week on the common and carried their muskets everywhere, in the fields, in shops, even in church." When they were mustered in March 1775, it "presented a revealing portrait of the community. This was a citizen army of rural neighbors. . . . The Concord militia included nearly everyone between the ages of sixteen and sixty." *Id.* at 69–70.

[208] Hardy, *supra* note 33, 9 Harv. J.L. & Pub. Pol'y at 590–91; Malcolm, *To Keep and Bear Arms, supra* note 33, at 145–46.

[209] Hardy, *supra* note 33, 9 Harv. J.L. & Pub. Pol'y at 592; Halbrook, *Right to Bear Arms, supra* note 56, at 16.

[210] 1 *Journals of Congress* 137 (July 6, 1775) (1800); *see* Halbrook, *Right to Bear Arms, supra* note 56, at 13–15; Hardy, *supra* note 33, 9 Harv. J.L. & Pub. Pol'y at 591.

[211] 1 *Mason Papers, supra* note 56, at 210–11.

free Government," and urged residents "from sixteen to fifty years of age" to choose officers, "provide themselves with good Firelocks," and train.[212] In April 1775, Mason addressed the Company and praised it as formed "for the great and useful purposes of defending our country, and preserving those inestimable rights which we inherit from our ancestors." In a time of "threatened . . . ruin of that constitution under which we were born," it was a security "that in case of absolute necessity, the people might be the better enabled to act in defence of their invaded liberty."[213]

Similar sentiments appeared in North Carolina. Soon after Lexington and Concord, the royal Governor denounced those urging people "to be prepared with Arms" and train under committees of safety.[214] But in July 1775, North Carolina's delegates to the Continental Congress urged the committees to "form yourselves into a Militia" in the exercise of "the Right of every *English* Subject to be prepared with Weapons for his Defense."[215]

In October 1775, Britain declared the colonies in rebellion,[216] but organizational efforts continued. John Adams, in his *Thoughts on Government* written in early 1776 in response to requests for advice, recommended a "Militia Law requiring all men, or with very few exceptions, besides cases of conscience, to be provided with arms and ammunition, to be trained at certain seasons." Such a law would be "always a wise institution" but was "in the present circumstances of our country indispensible."[217]

Many lauded the citizen militias that fought in the Revolution. American General Nathanael Greene, writing to Thomas Jefferson, remarked on the "Enterprize and Spirit" of "this Great Bulwark of Civil Liberty [that] promises Security and Independence to this Country."[218] Americans credited crucial early victories to the citizen militias, even while recognizing their limitations.[219] Well after the war,

---

[212] *Id.* at 212.

[213] *Id.* at 229–31.

[214] *See* Halbrook, *Right to Bear Arms, supra* note 56, at 29–30.

[215] Richard Caswell, William Hooper, & Joseph Hewes, *To the Committees of the Several Towns and Counties of the Province of North Carolina*, N.C. Gazette (Newburn), July 7, 1775, at 2, col. 3, *excerpted in* Halbrook, *Right to Bear Arms, supra* note 56, at 29.

[216] *See* 4 *Papers of John Adams* 78 n.6 (Robert J. Taylor ed., 1979) (editorial note).

[217] John Adams, *Thoughts on Government* (Apr. 1776), *reprinted in* 4 *id.* at 91. This pamphlet, written for political leaders in North Carolina, Virginia, and New Jersey, was widely reprinted and discussed for several years. *See id.* at 65, 68–72 (editorial note).

[218] Letter from Greene to Jefferson (Nov. 20, 1780), *in* 4 *Jefferson Papers, supra* note 62, at 130–31.

[219] *See, e.g.*, A Democratic Federalist, Penn. Herald, Oct. 17, 1787, *reprinted in* 2 *Ratification, supra* note 67, at 197 (arguing that "a well-regulated militia" is "sufficient for every purpose of internal defense," as shown by victories at Lexington and Bunker Hill); Va. Ratif. Conv., *in* 9 *Ratification, supra* note 67, at 981 (remarks of Edmund Randolph, June 6, 1788) ("I will pay the last tribute of gratitude to the militia of my country: They performed some of the most gallant feats during the last war, and acted as nobly as men enured to other avocations could be expected to do: But, Sir, it is

James Madison could argue in *The Federalist* that an oppressive army would be no match for citizen militias, as "[t]hose who are best acquainted with the late successful resistance of this country against the British arms" would recognize. He also pointed to "the advantage of being armed, which the Americans possess over the people of almost every other nation," governments in most of the world being "afraid to trust the people with arms."[220]

2. Early Constitutional Recognition of the Right

One product of this experience of the American Revolution was that several states included explicit right to bear arms provisions in declarations of rights that they adopted during the war. These appeared in Pennsylvania, North Carolina, Vermont, and Massachusetts. In the identical provisions of Pennsylvania and Vermont, the language plainly reaffirmed the established right of individuals to arm themselves for self-defense. In the provisions of North Carolina and Massachusetts, although the express scope of the right may have been narrower, the right still belonged to individuals—these state provisions could not have been intended to protect the states' prerogatives, nor did they restrict the right to participants in militia units. Other states, most notably Virginia, did not include any provision regarding the right to bear arms in their declarations but did praise "a well regulated Militia."[221]

Virginia. Virginia's Declaration of Rights, adopted a month before the Declaration of Independence, was the country's first. Section 13 provided:

> That a well regulated militia, composed of the body of the people, trained to arms, is the proper, natural, and safe defence of a free State: that standing armies, in time of peace, should be avoided, as dangerous to liberty; and that in all cases the military should be under strict subordination to, and governed by, the civil power.[222]

---

dangerous to look to them as our sole protectors."); *The Federalist No. 25*, at 161–62 (Alexander Hamilton) (praising militias' valor but emphasizing insufficiency for defense). General Greene recognized that the militia should "not [be] depended upon as a principal but employed as an Auxilliary." Letter to Jefferson, *reprinted in* 4 *Jefferson Papers*, *supra* note 62, at 131.

[220] *The Federalist No. 46*, at 321–22.

[221] The first constitutions of New Jersey, South Carolina, Georgia, and New York did not include separate bills of rights. Their constitutions did protect a few rights, but did not include the right to arms or general statements regarding the militia. *See* 1 Schwartz, *Bill of Rights*, *supra* note 67, at 256 (N.J. 1776); *id.* at 291 (Ga. 1777); *id.* at 301 (N.Y. 1777); *id.* at 325 (S.C. 1778). Georgia did provide for forming a militia battalion in any county with "two hundred and fifty men, and upwards, liable to bear arms," *id.* at 297, and New York declared the duty of all to provide personal service to protect society, *see id.* at 312, much as the Pennsylvania Declaration, discussed below, did. Connecticut and Rhode Island did not adopt new constitutions. *Id.* at 289.

[222] Va. Bill of Rights § 13 (1776), *reprinted in* 7 *Federal and State Constitutions*, *supra* note 78, at 3814.

This provision expressly recognizes the background definition of "militia" explained in Part II.C: It was not a specialized or select force, but rather a force of the people. Such an understanding of the militia is consistent with the right of individuals to have arms—particularly given that, as we have explained, the citizen militia was supposed to be "trained to" its members' private arms.[223] Significantly, the provision's primary author was George Mason,[224] whose public views have already been noted and who would play a leading role twelve years later, explained below, in authoring the proposal of Virginia's ratifying convention that placed together in a single article the individual right and this praise of the citizen militia.[225]

Pennsylvania. Pennsylvania adopted its Declaration of Rights in September 1776. Article 13, immediately following an article providing "[t]hat the people have a right to freedom of speech," read:

> That the people have a right to bear arms for the defence of themselves and the state; and as standing armies in the time of peace are dangerous to liberty, they ought not to be kept up; And that the military should be kept under strict subordination to, and governed by, the civil power.[226]

While following the same structure as Virginia's (of which the convention members were well aware[227]), this article replaced the praise of the well-regulated citizen militia with a right—a right of "the people," who, just as they had an individual right to speak, also had an individual right to "bear arms," for either of the dual purposes of defending "themselves and the state." The article does not restrict the right to those in militia service, which it does not mention and which Pennsylvania addressed separately: Article 8 broadly provided that "every member of society," receiving protection from it, was bound to contribute money and "his

---

[223] Regarding this point and the meaning of both "militia" and "well regulated militia," see above Parts II.C.2–4 and III.B.1, at note 196 (quoting Jefferson's *Notes on the State of Virginia*, *supra* note 56).

[224] *See* 1 *Mason Papers*, *supra* note 56, at 274–75, 286 (editorial notes); *id.* at 287 (final draft).

[225] Delaware, Maryland, and New Hampshire adapted Virginia's language, omitting definition of the militia and changing "free state" to "free government" while retaining the implicit connection between "a well regulated militia" and the avoidance of standing armies and military insubordination. *See* Del. Decl. of Rights §§ 18–20 (1776), *reprinted in* 5 *Founders' Constitution*, note 118, at 5, 6; Md. Decl. of Rights §§ 25–27 (1776), *reprinted in* 3 *Federal and State Constitutions*, *supra* note 78, at 1688; N.H. Const. pt. I, arts. 24–26 (1784), *reprinted in* 4 *Federal and State Constitutions*, *supra* note 78, at 2456. The Delaware Constitution also specially provided that "[t]o prevent any violence or force being used at . . . elections, no person shall come armed to any of them, and no muster of the militia shall be made on that day." Del. Const. art. XXVIII (1776), *reprinted in* 1 *Federal and State Constitutions*, *supra* note 78, at 567.

[226] *Reprinted in* 5 *Federal and State Constitutions*, *supra* note 78, at 3083.

[227] *See* 1 *Mason Papers*, *supra* note 56, at 276 (note discussing "the widespread and almost immediate influence of the Virginia Declaration of Rights on other nascent states," including Pennsylvania).

personal service when necessary," while allowing an exception for anyone "conscientiously scrupulous of bearing arms, . . . if he will pay [an] equivalent."[228] And the plan of government, adopted concurrently, provided for a militia of "[t]he freemen of this commonwealth and their sons."[229]

The plan of government also provided that persons could use their arms to hunt (without trespassing): "The inhabitants of this state shall have liberty to fowl and hunt in seasonable times on the lands they hold, and on all other lands therein not inclosed."[230] Regardless of the relevance of this provision to the contours of the right to bear arms (a question beyond the scope of this memorandum), the provision does seem to have been viewed as a practical security for, and thus a way of emphasizing the importance of, the right of individuals that Pennsylvania had elsewhere secured. The view that the English game laws—which had provided for disarming many in the name of the hunting privileges of a few—had been a pretext for undermining the right in practice was prevalent at the time. Thomas Paine had criticized the game laws in the *Pennsylvania Magazine* the year before Pennsylvania adopted its constitution, and one newspaper article, although recognizing that the newer game acts did not prohibit merely keeping a gun, argued that English aristocrats still used them to disarm commoners, by procuring witnesses to claim that defendants had used their arms for hunting.[231]

Pennsylvania held another convention from November 1789 through September 1790, as the Second Amendment was before the states for ratification. The resulting constitution retained essentially the same individual right. Section 21 of the declaration of rights, immediately following a section providing "[t]hat the citizens have a right" to assemble and petition, provided:

> That the right of the citizens to bear arms, in defence of themselves and the State, shall not be questioned.[232]

---

[228] 5 *Federal and State Constitutions, supra* note 78, at 3083. Such personal service would be difficult if one could not own private arms. This duty may have been broader than the obligation of militia duty, perhaps including the posse comitatus. *See generally The Federalist No. 29*, at 182–83 (Alexander Hamilton). New Hampshire's constitution, while praising the well-regulated militia, recognized this duty separately, N.H. Const. pt. I, arts. 12–13, *reprinted in* 4 *Federal and State Constitutions, supra* note 78, at 2455, although New York's connected the two, N.Y. Const. § 40 (1777), *reprinted in* 5 *id.* at 2637.

[229] Pa. Plan or Frame of Gov't § 5 (1776), *reprinted in* 5 *Federal and State Constitutions, supra* note 78, at 3084.

[230] *Id.* § 43, *reprinted in* 5 *Federal and State Constitutions, supra* note 78, at 3091.

[231] *See* Halbrook, *Right to Bear Arms, supra* note 56, at 23–25. Some in England shared this concern. *See* Schwoerer, *supra* note 168, 76 Chi.-Kent L. Rev. at 52–53.

[232] Pa. Const. art. IX, §§ 20 & 21, *reprinted in* 5 *Federal and State Constitutions, supra* note 78, at 3101. Section 22 addressed standing armies and civilian control of the military. Kentucky, admitted in 1791 as the fifteenth state, copied this language on the right verbatim. *See* Ky. Const. art. XII, § 23 (1792), *reprinted in* 3 *Federal and State Constitutions, supra* note 78, at 1275.

Separately, in the body of the constitution, the protection of conscientious objectors was combined with the provision relating to the citizen militia:

> The freemen of this commonwealth shall be armed and disciplined for its defence. Those who conscientiously scruple to bear arms shall not be compelled to do so, but shall pay an equivalent for personal service. The militia officers shall be appointed in such manner and for such time as shall be directed by law.[233]

Thus, the ***right*** to "bear arms" remained with individual people, now "the citizens," and existed for the dual purpose of facilitating the defense of individuals and the state. Neither purpose was expressly tied to, let alone limited to, service in the militia. And the *duty* of "freemen" to "bear arms," including possible exemption from that duty, was distinct and was tied to the militia. In both the 1776 and 1790 Pennsylvania constitutions, "bear arms" could and did bear both meanings.

North Carolina. North Carolina adopted its constitution and declaration of rights in December 1776. Article 17 of the declaration provided:

> That the people have a right to bear arms, for the defence of the State; and, as standing armies, in time of peace, are dangerous to liberty, they ought not to be kept up; and that the military should be kept under strict subordination to, and governed by, the civil power.[234]

This article mentions only the right of the people to bear arms for "the defence of the State." Regardless of the provision's scope, however, the right still belonged to individuals, just as the immediately following Article 18 set out a right of individuals in providing "[t]hat the people have a right to assemble together," and in contrast with Article 25's declaration, in delineating the state's boundaries, of "the essential rights of the collective body of the people" in the "property of the soil."[235] It would not have made sense, in the context of a state constitution, for a "right" of "the people" to protect only the prerogatives of the state. And the provision's text indicates that all of the people (not just those organized by the state into militia units) had a right to bear arms, at least in defense of the state. As an early North Carolina Supreme Court decision recognized, the right in Article 17 belonged "to every man indeed" and "secur[ed] to him a *right* of which he cannot

[233] Pa. Const. art. VI, § 2, *reprinted in* 5 *Federal and State Constitutions*, *supra* note 78, at 3099. Kentucky also copied this provision. *See* Ky. Const. art. VI, § 2, *reprinted in* 3 *Federal and State Constitutions*, *supra* note 78, at 1271.

[234] *Reprinted in* 5 *Federal and State Constitutions*, *supra* note 78, at 2788.

[235] *Id.*

be deprived," to be exercised "for the safety and protection of his country."[236] Moreover, by expressly protecting the right of the people to bear arms "for the defence of the State" (something that North Carolinians were then doing against the British), the drafters of the North Carolina Constitution do not appear to have intended to abrogate the arguably more modest individual English right.[237] Indeed, the president of the constitutional convention, who served on the committee that wrote the declaration, had been one of the three congressional delegates who the year before, as discussed above, had urged North Carolinians to exercise "the Right of every *English* Subject to be prepared with Weapons for his Defense."[238]

Vermont. The Vermont constitution approved in July 1777 provided that "the people have a right to bear arms for the defence of themselves and the State," in an article identical to Article 13 of Pennsylvania's Declaration.[239] As in Pennsylvania, this individual right immediately followed the individual right of "the people . . . to freedom of speech," and the constitution separately included a hunting guarantee, citizen militia provisions, and an exception for conscientious objectors.[240] All of these remained in Vermont's 1786 and 1793 constitutions.[241]

Massachusetts. Article 17 of the Massachusetts Declaration of Rights of 1780 provided:

> The people have a right to keep and to bear arms for the common defence. And as, in time of peace, armies are dangerous to liberty, they ought not to be maintained without the consent of the legislature; and

---

[236] *State v. Huntly*, 25 N.C. (3 Ired.) 418, 1843 WL 891, at *2. Another early decision recognized that the right of "free people of color" to bear arms might be abridged—but only because the court believed that they "cannot be considered as citizens," or at least not full citizens, not because of any exclusion from the militia (a subject the court did not mention). *State v. Newsom*, 27 N.C. (5 Ired.) 250, 1844 WL 1059, at *1, *2.

[237] See below note 239.

[238] This was Richard Caswell, who became the first governor. Another member of the committee also had been one of the three delegates. *See* Halbrook, *Right to Bear Arms*, *supra* note 56, at 29–31; *see also* 5 *Federal and State Constitutions*, *supra* note 78, at 2794.

[239] Vt. Const. ch. I, § 15, *reprinted in* 6 *Federal and State Constitutions*, *supra* note 78, at 3741. The constitution also asserted independence from New York. *Id.* at 3738–39 (preamble); *see* Halbrook, *Right to Bear Arms*, *supra* note 56, at 37 ("Recognition of bearing arms to defend the state was more radical than self-defense, since it justified action by armed private citizens to defend an incipient state from the constituted authorities of both New York and Great Britain."). The First Congress admitted Vermont as the fourteenth state, *see* Act of Feb. 18, 1791, 1 Stat. 191, in time for it to ratify the Bill of Rights, *see* 2 Schwartz, *Bill of Rights*, *supra* note 67, at 1202–03.

[240] Vt. Const. ch. I, § 14, *reprinted in* 6 *Federal and State Constitutions*, *supra* note 78, at 3741 (speech); *id.* § 9, at 3740–41 (duty of personal service, and conscientious objectors); *id.* ch. II, § 5, at 3742 (militia of "freemen . . . and their sons"); *id.* § 39, at 3748 (hunting).

[241] *See* Vt. Const. ch. I, §§ 10, 15 & 18 (1786), *reprinted in* 6 *id.* at 3753 (duty of personal service and conscientious objectors, speech, and arms, respectively); *id.* ch. II, § 19, at 3758 (militia, including all "inhabitants" rather than all freemen and their sons); *id.* § 37, at 3760 (hunting); Vt. Const. ch. I, arts. 9, 13 & 16 (1793), *reprinted in id.* at 3763–64 (duty of personal service and conscientious objectors, speech, and arms, respectively); *id.* ch. II, § 22, at 3768 (militia); *id.* § 40, at 3770 (hunting).

> the military power shall always be held in an exact subordination to the civil authority, and be governed by it.[242]

In addition, Article 1 announced as among the "natural, essential, and unalienable rights" of all men "the right of enjoying and defending their lives and liberties" and "of acquiring, possessing, and protecting property."[243] Massachusetts was the first state to add "keep" to "bear." But this double right was said to be "for the common defence," a phrase that arguably limits the purposes for which one might exercise it. Two towns had unsuccessfully proposed adding "their own and" before that phrase, one arguing that this change would make Article 17 "harmonize much better with" Article 1.[244]

Even assuming that the phrase "for the common defence" limited the purposes for which arms could be kept and borne, the "right" remained an individual one—residing in "the people," just as Article 19 set out an individual right in providing that "[t]he people have a right, in an orderly and peaceable manner, to assemble to consult upon the common good."[245] Nothing in Article 17 or any other provision connected the right to service in the militia, much less indicated that this "right" of the "people" belonged to the state or was intended to protect its prerogatives.[246] Moreover, the addition of the word "keep" to the right of the people reinforced the individual nature of the right, because, as explained above in Part II.B.1, the phrase "keep arms" commonly referred to individuals privately possessing their private arms.

The history of the provision reinforces this understanding of its text as securing an individual right. The principal draftsman was John Adams, joined by his cousin Samuel Adams and another individual.[247] As explained above, John Adams publicly acknowledged the individual right inherited from England both before and after he wrote the Declaration, and Samuel Adams both helped lead the Boston town meeting that had urged Bostonians to exercise that individual right

---

[242] *Reprinted in* 3 *Federal and State Constitutions*, *supra* note 78, at 1892.

[243] Mass. Const. pt. I, art. 1 (1780), *reprinted in id.* at 1889.

[244] *See* Halbrook, *Right to Bear Arms*, *supra* note 56, at 41–42.

[245] Mass. Const. pt. I, art. 19, *reprinted in* 3 *Federal and State Constitutions*, *supra* note 78, at 1892. An early decision of the state's supreme court, interpreting the Declaration's protection of the individual's "liberty of the press" as not protecting common law libel, drew a parallel to "the right to keep fire arms, which does not protect him who uses them for annoyance or destruction." *Commonwealth v. Blanding*, 20 Mass. 304, 338 (1825). Whether the court had in mind Article 17 or the right from England is unclear, but in either case it recognized a right of individuals to keep arms.

[246] In addition, the purposes of calling out the militia seem to have been narrower than whatever "for the common defence" signified, as the governor was authorized to call it out "for the special defence and safety of the commonwealth," which appears to have meant war, invasion, or rebellion. Mass. Const. pt. II, ch. 2, § 1, art. 7, *reprinted in* 3 *Federal and State Constitutions*, *supra* note 78, at 1901.

[247] 1 Schwartz, *Bill of Rights*, *supra* note 67, at 337. The only change between their draft and the final was the deletion of "standing" before "armies." *Id.* at 372 (draft); *id.* at 364 (deletion).

and publicly defended its resolution on the authority of the English Bill of Rights and Blackstone.[248] Much like Mason, Samuel Adams also would, during the ratification debate, urge that the Constitution protect that right, as we explain below.

Thus, the right of individual English subjects was transplanted to America. Americans also, from their experience in the American Revolution, came to emphasize the citizen militia, which they recognized was furthered by the individual right to private arms. But the English right as Americans came to understand it was not, as a result, somehow newly restricted to a person's service in that militia, much less to service in a select militia. Nor did early Americans see the right as a federalism protection (which would not have made sense in the context of *state* constitutions) or otherwise the property of the state rather than its citizens.

C. The Development of the Second Amendment

The proposed Constitution that emerged from the Constitutional Convention in 1787 did not have a bill of rights, notwithstanding a late effort by Mason, joined by Elbridge Gerry, to have one drawn up "with the aid of the State declarations."[249] It did contain a careful compromise regarding the militia. The federal government received, in Article I, Section 8, the powers to call out the militia "to execute the Laws of the Union, suppress Insurrections, and repel Invasions," to provide for "organizing, arming, and disciplining" it, and to govern any part of it in the service of the federal government (during which the President would be its Commander in Chief); states expressly retained the authority to appoint officers and to train the militia.[250]

---

[248] As with North Carolina's emphasis on the "defence of the State," Massachusetts's emphasis on the "common defence" may have represented the assertion of a right that went beyond the traditional English one. "Common" had been deleted from a similar clause ("for their common defence") in a draft of the English Declaration, perhaps at the urging of William of Orange or conservative Lords, who objected to suggestion of a popular right to check royal power. *See* Malcolm, *To Keep and Bear Arms*, *supra* note 33, at 119–21.

[249] Madison, *Notes of Debates*, *supra* note 44, at 630 (Sept. 12, 1787).

[250] U.S. Const. art. I, § 8, cls. 15 & 16, and art. II, § 2, cl. 1. The Ninth Circuit claims that there was "disagreement among the delegates" over whether Congress's power to arm the militias "should be exclusive or concurrent" with the states. *Silveira*, 312 F.3d at 1079. But the court only cites *Perpich v. Dep't of Defense*, 496 U.S. 334, 340 (1990), which does not support this claim; nor do the debates of the Convention, where the focus was on the extent of any federal authority to establish uniform discipline and regulation of the militia (including providing for arms), not on whether the states would retain concurrent authority in areas where federal power was granted. For the two chief debates, see Madison, *Notes of Debates*, *supra* note 44, at 478, 483–85 (Aug. 18, 1787); *id.* at 512–16 (Aug. 23, 1787). Similarly, the Third Circuit has cited, in support of the collective right view, a statement by Roger Sherman that states should retain power to use their militias for internal needs. *See United States v. Tot*, 131 F.2d 261, 266 (1942), *rev'd on other grounds*, 319 U.S. 463 (1943) (citing 5 *Elliot's Debates* 445 (2d ed. 1901)). We fail to see how this statement supports that view, particularly given that no one appears to have disagreed with Sherman; that he served on the committee that drafted what

Proposed bills of rights emerged from the ratifying conventions of several of the states. Many of these included protection for the right to arms—usually in language borrowed or adapted from the individual right to arms in the states' declarations of rights, and in any event always in language indicating an individual right. In those proposals, several states for the first time in a single constitutional provision both set out an individual right to arms and praised the citizen militia, uniting language from the different state declarations discussed above. In addition, some Anti-Federalists, concerned about the Constitution's allocation of powers over the militia, sought to protect the ability of the states to maintain effective militias. They proposed to do so expressly, in amendments using language similar to that of Article I, Section 8, and to be placed in the body of the Constitution, not in a bill of rights.[251]

Yet it was the former proposals that laid the foundation for the Second Amendment. And the latter proposals failed in the Federalist-controlled First Congress, which was, as many recognized at the time, willing to protect individual rights but not to alter the balance of power struck by the new Constitution between the states and the nascent federal government. Thus, the evidence points to an understanding of the Amendment as securing the individual right to arms already well established in America, rather than safeguarding the ability of states to establish well-regulated militias, whether through a "collective right" of states or a quasi-collective right of militiamen. Rather than "lay down any novel principles of government," the Second Amendment embodied the individual "guarant[ee] and immunit[y]" to which Americans were accustomed.[252]

1. Recommendations From the Ratification of the Original Constitution

Although the right of individuals to have arms was not a subject of much direct discussion in the ratification debates, two major topics are relevant. First, Anti-

became the final version of Article I, Section 8, Clause 16, Madison, *Notes of Debates* at 480, 485 (Aug. 18, 1787); *id.* at 494–95 (Aug. 21, 1787), and generally supported its compromise, *id.* at 513–14; and that he saw no need for amendments, *see A Countryman No. 2* (1787), *reprinted in* 14 *Ratification*, *supra* note 67, at 172 (John P. Kaminski & Gaspare J. Saladino eds., 1983); *A Countryman No. 3* (1787), *reprinted in id.* at 296; *A Citizen of New Haven* (1789), *reprinted in Creating the Bill of Rights*, *supra* note 82, at 220.

[251] The Ninth Circuit in *Silveira* did not mention this latter set of proposals, and the court presented the comments in the ratification debates most relevant to these separate proposals as if they instead related to the Second Amendment. *See* 312 F.3d at 1082–83; *see also id.* at 1078 (claiming without citation that "[t]he compromise that the convention eventually reached, which granted the federal government the dominant control over the national defense, led ultimately to the enactment of the counter-balancing Second Amendment").

[252] *Robertson*, 165 U.S. at 281 (discussing Bill of Rights in general); *see Silveira*, 328 F.3d at 584 (Kleinfeld, J., joined by Kozinski, O'Scannlain, and T.G. Nelson, JJ., dissenting from denial of rehearing en banc) ("The Second Amendment was not novel, but rather codified and expanded upon long established principles.").

Federalists objected to the absence of a bill of rights, often pointing to the English Bill of Rights (as well as the declarations of the states) as models.[253] The Federalists' response likewise recognized the English precedent, but sought to distinguish it on various grounds or to argue that many rights, such as the English Bill of Rights' ban on "cruel and unusual punishments," or "the liberty of the press" (which developed after the Bill), were too indefinite to provide dependable legal protections.[254]

Second, Anti-Federalists denounced the militia powers to be granted to the federal government, warning that it would destroy the militia through any number of means—by neglecting it, by creating a select militia and then neglecting the general militia, or (somewhat inconsistently[255]) by destroying the militia through onerous discipline and excessive deployment. The arguments from neglect rested on the premise that Congress's power of organizing, arming, and disciplining the militia would foreclose any such state power. If true, the militia might be left without any government ensuring its arming and training. The arguments also were premised on the common understanding of the "militia" as the citizen militia: The Federal Farmer, the leading Anti-Federalist essayist, admonished that "to preserve liberty, it is essential that the whole body of the people always possess arms, and be taught alike, especially when young, how to use them," and Patrick Henry, leader in the Virginia Ratifying Convention, warned, "The great object is, that every man be armed. . . . When this power is given up to Congress without limitation or bounds, how will your militia be armed?"[256] Anti-Federalists also warned that Congress would use its power to establish a standing army to trample

---

[253] *See, e.g.*, 2 *Complete Anti-Federalist*, *supra* note 101, at 7, 11 (public objections of Mason and Gerry); Va. Ratif. Conv., *reprinted in* 10 *Ratification*, *supra* note 67, at 1212 (remarks of Patrick Henry, June 12, 1788) (invoking English Bill and state declarations); Address by Sydney (Robert Yates) (1788), *reprinted in* 6 *Complete Anti-Federalist*, *supra* note 101, at 107, 109 (similar to Henry). One of the leading arguments of this point was by the Federal Farmer. *See Federal Farmer No. 16* (1788), *reprinted in* 2 *Complete Anti-Federalist*, *supra* note 101, at 323.

[254] *See, e.g.*, *The Federalist No. 84*, at 575–81 (Alexander Hamilton); *Marcus No. 1*, *Answer to Mr. Mason's Objections* (James Iredell) (1788), *reprinted in* 1 *Debate on the Constitution*, *supra* note 97, at 363–64; *Marcus No. 4* (1788), *reprinted in id.* at 387–90; *America, To the Dissenting Members of the late Convention of Pennsylvania* (Noah Webster) (1787), *reprinted in* 1 *Debate on the Constitution*, *supra* note 97, at 555–60.

[255] As one Federalist criticized Luther Martin, an Anti-Federalist who had been a delegate to the Constitutional Convention: "One hour you sported the opinion, that Congress, afraid of the militia resisting their measures, would neither arm nor organize them: and the next, as if men required no time to breathe between such contradictions, that they would harass them by long and unnecessary marches, till they wore down their spirit and rendered them fit subjects for despotism." *The Landholder No. 10* (1788), *reprinted in* 16 *Ratification*, *supra* note 67, at 265, 267 (John P. Kaminski & Gaspare J. Saladino eds., 1986).

[256] *Federal Farmer No. 18* (1788), *reprinted in* 2 *Complete Anti-Federalist*, *supra* note 101, at 342; Va. Ratif. Conv., *in* 10 *Ratification*, *supra* note 67, at 1276 (Henry, June 14, 1788).

traditional liberties, particularly after it had destroyed the militia.[257] The Federalists' response emphasized the same understanding of the citizen militia, asking how the federal government could tyrannize over a populace armed as America's was.[258] As already noted in Part II.D.2 above, they also argued that, in any event, the states would retain a concurrent power over their militias, including a power to arm them.[259]

Two separate categories of proposed amendments resulted from these two sets of arguments. Proposed amendments to protect the right to keep and bear arms not only were phrased as individual rights (even when accompanied by language concerning the militia and civilian control of the military) but also were distinct from proposals that would safeguard state powers over the militia or restrain federal power to create a standing army. (Restriction on standing armies would

[257] See, e.g., regarding all of these concerns, *John De Witt No.* 5 (1787), *reprinted in* 4 *Complete Anti-Federalist, supra* note 101, at 36–37 (warning that federal government would neglect to arm militia, not trusting the people, and enforce unjust laws through standing army); Pa. Ratif. Conv., *in* 2 *Ratification, supra* note 67, at 509 (remarks of John Smilie, Dec. 6, 1787) ("When a select militia is formed; the people in general may be disarmed."); *Federal Farmer No. 3* (1787), *reprinted in* 2 *Complete Anti-Federalist, supra* note 101, at 242 (discounting safeguard of armed "yeomanry of the people," whom Congress would undermine through creating select militia); *The Genuine Information Delivered to the Legislature of the State of Maryland Relative to the Proceedings of the General Convention Lately Held at Philadelphia; By Luther Martin, Esquire* (1788), *reprinted in* 2 *Complete Anti-Federalist, supra* note 101, at 59–60 (warning that Congress would use its militia and army powers "to *subvert* the *liberties* of the *States* and *their citizens*, since we [allow an unlimited standing army and,] by placing the militia under *its* power, enable it to leave the militia *totally unorganized, undisciplined*, and *even to disarm them*"); Va. Ratif. Conv., *in* 10 *Ratification, supra* note 67, at 1271 (remarks of Mason, June 14, 1788) (warning that Congress would "disarm the people" gradually, rather than "openly," by "totally disusing and neglecting the militia"). Henry repeatedly denounced the allegedly exclusive power. *See* 9 *Ratification, supra* note 67, at 957 (June 5) ("Of what service would militia be to you, when most probably you will not have a single musket in the State; for as arms are to be provided by Congress, they may or may not furnish them."); *id.* at 1066 (June 9) ("The power of arming the militia, and the means of purchasing arms, are taken from the States . . . . If Congress will not arm them, they will not be armed at all.").

[258] *See, e.g.*, *The Federalist No. 46*, at 321–22 (James Madison) (contrasting the "advantage of being armed, which the Americans possess," with the circumstances in "several kingdoms of Europe . . . [where] the governments are afraid to trust the people with arms"); *An American Citizen IV: On the Federal Government* (Tench Coxe) (1787), *reprinted in* 13 *Ratification, supra* note 67, at 433 (John P. Kaminski & Gaspare J. Saladino eds., 1981) (arguing that, if tyranny threatened, the "*friends to liberty* . . . using those arms which Providence has put into their hands, will make a solemn appeal '*to the power above*'"); A Citizen of America, *An Examination Into the Leading Principles of the Federal Constitution* (Noah Webster) (1787), *reprinted in* 1 *Debate on the Constitution, supra* note 97, at 155 ("Before a standing army can rule the people must be disarmed; as they are in almost every kingdom in Europe. The supreme power in America cannot enforce unjust laws by the sword; because the whole body of the people are armed").

[259] John Marshall, for example, provided a standard analysis: "The truth is, that when power is given to the General Legislature, if it was in the State Legislatures before, both shall exercise it; unless there be an incompatibility in the exercise by one, to that by the other; or negative words precluding the State Governments from it. But there are no negative words here. It rests therefore with the States." Va. Ratif. Conv., *in* 10 *Ratification, supra* note 67, at 1307 (June 16, 1788).

help ensure that the new government maintained the militia, by ensuring the government's dependence on it.)

Pennsylvania's Convention, the second to meet, ratified the Constitution by a 2 to 1 margin in December 1787, without proposing amendments.[260] A week later, 21 of the 23 dissenting delegates published their *Address and Reasons of Dissent* ("Minority Report"), including amendments that they had proposed but the convention had refused to consider. It drew heavily from the 1776 Pennsylvania Declaration of Rights. The proposal regarding arms was Article 7, immediately following one stating that "the people have a right to the freedom of speech," and it read as follows:

> That the people have a right to bear arms for the defence of themselves and their own State or the United States, or for the purpose of killing game; and no law shall be passed for disarming the people or any of them unless for crimes committed, or real danger of public injury from individuals; and as standing armies in the time of peace are dangerous to liberty, they ought not to be kept up; and that the military shall be kept under strict subordination to, and be governed by the civil powers.[261]

Article 8, immediately following, protected the right to hunt on one's private property and certain other lands.[262]

Separately, the Minority sought, in Article 11, both to restrict Congress's Article I, Section 8, Clause 16 powers over the militia and to protect state authority over it, by providing "[t]hat the power of organizing, arming and disciplining the militia (the manner of disciplining the militia to be prescribed by Congress), remain with the individual States."[263] They warned that, without *this* restriction, Congress's power over the militia could place "every man, probably from sixteen to sixty years of age" under Congress's power and military discipline—

---

[260] Delaware already had ratified unanimously. After Pennsylvania's vote, New Jersey, Georgia, and Connecticut ratified by large majorities. No proposed amendments emerged from these conventions. *See* 2 Schwartz, *Bill of Rights*, *supra* note 67, at 627, 674. Maryland ratified on April 26, 1788, without proposing amendments, although a committee had approved several, including a prohibition on subjecting the militia to martial law "except in time of war, invasion, or rebellion." The committee understood the militia to consist of "all men, able to bear arms," which would make martial law for the militia a pretext for applying it to the populace. *See id.* at 729–30, 734–35.

[261] 2 Schwartz, *Bill of Rights*, *supra* note 67, at 665. Tench Coxe, in a critique of the Minority, described this proposal as a "provision against disarming the people." *Philanthropos*, Penn. Gazette, 1788, *reprinted in* 15 *Ratification*, *supra* note 67, at 391, 393.

[262] 2 Schwartz, *Bill of Rights*, *supra* note 67, at 665. Noah Webster suggested that the Minority also propose "[t]hat Congress shall never restrain any inhabitant of America from eating and drinking, *at seasonable times*." His serious criticism of Article 8 was that it was useless because aimed at game laws, which had never existed in America. He did not comment on Article 7. *America*, Daily Advertiser, 1787, *reprinted in* 1 *Debate on the Constitution*, *supra* note 97, at 559–60.

[263] 2 Schwartz, *Bill of Rights*, *supra* note 67, at 665.

particularly "our young men, . . . as a select militia, composed of them, will best answer the purposes of government"—and also could leave conscientious objectors compelled to bear arms in the militia.[264] As in Pennsylvania's 1776 declaration and constitution, a right to bear arms was distinct from bearing arms in service to the government. There was no suggestion that the individual right somehow would directly guard the states' power, and this separate proposal and comment indicate that the Minority believed that it would not.

The Massachusetts Convention was the first to include with its ratification, in February 1788, a list of recommended amendments. The Federalists prepared and had John Hancock introduce the nine proposals to woo marginal Anti-Federalists. Samuel Adams, while supporting Hancock's list, also led an effort to add several rights that would appear in the First, Second, and Fourth Amendments, plus a ban on standing armies "unless when necessary for the defence of the United States, or of some one or more of them." Regarding arms, he proposed that the Constitution "be never construed to authorize Congress . . . to prevent the people of the United States, who are peaceable citizens, from keeping their own arms." This language indicated that the "people" consisted of the "citizens," who would, so long as they were peaceable, individually keep private arms. Adams's proposed additions were voted down, and the Convention then narrowly voted to ratify and to recommend the Federalists' list.[265]

Four months later, New Hampshire's Convention, also closely divided, adapted some of Adams's proposals.[266] It recommended the nine amendments that Massachusetts had, but added three: one calling for a supermajority before Congress could keep up a standing army in peacetime; the next barring Congress from making laws regarding religion or infringing the rights of conscience; and the final one providing that "Congress shall never disarm any Citizen unless such as are or have been in Actual Rebellion."[267] New Hampshire thus became the first state whose ratifying convention as a body recommended that the Constitution protect a right to arms. Again, the right belonged to the individual citizen.

Although New Hampshire had provided the crucial ninth state for the Constitution to take effect,[268] the convention of Virginia, occurring simultaneously and concluding four days later (on June 25, 1788), had particular importance, not only because of the possibility that Virginia would be the ninth state to ratify but also because of the state's significance, the prominence of its leaders, and the strength

[264] *Id.* at 671–72.

[265] *Id.* at 674–75, 681. South Carolina ratified in May 1788 without proposing any relevant amendments. *See id.* at 739, 756–57.

[266] The convention had adjourned in February 1788 to avoid a vote against ratification. When it reconvened in the summer, it ratified by a vote of 57 to 47. *See id.* at 758.

[267] *Id.* at 761; *see id.* at 758 (noting that the first nine New Hampshire amendments "were taken almost verbatim from those proposed by Massachusetts").

[268] *Id.* at 758. *See* U.S. Const. art. VII.

of the Anti-Federalists, led by Patrick Henry.[269] The convention did vote to ratify, but also recommended numerous amendments. Written by a committee of Mason, Henry, Madison, George Wythe, and John Marshall, twenty were proposed for a separate bill of rights and twenty for the body of the Constitution. Those in the former category amounted to the first full bill of rights proposed by a state convention, and most made their way into the federal Bill of Rights.[270]

The proposal regarding arms appeared in the bill, immediately after the "right[s]" of "the people" to assemble and petition and to speak, write, and publish. It was a synthesis from the leading state declarations, providing:

> That the people have a right to keep and bear arms; that a well-regulated militia, composed of the body of the people trained to arms, is the proper, natural, and safe defence of a free state; that standing armies, in time of peace, are dangerous to liberty, and therefore ought to be avoided, as far as the circumstances and protection of the community will admit; and that, in all cases, the military should be under strict subordination to, and governed by, the civil power.[271]

The two strands evident in the Revolutionary Era—an individual right to arms and high regard for the citizen militia—were brought together: The proposal combined an individual right to arms provision such as those from the Pennsylvania and Massachusetts Declarations with the praise of the militia from Virginia's. The "people" would have a right to keep and bear arms, and a well-regulated militia composed "of the *body* of the people"—the people as an organized whole—would protect "a free state." This language became the foundation for the Second Amendment. In addition, the combination of the two clauses indicates (as the differing first clauses of the analogous articles in the Virginia and Pennsylvania Declarations had done separately) that the individual right and the well-regulated militia *both* would contribute to the avoidance of standing armies and to civilian rule.

Only in its separate list of amendments for the body of the Constitution did the Virginia convention directly protect the power of states to maintain militias and restrict the federal power to raise standing armies. It recommended a supermajority vote for Congress to maintain a peacetime army (in the spirit of Samuel Adams and the New Hampshire Convention), and it sought to protect state power over the militia (much as the Pennsylvania Minority had) with the following provision:

---

[269] *See* 2 Schwartz, *Bill of Rights*, *supra* note 67, at 762, 764.

[270] *See id.* at 765–66.

[271] 2 Schwartz, *Bill of Rights*, *supra* note 67, at 842. Mason drafted this provision. *See* 9 *Ratification*, *supra* note 67, at 821 (reprinting Mason's draft). Two articles later, Virginia also proposed exemptions for those "religiously scrupulous of bearing arms," again borrowing from Pennsylvania's Declaration. 2 Schwartz, *Bill of Rights*, *supra* note 67, at 842.

> That each state respectively shall have the power to provide for organizing, arming, and disciplining its own militia, whensoever Congress shall omit or neglect to provide for the same.[272]

These distinct proposals confirm what is evident from the declarations included with the proposal for the bill of rights: The individual right of the people to keep and bear arms does not directly guard any power of states to maintain militias. (Much less does it guarantee against standing armies.) But it does *indirectly* further the policy of having a well-regulated militia of the body of the people, as well as that of mitigating the need for and risk from a standing army.

The New York Convention, voting just over a month after Virginia's (and ratifying by only 30–27), followed Virginia's model. The separate declaration of rights included both an individual right to keep and bear arms (immediately after the "right" of "the People" to free exercise of religion) and declarations regarding the militia and standing armies:

> That the People have a right to keep and bear Arms; that a well regulated Militia, including the body of the People capable of bearing arms, is the proper, natural, and safe defence of a free State.
>
> . . . .
>
> That standing Armies in time of Peace are dangerous to Liberty, and ought not to be kept up, except in Cases of necessity; and that at all times, the Military should be under strict Subordination to the civil Power.[273]

For the body of the Constitution, New York proposed, like New Hampshire and Virginia, an amendment requiring a supermajority for Congress to maintain a peacetime standing army. It did not propose express protection of state power over the militia.[274]

The force of Virginia's proposals is evident not only in New York's borrowing but also in the first North Carolina Convention. On August 1, 1788, North Carolina became the only state to decline to ratify until the Constitution had been amended to include a bill of rights (Rhode Island had declined even to call a convention), and it proposed verbatim the amendments that Virginia had proposed—including the individual right to keep and bear arms and the *separate* proposals, for the body of the Constitution, guarding state power over the militias and mandating supermajorities for standing armies. North Carolina's actions made

---

[272] 2 Schwartz, *Bill of Rights*, *supra* note 67, at 843.

[273] *Id.* at 912. New York did not propose any protection for conscientious objectors.

[274] *Id.* at 915, 918.

the momentum for a bill of rights "virtually irresistible," and, two months after Congress approved one, a new convention ratified.[275]

Every recommendation in these state conventions regarding the right to arms sought to protect an individual right—not a "right" to maintain well-regulated state militias, whether belonging to the states or to those serving in such entities (much less belonging just to those serving in well-regulated *select* militias). Virginia, New York, and North Carolina also appended declaratory clauses to the right suggesting that it would benefit the citizen militia, preserve the freedom of the state, and reduce the need for or risk from a standing army. But those states that wanted to protect state authority to maintain militias (Virginia and North Carolina) followed the lead of the Pennsylvania Minority by proposing separate amendments doing so directly, intended not for the bill of rights but for the body of the Constitution. Thus, regarding the right to arms, those who ratified the Constitution did nothing novel, but rather followed the path marked by the state declarations and the earlier right from England. They proposed an individual right, not a "right" of states and not a right restricted to their militias or militiamen. As the First Congress met, it had before it numerous proposals for an individual right to arms and a few proposals for safeguarding state militias by directly protecting state authority, but none for protecting that authority through a collective or quasi-collective "right" to arms.

2. The Drafting and Ratification of the Second Amendment

When the First Congress convened in 1789, Federalist Congressman James Madison moved quickly to win over marginal Anti-Federalists by responding to the calls for a bill of rights. The House soon approved seventeen amendments. The Senate reduced these to twelve, of which the states ratified the ten that form the Bill of Rights.

The Federalists, victorious in ratification and dominant in Congress, openly avoided any amendment that would materially alter the balance of power with the states or otherwise threaten legitimate federal powers. Thus, the amendments that Congress approved were devoted almost exclusively to protecting individual rights. Of the categories of proposals discussed in the previous subpart, only the first—the individual right of the people to keep and bear arms—received approval. The separate proposals for protecting state power to organize, discipline, and arm the militia and for restricting federal power to maintain standing armies failed.

President Washington set the stage in his inaugural address, urging Congress to consider amendments out of "a reverence for the characteristic rights of freemen" but "carefully avoid every alteration which might endanger the benefits of an

[275] *Id.* at 932–33, 968–69; Halbrook, *Right to Bear Arms*, *supra* note 56, at 33–34.

united and effective government."[276] Madison reiterated this view in introducing his proposals in June 1789:

> It will be a desirable thing to extinguish from the bosom of every member of the community, any apprehensions that there are those among his countrymen who wish to deprive them of the liberty for which they valiantly fought and honorably bled.
>
> . . . .
>
> I should be unwilling to see a door opened for a re-consideration of the whole structure of the government, for a re-consideration of the principles and the substance of the powers given . . . . But I do wish to see a door opened to consider, so far as to incorporate those provisions for the security of rights . . . .
>
> . . . .
>
> I believe that the great mass of the people who opposed [the Constitution], disliked it because it did not contain effectual provision against encroachments on particular rights, and those safeguards which they have been long accustomed to have interposed between them and the magistrate who exercised the sovereign power.[277]

Madison also urged Congress to "expressly declare the great rights of mankind" and provide "those securities for liberty" demanded by North Carolina and Rhode Island. In contrast, he was confident that those who opposed the Constitution's "structure," powers, or restrictions on state powers were a much smaller group.[278] Other congressmen similarly hoped that such an approach would win over many of the disaffected in various states.[279]

Anti-Federalist leaders recognized this focus on individual rights. Richard Henry Lee, one of Virginia's first senators, reported to Patrick Henry about a week before Madison's speech "that many of our amendments will not succeed, but my

---

[276] First Inaugural Address (Apr. 30, 1789), *reprinted in* 1 *A Compilation of the Messages and Papers of the Presidents* 43, 45 (James D. Richardson ed., 1897).

[277] Speech of Madison (June 8, 1789), *reprinted in Creating the Bill of Rights*, *supra* note 82, at 78–79.

[278] *Id.*

[279] *See* Letter from Rep. Fisher Ames to George R. Minot (July 23, 1789) (discussing North Carolina), *reprinted in Creating the Bill of Rights*, *supra* note 82, at 269; Letter from Rep. William L. Smith to Edward Rutledge (Aug. 9, 1789) (North Carolina; noting disposition of House to "agree to some, which will more effectually secure private rights"), *reprinted in id.* at 272–73; Letter from Rep. Frederick A. Muhlenberg to Benjamin Rush (Aug. 18, 1789) (Pennsylvania Minority), *reprinted in id.* at 280.

hopes are strong that such as may effectually secure civil liberty will not be refused."[280] Soon after Madison spoke, Virginia's other senator, William Grayson, wrote to Henry that Madison's proposals "altogether respected personal liberty."[281]

Among Madison's proposals was the following, which became the Second Amendment:

> The right of the people to keep and bear arms shall not be infringed; a well armed, and well regulated militia being the best security of a free country: but no person religiously scrupulous of bearing arms, shall be compelled to render military service in person.[282]

The first and second clauses resembled the proposals of the Virginia, New York, and North Carolina conventions, including by making the connection between the individual right and the militia. The first clause stated, as they had, a right both to keep and to bear arms, which belonged to "the people." Having made this into a full sentence, Madison made the second clause, which had been free-standing in the Virginia, New York, and North Carolina proposals, subordinate to the first. In shortening the second clause, he omitted the definition of the militia, just as Delaware, Maryland, and New Hampshire had done in their declarations of rights.[283] He also omitted the conventions' disparagement of standing armies and admonition to civilian rule, and appended protection for conscientious objectors, which the Pennsylvania Minority, Virginia, and North Carolina had separately requested. As the Pennsylvania and Vermont Declarations had shown even before ratification, there was no inconsistency in recognizing both an individual right to "bear arms" and an individual exemption from being compelled to "bear arms" in military service.

That Madison envisioned this proposed "right of the people" to secure an individual right is confirmed by the notes for his speech, in which he wrote that those provisions "relat[ing] to what may be called a bill of rights," including this one, "relate . . . to *private rights*";[284] by his using in his speech the same language to discuss both the rights of English subjects and those in his proposed bill;[285] and by

---

[280] Letter from Lee to Henry (May 28, 1789), *reprinted in Creating the Bill of Rights*, *supra* note 82, at 241.

[281] Letter from Grayson to Henry (June 12, 1789), *reprinted in id.* at 249. *See also* Letter from Joseph Jones to Madison (June 24, 1789), *reprinted in id.* at 253 (describing Madison's proposed amendments as well "calculated to secure the personal rights of the people").

[282] Madison Resolution (June 8, 1789), *reprinted in id.* at 12.

[283] See above Part III.B.2, at note 225 (discussing differences from Virginia Declaration).

[284] Notes for Speech in Congress (ca. June 8, 1789), *reprinted in* 12 *The Papers of James Madison* 193, 193 (Charles F. Hobson et al. eds., 1979) (emphasis added); *see id.* at 194–95; Speech of Madison, *reprinted in Creating the Bill of Rights*, *supra* note 82, at 80.

[285] *Compare* Speech of Madison, *reprinted in Creating the Bill of Rights*, *supra* note 82, at 80 (discussing "the declaration of rights" of England), *with id.* at 84 (concluding by describing his proposals "as a declaration of the rights of the people"). In his notes, although apparently not in his

the location in the body of the Constitution in which he proposed to place these amendments. He recommended that the right to arms, along with antecedents of the First, Third, Fourth, Eighth, Ninth, and portions of the Fifth and Sixth Amendments, be added in Article I, Section 9, immediately after clauses protecting three other individual rights: the writ of habeas corpus and the prohibitions against *ex post facto* laws and bills of attainder.[286] It is reasonable to assume that Madison viewed the additional rights as likewise belonging to the individual.[287] Had he instead intended to protect state militias (whether directly through a collective right or indirectly through a quasi-collective right), a more reasonable location would have been in or near the two clauses in Article I, Section 8, that granted congressional power over the militia, one of which already "reserv[ed] to the States" certain powers over the militia. And Madison likely would have drawn from the separate language that Virginia and others had proposed for just this purpose—but those proposals had the potential to threaten the balance of powers, at least by inviting disputes over whether the federal government had "neglect[ed]" the militia.

Others also understood Madison's proposal to secure an individual right to keep and bear arms. Leading Federalist Congressman Fisher Ames wrote: "Mr. Madison has introduced his long expected Amendments. . . . It contains a Bill of Rights . . . [including] the right of the people to bear arms."[288] Elsewhere he wrote: "The rights of conscience, of bearing arms, of changing the government, are declared to be inherent in the people."[289] Tench Coxe took the same view in his *Remarks on the First Part of the Amendments to the Federal Constitution*, published in the major cities. Writing as "A Pennsylvanian" (a pseudonym that he had used during the ratification debates), he explained the right that Madison's proposal protected as follows:

---

speech, he pointed out that the English right to arms was limited to Protestants. 12 *Madison Papers*, *supra* note 284, at 193–94.

[286] *See Creating the Bill of Rights*, *supra* note 82, at 12 (Madison's proposal); *id.* at 80, 84 (Madison's speech). His separate proposal of what would become the Tenth Amendment was to be placed between Articles 6 and 7, as its own article. *Id.* at 13–14.

[287] The arguable exception, as discussed above in Part II.D.1 regarding the Establishment Clause, was a prohibition on "any national religion." Madison proposed other amendments that did not relate to private rights, such as altering the ratio of representation in the House of Representatives and banning increases of legislator pay without an ensuing election, but he proposed to place these elsewhere in the Constitution. *Id.* at 12.

[288] Letter from Ames to Thomas Dwight (June 11, 1789), *reprinted in Creating the Bill of Rights*, *supra* note 82, at 247.

[289] Letter from Ames to George R. Minot (June 12, 1789), *reprinted in Creating the Bill of Rights*, *supra* note 82, at 247–48. The right of "changing the government" to which Ames referred was a provision, in a separate section of Madison's proposal, affirming the right of the people "to reform or change their government, whenever it be found adverse or inadequate to the purposes of its institution." Regarding such usage of the "the people," see Part II.A above.

> As civil rulers, not having their duty to the people duly before them, may attempt to tyrannize, and as the military forces which must be occasionally raised to defend our country, might pervert their power to the injury of their fellow citizens, the people are confirmed by the . . . article in their right to keep and bear their private arms.[290]

Coxe recognized that the "right" of "the people" belonged to the "citizens," who could both keep and bear "private" arms. He sent his *Remarks* to Madison the day that they were published, and Madison six days later returned thanks for his "explanatory strictures" and the "co-operation of your pen," noting from New York City that the *Remarks* "are already I find in the Gazettes here."[291] Neither Madison nor, it appears, anyone else disputed Coxe's interpretation.[292] Samuel Nasson, who had been an Anti-Federalist delegate to the Massachusetts Ratifying Convention, described the right similarly in a letter to a Federalist congressman from the state a month after Madison introduced his proposals:

> I find that Ammendments are once again on the Carpet. I hope that such may take place as will be for the Best Interest of the whole[.] A Bill of rights well secured that we the people may know how far we may Proceade in Every Department[,] then their will be no Dispute Between the people and rulers[.] [I]n that may be secured the right to keep arms for Common and Extraordinary Occations such as to secure ourselves against the wild Beast and also to amuse us by fowling and for our Defence against a Common Enemy[.] [Y]ou know to learn the Use of arms is all that can Save us from a forighn foe that may attempt to subdue us[,] for if we keep up the Use of arms and become acquainted with them we Shall allway be able to look them in the face that arise up against us[.][293]

---

[290] Philadelphia Fed. Gazette, June 18, 1789, at 2, *excerpted in* Kates, *supra* note 33, 82 Mich. L. Rev. at 224 & nn. 81–82. The *Remarks* were reprinted within three weeks in newspapers in Boston (on the front page of a special July 4 issue) and New York. *See* Stephen P. Halbrook & David B. Kopel, *Tench Coxe and the Right to Keep and Bear Arms, 1787–1823*, 7 Wm. & Mary Bill Rts. J. 347, 367 (1999).

[291] *See* Letter from Coxe to Madison (June 18, 1789), *reprinted in Creating the Bill of Rights*, *supra* note 82, at 252–53; Letter from Madison to Coxe (June 24, 1789), *reprinted in* 12 *Madison Papers*, *supra* note 284, at 257; *see also Creating the Bill of Rights*, *supra* note 82, at 254 (excerpting Madison's letter).

[292] *See* Halbrook, *That Every Man Be Armed*, *supra* note 33, at 77 (noting that author's "search of the literature of the time reveals that no writer disputed or contradicted Coxe's analysis").

[293] Letter from Nasson to Thatcher (July 9, 1789), *reprinted in Creating the Bill of Rights*, *supra* note 82, at 260–61 (sic); *see id.* at 309 (brief biography of Nasson).

Like Coxe and others, Nasson understood "the people" as distinct from the government, and included in "the right" of the people private ownership and private uses of arms.

In late July 1789, a committee, to which had been referred both Madison's proposals and all amendments that ratifying conventions had proposed, issued a revised draft. It provided:

> A well regulated militia, composed of the body of the people, being the best security of a free state, the right of the people to keep and bear arms shall not be infringed, but no person religiously scrupulous shall be compelled to bear arms.[294]

The Committee had left unchanged the text of Madison's independent clause stating the right. But it had inverted the first two clauses, modified the language regarding the militia to return it somewhat to what had been proposed by some of the state conventions (including by defining the militia), and revised the conscientious objector clause.

There is no reason to suppose that the mere reversal of order, or any of the other changes, had altered the right that Madison, and the ratifying conventions before him, had set out: The operative text of the independent clause was unchanged from Madison's draft, with the militia clause retaining its subordinate relationship; Madison had served on the committee, which does not seem to have had any serious disagreements over content;[295] and the committee had retained Madison's proposal that this amendment, along with the rest of the "Bill of Rights," be placed among the three pre-existing individual rights in Article I, Section 9, albeit moved forward one clause.[296] In the ensuing debates, no member of the House suggested that any change in the right had occurred. The Speaker of the House, from Pennsylvania, wrote to a leading fellow Federalist in the state that the committee's proposals "take[] in the principal Amendments which our Minority had so much at heart"; the Minority had, as discussed above, proposed an individual right to bear arms.[297] And an article in Boston, reprinted in Philadelphia, described the committee's proposal as containing "[e]very one of" the amendments "introduced to the convention of this common-

---

[294] *Creating the Bill of Rights*, *supra* note 82, at 30.

[295] *Id.* at 6, 102–03; *see* Letter from Madison to Wilson Cary Nicholas (Aug. 2, 1789), *reprinted in id.* at 271 (referring to "the concord" of the committee); Letter from Roger Sherman to Henry Gibbs (Aug. 4, 1789), *reprinted in id.* (another committee member, predicting that committee's proposals "will probably be harmless & Satisfactory to those who are fond of Bills of rights," although noting his desire to place them at the end of the Constitution).

[296] *See id.* at 30. The separate placement of what would become the Tenth Amendment remained unchanged, and Madison's other proposals, noted above, also remained separate.

[297] Letter from Rep. Frederick A. Muhlenberg to Benjamin Rush (Aug. 18, 1789), *reprinted in Creating the Bill of Rights*, *supra* note 82, at 280 (writing after the first day of debate that involved the arms provision, in which no changes were made, and describing proposed amendments to date as "nearly the same as" the committee "had reported them").

wealth by . . . Samuel Adams" (except the restriction against a standing army), including that "the said constitution be never construed . . . to prevent the people of the United States who are peaceable citizens, from keeping their own arms."[298] Clearly, the committee's proposed amendment on arms, like Madison's and like Adams's, was understood to protect an individual right.

In floor debate that began in mid-August, the focus was on the concluding exemption for conscientious objectors and thus on militia service rather than "the right of the people" that the committee's draft secured. Representative Gerry of Massachusetts, who had refused to sign the Constitution and was a leading Anti-Federalist,[299] objected that this final clause would enable the federal government to "declare who are those religiously scrupulous, and prevent them from bearing arms." This, he warned, "together with [Congress's] other powers," would enable Congress to "destroy the militia" and establish "a standing army, the bane of liberty."[300] He moved to narrow the clause, but after a debate, including an effort to delete it, the House approved the committee's draft. Immediately after, it resoundingly defeated another Anti-Federalist's motion to require a supermajority to authorize a standing army in peacetime.[301]

It does not appear from the debates that any congressman shared Gerry's concern, but, in any event, his concern seems more consistent with a view that the amendment secured an individual right than with the alternative views. Gerry presumed that the first two clauses—praising the well-regulated militia and setting out the right of the people—would not suffice to protect the militia in the face of affirmative federal efforts to undermine it. The individual right was inadequate to do so. That understanding is consistent with the individual right view, as we explained above in Part II.C. It also was the understanding, and concern, implicit in the dual recommendations of Virginia, North Carolina, and the Pennsylvania Minority, which sought separately to protect both state militia powers and the individual right to arms. In addition, if the "right of the people . . . to bear arms" meant some right restricted to serving in an organized militia, rather than a personal right, Gerry's concern would not have made sense: Persons whom Congress declared religiously scrupulous pursuant to the proposed amendment, although therefore not "*compelled* to bear arms" in the militia, still would, under a

[298] From the Bos. Indep. Chronicle, Phila. Indep. Gazetteer, Aug. 20, 1789, at 2, *excerpted in* Halbrook, *Right to Bear Arms*, *supra* note 56, at 45.

[299] At the Constitutional Convention, Gerry had bitterly opposed the federal powers over the militia in Article I, Section 8, Clause 16. Madison, *Notes of Debates*, *supra* note 44, at 513–16 (Aug. 23, 1787). Regarding his Anti-Federalist writings during ratification, *see* 1 Schwartz, *Bill of Rights*, *supra* note 67, at 464–65, 480–93, he had attended the Massachusetts Convention as an invited observer and helped lead the opposition, *id.* at 465. Presumably, therefore, he supported Samuel Adams's proposed amendments, even though he also desired additional ones. *See id.* at 486–89.

[300] Remarks of Gerry (Aug. 17, 1789), *reprinted in Creating the Bill of Rights*, *supra* note 82, at 182.

[301] *See Creating the Bill of Rights*, *supra* note 82, at 183–85.

quasi-collective right view of the other clauses of the amendment, have some ***right*** to do so, and thus Congress could not, as Gerry charged, "***prevent*** them" from serving.

After more debate over the conscientious objector clause on August 20, the House added back "in person" at the end and approved the draft.[302] It attached all of the amendments to the end of the Constitution rather than incorporating them, but no substantive change was intended.[303] The right of the people to keep and bear arms was the fifth of the seventeen proposed amendments that the House then sent to the Senate.[304]

An Anti-Federalist who during the ratification debates had written widely published essays as "Centinel" was enraged enough by the House's failure to restrict federal, and protect state, power that he took up his pen again, as Centinel Revived.[305] He denounced "the partial amendments making [sic] by Congress" and lamented that, although "many of these amendments are very proper and necessary, yet . . . the constitution is suffered to retain powers that may not only defeat their salutary operation, but may, and incontrovertibly will be so decisively injurious as to sweep away every vestige of liberty." He highlighted the Second Amendment for criticism:

> It is remarkable that this article only makes the observation, "that a well regulated militia, composed of the *body* of the people, is the best security of a free state"; it does not ordain, or constitutionally provide for, the establishment of such a one. The absolute command vested by other sections in Congress over the militia, are not in the least abridged by this amendment.[306]

---

302 *See id.* at 198–99. The addition may have been an effort to partially satisfy Representative Scott, by ensuring that Congress could at least require conscientious objectors to provide an equivalent. Unlike Gerry, he objected to the exemption because he worried that citizens, rather than Congress, would abuse it, with the result that "you can never depend upon your militia." He added, "This will lead to the violation of another article in the constitution, which secures to the people the right of keeping arms, as in this case you must have recourse to a standing army." *Id.* at 198. While this cryptic and elliptical comment conceivably might be construed to suggest a quasi-collective right, its meaning is far from clear, and we find little probative value in it. The Fifth Circuit in *Emerson* reasonably concluded that Scott's comment "does not plainly lend support to any of the Second Amendment models," 270 F.3d at 248, and the Ninth Circuit in *Silveira* did not cite it, *see* 312 F.3d at 1085–86.

303 *See Creating the Bill of Rights, supra* note 82, at 117–28 (debate of Aug. 13, 1789); *id.* at 197–98 (debate of Aug. 19, 1789).

304 *Id.* at 37–41.

305 "The most prolific and one of the best known of the Anti-Federalist essayists was the Centinel, whose essays appeared in the Philadelphia *Independent Gazetteer* and the Philadelphia *Freeman's Journal* and were widely reprinted." 2 *Complete Anti-Federalist, supra* note 101, at 130. He published twelve essays as Centinel Revived. *Id.*

306 *Centinel (Revived), No. 29* (1789), Phila. Indep. Gazetteer, Sept. 9, 1789, *quoted in Emerson,* 270 F.3d at 255.

Centinel understood the Second Amendment not to constrain Congress's Article I, Section 8 "absolute command" over the militia or otherwise secure any power of the states to maintain one (whether by creating a "right" of states or of the members of their organized militia units), and understood the Amendment's prefatory praise of the militia—a mere "observation"—not to have any operative effect. The reasonable inference is that he viewed the "right of the people to keep and bear arms" as one belonging to individuals.

The Senate reduced the House's proposed amendments to twelve in early September.[307] In so doing, it made three changes in what would become the Second Amendment: (1) deleting "composed of the body of the people," (2) replacing "the best" with "necessary to the," and (3) deleting the conscientious objector clause. It also voted down a motion to insert "for the common defense" immediately after "to keep and bear Arms."[308] The Senate deliberated in secret, and its minutes are conclusory, so it is difficult to discern the reasons for these changes. One could argue that some of them (deletion of the conscientious objector clause and rejection of the "common defense" clause) tend to support the individual right view of the Amendment, although contrary arguments are no doubt possible.[309] One also could argue that deletion of the definition of the militia cuts against the individual right view's reading of the prefatory language, although there, too, a counter-argument is possible.[310] Because of the lack of historical records and the multiple possible explanations, we are reluctant to attribute any material significance to these actions.

We do, however, find it significant that the Senate rejected a motion to add a separate amendment securing state power to organize, arm, and discipline the militias if Congress should "omit or neglect" to do so.[311] Notwithstanding the lack of historical records of the deliberations on this motion, the broader historical

---

[307] The Senate combined provisions (such as in creating what became the First and Fifth Amendments) and rejected House provisions regulating appeals to the Supreme Court; applying religion, speech, press, and criminal jury protections to the states; and prohibiting violations of the separation of powers. *See* 2 Schwartz, *Bill of Rights*, *supra* note 67, at 1145–47 (summarizing changes); *compare Creating the Bill of Rights*, *supra* note 82, at 37–41 (House proposals), *with id.* at 47–49 (Senate).

[308] *See Creating the Bill of Rights*, *supra* note 82, at 39 n.13; 2 Schwartz, *Bill of Rights*, *supra* note 67, at 1153–54 (Sen. Journal).

[309] *See* Uviller & Merkel, *supra* note 45, 76 Chi.-Kent L. Rev. at 507 (theorizing that vote on common defense clause was prompted by desire to avoid either redundancy or the objection that the amendment failed to protect militia service in defense of a state, as opposed to the "common" national defense). The deletion of the troublesome conscientious objector clause could have been simply because of a desire, as voiced in the House, to leave the matter to Congress's discretion, *see, e.g.*, Remarks of Rep. Benson (Aug. 17, 1789), *reprinted in Creating the Bill of Rights*, *supra* note 82, at 184, without affecting the right one way or the other.

[310] One could argue that the definition was considered superfluous. *See* 2 Schwartz, *Bill of Rights*, *supra* note 67, at 1145 (observing that Senate in its revisions of the House proposals generally "tighten[ed] up the language of the House version, striking out surplus wording and provisions."); Part II.C.2–4 (discussing meaning of "Militia" at the time).

[311] 2 Schwartz, *Bill of Rights*, *supra* note 67, at 1152 (Sen. Journal).

context suggests that, had Congress sought to secure the states' ability to maintain organized militia units, adopting this provision is how it would have done so. It is hard to ascribe this vote to a view that the proposed amendment was redundant with the right of the people to keep and bear arms: Not only are the texts of the two provisions markedly different, but also, as explained in the previous subpart, the Virginia and North Carolina Ratifying Conventions (from which the rejected language was directly taken) had made distinct proposals, one covering the right to arms and the other covering state power over the militia (the Pennsylvania Minority also had done this). In addition, the Senate was even more Federalist than the House (Lee and Grayson of Virginia being the only Anti-Federalists among the 22 senators).[312] As already noted, the Federalists were determined to avoid amendments affecting the federal-state balance of power and instead to focus on individual rights. If senators had thought that what became the Second Amendment had the effect of this rejected provision, one would have expected them to have refused to approve it as well. Finally, the two Anti-Federalist senators acknowledged that their efforts to obtain amendments affecting the federal-state balance had failed. Senator Lee, like Centinel, complained, in a letter to Patrick Henry, that the amendments were inadequate for "securing the due Authority of the States."[313] Senators Lee and Grayson jointly informed the Virginia legislature of their failure to secure the "Radical Amendments proposed by the Convention."[314] Thus, the Senate continued the House's approach—rejecting attempts to restrict congressional powers or augment state powers, while securing individual rights in the hope of creating a national consensus in favor of the new government.

On September 24, 1789, a conference committee agreed to some changes in the Senate's proposed amendments, but there was no change in (or effort to change) the Senate's version of what became the Second Amendment. Congress, through the President, then sent the twelve proposed amendments to the then-eleven states for ratification and to North Carolina and Rhode Island (which still had not ratified the Constitution).[315] The records of the state ratifying conventions are sparse and do not appear to provide any significant material concerning the meaning of the

---

[312] *See Creating the Bill of Rights*, *supra* note 82, at xii; Letter from Madison to Jefferson (Mar. 29, 1789), *reprinted in id.* at 225.

[313] Letter from Lee to Henry (Sept. 14, 1789), *reprinted in id.* at 295. The Senate also, like the House, had rejected a proposal to append to what became the Second Amendment a supermajority requirement for peacetime standing armies, a provision to help ensure that Congress would depend on and therefore provide for the militia. 2 Schwartz, *Bill of Rights*, *supra* note 67, at 1149 (Sen. Journal); *see Creating the Bill of Rights*, *supra* note 82, at 38–39 n.13.

[314] Letter from Lee and Grayson to the Speaker of the Virginia House of Delegates (Sept. 28, 1789), *reprinted in Creating the Bill of Rights*, *supra* note 82, at 299.

[315] *See id.* at 49–50 (Conference Committee Report and House Resolution); *id.* at 296–98 (various letters of Sept. 1789, including by Madison, detailing concerns with certain Senate revisions but not mentioning Second Amendment); 2 Schwartz, *Bill of Rights*, *supra* note 67, at 1171–73 (regarding presidential transmittal).

Second Amendment right.[316] The states approved ten of the twelve proposed amendments, and in March 1792, Secretary of State Jefferson officially declared the Bill of Rights ratified.[317]

The history in this subpart of the immediate development of the Second Amendment reveals a right consistent with, and developed from, the individual right to arms that had been inherited from England, recognized and invoked in revolutionary America, and codified to various extents in early state declarations of rights. In addition, the early states prized a well-regulated citizen militia, as some of their declarations recognized, and understood the individual right to arms to facilitate such a militia. The Second Amendment, following the lead of several of the ratifying conventions, reflects the contemporaneous understanding of this relationship; in so doing, it grants the right to "the people," not to the "Militia" (much less to members of select militia units), or to the "State." Nor does the history support limiting the right secured by the Amendment to any of these entities. Indeed, those who wanted to ensure that the states could have fully functioning militias proposed a separate amendment, expressly protecting state power. Their proposals failed.[318] Thus, the history of the Amendment, like its text, indicates that the Second Amendment's "right of the people to keep and bear Arms" is not collective or quasi-collective but rather is a personal right that belongs to individuals.

IV. The Early Interpretations

Our analysis of the Second Amendment's text and history in the two preceding parts of this memorandum is supported by the views of those who first interpreted the Amendment. In the generations immediately following its ratification, the three leading commentators to consider the Second Amendment each recognized that its right of the people to keep and bear arms belonged to individuals, not to states and not just to members of militias (whether of organized, select militia units or even of the citizen militia). Nearly all of the discussions of the antebellum courts, including in the leading cases, understood the right in the same way, whether they were considering the Second Amendment or similar provisions in

---

[316] *See* 2 Schwartz, *Bill of Rights*, *supra* note 67, at 1171–72 ("[W]e know practically nothing about what went on in the state legislatures during the ratification process" and "[e]ven the contemporary newspapers are virtually silent."); *Emerson*, 270 F.3d at 255 (without comment, omitting discussion of ratification); *Silveira*, 312 F.3d at 1086 (same).

[317] 2 Schwartz, *Bill of Rights*, *supra* note 67, at 1171, 1203. One of the two not then ratified was ratified in 1992 as the Twenty-Seventh Amendment, which relates to congressional pay. The other addressed the size of the House.

[318] And even if one believes, contrary to the historical record, that Anti-Federalists' concerns about the militia were resolved in their favor, the Anti-Federalists' insistence on the superiority of a citizen militia to a select militia, noted at the beginning of Part III.C, would lead to the understanding of the Amendment's prefatory clause that we set out in Part II.C, an understanding that is, as we explained, fully consistent with the individual right view of the Second Amendment.

state constitutions. This early understanding of a personal right continued at least through Reconstruction. The modern alternative views of the Second Amendment did not take hold until 1905, well over a century after the Amendment had been ratified.

A. The First Commentators

In the first few decades after the Second Amendment was drafted and ratified, each of the three leading commentators on the Constitution addressed it: St. George Tucker, William Rawle, and Joseph Story. Each agreed that it protects an individual right. Less prominent early commentators also concurred with this interpretation.

Tucker, a judge and law professor from Virginia, published in 1803 an edition of Blackstone's *Commentaries* to which he had added annotations and essays explaining the relation of American law, including the new Constitution, to England's. Tucker's Blackstone quickly became the leading American authority on both Blackstone and American law.[319]

Tucker addressed the Second Amendment at several points. He first did so, repeatedly, in his introductory *View of the Constitution of the United States*. He tied the federal right, as Blackstone had the English one, to the individual, natural right of self-defense and to the freedom of the state. After quoting the Amendment, he wrote:

> This may be considered as the true palladium of liberty . . . . The right of self defence is the first law of nature: in most governments it has been the study of rulers to confine this right within the narrowest limits possible. Wherever standing armies are kept up, and the right of the people to keep and bear arms is, under any colour or pretext whatsoever, prohibited, liberty, if not already annihilated, is on the brink of destruction.[320]

He condemned the use of the game laws in England as a pretext to disarm ordinary people—the "farmer, or inferior tradesman, or other person not qualified to kill game."[321] And he grouped the Second Amendment right with those of the First, confirming that all belonged to individuals:

---

[319] *See* Clyde N. Wilson, Forward, *in* St. George Tucker, *View of the Constitution of the United States, with Selected Writings* at viii–ix (1999); Paul Finkelman & David Cobin, An Introduction to St. George Tucker's *Blackstone's Commentaries*, *in* 1 Tucker's Blackstone, *supra* note 60, at v–xii; 1 *id.*, Editor's Preface at v.

[320] 1 Tucker's Blackstone, *supra* note 60, Note D, at 300 (ellipsis in original).

[321] *Id.*

> If, for example, a law be passed by congress, prohibiting the free exercise of religion, according to the dictates, or persuasions of a man's own conscience; or abridging the freedom of speech, or of the press; or the right of the people to assemble peaceably, or to keep and bear arms; it would, in any of these cases, be the province of the judiciary to pronounce whether any such act were constitutional, or not; and if not, to acquit the accused . . . .[322]

Second, in annotating Blackstone's description, in Book I, Chapter 1, of the individual English subject's right to have and use arms for self-defense (discussed above in Part III.A), Tucker praised the Second Amendment "right of the people" for being "without any qualification as to their condition or degree, as is the case in the British government" (under England's Bill of Rights) and again denounced the game laws, by which "the right of keeping arms is effectually taken away from the people of England."[323] Finally, in a note to one of Blackstone's (critical) discussions of the game laws, Tucker once more attacked them, because "it seems to be held" that no one but the very rich has "any right to keep a gun in his house" or "keep a gun for their defence," the result being that "the whole nation are completely disarmed, and left at the mercy of the government," and "the mass of the people" are kept "in a state of the most abject subjection." By contrast, "in America we may reasonably hope that the people will never cease to regard the right of keeping and bearing arms as the surest pledge of their liberty."[324]

In all of these discussions, the right belonged to individuals—to persons availing themselves of the natural, individual "right of self defence," to the "accused" seeking judicial review of a violation of the Second Amendment, and to "the mass" of ordinary people able to defend themselves because protected by the Second Amendment from class-based pretexts for disarmament. Tucker understood both the English and American rights to arms to belong to individuals, and he thought the latter more secure and broad-based.

Nowhere did Tucker suggest that the right of the people to keep and bear arms depended on a person's enrollment and exercise in the citizen militia (much less his membership in an organized, select militia unit) or that it was a "right" that belonged to state governments. He did elsewhere, in discussing the Militia Clauses, point out that the Second Amendment eliminated "all room for doubt, or

[322] *Id.* at 357; *see id.* at 315–16 (explaining that, whereas in England, "the game-laws, as was before observed, have been converted into the means of disarming the body of the people," and statutes have restricted assemblies, the Constitution will not "permit any prohibition of arms to the people; or of peaceable assemblies by them"); *id.* at 289 (describing hypothetical law "prohibiting any person from bearing arms" as violating the Second Amendment).

[323] 2 *id.* at *143–44 & nn. 40–41. *See also id.* at *145 n.42 (again criticizing game laws).

[324] 3 *id.* at *414 n.3; *see also* Parts III.A (discussing right to arms in England) & III.B.2 (discussing doubts whether the relaxation of English game laws in 1700s succeeded as a practical matter in enabling commoners to keep arms).

uneasiness" on whether the federal government could prohibit states from simply providing arms for their militias (doubt he rightly found questionable given that the original Constitution left a concurrent arming power in the states).[325] Tucker did not suggest here that he thought the Amendment had only this effect, and his other discussions confirm that he did not so understand it.

William Rawle of Pennsylvania published his *View of the Constitution of the United States of America* in 1825, with a second edition appearing in 1829. After having turned down President Washington's offer to be the first attorney general, he had served in the Pennsylvania Assembly when it ratified the Bill of Rights. His commentary, like Tucker's, gained wide prominence.[326]

Rawle analyzed the Second Amendment in a chapter entitled "Of the Restrictions on the Powers of Congress . . . [,] Restrictions on the Powers of States and Security to *the Rights of Individuals*," by which he meant, respectively, Article I, Section 9; Article I, Section 10; and the first eight amendments of the Bill of Rights.[327] He started with the Second Amendment's preface, giving to it, including the word "Militia," precisely the sense and significance that emerges from our analysis above, and making clear that the substantive right belonged to the ordinary citizen:

> In the second article, it is declared, that *a well regulated militia is necessary to the security of a free state*; a proposition from which few will dissent. Although in actual war, the services of regular troops are confessedly more valuable; yet, while peace prevails, and in the commencement of a war before a regular force can be raised, the militia form the palladium of the country. . . . That they should be well regulated, is judiciously added. . . . The duty of the state government is, to adopt such regulations as will tend to make good soldiers with the least interruptions of the ordinary and useful occupations of civil life. . . .
>
> The corollary, from the first position, is, that *the right of the people to keep and bear arms shall not be infringed.*

[325] 1 *id.* at 273. Tucker thought the federal powers in Article I, Section 8, Clause 16, to provide for "organizing" and "disciplining" the militia were exclusive, *id.* at 180–81, but that states retained "concurrent, though perhaps subordinate" powers to provide for "arming" their militias and "to call them forth when necessary for their internal defence," *id.* at 182, 183. His only other reference to the Second Amendment in connection with the militia was in a note to Blackstone's discussion of the militia, in which Tucker collected all references in the Constitution to the militia, along with the Third Amendment, Virginia laws, and the federal Militia Act. 2 *id.* at *409 n.1.

[326] *See* Hardy, *supra* note 33, 9 Harv. J.L. & Pub. Pol'y at 613. Rawle did agree to be United States Attorney for the District of Pennsylvania. *See, e.g., United States v. Fries*, 3 U.S. (3 Dall.) 515, 517 (C.C.D. Pa. 1799).

[327] William Rawle, *A View of the Constitution of the United States of America* 115 (2d ed. 1829; reprint 1970) (font altered; emphasis added).

> The prohibition is general. No clause in the Constitution could by any rule of construction be conceived to give to congress a power to disarm the people. Such a flagitious attempt could only be made under some general pretence by a state legislature. But if in any blind pursuit of inordinate power, either should attempt it, this amendment may be appealed to as a restraint on both.[328]

Both Rawle's language—the Amendment's prohibition "is general" and protects the arms of "the people"—and his view of the Second Amendment as applying to the states and *restricting* their power indicate that he saw the right as individual, not as collective or quasi-collective.

Two additional points further show that Rawle viewed the right as belonging to individuals. Like Tucker, he favorably contrasted the right of the people that the Second Amendment secured with the more selective individual right in England under the aristocratic game laws, including a summary of Blackstone's critique of those laws. In addition, he expressly recognized, as had Blackstone, Tucker, and, in varying degrees, the Pennsylvania Minority, Samuel Adams, and the New Hampshire Ratifying Convention, that the right provided no warrant to breach the peace, including by inciting reasonable fear of a breach.[329] This recognition indicates an individual right view because there is no need for ordinary criminal law to oversee either the actions of states in regulating their militias or the bearing of arms by members of a state's militia in connection with their service and under state regulation.

Rawle further explained the individual right view's understanding of the Second Amendment preface when discussing the President's limited power to command the militia. Although not mentioning the Amendment expressly, he noted: "In a people permitted and accustomed to bear arms, we have the rudiments of a militia, which properly consists of armed citizens, divided into military bands, and instructed at least in part in the use of arms for the purposes of war."[330] Thus, the "people" of the country, as individuals, keep and bear arms for private purposes; they also form the militia; and the former facilitates the latter, but only as a rudiment. That is why the individual right is a "corollary" from the need for a militia.

The same view appears in the influential 1833 *Commentaries on the Constitution of the United States* of Supreme Court Justice and law professor Joseph Story,

---

[328] *Id.* at 125–26.

[329] *Id.* at 126. Regarding Blackstone, see Part III.A above. For Tucker's annotations of some of Blackstone's discussions of improper uses of arms, *see* 5 Tucker's Blackstone, *supra* note 60, at *126, *142–49, *175. Regarding the Pennsylvania Minority, Adams, and New Hampshire, see Part III.C.1 above.

[330] Rawle, *View of the Constitution*, *supra* note 327, at 153. Significantly, in separately discussing the Militia Clauses of Article I, Section 8, Rawle made no mention of the Second Amendment. *Id.* at 111–12.

as well as in his later *Familiar Exposition* of the Constitution. The *Commentaries* appeared first in a three-volume set and then, a few months later, in a one-volume abridgement by Story (the "*Abridgement*").[331]

Story devoted a chapter of his *Abridgement* to the Bill of Rights. Before turning to its provisions, he recounted the debate over whether to add one and identified several purposes, all related to individual rights: (1) to prevent powers granted to the government from being exercised in a way "dangerous to the people"; (2) as part of "the muniments of freemen, showing their title to protection," to ensure against an "extravagant or undue extention of" powers granted; and (3) to protect minorities.[332] He then singled out those amendments that did not relate to judicial procedure (the First, Second, Third, Fourth, Eighth, Ninth, and Tenth) as those addressing "subjects properly belonging to a bill of rights."[333]

With regard to the Second Amendment, he first explained the importance of the militia for "a free country," including as a check on "domestic usurpations of power," and the hazards "for a free people" of keeping up "large military establishments and standing armies in time of peace." He linked these policies to the right: "The right of the citizens to keep, and bear arms has justly been considered, as the palladium of the liberties of a republic; since it offers a strong moral check against the usurpation and arbitrary power of rulers; and will generally, even if these are successful in the first instance, enable the people to resist and triumph over them."[334] In the unabridged version, he cited Tucker, Rawle, and the House of Representatives' first day of debate on the Amendment in support of this sentence.[335]

By paraphrasing the "right of the people" as the "right of the citizens"—not of states or members of their militias—as well as by citing Tucker and Rawle's discussions (including borrowing from Tucker's "palladium" language), Story left no doubt that he considered the right to belong to individuals. He reinforced this point in an additional paragraph in the unabridged version, citing both Blackstone's discussion of the "similar provision" in England—clearly an individual right, as explained above—and Tucker's discussion of what Story called the "defensive privilege" there.[336] In his *Familiar Exposition*, Story began his discus-

---

[331] Ronald D. Rotunda & John E. Nowak, Introduction, *in* Story, *Abridgement*, *supra* note 66, at xi–xiv.

[332] *Id.* §§ 980–982, at 696–97.

[333] *Id.* § 984, at 698; *see id.* §§ 985–1011, at 698–714.

[334] *Id.* § 1001, at 708.

[335] 3 Story, *Commentaries*, *supra* note 75, § 1890, at 746 n.1. In *United States v. Miller*, 307 U.S. 174, 182 n.3 (1939), the Supreme Court included this passage (from a later edition) in a string citation.

[336] 3 Story, *Commentaries*, *supra* note 75, § 1891, at 747. In a separate chapter, the full *Commentaries* also included an extended discussion of the Anti-Federalist charges leveled against the Militia Clauses, including the charge that the federal militia powers would be exclusive (which Story found unpersuasive). Story alluded to the failure of proposals explicitly to protect state militia powers. *Id.* §§ 1198–1202, at 83–87.

sion of the Amendment with an even more explicit statement: "One of the ordinary modes, by which tyrants accomplish their purposes without resistance, is, by disarming the people, and making it an offence to keep arms, and by substituting a regular army in the stead of a resort to the militia."[337]

Thus Story, like Tucker, Rawle, and others, recognized that the right that the Second Amendment secured was an individual one. He also saw, as they had, that this personal right was necessary for ensuring a well-regulated militia of the people. But he likewise recognized, consistent with the individual right view, that such a right was not sufficient for ensuring such an entity, wondering how it would be "practicable to keep the people duly armed without some organization," and lamenting the decline of militia discipline.[338]

Less prominent commentators shared Tucker, Rawle, and Story's view of the Second Amendment as securing an individual right. Most significant of these was probably Henry Tucker (son of St. George). In an 1831 commentary, he explained:

> The right of bearing arms—which with us is not limited and restrained by an arbitrary system of game laws as in England; but is practically enjoyed by every citizen, and is among his most valuable privileges, since it furnishes the means of resisting as a freeman ought, the inroads of usurpation.[339]

He also noted that the right inherited from England and expounded by Blackstone "is secured with us by" the Second Amendment.[340] And Jonathan Elliot, in his record of the ratification debates first published in the 1830s, provided an index of the Constitution that, under the heading "*Rights of the citizen* declared to be," listed each of the rights of the first nine amendments of the Bill of Rights, including "To keep and bear arms."[341] He grouped the right secured by the Second Amendment with the unquestionably individual rights secured by its neighbors. There was no entry in the index for the militia or its members, aside from reference to the congressional powers in Article I, Section 8, and none of his entries regarding the states included reference to the militia or the Second Amendment.[342] Thus, these early commentators were all consistent in recognizing that the Second

---

[337] Joseph Story, *A Familiar Exposition of the Constitution of the United States* § 450, at 319 (1840; reprint 1986).

[338] Story, *Abridgement*, *supra* note 66, § 1001, at 708–09.

[339] Henry St. George Tucker, *Commentaries on the Laws of Virginia* 43 (1831).

[340] *Id.*

[341] *The Debates in the Several State Conventions on the Adoption of the Federal Constitution* xv (Jonathan Elliot ed., 2d ed. 1836; reprint 1987).

[342] For additional antebellum commentators, see David B. Kopel, *The Second Amendment in the Nineteenth Century*, 1998 BYU L. Rev. 1359, 1399–1403, 1435–41; *see also id.* at 1397–98 (discussing Henry Tucker).

Amendment secures an individual right. They did not even mention possible alternative views, whether involving a collective or a quasi-collective "right."

B. The First Cases

Like the commentators, the early case law also treated the Second Amendment as securing a right of individuals, not a right of governments or those in its service. Without taking any position on the correctness of the courts' holdings or the constitutionality, under the Second Amendment, of any particular limitations on owning, carrying, or using firearms, we find it significant that these decisions consistently understood the right to be an individual one. The earliest cases, although not numerous, consistently recognized that the right to "bear" arms belonged to individuals, just as the right to "keep" them did. Judicial treatment became more common beginning in the 1840s, mostly because of new prohibitions on carrying weapons concealed. The courts upheld these prohibitions (some courts applying the Second Amendment and some applying similar state provisions), but in so doing they all recognized an individual right to arms: All of the decisions recognized an individual right to keep private arms; nearly all, including the leading cases, recognized a right of individuals to "bear" those arms for private purposes; and all recognized some manner of individual right to bear them. Most notably, the Supreme Court of Georgia twice unanimously ruled in favor of individuals on the basis of the Second Amendment.

1. Cases Before 1840

The first of the early cases is *Houston v. Moore*, in 1820. The Supreme Court, in upholding Pennsylvania's power to try a militiaman for failing to report for federal service in the War of 1812, recognized that states had concurrent power to regulate their militias at least when the militias were in the service of their state or in the absence of congressional regulation. Yet it did not mention the Second Amendment. Justice Story, in dissent, also recognized the concurrent power, and he noted that the Second Amendment was probably irrelevant to the question.[343] As we explained above in Part III.C.1, the Anti-Federalists who claimed to fear that the federal militia powers would not allow a concurrent state jurisdiction did not rely on the proposals for a right to arms to resolve their concern, but rather proposed separate amendments (which failed to pass). It appears that the Court in *Houston* similarly recognized that the Second Amendment did not guard state power to maintain militias, whether by creating a collective right of states or a quasi-collective right of militiamen to vindicate state power. Otherwise, one would

[343] *Houston v. Moore*, 18 U.S. (5 Wheat.) 1, 16–17, 21–22 (1820) (plurality opinion of Washington, J.); *see id.* at 34–36 (Johnson, J., concurring); *id.* at 50–53 (Story, J., dissenting). Story dissented on the ground that the militia law granted enforcement authority exclusively to federal courts. *Id.* at 71–72.

expect the Court to have discussed it. Thus, *Houston*, although far from conclusive, lends some support to an individual right view.

Second, in *Bliss v. Commonwealth* (1822), in what appears to be the first judicial interpretation of the right to bear arms in America, a divided highest court of Kentucky applied that state's constitutional protection of "the right of the citizens to bear arms in defense of themselves and the state," first adopted in 1792, to void a ban on wearing certain weapons concealed.[344] The state had argued that the ban merely restricted the manner of exercising the right. The court, although not citing authority, gave two primary reasons for rejecting this argument: (1) the right in 1792 included carrying weapons concealed, and (2) to recognize this one exception would leave no principled basis to reject others, eviscerating the right.[345] The court's specific holding was rejected thereafter—by courts[346] and by the people of Kentucky, who in their 1850 constitution added a clause allowing laws to prevent carrying concealed arms.[347] But the holding was rejected, not on the ground that it improperly recognized a right of individuals to "bear arms" (Kentucky's provision remained otherwise unchanged), but rather on the ground that *Bliss* erred in determining the right's scope. Thus *Bliss* confirms the individual nature of the right.

Third, several early references to the right or to "bearing arms" indicate that courts viewed the right as an individual one, or at least that an individual carrying weapons and not in militia service could be said to "bear arms." A Virginia appellate court in 1824, discussing that state's restrictions on the rights of free blacks—"many of which are inconsistent with the letter and spirit of the Constitution, both of this State and of the United States"—cited the restriction "upon their right to bear arms."[348] That the restriction involved their rights as individuals is evident from Tucker's summary of the Virginia laws.[349] In an 1829 libel case, the Supreme Court of Michigan (then a territory) drew a parallel between the freedoms of speech and press and the right of the people to bear arms to explain that

---

[344] 12 Ky. (2 Litt.) 90, 1822 WL 1085. The dissenting judge did not issue an opinion. *See id.* at *4.

[345] *Id.* at *2.

[346] The first court to depart from *Bliss*'s holding, the Indiana Supreme Court eleven years later in *State v. Mitchell*, 3 Blackf. 229, 1833 WL 2617, at *1, did not cite its neighboring court or otherwise explain itself, the entire opinion being as follows: "It was ***held*** in this case, that the statute of 1831, prohibiting all persons, except travelers, from wearing or carrying concealed weapons, is not unconstitutional." We discuss the later antebellum cases in the next subpart.

[347] *See* Ky. Const. art. XIII, § 25 (1850), *reprinted in* 3 *Federal and State Constitutions*, *supra* note 78, at 1314.

[348] *Aldridge v. Commonwealth*, 4 Va. (2 Va. Cas.) 447, 1824 WL 1072, at *3 (Va. Gen. Ct.).

[349] 5 Tucker's Blackstone, *supra* note 60, at *175 n.17, ¶ 7 (listing as among the "offences against the public police, or [e]conomy," the restriction against "any" black or mulatto "keeping or carrying any gun-powder, shot, club, or other weapon," including a "gun"). *See also Waters v. State*, 1 Gill. 302, 1843 WL 3024 (Md.) (explaining, with regard to free blacks, that "laws have been passed to prevent their migration to this State; to make it unlawful for them to bear arms; to guard even their religious assemblages with peculiar watchfulness.").

individual rights are not unlimited: "The constitution of the United States also grants to the citizen the right to keep and bear arms. But the grant of this privilege cannot be construed into the right in him who keeps a gun to destroy his neighbor."[350] And in a jury instruction while riding circuit in 1833, in a case unrelated to the militia, U.S. Supreme Court Justice Baldwin included the Amendment in a list of potentially relevant individual rights.[351]

Last of the earliest cases is the 1833 decision of the Supreme Court of Tennessee in *Simpson v. State*.[352] The question was the validity of a boilerplate indictment alleging that the defendant had appeared in a "public street and highway . . . arrayed in a warlike manner" and then "to the great terror and disturbance of divers good citizens . . . an affray did make . . . against the peace and dignity of the state."[353] The court held the indictment invalid because it alleged neither fighting (an element of "affray") nor any other act likely to have caused public terror and indictable at common law. The court reached this conclusion first by considering the common law, particularly as set out by Blackstone. But because there was some uncertainty regarding the common law, the court also relied on the 1796 Tennessee Constitution, which provided "that the freemen of this state have a right to keep and to bear arms for their common defence."[354] This right eliminated any doubt whether merely appearing in public armed could create "terror" and thus be criminal: "By this clause of the constitution, an express power is given and secured to all the free citizens of the state to keep and bear arms for their defence, without any qualification whatever as to their kind or nature."[355] The court recognized that individuals could "bear arms" for private purposes, just as they could "keep" them, and included self-defense within "their common defence." Thus, in the first four decades after the Founding, the courts were consistent in recognizing that the right to keep and bear arms was a right of individuals,

---

[350] *United States v. Sheldon*, 5 Blume Sup. Ct. Trans. 337, 1829 WL 3021, at *12 (Mich. Terr.). *See also Commonwealth v. Blanding*, 20 Mass. (3 Pick.) 304, 338 (1825) (invoking right to keep arms to draw same analogy).

[351] *Johnson v. Tompkins*, 13 F. Cas. 840, 850 (C.C.E.D. Pa. 1833) (No. 7,416).

[352] 13 Tenn. (5 Yer.) 356, 1833 WL 1227.

[353] 1833 WL 1227, at *1.

[354] *Id.* For more regarding the relevant common law, see the discussion in *State v. Huntly*, 25 N.C. (3 Ired.) 418, 1843 WL 891, at *2–3 (surveying common law and noting "that the carrying of a gun *per se* constitutes no offence"). *See also State v. Langford*, 10 N.C. (3 Hawks) 381, 1824 WL 380; 4 William Blackstone, *Commentaries* *149; 1 Hawkins, *Pleas of the Crown*, *supra* note 177, ch. 63, § 9, at 136. An English case that the court cited in *Huntly*, predating the English Declaration of Rights, had construed a seemingly restrictive medieval statute as only punishing "people who go armed to terrify the king's subjects," not all who go armed. *Sir John Knight's Case*, 87 Eng. Rep. 75, 76, 3 Mod. Rep. 117 (K.B. 1686). The court recognized that "now there be a general connivance to gentlemen to ride armed for their security," such that violating the statute required riding "malo animo." *Id.*, 90 Eng. Rep. 330, 330, Comberbach Rep. 38.

[355] 1833 WL 1227, at *1.

allowing both the keeping of private arms and the bearing of them for private purposes.

2. Cases From 1840 to the Civil War

The leading case from the antebellum period on the right to bear arms, and the first major decision, was *State v. Reid* in 1840. The Supreme Court of Alabama unanimously upheld the state's new ban on carrying guns or knives secretly, finding no violation of the provision in the state's 1819 constitution that "[e]very citizen has a right to bear arms, in defence of himself and the State."[356] In so doing, the court recognized that the provision's right to "bear arms" was a right of an individual, who could bear them to facilitate his self-defense. The court first looked to the origins of the right in the "provisions in favor of the liberty of the subject" in the English Declaration of Rights. Quoting the right of subjects to have arms for their defense, the court explained: "The evil which was intended to be remedied by the provision quoted, was a denial of the right of Protestants to have arms for their defence, and not an inhibition to wear them secretly."[357]

The court then adopted the state's factual argument that carrying weapons concealed did not facilitate self-defense but rather served the purpose of aggression and breaching the peace. The court elaborated in explaining the limits of the state's power to enact laws regulating "the manner in which arms shall be borne":

> A statute which, under the pretence of regulating, amounts to a destruction of the right, or which requires arms to be so borne as to render them wholly useless for the purpose of defence, would be clearly unconstitutional. But a law which is intended merely to promote personal security, and to put down lawless aggression and violence, and to that end inhibits the wearing of certain weapons, in such a manner as is calculated to exert an unhappy influence upon the moral feelings of the wearer, by making him less regardful of the personal security of others, does not come in collision with the constitution.[358]

The court thus rejected *Bliss*'s holding: "[The constitution] authorizes him to bear them for the purposes of defending himself and the State, and it is only when carried openly, that they can be efficiently used for defence."[359] If the need for defense were immediate, "there can be no necessity for concealing the weapon," and if it were not immediate, there were legal processes for securing protection. If

---

356 1 Ala. 612, 1840 WL 229, at *2.

357 1840 WL 229, at *2.

358 *Id.* at *3.

359 *Id.* at *5–6.

a defendant could prove that it was "indispensable to the right of defence" for him to conceal his weapon, the court might construe the statute not to apply, but Mr. Reid had not done so.[360]

Eighteen years later, the same court in *Owen v. State* reaffirmed *Reid* in recognizing the constitutionality of a similar statute (the legislature, perhaps prompted by *Reid*, had added an exception for those threatened with or reasonably fearing attack). In so doing, the court made explicit what had been implicit in *Reid*—that "carries" in the statute "was used as the synonym of 'bears.'"[361]

Soon after *Reid*, the Supreme Court of Georgia, in *Nunn v. State*, relied on *Reid*, as well as *Bliss*, in unanimously reversing a conviction for *openly* carrying a pistol. The court applied the Second Amendment, holding "that so far as the act . . . seeks to suppress the practice of carrying certain weapons *secretly*, . . . it is valid, inasmuch as it does not deprive the citizen of his *natural* right of self-defence, or of his constitutional right to keep and bear arms. But that so much of it, as contains a prohibition against bearing arms *openly*, is in conflict with the Constitution, and *void*."[362] As had *Reid*, *Nunn* looked for guidance to the right to have and use arms in England. The court viewed that right, the right of the Second Amendment, and the rights protected by the states' constitutions as all securing a personal right of individuals: "When, I would ask, did any legislative body in the Union have the right to deny to its citizens the privilege of keeping and bearing arms in defence of themselves and their country?" Likewise, "the Constitution of the United States, in declaring that the right of the people to keep and bear arms, should not be infringed, only reiterated a truth announced a century before, in the act of 1689."[363] This "right of the people" was just as "comprehensive" and "valuable" as those in the First, Fourth, Fifth, and Sixth Amendments.[364]

Like Rawle and Story, the *Nunn* court recognized the harmony between the Second Amendment's individual right and its preface: "[O]ur Constitution assigns as a reason why this right shall not be interfered with or in any manner abridged, that the free enjoyment of it will prepare and qualify *a well-regulated militia*, which are necessary to the security of a free State." More broadly:

> The right of the whole people, old and young, men, women and boys, and not militia only, to keep and bear arms of every descrip-

[360] *Id.* at *6–7; *see id.* at *1.

[361] 31 Ala. 387, 1858 WL 340, at *1, *2.

[362] 1 Ga. (1 Kelly) 243, 1846 WL 1167, at *11. Georgia's constitution did not expressly protect the right to arms. The court alluded to *Barron v. Mayor & City Council of Baltimore*, 32 U.S. (7 Pet.) 243 (1833), which held that the Takings Clause of the Fifth Amendment did not apply to the states and reasoned that none of the Bill of Rights did, but rejected it because of the court's own precedent, the Second Amendment's broad, non-restrictive language, and the fundamental importance of the right. 1846 WL 1167, at *9–10.

[363] *Id.* at *8.

[364] *Id.* at *10.

> tion, and not such merely as are used by the militia, shall not be infringed, curtailed, or broken in upon, in the smallest degree; and all this for the important end to be attained: the rearing up and qualifying a well-regulated militia, so vitally necessary to the security of a free State.[365]

The preface's reference to the militia as "necessary to the security of a free State" reinforced this understanding and helped convince the court that the Amendment also restricted the states: "If a well-regulated militia is *necessary* to the *security* of the State of Georgia and of the United States, is it competent for the General Assembly to take away this security, by disarming the people?" The right lay "at the bottom of every free government," state or federal.[366] As had Rawle, the court in *Nunn*, by concluding that the Amendment *restricted* the powers of the states, confirmed its view that the Amendment did not protect the powers of the states but rather protected the rights of their individual citizens.

Fifteen years later, the same court reported that *Nunn* had "been constantly adhered to," and unanimously applied it to reverse a jury instruction that, for a weapon to be carried openly, it had to be *entirely* uncovered. Because such carrying was "impossible," such an interpretation "would . . . prohibit the bearing of those arms altogether."[367]

The Louisiana Supreme Court took the same view of the Second Amendment as an individual right in a series of cases in the 1850s. In *State v. Chandler*, a murder defendant had sought an instruction that carrying weapons "either concealed or openly" could not be a crime consistent with the Constitution. The court affirmed the denial of the instruction. Like *Reid* and *Nunn*, the court saw no factual link between carrying weapons concealed and self-defense. But, also like them, it viewed open carrying of arms differently: "This is the right guaranteed by the Constitution of the United States, and which is calculated to incite men to a manly and noble defence of themselves, if necessary, and of their country."[368] Six years later, the court upheld a conviction for carrying a concealed weapon, finding no Second Amendment violation because "[t]he arms there spoken of are such as are borne by a people in war, or at least carried openly."[369] And two years after

[365] *Id.*

[366] *Id.* at *10, *9.

[367] *Stockdale v. State*, 32 Ga. 225, 1861 WL 1336, at *3. The Texas Supreme Court before the Civil War appears also to have viewed the Second Amendment as applying to the states and including an individual right to own arms and use them for self-defense and perhaps hunting. *See Choate v. Redding*, 18 Tex. 579, 1857 WL 5009, at *2; *Cockrum v. State*, 24 Tex. 394, 1859 WL 6446, at *6–8. In the latter case, in which the court rejected a constitutional challenge to a sentencing enhancement for homicide with a bowie knife, the court did not cite any authority, but the defendant had cited *Nunn, Reid, Bliss,* and *Mitchell.* 1859 WL 6446, at *3.

[368] 5 La. Ann. 489, 1850 WL 3838, at *1; *see id.* at *2 (discussing self-defense).

[369] *State v. Smith*, 11 La. Ann. 633, 1856 WL 4793, at *1.

that, the same court cited these decisions in upholding another such conviction, again treating the right as belonging to individuals and understanding "carry" to be synonymous with "bear": "The statute in question . . . . is a measure of police prohibiting only *a particular mode* of bearing arms which is found dangerous to the peace of society."[370]

Two other state court cases of this later antebellum period merit special mention. The first and more significant is *Aymette v. State*,[371] the second, *State v. Buzzard*.[372] In both, the court's holding was unremarkable—that bans on carrying weapons concealed were constitutional. But the courts' rationales were novel. While still recognizing a right to keep and to bear arms that belonged to individuals, these decisions sharply restricted the purposes for which arms could be borne. Unlike *Reid* and *Nunn*, neither case was cited until several years after the Civil War (and then usually just for their holdings), but *Aymette* acquired some prominence thereafter, and *Buzzard* is notable for one judge's separate opinion somewhat foreshadowing the collective and quasi-collective right views.

In *Aymette*, the Tennessee Supreme Court applied that state's 1834 Constitution, which provided "that the free white men of this State have a right to keep and bear arms for their common defence." (The only difference from the provision discussed in *Simpson* was the change of "freemen" to "free white men."[373]) In upholding the defendant's conviction for carrying a concealed bowie knife, the court limited the state right to "bear arms" to actions done "by the people in a body for their common defense."[374] Some have relied on *Aymette*'s reasoning in arguing against the individual right view of the Second Amendment. The Ninth Circuit in *Silveira*, for example, overlooking all of the antebellum cases discussed above, described *Aymette* as "the most significant judicial decision to construe the term 'bear arms'" and as concluding that the phrase "referred to the performance of a military function."[375] *Silveira* particularly relied on *Aymette*'s statement that "'[a] man in pursuit of deer, elk and buffaloes might carry his rifle every day for forty years, and yet it would never be said of him that he had borne arms.'"[376] Fairly read, however, *Aymette* does not contravene an individual right view of the Second Amendment.

First, even assuming for the sake of argument that *Aymette* read the Tennessee Constitution not to secure any individual right to bear arms, the decision has two

---

[370] *State v. Jumel*, 13 La. Ann. 399, 1858 WL 5151, at *1.

[371] 21 Tenn. (2 Hum.) 154, 1840 WL 1554.

[372] 4 Ark. (4 Pike) 18, 1842 WL 331.

[373] That change may have been prompted by Nat Turner's 1831 slave rebellion, which created fears of free blacks arming and inciting slaves. *See* Cottrol & Diamond, *supra* note 33, 80 Geo. L.J. at 337–38.

[374] 1840 WL 1554, at *3.

[375] 312 F.3d at 1073.

[376] *Id.* (quoting *Aymette*, 1840 WL 1554, at *5).

distinctive features that undermine its relevance to the Second Amendment. *Aymette*'s analysis rested heavily on the phrase "for their common defence" in the Tennessee provision, which is absent from the Second Amendment. The phrase pervades the court's brief analysis. The court defined "common" and even described the right to arms in the English Bill of Rights as if it included the word.[377] The court also relied on a conscientious objector clause that appeared elsewhere in the state constitution, citing it at the end of its opinion, in criticizing *Bliss*, to make "the case still more clear."[378] Yet no conscientious objector clause appears in the Second Amendment or even the Constitution.[379]

Second, and more importantly, *Aymette* does not reject an individual right either to keep or to bear arms, even though it may exclude individual self-defense from the meaning of "bear." The court was unequivocal on "keep": "The citizens have the unqualified right to keep the weapon," so long as it is a protected "arm."[380] It did describe "bear" as limited to "military use,"[381] but by that appears still to have contemplated a right that belonged to individuals rather than to the state or those engaged in its service.[382] The court did not mention the militia. Rather, the "military" bearing that it appears to have had in mind was the people, in an extreme case of governmental tyranny, independently bearing arms as a body to check the government. The court confined "bear" to the most radical of emergencies. Thus, it provided the following account of the English Revolution of 1688–1689:

---

[377] 1840 WL 1554, at *3; *see id.* at *2. As noted above in Part III.B.2, in discussing the Massachusetts Declaration of Rights, the phrase "common defense" is not necessarily inconsistent with a right to bear arms for private purposes.

[378] *Id.* at *5. Thus the Ninth Circuit was incorrect in contending that *Aymette* "reached its conclusion primarily because of" the conscientious objector provision, rather than the "common defense" language. *Silveira*, 312 F.3d at 1073. Furthermore, *Aymette*'s reliance on the conscientious objector provision was not persuasive, as our discussions of the Pennsylvania and Vermont declarations of rights (Part III.B.2) and proposals emerging from the Pennsylvania, Virginia, and North Carolina ratifying conventions (Part III.C.1) showed. *See also* Part II.B.2 (discussing meaning of "bear arms"). It was common in a single document to refer separately both to the right of individuals to "bear arms" and to exemption of individuals from the duty to "bear" them in the service of the government. In addition, the court's assertion that a hunter could never be said to "bear" arms, quoted above, is open to doubt, given the proposed Virginia law discussed in Part II.B.2 and the Pennsylvania Minority Report (*see* Parts II.B.2 and III.C.1), and, in any event, says nothing about persons "bearing" arms in self-defense. The court did not cite the decision of its southern neighbor in *Reid*, which appears to have been decided about six months before; it treated its previous discussion of the right in *Simpson* as dicta, 1840 WL 1554, at *5–6.

[379] See Part III.C.2 above (discussing conscientious objector clause in draft of Second Amendment).

[380] 1840 WL 1554, at *4. As we noted in the introduction of Part II.B, the Ninth Circuit, in reaffirming its collective right view, did not attempt to reconcile the right to "keep" arms with its view.

[381] *Id.* at *3, *5.

[382] *See id.* at *4 ("the citizens may bear [arms] for the common defence," but "the Legislature may prohibit such manner of wearing as would never be resorted to by persons engaged in the common defence") (emphasis added).

> [I]f the people had retained their arms, they would have been able, by a just and proper resistance to those oppressive measures, either to have caused the king to respect their rights, or surrender (as he was eventually compelled to do) the government into other hands. No private defence was contemplated, or would have availed anything. . . . [The right in the English Declaration means] that they may as a body rise up to defend their just rights, and compel their rulers to respect the laws. . . . The complaint was against the government. The grievances to which they were thus forced to submit were for the most part of a public character, and could have been redressed only by the people rising up for their common defence, to vindicate their rights.[383]

The court also wrote that the people "may keep arms to protect the public liberty, to keep in awe those in power, and to maintain the supremacy of the laws and the constitution." Citizens need to be prepared "to repel any encroachments upon their rights by those in authority," and the right "is a great political right. It respects the citizens, on the one hand, and the rulers on the other."[384]

Subsequent treatment by the same court confirms that *Aymette,* despite its narrow reading of "bear," still recognized an individual right. In *Andrews v. State,* a prominent case after the Civil War, the Tennessee Supreme Court interpreted the right of the "citizens of this State . . . to keep and bear arms for their common defense" under the state's 1870 constitution. It was not until after *Andrews* that *Aymette,* previously uncited, acquired any prominence.[385] The new constitution had added an exception granting to "the Legislature . . . power by law, to regulate the wearing of arms, with a view to prevent crime," which had been prompted by an

[383] *Id.* at *2.

[384] *Id.* at *3–4. Furthermore, even if one might read the court's rejection of an individual right to bear arms in "private defence" as foreclosing *any* individual right to bear arms, two aspects of the court's reasoning (in addition to its analysis of "bear") leave it open to question. First, the court's account of the English right, *see id.* at *2, was contrary to the text of the English Bill of Rights and Blackstone's exposition of an individual right to arms for self-defense, and failed to recognize that the individual English right was transplanted to America free of England's aristocratic restrictions, as Tucker, Rawle, Story, and others had recognized and praised. Second, faced with the defendant's provocatively absolute claim regarding the scope of the right, *see id.* at *1, the court responded with dichotomies between bearing arms by the body of the people for the common defense and "bearing" arms for hypothetical criminal purposes, such as terrifying people. In thus defining the question, the court defined away the well-established third possibility—bearing arms in legitimate self-defense—and overlooked background law prohibiting bearing weapons for the hypothesized purposes. *Compare id.* at *3–4, *with Simpson,* 1833 WL 1227, at *1; *State v. Huntly,* 25 N.C. (3 Ired.) 418, 1843 WL 891; 4 William Blackstone, *Commentaries* *145–47; *Reid,* 1840 WL 229, at *3, *5–6.

[385] *Andrews v. State,* 50 Tenn. (3 Heisk.) 165, 1871 WL 3579, at *6. *Andrews* was the first case in any jurisdiction to cite *Aymette* regarding the right to bear arms.

enduring dispute between partisans of *Aymette* and *Simpson*.[386] The statute at issue prohibited *any* public or private carrying of "a dirk, swordcane, Spanish stiletto, belt or pocket pistol or revolver."[387] Notwithstanding the added constitutional clause and the arguable implications of *Aymette*, the court held it unconstitutional as applied to certain revolvers.[388]

In reaching this holding, the court went far to assimilate *Aymette* to the reasoning of *Reid* and *Nunn*, even while technically retaining *Aymette*'s view of "bear."[389] It did so in three ways. First, it expressly reaffirmed that at least the right to "keep" belonged to individuals: The "right to bear arms for the common defense . . . may well be held to be a political right, or for protection and maintenance of such rights, intended to be guaranteed; but the right to keep them, with all that is implied fairly as an incident to this right, is a ***private individual right, guaranteed to the citizen, not the soldier***."[390] The court added, relying on Story, that it is "to be exercised and enjoyed by the citizen as such, and not by him as a soldier, or in defense solely of his political rights."[391]

Second, *Andrews* read "keep" expansively to include broad "incidental use," emphasizing that the goal of the right was to ensure that "the citizens making up the yeomanry of the land, the body of the militia," would be prepared when needed. Thus:

> The right to keep arms, necessarily involves the right to purchase them, to keep them in a state of efficiency for use, and to purchase and provide ammunition suitable for such arms, and to keep them in repair. And clearly for this purpose, a man would have the right to carry them to and from his home, and no one could claim that the Legislature had the right to punish him for it, without violating this clause of the Constitution.
>
> But farther than this, it must be held, that the right to keep arms involves, necessarily, the right to use such arms for all the ordinary

[386] *See id.* at *8 ("The Convention of 1870, knowing that there had been differences of opinion on this question, have conferred on the Legislature in this added clause, the right to regulate the wearing of arms, with a view to prevent crime"); *id.* at *13 ("Ever since the opinions were promulgated, it has been my deliberate conviction that the exposition of the Constitution . . . in *Simpson* . . . was much more correct than that . . . in *Aymette* . . . .") (Nelson, J., joined by Turley, J., dissenting in part).

[387] *Id.* at *3.

[388] *Id.* at *11.

[389] *Id.* at *10 (finding "much of interesting and able discussion of these questions" in *Bliss*, *Reid*, and *Nunn*; explaining that in *Reid* and *Nunn* "the general line of argument found in this opinion is maintained" and that the court had been "aided . . . greatly by the reasoning of these enlightened courts"); *id.* (describing *Aymette* as "hold[ing] the same ***general*** views" as the *Andrews* court) (emphasis added).

[390] *Id.* at *8 (emphasis added).

[391] *Id.* at *9.

> purposes, and in all the ordinary modes usual in the country, and to which arms are adapted, limited by the duties of a good citizen in times of peace . . . .

Because citizens needed to be able to "become familiar with" the use of arms "in times of peace, that they may the more efficiently use them in times of war, . . . the right to keep arms for this purpose involves the right to practice their use."[392] Use for "ordinary purposes" included a man taking his gun "from his room into the street to shoot a rabid dog that threatened his child"[393] and using them on one's property in lawful self-defense.[394] Such reasoning is in large measure the same as that taken by the traditional individual right view in explaining the relation between the Second Amendment's preface and operative text.

Third, consistently with its reading of "keep," the court also broadened "arms." *Aymette* had defined the word to include only such arms "as are usually employed in civilized warfare, and that constitute the ordinary military equipment."[395] *Andrews* explained it as follows: "[T]he idea of the Constitution is, the keeping and use of such arms as are useful either in warfare, or in preparing the citizen for their use in warfare, by training him as a citizen, to their use in times of peace."[396] The court took judicial notice "that the rifle of all descriptions, the shot gun, the musket, and repeater, are such arms."[397]

Thus, setting aside any distinctions based on the specific language of Tennessee's Constitution, the consequence of *Aymette*, taken together with *Andrews*, is that "bear arms" was defined more narrowly in those cases, and "keep arms" more broadly, than was usual. The net result seems to be not far from the traditional individual right view held at the Founding and reflected in the great weight of early authority.

The divided 1842 decision of the Arkansas Supreme Court in *Buzzard* did not, even after the Civil War, ever acquire the prominence of *Aymette*, and when cited

---

392 *Id.* at *6–7.

393 *Id.* at *11.

394 *Id.* at *13.

395 1840 WL 1554, at *3.

396 1871 WL 3579, at *9. The court elsewhere defined "arms" as those furthering the end of "the efficiency of the citizen as a soldier," *id.* at *7, and as including not only weapons "adapted to the usual equipment of the soldier" but also those "the use of which may render him more efficient as such," *id.* at *11. The term had to be "taken in connection with the fact that the citizen is to keep them as a citizen" and therefore included such "as are found to make up the usual arms of the country, and the use of which will properly train and render him efficient in defense of his own liberties, as well as of the State." *Id.* at *7.

397 *Id.* at *7; *id.* at *11. Two judges dissented in part, criticizing *Aymette* and taking a broader view than the majority based on *Simpson*, *Bliss*, Blackstone, and Tucker. *Id.* at *13–15 (Nelson, J., joined by Turney, J., dissenting in part). They argued that "for their common defense" was equivalent to "in defense of themselves and the State." *Id.* at *13–14. Similarly, "[t]he word 'bear' was not used alone in the military sense of carrying arms, but in the popular sense of wearing them in war or in peace." *Id.*

it was simply for its limited, uncontroversial holding, upholding a ban on carrying weapons concealed.[398] Nevertheless, coming four years before *Nunn*, it appears to have been the first judicial holding involving the Second Amendment, and one judge's concurring opinion was the first appearance of something suggesting a collective right or quasi-collective right view.

The reasoning of the leading opinion for the 2-1 court was similar to that of *Aymette*. The court addressed both the Second Amendment and the 1836 Arkansas Constitution, which, like Tennessee's, provided that "the free white men of this State shall have a right to keep and bear arms for their common defense."[399] Despite the textual differences between these two provisions (in particular the Arkansas provision's "for their common defense" language), the court treated them as the same.[400] Much like *Aymette*, albeit without distinguishing between "keep" and "bear," the court apparently recognized a right of individuals but gave it a limited scope.[401] The Arkansas court's post-war decisions confirmed that the right secured by the Arkansas Constitution belonged to individuals and included the right to bear arms for at least some private purposes.[402]

---

[398] *E.g.*, *Fife v. State*, 31 Ark. 455, 1876 WL 1562, at *3 (summarizing holding and then relying on *Aymette* and *Andrews*); *State v. Wilforth*, 74 Mo. 528, 1881 WL 10279, at *1 (including *Buzzard* in string citation with *Nunn*, *Jumel*, *Mitchell*, *Owen*, and *Reid*, and relying on *Reid*). *Buzzard* was first cited in 1872. *See State v. English*, 35 Tex. 473, 1872 WL 7422; *Carroll v. State*, 28 Ark. 99, 1872 WL 1104.

[399] *Buzzard*, 4 Ark. 18, 1842 WL 331, at *6.

[400] *See id.* (equating the two, and adopting a single rule for evaluating restrictions).

[401] *See id.* at *4 (explaining that "the militia, without arms . . . might be unable to resist, successfully, the effort of those who should conspire to overthrow the established institutions of the country, or subjugate their common liberties" and that "the people designed and expected to accomplish this object by the adoption of the article under consideration, which would forever invest them with a legal right to keep and bear arms for that purpose"); *id.* at *6 ("The act in question does not . . . detract anything from the power of the people to defend their free state and the established institutions of the country."); *see also id.* at *2 (expressly equating Second Amendment right with rights in First); *id.* at *7 (noting that *Reid* and *Mitchell* had upheld similar laws notwithstanding constitutional provisions expressly protecting bearing arms in self-defense). As in *Aymette*, the court was faced with an absolute claim that the right was subject to no restrictions, and responded similarly. *See id.* at *3, *5.

[402] *See Carroll*, 1872 WL 1104, at *2 (upholding conviction for carrying deadly weapon concealed and explaining *Buzzard* as holding that "a constitutional *right to bear arms in defense of person and property* does not prohibit the legislature from making such police regulations as may be necessary for the good of society, as to the manner in which such arms shall be borne"; adding that a "citizen" may not "use his own property or *bear his own arms* in such way as to injure the property or endanger the life of his fellow citizen") (emphases added); *Fife*, 1876 WL 1562, at *3, *4 (restating *Buzzard*'s holding, and upholding conviction for carrying pistol by construing statute only to apply to pistol that "is usually carried in the pocket, or of a size to be concealed about the person, and used in private quarrels, and brawls, and not such as is in ordinary use, and effective as a weapon of war, and useful and necessary for 'the common defence'"); *Wilson v. State*, 33 Ark. 557, 1878 WL 1301, at *2 (reversing conviction for carrying side arms, where trial court had refused jury instruction to acquit if pistol was "army size . . . such as are commonly used in warfare"; citing *Fife* and *Andrews* and explaining that "*to prohibit the citizen from wearing or carrying a war arm*, except upon his own premises or when on a journey . . . , or when acting as or in aid of an officer, *is an unwarranted restriction upon his constitutional right to keep and bear arms*") (emphases added).

Opinions of the Office of Legal Counsel in Volume 28

The concurring opinion cited no history or authority and, as far as we are aware, no court or even judge has ever cited it in interpreting a right to bear arms, whether secured by the Second Amendment or by any of the analogous provisions in state constitutions.[403] It did not present what would now be considered a standard collective right or quasi-collective right view. Whereas those views address the limits of federal power to interfere with state law, Judge Dickinson addressed the case from the opposite vantage point, stating the question as whether the state's ban on carrying weapons concealed "interfere[s] with any regulations made by Congress, as to the organizing, arming, or disciplining the militia, or in the manner in which that militia are either to keep or bear their arms."[404] In modern terminology, the judge seemed to recast the case as turning on possible federal preemption of the state law. The Second Amendment, in setting out what he described as "the power given the militia to keep and bear arms," merely rephrased the express federal powers in Article I, Section 8, Clause 16 of the Constitution, the Amendment being "but an assertion of that general right of sovereignty belonging to independent nations to regulate their military force."[405] The Amendment thus did not add any protection of *state* powers. That protection was implicit in Clause 16: "[T]he States *retain the power* to legislate in relation to arms and the mode of carrying and keeping them, provided its exercise is not repugnant to the previous grant to the Federal Government. . . . Could Congress authorize any and every person by express law, to carry deadly weapons concealed about his person, when not composing one of the militia, and not a part of the regulations ordained for their government?"[406]

The dissenting opinion employed the general rule for interpreting prefaces (discussed above in Part II.C.1), and the same reasoning as Rawle, Story, and *Nunn*, to explain the relation of the Amendment's preface to the right:

> Now, I take the expressions 'a well regulated militia being necessary for the security of a free State,' and the terms 'common defense,' to be the reasons assigned for the granting of the right, and not a restriction or limitation upon the right itself. . . . [W]hen was it contended before that the reason given for the establishment of a right or

---

[403] 1842 WL 331, at *7 (Dickinson, J., concurring). *See also* Kopel, *supra* note 342, 1998 BYU L. Rev. at 1425 ("The *Buzzard* concurrence's assertion that the right to arms was not individual vanished from American case law for the rest of the nineteenth century.").

[404] 1842 WL 331, at *7 (Dickinson, J.); *see id.* at *10 ("The act . . . does not, in my opinion, conflict with any of the powers of the General Government.").

[405] *Id.* at *7, *9. It is unclear what significance he gave to the state constitution's provision. *See id.* at *9.

[406] *Id.* at *8.

> its uninterrupted enjoyment not only limited the right itself, but restrained it to a single specific object?[407]

Judge Lacy also pointed to the Second Amendment's reference to a "free State": "To suppose that liberty cannot be in danger, except from a foreign foe or internal disorder, is virtually to deny the importance and necessity of written constitutions. . . . I cannot separate the political freedom of the State from the personal rights of its citizens."[408] He singled out the concurring opinion for granting the right to "the militia alone," and only at "the discretion of the Legislature"—a right "valueless and not worth preserving; for the State unquestionably possesses the power, without the grant, to arm the militia and direct how they shall be employed in cases of invasion or domestic insurrection. . . . [W]hy give that which is no right in itself and guarantees a privilege that is useless?"[409] Finally, the dissent explained the right much as Blackstone had, tying it to self-defense and pointing out that it was no more unlimited than the freedoms of speech and press.[410]

In sum, the activity of courts closest to the Founding tends to reinforce what the text and history establish—that the right secured by the Second Amendment belongs to individuals. No court questioned the private right to keep arms, and most recognized the traditional individual right to bear them. Two of the three state supreme courts to apply the Second Amendment (Georgia and Louisiana) repeatedly recognized a private right to bear arms for self-defense. The two cases taking the narrowest view of the right (both in states whose constitutions had "common defense" clauses in their right) were ignored, and even they recognized some manner of individual right. Only in an opinion of a single judge, which was and has continued to be ignored, did something like a quasi-collective or collective right understanding appear, but even that opinion did not view the Second Amendment as securing any right of states or of state (as opposed to federal) militias. On balance, then, the cases before the Civil War, like the first commentators, confirm that the text and history of the Second Amendment support the individual right view, not the collective right or quasi-collective right views.

C. Reconstruction

As the Civil War ended in 1865, southern governments enacted "black codes," which, among other things, either directly prohibited the newly freed slaves from keeping and bearing arms or imposed stringent permit systems. In addition, armed white mobs, sometimes including the militias, frequently disarmed the freed

---

[407] *Id.* at *10 (Lacy, J., dissenting).

[408] *Id.* at *14. *See also id.* (arguing that the right has at times "been the only means by which public liberty or the security of free States has been vindicated and maintained").

[409] *Id.* at *10.

[410] *Id.* at *12–14.

blacks.[411] Such practices, coupled with blacks' lack of citizenship, prompted the Thirty-Ninth Congress to take several actions securing the rights of the newly freed slaves and reaffirming the understanding that the right to keep and bear arms was a personal right.

The first action was enactment of the Civil Rights Act of 1866. One goal of many who sought its passage, noted by them and lamented by their opponents, appears to have been to secure to freedmen the Second Amendment's right to keep and bear arms. Both representatives and senators highlighted disarmament of blacks and argued that the Act, by making blacks citizens, would secure to them that right. Senator Trumbull, Chairman of the Judiciary Committee and a sponsor of the Act, explained that it would counteract those portions of the black codes that "prohibit any negro or mulatto from having fire-arms."[412] In the House, Representative Clarke quoted the Second Amendment and declared, "I shall insist that the reconstructed rebels of Mississippi respect the Constitution in their local laws"; he also decried that newly formed southern governments had been "allowed to rob and disarm our [black] veteran soldiers." Representative Raymond argued, in favor of the Act, that making blacks citizens would give to them "every right which you or I have," including "a right to bear arms."[413]

The second congressional action was passage of the Fourteenth Amendment in June 1866. Senator Pomeroy, in addressing an early draft, listed as among the "safeguards of liberty . . . under our Constitution" the right of "the freedman" to "bear arms for the defense of himself and family and his homestead," even suggesting that Congress's power to enforce the Thirteenth Amendment's ban on slavery might justify it in protecting this right in the South.[414] One of the Fourteenth Amendment's sponsors, in listing the rights of citizenship that its Privileges or Immunities Clause would extend to blacks, pointed to "the personal rights guaranteed and secured by the first eight amendments of the Constitution; such as the freedom of speech and of the press; . . . [and] the right to keep and to bear

---

[411] *See, e.g.*, Laws of Miss. ch. 23, § 1, at 165 (enacted Nov. 29, 1865), *reprinted in* Stephen P. Halbrook, *Freedmen, the Fourteenth Amendment, and the Right to Bear Arms, 1866–1876*, at 2 (1998). *See generally* Halbrook, *Freedmen* at 2–3, 5, 8–12, 15–16, 18–20, 22–23, 26–32, 34–37 (collecting reports of army and Freedmen's Bureau officers to President and Congress, petitions to Congress, and other public materials documenting attempts in former Confederacy in 1865 and 1866 to disarm blacks, including through legislation and by militias).

[412] Cong. Globe, 39th Cong., 1st Sess. 474 (1866). *See also id.* at 478 (Sen. Saulsbury, lamenting this effect of the Act). Regarding Trumbull, see Raoul Berger, *Government by Judiciary: The Transformation of the Fourteenth Amendment* 32 (2d ed. 1997).

[413] Cong. Globe at 1838–39 (Rep. Clarke); *id.* at 1266 (Rep. Raymond). *See also id.* at 1629 (Rep. Hart, explaining that Act would guarantee to free blacks "[a] government . . . where 'no law shall be made prohibiting the free exercise of religion'; where 'the right of the people to keep and bear arms shall not be infringed'").

[414] *Id.* at 1182.

arms."[415] The *New York Times* and other leading newspapers reprinted these comments, including the reference to the Second Amendment, and praised them.[416]

This history indicates that it was widely recognized that the right to keep and bear arms was to be protected by the Civil Rights Act and the Fourteenth Amendment, and that that right was understood to belong to individuals. For example, Raoul Berger, even while arguing against the view that the Fourteenth Amendment "incorporated" the Bill of Rights to apply to the states, explains that "all are agreed" that the Fourteenth Amendment aimed at least "to embody and protect" the Civil Rights Act of 1866; he contends that the Act, in turn, "intended to confer on the freedmen the auxiliary rights that would protect their 'life, liberty, and property'—no more." He quotes Blackstone's listing of these three principal rights and demonstrates Blackstone's prominence in the debates and in the denunciations of the black codes.[417] As explained above in Part III.A, Blackstone described five "auxiliary rights," and the right of individuals to have and use arms for their defense was one of them. Given the language of Section 1 of the Civil Rights Act, it may be that states simply could not discriminate against blacks in the right to keep and bear arms, not that the Second Amendment applied per se, but the point remains that there was a consensus that the right in question belonged to individuals and was a right *against* the state.[418]

Were there any remaining doubt on this question, Congress eliminated it a month after approving the Fourteenth Amendment, when it renewed the Freedmen's Bureau over President Andrew Johnson's veto. The act provided that wherever the courts were not open, or in any state that had not been restored to the Union, various rights, largely paralleling those in the Civil Rights Act, should "be secured to and enjoyed by all the citizens . . . without respect to race or color, or previous condition of slavery." Among these were "the right . . . to have full and equal benefit of all laws and proceedings concerning personal liberty, personal security, and the acquisition, enjoyment, and disposition of estate, real and personal, *including the constitutional right to bear arms*."[419] Congress thus not

---

[415] *Id.* at 2765 (Sen. Howard).

[416] *See* Halbrook, *Freedmen*, *supra* note 411, at 36 (collecting excerpts).

[417] Berger, *Government by Judiciary*, *supra* note 412, at 30, 30–39, 53–54. Berger does not specifically mention the right to keep and bear arms. *See, e.g.*, *id.* at 166–69 (addressing Sen. Howard's statement but omitting his listing of rights).

[418] Section 1 of the Civil Rights Act declares all those born in the United States to be citizens, grants "the same right, in every State and Territory in the United States . . . as is enjoyed by white citizens" with regard to certain enumerated aspects of property, contracting, and lawsuits, and guarantees "full and equal benefit of all laws and proceedings for the security of person and property." 14 Stat. 27, 27 (1866). In light of Blackstone's understanding and the context of the black codes, any laws regarding the ability to keep or bear arms would presumably be "laws . . . for the security of person and property" and therefore would need to be equal for all citizens regardless of color.

[419] Act of July 16, 1866, § 14, 14 Stat. 173, 176 (emphasis added). The President's reasons for his veto did not involve any disagreement with Congress regarding this right. *See* Veto Message (July 16, 1866), *reprinted in* 8 *Messages and Papers*, *supra* note 276, at 3620.

only enacted the understanding that the Second Amendment protected an individual right, including the right to "bear" arms, but also did so in a way that rested on Blackstone's exposition of the individual right to arms as a critical auxiliary to the three primary individual rights of life, liberty, and property.

Congress took the same view early in the following year, demonstrating not only its understanding that the right belonged to individuals but also the limited, indirect way in which it protected the states' militias. Responding to the southern militias' depredations against the freed blacks, Congress included in a bill, which the President signed, a provision "[t]hat all militia forces now organized or in service" in the states of the former Confederacy "be forthwith disbanded, and that the further organization, arming, or calling into service of the said militia forces, or any part thereof, is hereby prohibited."[420] Significantly, the bill's sponsor had agreed to strike "disarmed" after "disbanded," in the face of opposition from several (northern) senators that to disarm the citizens from whom the militia was drawn, rather than merely disbanding the militias, would violate the Second Amendment.[421] Congress's actions both in disbanding the southern states' militias and in not disarming their citizens show that it understood the Second Amendment right to protect individuals, not states or their militias.[422] Thus, from the Founding through the Civil War, the overwhelming understanding of the right of the people to keep and bear arms was that it was a right that belonged to individuals.

D. Beyond Reconstruction

As already suggested by our discussions above of *Andrews* and cases citing *Buzzard*, the understanding of the right to keep and bear arms as an individual right continued beyond the Civil War and Reconstruction. Although we do not provide an exhaustive survey of the post-war period, we find it significant that the modern alternative views of the right did not take hold until the twentieth century, well over a century after the Second Amendment was ratified. Before that, the

---

[420] Act of Mar. 2, 1867, § 6, 14 Stat. 485, 487. The President did inform the House that he was signing under "protest" because this provision, and another to which he objected, were included in an essential appropriation bill. *See* Letter to the House of Representatives (Mar. 2, 1867), *reprinted in* 8 *Messages and Papers*, *supra* note 276, at 3670. Regarding the militia provision, he objected that it "denies to ten States of this Union their constitutional right to protect themselves in any emergency by means of their own militia." It may be that in his constitutional objection he had in mind Article I, Section 10's implicit recognition of the prerogative of states to defend themselves with their militias in cases of invasion or imminent danger. See Part II.D.2 above (discussing ways in which original Constitution recognizes that states will have and be able to use militias).

[421] The Senate debate is summarized from the Congressional Globe in Halbrook, *Freedmen*, *supra* note 411, at 68–69.

[422] *See id.* at 69 ("Astonishingly, while still waving the bloody shirt and depriving Southerners of suffrage, Republicans were unwilling to deny the right to have arms to ex-Confederates."); Nelson Lund, Book Review, *Outsider Voices on Guns and the Constitution*, 17 Const. Comm. 701, 713 (2000) (reviewing Halbrook) ("This incident perfectly illustrates why the Second Amendment had been adopted in the first place.").

views of the leading constitutional law scholar of the period, Thomas Cooley, were in accord with his predecessors Tucker, Rawle, and Story, in recognizing an individual right. And the Supreme Court, although making no holding regarding the substance of the Amendment, suggested in dicta that it protected an individual right.

Cooley's *General Principles of Constitutional Law*, first published in 1880, gained a prominence on the level of the works of his predecessors.[423] As had the antebellum commentators, he espoused the individual right view of the Second Amendment. After quoting the Amendment, noting that it was a "modification and enlargement from the English Bill of Rights," and citing Tucker, Cooley added the following:

> *The Right is General.*—It might be supposed from the phraseology of this provision that the right to keep and bear arms was only guaranteed to the militia; but this would be an interpretation not warranted by the intent. . . . [I]f the right were limited to those enrolled [in the militia, a number that the government could constrict], the purpose of this guaranty might be defeated altogether by the action or neglect to act of the government it was meant to hold in check. The meaning of the provision undoubtedly is, that the people, from whom the militia must be taken, shall have the right to keep and bear arms, and they need no permission or regulation of law for the purpose. But this enables the government to have a well-regulated militia; for to bear arms implies something more than the mere keeping; it implies the learning to handle and use them in a way that makes those who keep them ready for their efficient use; in other words, it implies the right to meet for voluntary discipline in arms, observing in doing so the laws of public order.[424]

Cooley's rejection of any collective right and quasi-collective right view is consistent with the understanding of the Amendment's prefatory clause that is evident from the Founding and had been reiterated before the Civil War by Rawle, Story, and *Nunn*. Even Cooley's heading echoed Rawle's statement over fifty years earlier: "The prohibition is general."[425] Cooley likewise treated *both* keeping and bearing as private rights of citizens, and recognized that the right has limita-

---

[423] *See supra* note 41; Kates, *supra* note 33, 82 Mich. L. Rev. at 243. Among Cooley's many works was to prepare the fourth edition of Story's unabridged *Commentaries*, published in 1873.

[424] Cooley, *General Principles*, *supra* note 41, at 271. Cooley cited 1 Tucker's Blackstone, *supra* note 60, at 300, which praises the right in the Second Amendment as "the true palladium of liberty" and, paralleling Blackstone, ties it to the natural "right of self defence." See Part IV.A above.

[425] Rawle, *View of the Constitution*, *supra* note 327, at 125, discussed above in Part IV.A.

tions ("the laws of public order"), just as any other individual right does.[426] Conversely, in discussing the Militia Clauses of Article I, Section 8, in a separate part of his treatise, he made no mention of the Second Amendment.[427]

Cooley reiterated this individual right interpretation in his even more celebrated *Treatise on the Constitutional Limitations*, first published in 1868.[428] Among the clauses common in state constitutions, he explained, were "[t]hose declaratory of the fundamental rights of the citizen," among which were freedom of speech and of the press and "that every man may bear arms for the defence of himself and the State."[429] In a later chapter he included the right among the "the constitutional protections to personal liberty": "Among the other defences to personal liberty should be mentioned the right of the people to keep and bear arms." He explained the right's English origins, noted the importance for a "well-regulated militia" of "the people" being "trained to bearing arms," praised the lack of legislation "regulat[ing] this right," and cited *Bliss*, *Nunn*, and a case concerning the right of self-defense.[430] Finally, in elsewhere explaining the scope of a state's concurrent power to organize and discipline the militia, Cooley simply cited *Houston v. Moore*, not mentioning the Second Amendment.[431] Like the Court, he apparently did not see the Amendment as relevant to the scope of the state's power to maintain a militia.

The Supreme Court did not address the substance of the Second Amendment during this period, because of its view that the Bill of Rights, including the Second Amendment, did not apply to the states.[432] In *Robertson v. Baldwin*, however, the Court invoked the history of, and limitations on, the various rights in the Bill of Rights, including the Second Amendment, to illustrate and defend a holding regarding the limitations on the Thirteenth Amendment's ban on slavery:

> The law is perfectly well settled that the first ten amendments to the Constitution, commonly known as the Bill of Rights, were not intend-

---

[426] He added, citing *Andrews* (which had not interpreted the Second Amendment), that the Amendment protected the keeping of arms "suitable for the general defence of the community against invasion or oppression," whereas "the secret carrying of those suited merely to deadly individual encounters may be prohibited." Cooley, *General Principles*, *supra* note 41, at 271–72.

[427] *Id.* at 88–89.

[428] *See* Kopel, *supra* note 342, 1998 BYU L. Rev. at 1462.

[429] Thomas Cooley, *A Treatise on the Constitutional Limitations Which Rest Upon the Legislative Power of the States of the American Union* 35–36 (1868).

[430] *Id.* at 350; *see id.* at 295 (chapter title). *Miller* cited this section. *See* 307 U.S. at 182 n.3 (citing "Cooley's Constitutional Limitations, Vol. 1, p. 729," likely the 8th edition, published well after Cooley's death).

[431] Cooley, *Constitutional Limitations*, *supra* note 429, at 18.

[432] *See Presser v. Illinois*, 116 U.S. 252, 264–65 (1886); *see also United States v. Cruikshank*, 92 U.S. 542, 553 (1876); *Logan v. United States*, 144 U.S. 263, 286–87 (1892); *Maxwell v. Dow*, 176 U.S. 581, 597 (1900). As noted above in Part I, the federal government did not regulate private firearms until 1934.

> ed to lay down any novel principles of government, but simply to embody certain guaranties and immunities which we had inherited from our English ancestors, and which had from time immemorial been subject to certain well-recognized exceptions arising from the necessities of the case. In incorporating these principles into the fundamental law there was no intention of disregarding the exceptions, which continued to be recognized as if they had been formally expressed. Thus, the freedom of speech and of the press (art. 1) does not permit the publication of libels, blasphemous or indecent articles, or other publications injurious to public morals or private reputation; [and] the right of the people to keep and bear arms (art. 2) is not infringed by laws prohibiting the carrying of concealed weapons . . . .[433]

The Court added similar illustrations from the Fifth and Sixth Amendments. The Court thus suggested that the Second Amendment protected an individual right, both by treating it in parallel with the individual rights in the rest of the Bill of Rights and by pointing to the right's English origins.

Not until 1905 was a view rejecting the individual right view truly born, and then in a decision interpreting not the Second Amendment but rather a provision in a state constitution. In *City of Salina v. Blaksley*, the Kansas Supreme Court held that a clause in the Kansas Bill of Rights, providing that "'[t]he people have the right to bear arms for their defence and security,'" referred only "to the people as a collective body" and dealt "exclusively with the military. Individual rights are not considered in this section." Rather, the "people shall exercise this right" through the *power of their legislature*, set out in the body of the state constitution, to organize, equip, and discipline the militia. The right extended "only to the right to bear arms as a member of the state militia, or some other military organization provided for by law."[434] The court seems to have been influenced by a provision in the state constitution admonishing against standing armies in time of peace, and praising civilian control of the military, that immediately followed the text of the right.[435] The court also, without citing historical authority and with little explanation, pointed to the Second Amendment as analogous and reinforcing its reading.[436] *Salina*'s novelty was

[433] 165 U.S. 275, 281–82 (1897).

[434] 83 P. 619, 620 (Kan. 1905).

[435] *See id.* As shown in Parts III.B.2 and III.C.1, however, there was nothing unusual in combining such declarations with an individual right to arms.

[436] *See Blaksley*, 83 P. at 620. The Fifth Circuit in *Emerson* criticized *Salina*, to the extent that it was endorsing a quasi-collective right view, as "constru[ing] the constitutional provision as saying no more than that the citizen has a right to do that which the state orders him to do and thus neither grants the citizen any right nor in any way restricts the power of the state." It found such a criticism "especially applicable to the theory that such *state* constitutional provisions grant rights only to the state," noting that *Salina* did "not appear even to recognize, much less attempt to justify, the anomaly of construing a constitutional declaration of rights as conferring rights only on the state which had them anyway." 270 F.3d at 231 n.30 (emphasis added). In the context of the right to keep and bear arms in

District of Columbia, et al. v Dick Anthony Heller
(2008)

The Supreme Court decision in the 1939 *Miller* case was the defining case regarding the Second Amendment for several decades. Critics of the decision argued that the court had been in error in not recognizing the military uses of short-barreled shotguns, and they further argued that the reliance of the court in *Miller* on a connection between the right to keep and bear arms and militia or military service was not in keeping with either the language or the original intent of the Second Amendment. However, multiple obstacles stood in the way of bringing another Second Amendment case before the Supreme Court. One of the major hurdles to be overcome was the patchwork application of the Bill of Rights (the first ten amendments to the Constitution) to the states. Rather than simply saying outright that all the provisions of the Bill of Rights applied to the states and to state laws as well as to the federal government and federal laws. Instead, the Supreme Court ruled on each right individually, as cases came before them. The Second Amendment had not been "incorporated" under the 14th Amendment[6], which meant that cases involving the right to keep and bear arms under state laws were not subject to precedents established under federal law.

The situation came to a head when the Cato Institute decided that the time was ripe to further legal examination of the Right to Keep and Bear Arms. To do that, they assembled a group of people who were situated such that they could claim to be unfairly burdened by a District of Columbia (which is a federal enclave, not part of any state, and thus governed entirely by federal laws) law that prohibited the keeping of a loaded or operational firearm within a private home. The group put together by attorneys for the Cato Institute originally included six plaintiffs.

---

[6] Section 1 of the 14th Amendment to the Constitution says, "All persons born or naturalized in the United States, and subject to the jurisdiction thereof, are citizens of the United States and of the state wherein they reside. No state shall make or enforce any law which shall abridge the privileges or immunities of citizens of the United States; nor shall any state deprive any person of life, liberty, or property, without due process of law; nor deny to any person within its jurisdiction the equal protection of the laws."

The six plaintiffs filed their initial lawsuit in the federal District Court for the District of Columbia in February of 2003. The judge dismissed the case, upon which the plaintiffs appealed to the Circuit Court of Appeals. A three-judge panel of the Circuit Court heard the appeal and, by a 2–1 vote, ruled to overturn the lower court's decision. The Circuit Court decision held that the District of Columbia law was unconstitutional. The defendant District of Columbia petitioned the Circuit Court for a re-hearing "en banc," which means before the entire panel of judges rather than a subcommittee of three. The Circuit Court declined the request for a re-hearing.

The defendant District of Columbia and the mayor then appealed to the Supreme Court, which granted *Certiorari* (meaning they agreed to hear the case) on November 20, 2007. Prior to the oral hearing, numerous interested parties on both sides of the gun control argument submitted friend-of-the-court (*amicus curiae*) briefs. Oral arguments were heard on March 18, 2008. The Supreme Court released its decision, with the majority position written by the late Justice Antonin Scalia, on June 26, 2008. By a 5–4 vote, the Supreme Court agreed that the Second Amendment protected an individual right, not connected to militia or military service, to keep a functional firearm in the home.

Dissents were filed by Justice John P. Stevens, with David Souter, Ruth Bader Ginsberg, and Stephen Breyer; and by Justice Stephen Breyer, with John P. Stevens, David Souter, and Ruth Bader Ginsberg.

Impact

Justice Scalia's majority opinion was extensive, and discussed both the history of the right to keep and bear arms and the linguistic and grammatical construction of the Second Amendment itself. The importance of the decision is summarized in the following key points:

- The Second Amendment protects an individual right to possess a firearm unconnected with service in a militia, and to use that arm for traditionally lawful purposes, such as self-defense within the home.[7]
- The decision held that the Right to Keep and Bear Arms is not unlimited, but it made no attempt to establish what the limits of "reasonable regulation" are or might be other than allowing that the prohibition against carrying firearms in schools and similar "sensitive" places were not immediately rendered null and void. Constitutional scholars generally agree that the language Justice Scalia chose in this regard simply means that other gun control regulations must be litigated and decided separately, on their own merits.
- The District of Columbia handgun ban and trigger lock requirement were ruled unconstitutional.

[7] District of Columbia, et al. v Dick Anthony Heller, pp. 2-53

The key point that came out of the *Heller* decision is that the question of whether the Second Amendment protects an individual right to keep and bear arms or only a collective right was finally decided; the right is an individual right.

However, because the lawsuit was brought in the District of Columbia under federal law and the Second Amendment had not at that time been incorporated to apply to the states, the overall, national impact of the ruling was simultaneously earth-shattering and yet inconsequential. That did not change until the *McDonald* case, in 2016.

Note: Because of mechanical issues affecting the production of paperback books, I learned that the size of this book if it included the full and complete text of all the documents discussed exceeded the maximum page count by more than 200 pages. That meant that something had to be omitted. Because dissenting opinions in Supreme Court decisions are not binding legal precedent, I reluctantly made the decision to omit the dissenting opinions from this decision.

Dissenting opinions are not binding legal authority, but they can be of interest to legal scholars. For anyone who wishes to read the dissenting opinions, an official copy of the complete decision can be found on-line at: https://www.supremecourt.gov/opinions/07pdf/07-290.pdf

Syllabus

DISTRICT OF COLUMBIA ET AL. *v.* HELLER

CERTIORARI TO THE UNITED STATES COURT OF APPEALS FOR THE DISTRICT OF COLUMBIA CIRCUIT

No. 07–290. Argued March 18, 2008—Decided June 26, 2008

District of Columbia law bans handgun possession by making it a crime to carry an unregistered firearm and prohibiting the registration of handguns; provides separately that no person may carry an unlicensed handgun, but authorizes the police chief to issue 1-year licenses; and requires residents to keep lawfully owned firearms unloaded and disassembled or bound by a trigger lock or similar device. Respondent Heller, a D. C. special policeman, applied to register a handgun he wished to keep at home, but the District refused. He filed this suit seeking, on Second Amendment grounds, to enjoin the city from enforcing the bar on handgun registration, the licensing requirement insofar as it prohibits carrying an unlicensed firearm in the home, and the trigger-lock requirement insofar as it prohibits the use of functional firearms in the home. The District Court dismissed the suit, but the D. C. Circuit reversed, holding that the Second Amendment protects an individual's right to possess firearms and that the city's total ban on handguns, as well as its requirement that firearms in the home be kept nonfunctional even when necessary for self-defense, violated that right.

Held:

1. The Second Amendment protects an individual right to possess a firearm unconnected with service in a militia, and to use that arm for traditionally lawful purposes, such as self-defense within the home. Pp. 576–626.

(a) The Amendment's prefatory clause announces a purpose, but does not limit or expand the scope of the second part, the operative clause. The operative clause's text and history demonstrate that it connotes an individual right to keep and bear arms. Pp. 576–595.

(b) The prefatory clause comports with the Court's interpretation of the operative clause. The "militia" comprised all males physically capable of acting in concert for the common defense. The Antifederalists feared that the Federal Government would disarm the people in order to disable this citizens' militia, enabling a politicized standing army or a select militia to rule. The response was to deny Congress power to abridge the ancient right of individuals to keep and bear arms, so that the ideal of a citizens' militia would be preserved. Pp. 595–600.

(c) The Court's interpretation is confirmed by analogous arms-bearing rights in state constitutions that preceded and immediately followed the Second Amendment. Pp. 600–603.

(d) The Second Amendment's drafting history, while of dubious interpretive worth, reveals three state Second Amendment proposals that unequivocally referred to an individual right to bear arms. Pp. 603–605.

(e) Interpretation of the Second Amendment by scholars, courts, and legislators, from immediately after its ratification through the late 19th century, also supports the Court's conclusion. Pp. 605–619.

(f) None of the Court's precedents forecloses the Court's interpretation. Neither *United States* v. *Cruikshank*, 92 U. S. 542, 553, nor *Presser* v. *Illinois*, 116 U. S. 252, 264–265, refutes the individual-rights interpretation. *United States* v. *Miller*, 307 U. S. 174, does not limit the right to keep and bear arms to militia purposes, but rather limits the type of weapon to which the right applies to those used by the militia, *i. e.*, those in common use for lawful purposes. Pp. 619–626.

2. Like most rights, the Second Amendment right is not unlimited. It is not a right to keep and carry any weapon whatsoever in any manner whatsoever and for whatever purpose: For example, concealed weapons prohibitions have been upheld under the Amendment or state analogues. The Court's opinion should not be taken to cast doubt on longstanding prohibitions on the possession of firearms by felons and the mentally ill, or laws forbidding the carrying of firearms in sensitive places such as schools and government buildings, or laws imposing conditions and qualifications on the commercial sale of arms. *Miller*'s holding that the sorts of weapons protected are those "in common use at the time" finds support in the historical tradition of prohibiting the carrying of dangerous and unusual weapons. Pp. 626–628.

3. The handgun ban and the trigger-lock requirement (as applied to self-defense) violate the Second Amendment. The District's total ban on handgun possession in the home amounts to a prohibition on an entire class of "arms" that Americans overwhelmingly choose for the lawful purpose of self-defense. Under any of the standards of scrutiny the Court has applied to enumerated constitutional rights, this prohibition—in the place where the importance of the lawful defense of self, family, and property is most acute—would fail constitutional muster. Similarly, the requirement that any lawful firearm in the home be disassembled or bound by a trigger lock makes it impossible for citizens to use arms for the core lawful purpose of self-defense and is hence unconstitutional. Because Heller conceded at oral argument that the D. C. licensing law is permissible if it is not enforced arbitrarily and capriciously, the Court assumes that a license will satisfy his prayer for relief and

does not address the licensing requirement. Assuming he is not disqualified from exercising Second Amendment rights, the District must permit Heller to register his handgun and must issue him a license to carry it in the home. Pp. 628–636.

478 F. 3d 370, affirmed.

SCALIA, J., delivered the opinion of the Court, in which ROBERTS, C. J., and KENNEDY, THOMAS, and ALITO, JJ., joined. STEVENS, J., filed a dissenting opinion, in which SOUTER, GINSBURG, and BREYER, JJ., joined, *post*, p. 636. BREYER, J., filed a dissenting opinion, in which STEVENS, SOUTER, and GINSBURG, JJ., joined, *post*, p. 681.

Walter Dellinger argued the cause for petitioners. With him on the briefs were *Peter J. Nickles*, Attorney General for the District of Columbia, *Linda Singer*, former Attorney General for the District of Columbia, *Alan B. Morrison*, *Todd S. Kim*, Solicitor General, *Donna M. Murasky*, Deputy Solicitor General, *Lutz Alexander Prager*, *Robert A. Long, Jr.*, *Jonathan L. Marcus*, *Thomas C. Goldstein*, *Matthew M. Shors*, and *Mark S. Davies*.

Alan Gura argued the cause for respondent. With him on the brief were *Robert A. Levy* and *Clark M. Neily III*.

Former *Solicitor General Clement* argued the cause for the United States as *amicus curiae* urging affirmance. With him on the brief were *Acting Solicitor General Garre*, *Assistant Attorney General Fisher*, *Acting Assistant Attorney General Bucholtz*, *Malcolm L. Stewart*, and *Stephen R. Rubenstein*.*

---

*Briefs of *amici curiae* urging reversal were filed for the City of Chicago et al. by *Andrew L. Frey*, *David M. Gossett*, *Benna Ruth Solomon*, *Patrick J. Rocks*, and *Lee Ann Lowder;* for the American Academy of Pediatrics et al. by *Bert H. Deixler* and *Lary Alan Rappaport;* for the American Bar Association by *William H. Neukom*, *Robert N. Weiner*, and *John A. Freedman;* for the American Jewish Committee et al. by *Jeffrey A. Lamken*, *Allyson N. Ho*, *D. Randall Benn*, *Jeffrey L. Kessler*, *William C. Heuer*, *Robert E. Cortes*, and *Sayre Weaver;* for the Brady Center to Prevent Gun Violence et al. by *John Payton*, *Jonathan G. Cedarbaum*, *Dennis A. Henigan*, *Brian J. Siebel*, and *Jonathan E. Lowy;* for the DC Appleseed Center for Law and Justice et al. by *Jonathan S. Franklin;* for

JUSTICE SCALIA delivered the opinion of the Court.

We consider whether a District of Columbia prohibition on the possession of usable handguns in the home violates the Second Amendment to the Constitution.

District Attorneys by *Alexis S. Coll-Very, Simona G. Strauss,* the *Honorable Robert M. Morgenthau, Mark Dwyer,* the *Honorable Charles J. Hynes,* and *Laurie L. Levenson;* for Former Department of Justice Officials by *Messrs. Long* and *Marcus;* for Major American Cities et al. by *Jeffrey L. Bleich, George A. Nilson, William R. Phelan, Jr., Debra Lynn Gonzales, Michael A. Cardozo, Leonard J. Koerner, Richard Feder, Dennis J. Herrera, Danny Chou,* and *John Daniel Reaves;* for Members of Congress by *Scott E. Gant* and *Christopher L. Hayes;* for the NAACP Legal Defense & Educational Fund, Inc., by *Theodore M. Shaw, Jacqueline A. Berrien, Victor A. Bolden, Debo P. Adegbile, Michael B. de Leeuw,* and *Darcy M. Goddard;* for the National Network to End Domestic Violence et al. by *Bruce D. Sokler;* for Professors of Criminal Justice by *Albert W. Wallis;* for Professors of Linguistics and English by *Charles M. Dyke, Charles M. English, Jeffrey R. Gans, Elizabeth M. Walsh,* and *Frederick L. Whitmer;* for the Violence Policy Center et al. by *Daniel G. Jarcho;* and for Jack N. Rakove et al. by *Carl T. Bogus.*

Briefs of *amici curiae* urging affirmance were filed for the State of New York et al. by *Andrew M. Cuomo,* Attorney General of New York, *Barbara D. Underwood,* Solicitor General, *Michelle Aronowitz,* Deputy Solicitor General, *Sasha Samberg-Champion,* Assistant Solicitor General, by *Roberto J. Sánchez-Ramos,* Secretary of Justice of Puerto Rico, and by the Attorneys General for their respective States as follows: *Mark J. Bennett* of Hawaii, *Douglas F. Gansler* of Maryland, *Martha Coakley* of Massachusetts, and *Anne Milgram* of New Jersey; for the State of Texas et al. by *Greg Abbott,* Attorney General of Texas, *R. Ted Cruz,* Solicitor General, *Kent C. Sullivan,* First Assistant Attorney General, *David S. Morales,* Deputy Attorney General for Civil Litigation, *Sean D. Jordan,* Deputy Solicitor General, *Michael P. Murphy,* Assistant Solicitor General, and by the Attorneys General for their respective States as follows: *Troy King* of Alabama, *Talis J. Colberg* of Alaska, *Dustin McDaniel* of Arkansas, *John W. Suthers* of Colorado, *Bill McCollum* of Florida, *Thurbert E. Baker* of Georgia, *Lawrence G. Wasden* of Idaho, *Steve Carter* of Indiana, *Stephen N. Six* of Kansas, *Jack Conway* of Kentucky, *James D. Caldwell* of Louisiana, *Michael A. Cox* of Michigan, *Lori Swanson* of Minnesota, *Jim Hood* of Mississippi, *Jeremiah W. (Jay) Nixon* of Missouri, *Mike McGrath* of Montana, *Jon Bruning* of Nebraska, *Kelly A. Ayotte* of New Hampshire, *Gary K. King* of New Mexico, *Wayne Stenehjem* of North Dakota, *Marc*

I

The District of Columbia generally prohibits the possession of handguns. It is a crime to carry an unregistered

---

Dann of Ohio, *W. A. Drew Edmondson* of Oklahoma, *Thomas W. Corbett, Jr.*, of Pennsylvania, *Henry McMaster* of South Carolina, *Lawrence E. Long* of South Dakota, *Mark L. Shurtleff* of Utah, *Robert F. McDonnell* of Virginia, *Robert M. McKenna* of Washington, *Darrell V. McGraw, Jr.*, of West Virginia, and *Bruce A. Salzburg* of Wyoming; for the State of Wisconsin by *J. B. Van Hollen*, Attorney General of Wisconsin, and *Christopher G. Wren* and *Steven P. Means*, Assistant Attorneys General; for Academics et al. by *Richard E. Gardiner;* for Academics for the Second Amendment by *David T. Hardy, Joseph Edward Olson, Daniel D. Polsby, Henry C. Karlson, Randy E. Barnett,* and *Michael Ian Krauss;* for the Alaska Outdoor Council et al. by *Jack Brian McGee;* for the American Center for Law and Justice by *Jay Alan Sekulow, Stuart J. Roth, Colby M. May,* and *James M. Henderson, Sr.;* for the American Civil Rights Union by *Peter J. Ferrara;* for the American Legislative Exchange by *Robert Dowlut;* for the Association of American Physicians and Surgeons, Inc., by *Andrew L. Schlafly;* for the Cato Institute et al. by *C. Kevin Marshall;* for the Center for Individual Freedom by *Renee L. Giachino;* for the Citizens Committee for the Right to Keep and Bear Arms et al. by *Jeffrey B. Teichert;* for the Congress of Racial Equality by *Stefan Bijan Tahmassebi;* for Criminologists et al. by *Marc James Ayers* and *Don B. Kates;* for Disabled Veterans for Self-Defense et al. by *James H. Warner;* for the Eagle Forum Education & Legal Defense Fund by *Douglas G. Smith;* for the Foundation for Free Expression by *Deborah J. Dewart* and *James L. Hirsen;* for the Foundation for Moral Law by *Gregory M. Jones* and *Benjamin D. DuPré;* for the Goldwater Institute by *Bradford A. Berenson, Ileana Maria Ciobanu,* and *Clint Bolick;* for Grass Roots of South Carolina, Inc., by *R. Jeffords Barham;* for Gun Owners of America, Inc., et al. by *Herbert W. Titus* and *William J. Olson;* for the Heartland Institute by *Richard K. Willard;* for the Institute for Justice by *Erik S. Jaffe, William H. Mellor,* and *Steven M. Simpson;* for the International Law Enforcement Educators and Trainers Association et al. by *David B. Kopel* and *C. D. Michel;* for International Scholars by *James R. Schaller;* for Jews for the Preservation of Firearms Ownership by *Daniel L. Schmutter;* for the Libertarian National Committee, Inc., by *Bob Barr;* for the Maricopa County Attorney's Office et al. by *Daryl Manhart, Andrew P. Thomas, Arthur E. Mallory, Hy Forgeron,* and *Bryan A. Skoric;* for the Mountain States Legal Foundation by *William Perry Pendley;* for the National Rifle Association et al. by *Stephen D. Poss, Kevin P. Martin,* firearm, and the registration of handguns is prohibited. See D. C. Code §§ 7–2501.01(12), 7–2502.01(a), 7–2502.02(a)(4) (2001). Wholly apart from that prohibition, no person may carry a handgun without a license, but the chief of police may issue licenses for 1-year periods. See §§ 22–4504(a), 22–4506. District of Columbia law also requires residents to keep their lawfully owned firearms, such as registered long guns, "unloaded and disassembled or bound by a trigger lock or similar device" unless they are located in a place of business or are being used for lawful recreational activities. See § 7–2507.02.[1]

Respondent Dick Heller is a D. C. special police officer authorized to carry a handgun while on duty at the Thurgood Marshall Judiciary Building. He applied for a registration certificate for a handgun that he wished to keep at home, but the District refused. He thereafter filed a lawsuit in the Federal District Court for the District of Columbia seeking,

---

and *Scott B. Nardi;* for the National Shooting Sports Foundation, Inc., by *Lawrence G. Keane, Christopher P. Johnson,* and *Kanchana Wangkeo Leung;* for Ohio Concealed Carry Permitholders et al. by *Jeanette M. Moll;* for the Paragon Foundation, Inc., by *Paul M. Kienzle III;* for Pink Pistols et al. by *Michael B. Minton;* for Retired Military Officers by *Andrew G. McBride;* for the Rutherford Institute by *John W. Whitehead;* for the Second Amendment Foundation by *Nelson Lund;* for the Southeastern Legal Foundation, Inc., et al. by *Shannon Lee Goessling;* for State Firearm Associations by *David J. Schenck;* for Virginia1774.org by *Richard E. Hill, Jr.;* for Major General John D. Altenburg, Jr., et al. by *C. Allen Foster, Robert P. Charrow, John D. Altenburg, Jr.,* and *John P. Einwechter;* for Dr. Suzanna Gratia Hupp, D. C., et al. by *Kelly J. Shackelford;* for the President *Pro Tempore* of the Senate of Pennsylvania Joseph B. Scarnati III by *John P. Krill, Jr.,* and *Linda J. Shorey;* and for 55 Members of the United States Senate et al. by *Stephen P. Halbrook.*

Briefs of *amici curiae* were filed for the American Public Health Association et al. by *Alison M. Tucher;* for GeorgiaCarry.Org, Inc., by *John R. Monroe* and *Edward A. Stone;* for Erwin Chemerinsky et al. by *Mr. Chemerinsky, pro se;* and for 126 Women State Legislators et al. by *M. Carol Bambery.*

[1] There are minor exceptions to all of these prohibitions, none of which is relevant here.

on Second Amendment grounds, to enjoin the city from enforcing the bar on the registration of handguns, the licensing requirement insofar as it prohibits the carrying of a firearm in the home without a license, and the trigger-lock requirement insofar as it prohibits the use of "functional firearms within the home." App. 59a. The District Court dismissed respondent's complaint, see *Parker* v. *District of Columbia*, 311 F. Supp. 2d 103, 109 (2004). The Court of Appeals for the District of Columbia Circuit, construing his complaint as seeking the right to render a firearm operable and carry it about his home in that condition only when necessary for self-defense,[2] reversed, see *Parker* v. *District of Columbia*, 478 F. 3d 370, 401 (2007). It held that the Second Amendment protects an individual right to possess firearms and that the city's total ban on handguns, as well as its requirement that firearms in the home be kept nonfunctional even when necessary for self-defense, violated that right. See *id.*, at 395, 399–401. The Court of Appeals directed the District Court to enter summary judgment for respondent.

We granted certiorari. 552 U. S. 1035 (2007).

II

We turn first to the meaning of the Second Amendment.

A

The Second Amendment provides: "A well regulated Militia, being necessary to the security of a free State, the right of the people to keep and bear Arms, shall not be infringed." In interpreting this text, we are guided by the principle that "[t]he Constitution was written to be understood by the voters; its words and phrases were used in their normal and ordinary as distinguished from technical meaning." *United States* v. *Sprague*, 282 U. S. 716, 731 (1931); see also *Gibbons* v. *Ogden*, 9 Wheat. 1, 188 (1824). Normal meaning may of

[2] That construction has not been challenged here.

course include an idiomatic meaning, but it excludes secret or technical meanings that would not have been known to ordinary citizens in the founding generation.

The two sides in this case have set out very different interpretations of the Amendment. Petitioners and today's dissenting Justices believe that it protects only the right to possess and carry a firearm in connection with militia service. See Brief for Petitioners 11–12; *post*, at 636–637 (STEVENS, J., dissenting). Respondent argues that it protects an individual right to possess a firearm unconnected with service in a militia, and to use that arm for traditionally lawful purposes, such as self-defense within the home. See Brief for Respondent 2–4.

The Second Amendment is naturally divided into two parts: its prefatory clause and its operative clause. The former does not limit the latter grammatically, but rather announces a purpose. The Amendment could be rephrased, "Because a well regulated Militia is necessary to the security of a free State, the right of the people to keep and bear Arms shall not be infringed." See J. Tiffany, A Treatise on Government and Constitutional Law § 585, p. 394 (1867); Brief for Professors of Linguistics and English as *Amici Curiae* 3 (hereinafter Linguists' Brief). Although this structure of the Second Amendment is unique in our Constitution, other legal documents of the founding era, particularly individual-rights provisions of state constitutions, commonly included a prefatory statement of purpose. See generally Volokh, The Commonplace Second Amendment, 73 N. Y. U. L. Rev. 793, 814–821 (1998).

Logic demands that there be a link between the stated purpose and the command. The Second Amendment would be nonsensical if it read, "A well regulated Militia, being necessary to the security of a free State, the right of the people to petition for redress of grievances shall not be infringed." That requirement of logical connection may cause a prefatory clause to resolve an ambiguity in the operative clause.

("The separation of church and state being an important objective, the teachings of canons shall have no place in our jurisprudence." The preface makes clear that the operative clause refers not to canons of interpretation but to clergymen.) But apart from that clarifying function, a prefatory clause does not limit or expand the scope of the operative clause. See F. Dwarris, A General Treatise on Statutes 268–269 (P. Potter ed. 1871); T. Sedgwick, The Interpretation and Construction of Statutory and Constitutional Law 42–45 (2d ed. 1874).[3] "'It is nothing unusual in acts . . . for the enacting part to go beyond the preamble; the remedy often extends beyond the particular act or mischief which first suggested the necessity of the law.'" J. Bishop, Commentaries on Written Laws and Their Interpretation § 51, p. 49 (1882) (quoting *Rex* v. *Marks*, 3 East 157, 165, 102 Eng. Rep. 557, 560 (K. B. 1802)). Therefore, while we will begin our textual analysis with the operative clause, we will return to the prefatory clause to ensure that our reading of the operative clause is consistent with the announced purpose.[4]

---

[3] As Sutherland explains, the key 18th-century English case on the effect of preambles, *Copeman* v. *Gallant*, 1 P. Wms. 314, 24 Eng. Rep. 404 (1716), stated that "the preamble could not be used to restrict the effect of the words used in the purview." 2A N. Singer, Sutherland on Statutory Construction § 47.04, pp. 145–146 (rev. 5th ed. 1992). This rule was modified in England in an 1826 case to give more importance to the preamble, but in America "the settled principle of law is that the preamble cannot control the enacting part of the statute in cases where the enacting part is expressed in clear, unambiguous terms." *Id.*, at 146.

JUSTICE STEVENS says that we violate the general rule that every clause in a statute must have effect. *Post*, at 643. But where the text of a clause itself indicates that it does not have operative effect, such as "whereas" clauses in federal legislation or the Constitution's preamble, a court has no license to make it do what it was not designed to do. Or to put the point differently, operative provisions should be given effect as operative provisions, and prologues as prologues.

[4] JUSTICE STEVENS criticizes us for discussing the prologue last. *Ibid.* But if a prologue can be used only to clarify an ambiguous operative provision, surely the first step must be to determine whether the operative

1. Operative Clause.

a. "Right of the People." The first salient feature of the operative clause is that it codifies a "right of the people." The unamended Constitution and the Bill of Rights use the phrase "right of the people" two other times, in the First Amendment's Assembly-and-Petition Clause and in the Fourth Amendment's Search-and-Seizure Clause. The Ninth Amendment uses very similar terminology ("The enumeration in the Constitution, of certain rights, shall not be construed to deny or disparage others retained by the people"). All three of these instances unambiguously refer to individual rights, not "collective" rights, or rights that may be exercised only through participation in some corporate body.[5]

Three provisions of the Constitution refer to "the people" in a context other than "rights"—the famous preamble ("We the people"), § 2 of Article I (providing that "the people" will choose members of the House), and the Tenth Amendment (providing that those powers not given the Federal Government remain with "the States" or "the people"). Those provisions arguably refer to "the people" acting collectively—

---

provision is ambiguous. It might be argued, we suppose, that the prologue itself should be one of the factors that go into the determination of whether the operative provision is ambiguous—but that would cause the prologue to be used to produce ambiguity rather than just to resolve it. In any event, even if we considered the prologue *along with* the operative provision we would reach the same result we do today, since (as we explain) our interpretation of "the right of the people to keep and bear arms" furthers the purpose of an effective militia no less than (indeed, more than) the dissent's interpretation. See *infra*, at 599–600.

[5] JUSTICE STEVENS is of course correct, *post*, at 645, that the right to assemble cannot be exercised alone, but it is still an individual right, and not one conditioned upon membership in some defined "assembly," as he contends the right to bear arms is conditioned upon membership in a defined militia. And JUSTICE STEVENS is dead wrong to think that the right to petition is "primarily collective in nature." *Ibid.* See *McDonald* v. *Smith*, 472 U. S. 479, 482–484 (1985) (describing historical origins of right to petition).

but they deal with the exercise or reservation of powers, not rights. Nowhere else in the Constitution does a "right" attributed to "the people" refer to anything other than an individual right.[6]

What is more, in all six other provisions of the Constitution that mention "the people," the term unambiguously refers to all members of the political community, not an unspecified subset. As we said in *United States* v. *Verdugo-Urquidez,* 494 U. S. 259, 265 (1990):

> "'[T]he people' seems to have been a term of art employed in select parts of the Constitution. . . . [Its uses] sugges[t] that 'the people' protected by the Fourth Amendment, and by the First and Second Amendments, and to whom rights and powers are reserved in the Ninth and Tenth Amendments, refers to a class of persons who are part of a national community or who have otherwise developed sufficient connection with this country to be considered part of that community."

This contrasts markedly with the phrase "the militia" in the prefatory clause. As we will describe below, the "militia" in colonial America consisted of a subset of "the people"—those who were male, able bodied, and within a certain age range. Reading the Second Amendment as protecting only the right

[6] If we look to other founding-era documents, we find that some state constitutions used the term "the people" to refer to the people collectively, in contrast to "citizen," which was used to invoke individual rights. See Heyman, Natural Rights and the Second Amendment, in The Second Amendment in Law and History 179, 193–195 (C. Bogus ed. 2000) (hereinafter Bogus). But that usage was not remotely uniform. See, *e. g.*, N. C. Declaration of Rights § XIV (1776), in 5 The Federal and State Constitutions, Colonial Charters, and Other Organic Laws 2787, 2788 (F. Thorpe ed. 1909) (hereinafter Thorpe) (jury trial); Md. Declaration of Rights § XVIII (1776), in 3 *id.*, at 1686, 1688 (vicinage requirement); Vt. Declaration of Rights, ch. 1, § XI (1777), in 6 *id.*, at 3737, 3741 (searches and seizures); Pa. Declaration of Rights § XII (1776), in 5 *id.*, at 3082, 3083 (free speech). And, most importantly, it was clearly not the terminology used in the Federal Constitution, given the First, Fourth, and Ninth Amendments.

to "keep and bear Arms" in an organized militia therefore fits poorly with the operative clause's description of the holder of that right as "the people."

We start therefore with a strong presumption that the Second Amendment right is exercised individually and belongs to all Americans.

b. "Keep and Bear Arms." We move now from the holder of the right—"the people"—to the substance of the right: "to keep and bear Arms."

Before addressing the verbs "keep" and "bear," we interpret their object: "Arms." The 18th-century meaning is no different from the meaning today. The 1773 edition of Samuel Johnson's dictionary defined "arms" as "[w]eapons of offence, or armour of defence." 1 Dictionary of the English Language 106 (4th ed.) (reprinted 1978) (hereinafter Johnson). Timothy Cunningham's important 1771 legal dictionary defined "arms" as "any thing that a man wears for his defence, or takes into his hands, or useth in wrath to cast at or strike another." 1 A New and Complete Law Dictionary; see also N. Webster, American Dictionary of the English Language (1828) (reprinted 1989) (hereinafter Webster) (similar).

The term was applied, then as now, to weapons that were not specifically designed for military use and were not employed in a military capacity. For instance, Cunningham's legal dictionary gave as an example of usage: "Servants and labourers shall use bows and arrows on *Sundays,* &c. and not bear other arms." See also, *e. g.,* An Act for the trial of Negroes, 1797 Del. Laws ch. XLIII, §6, in 1 First Laws of the State of Delaware 102, 104 (J. Cushing ed. 1981 (pt. 1)); see generally *State* v. *Duke,* 42 Tex. 455, 458 (1874) (citing decisions of state courts construing "arms"). Although one founding-era thesaurus limited "arms" (as opposed to "weapons") to "instruments of offence *generally* made use of in war," even that source stated that all firearms constituted "arms." 1 J. Trusler, The Distinction Between Words Esteemed Synonymous in the English Language 37 (3d ed. 1794) (emphasis added).

Some have made the argument, bordering on the frivolous, that only those arms in existence in the 18th century are protected by the Second Amendment. We do not interpret constitutional rights that way. Just as the First Amendment protects modern forms of communications, *e. g., Reno* v. *American Civil Liberties Union,* 521 U. S. 844, 849 (1997), and the Fourth Amendment applies to modern forms of search, *e. g., Kyllo* v. *United States,* 533 U. S. 27, 35–36 (2001), the Second Amendment extends, prima facie, to all instruments that constitute bearable arms, even those that were not in existence at the time of the founding.

We turn to the phrases "keep arms" and "bear arms." Johnson defined "keep" as, most relevantly, "[t]o retain; not to lose," and "[t]o have in custody." Johnson 1095. Webster defined it as "[t]o hold; to retain in one's power or possession." No party has apprised us of an idiomatic meaning of "keep Arms." Thus, the most natural reading of "keep Arms" in the Second Amendment is to "have weapons."

The phrase "keep arms" was not prevalent in the written documents of the founding period that we have found, but there are a few examples, all of which favor viewing the right to "keep Arms" as an individual right unconnected with militia service. William Blackstone, for example, wrote that Catholics convicted of not attending service in the Church of England suffered certain penalties, one of which was that they were not permitted to "keep arms in their houses." 4 Commentaries on the Laws of England 55 (1769) (hereinafter Blackstone); see also 1 W. & M., ch. 15, §4, in 3 Eng. Stat. at Large 422 (1689) ("[N]o Papist . . . shall or may have or keep in his House . . . any Arms . . . "); 1 W. Hawkins, Treatise on the Pleas of the Crown 26 (1771) (similar). Petitioners point to militia laws of the founding period that required militia members to "keep" arms in connection with militia service, and they conclude from this that the phrase "keep Arms" has a militia-related connotation. See Brief for Petitioners 16–17 (citing laws of Delaware, New Jersey, and Virginia). This is rather like saying that, since there are many statutes that authorize aggrieved employees to "file complaints" with federal agencies, the phrase "file complaints" has an employment-related connotation. "Keep arms" was simply a common way of referring to possessing arms, for militiamen *and everyone else.*[7]

[7] See, *e. g.*, 3 A Compleat Collection of State-Tryals 185 (1719) ("Hath not every Subject power to keep Arms, as well as Servants in his House for defence of his Person?"); T. Wood, A New Institute of the Imperial or Civil Law 282 (4th ed. corrected 1730) ("Those are guilty of *publick* Force, who keep Arms in their Houses, and make use of them otherwise than upon Journeys or Hunting, or for Sale . . . "); A Collection of All the Acts of Assembly, Now in Force, in the Colony of Virginia 596 (1733) ("Free Negros, Mulattos, or Indians, and Owners of Slaves, seated at Frontier Plantations, may obtain Licence from a Justice of Peace, for keeping Arms, &c."); J. Ayliffe, A New Pandect of *Roman* Civil Law 195 (1734) ("Yet a Person might keep Arms in his House, or on his Estate, on the Account of Hunting, Navigation, Travelling, and on the Score of Selling them in the way of Trade or Commerce, or such Arms as accrued to him by way of Inheritance"); J. Trusler, A Concise View of the Common Law and Statute Law of England 270 (1781) ("[I]f [papists] keep arms in their houses, such arms may be seized by a justice of the peace"); Some Considerations on the Game Laws 54 (1796) ("Who has been deprived by [the law] of keeping arms for his own defence? What law forbids the veriest pauper, if he can raise a sum sufficient for the purchase of it, from mounting his Gun on his Chimney Piece . . . ?"); 3 B. Wilson, The Works of the Honourable James Wilson 84 (1804) (with reference to state constitutional right: "This is one of our many renewals of the Saxon regulations. 'They were bound,' says Mr. Selden, 'to keep arms for the preservation of the kingdom, and of their own persons'"); W. Duer, Outlines of the Constitutional Jurisprudence of the United States 31–32 (1833) (with reference to colonists' English rights: "The right of every individual to keep arms for his defence, suitable to his condition and degree; which was the public allowance, under due restrictions of the natural right of resistance and self-preservation"); 3 R. Burn, Justice of the Peace and Parish Officer 88 (29th ed. 1845) ("It is, however, laid down by Serjeant *Hawkins*, . . . that

At the time of the founding, as now, to "bear" meant to "carry." See Johnson 161; Webster; T. Sheridan, A Complete Dictionary of the English Language (1796); 2 Oxford English Dictionary 20 (2d ed. 1989) (hereinafter Oxford). When used with "arms," however, the term has a meaning that refers to carrying for a particular purpose—confrontation. In *Muscarello* v. *United States,* 524 U. S. 125 (1998), in the course of analyzing the meaning of "carries a firearm" in a federal criminal statute, JUSTICE GINSBURG wrote that "[s]urely a most familiar meaning is, as the Constitution's Second Amendment . . . indicate[s]: 'wear, bear, or carry . . . upon the person or in the clothing or in a pocket, for the purpose . . . of being armed and ready for offensive or defensive action in a case of conflict with another person.'" *Id.,* at 143 (dissenting opinion) (quoting Black's Law Dictionary 214 (6th ed. 1990)). We think that JUSTICE GINSBURG accurately captured the natural meaning of "bear arms." Although the phrase implies that the carrying of the weapon is for the purpose of "offensive or defensive action," it in no way connotes participation in a structured military organization.

From our review of founding-era sources, we conclude that this natural meaning was also the meaning that "bear arms" had in the 18th century. In numerous instances, "bear arms" was unambiguously used to refer to the carrying of weapons outside of an organized militia. The most prominent examples are those most relevant to the Second Amendment: nine state constitutional provisions written in the 18th century or the first two decades of the 19th, which enshrined a right of citizens to "bear arms in defense of themselves and the state" or "bear arms in defense of himself and

---

if a lessee, after the end of the term, keep arms in his house to oppose the entry of the lessor, . . . "); *State* v. *Dempsey,* 31 N. C. 384, 385 (1849) (citing 1840 state law making it a misdemeanor for a member of certain racial groups "to carry about his person or keep in his house any shot gun or other arms").

the state."[8] It is clear from those formulations that "bear arms" did not refer only to carrying a weapon in an organized military unit. Justice James Wilson interpreted the Pennsylvania Constitution's arms-bearing right, for example, as a recognition of the natural right of defense "of one's person or house"—what he called the law of "self preservation." 2 Collected Works of James Wilson 1142, and n. x (K. Hall & M. Hall eds. 2007) (citing Pa. Const., Art. IX, § 21 (1790)); see also T. Walker, Introduction to American Law 198 (1837) ("Thus the right of self-defence [is] guaranteed by the [Ohio] constitution"); see also *id.*, at 157 (equating Second Amendment with that provision of the Ohio Constitution). That was also the interpretation of those state constitutional provisions adopted by pre-Civil War state courts.[9] These pro-

[8] See Pa. Declaration of Rights § XIII, in 5 Thorpe 3083 ("That the people have a right to bear arms for the defence of themselves and the state . . . "); Vt. Declaration of Rights, ch. 1, § XV, in 6 *id.*, at 3741 ("That the people have a right to bear arms for the defence of themselves and the State . . . "); Ky. Const., Art. XII, § 23 (1792), in 3 *id.*, at 1264, 1275 ("That the right of the citizens to bear arms in defence of themselves and the State shall not be questioned"); Ohio Const., Art. VIII, § 20 (1802), in 5 *id.*, at 2901, 2911 ("That the people have a right to bear arms for the defence of themselves and the State . . . "); Ind. Const., Art. I, § 20 (1816), in 2 *id.*, at 1057, 1059 ("That the people have a right to bear arms for the defense of themselves and the State . . . "); Miss. Const., Art. I, § 23 (1817), in 4 *id.*, at 2032, 2034 ("Every citizen has a right to bear arms, in defence of himself and the State"); Conn. Const., Art. First, § 17 (1818), in 1 *id.*, at 536, 538 ("Every citizen has a right to bear arms in defense of himself and the state"); Ala. Const., Art. I, § 23 (1819), in *id.*, at 96, 98 ("Every citizen has a right to bear arms in defence of himself and the State"); Mo. Const., Art. XIII, § 3 (1820), in 4 *id.*, at 2150, 2163 ("[T]hat their right to bear arms in defence of themselves and of the State cannot be questioned"). See generally Volokh, State Constitutional Rights to Keep and Bear Arms, 11 Tex. Rev. L. & Politics 191 (2006).

[9] See *Bliss* v. *Commonwealth*, 2 Litt. 90, 91–92 (Ky. 1822); *State* v. *Reid*, 1 Ala. 612, 616–617 (1840); *State* v. *Schoultz*, 25 Mo. 128, 155 (1857); see also *Simpson* v. *State*, 5 Yer. 356, 360 (Tenn. 1833) (interpreting similar provision with " 'common defence' " purpose); *State* v. *Huntly*, 25 N. C. 418, 422–423 (1843) (same); cf. *Nunn* v. *State*, 1 Ga. 243, 250–251 (1846) (con-

visions demonstrate—again, in the most analogous linguistic context—that "bear arms" was not limited to the carrying of arms in a militia.

The phrase "bear Arms" also had at the time of the founding an idiomatic meaning that was significantly different from its natural meaning: "to serve as a soldier, do military service, fight" or "to wage war." See Linguists' Brief 18; *post,* at 646 (STEVENS, J., dissenting). But it *unequivocally* bore that idiomatic meaning only when followed by the preposition "against," which was in turn followed by the target of the hostilities. See 2 Oxford 21. (That is how, for example, our Declaration of Independence ¶ 28 used the phrase: "He has constrained our fellow Citizens taken Captive on the high Seas to bear Arms against their Country . . . .") Every example given by petitioners' *amici* for the idiomatic meaning of "bear arms" from the founding period either includes the preposition "against" or is not clearly idiomatic. See Linguists' Brief 18–23. Without the preposition, "bear arms" normally meant (as it continues to mean today) what JUSTICE GINSBURG's opinion in *Muscarello* said.

In any event, the meaning of "bear arms" that petitioners and JUSTICE STEVENS propose is *not even* the (sometimes) idiomatic meaning. Rather, they manufacture a hybrid definition, whereby "bear arms" connotes the actual carrying of arms (and therefore is not really an idiom) but only in the service of an organized militia. No dictionary has ever adopted that definition, and we have been apprised of no source that indicates that it carried that meaning at the time of the founding. But it is easy to see why petitioners and the dissent are driven to the hybrid definition. Giving "bear Arms" its idiomatic meaning would cause the protected right to consist of the right to be a soldier or to wage war—an absurdity that no commentator has ever endorsed. See L. Levy, Origins of the Bill of Rights 135 (1999). Worse still,

struing Second Amendment); *State* v. *Chandler,* 5 La. Ann. 489, 489–490 (1850) (same).

the phrase "keep and bear Arms" would be incoherent. The word "Arms" would have two different meanings at once: "weapons" (as the object of "keep") and (as the object of "bear") one-half of an idiom. It would be rather like saying "He filled and kicked the bucket" to mean "He filled the bucket and died." Grotesque.

Petitioners justify their limitation of "bear arms" to the military context by pointing out the unremarkable fact that it was often used in that context—the same mistake they made with respect to "keep arms." It is especially unremarkable that the phrase was often used in a military context in the federal legal sources (such as records of congressional debate) that have been the focus of petitioners' inquiry. Those sources would have had little occasion to use it *except* in discussions about the standing army and the militia. And the phrases used primarily in those military discussions include not only "bear arms" but also "carry arms," "possess arms," and "have arms"—though no one thinks that those *other* phrases also had special military meanings. See Barnett, Was the Right to Keep and Bear Arms Conditioned on Service in an Organized Militia? 83 Texas L. Rev. 237, 261 (2004). The common references to those "fit to bear arms" in congressional discussions about the militia are matched by use of the same phrase in the few nonmilitary federal contexts where the concept would be relevant. See, *e. g.*, 30 Journals of Continental Congress 349–351 (J. Fitzpatrick ed. 1934). Other legal sources frequently used "bear arms" in nonmilitary contexts.[10] Cunningham's legal dictionary, cited

---

[10] See J. Brydall, Privilegia Magnatud apud Anglos 14 (1704) (Privilege XXXIII) ("In the 21st Year of King Edward the Third, a Proclamation Issued, that no Person should bear any Arms within London, and the Suburbs"); J. Bond, A Compleat Guide to Justices of the Peace 43 (3d ed. 1707) ("Sheriffs, and all other Officers in executing their Offices, and all other persons pursuing Hu[e] and Cry may lawfully bear Arms"); 1 An Abridgment of the Public Statutes in Force and Use Relative to Scotland (1755) (entry for "Arms": "And if any person above described shall have in his custody, use, or bear arms, being thereof convicted before one justice of

above, gave as an example of its usage a sentence unrelated to military affairs ("Servants and labourers shall use bows and arrows on *Sundays*, &c. and not bear other arms"). And if one looks beyond legal sources, "bear arms" was frequently used in nonmilitary contexts. See Cramer & Olson, What Did "Bear Arms" Mean in the Second Amendment? 6 Georgetown J. L. & Pub. Pol'y 511 (2008) (identifying numerous nonmilitary uses of "bear arms" from the founding period).

JUSTICE STEVENS points to a study by *amici* supposedly showing that the phrase "bear arms" was most frequently used in the military context. See *post*, at 647–648, n. 9; Linguists' Brief 24. Of course, as we have said, the fact that the phrase was commonly used in a particular context does not show that it is limited to that context, and, in any event, we have given many sources where the phrase was used in nonmilitary contexts. Moreover, the study's collection appears to include (who knows how many times) the idiomatic phrase "bear arms against," which is irrelevant. The *amici* also dismiss examples such as "'bear arms . . . for the purpose of killing game'" because those uses are "expressly

---

peace, or other judge competent, summarily, he shall for the first offense forfeit all such arms" (citing 1 Geo., ch. 54, § 1, in 5 Eng. Stat. at Large 90 (1668))); Statute Law of Scotland Abridged 132–133 (2d ed. 1769) ("Acts for disarming the highlands" but "exempting those who have particular licenses to bear arms"); E. de Vattel, The Law of Nations, or, Principles of the Law of Nature 144 (1792) ("Since custom has allowed persons of rank and gentlemen of the army to bear arms in time of peace, strict care should be taken that none but these should be allowed to wear swords"); E. Roche, Proceedings of a Court-Martial, Held at the Council-Chamber, in the City of Cork 3 (1798) (charge VI: "With having held traitorous conferences, and with having conspired, with the like intent, for the purpose of attacking and despoiling of the arms of several of the King's subjects, qualified by law to bear arms"); C. Humphreys, A Compendium of the Common Law in Force in Kentucky 482 (1822) ("[I]n this country the constitution guarranties to all persons the right to bear arms; then it can only be a crime to exercise this right in such a manner, as to terrify people unnecessarily").

qualified." Linguists' Brief 24. (JUSTICE STEVENS uses the same excuse for dismissing the state constitutional provisions analogous to the Second Amendment that identify private-use purposes for which the individual right can be asserted. See *post*, at 647.) That analysis is faulty. A purposive qualifying phrase that contradicts the word or phrase it modifies is unknown this side of the looking glass (except, apparently, in some courses on linguistics). If "bear arms" means, as we think, simply the carrying of arms, a modifier can limit the purpose of the carriage ("for the purpose of self-defense" or "to make war against the King"). But if "bear arms" means, as the petitioners and the dissent think, the carrying of arms only for military purposes, one simply cannot add "for the purpose of killing game." The right "to carry arms in the militia for the purpose of killing game" is worthy of the Mad Hatter. Thus, these purposive qualifying phrases positively establish that "to bear arms" is not limited to military use.[11]

JUSTICE STEVENS places great weight on James Madison's inclusion of a conscientious-objector clause in his original draft of the Second Amendment: "but no person religiously scrupulous of bearing arms, shall be compelled to render military service in person." Creating the Bill of Rights 12 (H. Veit, K. Bowling, & C. Bickford eds. 1991) (hereinafter Veit). He argues that this clause establishes that the drafters of the Second Amendment intended "bear Arms" to refer only

---

[11] JUSTICE STEVENS contends, *post*, at 650, that since we assert that adding "against" to "bear arms" gives it a military meaning we must concede that adding a purposive qualifying phrase to "bear arms" can alter its meaning. But the difference is that we do not maintain that "against" *alters* the meaning of "bear arms" but merely that it *clarifies* which of various meanings (one of which is military) is intended. JUSTICE STEVENS, however, argues that "[t]he term 'bear arms' is a familiar idiom; when used unadorned by any additional words, its meaning is 'to serve as a soldier, do military service, fight.'" *Post*, at 646. He therefore must establish that adding a contradictory purposive phrase can *alter* a word's meaning.

to military service. See *post,* at 660–661. It is always perilous to derive the meaning of an adopted provision from another provision deleted in the drafting process.[12] In any case, what JUSTICE STEVENS would conclude from the deleted provision does not follow. It was not meant to exempt from military service those who objected to going to war but had no scruples about personal gunfights. Quakers opposed the use of arms not just for militia service, but for any violent purpose whatsoever—so much so that Quaker frontiersmen were forbidden to use arms to defend their families, even though "[i]n such circumstances the temptation to seize a hunting rifle or knife in self-defense . . . must sometimes have been almost overwhelming." P. Brock, Pacifism in the United States 359 (1968); see M. Hirst, The Quakers in Peace and War 336–339 (1923); 3 T. Clarkson, Portraiture of Quakerism 103–104 (3d ed. 1807). The Pennsylvania Militia Act of 1757 exempted from service those *"scrupling the use of arms"*—a phrase that no one contends had an idiomatic meaning. See 5 Stat. at Large of Pa. 613 (J. Mitchell & H. Flanders comm'rs 1898) (emphasis in original). Thus, the most natural interpretation of Madison's deleted text is that those opposed to carrying weapons for potential violent confrontation would not be "compelled to render military service," in which such carrying would be required.[13]

---

[12] JUSTICE STEVENS finds support for his legislative history inference from the recorded views of one Antifederalist member of the House. *Post,* at 660, n. 25. "The claim that the best or most representative reading of the [language of the] amendments would conform to the understanding and concerns of [the Antifederalists] is . . . highly problematic." Rakove, The Second Amendment: The Highest Stage of Originalism, in Bogus 74, 81.

[13] The same applies to the conscientious-objector amendments proposed by Virginia and North Carolina, which said: "That any person religiously scrupulous of bearing arms ought to be exempted upon payment of an equivalent to employ another to bear arms in his stead." See Veit 19; 4 J. Eliot, The Debates in the Several State Constitutions on the Adoption

Finally, JUSTICE STEVENS suggests that "keep and bear Arms" was some sort of term of art, presumably akin to "hue and cry" or "cease and desist." (This suggestion usefully evades the problem that there is no evidence whatsoever to support a military reading of "keep arms.") JUSTICE STEVENS believes that the unitary meaning of "keep and bear Arms" is established by the Second Amendment's calling it a "right" (singular) rather than "rights" (plural). See *post*, at 651. There is nothing to this. State constitutions of the founding period routinely grouped multiple (related) guarantees under a singular "right," and the First Amendment protects the "right [singular] of the people peaceably to assemble, and to petition the Government for a redress of grievances." See, *e. g.*, Pa. Declaration of Rights §§ IX, XII, XVI, in 5 Thorpe 3083–3084; Ohio Const., Art. VIII, §§ 11, 19 (1802), in *id.*, at 2910–2911.[14] And even if "keep and bear Arms" were a unitary phrase, we find no evidence that it bore a military meaning. Although the phrase was not at all common (which would be unusual for a term of art), we have found instances of its use with a clearly nonmilitary connotation. In a 1780 debate in the House of Lords, for example, Lord Richmond described an order to disarm pri-

---

of the Federal Constitution 243, 244 (2d ed. 1836) (reprinted 1941). Certainly their second use of the phrase ("bear arms in his stead") refers, by reason of context, to compulsory bearing of arms for military duty. But their first use of the phrase ("any person religiously scrupulous of bearing arms") assuredly did not refer to people whose God allowed them to bear arms for defense of themselves but not for defense of their country.

[14] Faced with this clear historical usage, JUSTICE STEVENS resorts to the bizarre argument that because the word "to" is not included before "bear" (whereas it is included before "petition" in the First Amendment), the unitary meaning of "'to keep and bear'" is established. *Post*, at 651, n. 13. We have never heard of the proposition that omitting repetition of the "to" causes two verbs with different meanings to become one. A promise "to support and to defend the Constitution of the United States" is not a whit different from a promise "to support and defend the Constitution of the United States."

vate citizens (not militia members) as "a violation of the constitutional right of Protestant subjects to keep and bear arms for their own defence." 49 The London Magazine or Gentleman's Monthly Intelligencer 467 (1780). In response, another member of Parliament referred to "the right of bearing arms for personal defence," making clear that no special military meaning for "keep and bear arms" was intended in the discussion. *Id.*, at 467–468.[15]

c. Meaning of the Operative Clause. Putting all of these textual elements together, we find that they guarantee the individual right to possess and carry weapons in case of confrontation. This meaning is strongly confirmed by the historical background of the Second Amendment. We look to this because it has always been widely understood that the Second Amendment, like the First and Fourth Amendments, codified a *pre-existing* right. The very text of the Second Amendment implicitly recognizes the pre-existence of the right and declares only that it "shall not be infringed." As we said in *United States* v. *Cruikshank*, 92 U. S. 542, 553 (1876), "[t]his is not a right granted by the Constitution. Neither is it in any manner dependent upon that instrument for its existence. The second amendment declares that it shall not be infringed . . . ."[16]

Between the Restoration and the Glorious Revolution, the Stuart Kings Charles II and James II succeeded in using select militias loyal to them to suppress political dissidents, in part by disarming their opponents. See J. Malcolm, To Keep and Bear Arms 31–53 (1994) (hereinafter Malcolm); L. Schwoerer, The Declaration of Rights, 1689, p. 76 (1981).

---

[15] Cf. 21 Geo. II, ch. 34, §3, in 7 Eng. Stat. at Large 126 (1748) ("That the Prohibition contained . . . in this Act, of having, keeping, bearing, or wearing any Arms or Warlike Weapons . . . shall not extend . . . to any Officers or their Assistants, employed in the Execution of Justice . . . ").

[16] Contrary to JUSTICE STEVENS' wholly unsupported assertion, *post*, at 636, 652, there was no pre-existing right in English law "to use weapons for certain military purposes" or to use arms in an organized militia.

Under the auspices of the 1671 Game Act, for example, the Catholic Charles II had ordered general disarmaments of regions home to his Protestant enemies. See Malcolm 103–106. These experiences caused Englishmen to be extremely wary of concentrated military forces run by the state and to be jealous of their arms. They accordingly obtained an assurance from William and Mary, in the Declaration of Right (which was codified as the English Bill of Rights), that Protestants would never be disarmed: "That the Subjects which are Protestants, may have Arms for their Defence suitable to their Conditions, and as allowed by Law." 1 W. & M., ch. 2, § 7, in 3 Eng. Stat. at Large 441. This right has long been understood to be the predecessor to our Second Amendment. See E. Dumbauld, The Bill of Rights and What It Means Today 51 (1957); W. Rawle, A View of the Constitution of the United States of America 122 (1825) (hereinafter Rawle). It was clearly an individual right, having nothing whatever to do with service in a militia. To be sure, it was an individual right not available to the whole population, given that it was restricted to Protestants, and like all written English rights it was held only against the Crown, not Parliament. See Schwoerer, To Hold and Bear Arms: The English Perspective, in Bogus 207, 218; but see 3 J. Story, Commentaries on the Constitution of the United States § 1858 (1833) (hereinafter Story) (contending that the "right to bear arms" is a "limitatio[n] upon the power of parliament" as well). But it was secured to them as individuals, according to "libertarian political principles," not as members of a fighting force. Schwoerer, Declaration of Rights, at 283; see also *id.*, at 78; G. Jellinek, The Declaration of the Rights of Man and of Citizens 49, and n. 7 (1901) (reprinted 1979).

By the time of the founding, the right to have arms had become fundamental for English subjects. See Malcolm 122–134. Blackstone, whose works, we have said, "constituted the preeminent authority on English law for the founding generation," *Alden* v. *Maine*, 527 U. S. 706, 715 (1999), cited the arms provision of the Bill of Rights as one of the fundamental rights of Englishmen. See 1 Blackstone 136, 139–140 (1765). His description of it cannot possibly be thought to tie it to militia or military service. It was, he said, "the natural right of resistance and self-preservation," *id.*, at 139, and "the right of having and using arms for self-preservation and defence," *id.*, at 140; see also 3 *id.*, at 2–4 (1768). Other contemporary authorities concurred. See G. Sharp, Tracts, Concerning the Ancient and Only True Legal Means of National Defence, by a Free Militia 17–18, 27 (3d ed. 1782); 2 J. de Lolme, The Rise and Progress of the English Constitution 886–887 (1784) (A. Stephens ed. 1838); W. Blizard, Desultory Reflections on Police 59–60 (1785). Thus, the right secured in 1689 as a result of the Stuarts' abuses was by the time of the founding understood to be an individual right protecting against both public and private violence.

And, of course, what the Stuarts had tried to do to their political enemies, George III had tried to do to the colonists. In the tumultuous decades of the 1760's and 1770's, the Crown began to disarm the inhabitants of the most rebellious areas. That provoked polemical reactions by Americans invoking their rights as Englishmen to keep arms. A New York article of April 1769 said that "[i]t is a natural right which the people have reserved to themselves, confirmed by the Bill of Rights, to keep arms for their own defence." A Journal of the Times: Mar. 17, New York Journal, Supp. 1, Apr. 13, 1769, in Boston Under Military Rule 79 (O. Dickerson ed. 1936) (reprinted 1970); see also, *e. g.*, Shippen, Boston Gazette, Jan. 30, 1769, in 1 The Writings of Samuel Adams 299 (H. Cushing ed. 1904) (reprinted 1968). They understood the right to enable individuals to defend themselves. As the most important early American edition of Blackstone's Commentaries (by the law professor and former Antifederalist St. George Tucker) made clear in the notes to the description of the arms right, Americans understood the "right of self-preservation" as permitting a citizen to "repe[l] force by force" when "the intervention of society in his behalf, may be too late to prevent an injury." 1 Blackstone's Commentaries 145–146, n. 42 (1803) (hereinafter Tucker's Blackstone). See also W. Duer, Outlines of the Constitutional Jurisprudence of the United States 31–32 (1833).

There seems to us no doubt, on the basis of both text and history, that the Second Amendment conferred an individual right to keep and bear arms. Of course the right was not unlimited, just as the First Amendment's right of free speech was not, see, *e. g., United States* v. *Williams,* 553 U. S. 285 (2008). Thus, we do not read the Second Amendment to protect the right of citizens to carry arms for *any sort* of confrontation, just as we do not read the First Amendment to protect the right of citizens to speak for *any purpose.* Before turning to limitations upon the individual right, however, we must determine whether the prefatory clause of the Second Amendment comports with our interpretation of the operative clause.

2. Prefatory Clause.

The prefatory clause reads: "A well regulated Militia, being necessary to the security of a free State . . . ."

a. "Well-Regulated Militia." In *United States* v. *Miller,* 307 U. S. 174, 179 (1939), we explained that "the Militia comprised all males physically capable of acting in concert for the common defense." That definition comports with founding-era sources. See, *e. g.,* Webster ("The militia of a country are the able bodied men organized into companies, regiments and brigades . . . and required by law to attend military exercises on certain days only, but at other times left to pursue their usual occupations"); The Federalist No. 46, pp. 329, 334 (B. Wright ed. 1961) (J. Madison) ("near half a million of citizens with arms in their hands"); Letter to Destutt de Tracy (Jan. 26, 1811), in The Portable Thomas

Jefferson 520, 524 (M. Peterson ed. 1975) ("the militia of the State, that is to say, of every man in it able to bear arms").

Petitioners take a seemingly narrower view of the militia, stating that "[m]ilitias are the state- and congressionally-regulated military forces described in the Militia Clauses (art. I, § 8, cls. 15–16)." Brief for Petitioners 12. Although we agree with petitioners' interpretive assumption that "militia" means the same thing in Article I and the Second Amendment, we believe that petitioners identify the wrong thing, namely, the organized militia. Unlike armies and navies, which Congress is given the power to create ("to raise . . . Armies"; "to provide . . . a Navy," Art. I, § 8, cls. 12–13), the militia is assumed by Article I already to be *in existence.* Congress is given the power to "provide for calling forth the Militia," § 8, cl. 15; and the power not to create, but to "organiz[e]" it—and not to organize "a" militia, which is what one would expect if the militia were to be a federal creation, but to organize "the" militia, connoting a body already in existence, *ibid.*, cl. 16. This is fully consistent with the ordinary definition of the militia as all able-bodied men. From that pool, Congress has plenary power to organize the units that will make up an effective fighting force. That is what Congress did in the first Militia Act, which specified that "each and every free able-bodied white male citizen of the respective states, resident therein, who is or shall be of the age of eighteen years, and under the age of forty-five years (except as is herein after excepted) shall severally and respectively be enrolled in the militia." Act of May 8, 1792, 1 Stat. 271. To be sure, Congress need not conscript every able-bodied man into the militia, because nothing in Article I suggests that in exercising its power to organize, discipline, and arm the militia, Congress must focus upon the entire body. Although the militia consists of all able-bodied men, the federally organized militia may consist of a subset of them.

Finally, the adjective "well-regulated" implies nothing more than the imposition of proper discipline and training. See Johnson 1619 ("Regulate": "To adjust by rule or method"); Rawle 121–122; cf. Va. Declaration of Rights § 13 (1776), in 7 Thorpe 3812, 3814 (referring to "a well-regulated militia, composed of the body of the people, trained to arms").

b. "Security of a Free State." The phrase "security of a free State" meant "security of a free polity," not security of each of the several States as the dissent below argued, see 478 F. 3d, at 405, and n. 10. Joseph Story wrote in his treatise on the Constitution that "the word 'state' is used in various senses [and in] its most enlarged sense it means the people composing a particular nation or community." 1 Story § 208; see also 3 *id.*, § 1890 (in reference to the Second Amendment's prefatory clause: "The militia is the natural defence of a free country"). It is true that the term "State" elsewhere in the Constitution refers to individual States, but the phrase "security of a free State" and close variations seem to have been terms of art in 18th-century political discourse, meaning a " 'free country' " or free polity. See Volokh, "Necessary to the Security of a Free State," 83 Notre Dame L. Rev. 1, 5 (2007); see, *e. g.*, 4 Blackstone 151 (1769); Brutus Essay III (Nov. 15, 1787), in The Essential Antifederalist 251, 253 (W. Allen & G. Lloyd eds., 2d ed. 2002). Moreover, the other instances of "state" in the Constitution are typically accompanied by modifiers making clear that the reference is to the several States—"each state," "several states," "any state," "that state," "particular states," "one state," "no state." And the presence of the term "foreign state" in Article I and Article III shows that the word "state" did not have a single meaning in the Constitution.

There are many reasons why the militia was thought to be "necessary to the security of a free State." See 3 Story § 1890. First, of course, it is useful in repelling invasions and suppressing insurrections. Second, it renders large standing armies unnecessary—an argument that Alexander Hamilton made in favor of federal control over the militia. The Federalist No. 29, pp. 226, 227 (B. Wright ed. 1961). Third, when the able-bodied men of a nation are trained in arms and organized, they are better able to resist tyranny.

3. Relationship Between Prefatory Clause and Operative Clause.

We reach the question, then: Does the preface fit with an operative clause that creates an individual right to keep and bear arms? It fits perfectly, once one knows the history that the founding generation knew and that we have described above. That history showed that the way tyrants had eliminated a militia consisting of all the able-bodied men was not by banning the militia but simply by taking away the people's arms, enabling a select militia or standing army to suppress political opponents. This is what had occurred in England that prompted codification of the right to have arms in the English Bill of Rights.

The debate with respect to the right to keep and bear arms, as with other guarantees in the Bill of Rights, was not over whether it was desirable (all agreed that it was) but over whether it needed to be codified in the Constitution. During the 1788 ratification debates, the fear that the Federal Government would disarm the people in order to impose rule through a standing army or select militia was pervasive in Antifederalist rhetoric. See, *e. g.*, Letters from The Federal Farmer III (Oct. 10, 1787), in 2 The Complete Anti-Federalist 234, 242 (H. Storing ed. 1981). John Smilie, for example, worried not only that Congress's "command of the militia" could be used to create a "select militia," or to have "no militia at all," but also, as a separate concern, that "[w]hen a select militia is formed; the people in general may be disarmed." 2 Documentary History of the Ratification of the Constitution 508–509 (M. Jensen ed. 1976) (hereinafter

Documentary Hist.). Federalists responded that because Congress was given no power to abridge the ancient right of individuals to keep and bear arms, such a force could never oppress the people. See, *e. g.*, A Pennsylvanian III (Feb. 20, 1788), in The Origin of the Second Amendment 275, 276 (D. Young ed., 2d ed. 2001) (hereinafter Young); White, To the Citizens of Virginia (Feb. 22, 1788), in *id.*, at 280, 281; A Citizen of America (Oct. 10, 1787), in *id.*, at 38, 40; Foreign Spectator, Remarks on the Amendments to the Federal Constitution, Nov. 7, 1788, in *id.*, at 556. It was understood across the political spectrum that the right helped to secure the ideal of a citizen militia, which might be necessary to oppose an oppressive military force if the constitutional order broke down.

It is therefore entirely sensible that the Second Amendment's prefatory clause announces the purpose for which the right was codified: to prevent elimination of the militia. The prefatory clause does not suggest that preserving the militia was the only reason Americans valued the ancient right; most undoubtedly thought it even more important for self-defense and hunting. But the threat that the new Federal Government would destroy the citizens' militia by taking away their arms was the reason that right—unlike some other English rights—was codified in a written Constitution. JUSTICE BREYER's assertion that individual self-defense is merely a "subsidiary interest" of the right to keep and bear arms, see *post*, at 714 (dissenting opinion), is profoundly mistaken. He bases that assertion solely upon the prologue—but that can only show that self-defense had little to do with the right's *codification;* it was the *central component* of the right itself.

Besides ignoring the historical reality that the Second Amendment was not intended to lay down a "novel principl[e]" but rather codified a right "inherited from our English ancestors," *Robertson* v. *Baldwin*, 165 U. S. 275, 281 (1897), petitioners' interpretation does not even achieve the narrower purpose that prompted codification of the right. If, as they believe, the Second Amendment right is no more than the right to keep and use weapons as a member of an organized militia, see Brief for Petitioners 8—if, that is, the *organized* militia is the sole institutional beneficiary of the Second Amendment's guarantee—it does not assure the existence of a "citizens' militia" as a safeguard against tyranny. For Congress retains plenary authority to organize the militia, which must include the authority to say who will belong to the organized force.[17] That is why the first Militia Act's requirement that only whites enroll caused States to amend their militia laws to exclude free blacks. See Siegel, The Federal Government's Power to Enact Color-Conscious Laws, 92 Nw. U. L. Rev. 477, 521–525 (1998). Thus, if petitioners are correct, the Second Amendment protects citizens' right to use a gun in an organization from which Congress has plenary authority to exclude them. It guarantees a select militia of the sort the Stuart kings found useful, but not the people's militia that was the concern of the founding generation.

B

Our interpretation is confirmed by analogous arms-bearing rights in state constitutions that preceded and im-

[17] Article I, § 8, cl. 16, of the Constitution gives Congress the power

"[t]o provide for organizing, arming, and disciplining, the Militia, and for governing such Part of them as may be employed in the Service of the United States, reserving to the States respectively, the Appointment of the Officers, and the Authority of training the Militia according to the discipline prescribed by Congress."

It could not be clearer that Congress's "organizing" power, unlike its "governing" power, can be invoked even for that part of the militia not "employed in the Service of the United States." JUSTICE STEVENS provides no support whatever for his contrary view, see *post*, at 654, n. 20. Both the Federalists and Antifederalists read the provision as it was written, to permit the creation of a "select" militia. See The Federalist No. 29, pp. 226, 227 (B. Wright ed. 1961); Centinel, Revived, No. XXIX, Philadelphia Independent Gazetteer, Sept. 9, 1789, in Young 711, 712.

mediately followed adoption of the Second Amendment. Four States adopted analogues to the Federal Second Amendment in the period between independence and the ratification of the Bill of Rights. Two of them—Pennsylvania and Vermont—clearly adopted individual rights unconnected to militia service. Pennsylvania's Declaration of Rights of 1776 said: "That the people have a right to bear arms *for the defence of themselves* and the state . . . ." § XIII, in 5 Thorpe 3082, 3083 (emphasis added). In 1777, Vermont adopted the identical provision, except for inconsequential differences in punctuation and capitalization. See Vt. Const., ch. 1, § XV, in 6 *id.*, at 3741.

North Carolina also codified a right to bear arms in 1776: "That the people have a right to bear arms, for the defence of the State . . . ." Declaration of Rights § XVII, in 5 *id.*, at 2787, 2788. This could plausibly be read to support only a right to bear arms in a militia—but that is a peculiar way to make the point in a constitution that elsewhere repeatedly mentions the militia explicitly. See N. C. Const., §§ XIV, XVIII, XXXV, in *id.*, at 2789, 2791, 2793. Many colonial statutes required individual arms bearing for public-safety reasons—such as the 1770 Georgia law that "for the security and *defence of this province* from internal dangers and insurrections" required those men who qualified for militia duty individually "to carry fire arms" "to places of public worship." 19 Colonial Records of the State of Georgia 137–139 (A. Candler ed. 1911 (pt. 1)) (emphasis added). That broad public-safety understanding was the connotation given to the North Carolina right by that State's Supreme Court in 1843. See *State* v. *Huntly*, 25 N. C. 418, 422–423.

The 1780 Massachusetts Constitution presented another variation on the theme: "The people have a right to keep and to bear arms for the common defence. . . . " Pt. First, Art. XVII, in 3 Thorpe 1888, 1892. Once again, if one gives narrow meaning to the phrase "common defence" this can be thought to limit the right to the bearing of arms in a state-organized military force. But once again the State's highest court thought otherwise. Writing for the court in an 1825 libel case, Chief Justice Parker wrote: "The liberty of the press was to be unrestrained, but he who used it was to be responsible in cases of its abuse; like the right to keep fire arms, which does not protect him who uses them for annoyance or destruction." *Commonwealth* v. *Blanding,* 20 Mass. 304, 313–314. The analogy makes no sense if firearms could not be used for any individual purpose at all. See also Kates, Handgun Prohibition and the Original Meaning of the Second Amendment, 82 Mich. L. Rev. 204, 244 (1983) (19th-century courts never read "common defence" to limit the use of weapons to militia service).

We therefore believe that the most likely reading of all four of these pre-Second Amendment state constitutional provisions is that they secured an individual right to bear arms for defensive purposes. Other States did not include rights to bear arms in their pre-1789 constitutions—although in Virginia a Second Amendment analogue was proposed (unsuccessfully) by Thomas Jefferson. (It read: "No freeman shall ever be debarred the use of arms [within his own lands or tenements]."[18] 1 The Papers of Thomas Jefferson 344 (J. Boyd ed. 1950).)

Between 1789 and 1820, nine States adopted Second Amendment analogues. Four of them—Kentucky, Ohio, Indiana, and Missouri—referred to the right of the people to "bear arms in defence of themselves and the State." See n. 8, *supra.* Another three States—Mississippi, Connecticut, and Alabama—used the even more individualistic phrasing that each citizen has the "right to bear arms in defence of himself and the State." See *ibid.* Finally, two States—Tennessee and Maine—used the "common defence" language

---

[18] JUSTICE STEVENS says that the drafters of the Virginia Declaration of Rights rejected this proposal and adopted "instead" a provision written by George Mason stressing the importance of the militia. See *post,* at 659, and n. 24. There is no evidence that the drafters regarded the Mason proposal as a substitute for the Jefferson proposal.

of Massachusetts. See Tenn. Const., Art. XI, § 26 (1796), in 6 Thorpe 3414, 3424; Me. Const., Art. I, § 16 (1819), in 3 *id.*, at 1646, 1648. That of the nine state constitutional protections for the right to bear arms enacted immediately after 1789 at least seven unequivocally protected an individual citizen's right to self-defense is strong evidence that that is how the founding generation conceived of the right. And with one possible exception that we discuss in Part II–D–2, 19th-century courts and commentators interpreted these state constitutional provisions to protect an individual right to use arms for self-defense. See n. 9, *supra; Simpson* v. *State*, 5 Yer. 356, 360 (Tenn. 1833).

The historical narrative that petitioners must endorse would thus treat the Federal Second Amendment as an odd outlier, protecting a right unknown in state constitutions or at English common law, based on little more than an overreading of the prefatory clause.

C

JUSTICE STEVENS relies on the drafting history of the Second Amendment—the various proposals in the state conventions and the debates in Congress. It is dubious to rely on such history to interpret a text that was widely understood to codify a pre-existing right, rather than to fashion a new one. But even assuming that this legislative history is relevant, JUSTICE STEVENS flatly misreads the historical record.

It is true, as JUSTICE STEVENS says, that there was concern that the Federal Government would abolish the institution of the state militia. See *post*, at 655. That concern found expression, however, *not* in the various Second Amendment precursors proposed in the state conventions, but in separate structural provisions that would have given the States concurrent and seemingly non-pre-emptible authority to organize, discipline, and arm the militia when the Federal Government failed to do so. See Veit 17, 20 (Virginia proposal); 4 J. Eliot, The Debates in the Several State

Conventions on the Adoption of the Federal Constitution 244, 245 (2d ed. 1836) (reprinted 1941) (North Carolina proposal); see also 2 Documentary Hist. 624 (Pennsylvania minority's proposal). The Second Amendment precursors, by contrast, referred to the individual English right already codified in two (and probably four) state constitutions. The Federalist-dominated first Congress chose to reject virtually all major structural revisions favored by the Antifederalists, including the proposed militia amendments. Rather, it adopted primarily the popular and uncontroversial (though, in the Federalists' view, unnecessary) individual-rights amendments. The Second Amendment right, protecting only individuals' liberty to keep and carry arms, did nothing to assuage Antifederalists' concerns about federal control of the militia. See, *e. g.*, Centinel, Revived, No. XXIX, Philadelphia Independent Gazetteer, Sept. 9, 1789, in Young 711, 712.

JUSTICE STEVENS thinks it significant that the Virginia, New York, and North Carolina Second Amendment proposals were "embedded . . . within a group of principles that are distinctly military in meaning," such as statements about the danger of standing armies. *Post,* at 657. But so was the highly influential minority proposal in Pennsylvania, yet that proposal, with its reference to hunting, plainly referred to an individual right. See 2 Documentary Hist. 624. Other than that erroneous point, JUSTICE STEVENS has brought forward absolutely no evidence that those proposals conferred only a right to carry arms in a militia. By contrast, New Hampshire's proposal, the Pennsylvania minority's proposal, and Samuel Adams' proposal in Massachusetts unequivocally referred to individual rights, as did two state constitutional provisions at the time. See Veit 16, 17 (New Hampshire proposal); 6 Documentary Hist. 1452, 1453 (J. Kaminski & G. Saladino eds. 2000) (Samuel Adams' proposal). JUSTICE STEVENS' view thus relies on the proposition, unsupported by any evidence, that different people of the founding period had vastly different conceptions of the right to keep and bear arms. That simply does not comport with our longstanding view that the Bill of Rights codified venerable, widely understood liberties.

D

We now address how the Second Amendment was interpreted from immediately after its ratification through the end of the 19th century. Before proceeding, however, we take issue with JUSTICE STEVENS' equating of these sources with postenactment legislative history, a comparison that betrays a fundamental misunderstanding of a court's interpretive task. See *post*, at 662, n. 28. " '[L]egislative history,' " of course, refers to the preenactment statements of those who drafted or voted for a law; it is considered persuasive by some, not because they reflect the general understanding of the disputed terms, but because the legislators who heard or read those statements presumably voted with that understanding. *Ibid.* "[P]ostenactment legislative history," *ibid.*, a deprecatory contradiction in terms, refers to statements of those who drafted or voted for the law that are made after its enactment and hence could have had no effect on the congressional vote. It most certainly does not refer to the examination of a variety of legal and other sources to determine *the public understanding* of a legal text in the period after its enactment or ratification. That sort of inquiry is a critical tool of constitutional interpretation. As we will show, virtually all interpreters of the Second Amendment in the century after its enactment interpreted the Amendment as we do.

1. Postratification Commentary.

Three important founding-era legal scholars interpreted the Second Amendment in published writings. All three understood it to protect an individual right unconnected with militia service.

St. George Tucker's version of Blackstone's Commentaries, as we explained above, conceived of the Blackstonian arms right as necessary for self-defense. He equated that right, absent the religious and class-based restrictions, with the Second Amendment. See 2 Tucker's Blackstone 143. In Note D, entitled, "View of the Constitution of the United States," Tucker elaborated on the Second Amendment: "This may be considered as the true palladium of liberty . . . . The right to self defence is the first law of nature: in most governments it has been the study of rulers to confine the right within the narrowest limits possible. Wherever standing armies are kept up, and the right of the people to keep and bear arms is, under any colour or pretext whatsoever, prohibited, liberty, if not already annihilated, is on the brink of destruction." 1 *id.*, at App. 300 (ellipsis in original). He believed that the English game laws had abridged the right by prohibiting "keeping a gun or other engine for the destruction of game." *Ibid.;* see also 2 *id.*, at 143, and nn. 40 and 41. He later grouped the right with some of the individual rights included in the First Amendment and said that if "a law be passed by congress, prohibiting" any of those rights, it would "be the province of the judiciary to pronounce whether any such act were constitutional, or not; and if not, to acquit the accused . . . ." 1 *id.*, at App. 357. It is unlikely that Tucker was referring to a person's being "accused" of violating a law making it a crime to bear arms in a state militia.[19]

---

[19] JUSTICE STEVENS quotes some of Tucker's unpublished notes, which he claims show that Tucker had ambiguous views about the Second Amendment. See *post*, at 666, and n. 32. But it is clear from the notes that Tucker located the power of States to arm their militias in the *Tenth* Amendment, and that he cited the Second Amendment for the proposition that such armament could not run afoul of any power of the Federal Government (since the Amendment prohibits Congress from ordering disarmament). Nothing in the passage implies that the Second Amendment pertains only to the carrying of arms in the organized militia.

In 1825, William Rawle, a prominent lawyer who had been a member of the Pennsylvania Assembly that ratified the Bill of Rights, published an influential treatise, which analyzed the Second Amendment as follows:

> "The first [principle] is a declaration that a well regulated militia is necessary to the security of a free state; a proposition from which few will dissent. . . .
>
> "The corollary, from the first position is, that the right of the people to keep and bear arms shall not be infringed.
>
> "The prohibition is general. No clause in the constitution could by any rule of construction be conceived to give to congress a power to disarm the people. Such a flagitious attempt could only be made under some general pretence by a state legislature. But if in any blind pursuit of inordinate power, either should attempt it, this amendment may be appealed to as a restraint on both." Rawle 121–122.[20]

Like Tucker, Rawle regarded the English game laws as violating the right codified in the Second Amendment. See *id.*, at 122–123. Rawle clearly differentiated between the people's right to bear arms and their service in a militia: "In a people permitted and accustomed to bear arms, we have the rudiments of a militia, which properly consists of armed citizens, divided into military bands, and instructed at least in part, in the use of arms for the purposes of war." *Id.*, at 140. Rawle further said that the Second Amendment right ought not "be abused to the disturbance of the public peace," such as by assembling with other armed individuals "for an

---

[20] Rawle, writing before our decision in *Barron ex rel. Tiernan* v. *Mayor of Baltimore*, 7 Pet. 243 (1833), believed that the Second Amendment could be applied against the States. Such a belief would of course be nonsensical on petitioners' view that it protected only a right to possess and carry arms when conscripted by the State itself into militia service.

unlawful purpose"—statements that make no sense if the right does not extend to *any* individual purpose. *Id.*, at 123.

Joseph Story published his famous Commentaries on the Constitution of the United States in 1833. JUSTICE STEVENS suggests that "[t]here is not so much as a whisper" in Story's explanation of the Second Amendment that favors the individual-rights view. *Post*, at 668. That is wrong. Story explained that the English Bill of Rights had also included a "right to bear arms," a right that, as we have discussed, had nothing to do with militia service. 3 Story § 1858. He then equated the English right with the Second Amendment:

> "§ 1891. A similar provision [to the Second Amendment] in favour of protestants (for to them it is confined) is to be found in the bill of rights of 1688, it being declared, 'that the subjects, which are protestants, may have arms for their defence suitable to their condition, and as allowed by law.' But under various pretences the effect of this provision has been greatly narrowed; and it is at present in England more nominal than real, as a defensive privilege." (Footnotes omitted.)

This comparison to the Declaration of Right would not make sense if the Second Amendment right was the right to use a gun in a militia, which was plainly not what the English right protected. As the Tennessee Supreme Court recognized 38 years after Story wrote his Commentaries, "[t]he passage from Story, shows clearly that this right was intended . . . and was guaranteed to, and to be exercised and enjoyed by the citizen as such, and not by him as a soldier, or in defense solely of his political rights." *Andrews* v. *State*, 50 Tenn. 165, 183–184 (1871). Story's Commentaries also cite as support Tucker and Rawle, both of whom clearly viewed the right as unconnected to militia service. See 3 Story § 1890, n. 2, § 1891, n. 3. In addition, in a shorter 1840 work Story wrote: "One of the ordinary modes, by which tyrants accomplish their purposes without resistance, is, by disarming the people, and making it an offence to keep arms, and by substituting a regular army in the stead of a resort to the militia." A Familiar Exposition of the Constitution of the United States § 450 (reprinted 1986).

Antislavery advocates routinely invoked the right to bear arms for self-defense. Joel Tiffany, for example, citing Blackstone's description of the right, wrote that "the right to keep and bear arms, also implies the right to use them if necessary in self defence; without this right to use the guaranty would have hardly been worth the paper it consumed." A Treatise on the Unconstitutionality of American Slavery 117–118 (1849); see also L. Spooner, The Unconstitutionality of Slavery 116 (1845) (right enables "personal defence"). In his famous Senate speech about the 1856 "Bleeding Kansas" conflict, Charles Sumner proclaimed:

> "The rifle has ever been the companion of the pioneer and, under God, his tutelary protector against the red man and the beast of the forest. Never was this efficient weapon more needed in just self-defense, than now in Kansas, and at least one article in our National Constitution must be blotted out, before the complete right to it can in any way be impeached. And yet such is the madness of the hour, that, in defiance of the solemn guarantee, embodied in the Amendments to the Constitution, that 'the right of the people to keep and bear arms shall not be infringed,' the people of Kansas have been arraigned for keeping and bearing them, and the Senator from South Carolina has had the face to say openly, on this floor, that they should be disarmed—of course, that the fanatics of Slavery, his allies and constituents, may meet no impediment." The Crime Against Kansas, May 19–20, 1856, in American Speeches: Political Oratory From the Revolution to the Civil War 553, 606–607 (T. Widmer ed. 2006).

We have found only one early-19th-century commentator who clearly conditioned the right to keep and bear arms upon service in the militia—and he recognized that the prevailing view was to the contrary. "The provision of the constitution, declaring the right of the people to keep and bear arms, &c. was probably intended to apply to the right of the people to bear arms for such [militia-related] purposes only, and not to prevent congress or the legislatures of the different states from enacting laws to prevent the citizens from always going armed. A different construction however has been given to it." B. Oliver, The Rights of an American Citizen 177 (1832).

2. Pre-Civil War Case Law.

The 19th-century cases that interpreted the Second Amendment universally support an individual right unconnected to militia service. In *Houston* v. *Moore*, 5 Wheat. 1, 24 (1820), this Court held that States have concurrent power over the militia, at least where not pre-empted by Congress. Agreeing in dissent that States could "organize, arm, and discipline" the militia in the absence of conflicting federal regulation, Justice Story said that the Second Amendment "may not, perhaps, be thought to have any important bearing on this point. If it have, it confirms and illustrates, rather than impugns the reasoning already suggested." *Id.*, at 51–53. Of course, if the Amendment simply "protect[ed] the right of the people of each of the several States to maintain a well-regulated militia," *post*, at 637 (STEVENS, J., dissenting), it would have enormous and obvious bearing on the point. But the Court and Story derived the States' power over the militia from the nonexclusive nature of federal power, not from the Second Amendment, whose preamble merely "confirms and illustrates" the importance of the militia. Even clearer was Justice Baldwin. In the famous fugitive-slave case of *Johnson* v. *Tompkins*, 13 F. Cas. 840,

850, 852 (CC Pa. 1833), Baldwin, sitting as a Circuit Judge, cited both the Second Amendment and the Pennsylvania analogue for his conclusion that a citizen has "a right to carry arms in defence of his property or person, and to use them, if either were assailed with such force, numbers or violence as made it necessary for the protection or safety of either."

Many early-19th century state cases indicated that the Second Amendment right to bear arms was an individual right unconnected to militia service, though subject to certain restrictions. A Virginia case in 1824 holding that the Constitution did not extend to free blacks explained: "[N]umerous restrictions imposed on [blacks] in our Statute Book, many of which are inconsistent with the letter and spirit of the Constitution, both of this State and of the United States as respects the free whites, demonstrate, that, here, those instruments have not been considered to extend equally to both classes of our population. We will only instance the restriction upon the migration of free blacks into this State, and upon their right to bear arms." *Aldridge* v. *Commonwealth*, 2 Va. Cas. 447, 449 (Gen. Ct.). The claim was obviously not that blacks were prevented from carrying guns in the militia.[21] See also *Waters* v. *State*, 1 Gill 302, 309 (Md.

[21] JUSTICE STEVENS suggests that this is not obvious because free blacks in Virginia had been required to muster without arms. See *post*, at 663, n. 29 (citing Siegel, The Federal Government's Power to Enact Color-Conscious Laws, 92 Nw. U. L. Rev. 477, 497 (1998)). But that could not have been the type of law referred to in *Aldridge*, because that practice had stopped 30 years earlier when blacks were excluded entirely from the militia by the first Militia Act. See Siegel, *supra*, at 498, n. 120. JUSTICE STEVENS further suggests that laws barring blacks from militia service could have been said to violate the "right to bear arms." But under JUSTICE STEVENS' reading of the Second Amendment (we think), the protected right is the right to carry arms to the extent one is enrolled in the militia, not the right *to be in the militia*. Perhaps JUSTICE STEVENS really does adopt the full-blown idiomatic meaning of "bear arms," in which case every man and woman in this country has a right "to be a soldier" or even "to wage war." In any case, it is clear to us that *Al-*

1843) (because free blacks were treated as a "dangerous population," "laws have been passed to prevent their migration into this State; to make it unlawful for them to bear arms; to guard even their religious assemblages with peculiar watchfulness"). An 1829 decision by the Supreme Court of Michigan said: "The constitution of the United States also grants to the citizen the right to keep and bear arms. But the grant of this privilege cannot be construed into the right in him who keeps a gun to destroy his neighbor. No rights are intended to be granted by the constitution for an unlawful or unjustifiable purpose." *United States* v. *Sheldon,* in 5 Transactions of the Supreme Court of the Territory of Michigan 337, 346 (W. Blume ed. 1940) (hereinafter Blume). It is not possible to read this as discussing anything other than an individual right unconnected to militia service. If it did have to do with militia service, the limitation upon it would not be any "unlawful or unjustifiable purpose," but any nonmilitary purpose whatsoever.

In *Nunn* v. *State,* 1 Ga. 243, 251 (1846), the Georgia Supreme Court construed the Second Amendment as protecting the "*natural* right of self-defence" and therefore struck down a ban on carrying pistols openly. Its opinion perfectly captured the way in which the operative clause of the Second Amendment furthers the purpose announced in the prefatory clause, in continuity with the English right:

> "The right of the whole people, old and young, men, women and boys, and not militia only, to keep and bear *arms* of every description, and not *such* merely as are used by the *militia,* shall not be *infringed,* curtailed, or broken in upon, in the smallest degree; and all this for the important end to be attained: the rearing up and qualifying a well-regulated militia, so vitally necessary

---

dridge's allusion to the existing Virginia "restriction" upon the right of free blacks "to bear arms" could only have referred to "laws prohibiting free blacks from keeping weapons," Siegel, *supra,* at 497–498.

> to the security of a free State. Our opinion is, that any law, State or Federal, is repugnant to the Constitution, and void, which contravenes this *right,* originally belonging to our forefathers, trampled under foot by Charles I. and his two wicked sons and successors, reestablished by the revolution of 1688, conveyed to this land of liberty by the colonists, and finally incorporated conspicuously in our own *Magna Charta!*" *Ibid.*

Likewise, in *State* v. *Chandler,* 5 La. Ann. 489, 490 (1850), the Louisiana Supreme Court held that citizens had a right to carry arms openly: "This is the right guaranteed by the Constitution of the United States, and which is calculated to incite men to a manly and noble defence of themselves, if necessary, and of their country, without any tendency to secret advantages and unmanly assassinations."

Those who believe that the Second Amendment preserves only a militia-centered right place great reliance on the Tennessee Supreme Court's 1840 decision in *Aymette* v. *State,* 21 Tenn. 154. The case does not stand for that broad proposition; in fact, the case does not mention the word "militia" at all, except in its quoting of the Second Amendment. *Aymette* held that the state constitutional guarantee of the right to "bear" arms did not prohibit the banning of concealed weapons. The opinion first recognized that both the state right and the federal right were descendents of the 1689 English right, but (erroneously, and contrary to virtually all other authorities) read that right to refer only to "protect[ion of] the public liberty" and "keep[ing] in awe those who are in power," *id.,* at 158. The court then adopted a sort of middle position, whereby citizens were permitted to carry arms openly, unconnected with any service in a formal militia, but were given the right to use them only for the military purpose of banding together to oppose tyranny. This odd reading of the right is, to be sure, not the one we adopt—but it is not petitioners' reading either. More importantly, seven years earlier the Tennessee Supreme Court had treated the state constitutional provision as conferring a right "to all the free citizens of the State to keep and bear arms for their defence," *Simpson,* 5 Yer., at 360; and 21 years later the court held that the "keep" portion of the state constitutional right included the right to personal self-defense: "[T]he right to keep arms involves, necessarily, the right to use such arms for all the ordinary purposes, and in all the ordinary modes usual in the country, and to which arms are adapted, limited by the duties of a good citizen in times of peace." *Andrews,* 50 Tenn., at 178–179; see also *ibid.* (equating state provision with Second Amendment).

3. Post-Civil War Legislation.

In the aftermath of the Civil War, there was an outpouring of discussion of the Second Amendment in Congress and in public discourse, as people debated whether and how to secure constitutional rights for newly free slaves. See generally S. Halbrook, Freedmen, the Fourteenth Amendment, and the Right to Bear Arms, 1866–1876 (1998) (hereinafter Halbrook); Brief for Institute for Justice as *Amicus Curiae.* Since those discussions took place 75 years after the ratification of the Second Amendment, they do not provide as much insight into its original meaning as earlier sources. Yet those born and educated in the early 19th century faced a widespread effort to limit arms ownership by a large number of citizens; their understanding of the origins and continuing significance of the Amendment is instructive.

Blacks were routinely disarmed by Southern States after the Civil War. Those who opposed these injustices frequently stated that they infringed blacks' constitutional right to keep and bear arms. Needless to say, the claim was not that blacks were being prohibited from carrying arms in an organized state militia. A Report of the Commission of the Freedmen's Bureau in 1866 stated plainly: "[T]he civil law [of Kentucky] prohibits the colored man from bearing arms. . . . Their arms are taken from them by the civil authorities. . . . Thus, the right of the people to keep and bear arms as provided in the Constitution is *infringed.*" H. R. Exec. Doc. No. 70, 39th Cong., 1st Sess., 233, 236. A joint congressional Report decried:

> "[I]n some parts of [South Carolina,] armed parties are, without proper authority, engaged in seizing all firearms found in the hands of the freedmen. Such conduct is in plain and direct violation of their personal rights as guaranteed by the Constitution of the United States, which declares that 'the right of the people to keep and bear arms shall not be infringed.' The freedmen of South Carolina have shown by their peaceful and orderly conduct that they can safely be trusted with firearms, and they need them to kill game for subsistence, and to protect their crops from destruction by birds and animals." Joint Comm. on Reconstruction, H. R. Rep. No. 30, 39th Cong., 1st Sess., pt. 2, p. 229 (1866) (Proposed Circular of Brigadier General R. Saxton).

The view expressed in these statements was widely reported and was apparently widely held. For example, an editorial in The Loyal Georgian (Augusta) on February 3, 1866, assured blacks that "[a]ll men, without distinction of color, have the right to keep and bear arms to defend their homes, families or themselves." Halbrook 19.

Congress enacted the Freedmen's Bureau Act on July 16, 1866. Section 14 stated:

> "[T]he right . . . to have full and equal benefit of all laws and proceedings concerning personal liberty, personal security, and the acquisition, enjoyment, and disposition of estate, real and personal, including the constitutional right to bear arms, shall be secured to and enjoyed by all the citizens . . . without respect to race or color, or previous condition of slavery. . . . " 14 Stat. 176–177.

The understanding that the Second Amendment gave freed blacks the right to keep and bear arms was reflected in congressional discussion of the bill, with even an opponent of it saying that the founding generation "were for every man bearing his arms about him and keeping them in his house, his castle, for his own defense." Cong. Globe, 39th Cong., 1st Sess., 362, 371 (1866) (Sen. Davis).

Similar discussion attended the passage of the Civil Rights Act of 1871 and the Fourteenth Amendment. For example, Representative Butler said of the Act: "Section eight is intended to enforce the well-known constitutional provision guaranteeing the right of the citizen to 'keep and bear arms,' and provides that whoever shall take away, by force or violence, or by threats and intimidation, the arms and weapons which any person may have for his defense, shall be deemed guilty of larceny of the same." H. R. Rep. No. 37, 41st Cong., 3d Sess., 7–8 (1871). With respect to the proposed Amendment, Senator Pomeroy described as one of the three "indispensable" "safeguards of liberty . . . under the Constitution" a man's "right to bear arms for the defense of himself and family and his homestead." Cong. Globe, 39th Cong., 1st Sess., 1182 (1866). Representative Nye thought the Fourteenth Amendment unnecessary because "[a]s citizens of the United States [blacks] have equal right to protection, and to keep and bear arms for self-defense." *Id.*, at 1073.

It was plainly the understanding in the post-Civil War Congress that the Second Amendment protected an individual right to use arms for self-defense.

4. Post-Civil War Commentators.

Every late-19th-century legal scholar that we have read interpreted the Second Amendment to secure an individual right unconnected with militia service. The most famous was the judge and professor Thomas Cooley, who wrote a massively popular 1868 Treatise on Constitutional Limitations. Concerning the Second Amendment it said:

> "Among the other defences to personal liberty should be mentioned the right of the people to keep and bear

> arms. . . . The alternative to a standing army is 'a well-regulated militia,' but this cannot exist unless the people are trained to bearing arms. How far it is in the power of the legislature to regulate this right, we shall not undertake to say, as happily there has been very little occasion to discuss that subject by the courts." *Id.*, at 350.

That Cooley understood the right not as connected to militia service, but as securing the militia by ensuring a populace familiar with arms, is made even clearer in his 1880 work, General Principles of Constitutional Law. The Second Amendment, he said, "was adopted with some modification and enlargement from the English Bill of Rights of 1688, where it stood as a protest against arbitrary action of the overturned dynasty in disarming the people." *Id.*, at 270. In a section entitled "The Right in General," he continued:

> "It might be supposed from the phraseology of this provision that the right to keep and bear arms was only guaranteed to the militia; but this would be an interpretation not warranted by the intent. The militia, as has been elsewhere explained, consists of those persons who, under the law, are liable to the performance of military duty, and are officered and enrolled for service when called upon. But the law may make provision for the enrolment of all who are fit to perform military duty, or of a small number only, or it may wholly omit to make any provision at all; and if the right were limited to those enrolled, the purpose of this guaranty might be defeated altogether by the action or neglect to act of the government it was meant to hold in check. The meaning of the provision undoubtedly is, that the people, from whom the militia must be taken, shall have the right to keep and bear arms; and they need no permission or regulation of law for the purpose. But this enables government to have a well-regulated militia; for to bear arms implies something more than the mere keeping; it

> implies the learning to handle and use them in a way that makes those who keep them ready for their efficient use; in other words, it implies the right to meet for voluntary discipline in arms, observing in doing so the laws of public order." *Id.*, at 271.

All other post-Civil War 19th-century sources we have found concurred with Cooley. One example from each decade will convey the general flavor:

> "[The purpose of the Second Amendment is] to secure a well-armed militia. . . . But a militia would be useless unless the citizens were enabled to exercise themselves in the use of warlike weapons. To preserve this privilege, and to secure to the people the ability to oppose themselves in military force against the usurpations of government, as well as against enemies from without, that government is forbidden by any law or proceeding to invade or destroy the right to keep and bear arms. . . . The clause is analogous to the one securing the freedom of speech and of the press. Freedom, not license, is secured; the fair use, not the libellous abuse, is protected." J. Pomeroy, An Introduction to the Constitutional Law of the United States § 239, pp. 152–153 (1868) (hereinafter Pomeroy).
>
> "As the Constitution of the United States, and the constitutions of several of the states, in terms more or less comprehensive, declare the right of the people to keep and bear arms, it has been a subject of grave discussion, in some of the state courts, whether a statute prohibiting persons, when not on a journey, or as travellers, from *wearing or carrying concealed weapons*, be constitutional. There has been a great difference of opinion on the question." 2 J. Kent, Commentaries on American Law *340, n. 2 (O. Holmes ed., 12th ed. 1873) (hereinafter Kent).

"Some general knowledge of firearms is important to the public welfare; because it would be impossible, in case of war, to organize promptly an efficient force of volunteers unless the people had some familiarity with weapons of war. The Constitution secures the right of the people to keep and bear arms. No doubt, a citizen who keeps a gun or pistol under judicious precautions, practises in safe places the use of it, and in due time teaches his sons to do the same, exercises his individual right. No doubt, a person whose residence or duties involve peculiar peril may keep a pistol for prudent self-defence." B. Abbott, Judge and Jury: A Popular Explanation of the Leading Topics in the Law of the Land 333 (1880) (hereinafter Abbott).

"The right to bear arms has always been the distinctive privilege of freemen. Aside from any necessity of self-protection to the person, it represents among all nations power coupled with the exercise of a certain jurisdiction. . . . [I]t was not necessary that the right to bear arms should be granted in the Constitution, for it had always existed." J. Ordronaux, Constitutional Legislation in the United States 241–242 (1891).

E

We now ask whether any of our precedents forecloses the conclusions we have reached about the meaning of the Second Amendment.

United States v. *Cruikshank*, 92 U. S. 542, in the course of vacating the convictions of members of a white mob for depriving blacks of their right to keep and bear arms, held that the Second Amendment does not by its own force apply to anyone other than the Federal Government. The opinion explained that the right "is not a right granted by the Constitution [or] in any manner dependent upon that instrument for its existence. The second amendment . . . means no more than that it shall not be infringed by Congress." *Id.*, at 553. States, we said, were free to restrict or protect the right under their police powers. The limited discussion of the Second Amendment in *Cruikshank* supports, if anything, the individual-rights interpretation. There was no claim in *Cruikshank* that the victims had been deprived of their right to carry arms in a militia; indeed, the Governor had disbanded the local militia unit the year before the mob's attack, see C. Lane, The Day Freedom Died 62 (2008). We described the right protected by the Second Amendment as "'bearing arms for a lawful purpose'"[22] and said that "the people [must] look for their protection against any violation by their fellow-citizens of the rights it recognizes" to the States' police power. 92 U. S., at 553. That discussion makes little sense if it is only a right to bear arms in a state militia.[23]

Presser v. *Illinois*, 116 U. S. 252 (1886), held that the right to keep and bear arms was not violated by a law that forbade "bodies of men to associate together as military organizations, or to drill or parade with arms in cities and towns unless authorized by law." *Id.*, at 264–265. This does not refute the individual-rights interpretation of the Amendment; no one supporting that interpretation has contended that States may not ban such groups. JUSTICE STEVENS

[22] JUSTICE STEVENS' accusation that this is "not accurate," *post*, at 673, is wrong. It is true it was the indictment that described the right as "bearing arms for a lawful purpose." But, in explicit reference to the right described in the indictment, the Court stated that "[t]he second amendment declares that it [*i. e.*, the right of bearing arms for a lawful purpose] shall not be infringed." 92 U. S., at 553.

[23] With respect to *Cruikshank*'s continuing validity on incorporation, a question not presented by this case, we note that *Cruikshank* also said that the First Amendment did not apply against the States and did not engage in the sort of Fourteenth Amendment inquiry required by our later cases. Our later decisions in *Presser* v. *Illinois*, 116 U. S. 252, 265 (1886), and *Miller* v. *Texas*, 153 U. S. 535, 538 (1894), reaffirmed that the Second Amendment applies only to the Federal Government.

presses *Presser* into service to support his view that the right to bear arms is limited to service in the militia by joining *Presser*'s brief discussion of the Second Amendment with a later portion of the opinion making the seemingly relevant (to the Second Amendment) point that the plaintiff was not a member of the state militia. Unfortunately for JUSTICE STEVENS' argument, that later portion deals with the *Fourteenth Amendment;* it was the *Fourteenth Amendment* to which the plaintiff's nonmembership in the militia was relevant. Thus, JUSTICE STEVENS' statement that *Presser* "suggested that . . . nothing in the Constitution protected the use of arms outside the context of a militia," *post,* at 674–675, is simply wrong. *Presser* said nothing about the Second Amendment's meaning or scope, beyond the fact that it does not prevent the prohibition of private paramilitary organizations.

JUSTICE STEVENS places overwhelming reliance upon this Court's decision in *Miller,* 307 U. S. 174. "[H]undreds of judges," we are told, "have relied on the view of the Amendment we endorsed there," *post,* at 638, and "[e]ven if the textual and historical arguments on both sides of the issue were evenly balanced, respect for the well-settled views of all of our predecessors on this Court, and for the rule of law itself . . . would prevent most jurists from endorsing such a dramatic upheaval in the law," *post,* at 639. And what is, according to JUSTICE STEVENS, the holding of *Miller* that demands such obeisance? That the Second Amendment "protects the right to keep and bear arms for certain military purposes, but that it does not curtail the Legislature's power to regulate the nonmilitary use and ownership of weapons." *Post,* at 637.

Nothing so clearly demonstrates the weakness of JUSTICE STEVENS' case. *Miller* did not hold that and cannot possibly be read to have held that. The judgment in the case upheld against a Second Amendment challenge two men's federal indictment for transporting an unregistered short-barreled shotgun in interstate commerce, in violation of the National Firearms Act, 48 Stat. 1236. It is entirely clear that the Court's basis for saying that the Second Amendment did not apply was *not* that the defendants were "bear[ing] arms" not "for . . . military purposes" but for "nonmilitary use," *post,* at 637. Rather, it was that the *type of weapon at issue* was not eligible for Second Amendment protection: "In the absence of any evidence tending to show that the possession or use of a [short-barreled shotgun] at this time has some reasonable relationship to the preservation or efficiency of a well regulated militia, we cannot say that the Second Amendment guarantees the right to keep and bear *such an instrument.*" 307 U. S., at 178 (emphasis added). "Certainly," the Court continued, "it is not within judicial notice that this weapon is any part of the ordinary military equipment or that its use could contribute to the common defense." *Ibid.* Beyond that, the opinion provided no explanation of the content of the right.

This holding is not only consistent with, but positively suggests, that the Second Amendment confers an individual right to keep and bear arms (though only arms that "have some reasonable relationship to the preservation or efficiency of a well regulated militia"). Had the Court believed that the Second Amendment protects only those serving in the militia, it would have been odd to examine the character of the weapon rather than simply note that the two crooks were not militiamen. JUSTICE STEVENS can say again and again that *Miller* did not "turn on the difference between muskets and sawed-off shotguns; it turned, rather, on the basic difference between the military and nonmilitary use and possession of guns," *post,* at 677, but the words of the opinion prove otherwise. The most JUSTICE STEVENS can plausibly claim for *Miller* is that it declined to decide the nature of the Second Amendment right, despite the Solicitor General's argument (made in the alternative) that the right was collective, see Brief for United States, O. T. 1938,

No. 696, pp. 4–5. *Miller* stands only for the proposition that the Second Amendment right, whatever its nature, extends only to certain types of weapons.

It is particularly wrongheaded to read *Miller* for more than what it said, because the case did not even purport to be a thorough examination of the Second Amendment. JUSTICE STEVENS claims, *post*, at 676–677, that the opinion reached its conclusion "[a]fter reviewing many of the same sources that are discussed at greater length by the Court today." Not many, which was not entirely the Court's fault. The defendants made no appearance in the case, neither filing a brief nor appearing at oral argument; the Court heard from no one but the Government (reason enough, one would think, not to make that case the beginning and the end of this Court's consideration of the Second Amendment). See Frye, The Peculiar Story of *United States* v. *Miller*, 3 N. Y. U. J. L. & Liberty 48, 65–68 (2008). The Government's brief spent two pages discussing English legal sources, concluding "that at least the carrying of weapons without lawful occasion or excuse was always a crime" and that (because of the class-based restrictions and the prohibition on terrorizing people with dangerous or unusual weapons) "the early English law did not guarantee an unrestricted right to bear arms." Brief for United States, O. T. 1938, No. 696, at 9–11. It then went on to rely primarily on the discussion of the English right to bear arms in *Aymette* v. *State*, 21 Tenn. 154, for the proposition that the only uses of arms protected by the Second Amendment are those that relate to the militia, not self-defense. See Brief for United States, O. T. 1938, No. 696, at 12–18. The final section of the brief recognized that "some courts have said that the right to bear arms includes the right of the individual to have them for the protection of his person and property," and launched an alternative argument that "weapons which are commonly used by criminals," such as sawed-off shotguns, are not protected. See *id.*, at 18–21. The Government's *Miller* brief thus provided scant discussion of the history of the Second Amendment—and the Court was presented with no counterdiscussion. As for the text of the Court's opinion itself, that discusses *none* of the history of the Second Amendment. It assumes from the prologue that the Amendment was designed to preserve the militia, 307 U. S., at 178 (which we do not dispute), and then reviews some historical materials dealing with the nature of the militia, and in particular with the nature of the arms their members were expected to possess, *id.*, at 178–182. Not a word *(not a word)* about the history of the Second Amendment. This is the mighty rock upon which the dissent rests its case.[24]

We may as well consider at this point (for we will have to consider eventually) *what* types of weapons *Miller* permits. Read in isolation, *Miller*'s phrase "part of ordinary military equipment" could mean that only those weapons useful in warfare are protected. That would be a startling reading of the opinion, since it would mean that the National Firearms Act's restrictions on machineguns (not challenged in *Miller*) might be unconstitutional, machineguns being useful in warfare in 1939. We think that *Miller*'s "ordinary military equipment" language must be read in tandem with what comes after: "[O]rdinarily when called for [militia] service [able-bodied] men were expected to appear bearing arms supplied by themselves and of the kind in common use at the time." 307 U. S., at 179. The traditional militia was formed from a pool of men bringing arms "in common use at the time" for lawful purposes like self-defense. "In the colonial

---

[24] As for the "hundreds of judges," *post*, at 638, who have relied on the view of the Second Amendment JUSTICE STEVENS claims we endorsed in *Miller*: If so, they overread *Miller*. And their erroneous reliance upon an uncontested and virtually unreasoned case cannot nullify the reliance of millions of Americans (as our historical analysis has shown) upon the true meaning of the right to keep and bear arms. In any event, it should not be thought that the cases decided by these judges would necessarily have come out differently under a proper interpretation of the right.

and revolutionary war era, [small-arms] weapons used by militiamen and weapons used in defense of person and home were one and the same." *State* v. *Kessler*, 289 Ore. 359, 368, 614 P. 2d 94, 98 (1980) (citing G. Neumann, Swords and Blades of the American Revolution 6–15, 252–254 (1973)). Indeed, that is precisely the way in which the Second Amendment's operative clause furthers the purpose announced in its preface. We therefore read *Miller* to say only that the Second Amendment does not protect those weapons not typically possessed by law-abiding citizens for lawful purposes, such as short-barreled shotguns. That accords with the historical understanding of the scope of the right, see Part III, *infra*.[25]

We conclude that nothing in our precedents forecloses our adoption of the original understanding of the Second Amendment. It should be unsurprising that such a significant matter has been for so long judicially unresolved. For most of our history, the Bill of Rights was not thought applicable to the States, and the Federal Government did not significantly regulate the possession of firearms by law-abiding citizens. Other provisions of the Bill of Rights have similarly remained unilluminated for lengthy periods. This Court first

---

[25] *Miller* was briefly mentioned in our decision in *Lewis* v. *United States*, 445 U. S. 55 (1980), an appeal from a conviction for being a felon in possession of a firearm. The challenge was based on the contention that the prior felony conviction had been unconstitutional. No Second Amendment claim was raised or briefed by any party. In the course of rejecting the asserted challenge, the Court commented gratuitously, in a footnote, that "[t]hese legislative restrictions on the use of firearms are neither based upon constitutionally suspect criteria, nor do they trench upon any constitutionally protected liberties. See *United States* v. *Miller* . . . (the Second Amendment guarantees no right to keep and bear a firearm that does not have 'some reasonable relationship to the preservation or efficiency of a well regulated militia')." *Id.*, at 65–66, n. 8. The footnote then cites several Court of Appeals cases to the same effect. It is inconceivable that we would rest our interpretation of the basic meaning of any guarantee of the Bill of Rights upon such a footnoted dictum in a case where the point was not at issue and was not argued.

held a law to violate the First Amendment's guarantee of freedom of speech in 1931, almost 150 years after the Amendment was ratified, see *Near* v. *Minnesota ex rel. Olson*, 283 U. S. 697 (1931), and it was not until after World War II that we held a law invalid under the Establishment Clause, see *Illinois ex rel. McCollum* v. *Board of Ed. of School Dist. No. 71, Champaign Cty.*, 333 U. S. 203 (1948). Even a question as basic as the scope of proscribable libel was not addressed by this Court until 1964, nearly two centuries after the founding. See *New York Times Co.* v. *Sullivan*, 376 U. S. 254 (1964). It is demonstrably not true that, as JUSTICE STEVENS claims, *post*, at 676, "for most of our history, the invalidity of Second-Amendment-based objections to firearms regulations has been well settled and uncontroversial." For most of our history the question did not present itself.

III

Like most rights, the right secured by the Second Amendment is not unlimited. From Blackstone through the 19th-century cases, commentators and courts routinely explained that the right was not a right to keep and carry any weapon whatsoever in any manner whatsoever and for whatever purpose. See, *e. g.*, *Sheldon*, in 5 Blume 346; Rawle 123; Pomeroy 152–153; Abbott 333. For example, the majority of the 19th-century courts to consider the question held that prohibitions on carrying concealed weapons were lawful under the Second Amendment or state analogues. See, *e. g.*, *State* v. *Chandler*, 5 La. Ann., at 489–490; *Nunn* v. *State*, 1 Ga., at 251; see generally 2 Kent *340, n. 2; The American Students' Blackstone 84, n. 11 (G. Chase ed. 1884). Although we do not undertake an exhaustive historical analysis today of the full scope of the Second Amendment, nothing in our opinion should be taken to cast doubt on longstanding prohibitions on the possession of firearms by felons and the mentally ill, or laws forbidding the carrying of firearms in sensitive places such as schools and government buildings, or laws imposing conditions and qualifications on the commercial sale of arms.[26]

We also recognize another important limitation on the right to keep and carry arms. *Miller* said, as we have explained, that the sorts of weapons protected were those "in common use at the time." 307 U. S., at 179. We think that limitation is fairly supported by the historical tradition of prohibiting the carrying of "dangerous and unusual weapons." See 4 Blackstone 148–149 (1769); 3 B. Wilson, Works of the Honourable James Wilson 79 (1804); J. Dunlap, The New-York Justice 8 (1815); C. Humphreys, A Compendium of the Common Law in Force in Kentucky 482 (1822); 1 W. Russell, A Treatise on Crimes and Indictable Misdemeanors 271–272 (1831); H. Stephen, Summary of the Criminal Law 48 (1840); E. Lewis, An Abridgment of the Criminal Law of the United States 64 (1847); F. Wharton, A Treatise on the Criminal Law of the United States 726 (1852). See also *State* v. *Langford,* 10 N. C. 381, 383–384 (1824); *O'Neill* v. *State,* 16 Ala. 65, 67 (1849); *English* v. *State,* 35 Tex. 473, 476 (1871); *State* v. *Lanier,* 71 N. C. 288, 289 (1874).

It may be objected that if weapons that are most useful in military service—M–16 rifles and the like—may be banned, then the Second Amendment right is completely detached from the prefatory clause. But as we have said, the conception of the militia at the time of the Second Amendment's ratification was the body of all citizens capable of military service, who would bring the sorts of lawful weapons that they possessed at home to militia duty. It may well be true today that a militia, to be as effective as militias in the 18th century, would require sophisticated arms that are highly unusual in society at large. Indeed, it may be true that no amount of small arms could be useful against modern-day bombers and tanks. But the fact that modern developments have limited the degree of fit between the prefatory clause

[26] We identify these presumptively lawful regulatory measures only as examples; our list does not purport to be exhaustive.

and the protected right cannot change our interpretation of the right.

IV

We turn finally to the law at issue here. As we have said, the law totally bans handgun possession in the home. It also requires that any lawful firearm in the home be disassembled or bound by a trigger lock at all times, rendering it inoperable.

As the quotations earlier in this opinion demonstrate, the inherent right of self-defense has been central to the Second Amendment right. The handgun ban amounts to a prohibition of an entire class of "arms" that is overwhelmingly chosen by American society for that lawful purpose. The prohibition extends, moreover, to the home, where the need for defense of self, family, and property is most acute. Under any of the standards of scrutiny that we have applied to enumerated constitutional rights,[27] banning from the home "the most preferred firearm in the nation to 'keep' and use for

---

[27] JUSTICE BREYER correctly notes that this law, like almost all laws, would pass rational-basis scrutiny. *Post*, at 687–688. But rational-basis scrutiny is a mode of analysis we have used when evaluating laws under constitutional commands that are themselves prohibitions on irrational laws. See, *e. g., Engquist* v. *Oregon Dept. of Agriculture*, 553 U. S. 591, 602 (2008). In those cases, "rational basis" is not just the standard of scrutiny, but the very substance of the constitutional guarantee. Obviously, the same test could not be used to evaluate the extent to which a legislature may regulate a specific, enumerated right, be it the freedom of speech, the guarantee against double jeopardy, the right to counsel, or the right to keep and bear arms. See *United States* v. *Carolene Products Co.*, 304 U. S. 144, 152, n. 4 (1938) ("There may be narrower scope for operation of the presumption of constitutionality [*i. e.*, narrower than that provided by rational-basis review] when legislation appears on its face to be within a specific prohibition of the Constitution, such as those of the first ten amendments . . . "). If all that was required to overcome the right to keep and bear arms was a rational basis, the Second Amendment would be redundant with the separate constitutional prohibitions on irrational laws, and would have no effect.

protection of one's home and family," 478 F. 3d, at 400, would fail constitutional muster.

Few laws in the history of our Nation have come close to the severe restriction of the District's handgun ban. And some of those few have been struck down. In *Nunn* v. *State*, the Georgia Supreme Court struck down a prohibition on carrying pistols openly (even though it upheld a prohibition on carrying concealed weapons). See 1 Ga., at 251. In *Andrews* v. *State*, the Tennessee Supreme Court likewise held that a statute that forbade openly carrying a pistol "publicly or privately, without regard to time or place, or circumstances," 50 Tenn., at 187, violated the state constitutional provision (which the court equated with the Second Amendment). That was so even though the statute did not restrict the carrying of long guns. *Ibid.* See also *State* v. *Reid*, 1 Ala. 612, 616–617 (1840) ("A statute which, under the pretence of regulating, amounts to a destruction of the right, or which requires arms to be so borne as to render them wholly useless for the purpose of defence, would be clearly unconstitutional").

It is no answer to say, as petitioners do, that it is permissible to ban the possession of handguns so long as the possession of other firearms (*i. e.*, long guns) is allowed. It is enough to note, as we have observed, that the American people have considered the handgun to be the quintessential self-defense weapon. There are many reasons that a citizen may prefer a handgun for home defense: It is easier to store in a location that is readily accessible in an emergency; it cannot easily be redirected or wrestled away by an attacker; it is easier to use for those without the upper-body strength to lift and aim a long gun; it can be pointed at a burglar with one hand while the other hand dials the police. Whatever the reason, handguns are the most popular weapon chosen by Americans for self-defense in the home, and a complete prohibition of their use is invalid.

We must also address the District's requirement (as applied to respondent's handgun) that firearms in the home be rendered and kept inoperable at all times. This makes it impossible for citizens to use them for the core lawful purpose of self-defense and is hence unconstitutional. The District argues that we should interpret this element of the statute to contain an exception for self-defense. See Brief for Petitioners 56–57. But we think that is precluded by the unequivocal text, and by the presence of certain other enumerated exceptions: "Except for law enforcement personnel . . . , each registrant shall keep any firearm in his possession unloaded and disassembled or bound by a trigger lock or similar device unless such firearm is kept at his place of business, or while being used for lawful recreational purposes within the District of Columbia." D. C. Code § 7-2507.02. The nonexistence of a self-defense exception is also suggested by the D. C. Court of Appeals' statement that the statute forbids residents to use firearms to stop intruders, see *McIntosh* v. *Washington*, 395 A. 2d 744, 755–756 (1978).[28]

Apart from his challenge to the handgun ban and the trigger-lock requirement respondent asked the District Court to enjoin petitioners from enforcing the separate licensing requirement "in such a manner as to forbid the carrying of a firearm within one's home or possessed land without a license." App. 59a. The Court of Appeals did not invalidate the licensing requirement, but held only that the District "may not prevent [a handgun] from being moved throughout one's house." 478 F. 3d, at 400. It then ordered the District Court to enter summary judgment "consistent

---

[28] *McIntosh* upheld the law against a claim that it violated the Equal Protection Clause by arbitrarily distinguishing between residences and businesses. See 395 A. 2d, at 755. One of the rational bases listed for that distinction was the legislative finding "that for each intruder stopped by a firearm there are four gun-related accidents within the home." *Ibid.* That tradeoff would not bear mention if the statute did not prevent stopping intruders by firearms.

with [respondent's] prayer for relief." *Id.*, at 401. Before this Court petitioners have stated that "if the handgun ban is struck down and respondent registers a handgun, he could obtain a license, assuming he is not otherwise disqualified," by which they apparently mean if he is not a felon and is not insane. Brief for Petitioners 58. Respondent conceded at oral argument that he does not "have a problem with . . . licensing" and that the District's law is permissible so long as it is "not enforced in an arbitrary and capricious manner." Tr. of Oral Arg. 74–75. We therefore assume that petitioners' issuance of a license will satisfy respondent's prayer for relief and do not address the licensing requirement.

JUSTICE BREYER has devoted most of his separate dissent to the handgun ban. He says that, even assuming the Second Amendment is a personal guarantee of the right to bear arms, the District's prohibition is valid. He first tries to establish this by founding-era historical precedent, pointing to various restrictive laws in the colonial period. These demonstrate, in his view, that the District's law "imposes a burden upon gun owners that seems proportionately no greater than restrictions in existence at the time the Second Amendment was adopted." *Post*, at 682. Of the laws he cites, only one offers even marginal support for his assertion. A 1783 Massachusetts law forbade the residents of Boston to "take into" or "receive into" "any Dwelling-House, Stable, Barn, Out-house, Ware-house, Store, Shop or other Building" loaded firearms, and permitted the seizure of any loaded firearms that "shall be found" there. Act of Mar. 1, 1783, ch. XIII, 1783 Mass. Acts p. 218. That statute's text and its prologue, which makes clear that the purpose of the prohibition was to eliminate the danger to firefighters posed by the "depositing of loaded Arms" in buildings, give reason to doubt that colonial Boston authorities would have enforced that general prohibition against someone who temporarily loaded a firearm to confront an intruder (despite the law's application in that case). In any case, we would not stake our interpretation of the Second Amendment upon a single law, in effect in a single city, that contradicts the overwhelming weight of other evidence regarding the right to keep and bear arms for defense of the home. The other laws JUSTICE BREYER cites are gunpowder-storage laws that he concedes did not clearly prohibit loaded weapons, but required only that excess gunpowder be kept in a special container or on the top floor of the home. *Post,* at 686. Nothing about those fire-safety laws undermines our analysis; they do not remotely burden the right of self-defense as much as an absolute ban on handguns. Nor, correspondingly, does our analysis suggest the invalidity of laws regulating the storage of firearms to prevent accidents.

JUSTICE BREYER points to other founding-era laws that he says "restricted the firing of guns within the city limits to at least some degree" in Boston, Philadelphia, and New York. *Post,* at 683 (citing Churchill, Gun Regulation, the Police Power, and the Right to Keep Arms in Early America, 25 Law & Hist. Rev. 139, 162 (2007)). Those laws provide no support for the severe restriction in the present case. The New York law levied a fine of 20 shillings on anyone who fired a gun in certain places (including houses) on New Year's Eve and the first two days of January, and was aimed at preventing the "great Damages . . . frequently done on [those days] by persons going House to House, with Guns and other Fire Arms and being often intoxicated with Liquor." Ch. 1501, 5 Colonial Laws of New York 244–246 (1894). It is inconceivable that this law would have been enforced against a person exercising his right to self-defense on New Year's Day against such drunken hooligans. The Pennsylvania law to which JUSTICE BREYER refers levied a fine of five shillings on one who fired a gun or set off fireworks in Philadelphia without first obtaining a license from the Governor. See Act of Aug. 26, 1721, ch. CCXLV, § IV, in 3 Stat. at Large of Pa. 253–254 (1896). Given Justice Wilson's explanation that the right to self-defense with arms was protected by the Pennsylvania Constitution, it is unlikely that this law (which in any event amounted to at most a licensing regime) would have been enforced against a person who used firearms for self-defense. JUSTICE BREYER cites a Rhode Island law that simply levied a 5-shilling fine on those who fired guns in *streets* and *taverns*, a law obviously inapplicable to this case. See An Act for preventing Mischief being done in the town of *Newport*, or in any other Town in this Government, 1731 Rhode Island Session Laws pp. 240–241. Finally, JUSTICE BREYER points to a Massachusetts law similar to the Pennsylvania law, prohibiting "discharg[ing] any Gun or Pistol charged with Shot or Ball in the Town of *Boston*." Act of May 28, 1746, ch. X, Acts and Laws of Mass. Bay p. 208. It is again implausible that this would have been enforced against a citizen acting in self-defense, particularly given its preambulatory reference to "the *indiscreet* firing of Guns." *Ibid.* (preamble) (emphasis added).

A broader point about the laws that JUSTICE BREYER cites: All of them punished the discharge (or loading) of guns with a small fine and forfeiture of the weapon (or in a few cases a very brief stay in the local jail), not with significant criminal penalties.[29] They are akin to modern penalties for minor public-safety infractions like speeding or jaywalking. And although such public-safety laws may not contain exceptions for self-defense, it is inconceivable that the threat of a jaywalking ticket would deter someone from disregarding a "Do Not Walk" sign in order to flee an attacker, or that the government would enforce those laws under such circumstances. Likewise, we do not think that a law imposing a

---

[29] The Supreme Court of Pennsylvania described the amount of five shillings in a contract matter in 1792 as "nominal consideration." *Morris's Lessee* v. *Smith*, 4 Dall. 119, 120 (Pa. 1792). Many of the laws cited punished violation with fine in a similar amount; the 1783 Massachusetts gunpowder-storage law carried a somewhat larger fine of £10 (200 shillings) and forfeiture of the weapon.

5-shilling fine and forfeiture of the gun would have prevented a person in the founding era from using a gun to protect himself or his family from violence, or that if he did so the law would be enforced against him. The District law, by contrast, far from imposing a minor fine, threatens citizens with a year in prison (five years for a second violation) for even obtaining a gun in the first place. See D. C. Code § 7–2507.06.

JUSTICE BREYER moves on to make a broad jurisprudential point: He criticizes us for declining to establish a level of scrutiny for evaluating Second Amendment restrictions. He proposes, explicitly at least, none of the traditionally expressed levels (strict scrutiny, intermediate scrutiny, rational basis), but rather a judge-empowering "interest-balancing inquiry" that "asks whether the statute burdens a protected interest in a way or to an extent that is out of proportion to the statute's salutary effects upon other important governmental interests." *Post*, at 689–690. After an exhaustive discussion of the arguments for and against gun control, JUSTICE BREYER arrives at his interest-balanced answer: Because handgun violence is a problem, because the law is limited to an urban area, and because there were somewhat similar restrictions in the founding period (a false proposition that we have already discussed), the interest-balancing inquiry results in the constitutionality of the handgun ban. QED.

We know of no other enumerated constitutional right whose core protection has been subjected to a freestanding "interest-balancing" approach. The very enumeration of the right takes out of the hands of government—even the Third Branch of Government—the power to decide on a case-by-case basis whether the right is *really worth* insisting upon. A constitutional guarantee subject to future judges' assessments of its usefulness is no constitutional guarantee at all. Constitutional rights are enshrined with the scope they were understood to have when the people adopted them, whether or not future legislatures or (yes) even future judges think that scope too broad. We would not apply an "interest-balancing" approach to the prohibition of a peaceful neo-Nazi march through Skokie. See *National Socialist Party of America* v. *Skokie*, 432 U. S. 43 (1977) *(per curiam).* The First Amendment contains the freedom-of-speech guarantee that the people ratified, which included exceptions for obscenity, libel, and disclosure of state secrets, but not for the expression of extremely unpopular and wrongheaded views. The Second Amendment is no different. Like the First, it is the very *product* of an interest balancing by the people—which JUSTICE BREYER would now conduct for them anew. And whatever else it leaves to future evaluation, it surely elevates above all other interests the right of law-abiding, responsible citizens to use arms in defense of hearth and home.

JUSTICE BREYER chides us for leaving so many applications of the right to keep and bear arms in doubt, and for not providing extensive historical justification for those regulations of the right that we describe as permissible. See *post*, at 720–721. But since this case represents this Court's first in-depth examination of the Second Amendment, one should not expect it to clarify the entire field, any more than *Reynolds* v. *United States*, 98 U. S. 145 (1879), our first in-depth Free Exercise Clause case, left that area in a state of utter certainty. And there will be time enough to expound upon the historical justifications for the exceptions we have mentioned if and when those exceptions come before us.

In sum, we hold that the District's ban on handgun possession in the home violates the Second Amendment, as does its prohibition against rendering any lawful firearm in the home operable for the purpose of immediate self-defense. Assuming that Heller is not disqualified from the exercise of Second Amendment rights, the District must permit him to register his handgun and must issue him a license to carry it in the home.

* * *

We are aware of the problem of handgun violence in this country, and we take seriously the concerns raised by the many *amici* who believe that prohibition of handgun ownership is a solution. The Constitution leaves the District of Columbia a variety of tools for combating that problem, including some measures regulating handguns, see *supra*, at 626–627, and n. 26. But the enshrinement of constitutional rights necessarily takes certain policy choices off the table. These include the absolute prohibition of handguns held and used for self-defense in the home. Undoubtedly some think that the Second Amendment is outmoded in a society where our standing army is the pride of our Nation, where well-trained police forces provide personal security, and where gun violence is a serious problem. That is perhaps debatable, but what is not debatable is that it is not the role of this Court to pronounce the Second Amendment extinct.

We affirm the judgment of the Court of Appeals.

It is so ordered.

JUSTICE STEVENS, with whom JUSTICE SOUTER, JUSTICE GINSBURG, and JUSTICE BREYER join, dissenting.

The question presented by this case is not whether the Second Amendment protects a "collective right" or an "individual right." Surely it protects a right that can be enforced by individuals. But a conclusion that the Second Amendment protects an individual right does not tell us anything about the scope of that right.

Guns are used to hunt, for self-defense, to commit crimes, for sporting activities, and to perform military duties. The Second Amendment plainly does not protect the right to use a gun to rob a bank; it is equally clear that it *does* encompass the right to use weapons for certain military purposes. Whether it also protects the right to possess and use guns for nonmilitary purposes like hunting and personal self-

Otis McDonald, et al. v City of Chicago, Illinois, et al.
2010

The Supreme Court decision in *District of Columbia, et al. v Dick Anthony Heller* established that, as a matter of law, the right to keep and bear arms referred to in the Second Amendment is an individual right. However, *Heller* did not establish that the constitutional prohibition on infringing the right applied to the states as well as to the federal government. It would require another lawsuit to answer that question.

That case came two years after the *Heller* decision: *Otis McDonald, et al. v City of Chicago, Illinois, et al.* The plaintiff, Otis McDonald, was a retired person who lived in a neighborhood of Chicago that was deteriorating. As a result of multiple break-ins at his home, Mr. McDonald wanted a firearm for protection. He legally owned shotguns for hunting but he felt that a handgun was more suitable for self defense inside a home. However, the City of Chicago had enacted a ban on privately owned handguns in 1982. The City also required that all privately owned firearms be registered. Because of the 1982 handgun ban, Mr. McDonald was unable to register a handgun. This, he would argue in court, deprived him of the right to keep a handgun in the home for self defense—which was exactly the right that the Supreme Court had affirmed two years earlier, in the *Heller* case.

In the case, Otis McDonald was the lead plaintiff. He was joined by three other plaintiffs, all of whom were residents of Chicago and all of whom wished to keep a handgun in their homes for the purpose of self-defense. The federal District Court dismissed the case on the grounds that the *Heller* case had not made the Second Amendment binding against the states, and that a previous decision by the Seventh Circuit Court of Appeals had ruled that Chicago's handgun ban was constitutional. The District Court's view was that it had to follow established precedent. On appeal, the Seventh Circuit Court of Appeals upheld the decision of the District Court. The stage was set.

The *McDonald* plaintiffs appealed to the Supreme Court, which granted *Certiorari* on September 30, 2009. Oral arguments were heard on March 2, 2010, and the decision was handed down on June 28, 2010. As had been the case in the *Heller* case, the decision was a 5–4 split in favor of McDonald and the other plaintiffs.

Impact

The ruling in *McDonald* held that the Second Amendment does apply to the states, which meant that the Chicago law prohibiting residents from keeping a handgun in the home for self defense was in violation of the ruling two years prior in the *Heller* case.

Four of the justices in the majority agreed that the Second Amendment was incorporated against the states because of a clause in the 14th Amendment that addressed Due Process. Justice Clarence Thomas, although he agreed that the Second Amendment was incorporated under the 14th Amendment, wrote a concurring opinion in which he cited the Privileges or Immunities clause as the reason why it should be incorporated.

The Second Amendment was drafted in 1789 and ratified December 15, 1791. It took 218 years before it was finally established that the Right to Keep and Bear Arms is a right shared by all citizens, of all the states.

Note: Because of mechanical issues affecting the production of paperback books, I learned that the size of this book if it included the full and complete text of all the documents discussed exceeded the maximum page count by more than 200 pages. That meant that something had to be omitted. Because dissenting opinions in Supreme Court decisions are not binding legal precedent, I reluctantly made the decision to omit the dissenting opinions from this decision.

Dissenting opinions are not binding legal authority, but they can be of interest to legal scholars. For anyone who wishes to read the dissenting opinions, an official copy of the complete decision can be found on-line at: https://www.supremecourt.gov/opinions/09pdf/08-1521.pdf

Syllabus

McDONALD ET AL. *v.* CITY OF CHICAGO, ILLINOIS, ET AL.

CERTIORARI TO THE UNITED STATES COURT OF APPEALS FOR THE SEVENTH CIRCUIT

No. 08–1521. Argued March 2, 2010—Decided June 28, 2010

Two years ago, in *District of Columbia* v. *Heller*, 554 U. S. 570, this Court held that the Second Amendment protects the right to keep and bear arms for the purpose of self-defense and struck down a District of Columbia law that banned the possession of handguns in the home. Chicago (hereinafter City) and the village of Oak Park, a Chicago suburb, have laws effectively banning handgun possession by almost all private citizens. After *Heller*, petitioners filed this federal suit against the City, which was consolidated with two related actions, alleging that the City's handgun ban has left them vulnerable to criminals. They sought a declaration that the ban and several related City ordinances violate the Second and Fourteenth Amendments. Rejecting petitioners' argument that the ordinances are unconstitutional, the court noted that the Seventh Circuit previously had upheld the constitutionality of a handgun ban, that *Heller* had explicitly refrained from opining on whether the Second Amendment applied to the States, and that the court had a duty to follow established Circuit precedent. The Seventh Circuit affirmed, relying on three 19th-century cases—*United States* v. *Cruikshank*, 92 U. S. 542, *Presser* v. *Illinois*, 116 U. S. 252, and *Miller* v. *Texas*, 153 U. S. 535—which were decided in the wake of this Court's interpretation of the Fourteenth Amendment's Privileges or Immunities Clause in the *Slaughter-House Cases*, 16 Wall. 36.

Held: The judgment is reversed, and the case is remanded.

567 F. 3d 856, reversed and remanded.

JUSTICE ALITO delivered the opinion of the Court with respect to Parts I, II–A, II–B, II–D, and III, concluding that the Fourteenth Amendment incorporates the Second Amendment right, recognized in *Heller*, to keep and bear arms for the purpose of self-defense. Pp. 753–758, 759–780.

(a) Petitioners base their case on two submissions. Primarily, they argue that the right to keep and bear arms is protected by the Privileges or Immunities Clause of the Fourteenth Amendment and that the *Slaughter-House Cases'* narrow interpretation of the Clause should now be rejected. As a secondary argument, they contend that the Fourteenth Amendment's Due Process Clause incorporates the Second

Amendment right. Chicago and Oak Park (municipal respondents) maintain that a right set out in the Bill of Rights applies to the States only when it is an indispensable attribute of *any* "'civilized'" legal system. If it is possible to imagine a civilized country that does not recognize the right, municipal respondents assert, that right is not protected by due process. And since there are civilized countries that ban or strictly regulate the private possession of handguns, they maintain that due process does not preclude such measures. P. 753.

(b) The Bill of Rights, including the Second Amendment, originally applied only to the Federal Government, not to the States, see, *e. g., Barron ex rel. Tiernan* v. *Mayor of Baltimore*, 7 Pet. 243, 247, but the constitutional Amendments adopted in the Civil War's aftermath fundamentally altered the federal system. Four years after the adoption of the Fourteenth Amendment, this Court held in the *Slaughter-House Cases* that the Privileges or Immunities Clause protects only those rights "which owe their existence to the Federal government, its National character, its Constitution, or its laws," 16 Wall., at 79, and that the fundamental rights predating the creation of the Federal Government were not protected by the Clause, *id.*, at 76. Under this narrow reading, the Court held that the Privileges or Immunities Clause protects only very limited rights. *Id.*, at 79–80. Subsequently, the Court held that the Second Amendment applies only to the Federal Government in *Cruikshank, supra, Presser, supra,* and *Miller, supra,* the decisions on which the Seventh Circuit relied in this case. Pp. 754–758.

(c) Whether the Second Amendment right to keep and bear arms applies to the States is considered in light of the Court's precedents applying the Bill of Rights' protections to the States. Pp. 759–766.

(1) In the late 19th century, the Court began to hold that the Due Process Clause prohibits the States from infringing Bill of Rights protections. See, *e. g., Hurtado* v. *California*, 110 U. S. 516. Five features of the approach taken during the ensuing era are noted. First, the Court viewed the due process question as entirely separate from the question whether a right was a privilege or immunity of national citizenship. See *Twining* v. *New Jersey*, 211 U. S. 78, 99. Second, the Court explained that the only rights due process protected against state infringement were those "of such a nature that they are included in the conception of due process of law." *Ibid.* Third, some cases during this era "can be seen as having asked . . . if a civilized system could be imagined that would not accord the particular protection" asserted therein. *Duncan* v. *Louisiana*, 391 U. S. 145, 149, n. 14. Fourth, the Court did not hesitate to hold that a Bill of Rights guarantee failed to meet the test for Due Process Clause protection, finding, *e. g.*, that freedom of speech and press qualified, *Gitlow* v. *New York*, 268 U. S. 652,

666; *Near* v. *Minnesota ex rel. Olson,* 283 U. S. 697, but the grand jury indictment requirement did not, *Hurtado, supra.* Finally, even when such a right was held to fall within the conception of due process, the protection or remedies afforded against state infringement sometimes differed from those provided against abridgment by the Federal Government. Pp. 759–761.

(2) Justice Black championed the alternative theory that § 1 of the Fourteenth Amendment totally incorporated all of the Bill of Rights' provisions, see, *e. g., Adamson* v. *California,* 332 U. S. 46, 71–72 (Black, J., dissenting), but the Court never has embraced that theory. Pp. 761–763.

(3) The Court eventually moved in the direction advocated by Justice Black, by adopting a theory of selective incorporation by which the Due Process Clause incorporates particular rights contained in the first eight Amendments. See, *e. g., Gideon* v. *Wainwright,* 372 U. S. 335, 341. These decisions abandoned three of the characteristics of the earlier period. The Court clarified that the governing standard is whether a particular Bill of Rights protection is fundamental to our Nation's particular scheme of ordered liberty and system of justice. *Duncan, supra,* at 149, n. 14. The Court eventually held that almost all of the Bill of Rights' guarantees met the requirements for protection under the Due Process Clause. The Court also held that Bill of Rights protections must "all . . . be enforced against the States under the Fourteenth Amendment according to the same standards that protect those personal rights against federal encroachment." *Malloy* v. *Hogan,* 378 U. S. 1, 10. Under this approach, the Court overruled earlier decisions holding that particular Bill of Rights guarantees or remedies did not apply to the States. See, *e. g., Gideon, supra,* which overruled *Betts* v. *Brady,* 316 U. S. 455. Pp. 763–766.

(d) The Fourteenth Amendment makes the Second Amendment right to keep and bear arms fully applicable to the States. Pp. 767–780.

(1) The Court must decide whether that right is fundamental to the Nation's scheme of ordered liberty, *Duncan, supra,* at 149, or, as the Court has said in a related context, whether it is "deeply rooted in this Nation's history and tradition," *Washington* v. *Glucksberg,* 521 U. S. 702, 721. *Heller* points unmistakably to the answer. Self-defense is a basic right, recognized by many legal systems from ancient times to the present, and the *Heller* Court held that individual self-defense is "the central component" of the Second Amendment right. 554 U. S., at 599. Explaining that "the need for defense of self, family, and property is most acute" in the home, *id.,* at 628, the Court found that this right applies to handguns because they are "the most preferred firearm in the nation to 'keep' and use for protection of one's home and family," *id.,* at

628–629. It thus concluded that citizens must be permitted "to use [handguns] for the core lawful purpose of self-defense." *Id.*, at 630. *Heller* also clarifies that this right is "deeply rooted in this Nation's history and tradition," *Glucksberg, supra*, at 721. *Heller* explored the right's origins in English law and noted the esteem with which the right was regarded during the colonial era and at the time of the ratification of the Bill of Rights. This is powerful evidence that the right was regarded as fundamental in the sense relevant here. That understanding persisted in the years immediately following the Bill of Rights' ratification and is confirmed by the state constitutions of that era, which protected the right to keep and bear arms. Pp. 767–770.

(2) A survey of the contemporaneous history also demonstrates clearly that the Fourteenth Amendment's Framers and ratifiers counted the right to keep and bear arms among those fundamental rights necessary to the Nation's system of ordered liberty. Pp. 770–780.

(i) By the 1850's, the fear that the National Government would disarm the universal militia had largely faded, but the right to keep and bear arms was highly valued for self-defense. Abolitionist authors wrote in support of the right, and attempts to disarm "Free-Soilers" in "Bloody Kansas" met with outrage that the constitutional right to keep and bear arms had been taken from the people. After the Civil War, the Southern States engaged in systematic efforts to disarm and injure African-Americans, see *Heller, supra*, at 614–615. These injustices prompted the 39th Congress to pass the Freedmen's Bureau Act of 1866 and the Civil Rights Act of 1866 to protect the right to keep and bear arms. Congress, however, ultimately deemed these legislative remedies insufficient, and approved the Fourteenth Amendment. Today, it is generally accepted that that Amendment was understood to provide a constitutional basis for protecting the rights set out in the Civil Rights Act. See *General Building Contractors Assn., Inc.* v. *Pennsylvania*, 458 U. S. 375, 389. In congressional debates on the proposed Amendment, its legislative proponents in the 39th Congress referred to the right to keep and bear arms as a fundamental right deserving of protection. Evidence from the period immediately following the Amendment's ratification confirms that that right was considered fundamental. Pp. 770–778.

(ii) Despite all this evidence, municipal respondents argue that Members of Congress overwhelmingly viewed § 1 of the Fourteenth Amendment as purely an antidiscrimination rule. But while § 1 does contain an antidiscrimination rule, *i. e.*, the Equal Protection Clause, it can hardly be said that the section does no more than prohibit discrimination. If what municipal respondents mean is that the Second Amendment should be singled out for special—and specially unfavorable—

treatment, the Court rejects the suggestion. The right to keep and bear arms must be regarded as a substantive guarantee, not a prohibition that could be ignored so long as the States legislated in an even-handed manner. Pp. 778–780.

JUSTICE ALITO, joined by THE CHIEF JUSTICE, JUSTICE SCALIA, and JUSTICE KENNEDY, concluded, in Parts II–C, IV, and V, that the Fourteenth Amendment's Due Process Clause incorporates the Second Amendment right recognized in *Heller*. Pp. 758–759, 780–791.

(a) Petitioners argue that the Second Amendment right is one of the "privileges or immunities of citizens of the United States." There is no need to reconsider the Court's interpretation of the Privileges or Immunities Clause in the *Slaughter-House Cases* because, for many decades, the Court has analyzed the question whether particular rights are protected against state infringement under the Fourteenth Amendment's Due Process Clause. Pp. 758–759.

(b) Municipal respondents' remaining arguments are rejected because they are at war with *Heller*'s central holding. In effect, they ask the Court to hold the right to keep and bear arms as subject to a different body of rules for incorporation than the other Bill of Rights guarantees. Pp. 780–787.

(c) The dissents' objections are addressed and rejected. Pp. 787–791.

JUSTICE THOMAS agreed that the Fourteenth Amendment makes the Second Amendment right to keep and bear arms that was recognized in *District of Columbia* v. *Heller*, 554 U. S. 570, fully applicable to the States. However, he asserted, there is a path to this conclusion that is more straightforward and more faithful to the Second Amendment's text and history. The Court is correct in describing the Second Amendment right as "fundamental" to the American scheme of ordered liberty, *Duncan* v. *Louisiana*, 391 U. S. 145, 149, and "deeply rooted in this Nation's history and tradition," *Washington* v. *Glucksberg*, 521 U. S. 702, 721. But the Fourteenth Amendment's Due Process Clause, which speaks only to "process," cannot impose the type of substantive restraint on state legislation that the Court asserts. Rather, the right to keep and bear arms is enforceable against the States because it is a privilege of American citizenship recognized by § 1 of the Fourteenth Amendment, which provides, *inter alia:* "No State shall make or enforce any law which shall abridge the privileges or immunities of citizens of the United States." In interpreting this language, it is important to recall that constitutional provisions are " 'written to be understood by the voters.' " *Heller*, 554 U. S., at 576. The objective of this inquiry is to discern what "ordinary citizens" at the time of the Fourteenth Amendment's ratification would have understood that Amendment's Privileges or Immunities Clause to mean. *Id.*, at 577. A survey of contemporary legal authorities plainly shows that, at that time, the ratifying public understood the Clause to protect constitutionally enumerated rights, including the right to keep and bear arms. Pp. 805–838.

ALITO, J., announced the judgment of the Court and delivered the opinion of the Court with respect to Parts I, II–A, II–B, II–D, and III, in which ROBERTS, C. J., and SCALIA, KENNEDY, and THOMAS, JJ., joined, and an opinion with respect to Parts II–C, IV, and V, in which ROBERTS, C. J., and SCALIA and KENNEDY, JJ., joined. SCALIA, J., filed a concurring opinion, *post*, p. 791. THOMAS, J., filed an opinion concurring in part and concurring in the judgment, *post*, p. 805. STEVENS, J., filed a dissenting opinion, *post*, p. 858. BREYER, J., filed a dissenting opinion, in which GINSBURG and SOTOMAYOR, JJ., joined, *post*, p. 912.

Alan Gura argued the cause for petitioners. With him on the briefs was *David G. Sigale*. *Paul D. Clement* argued the cause for the National Rifle Association of America, Inc., et al., respondents in support of petitioners. On the briefs were *Stephen D. Poss, Kevin P. Martin, Scott B. Nardi, Joshua S. Lipshutz,* and *Stephen P. Halbrook*.

James A. Feldman argued the cause for respondent City of Chicago et al. With him on the brief were *Benna Ruth Solomon, Myriam Zreczny Kasper, Suzanne M. Loose,* and *Andrew W. Worseck*.*

---

*Briefs of *amici curiae* urging reversal were filed for the State of Texas et al. by *Greg Abbott*, Attorney General of Texas, *James C. Ho*, Solicitor General, *C. Andrew Weber*, First Assistant Attorney General, *David S. Morales*, Deputy Attorney General, *Sean D. Jordan*, Deputy Solicitor General, and *Candice N. Hance*, Assistant Attorney General, and by the Attorneys General for their respective States as follows: *Troy King* of Alabama, *Daniel S. Sullivan* of Alaska, *Terry Goddard* of Arizona, *Dustin McDaniel* of Arkansas, *John W. Suthers* of Colorado, *Bill McCollum* of Florida, *Thurbert E. Baker* of Georgia, *Lawrence G. Wasden* of Idaho, *Gregory F. Zoeller* of Indiana, *Steve Six* of Kansas, *Jack Conway* of Kentucky, *James D. "Buddy" Caldwell* of Louisiana, *Janet T. Mills* of Maine, *Michael A. Cox* of Michigan, *Lori Swanson* of Minnesota, *Jim Hood* of Mississippi, *Chris Koster* of Missouri, *Steve Bullock* of Montana, *Jon Bruning* of Nebraska, *Catherine Cortez Masto* of Nevada, *Michael A. Delaney* of New Hampshire, *Gary K. King* of New Mexico, *Roy Cooper* of North Carolina, *Wayne Stenehjem* of North Dakota, *Richard Cordray* of Ohio, *W. A. Drew*

JUSTICE ALITO announced the judgment of the Court and delivered the opinion of the Court with respect to Parts I, II–A, II–B, II–D, and III, in which THE CHIEF JUSTICE, JUS-

---

Edmondson of Oklahoma, *Thomas W. Corbett, Jr.*, of Pennsylvania, *Patrick C. Lynch* of Rhode Island, *Henry McMaster* of South Carolina, *Marty J. Jackley* of South Dakota, *Robert E. Cooper, Jr.*, of Tennessee, *Mark L. Shurtleff* of Utah, *William C. Mims* of Virginia, *Robert M. McKenna* of Washington, *Darrell V. McGraw, Jr.*, of West Virginia, *J. B. Van Hollen* of Wisconsin, and *Bruce A. Salzburg* of Wyoming; for Academics for the Second Amendment by *Joseph Edward Olson* and *David T. Hardy;* for the American Center for Law and Justice by *Jay Alan Sekulow, Stuart J. Roth, Colby M. May, James M. Henderson, Sr.*, and *John P. Tuskey;* for the American Civil Rights Union et al. by *Peter J. Ferrara;* for the American Legislative Exchange Council by *Rick A. Haberman* and *K. Scott Hamilton;* for Appellants from the Ninth Circuit Incorporation Case of *Nordyke v. King* et al. by *Donald E. J. Kilmer, Jr.*, and *Jason A. Davis;* for Arms Keepers by *Andrew T. Hyman;* for the Buckeye Firearms Foundation, Inc., et al. by *L. Kenneth Hanson III;* for the Calguns Foundation, Inc., by *Erik S. Jaffe;* for the Cato Institute et al. by *M. Reed Hopper, Timothy Sandefur, Robert A. Levy*, and *Ilya Shapiro;* for Constitutional Law Professors by *Douglas T. Kendall, Elizabeth B. Wydra*, and *David H. Gans;* for the Foundation for Moral Law by *John A. Eidsmoe* and *Benjamin D. DuPré;* for Gun Owners of America, Inc., et al. by *William J. Olson, Herbert W. Titus*, and *John S. Miles;* for the Heartland Institute by *Nancy Lee Carlson;* for the International Law Enforcement Educators and Trainers Association et al. by *David B. Kopel;* for Jews for the Preservation of Firearms Ownership by *Daniel L. Schmutter;* for the Maryland Arms Collectors' Association, Inc., by *Don B. Kates;* for the National Shooting Sports Foundation, Inc., by *Lawrence G. Keane, Christopher P. Johnson*, and *Laurin B. Grollman;* for the Paragon Foundation, Inc., by *Paul M. Kienzle III;* for Professors of Philosophy et al. by *Marc James Ayers* and *Mr. Kates;* for Rocky Mountain Gun Owners et al. by *Steven J. Lechner;* for Safari Club International by *Douglas S. Burdin* and *Anna M. Seidman;* for State Firearm Associations by *James W. Hryekewicz;* for State Legislators by *John Parker Sweeney* and *T. Sky Woodward;* for Thirty-Four California District Attorneys et al. by *C. D. Michel, Glenn S. McRoberts*, and *Hillary J. Green;* for Women State Legislators et al. by *Sarah Anne Gervase* and *M. Carol Bambery;* and for Senator Kay Bailey Hutchison et al. by *Mr. Clement, Jeffrey S. Bucholtz*, and *Adam Conrad.*

Briefs of *amici curiae* urging affirmance were filed for the State of Illinois et al. by *Lisa Madigan*, Attorney General of Illinois, *Michael A.*

TICE SCALIA, JUSTICE KENNEDY, and JUSTICE THOMAS join, and an opinion with respect to Parts II–C, IV, and V, in which THE CHIEF JUSTICE, JUSTICE SCALIA, and JUSTICE KENNEDY join.

Two years ago, in *District of Columbia* v. *Heller*, 554 U. S. 570 (2008), we held that the Second Amendment protects the

---

Scodro, Solicitor General, *Jane Elinor Notz*, Deputy Solicitor General, and *David A. Simpson*, Assistant Attorney General, and by the Attorneys General for their respective States as follows: *Douglas F. Gansler* of Maryland and *Anne Milgram* of New Jersey; for American Cities et al. by *Henry C. Su, Jerrold J. Ganzfried, Anita Alvarez, Paul A. Castiglione, Dennis J. Herrera, Jean Boler, Linda Meng, George A. Nilson, William R. Phelan, Jr., Randy Riddle,* and *Matthew D. Ruyak;* for the Anti-Defamation League by *Leonard M. Niehoff, Martin E. Karlinsky, Mark S. Finkelstein, Steven M. Freeman,* and *Steven C. Sheinberg;* for the Association of Prosecuting Attorneys et al. by *Clifford M. Sloan* and *Geoffrey M. Wyatt;* for Historians on Early American Legal, Constitutional, and Pennsylvania History by *Roderick M. Thompson;* for the Oak Park Citizens Committee for Handgun Control by *Robert N. Hochman, Carter G. Phillips, Jeffrey T. Green,* and *Christopher G. Walsh, Jr.;* for Professors of Criminal Justice by *Elizabeth A. Ritvo, Amanda Buck Varella,* and *Albert W. Wallis;* for Thirty-Four Professional Historians and Legal Historians by *Matthew M. Shors;* for the United States Conference of Mayors by *Lawrence Rosenthal* and *John Daniel Reaves;* for the Villages of Winnetka and Skokie, Illinois, et al. by *David T. Goldberg, Sean H. Donahue, Charles W. Thompson, Jr.,* and *Katherine S. Janega;* and for Representative Carolyn McCarthy et al. by *Jennifer Milici* and *Christopher L. Hayes.*

Briefs of *amici curiae* were filed for the American Public Health Association et al. by *Julie D. Cantor* and *H. Philip Grossman;* for the Board of Education of the City of Chicago et al. by *Charles M. Dyke;* for the Brady Center to Prevent Gun Violence et al. by *A. Stephen Hut, Jr., Paul R. Q. Wolfson, D. Hien Tran, Jonathan E. Lowy,* and *Daniel R. Vice;* for the Center for Constitutional Jurisprudence by *Anthony T. Caso, John C. Eastman,* and *Edwin Meese III;* for the Eagle Forum Education and Legal Defense Fund by *Andrew L. Schlafly;* for the Educational Fund to Stop Gun Violence by *John E. Schreiber;* for English/Early American Historians by *Robert A. Goodin* and *Francine T. Radford;* for the Goldwater Institute et al. by *Clint Bolick, Nicholas C. Dranias,* and *Benjamin Barr;* for Historians and Legal Scholars by *Linda T. Coberly;* for the Institute for Jusright to keep and bear arms for the purpose of self-defense, and we struck down a District of Columbia law that banned the possession of handguns in the home. The city of Chicago (Chicago or City) and the village of Oak Park, a Chicago suburb, have laws that are similar to the District of Columbia's, but Chicago and Oak Park argue that their laws are constitutional because the Second Amendment has no application to the States. We have previously held that most of the provisions of the Bill of Rights apply with full force to both the Federal Government and the States. Applying the standard that is well established in our case law, we hold that the Second Amendment right is fully applicable to the States.

I

Otis McDonald, Adam Orlov, Colleen Lawson, and David Lawson (Chicago petitioners) are Chicago residents who would like to keep handguns in their homes for self-defense but are prohibited from doing so by Chicago's firearms laws. A City ordinance provides that "[n]o person shall . . . possess . . . any firearm unless such person is the holder of a valid registration certificate for such firearm." Chicago, Ill., Municipal Code § 8–20–040(a) (2009). The Code then prohibits registration of most handguns, thus effectively banning handgun possession by almost all private citizens who reside in the City. § 8–20–050(c). Like Chicago, Oak Park makes it "unlawful for any person to possess . . . any firearm," a term that includes "pistols, revolvers, guns and small arms . . . commonly known as handguns." Oak Park, Ill., Village Code §§ 27–2–1 (2007), 27–1–1 (2009).

Chicago enacted its handgun ban to protect its residents "from the loss of property and injury or death from fire-

---

tice by *William H. Mellor, Clark M. Neily III,* and *Robert J. McNamara;* for Law Professor and Students by *Douglas A. Berman, pro se,* and *William B. Saxbe;* for the NAACP Legal Defense & Educational Fund, Inc., by *John Payton, Debo P. Adegbile, Dale E. Ho,* and *Joshua Civin;* and for the Rutherford Institute by *John W. Whitehead.*

arms." See Chicago, Ill., Journal of Proceedings of the City Council, p. 10049 (Mar. 19, 1982). The Chicago petitioners and their *amici*, however, argue that the handgun ban has left them vulnerable to criminals. Chicago Police Department statistics, we are told, reveal that the City's handgun murder rate has actually increased since the ban was enacted[1] and that Chicago residents now face one of the highest murder rates in the country and rates of other violent crimes that exceed the average in comparable cities.[2]

Several of the Chicago petitioners have been the targets of threats and violence. For instance, Otis McDonald, who is in his late seventies, lives in a high-crime neighborhood. He is a community activist involved with alternative policing strategies, and his efforts to improve his neighborhood have subjected him to violent threats from drug dealers. App. 16–17; Brief for State Firearm Associations as *Amici Curiae* 20–21; Brief for State of Texas et al. as *Amici Curiae* 7–8. Colleen Lawson is a Chicago resident whose home has been targeted by burglars. "In Mrs. Lawson's judgment, possessing a handgun in Chicago would decrease her chances of suffering serious injury or death should she ever be threatened again in her home."[3] McDonald, Lawson, and the other Chicago petitioners own handguns that they store outside of the city limits, but they would like to keep their handguns in their homes for protection. See App. 16–19, 43–44 (McDonald), 20–24 (C. Lawson), 19, 36 (Orlov), 20–21, 40 (D. Lawson).

---

[1] See Brief for Heartland Institute as *Amicus Curiae* 6–7 (noting that handgun murder rate per 100,000 persons was 9.65 in 1983 and 13.88 in 2008).

[2] Brief for Buckeye Firearms Foundation, Inc., et al. as *Amici Curiae* 8–9 ("In 2002 and again in 2008, Chicago had more murders than any other city in the U. S., including the much larger Los Angeles and New York" (internal quotation marks omitted)); see also Brief for International Law Enforcement Educators and Trainers Association et al. as *Amici Curiae* 17–21, and App. A (providing comparisons of Chicago's rates of assault, murder, and robbery to average crime rates in 24 other large cities).

[3] Brief for Women State Legislators et al. as *Amici Curiae* 2.

After our decision in *Heller,* the Chicago petitioners and two groups[4] filed suit against the City in the United States District Court for the Northern District of Illinois. They sought a declaration that the handgun ban and several related Chicago ordinances violate the Second and Fourteenth Amendments to the United States Constitution. Another action challenging the Oak Park law was filed in the same District Court by the National Rifle Association (NRA) and two Oak Park residents. In addition, the NRA and others filed a third action challenging the Chicago ordinances. All three cases were assigned to the same District Judge.

The District Court rejected plaintiffs' argument that the Chicago and Oak Park laws are unconstitutional. See App. 83–84; *NRA, Inc.* v. *Oak Park,* 617 F. Supp. 2d 752, 754 (ND Ill. 2008). The court noted that the Seventh Circuit had "squarely upheld the constitutionality of a ban on handguns a quarter century ago," *id.,* at 753 (citing *Quilici* v. *Morton Grove,* 695 F. 2d 261 (CA7 1982)), and that *Heller* had explicitly refrained from "opin[ing] on the subject of incorporation vel non of the Second Amendment," *NRA,* 617 F. Supp. 2d, at 754. The court observed that a district judge has a "duty to follow established precedent in the Court of Appeals to which he or she is beholden, even though the logic of more recent caselaw may point in a different direction." *Id.,* at 753.

The Seventh Circuit affirmed, relying on three 19th-century cases—*United States* v. *Cruikshank,* 92 U. S. 542 (1876), *Presser* v. *Illinois,* 116 U. S. 252 (1886), and *Miller* v. *Texas,* 153 U. S. 535 (1894)—that were decided in the wake of this Court's interpretation of the Privileges or Immunities Clause of the Fourteenth Amendment in the *Slaughter-House Cases,* 16 Wall. 36 (1873). The Seventh Circuit described the rationale of those cases as "defunct" and recognized that they did not consider the question whether the

[4] The Illinois State Rifle Association and the Second Amendment Foundation, Inc.

Fourteenth Amendment's Due Process Clause incorporates the Second Amendment right to keep and bear arms. *NRA, Inc.* v. *Chicago*, 567 F. 3d 856, 857, 858 (2009). Nevertheless, the Seventh Circuit observed that it was obligated to follow Supreme Court precedents that have "direct application," and it declined to predict how the Second Amendment would fare under this Court's modern "selective incorporation" approach. *Id.*, at 857–858 (internal quotation marks omitted).

We granted certiorari. 557 U. S. 965 (2009).

II

A

Petitioners argue that the Chicago and Oak Park laws violate the right to keep and bear arms for two reasons. Petitioners' primary submission is that this right is among the "privileges or immunities of citizens of the United States" and that the narrow interpretation of the Privileges or Immunities Clause adopted in the *Slaughter-House Cases, supra,* should now be rejected. As a secondary argument, petitioners contend that the Fourteenth Amendment's Due Process Clause "incorporates" the Second Amendment right.

Chicago and Oak Park (municipal respondents) maintain that a right set out in the Bill of Rights applies to the States only if that right is an indispensable attribute of *any* " 'civilized' " legal system. Brief for Municipal Respondents 9. If it is possible to imagine a civilized country that does not recognize the right, the municipal respondents tell us, then that right is not protected by due process. *Ibid.* And since there are civilized countries that ban or strictly regulate the private possession of handguns, the municipal respondents maintain that due process does not preclude such measures. *Id.*, at 21–23. In light of the parties' far-reaching arguments, we begin by recounting this Court's analysis over the years of the relationship between the provisions of the Bill of Rights and the States.

B

The Bill of Rights, including the Second Amendment, originally applied only to the Federal Government. In *Barron ex rel. Tiernan* v. *Mayor of Baltimore,* 7 Pet. 243 (1833), the Court, in an opinion by Chief Justice Marshall, explained that this question was "of great importance" but "not of much difficulty." *Id.,* at 247. In less than four pages, the Court firmly rejected the proposition that the first eight Amendments operate as limitations on the States, holding that they apply only to the Federal Government. See also *Lessee of Livingston* v. *Moore,* 7 Pet. 469, 551–552 (1833) ("[I]t is now settled that those amendments [in the Bill of Rights] do not extend to the states").

The constitutional Amendments adopted in the aftermath of the Civil War fundamentally altered our country's federal system. The provision at issue in this case, § 1 of the Fourteenth Amendment, provides, among other things, that a State may not abridge "the privileges or immunities of citizens of the United States" or deprive "any person of life, liberty, or property, without due process of law."

Four years after the adoption of the Fourteenth Amendment, this Court was asked to interpret the Amendment's reference to "the privileges or immunities of citizens of the United States." The *Slaughter-House Cases, supra,* involved challenges to a Louisiana law permitting the creation of a state-sanctioned monopoly on the butchering of animals within the city of New Orleans. Justice Samuel Miller's opinion for the Court concluded that the Privileges or Immunities Clause protects only those rights "which owe their existence to the Federal government, its National character, its Constitution, or its laws." *Id.,* at 79. The Court held that other fundamental rights—rights that predated the creation of the Federal Government and that "the State governments were created to establish and secure"—were not protected by the Clause. *Id.,* at 76.

In drawing a sharp distinction between the rights of federal and state citizenship, the Court relied on two principal arguments. First, the Court emphasized that the Fourteenth Amendment's Privileges or Immunities Clause spoke of "the privileges or immunities of *citizens of the United States*," and the Court contrasted this phrasing with the wording in the first sentence of the Fourteenth Amendment and in the Privileges and Immunities Clause of Article IV, both of which refer to *state* citizenship.[5] (Emphasis added.) Second, the Court stated that a contrary reading would "radically chang[e] the whole theory of the relations of the State and Federal governments to each other and of both these governments to the people," and the Court refused to conclude that such a change had been made "in the absence of language which expresses such a purpose too clearly to admit of doubt." *Id.*, at 78. Finding the phrase "privileges or immunities of citizens of the United States" lacking by this high standard, the Court reasoned that the phrase must mean something more limited.

Under the Court's narrow reading, the Privileges or Immunities Clause protects such things as the right

> "to come to the seat of government to assert any claim [a citizen] may have upon that government, to transact any business he may have with it, to seek its protection, to share its offices, to engage in administering its functions . . . [and to] become a citizen of any State of the Union by a *bonâ fide* residence therein, with the same rights as other citizens of that State." *Id.*, at 79–80 (internal quotation marks omitted).

---

[5] The first sentence of the Fourteenth Amendment makes "[a]ll persons born or naturalized in the United States and subject to the jurisdiction thereof . . . citizens of the United States *and of the State wherein they reside.*" (Emphasis added.) The Privileges and Immunities Clause of Article IV provides that "[t]he Citizens of each State shall be entitled to all Privileges and Immunities of *Citizens in the several States.*" (Emphasis added.)

Finding no constitutional protection against state intrusion of the kind envisioned by the Louisiana statute, the Court upheld the statute. Four Justices dissented. Justice Field, joined by Chief Justice Chase and Justices Swayne and Bradley, criticized the majority for reducing the Fourteenth Amendment's Privileges or Immunities Clause to "a vain and idle enactment, which accomplished nothing, and most unnecessarily excited Congress and the people on its passage." *Id.*, at 96; see also *id.*, at 104. Justice Field opined that the Privileges or Immunities Clause protects rights that are "in their nature . . . fundamental," including the right of every man to pursue his profession without the imposition of unequal or discriminatory restrictions. *Id.*, at 96–97 (internal quotation marks omitted). Justice Bradley's dissent observed that "we are not bound to resort to implication . . . to find an authoritative declaration of some of the most important privileges and immunities of citizens of the United States. It is in the Constitution itself." *Id.*, at 118. Justice Bradley would have construed the Privileges or Immunities Clause to include those rights enumerated in the Constitution as well as some unenumerated rights. *Id.*, at 119. Justice Swayne described the majority's narrow reading of the Privileges or Immunities Clause as "turn[ing] . . . what was meant for bread into a stone." *Id.*, at 129 (dissenting opinion).

Today, many legal scholars dispute the correctness of the narrow *Slaughter-House* interpretation. See, *e. g., Saenz* v. *Roe,* 526 U. S. 489, 522, n. 1, 527 (1999) (THOMAS, J., dissenting) (scholars of the Fourteenth Amendment agree "that the Clause does not mean what the Court said it meant in 1873"); Amar, Substance and Method in the Year 2000, 28 Pepperdine L. Rev. 601, 631, n. 178 (2001) ("Virtually no serious modern scholar—left, right, and center—thinks that this [interpretation] is a plausible reading of the Amendment"); Brief for Constitutional Law Professors as *Amici Curiae* 33 (claiming an "overwhelming consensus among leading constitutional scholars" that the opinion is "egregiously wrong"); C. Black, A New Birth of Freedom 74–75 (1997).

Three years after the decision in the *Slaughter-House Cases*, the Court decided *Cruikshank*, the first of the three 19th-century cases on which the Seventh Circuit relied. 92 U. S. 542. In that case, the Court reviewed convictions stemming from the infamous Colfax Massacre in Louisiana on Easter Sunday 1873. Dozens of blacks, many unarmed, were slaughtered by a rival band of armed white men.[6] Cruikshank himself allegedly marched unarmed African-American prisoners through the streets and then had them summarily executed.[7] Ninety-seven men were indicted for participating in the massacre, but only nine went to trial. Six of the nine were acquitted of all charges; the remaining three were acquitted of murder but convicted under the Enforcement Act of 1870, 16 Stat. 140, for banding and conspiring together to deprive their victims of various constitutional rights, including the right to bear arms.[8]

The Court reversed all of the convictions, including those relating to the deprivation of the victims' right to bear arms. *Cruikshank*, 92 U. S., at 553, 559. The Court wrote that the right of bearing arms for a lawful purpose "is not a right granted by the Constitution" and is not "in any manner dependent upon that instrument for its existence." *Id.*, at 553. "The second amendment," the Court continued, "declares that it shall not be infringed; but this . . . means no more than that it shall not be infringed by Congress." *Ibid.* "Our later decisions in *Presser* v. *Illinois*, 116 U. S. 252, 265

---

[6] See C. Lane, The Day Freedom Died 265–266 (2008); see also Brief for NAACP Legal Defense & Education Fund, Inc., as *Amicus Curiae* 3, and n. 2.

[7] See Lane, *supra*, at 106.

[8] *United States* v. *Cruikshank*, 92 U. S. 542, 544–545 (statement of the case), 548, 553 (opinion of the Court) (1876); Lawrence, Civil Rights and Criminal Wrongs: The Mens Rea of Federal Civil Rights Crimes, 67 Tulane L. Rev. 2113, 2153 (1993).

(1886), and *Miller* v. *Texas,* 153 U. S. 535, 538 (1894), reaffirmed that the Second Amendment applies only to the Federal Government." *Heller,* 554 U. S., at 620, n. 23.

C

As previously noted, the Seventh Circuit concluded that *Cruikshank, Presser,* and *Miller* doomed petitioners' claims at the Court of Appeals level. Petitioners argue, however, that we should overrule those decisions and hold that the right to keep and bear arms is one of the "privileges or immunities of citizens of the United States." In petitioners' view, the Privileges or Immunities Clause protects all of the rights set out in the Bill of Rights, as well as some others, see Brief for Petitioners 10, 14, 15–21, but petitioners are unable to identify the Clause's full scope, Tr. of Oral Arg. 5–6, 8–11. Nor is there any consensus on that question among the scholars who agree that the *Slaughter-House Cases'* interpretation is flawed. See *Saenz, supra,* at 522, n. 1 (THOMAS, J., dissenting).

We see no need to reconsider that interpretation here. For many decades, the question of the rights protected by the Fourteenth Amendment against state infringement has been analyzed under the Due Process Clause of that Amendment and not under the Privileges or Immunities Clause. We therefore decline to disturb the *Slaughter-House* holding.

At the same time, however, this Court's decisions in *Cruikshank, Presser,* and *Miller* do not preclude us from considering whether the Due Process Clause of the Fourteenth Amendment makes the Second Amendment right binding on the States. See *Heller,* 554 U. S., at 620, n. 23. None of those cases "engage[d] in the sort of Fourteenth Amendment inquiry required by our later cases." *Ibid.* As explained more fully below, *Cruikshank, Presser,* and *Miller* all preceded the era in which the Court began the process of "selective incorporation" under the Due Process Clause, and we have never previously addressed the question whether the right to keep and bear arms applies to the States under that theory.

Indeed, *Cruikshank* has not prevented us from holding that other rights that were at issue in that case are binding on the States through the Due Process Clause. In *Cruikshank,* the Court held that the general "right of the people peaceably to assemble for lawful purposes," which is protected by the First Amendment, applied only against the Federal Government and not against the States. See 92 U. S., at 551–552. Nonetheless, over 60 years later the Court held that the right of peaceful assembly was a "fundamental righ[t] . . . safeguarded by the due process clause of the Fourteenth Amendment." *De Jonge* v. *Oregon,* 299 U. S. 353, 364 (1937). We follow the same path here and thus consider whether the right to keep and bear arms applies to the States under the Due Process Clause.

D

1

In the late 19th century, the Court began to consider whether the Due Process Clause prohibits the States from infringing rights set out in the Bill of Rights. See *Hurtado* v. *California,* 110 U. S. 516 (1884) (due process does not require grand jury indictment); *Chicago, B. & Q. R. Co.* v. *Chicago,* 166 U. S. 226 (1897) (due process prohibits States from taking of private property for public use without just compensation). Five features of the approach taken during the ensuing era should be noted.

First, the Court viewed the due process question as entirely separate from the question whether a right was a privilege or immunity of national citizenship. See *Twining* v. *New Jersey,* 211 U. S. 78, 99 (1908).

Second, the Court explained that the only rights protected against state infringement by the Due Process Clause were those rights "of such a nature that they are included in the conception of due process of law." *Ibid.* See also, *e. g., Ad-*

amson v. *California,* 332 U. S. 46 (1947); *Betts* v. *Brady,* 316 U. S. 455 (1942); *Palko* v. *Connecticut,* 302 U. S. 319 (1937); *Grosjean* v. *American Press Co.,* 297 U. S. 233 (1936); *Powell* v. *Alabama,* 287 U. S. 45 (1932). While it was "possible that some of the personal rights safeguarded by the first eight Amendments against National action [might] also be safeguarded against state action," the Court stated, this was "not because those rights are enumerated in the first eight Amendments." *Twining,* 211 U. S., at 99.

The Court used different formulations in describing the boundaries of due process. For example, in *Twining,* the Court referred to "immutable principles of justice which inhere in the very idea of free government which no member of the Union may disregard." *Id.,* at 102 (internal quotation marks omitted). In *Snyder* v. *Massachusetts,* 291 U. S. 97, 105 (1934), the Court spoke of rights that are "so rooted in the traditions and conscience of our people as to be ranked as fundamental." And in *Palko,* the Court famously said that due process protects those rights that are "the very essence of a scheme of ordered liberty" and essential to "a fair and enlightened system of justice." 302 U. S., at 325.

Third, in some cases decided during this era the Court "can be seen as having asked, when inquiring into whether some particular procedural safeguard was required of a State, if a civilized system could be imagined that would not accord the particular protection." *Duncan* v. *Louisiana,* 391 U. S. 145, 149, n. 14 (1968). Thus, in holding that due process prohibits a State from taking private property without just compensation, the Court described the right as "a principle of natural equity, recognized by all temperate and civilized governments, from a deep and universal sense of its justice." *Chicago, B. & Q. R. Co., supra,* at 238. Similarly, the Court found that due process did not provide a right against compelled incrimination in part because this right "has no place in the jurisprudence of civilized and free countries outside the domain of the common law." *Twining, supra,* at 113.

Fourth, the Court during this era was not hesitant to hold that a right set out in the Bill of Rights failed to meet the test for inclusion within the protection of the Due Process Clause. The Court found that some such rights qualified. See, *e. g., Gitlow* v. *New York,* 268 U. S. 652, 666 (1925) (freedom of speech and press); *Near* v. *Minnesota ex rel. Olson,* 283 U. S. 697 (1931) (same); *Powell, supra* (assistance of counsel in capital cases); *De Jonge, supra* (freedom of assembly); *Cantwell* v. *Connecticut,* 310 U. S. 296 (1940) (free exercise of religion). But others did not. See, *e. g., Hurtado, supra* (grand jury indictment requirement); *Twining, supra* (privilege against self-incrimination).

Finally, even when a right set out in the Bill of Rights was held to fall within the conception of due process, the protection or remedies afforded against state infringement sometimes differed from the protection or remedies provided against abridgment by the Federal Government. To give one example, in *Betts* the Court held that, although the Sixth Amendment required the appointment of counsel in all federal criminal cases in which the defendant was unable to retain an attorney, the Due Process Clause required appointment of counsel in state criminal proceedings only where "want of counsel in [the] particular case . . . result[ed] in a conviction lacking in . . . fundamental fairness." 316 U. S., at 473. Similarly, in *Wolf* v. *Colorado,* 338 U. S. 25 (1949), the Court held that the "core of the Fourth Amendment" was implicit in the concept of ordered liberty and thus "enforceable against the States through the Due Process Clause" but that the exclusionary rule, which applied in federal cases, did not apply to the States. *Id.,* at 27–28, 33.

2

An alternative theory regarding the relationship between the Bill of Rights and § 1 of the Fourteenth Amendment was championed by Justice Black. This theory held that § 1 of the Fourteenth Amendment totally incorporated all of the provisions of the Bill of Rights. See, *e. g., Adamson, supra,* at 71–72 (Black, J., dissenting); *Duncan, supra,* at 166 (Black, J., concurring). As Justice Black noted, the chief congressional proponents of the Fourteenth Amendment espoused the view that the Amendment made the Bill of Rights applicable to the States and, in so doing, overruled this Court's decision in *Barron.*[9] *Adamson, supra,* at 72 (dissenting opinion).[10] None-

[9] Senator Jacob Howard, who spoke on behalf of the Joint Committee on Reconstruction and sponsored the Amendment in the Senate, stated that the Amendment protected all of "the personal rights guarantied and secured by the first eight amendments of the Constitution." Cong. Globe, 39th Cong., 1st Sess., 2765 (1866) (hereinafter 39th Cong. Globe). Representative John Bingham, the principal author of the text of § 1, said that the Amendment would "arm the Congress . . . with the power to enforce the bill of rights as it stands in the Constitution today." *Id.,* at 1088; see also *id.,* at 1089–1090; A. Amar, The Bill of Rights: Creation and Reconstruction 183 (1998) (hereinafter Amar, Bill of Rights). After ratification of the Amendment, Bingham maintained the view that the rights guaranteed by § 1 of the Fourteenth Amendment "are chiefly defined in the first eight amendments to the Constitution of the United States." Cong. Globe, 42d Cong., 1st Sess., App. 84 (1871). Finally, Representative Thaddeus Stevens, the political leader of the House and acting chairman of the Joint Committee on Reconstruction, stated during the debates on the Amendment that "the Constitution limits only the action of Congress, and is not a limitation on the States. This amendment supplies that defect, and allows Congress to correct the unjust legislation of the States." 39th Cong. Globe 2459; see also M. Curtis, No State Shall Abridge: The Fourteenth Amendment and the Bill of Rights 112 (1986) (counting at least 30 statements during the debates in Congress interpreting § 1 to incorporate the Bill of Rights); Brief for Constitutional Law Professors as *Amici Curiae* 20 (collecting authorities and stating that "[n]ot a single senator or representative disputed [the incorporationist] understanding" of the Fourteenth Amendment).

[10] The municipal respondents and some of their *amici* dispute the significance of these statements. They contend that the phrase "privileges or immunities" is not naturally read to mean the rights set out in the first eight Amendments, see Brief for Historians et al. as *Amici Curiae* 13–16, and that "there is 'support in the legislative history for no fewer than four

theless, the Court never has embraced Justice Black's "total incorporation" theory.

3

While Justice Black's theory was never adopted, the Court eventually moved in that direction by initiating what has been called a process of "selective incorporation," *i. e.*, the Court began to hold that the Due Process Clause fully incorporates particular rights contained in the first eight Amendments. See, *e. g.*, *Gideon* v. *Wainwright*, 372 U. S. 335, 341 (1963); *Malloy* v. *Hogan*, 378 U. S. 1, 5–6 (1964); *Pointer* v. *Texas*, 380 U. S. 400, 403–404 (1965); *Washington* v. *Texas*, 388 U. S. 14, 18 (1967); *Duncan*, 391 U. S., at 147–148; *Benton* v. *Maryland*, 395 U. S. 784, 794 (1969).

---

interpretations of the . . . Privileges or Immunities Clause,'" Brief for Municipal Respondents 69 (quoting Currie, The Reconstruction Congress, 75 U. Chi. L. Rev. 383, 406 (2008); brackets omitted). They question whether there is sound evidence of "'any strong public awareness of nationalizing the *entire* Bill of Rights.'" Brief for Municipal Respondents 69 (quoting Wildenthal, Nationalizing the Bill of Rights: Revisiting the Original Understanding of the Fourteenth Amendment in 1866–67, 68 Ohio St. L. J. 1509, 1600 (2007)). Scholars have also disputed the total incorporation theory. See, *e. g.*, Fairman, Does the Fourteenth Amendment Incorporate the Bill of Rights? 2 Stan. L. Rev. 5 (1949); Berger, Incorporation of the Bill of Rights in the Fourteenth Amendment: A Nine-Lived Cat, 42 Ohio St. L. J. 435 (1981).

Proponents of the view that § 1 of the Fourteenth Amendment makes all of the provisions of the Bill of Rights applicable to the States respond that the terms privileges, immunities, and rights were used interchangeably at the time, see, *e. g.*, Curtis, *supra*, at 64–65, and that the position taken by the leading congressional proponents of the Amendment was widely publicized and understood, see, *e. g.*, Wildenthal, *supra*, at 1564–1565, 1590; Hardy, Original Popular Understanding of the Fourteenth Amendment as Reflected in the Print Media of 1866–1868, 30 Whittier L. Rev. 695 (2009). A number of scholars have found support for the total incorporation of the Bill of Rights. See Curtis, *supra*, at 57–130; Aynes, On Misreading John Bingham and the Fourteenth Amendment, 103 Yale L. J. 57, 61 (1993); see also Amar, Bill of Rights 181–230. We take no position with respect to this academic debate.

The decisions during this time abandoned three of the previously noted characteristics of the earlier period.[11] The Court made it clear that the governing standard is not whether *any* "civilized system [can] be imagined that would not accord the particular protection." *Duncan*, 391 U. S., at 149, n. 14. Instead, the Court inquired whether a particular Bill of Rights guarantee is fundamental to *our* scheme of ordered liberty and system of justice. *Id.*, at 149, and n. 14; see also *id.*, at 148 (referring to those "fundamental principles of liberty and justice which lie at the base of all *our* civil and political institutions" (emphasis added; internal quotation marks omitted)).

The Court also shed any reluctance to hold that rights guaranteed by the Bill of Rights met the requirements for protection under the Due Process Clause. The Court eventually incorporated almost all of the provisions of the Bill of Rights.[12]

---

[11] By contrast, the Court has never retreated from the proposition that the Privileges or Immunities Clause and the Due Process Clause present different questions. And in recent cases addressing unenumerated rights, we have required that a right also be "implicit in the concept of ordered liberty." See, *e. g.*, *Washington* v. *Glucksberg*, 521 U. S. 702, 721 (1997) (internal quotation marks omitted).

[12] With respect to the First Amendment, see *Everson* v. *Board of Ed. of Ewing*, 330 U. S. 1 (1947) (Establishment Clause); *Cantwell* v. *Connecticut*, 310 U. S. 296 (1940) (Free Exercise Clause); *De Jonge* v. *Oregon*, 299 U. S. 353 (1937) (freedom of assembly); *Gitlow* v. *New York*, 268 U. S. 652 (1925) (free speech); *Near* v. *Minnesota ex rel. Olson*, 283 U. S. 697 (1931) (freedom of the press).

With respect to the Fourth Amendment, see *Aguilar* v. *Texas*, 378 U. S. 108 (1964) (warrant requirement); *Mapp* v. *Ohio*, 367 U. S. 643 (1961) (exclusionary rule); *Wolf* v. *Colorado*, 338 U. S. 25 (1949) (freedom from unreasonable searches and seizures).

With respect to the Fifth Amendment, see *Benton* v. *Maryland*, 395 U. S. 784 (1969) (Double Jeopardy Clause); *Malloy* v. *Hogan*, 378 U. S. 1 (1964) (privilege against self-incrimination); *Chicago, B. & Q. R. Co.* v. *Chicago*, 166 U. S. 226 (1897) (Just Compensation Clause).

With respect to the Sixth Amendment, see *Duncan* v. *Louisiana*, 391 U. S. 145 (1968) (trial by jury in criminal cases); *Washington* v. *Texas*, 388 U. S. 14 (1967) (compulsory process); *Klopfer* v. *North Carolina*, 386

Only a handful of the Bill of Rights protections remain unincorporated.[13]

Finally, the Court abandoned "the notion that the Fourteenth Amendment applies to the States only a watered-down, subjective version of the individual guarantees of the Bill of Rights," stating that it would be "incongruous" to apply different standards "depending on whether the claim was asserted in a state or federal court." *Malloy*, 378 U. S., at 10–11 (internal quotation marks omitted). Instead, the Court decisively held that incorporated Bill of Rights protections "are all to be enforced against the States under the Fourteenth Amendment according to the same standards that protect those personal rights against federal encroachment." *Id.*, at 10; see also *Mapp* v. *Ohio*, 367 U. S. 643, 655–656 (1961); *Ker* v. *California*, 374 U. S. 23, 33–34 (1963);

U. S. 213 (1967) (speedy trial); *Pointer* v. *Texas*, 380 U. S. 400 (1965) (right to confront adverse witness); *Gideon* v. *Wainwright*, 372 U. S. 335 (1963) (assistance of counsel); *In re Oliver*, 333 U. S. 257 (1948) (right to a public trial).

With respect to the Eighth Amendment, see *Robinson* v. *California*, 370 U. S. 660 (1962) (cruel and unusual punishment); *Schilb* v. *Kuebel*, 404 U. S. 357 (1971) (prohibition against excessive bail (assumed)).

[13] In addition to the right to keep and bear arms (and the Sixth Amendment right to a unanimous jury verdict, see n. 14, *infra*), the only rights not fully incorporated are (1) the Third Amendment's protection against quartering of soldiers; (2) the Fifth Amendment's grand jury indictment requirement; (3) the Seventh Amendment right to a jury trial in civil cases; and (4) the Eighth Amendment's prohibition on excessive fines.

We never have decided whether the Third Amendment or the Eighth Amendment's prohibition of excessive fines applies to the States through the Due Process Clause. See *Browning-Ferris Industries of Vt., Inc.* v. *Kelco Disposal, Inc.*, 492 U. S. 257, 276, n. 22 (1989) (declining to decide whether the excessive-fines protection applies to the States); see also *Engblom* v. *Carey*, 677 F. 2d 957, 961 (CA2 1982) (holding as a matter of first impression that the "Third Amendment is incorporated into the Fourteenth Amendment for application to the states").

Our governing decisions regarding the Grand Jury Clause of the Fifth Amendment and the Seventh Amendment's civil jury requirement long predate the era of selective incorporation.

Aguilar v. *Texas,* 378 U. S. 108, 110 (1964); *Pointer,* 380 U. S., at 406; *Duncan, supra,* at 149, 157–158; *Benton,* 395 U. S., at 794–795; *Wallace* v. *Jaffree,* 472 U. S. 38, 48–49 (1985).[14]

Employing this approach, the Court overruled earlier decisions in which it had held that particular Bill of Rights guarantees or remedies did not apply to the States. See, *e. g., Mapp, supra* (overruling in part *Wolf,* 338 U. S. 25); *Gideon,* 372 U. S. 335 (overruling *Betts,* 316 U. S. 455); *Malloy, supra* (overruling *Adamson,* 332 U. S. 46, and *Twining,* 211 U. S. 78); *Benton,* 395 U. S., at 794 (overruling *Palko,* 302 U. S. 319).

---

[14] There is one exception to this general rule. The Court has held that although the Sixth Amendment right to trial by jury requires a unanimous jury verdict in federal criminal trials, it does not require a unanimous jury verdict in state criminal trials. See *Apodaca* v. *Oregon,* 406 U. S. 404 (1972); see also *Johnson* v. *Louisiana,* 406 U. S. 356 (1972) (holding that the Due Process Clause does not require unanimous jury verdicts in state criminal trials). But that ruling was the result of an unusual division among the Justices, not an endorsement of the two-track approach to incorporation. In *Apodaca,* eight Justices agreed that the Sixth Amendment applies identically to both the Federal Government and the States. See *Johnson, supra,* at 395 (Brennan, J., dissenting). Nonetheless, among those eight, four Justices took the view that the Sixth Amendment does not require unanimous jury verdicts in either federal or state criminal trials, *Apodaca,* 406 U. S., at 406 (plurality opinion), and four other Justices took the view that the Sixth Amendment requires unanimous jury verdicts in federal and state criminal trials, *id.,* at 414–415 (Stewart, J., dissenting); *Johnson, supra,* at 381–382 (Douglas, J., dissenting). Justice Powell's concurrence in the judgment broke the tie, and he concluded that the Sixth Amendment requires juror unanimity in federal, but not state, cases. *Apodaca,* therefore, does not undermine the well-established rule that incorporated Bill of Rights protections apply identically to the States and the Federal Government. See *Johnson, supra,* at 395–396 (Brennan, J., dissenting) ("In any event, the affirmance must not obscure that the majority of the Court remains of the view that, as in the case of every specific of the Bill of Rights that extends to the States, the Sixth Amendment's jury trial guarantee, however it is to be construed, has identical application against both State and Federal Governments" (footnote omitted)).

III

With this framework in mind, we now turn directly to the question whether the Second Amendment right to keep and bear arms is incorporated in the concept of due process. In answering that question, as just explained, we must decide whether the right to keep and bear arms is fundamental to *our* scheme of ordered liberty, *Duncan*, 391 U. S., at 149, or as we have said in a related context, whether this right is "deeply rooted in this Nation's history and tradition," *Washington* v. *Glucksberg*, 521 U. S. 702, 721 (1997) (internal quotation marks omitted).

A

Our decision in *Heller* points unmistakably to the answer. Self-defense is a basic right, recognized by many legal systems from ancient times to the present day,[15] and in *Heller*, we held that individual self-defense is "the *central component*" of the Second Amendment right. 554 U. S., at 599; see also *id.*, at 628 (stating that the "inherent right of self-defense has been central to the Second Amendment right"). Explaining that "the need for defense of self, family, and property is most acute" in the home, *ibid.*, we found that this right applies to handguns because they are "the most preferred firearm in the nation to 'keep' and use for protection of one's home and family," *id.*, at 628–629 (some internal quotation marks omitted); see also *id.*, at 628 (noting that handguns are "overwhelmingly chosen by American society for [the] lawful purpose" of self-defense); *id.*, at 629 ("[T]he American people have considered the handgun to be the quintessential self-defense weapon"). Thus, we concluded,

---

[15] Citing Jewish, Greek, and Roman law, Blackstone wrote that if a person killed an attacker, "the slayer is in no kind of fault whatsoever, not even in the minutest degree; and is therefore to be totally acquitted and discharged, with commendation rather than blame." 4 W. Blackstone, Commentaries on the Laws of England 182 (1769).

citizens must be permitted "to use [handguns] for the core lawful purpose of self-defense." *Id.*, at 630.

Heller makes it clear that this right is "deeply rooted in this Nation's history and tradition." *Glucksberg, supra,* at 721 (internal quotation marks omitted). *Heller* explored the right's origins, noting that the 1689 English Bill of Rights explicitly protected a right to keep arms for self-defense, 554 U. S., at 592–593, and that by 1765, Blackstone was able to assert that the right to keep and bear arms was "one of the fundamental rights of Englishmen," *id.*, at 594.

Blackstone's assessment was shared by the American colonists. As we noted in *Heller,* King George III's attempt to disarm the colonists in the 1760's and 1770's "provoked polemical reactions by Americans invoking their rights as Englishmen to keep arms."[16] *Ibid.;* see also L. Levy, Origins of the Bill of Rights 137–143 (1999) (hereinafter Levy).

The right to keep and bear arms was considered no less fundamental by those who drafted and ratified the Bill of Rights. "During the 1788 ratification debates, the fear that the federal government would disarm the people in order to impose rule through a standing army or select militia was pervasive in Antifederalist rhetoric." *Heller, supra,* at 598 (citing Letters from The Federal Farmer III (Oct. 10, 1787), in 2 The Complete Anti-Federalist 234, 242 (H. Storing ed. 1981)); see also Federal Farmer: An Additional Number of Letters to the Republican, Letter XVIII (Jan. 25, 1788), in 17 Documentary History of the Ratification of the Constitution 360, 362–363 (J. Kaminski & G. Saladino eds. 1995); S. Halbrook, The Founders' Second Amendment 171–278

---

[16] For example, an article in the Boston Evening Post stated: "For it is certainly beyond human art and sophistry, to prove the British subjects, to whom the priviledge of possessing arms is expressly recognized by the Bill of Rights, and, who live in a province where the law requires them to be equip'd with arms, &c. are guilty of an illegal act, in calling upon one another to be provided with them, as the law directs." Boston Evening Post, Feb. 6, 1769, in Boston Under Military Rule 1768–1769, p. 61 (1936) (emphasis deleted).

(2008). Federalists responded, not by arguing that the right was insufficiently important to warrant protection but by contending that the right was adequately protected by the Constitution's assignment of only limited powers to the Federal Government. *Heller, supra,* at 599; cf. The Federalist No. 46, p. 296 (C. Rossiter ed. 1961) (J. Madison). Thus, Antifederalists and Federalists alike agreed that the right to bear arms was fundamental to the newly formed system of government. See Levy 143–149; J. Malcolm, To Keep and Bear Arms: The Origins of an Anglo-American Right 155–164 (1994). But those who were fearful that the new Federal Government would infringe traditional rights such as the right to keep and bear arms insisted on the adoption of the Bill of Rights as a condition for ratification of the Constitution. See 1 Debates in the Several State Conventions on the Adoption of the Federal Constitution 327–331 (J. Elliot 2d ed. 1854); 3 *id.*, at 657–661; 4 *id.*, at 242–246, 248–249; see also Levy 26–34; 1 A. Kelly, W. Harbison, & H. Belz, The American Constitution: Its Origins and Development 110, 118 (7th ed. 1991). This is surely powerful evidence that the right was regarded as fundamental in the sense relevant here.

This understanding persisted in the years immediately following the ratification of the Bill of Rights. In addition to the four States that had adopted Second Amendment analogues before ratification, nine more States adopted state constitutional provisions protecting an individual right to keep and bear arms between 1789 and 1820. *Heller, supra,* at 600–603. Founding-era legal commentators confirmed the importance of the right to early Americans. St. George Tucker, for example, described the right to keep and bear arms as "the true palladium of liberty" and explained that prohibitions on the right would place liberty "on the brink of destruction." 1 Blackstone's Commentaries, Editor's App. 300 (S. Tucker ed. 1803); see also W. Rawle, A View of the Constitution of the United States of America 125–126 (2d ed. 1829); 3 J. Story, Commentaries on the Constitution of the United States § 1890, p. 746 (1833) ("The right of the citizens to keep and bear arms has justly been considered, as the palladium of the liberties of a republic; since it offers a strong moral check against the usurpation and arbitrary power of rulers; and will generally, even if these are successful in the first instance, enable the people to resist and triumph over them").

B

1

By the 1850's, the perceived threat that had prompted the inclusion of the Second Amendment in the Bill of Rights—the fear that the National Government would disarm the universal militia—had largely faded as a popular concern, but the right to keep and bear arms was highly valued for purposes of self-defense. See M. Doubler, Civilian in Peace, Soldier in War 87–90 (2003); Amar, Bill of Rights 258–259. Abolitionist authors wrote in support of the right. See L. Spooner, The Unconstitutionality of Slavery 66 (1860); J. Tiffany, A Treatise on the Unconstitutionality of American Slavery 117–118 (1849). And when attempts were made to disarm "Free-Soilers" in "Bloody Kansas," Senator Charles Sumner, who later played a leading role in the adoption of the Fourteenth Amendment, proclaimed that "[n]ever was [the rifle] more needed in just self-defense than now in Kansas." The Crime Against Kansas: The Apologies for the Crime: The True Remedy, Speech of Hon. Charles Sumner in the Senate of the United States 64–65 (1856). Indeed, the 1856 Republican Party Platform protested that in Kansas the constitutional rights of the people had been "fraudulently and violently taken from them" and the "right of the people to keep and bear arms" had been "infringed." National Party Platforms 1840–1972, p. 27 (D. Johnson & K. Porter comp. 5th ed. 1973).[17]

---

[17] Abolitionists and Republicans were not alone in believing that the right to keep and bear arms was a fundamental right. The 1864 Democratic Party Platform complained that the confiscation of firearms by

After the Civil War, many of the over 180,000 African-Americans who served in the Union Army returned to the States of the old Confederacy, where systematic efforts were made to disarm them and other blacks. See *Heller*, 554 U. S., at 614; E. Foner, Reconstruction: America's Unfinished Revolution 1863–1877, p. 8 (1988) (hereinafter Foner). The laws of some States formally prohibited African-Americans from possessing firearms. For example, a Mississippi law provided that "no freedman, free negro or mulatto, not in the military service of the United States government, and not licensed so to do by the board of police of his or her county, shall keep or carry fire-arms of any kind, or any ammunition, dirk or bowie knife." Certain Offenses of Freedmen, 1865 Miss. Laws p. 165, § 1, in 1 Documentary History of Reconstruction 289 (W. Fleming ed. 1950); see also Regulations for Freedmen in Louisiana, in *id.*, at 279–280; H. R. Exec. Doc. No. 70, 39th Cong., 1st Sess., 233, 236 (1866) (describing a Kentucky law); E. McPherson, The Political History of the United States of America During the Period of Reconstruction 40 (1871) (describing a Florida law); *id.*, at 33 (describing an Alabama law).[18]

Union troops occupying parts of the South constituted "the interference with and denial of the right of the people to bear arms in their defense." National Party Platforms 1840–1972, at 34.

[18] In South Carolina, prominent black citizens held a convention to address the State's Black Code. They drafted a memorial to Congress, in which they included a plea for protection of their constitutional right to keep and bear arms: "'We ask that, inasmuch as the Constitution of the United States explicitly declares that the right to keep and bear arms shall not be infringed . . . that the late efforts of the Legislature of this State to pass an act to deprive us [of] arms be forbidden, as a plain violation of the Constitution.'" S. Halbrook, Freedmen, The Fourteenth Amendment, and The Right to Bear Arms, 1866–1876, p. 9 (1998) (hereinafter Halbrook, Freedmen) (quoting 2 Proceedings of the Black State Conventions, 1840–1865, p. 302 (P. Foner & G. Walker eds. 1980)). Senator Charles Sumner relayed the memorial to the Senate and described the memorial as a request that black citizens "have the constitutional protection in keeping arms." 39th Cong. Globe 337.

Throughout the South, armed parties, often consisting of ex-Confederate soldiers serving in the state militias, forcibly took firearms from newly freed slaves. In the first session of the 39th Congress, Senator Henry Wilson told his colleagues: "In Mississippi rebel State forces, men who were in the rebel armies, are traversing the State, visiting the freedmen, disarming them, perpetrating murders and outrages upon them; and the same things are done in other sections of the country." 39th Cong. Globe 40 (1865). The Report of the Joint Committee on Reconstruction—which was widely reprinted in the press and distributed by Members of the 39th Congress to their constituents shortly after Congress approved the Fourteenth Amendment[19]—contained numerous examples of such abuses. See, *e. g.*, H. R. Rep. No. 30, 39th Cong., 1st Sess., pt. 2, pp. 219, 229, 272, pt. 3, pp. 46, 140, pt. 4, pp. 49–50 (1866); see also S. Exec. Doc. No. 2, 39th Cong., 1st Sess., 23–24, 26, 36 (1865). In one town, the "marshal [took] all arms from returned colored soldiers, and [was] very prompt in shooting the blacks whenever an opportunity occur[red]." H. R. Exec. Doc. No. 70, at 238 (internal quotation marks omitted). As Senator Wilson put it during the debate on a failed proposal to disband Southern militias: "There is one unbroken chain of testimony from all people that are loyal to this country, that the greatest outrages are perpetrated by armed men who go up and down the country searching houses, disarming people, committing outrages of every kind and description." 39th Cong. Globe 915 (1866).[20]

---

[19] See B. Kendrick, Journal of the Joint Committee of Fifteen on Reconstruction 265–266 (1914); *Adamson* v. *California*, 332 U. S. 46, 108–109 (1947) (appendix to dissenting opinion of Black, J.).

[20] Disarmament by bands of former Confederate soldiers eventually gave way to attacks by the Ku Klux Klan. In debates over the later enacted Enforcement Act of 1870, Senator John Pool observed that the Klan would "order the colored men to give up their arms; saying that everybody would be Kukluxed in whose house fire-arms were found." Cong. Globe, 41st Cong., 2d Sess., 2719 (1870); see also H. R. Exec. Doc. No. 268, 42d Cong., 2d Sess., 2 (1872).

Union Army commanders took steps to secure the right of all citizens to keep and bear arms,[21] but the 39th Congress concluded that legislative action was necessary. Its efforts to safeguard the right to keep and bear arms demonstrate that the right was still recognized to be fundamental.

The most explicit evidence of Congress' aim appears in § 14 of the Freedmen's Bureau Act of 1866, which provided that "the right . . . to have full and equal benefit of all laws and proceedings concerning personal liberty, personal security, and the acquisition, enjoyment, and disposition of estate, real and personal, *including the constitutional right to bear arms,* shall be secured to and enjoyed by all the citizens . . . without respect to race or color, or previous condition of slavery." 14 Stat. 176–177 (emphasis added).[22] Section 14 thus explicitly guaranteed that "all the citizens," black and white, would have "the constitutional right to bear arms."

---

[21] For example, the occupying Union commander in South Carolina issued an order stating that "[t]he constitutional rights of all loyal and well disposed inhabitants to bear arms, will not be infringed." General Order No. 1, Department of South Carolina, January 1, 1866, in 1 Documentary History of Reconstruction 208 (W. Fleming ed. 1950). Union officials in Georgia issued a similar order, declaring that " '[a]ll men, without the distinction of color, have the right to keep arms to defend their homes, families or themselves.' " Cramer, Johnson, & Mocsary, "This Right is Not Allowed by Governments That Are Afraid of The People": The Public Meaning of the Second Amendment When the Fourteenth Amendment Was Ratified, 17 Geo. Mason L. Rev. 823, 854 (2010) (hereinafter Cramer) (quoting Right To Bear Arms, Phila., Pa., Christian Recorder, Feb. 24, 1866, pp. 1–2). In addition, when made aware of attempts by armed parties to disarm blacks, the head of the Freedmen's Bureau in Alabama "made public [his] determination to maintain the right of the negro to keep and to bear arms, and [his] disposition to send an armed force into any neighborhood in which that right should be systematically interfered with." Joint Committee on Reconstruction, H. R. Rep. No. 30, 39th Cong., 1st Sess., pt. 3, p. 140 (1866).

[22] The Freedmen's Bureau bill was amended to include an express reference to the right to keep and bear arms, see 39th Cong. Globe 654 (Rep. Thomas Eliot), even though at least some Members believed that the unamended version alone would have protected the right, see *id.,* at 743 (Sen. Lyman Trumbull).

The Civil Rights Act of 1866, 14 Stat. 27, which was considered at the same time as the Freedmen's Bureau Act, similarly sought to protect the right of all citizens to keep and bear arms.[23] Section 1 of the Civil Rights Act guaranteed the "full and equal benefit of all laws and proceedings for the security of person and property, as is enjoyed by white citizens." *Ibid.* This language was virtually identical to language in § 14 of the Freedmen's Bureau Act, 14 Stat. 176 ("the right . . . to have full and equal benefit of all laws and proceedings concerning personal liberty, personal security, and the acquisition, enjoyment, and disposition of estate, real and personal"). And as noted, the latter provision went on to explain that one of the "laws and proceedings concerning personal liberty, personal security, and the acquisition, enjoyment, and disposition of estate, real and personal" was "the constitutional right to bear arms." *Ibid.* Representative Bingham believed that the Civil Rights Act protected the same rights as enumerated in the Freedmen's Bureau bill, which of course explicitly mentioned the right to keep

[23] There can be no doubt that the principal proponents of the Civil Rights Act of 1866 meant to end the disarmament of African-Americans in the South. In introducing the bill, Senator Trumbull described its purpose as securing to blacks the "privileges which are essential to freemen." *Id.*, at 474. He then pointed to the previously described Mississippi law that "prohibit[ed] any negro or mulatto from having fire-arms" and explained that the bill would "destroy" such laws. *Ibid.* Similarly, Representative Sidney Clarke cited disarmament of freedmen in Alabama and Mississippi as a reason to support the Civil Rights Act and to continue to deny Alabama and Mississippi representation in Congress: "I regret, sir, that justice compels me to say, to the disgrace of the Federal Government, that the 'reconstructed' State authorities of Mississippi were allowed to rob and disarm our veteran soldiers and arm the rebels fresh from the field of treasonable strife. Sir, the disarmed loyalists of Alabama, Mississippi, and Louisiana are powerless to-day, and oppressed by the pardoned and encouraged rebels of those States. They appeal to the American Congress for protection. In response to this appeal I shall vote for every just measure of protection, for I do not intend to be among the treacherous violators of the solemn pledge of the nation." *Id.*, at 1838–1839.

and bear arms. 39th Cong. Globe 1292. The unavoidable conclusion is that the Civil Rights Act, like the Freedmen's Bureau Act, aimed to protect "the constitutional right to bear arms" and not simply to prohibit discrimination. See also Amar, Bill of Rights 264–265 (noting that one of the "core purposes of the Civil Rights Act of 1866 and of the Fourteenth Amendment was to redress the grievances" of freedmen who had been stripped of their arms and to "affirm the full and equal right of every citizen to self-defense").

Congress, however, ultimately deemed these legislative remedies insufficient. Southern resistance, Presidential vetoes, and this Court's pre-Civil-War precedent persuaded Congress that a constitutional amendment was necessary to provide full protection for the rights of blacks.[24] Today, it is generally accepted that the Fourteenth Amendment was understood to provide a constitutional basis for protecting the rights set out in the Civil Rights Act of 1866. See *General Building Contractors Assn., Inc.* v. *Pennsylvania*, 458 U. S. 375, 389 (1982); see also Amar, Bill of Rights 187; Calabresi & Fine, Two Cheers for Professor Balkin's Originalism, 103 Nw. U. L. Rev. 663, 669–670 (2009).

In debating the Fourteenth Amendment, the 39th Congress referred to the right to keep and bear arms as a fundamental right deserving of protection. Senator Samuel Pomeroy described three "indispensable" "safeguards of liberty under our form of Government." 39th Cong. Globe 1182. One of these, he said, was the right to keep and bear arms:

> "Every man . . . should have the right to bear arms for the defense of himself and family and his homestead. And if the cabin door of the freedman is broken open

---

[24] For example, at least one Southern court had held the Civil Rights Act to be unconstitutional. That court did so, moreover, in the course of upholding the conviction of an African-American man for violating Mississippi's law against firearm possession by freedmen. See Decision of Chief Justice Handy, Declaring the Civil Rights Bill Unconstitutional, N. Y. Times, Oct. 26, 1866, p. 2, col. 3.

> and the intruder enters for purposes as vile as were known to slavery, then should a well-loaded musket be in the hand of the occupant to send the polluted wretch to another world, where his wretchedness will forever remain complete." *Ibid.*

Even those who thought the Fourteenth Amendment unnecessary believed that blacks, as citizens, "have equal right to protection, and to keep and bear arms for self-defense." *Id.*, at 1073 (Sen. James Nye); see also Foner 258–259.[25]

Evidence from the period immediately following the ratification of the Fourteenth Amendment only confirms that the right to keep and bear arms was considered fundamental. In an 1868 speech addressing the disarmament of freedmen, Representative Stevens emphasized the necessity of the right: "Disarm a community and you rob them of the means of defending life. Take away their weapons of defense and you take away the inalienable right of defending liberty." "The fourteenth amendment, now so happily adopted, settles the whole question." Cong. Globe, 40th Cong., 2d Sess., 1967. And in debating the Civil Rights Act of 1871, Congress routinely referred to the right to keep and bear arms and decried the continued disarmament of blacks in the South. See Halbrook, Freedmen 120–131. Finally, legal commentators from the period emphasized the fundamental nature of the right. See, *e. g.*, T. Farrar, Manual of the Constitution of the United States of America § 118, p. 145 (1867);

---

[25] Other Members of the 39th Congress stressed the importance of the right to keep and bear arms in discussing other measures. In speaking generally on Reconstruction, Representative Roswell Hart listed the " 'right of the people to keep and bear arms' " as among those rights necessary to a "republican form of government." 39th Cong. Globe 1629. Similarly, in objecting to a bill designed to disarm Southern militias, Senator Willard Saulsbury argued that such a measure would violate the Second Amendment. *Id.*, at 914–915. Indeed, the bill "ultimately passed in a form that disbanded militias but maintained the right of individuals to their private firearms." Cramer 858.

J. Pomeroy, An Introduction to the Constitutional Law of the United States § 239, pp. 152–153 (3d ed. 1875).

The right to keep and bear arms was also widely protected by state constitutions at the time when the Fourteenth Amendment was ratified. In 1868, 22 of the 37 States in the Union had state constitutional provisions explicitly protecting the right to keep and bear arms. See Calabresi & Agudo, Individual Rights Under State Constitutions When the Fourteenth Amendment Was Ratified in 1868: What Rights Are Deeply Rooted in American History and Tradition? 87 Texas L. Rev. 7, 50 (2008).[26] Quite a few of these state constitutional guarantees, moreover, explicitly protected the right to keep and bear arms as an individual right to self-defense. See Ala. Const., Art. I, § 28 (1868); Conn. Const., Art. I, § 17 (1818); Ky. Const., Art. XIII, § 25 (1850); Mich. Const., Art. XVIII, § 7 (1850); Miss. Const., Art. I, § 15 (1868); Mo. Const., Art. I, § 8 (1865); Tex. Const., Art. I, § 13 (1869); see also Mont. Const., Art. III, § 13 (1889); Wash. Const., Art. I, § 24 (1889); Wyo. Const., Art. I, § 24 (1889); see also *State* v. *McAdams*, 714 P. 2d 1236, 1238 (Wyo. 1986). What is more, state constitutions adopted during the Reconstruction era by former Confederate States included a right to keep and bear arms. See, *e. g.*, Ark. Const., Art. I, § 5 (1868); Miss. Const., Art. I, § 15 (1868); Tex. Const., Art. I, § 13 (1869). A clear majority of the States in 1868, therefore, recognized the right to keep and bear arms as being among the foundational rights necessary to our system of government.[27]

---

[26] More generally worded provisions in the constitutions of seven other States may also have encompassed a right to bear arms. See Calabresi & Agudo, 87 Texas L. Rev., at 52.

[27] These state constitutional protections often reflected a lack of law enforcement in many sections of the country. In the frontier towns that did not have an effective police force, law enforcement often could not pursue criminals beyond the town borders. See Brief for Rocky Mountain Gun Owners et al. as *Amici Curiae* 15. Settlers in the West and elsewhere, therefore, were left to "repe[l] force by force when the intervention of

In sum, it is clear that the Framers and ratifiers of the Fourteenth Amendment counted the right to keep and bear arms among those fundamental rights necessary to our system of ordered liberty.

2

Despite all this evidence, municipal respondents contend that Congress, in the years immediately following the Civil War, merely sought to outlaw "discriminatory measures taken against freedmen, which it addressed by adopting a non-discrimination principle" and that even an outright ban on the possession of firearms was regarded as acceptable, "so long as it was not done in a discriminatory manner." Brief for Municipal Respondents 7. They argue that Members of Congress overwhelmingly viewed § 1 of the Fourteenth Amendment "as an antidiscrimination rule," and they cite statements to the effect that the section would outlaw discriminatory measures. *Id.*, at 64. This argument is implausible.

First, while § 1 of the Fourteenth Amendment contains "an antidiscrimination rule," namely, the Equal Protection Clause, municipal respondents can hardly mean that § 1 does no more than prohibit discrimination. If that were so, then the First Amendment, as applied to the States, would not prohibit nondiscriminatory abridgments of the rights to freedom of speech or freedom of religion; the Fourth Amendment, as applied to the States, would not prohibit all unreasonable searches and seizures but only discriminatory searches and seizures—and so on. We assume that this is not municipal respondents' view, so what they must mean is that the Second Amendment should be singled out for

---

society . . . [was] too late to prevent an injury." *District of Columbia* v. *Heller*, 554 U. S. 570, 595 (2008) (internal quotation marks omitted). The settlers' dependence on game for food and economic livelihood, moreover, undoubtedly undergirded these state constitutional guarantees. See *id.*, at 599, 609, 615.

special—and specially unfavorable—treatment. We reject that suggestion.

Second, municipal respondents' argument ignores the clear terms of the Freedmen's Bureau Act of 1866, which acknowledged the existence of the right to bear arms. If that law had used language such as "the equal benefit of laws concerning the bearing of arms," it would be possible to interpret it as simply a prohibition of racial discrimination. But § 14 speaks of and protects "the constitutional right to bear arms," an unmistakable reference to the right protected by the Second Amendment. And it protects the "full and equal benefit" of this right in the States. 14 Stat. 176–177. It would have been nonsensical for Congress to guarantee the full and equal benefit of a constitutional right that does not exist.

Third, if the 39th Congress had outlawed only those laws that discriminate on the basis of race or previous condition of servitude, African-Americans in the South would likely have remained vulnerable to attack by many of their worst abusers: the state militia and state peace officers. In the years immediately following the Civil War, a law banning the possession of guns by all private citizens would have been nondiscriminatory only in the formal sense. Any such law—like the Chicago and Oak Park ordinances challenged here—presumably would have permitted the possession of guns by those acting under the authority of the State and would thus have left firearms in the hands of the militia and local peace officers. And as the Report of the Joint Committee on Reconstruction revealed, see *supra*, at 772, those groups were widely involved in harassing blacks in the South.

Fourth, municipal respondents' purely antidiscrimination theory of the Fourteenth Amendment disregards the plight of whites in the South who opposed the Black Codes. If the 39th Congress and the ratifying public had simply prohibited racial discrimination with respect to the bearing of arms, opponents of the Black Codes would have been left without the means of self-defense—as had abolitionists in Kansas in the 1850's.

Fifth, the 39th Congress' response to proposals to disband and disarm the Southern militias is instructive. Despite recognizing and deploring the abuses of these militias, the 39th Congress balked at a proposal to disarm them. See 39th Cong. Globe 914; Halbrook, Freedmen 20–21. Disarmament, it was argued, would violate the members' right to bear arms, and it was ultimately decided to disband the militias but not to disarm their members. See Act of Mar. 2, 1867, § 6, 14 Stat. 487; Halbrook, Freedmen 68–69; Cramer 858–861. It cannot be doubted that the right to bear arms was regarded as a substantive guarantee, not a prohibition that could be ignored so long as the States legislated in an evenhanded manner.

IV

Municipal respondents' remaining arguments are at war with our central holding in *Heller:* that the Second Amendment protects a personal right to keep and bear arms for lawful purposes, most notably for self-defense within the home. Municipal respondents, in effect, ask us to treat the right recognized in *Heller* as a second-class right, subject to an entirely different body of rules than the other Bill of Rights guarantees that we have held to be incorporated into the Due Process Clause.

Municipal respondents' main argument is nothing less than a plea to disregard 50 years of incorporation precedent and return (presumably for this case only) to a bygone era. Municipal respondents submit that the Due Process Clause protects only those rights "'recognized by all temperate and civilized governments, from a deep and universal sense of [their] justice.'" Brief for Municipal Respondents 9 (quoting *Chicago, B. & Q. R. Co.*, 166 U. S., at 238). According to municipal respondents, if it is possible to imagine *any* civilized legal system that does not recognize a particular right, then the Due Process Clause does not make that right binding on the States. Brief for Municipal Respondents 9. Therefore, municipal respondents continue, because such countries as England, Canada, Australia, Japan, Denmark, Finland, Luxembourg, and New Zealand either ban or severely limit handgun ownership, it must follow that no right to possess such weapons is protected by the Fourteenth Amendment. *Id.*, at 21–23.

This line of argument is, of course, inconsistent with the long-established standard we apply in incorporation cases. See *Duncan*, 391 U. S., at 149, and n. 14. And the present-day implications of municipal respondents' argument are stunning. For example, many of the rights that our Bill of Rights provides for persons accused of criminal offenses are virtually unique to this country.[28] If *our* understanding of the right to a jury trial, the right against self-incrimination,

[28] For example, the United States affords criminal jury trials far more broadly than other countries. See, *e. g.*, Van Kessel, Adversary Excesses in the American Criminal Trial, 67 Notre Dame L. Rev. 403 (1992); Leib, A Comparison of Criminal Jury Decision Rules in Democratic Countries, 5 Ohio St. J. Crim. L. 629, 630 (2008); Henderson, The Wrongs of Victim's Rights, 37 Stan. L. Rev. 937, 1003, n. 296 (1985); see also *Roper* v. *Simmons*, 543 U. S. 551, 624 (2005) (SCALIA, J., dissenting) ("In many significant respects the laws of most other countries differ from our law—including . . . such explicit provisions of our Constitution as the right to jury trial"). Similarly, our rules governing pretrial interrogation differ from those in countries sharing a similar legal heritage. See Dept. of Justice, Office of Legal Policy, Report to the Attorney General on the Law of Pretrial Interrogation: Truth in Criminal Justice Report No. 1 (Feb. 12, 1986), reprinted in 22 U. Mich. J. L. Ref. 437, 534–542 (1989) (comparing the system envisioned by *Miranda* v. *Arizona*, 384 U. S. 436 (1966), with rights afforded by England, Scotland, Canada, India, France, and Germany). And the "Court-pronounced exclusionary rule . . . is distinctively American." *Roper*, *supra*, at 624 (SCALIA, J., dissenting) (citing *Bivens* v. *Six Unknown Fed. Narcotics Agents*, 403 U. S. 388, 415 (1971) (Burger, C. J., dissenting) (noting that exclusionary rule was "unique to American jurisprudence" (internal quotation marks omitted))); see also Sklansky, Anti-Inquisitorialism, 122 Harv. L. Rev. 1634, 1648–1656, 1689–1693 (2009) (discussing the differences between American and European confrontation rules).

and the right to counsel were necessary attributes of *any* civilized country, it would follow that the United States is the only civilized Nation in the world.

Municipal respondents attempt to salvage their position by suggesting that their argument applies only to substantive as opposed to procedural rights. Brief for Municipal Respondents 10, n. 3. But even in this trimmed form, municipal respondents' argument flies in the face of more than a half century of precedent. For example, in *Everson* v. *Board of Ed. of Ewing,* 330 U. S. 1, 8 (1947), the Court held that the Fourteenth Amendment incorporates the Establishment Clause of the First Amendment. Yet several of the countries that municipal respondents recognize as civilized have established state churches.[29] If we were to adopt municipal respondents' theory, all of this Court's Establishment Clause precedents involving actions taken by state and local governments would go by the boards.

Municipal respondents maintain that the Second Amendment differs from all of the other provisions of the Bill of Rights because it concerns the right to possess a deadly implement and thus has implications for public safety. Brief for Municipal Respondents 11. And they note that there is intense disagreement on the question whether the private

[29] England and Denmark have state churches. See Torke, The English Religious Establishment, 12 J. Law & Religion 399, 417–427 (1995–1996) (describing legal status of Church of England); Constitutional Act of Denmark, pt. I, § 4 (1953) ("The Evangelical Lutheran Church shall be the Established Church of Denmark"). The Evangelical Lutheran Church of Finland has attributes of a state church. See Christensen, Is the Lutheran Church Still the State Church? An Analysis of Church-State Relations in Finland, 1995 B. Y. U. L. Rev. 585, 596–600 (describing status of church under Finnish law). The Web site of the Evangelical Lutheran Church of Finland states that the church may be usefully described as both a "state church" and a "folk church." See J. Seppo, The Current Condition of Church-State Relations in Finland (2004), online at http://evl.fi/EVLen.nsf/Documents/838DDBEF4A28712AC225730F001F7C67?OpenDocument&lang=EN (all Internet materials as visited June 23, 2010, and available in Clerk of Court's case file).

possession of guns in the home increases or decreases gun deaths and injuries. *Id.*, at 11, 13–17.

The right to keep and bear arms, however, is not the only constitutional right that has controversial public safety implications. All of the constitutional provisions that impose restrictions on law enforcement and on the prosecution of crimes fall into the same category. See, *e. g., Hudson* v. *Michigan*, 547 U. S. 586, 591 (2006) ("The exclusionary rule generates 'substantial social costs,' *United States* v. *Leon*, 468 U. S. 897, 907 (1984), which sometimes include setting the guilty free and the dangerous at large"); *Barker* v. *Wingo*, 407 U. S. 514, 522 (1972) (reflecting on the serious consequences of dismissal for a speedy trial violation, which means "a defendant who may be guilty of a serious crime will go free"); *Miranda* v. *Arizona*, 384 U. S. 436, 517 (1966) (Harlan, J., dissenting); *id.*, at 542 (White, J., dissenting) (objecting that the Court's rule "[i]n some unknown number of cases . . . will return a killer, a rapist or other criminal to the streets . . . to repeat his crime"); *Mapp*, 367 U. S., at 659. Municipal respondents cite no case in which we have refrained from holding that a provision of the Bill of Rights is binding on the States on the ground that the right at issue has disputed public safety implications.

We likewise reject municipal respondents' argument that we should depart from our established incorporation methodology on the ground that making the Second Amendment binding on the States and their subdivisions is inconsistent with principles of federalism and will stifle experimentation. Municipal respondents point out—quite correctly—that conditions and problems differ from locality to locality and that citizens in different jurisdictions have divergent views on the issue of gun control. Municipal respondents therefore urge us to allow state and local governments to enact any gun control law that they deem to be reasonable, including a complete ban on the possession of handguns in the home for self-defense. Brief for Municipal Respondents 18–20, 23.

There is nothing new in the argument that, in order to respect federalism and allow useful state experimentation, a federal constitutional right should not be fully binding on the States. This argument was made repeatedly and eloquently by Members of this Court who rejected the concept of incorporation and urged retention of the two-track approach to incorporation. Throughout the era of "selective incorporation," Justice Harlan in particular, invoking the values of federalism and state experimentation, fought a determined rearguard action to preserve the two-track approach. See, *e. g., Roth* v. *United States,* 354 U. S. 476, 500–503 (1957) (Harlan, J., concurring in result in part and dissenting in part); *Mapp, supra,* at 678–680 (Harlan, J., dissenting); *Gideon,* 372 U. S., at 352 (Harlan, J., concurring); *Malloy,* 378 U. S., at 14–33 (Harlan, J., dissenting); *Pointer,* 380 U. S., at 408–409 (Harlan, J., concurring in result); *Washington,* 388 U. S., at 23–24 (Harlan, J., concurring in result); *Duncan,* 391 U. S., at 171–193 (Harlan, J., dissenting); *Benton,* 395 U. S., at 808–809 (Harlan, J., dissenting); *Williams* v. *Florida,* 399 U. S. 78, 117 (1970) (Harlan, J., dissenting in part and concurring in result in part).

Time and again, however, those pleas failed. Unless we turn back the clock or adopt a special incorporation test applicable only to the Second Amendment, municipal respondents' argument must be rejected. Under our precedents, if a Bill of Rights guarantee is fundamental from an American perspective, then, unless *stare decisis* counsels otherwise,[30]

[30] As noted above, see n. 13, *supra,* cases that predate the era of selective incorporation held that the Grand Jury Clause of the Fifth Amendment and the Seventh Amendment's civil jury requirement do not apply to the States. See *Hurtado* v. *California,* 110 U. S. 516 (1884) (indictment); *Minneapolis & St. Louis R. Co.* v. *Bombolis,* 241 U. S. 211 (1916) (civil jury).

As a result of *Hurtado,* most States do not require a grand jury indictment in all felony cases, and many have no grand juries. See Dept. of Justice, Office of Justice Programs, Bureau of Justice Statistics, D. Rottman & S. Strickland, State Court Organization 2004, pp. 213, 215–217 that guarantee is fully binding on the States and thus *limits* (but by no means eliminates) their ability to devise solutions to social problems that suit local needs and values. As noted by the 38 States that have appeared in this case as *amici* supporting petitioners, "[s]tate and local experimentation with reasonable firearms regulations will continue under the Second Amendment." Brief for State of Texas et al. 23.

Municipal respondents and their *amici* complain that incorporation of the Second Amendment right will lead to extensive and costly litigation, but this argument applies with even greater force to constitutional rights and remedies that have already been held to be binding on the States. Consider the exclusionary rule. Although the exclusionary rule "is not an individual right," *Herring* v. *United States,* 555 U. S. 135, 141 (2009), but a "judicially created rule," *id.,* at 139, this Court made the rule applicable to the States. See *Mapp, supra,* at 660. The exclusionary rule is said to result in "tens of thousands of contested suppression motions each year." Stuntz, The Virtues and Vices of the Exclusionary Rule, 20 Harv. J. L. & Pub. Pol'y 443, 444 (1997).

Municipal respondents assert that, although most state constitutions protect firearms rights, state courts have held that these rights are subject to "interest-balancing" and have sustained a variety of restrictions. Brief for Municipal Respondents 23–31. In *Heller,* however, we expressly rejected the argument that the scope of the Second Amendment right should be determined by judicial interest balancing, 554 U. S., at 633–635, and this Court decades ago

---

(2006) (Table 38), online at http://bjs.ojp.usdoj.gov/content/pub/pdf/sco04.pdf.

As a result of *Bombolis,* cases that would otherwise fall within the Seventh Amendment are now tried without a jury in state small claims courts. See, *e. g., Cheung* v. *Eighth Judicial Dist. Court,* 121 Nev. 867, 124 P. 3d 550 (2005) (no right to jury trial in small claims court under Nevada Constitution).

abandoned "the notion that the Fourteenth Amendment applies to the States only a watered-down, subjective version of the individual guarantees of the Bill of Rights," *Malloy, supra,* at 10–11 (internal quotation marks omitted).

As evidence that the Fourteenth Amendment has not historically been understood to restrict the authority of the States to regulate firearms, municipal respondents and supporting *amici* cite a variety of state and local firearms laws that courts have upheld. But what is most striking about their research is the paucity of precedent sustaining bans comparable to those at issue here and in *Heller.* Municipal respondents cite precisely one case (from the late 20th century) in which such a ban was sustained. See Brief for Municipal Respondents 26–27 (citing *Kalodimos* v. *Morton Grove,* 103 Ill. 2d 483, 470 N. E. 2d 266 (1984)); see also Reply Brief for Respondent NRA et al. 23, n. 7 (asserting that no other court has ever upheld a complete ban on the possession of handguns). It is important to keep in mind that *Heller,* while striking down a law that prohibited the possession of handguns in the home, recognized that the right to keep and bear arms is not "a right to keep and carry any weapon whatsoever in any manner whatsoever and for whatever purpose." 554 U. S., at 626. We made it clear in *Heller* that our holding did not cast doubt on such longstanding regulatory measures as "prohibitions on the possession of firearms by felons and the mentally ill," "laws forbidding the carrying of firearms in sensitive places such as schools and government buildings, or laws imposing conditions and qualifications on the commercial sale of arms." *Id.,* at 626–627. We repeat those assurances here. Despite municipal respondents' doomsday proclamations, incorporation does not imperil every law regulating firearms.

Municipal respondents argue, finally, that the right to keep and bear arms is unique among the rights set out in the first eight Amendments "because the reason for codifying the Second Amendment (to protect the militia) differs from the purpose (primarily, to use firearms to engage in self-defense) that is claimed to make the right implicit in the concept of ordered liberty." Brief for Municipal Respondents 36–37. Municipal respondents suggest that the Second Amendment right differs from the rights heretofore incorporated because the latter were "valued for [their] own sake." *Id.*, at 33. But we have never previously suggested that incorporation of a right turns on whether it has intrinsic as opposed to instrumental value, and quite a few of the rights previously held to be incorporated—for example the right to counsel and the right to confront and subpoena witnesses—are clearly instrumental by any measure. Moreover, this contention repackages one of the chief arguments that we rejected in *Heller, i. e.*, that the scope of the Second Amendment right is defined by the immediate threat that led to the inclusion of that right in the Bill of Rights. In *Heller*, we recognized that the codification of this right was prompted by fear that the Federal Government would disarm and thus disable the militias, but we rejected the suggestion that the right was valued only as a means of preserving the militias. 554 U. S., at 598–599. On the contrary, we stressed that the right was also valued because the possession of firearms was thought to be essential for self-defense. As we put it, self-defense was "the *central component* of the right itself." *Id.*, at 599.

V

A

We turn, finally, to the two dissenting opinions. JUSTICE STEVENS' eloquent opinion covers ground already addressed, and therefore little need be added in response. JUSTICE STEVENS would "'ground the prohibitions against state action squarely on due process, without intermediate reliance on any of the first eight Amendments.'" *Post*, at 865 (quoting *Malloy*, 378 U. S., at 24 (Harlan, J., dissenting)). The question presented in this case, in his view, "is whether the particular right asserted by petitioners applies to the States because of the Fourteenth Amendment itself, standing on its own bottom." *Post,* at 883. He would hold that "[t]he rights protected against state infringement by the Fourteenth Amendment's Due Process Clause need not be identical in shape or scope to the rights protected against Federal Government infringement by the various provisions of the Bill of Rights." *Post,* at 866.

As we have explained, the Court, for the past half century, has moved away from the two-track approach. If we were now to accept JUSTICE STEVENS' theory across the board, decades of decisions would be undermined. We assume that this is not what is proposed. What is urged instead, it appears, is that this theory be revived solely for the individual right that *Heller* recognized, over vigorous dissents.

The relationship between the Bill of Rights' guarantees and the States must be governed by a single, neutral principle. It is far too late to exhume what Justice Brennan, writing for the Court 46 years ago, derided as "the notion that the Fourteenth Amendment applies to the States only a watered-down, subjective version of the individual guarantees of the Bill of Rights." *Malloy, supra,* at 10–11 (internal quotation marks omitted).

B

JUSTICE BREYER's dissent makes several points to which we briefly respond. To begin, while there is certainly room for disagreement about *Heller*'s analysis of the history of the right to keep and bear arms, nothing written since *Heller* persuades us to reopen the question there decided. Few other questions of original meaning have been as thoroughly explored.

JUSTICE BREYER's conclusion that the Fourteenth Amendment does not incorporate the right to keep and bear arms appears to rest primarily on four factors: First, "there is no popular consensus" that the right is fundamental, *post,* at

920; second, the right does not protect minorities or persons neglected by those holding political power, *post*, at 921–922; third, incorporation of the Second Amendment right would "amount to a significant incursion on a traditional and important area of state concern, altering the constitutional relationship between the States and the Federal Government" and preventing local variations, *ibid.;* and fourth, determining the scope of the Second Amendment right in cases involving state and local laws will force judges to answer difficult empirical questions regarding matters that are outside their area of expertise, *post*, at 922–927. Even if we believed that these factors were relevant to the incorporation inquiry, none of these factors undermines the case for incorporation of the right to keep and bear arms for self-defense.

First, we have never held that a provision of the Bill of Rights applies to the States only if there is a "popular consensus" that the right is fundamental, and we see no basis for such a rule. But in this case, as it turns out, there is evidence of such a consensus. An *amicus* brief submitted by 58 Members of the Senate and 251 Members of the House of Representatives urges us to hold that the right to keep and bear arms is fundamental. See Brief for Senator Kay Bailey Hutchison et al. 4. Another brief submitted by 38 States takes the same position. Brief for State of Texas et al. 6.

Second, petitioners and many others who live in high-crime areas dispute the proposition that the Second Amendment right does not protect minorities and those lacking political clout. The plight of Chicagoans living in high-crime areas was recently highlighted when two Illinois legislators representing Chicago districts called on the Governor to deploy the Illinois National Guard to patrol the City's streets.[31] The legislators noted that the number of Chicago homicide victims during the current year equaled the number of

[31] See Mack & Burnette, 2 Lawmakers to Quinn: Send the Guard to Chicago, Chicago Tribune, Apr. 26, 2010, p. 6.

American soldiers killed during that same period in Afghanistan and Iraq and that 80% of the Chicago victims were black.[32] *Amici* supporting incorporation of the right to keep and bear arms contend that the right is especially important for women and members of other groups that may be especially vulnerable to violent crime.[33] If, as petitioners believe, their safety and the safety of other law-abiding members of the community would be enhanced by the possession of handguns in the home for self-defense, then the Second Amendment right protects the rights of minorities and other residents of high-crime areas whose needs are not being met by elected public officials.

Third, JUSTICE BREYER is correct that incorporation of the Second Amendment right will to some extent limit the legislative freedom of the States, but this is always true when a Bill of Rights provision is incorporated. Incorporation always restricts experimentation and local variations, but that has not stopped the Court from incorporating virtually every other provision of the Bill of Rights. "[T]he enshrinement of constitutional rights necessarily takes certain policy choices off the table." *Heller*, 554 U. S., at 636. This conclusion is no more remarkable with respect to the Second Amendment than it is with respect to all the other limitations on state power found in the Constitution.

Finally, JUSTICE BREYER is incorrect that incorporation will require judges to assess the costs and benefits of fire-

---

[32] Janssen & Knowles, Send in Troops? Chicago Sun-Times, Apr. 26, 2010, p. 2; see also Brief for NAACP Legal Defense & Educational Fund, Inc., as *Amicus Curiae* 5, n. 4 (stating that in 2008, almost three out of every four homicide victims in Chicago were African-Americans); *id.*, at 5–6 (noting that "each year [in Chicago], many times more African Americans are murdered by assailants wielding guns than were killed during the Colfax massacre" (footnote omitted)).

[33] See Brief for Women State Legislators et al. 9–10, 14–15; Brief for Jews for the Preservation of Firearms Ownership 3–4; see also Brief for Pink Pistols et al. in *District of Columbia* v. *Heller*, O. T. 2007, No. 07–290, pp. 5–11.

arms restrictions and thus to make difficult empirical judgments in an area in which they lack expertise. As we have noted, while his opinion in *Heller* recommended an interest-balancing test, the Court specifically rejected that suggestion. See *supra*, at 785–786. "The very enumeration of the right takes out of the hands of government—even the Third Branch of Government—the power to decide on a case-by-case basis whether the right is *really worth* insisting upon." *Heller*, *supra*, at 634.

* * *

In *Heller*, we held that the Second Amendment protects the right to possess a handgun in the home for the purpose of self-defense. Unless considerations of *stare decisis* counsel otherwise, a provision of the Bill of Rights that protects a right that is fundamental from an American perspective applies equally to the Federal Government and the States. See *Duncan*, 391 U. S., at 149, and n. 14. We therefore hold that the Due Process Clause of the Fourteenth Amendment incorporates the Second Amendment right recognized in *Heller*. The judgment of the Court of Appeals is reversed, and the case is remanded for further proceedings.

It is so ordered.

JUSTICE SCALIA, concurring.

I join the Court's opinion. Despite my misgivings about substantive due process as an original matter, I have acquiesced in the Court's incorporation of certain guarantees in the Bill of Rights "because it is both long established and narrowly limited." *Albright* v. *Oliver*, 510 U. S. 266, 275 (1994) (SCALIA, J., concurring). This case does not require me to reconsider that view, since straightforward application of settled doctrine suffices to decide it.

I write separately only to respond to some aspects of JUSTICE STEVENS' dissent. Not that aspect which disagrees with the majority's application of our precedents to this case, which is fully covered by the Court's opinion. But much of what JUSTICE STEVENS writes is a broad condemnation of the theory of interpretation which underlies the Court's opinion, a theory that makes the traditions of our people paramount. He proposes a different theory, which he claims is more "cautiou[s]" and respectful of proper limits on the judicial role. *Post,* at 912. It is that claim I wish to address.

I

A

After stressing the substantive dimension of what he has renamed the "liberty clause," *post,* at 861–864,[1] JUSTICE STEVENS proceeds to urge readoption of the theory of incorporation articulated in *Palko* v. *Connecticut,* 302 U. S. 319, 325 (1937), see *post,* at 871–877. But in fact he does not favor application of that theory at all. For whether *Palko* requires only that "a fair and enlightened system of justice would be impossible without" the right sought to be incorporated, 302 U. S., at 325, or requires in addition that the right be rooted in the "traditions and conscience of our people," *ibid.* (internal quotation marks omitted), many of the rights JUSTICE STEVENS thinks are incorporated could not pass muster under either test: abortion, *post,* at 864 (citing *Planned Parenthood of Southeastern Pa.* v. *Casey,* 505 U. S. 833, 847 (1992)); homosexual sodomy, *post,* at 873 (citing *Lawrence* v. *Texas,* 539 U. S. 558, 572 (2003)); the right to have excluded from criminal trials evidence obtained in violation of the Fourth Amendment, *post,* at 875 (citing *Mapp* v. *Ohio,* 367 U. S. 643, 650, 655–657 (1961)); and the right to teach one's

[1] I do not entirely understand JUSTICE STEVENS' renaming of the Due Process Clause. What we call it, of course, does not change what the Clause says, but shorthand should not obscure what it says. Accepting for argument's sake the shift in emphasis—from avoiding certain deprivations without that "process" which is "due," to avoiding the deprivations themselves—the Clause applies not just to deprivations of "liberty," but also to deprivations of "life" and even "property."

children foreign languages, *post,* at 864 (citing *Meyer* v. *Nebraska,* 262 U. S. 390, 399–403 (1923)), among others.

That Justice Stevens is not applying any version of *Palko* is clear from comparing, on the one hand, the rights he believes *are* covered, with, on the other hand, his conclusion that the right to keep and bear arms is *not* covered. Rights that pass his test include not just those "relating to marriage, procreation, contraception, family relationships, and child rearing and education," but also rights against "[g]overnment action that shocks the conscience, pointlessly infringes settled expectations, trespasses into sensitive private realms or life choices without adequate justification, [or] perpetrates gross injustice." *Post,* at 879 (internal quotation marks omitted). Not *all* such rights are in, however, since only "*some* fundamental aspects of personhood, dignity, and the like" are protected, *post,* at 880 (emphasis added). Exactly what is covered is not clear. But whatever else is in, he *knows* that the right to keep and bear arms is out, despite its being as "deeply rooted in this Nation's history and tradition," *Washington* v. *Glucksberg,* 521 U. S. 702, 721 (1997) (internal quotation marks omitted), as a right can be, see *District of Columbia* v. *Heller,* 554 U. S. 570, 593–595, 599, 603, 614–616 (2008). I can find no other explanation for such certitude except that Justice Stevens, despite his forswearing of "personal and private notions," *post,* at 878 (internal quotation marks omitted), deeply believes it should be out.

The subjective nature of Justice Stevens' standard is also apparent from his claim that it is the courts' prerogative—indeed their *duty*—to update the Due Process Clause so that it encompasses new freedoms the Framers were too narrowminded to imagine, *post,* at 875–877, and n. 21. Courts, he proclaims, must "do justice to [the Clause's] urgent call and its open texture" by exercising the "interpretive discretion the latter embodies." *Post,* at 877. (Why the *people* are not up to the task of deciding what new rights to protect, even though it is *they* who are authorized to make changes, see U. S. Const., Art. V, is never explained.[2]) And it would be "judicial abdication" for a judge to "tur[n] his back" on *his* task of determining what the Fourteenth Amendment covers by "outsourc[ing]" the job to "historical sentiment," *post,* at 876, 877—that is, by being guided by what the American people throughout our history have thought. It is only we judges, exercising our "own reasoned judgment," *post,* at 872, who can be entrusted with deciding the Due Process Clause's scope—which rights serve the Amendment's "central values," *post,* at 880—which basically means picking the rights we want to protect and discarding those we do not.

B

JUSTICE STEVENS resists this description, insisting that his approach provides plenty of "guideposts" and "constraints" to keep courts from "injecting excessive subjectivity" into the process.[3] *Post,* at 877, 878. Plenty indeed—and

[2] JUSTICE STEVENS insists that he would not make courts the *sole* interpreters of the "liberty clause"; he graciously invites "[a]ll Americans" to ponder what the Clause means to them today. *Post,* at 877, n. 22. The problem is that in his approach the people's ponderings do not matter, since whatever the people decide, courts have the last word.

[3] JUSTICE BREYER is not worried by that prospect. His interpretive approach applied to incorporation of the Second Amendment includes consideration of such factors as "the extent to which incorporation will further other, perhaps more basic, constitutional aims; and the extent to which incorporation will advance or hinder the Constitution's structural aims"; whether recognizing a particular right will "further the Constitution's effort to ensure that the government treats each individual with equal respect" or will "help maintain the democratic form of government"; whether it is "inconsistent . . . with the Constitution's efforts to create governmental institutions well suited to the carrying out of its constitutional promises"; whether it fits with "the Framers' basic reason for believing the Court ought to have the power of judicial review"; courts' comparative advantage in answering empirical questions that may be involved in applying the right; and whether there is a "strong offsetting justification" for removing a decision from the democratic process. *Post,* at 918, 922–927 (dissenting opinion).

that alone is a problem. The ability of omnidirectional guideposts to constrain is inversely proportional to their number. But even individually, each lodestar or limitation he lists either is incapable of restraining judicial whimsy or cannot be squared with the precedents he seeks to preserve.

He begins with a brief nod to history, *post,* at 877–878, but as he has just made clear, he thinks historical inquiry unavailing, *post,* at 874–877. Moreover, trusting the meaning of the Due Process Clause to what has historically been protected is circular, see *post,* at 875–876, since that would mean no *new* rights could get in.

JUSTICE STEVENS moves on to the "most basic" constraint on subjectivity his theory offers: that he would "esche[w] attempts to provide any all-purpose, top-down, totalizing theory of 'liberty.'" *Post,* at 878. The notion that the absence of a coherent theory of the Due Process Clause will somehow *curtail* judicial caprice is at war with reason. Indeterminacy means opportunity for courts to impose whatever rule they like; it is the problem, not the solution. The idea that interpretive pluralism would *reduce* courts' ability to impose their will on the ignorant masses is not merely naive, but absurd. If there are no right answers, there are no wrong answers either.

JUSTICE STEVENS also argues that requiring courts to show "respect for the democratic process" should serve as a constraint. *Post,* at 880. That is true, but JUSTICE STEVENS would have them show respect in an extraordinary manner. In his view, if a right "is already being given careful consideration in, and subjected to ongoing calibration by, the States, judicial enforcement may not be appropriate." *Ibid.* In other words, a right, such as the right to keep and bear arms, that has long been recognized but on which the States are considering restrictions, apparently deserves *less* protection, while a privilege the political branches (instruments of the democratic process) have withheld entirely and continue to withhold, deserves *more.* That topsy-turvy approach conveniently accomplishes the objective of ensuring that the rights this Court held protected in *Casey*, *Lawrence*, and other such cases fit the theory—but at the cost of insulting rather than respecting the democratic process.

The next constraint JUSTICE STEVENS suggests is harder to evaluate. He describes as "an important tool for guiding judicial discretion" "sensitivity to the interaction between the intrinsic aspects of liberty and the practical realities of contemporary society." *Post*, at 880. I cannot say whether that sensitivity will really guide judges because I have no idea what it is. Is it some sixth sense instilled in judges when they ascend to the bench? Or does it mean judges are more constrained when they agonize about the cosmic conflict between liberty and its potentially harmful consequences? Attempting to give the concept more precision, JUSTICE STEVENS explains that "sensitivity is an aspect of a deeper principle: the need to approach our work with humility and caution." *Post*, at 881. Both traits are undeniably admirable, though what relation they bear to sensitivity is a mystery. But it makes no difference, for the first case JUSTICE STEVENS cites in support, see *ibid.*, *Casey*, 505 U. S., at 849, dispels any illusion that he has a meaningful form of judicial modesty in mind.

JUSTICE STEVENS offers no examples to illustrate the next constraint: *stare decisis*, *post*, at 881. But his view of it is surely not very confining, since he holds out as a "canonical" exemplar of the proper approach, see *post*, at 873, 909, *Lawrence*, which overruled a case decided a mere 17 years earlier, *Bowers* v. *Hardwick*, 478 U. S. 186 (1986), see 539 U. S., at 578 (it "was not correct when it was decided, and it is not correct today"). Moreover, JUSTICE STEVENS would apply that constraint unevenly: He apparently approves those Warren Court cases that adopted jot-for-jot incorporation of procedural protections for criminal defendants, *post*, at 868, but would abandon those Warren Court rulings that undercut his approach to substantive rights, on the basis that we have "cut back" on cases from that era before, *post,* at 869.

JUSTICE STEVENS also relies on the requirement of a "careful description of the asserted fundamental liberty interest" to limit judicial discretion. *Post,* at 882 (internal quotation marks omitted). I certainly agree with that requirement, see *Reno* v. *Flores,* 507 U. S. 292, 302 (1993), though some cases JUSTICE STEVENS approves have not applied it seriously, see, *e. g., Lawrence, supra,* at 562 ("The instant case involves liberty of the person both in its spatial and in its more transcendent dimensions"). But if the "careful description" requirement is used in the manner we have hitherto employed, then the enterprise of determining the Due Process Clause's "conceptual core," *post,* at 879, is a waste of time. In the cases he cites we sought a careful, specific description of the right at issue in order to determine *whether that right, thus narrowly defined, was fundamental.* See, *e. g., Glucksberg,* 521 U. S., at 722–728; *Reno, supra,* at 302–306; *Collins* v. *Harker Heights,* 503 U. S. 115, 125–129 (1992); *Cruzan* v. *Director, Mo. Dept. of Health,* 497 U. S. 261, 269–279 (1990); see also *Vacco* v. *Quill,* 521 U. S. 793, 801–808 (1997). The threshold step of defining the asserted right with precision is entirely unnecessary, however, if (as JUSTICE STEVENS maintains) the "conceptual core" of the "liberty clause," *post,* at 879, includes a number of capacious, hazily defined categories. There is no need to define the right with much precision in order to conclude that it pertains to the plaintiff's "ability independently to define [his] identity," his "right to make certain unusually important decisions that will affect his own, or his family's, destiny," or some aspect of his "[s]elf-determination, bodily integrity, freedom of conscience, intimate relationships, political equality, dignity [or] respect." *Post,* at 879, 880 (internal quotation marks omitted). JUSTICE STEVENS must therefore have in mind some other use for the careful-description requirement—perhaps just as a means of ensuring that courts "procee[d] slowly and incrementally," *post*, at 881. But that could be achieved just as well by having them draft their opinions in longhand.[4]

II

If JUSTICE STEVENS' account of the constraints of his approach did not demonstrate that they do not exist, his application of that approach to the case before us leaves no doubt. He offers several reasons for concluding that the Second Amendment right to keep and bear arms is not fundamental enough to be applied against the States.[5] None is persuasive, but more pertinent to my purpose, each is either intrinsically indeterminate, would preclude incorporation of rights we have already held incorporated, or both. His approach

---

[4] After defending the careful-description criterion, JUSTICE STEVENS quickly retreats and cautions courts not to apply it too stringently. *Post*, at 882. Describing a right *too* specifically risks robbing it of its "universal valence and a moral force it might otherwise have," *ibid.*, and "loads the dice against its recognition," *post*, at 882, n. 25 (internal quotation marks omitted). *That* must be avoided, since it endangers rights JUSTICE STEVENS *does* like. See *ibid.* (discussing *Lawrence* v. *Texas*, 539 U. S. 558 (2003)). To make sure *those* rights get in, we must leave leeway in our description, so that a right that has not itself been recognized as fundamental can ride the coattails of one that has been.

[5] JUSTICE STEVENS claims that I mischaracterize his argument by referring to the Second Amendment right to keep and bear arms, instead of "the interest in keeping a firearm of one's choosing in the home," the right he says petitioners assert. *Post*, at 894, n. 36. But it is precisely the "Second Amendment right to keep and bear arms" that petitioners argue is incorporated by the Due Process Clause. See, *e. g.*, Pet. for Cert. i. Under JUSTICE STEVENS' own approach, that should end the matter. See *post*, at 882 ("[W]e must pay close attention to the precise liberty interest the litigants have asked us to vindicate"). In any event, the demise of watered-down incorporation, see *ante*, at 765–766, means that we no longer subdivide Bill of Rights guarantees into their theoretical components, only some of which apply to the States. The First Amendment freedom of speech is incorporated—not the freedom to speak on Fridays, or to speak about philosophy.

therefore does nothing to stop a judge from arriving at any conclusion he sets out to reach.

JUSTICE STEVENS begins with the odd assertion that "firearms have a fundamentally ambivalent relationship to liberty," since sometimes they are used to cause (or sometimes accidentally produce) injury to others. *Post,* at 891. The source of the rule that only nonambivalent liberties deserve due process protection is never explained—proof that judges applying JUSTICE STEVENS' approach can add new elements to the test as they see fit. The criterion, moreover, is inherently manipulable. Surely JUSTICE STEVENS does not mean that the Clause covers only rights that have *zero* harmful effect on *anyone.* Otherwise even the First Amendment is out. Maybe what he means is that the right to keep and bear arms imposes *too great* a risk to others' physical well-being. But as the plurality explains, *ante,* at 782–783, other rights we have already held incorporated pose similarly substantial risks to public safety. In all events, JUSTICE STEVENS supplies neither a standard for how severe the impairment on others' liberty must be for a right to be disqualified, nor (of course) any method of measuring the severity.

JUSTICE STEVENS next suggests that the Second Amendment right is not fundamental because it is "different in kind" from other rights we have recognized. *Post,* at 893. In one respect, of course, the right to keep and bear arms *is* different from some other rights we have held the Clause protects and he would recognize: It is deeply grounded in our Nation's history and tradition. But JUSTICE STEVENS has a different distinction in mind: Even though he does "not doubt for a moment that many Americans . . . see [firearms] as critical to their way of life as well as to their security," he pronounces that owning a handgun is not "critical to leading a life of autonomy, dignity, or political equality."[6] *Ibid.*

[6] JUSTICE STEVENS goes a step further still, suggesting that the right to keep and bear arms is not protected by the "liberty clause" because it

Who says? Deciding what is essential to an enlightened, liberty-filled life is an inherently political, moral judgment—the antithesis of an objective approach that reaches conclusions by applying neutral rules to verifiable evidence.[7]

No determination of what rights the Constitution of the United States covers would be complete, of course, without a survey of what *other* countries do. *Post,* at 895–896. When it comes to guns, JUSTICE STEVENS explains, our Nation is *already* an outlier among "advanced democracies"; not even our "oldest allies" protect as robust a right as we do, and we should not widen the gap. *Ibid.* Never mind that he explains neither which countries qualify as "advanced democracies" nor why others are irrelevant. For there is an even clearer indication that this criterion lets judges pick which rights States must respect and those they can ignore: As the plurality shows, *ante,* at 781–782, and nn. 28–29, this follow-the-foreign-crowd requirement would foreclose rights

---

is not really a liberty at all, but a "property right." *Post,* at 894. Never mind that the right to bear arms sounds mighty like a liberty; and never mind that the "liberty clause" is really a Due Process Clause which explicitly protects "property," see *United States* v. *Carlton,* 512 U. S. 26, 41–42 (1994) (SCALIA, J., concurring in judgment). JUSTICE STEVENS' theory cannot explain why the Takings Clause, which unquestionably protects property, has been incorporated, see *Chicago, B. & Q. R. Co.* v. *Chicago,* 166 U. S. 226, 241 (1897), in a decision he appears to accept, *post,* at 871, n. 14.

[7] As JUSTICE STEVENS notes, see *post,* at 906–907, I accept as a matter of *stare decisis* the requirement that to be fundamental for purposes of the Due Process Clause, a right must be "implicit in the concept of ordered liberty," *Lawrence, supra,* at 593, n. 3 (SCALIA, J., dissenting) (internal quotation marks omitted). But that inquiry provides infinitely less scope for judicial invention when conducted under the Court's approach, since the field of candidates is *immensely* narrowed by the prior requirement that a right be rooted in this country's traditions. JUSTICE STEVENS, on the other hand, is free to scan the universe for rights that he thinks "implicit in the concept," etc. The point JUSTICE STEVENS makes here is merely one example of his demand that a historical approach to the Constitution prove itself, not merely much better than his in restraining judicial invention, but utterly perfect in doing so. See Part III, *infra.*

that we have held (and JUSTICE STEVENS accepts) are incorporated, but that other "advanced" nations do not recognize—from the exclusionary rule to the Establishment Clause. A judge applying JUSTICE STEVENS' approach must either throw all of those rights overboard or, as cases JUSTICE STEVENS approves have done in considering unenumerated rights, simply ignore foreign law when it undermines the desired conclusion, see, *e. g., Casey,* 505 U. S. 833 (making no mention of foreign law).

JUSTICE STEVENS also argues that since the right to keep and bear arms was *codified* for the purpose of "prevent[ing] elimination of the militia," it should be viewed as " 'a federalism provision' " logically incapable of incorporation. *Post,* at 897 (quoting *Elk Grove Unified School Dist.* v. *Newdow,* 542 U. S. 1, 45 (2004) (THOMAS, J., concurring in judgment); some internal quotation marks omitted). This criterion, too, evidently applies only when judges want it to. The opinion JUSTICE STEVENS quotes for the "federalism provision" principle, JUSTICE THOMAS's concurrence in *Newdow,* argued that incorporation of the Establishment Clause "makes little sense" because that Clause was originally understood as a limit on congressional interference with state establishments of religion. *Id.,* at 49–51. JUSTICE STEVENS, of course, has no problem with applying the Establishment Clause to the States. See, *e. g., id.,* at 8, n. 4 (opinion for the Court by STEVENS, J.) (acknowledging that the Establishment Clause "appl[ies] to the States by incorporation into the Fourteenth Amendment"). While he insists *that* Clause is not a "federalism provision," *post,* at 897, n. 40, he does not explain why *it* is not, but the right to keep and bear arms *is* (even though only the latter refers to a "right of the people"). The "federalism" argument prevents the incorporation of only *certain* rights.

JUSTICE STEVENS next argues that even if the right to keep and bear arms is "deeply rooted in some important senses," the roots of States' efforts to regulate guns run just as deep. *Post,* at 899 (internal quotation marks omitted).

But this too is true of other rights we have held incorporated. No fundamental right—not even the First Amendment—is absolute. The traditional restrictions go to show the scope of the right, not its lack of fundamental character. At least that is what they show (JUSTICE STEVENS would agree) for *other* rights. Once again, principles are applied selectively.

JUSTICE STEVENS' final reason for rejecting incorporation of the Second Amendment reveals, more clearly than any of the others, the game that is afoot. Assuming that there is a "plausible constitutional basis" for holding that the right to keep and bear arms is incorporated, he asserts that we ought not to do so *for prudential reasons. Post,* at 902. Even if we had the authority to withhold rights that are within the Constitution's command (and we assuredly do not), two of the reasons JUSTICE STEVENS gives for abstention show just how much power he would hand to judges. The States' "right to experiment" with solutions to the problem of gun violence, he says, is at its apex here because "the best solution is far from clear." *Post,* at 902–903 (internal quotation marks omitted). That is true of most serious social problems—whether, for example, "the best solution" for rampant crime is to admit confessions unless they are affirmatively shown to have been coerced, but see *Miranda* v. *Arizona,* 384 U. S. 436, 444–445 (1966), or to permit jurors to impose the death penalty without a requirement that they be free to consider "any relevant mitigating factor," see *Eddings* v. *Oklahoma,* 455 U. S. 104, 112 (1982), which in turn leads to the conclusion that defense counsel has provided inadequate defense if he has not conducted a "reasonable investigation" into potentially mitigating factors, see, *e. g., Wiggins* v. *Smith,* 539 U. S. 510, 534 (2003), inquiry into which question tends to destroy any prospect of prompt justice, see, *e. g., Wong* v. *Belmontes,* 558 U. S. 15 (2009) *(per curiam)* (reversing grant of habeas relief for sentencing on a crime committed in 1981). The obviousness of the optimal answer is in the eye of the beholder. The implication of JUSTICE STEVENS' call for abstention is that if We The Court conclude that They The People's answers to a problem are silly, we are free to "interven[e]," *post*, at 902, but if we too are uncertain of the right answer, or merely think the States may be on to something, we can loosen the leash.

A second reason JUSTICE STEVENS says we should abstain is that the States have shown they are "capable" of protecting the right at issue, and if anything have protected it too much. *Post*, at 904. That reflects an assumption that judges can distinguish between a *proper* democratic decision to leave things alone (which we should honor), and a case of democratic market failure (which we should step in to correct). I would not—and no judge should—presume to have that sort of omniscience, which seems to me far more "arrogant," *post*, at 896, than confining courts' focus to our own national heritage.

III

JUSTICE STEVENS' response to this concurrence, *post*, at 906–911, makes the usual rejoinder of "living Constitution" advocates to the criticism that it empowers judges to eliminate or expand what the people have prescribed: The traditional, historically focused method, he says, reposes discretion in judges as well.[8] Historical analysis can be difficult; it sometimes requires resolving threshold questions, and making nu-

[8] JUSTICE STEVENS also asserts that his approach is "more faithful to this Nation's constitutional history" and to "the values and commitments of the American people, as they stand today," *post*, at 909. But what he asserts to be the proof of this is that his approach aligns (no surprise) with those cases he approves (and dubs "canonical," *ibid.*). Cases he disfavors are discarded as "hardly bind[ing]" "excesses," *post*, at 869, or less "enduring," *post*, at 873, n. 16. Not proven. Moreover, whatever relevance JUSTICE STEVENS ascribes to current "values and commitments of the American people" (and that is unclear, see *post*, at 903–904, n. 47), it is hard to see how it shows fidelity to them that he disapproves a different subset of old cases than the Court does.

anced judgments about which evidence to consult and how to interpret it.

I will stipulate to that.[9] But the question to be decided is not whether the historically focused method is a *perfect means* of restraining aristocratic judicial Constitution-writing; but whether it is the *best means available* in an imperfect world. Or indeed, even more narrowly than that: whether it is demonstrably much better than what JUSTICE STEVENS proposes. I think it beyond all serious dispute that it is much less subjective, and intrudes much less upon the democratic process. It is less subjective because it depends upon a body of evidence susceptible of reasoned analysis rather than a variety of vague ethico-political First Principles whose combined conclusion can be found to point in any direction the judges favor. In the most controversial matters brought before this Court—for example, the constitutionality of prohibiting abortion, assisted suicide, or homosexual sodomy, or the constitutionality of the death penalty—*any* historical methodology, under *any* plausible standard of proof, would lead to the same conclusion.[10] Moreover, the methodological differences that divide historians, and the varying interpretive assumptions they bring to their work, *post*, at 907–908, are nothing compared to the differences among the American people (though perhaps not among graduates of prestigious law schools) with regard to the moral judgments JUSTICE STEVENS would have courts pronounce. And whether or not special expertise is needed

---

[9] That is not to say that every historical question on which there is room for debate is indeterminate, or that every question on which historians disagree is equally balanced. Cf. *post*, at 907–908. For example, the historical analysis of the principal dissent in *Heller* is as valid as the Court's only in a two-dimensional world that conflates length and depth.

[10] By the way, JUSTICE STEVENS greatly magnifies the difficulty of a historical approach by suggesting that it was *my* burden in *Lawrence* to show the "ancient roots of proscriptions against sodomy," *post*, at 908 (internal quotation marks omitted). *Au contraire*, it was *his* burden (in the opinion he joined) to show the ancient roots of the right of sodomy.

to answer historical questions, judges most certainly have no "comparative . . . advantage," *post*, at 880 (internal quotation marks omitted), in resolving moral disputes. What is more, his approach would not eliminate, but multiply, the hard questions courts must confront, since he would not *replace* history with moral philosophy, but would have courts consider *both*.

And the Court's approach intrudes less upon the democratic process because the rights it acknowledges are those established by a constitutional history formed by democratic decisions; and the rights it fails to acknowledge are left to be democratically adopted or rejected by the people, with the assurance that their decision is not subject to judicial revision. JUSTICE STEVENS' approach, on the other hand, deprives the people of that power, since whatever the Constitution and laws may say, the list of protected rights will be whatever courts wish it to be. After all, he notes, the people have been wrong before, *post*, at 910, and courts may conclude they are wrong in the future. JUSTICE STEVENS abhors a system in which "majorities or powerful interest groups always get their way," *post*, at 911, but replaces it with a system in which unelected and life-tenured judges always get their way. That such usurpation is effected unabashedly, see *post*, at 908—with "the judge's cards . . . laid on the table," *ibid.*—makes it even worse. In a vibrant democracy, usurpation should have to be accomplished in the dark. It is JUSTICE STEVENS' approach, not the Court's, that puts democracy in peril.

JUSTICE THOMAS, concurring in part and concurring in the judgment.

I agree with the Court that the Fourteenth Amendment makes the right to keep and bear arms set forth in the Second Amendment "fully applicable to the States." *Ante*, at 750. I write separately because I believe there is a more straightforward path to this conclusion, one that is more faithful to the Fourteenth Amendment's text and history. I therefore do not join Parts II–C, IV, and V of the principal opinion.

Applying what is now a well-settled test, the Court concludes that the right to keep and bear arms applies to the States through the Fourteenth Amendment's Due Process Clause because it is "fundamental" to the American "scheme of ordered liberty," *ante,* at 767 (citing *Duncan* v. *Louisiana,* 391 U. S. 145, 149 (1968)), and " 'deeply rooted in this Nation's history and tradition,' " *ante,* at 767 (quoting *Washington* v. *Glucksberg,* 521 U. S. 702, 721 (1997)). I agree with that description of the right. But I cannot agree that it is enforceable against the States through a Clause that speaks only to "process." Instead, the right to keep and bear arms is a privilege of American citizenship that applies to the States through the Fourteenth Amendment's Privileges or Immunities Clause.

I

In *District of Columbia* v. *Heller,* 554 U. S. 570 (2008), this Court held that the Second Amendment protects an individual right to keep and bear arms for the purpose of self-defense, striking down a District of Columbia ordinance that banned the possession of handguns in the home. *Id.,* at 635. The question in this case is whether the Constitution protects that right against abridgment by the States.

As the Court explains, if this case were litigated before the Fourteenth Amendment's adoption in 1868, the answer to that question would be simple. In *Barron ex rel. Tiernan* v. *Mayor of Baltimore,* 7 Pet. 243 (1833), this Court held that the Bill of Rights applied only to the Federal Government. Writing for the Court, Chief Justice Marshall recalled that the founding generation added the first eight Amendments to the Constitution in response to Antifederalist concerns regarding the extent of federal—not state—power, and held that if "the framers of these amendments [had] intended them to be limitations on the powers of the state governments," "they would have declared this purpose in plain and intelligible language." *Id.*, at 250. Finding no such language in the Bill of Rights, Chief Justice Marshall held that it did not in any way restrict state authority. *Id.*, at 248–250; see *Lessee of Livingston* v. *Moore*, 7 Pet. 469, 551–552 (1833) (reaffirming *Barron*'s holding); *Permoli* v. *Municipality No. 1 of New Orleans*, 3 How. 589, 609–610 (1845) (same).

Nearly three decades after *Barron*, the Nation was splintered by a civil war fought principally over the question of slavery. As was evident to many throughout our Nation's early history, slavery, and the measures designed to protect it, were irreconcilable with the principles of equality, government by consent, and inalienable rights proclaimed by the Declaration of Independence and embedded in our constitutional structure. See, *e. g.*, 3 Records of the Federal Convention of 1787, p. 212 (M. Farrand ed. 1911) (remarks of Luther Martin) ("[S]lavery is inconsistent with the genius of republicanism, and has a tendency to destroy those principles on which it is supported, as it lessens the sense of the equal rights of mankind" (emphasis deleted)); A. Lincoln, Speech at Peoria, Ill. (Oct. 16, 1854), reprinted in 2 The Collected Works of Abraham Lincoln 266 (R. Basler ed. 1953) ("[N]o man is good enough to govern another man, *without that other's consent*. I say this is the leading principle—the sheet anchor of American republicanism. . . . Now the relation of masters and slaves is, *pro tanto*, a total violation of this principle").

After the war, a series of constitutional amendments were adopted to repair the Nation from the damage slavery had caused. The provision at issue here, § 1 of the Fourteenth Amendment, significantly altered our system of government. The first sentence of that section provides that "[a]ll persons born or naturalized in the United States and subject to the jurisdiction thereof, are citizens of the United States and of the State wherein they reside." This unambiguously overruled this Court's contrary holding in *Dred Scott* v. *Sand-*

ford, 19 How. 393 (1857), that the Constitution did not recognize black Americans as citizens of the United States or their own State. *Id.*, at 405–406.

The meaning of § 1's next sentence has divided this Court for many years. That sentence begins with the command that "[n]o State shall make or enforce any law which shall abridge the privileges or immunities of citizens of the United States." On its face, this appears to grant the persons just made United States citizens a certain collection of rights—*i. e.*, privileges or immunities—attributable to that status.

This Court's precedents accept that point, but define the relevant collection of rights quite narrowly. In the *Slaughter-House Cases*, 16 Wall. 36 (1873), decided just five years after the Fourteenth Amendment's adoption, the Court interpreted this text, now known as the Privileges or Immunities Clause, for the first time. In a closely divided decision, the Court drew a sharp distinction between the privileges and immunities of state citizenship and those of federal citizenship, and held that the Privileges or Immunities Clause protected only the latter category of rights from state abridgment. *Id.*, at 78. The Court defined that category to include only those rights "which owe their existence to the Federal government, its National character, its Constitution, or its laws." *Id.*, at 79. This arguably left open the possibility that certain individual rights enumerated in the Constitution could be considered privileges or immunities of federal citizenship. See *ibid.* (listing "[t]he right to peaceably assemble" and "the privilege of the writ of *habeas corpus*" as rights potentially protected by the Privileges or Immunities Clause). But the Court soon rejected that proposition, interpreting the Privileges or Immunities Clause even more narrowly in its later cases.

Chief among those cases is *United States* v. *Cruikshank*, 92 U. S. 542 (1876). There, the Court held that members of a white militia who had brutally murdered as many as 165 black Louisianians congregating outside a courthouse had not deprived the victims of their privileges as American citizens to peaceably assemble or to keep and bear arms. *Ibid.;* see L. Keith, The Colfax Massacre 109 (2008). According to the Court, the right to peaceably assemble codified in the First Amendment was not a privilege of United States citizenship because "[t]he right . . . existed long *before* the adoption of the Constitution." 92 U. S., at 551 (emphasis added). Similarly, the Court held that the right to keep and bear arms was not a privilege of United States citizenship because it was not "in any manner dependent upon that instrument for its existence." *Id.*, at 553. In other words, the reason the Framers codified the right to bear arms in the Second Amendment—its nature as an inalienable right that pre-existed the Constitution's adoption—was the very reason citizens could not enforce it against States through the Fourteenth.

That circular reasoning effectively has been the Court's last word on the Privileges or Immunities Clause.[1] In the intervening years, the Court has held that the Clause prevents state abridgment of only a handful of rights, such as the right to travel, see *Saenz* v. *Roe*, 526 U. S. 489, 503 (1999), that are not readily described as essential to liberty.

As a consequence of this Court's marginalization of the Clause, litigants seeking federal protection of fundamental rights turned to the remainder of § 1 in search of an alternative fount of such rights. They found one in a most curious place—that section's command that every State guarantee "due process" to any person before depriving him of "life, liberty, or property." At first, litigants argued that this Due Process Clause "incorporated" certain procedural rights codified in the Bill of Rights against the States. The Court

[1] In the two decades after *United States* v. *Cruikshank*, 92 U. S. 542 (1876), was decided, this Court twice reaffirmed its holding that the Privileges or Immunities Clause does not apply the Second Amendment to the States. *Presser* v. *Illinois*, 116 U. S. 252, 266–267 (1886); *Miller* v. *Texas*, 153 U. S. 535 (1894).

generally rejected those claims, however, on the theory that the rights in question were not sufficiently "fundamental" to warrant such treatment. See, *e. g., Hurtado* v. *California,* 110 U. S. 516 (1884) (grand jury indictment requirement); *Maxwell* v. *Dow,* 176 U. S. 581 (1900) (12-person jury requirement); *Twining* v. *New Jersey,* 211 U. S. 78 (1908) (privilege against self-incrimination).

That changed with time. The Court came to conclude that certain Bill of Rights guarantees *were* sufficiently fundamental to fall within § 1's guarantee of "due process." These included not only procedural protections listed in the first eight Amendments, see, *e. g., Benton* v. *Maryland,* 395 U. S. 784 (1969) (protection against double jeopardy), but substantive rights as well, see, *e. g., Gitlow* v. *New York,* 268 U. S. 652, 666 (1925) (right to free speech); *Near* v. *Minnesota ex rel. Olson,* 283 U. S. 697, 707 (1931) (same). In the process of incorporating these rights against the States, the Court often applied them differently against the States than against the Federal Government on the theory that only those "fundamental" aspects of the right required Due Process Clause protection. See, *e. g., Betts* v. *Brady,* 316 U. S. 455, 473 (1942) (holding that the Sixth Amendment required the appointment of counsel in all federal criminal cases in which the defendant was unable to retain an attorney, but that the Due Process Clause required appointment of counsel in state criminal cases only where "want of counsel . . . result[ed] in a conviction lacking in . . . fundamental fairness"). In more recent years, this Court has "abandoned the notion" that the guarantees in the Bill of Rights apply differently when incorporated against the States than they do when applied to the Federal Government. *Ante,* at 765 (opinion of the Court) (internal quotation marks omitted). But our cases continue to adhere to the view that a right is incorporated through the Due Process Clause only if it is sufficiently "fundamental," *ante,* at 784–785, 789–791 (plurality opinion)—a term the Court has long struggled to define.

While this Court has at times concluded that a right gains "fundamental" status only if it is essential to the American "scheme of ordered liberty" or "'deeply rooted in this Nation's history and tradition,'" *ante*, at 767 (opinion of the Court) (quoting *Glucksberg*, 521 U. S., at 721), the Court has just as often held that a right warrants Due Process Clause protection if it satisfies a far less measurable range of criteria, see *Lawrence* v. *Texas*, 539 U. S. 558, 562 (2003) (concluding that the Due Process Clause protects "liberty of the person both in its spatial and in its more transcendent dimensions"). Using the latter approach, the Court has determined that the Due Process Clause applies rights against the States that are not mentioned in the Constitution at all, even without seriously arguing that the Clause was originally understood to protect such rights. See, *e. g.*, *Lochner* v. *New York*, 198 U. S. 45 (1905); *Roe* v. *Wade*, 410 U. S. 113 (1973); *Lawrence*, *supra*.

All of this is a legal fiction. The notion that a constitutional provision that guarantees only "process" before a person is deprived of life, liberty, or property could define the substance of those rights strains credulity for even the most casual user of words. Moreover, this fiction is a particularly dangerous one. The one theme that links the Court's substantive due process precedents together is their lack of a guiding principle to distinguish "fundamental" rights that warrant protection from nonfundamental rights that do not. Today's decision illustrates the point. Replaying a debate that has endured from the inception of the Court's substantive due process jurisprudence, the dissents laud the "flexibility" in this Court's substantive due process doctrine, *post*, at 871 (opinion of STEVENS, J.); see *post*, at 918–919 (opinion of BREYER, J.), while the plurality makes yet another effort to impose principled restraints on its exercise, see *ante*, at 780–787. But neither side argues that the meaning they attribute to the Due Process Clause was consistent with public understanding at the time of its ratification.

To be sure, the plurality's effort to cabin the exercise of judicial discretion under the Due Process Clause by focusing its inquiry on those rights deeply rooted in American history and tradition invites less opportunity for abuse than the alternatives. See *post,* at 918 (BREYER, J., dissenting) (arguing that rights should be incorporated against the States through the Due Process Clause if they are "well suited to the carrying out of . . . constitutional promises"); *post,* at 878 (STEVENS, J., dissenting) (warning that there is no "all-purpose, top-down, totalizing theory of 'liberty'" protected by the Due Process Clause). But any serious argument over the scope of the Due Process Clause must acknowledge that neither its text nor its history suggests that it protects the many substantive rights this Court's cases now claim it does.

I cannot accept a theory of constitutional interpretation that rests on such tenuous footing. This Court's substantive due process framework fails to account for both the text of the Fourteenth Amendment and the history that led to its adoption, filling that gap with a jurisprudence devoid of a guiding principle. I believe the original meaning of the Fourteenth Amendment offers a superior alternative, and that a return to that meaning would allow this Court to enforce the rights the Fourteenth Amendment is designed to protect with greater clarity and predictability than the substantive due process framework has so far managed.

I acknowledge the volume of precedents that have been built upon the substantive due process framework, and I further acknowledge the importance of *stare decisis* to the stability of our Nation's legal system. But *stare decisis* is only an "adjunct" of our duty as judges to decide by our best lights what the Constitution means. *Planned Parenthood of Southeastern Pa.* v. *Casey,* 505 U. S. 833, 963 (1992) (Rehnquist, C. J., concurring in judgment in part and dissenting in part). It is not "an inexorable command." *Lawrence, supra,* at 577. Moreover, as judges, we interpret the Constitution one case or controversy at a time. The question presented in this case is not whether our entire Fourteenth Amendment jurisprudence must be preserved or revised, but only whether, and to what extent, a particular Clause in the Constitution protects the particular right at issue here. With the inquiry appropriately narrowed, I believe this case presents an opportunity to reexamine, and begin the process of restoring, the meaning of the Fourteenth Amendment agreed upon by those who ratified it.

II

"It cannot be presumed that any clause in the constitution is intended to be without effect." *Marbury* v. *Madison*, 1 Cranch 137, 174 (1803) (opinion for the Court by Marshall, C. J.). Because the Court's Privileges or Immunities Clause precedents have presumed just that, I set them aside for the moment and begin with the text.

The Privileges or Immunities Clause of the Fourteenth Amendment declares that "[n]o State . . . shall abridge the privileges or immunities of citizens of the United States." In interpreting this language, it is important to recall that constitutional provisions are "'written to be understood by the voters.'" *Heller*, 554 U. S., at 576 (quoting *United States* v. *Sprague*, 282 U. S. 716, 731 (1931)). Thus, the objective of this inquiry is to discern what "ordinary citizens" at the time of ratification would have understood the Privileges or Immunities Clause to mean. 554 U. S., at 577.

A

1

At the time of Reconstruction, the terms "privileges" and "immunities" had an established meaning as synonyms for "rights." The two words, standing alone or paired together, were used interchangeably with the words "rights," "liberties," and "freedoms," and had been since the time of Blackstone. See 1 W. Blackstone, Commentaries *129 (describing the "rights and liberties" of Englishmen as "private immunities" and "civil privileges"). A number of antebellum judicial decisions used the terms in this manner. See, *e. g., Magill* v. *Brown*, 16 F. Cas. 408, 428 (No. 8,952) (CC ED Pa. 1833) (Baldwin, J.) ("The words 'privileges and immunities' relate to the rights of persons, place or property; a privilege is a peculiar right, a private law, conceded to particular persons or places"). In addition, dictionary definitions confirm that the public shared this understanding. See, *e. g.*, 2 N. Webster, An American Dictionary of the English Language 1039 (C. Goodrich & N. Porter rev. 1865) (defining "privilege" as "a right or immunity not enjoyed by others or by all" and listing among its synonyms the words "immunity," "franchise," "right," and "liberty"); 1 *id.*, at 661 (defining "immunity" as "[f]reedom from an obligation" or "particular privilege"); 2 *id.*, at 1140 (defining "right" as "[p]rivilege or immunity granted by authority").[2]

The fact that a particular interest was designated as a "privilege" or "immunity," rather than a "right," "liberty," or "freedom," revealed little about its substance. Blackstone, for example, used the terms "privileges" and "immunities" to describe both the inalienable rights of individuals and the positive-law rights of corporations. See 1 Commentaries, at *129 (describing "private immunities" as a "*residuum* of natural liberty," and "civil privileges" as those "which society hath engaged to provide, in lieu of the natural liberties so given up by individuals"); *id.*, at *468 (stating that a corporate charter enables a corporation to "establish

[2] See also 2 C. Richardson, A New Dictionary of the English Language 1512 (1839) (defining "privilege" as "an appropriate or peculiar law or rule or right; a peculiar immunity, liberty, or franchise"); 1 *id.*, at 1056 (defining "immunity" as "[f]reedom or exemption, (from duties,) liberty, privilege"); The Philadelphia School Dictionary; or Expositor of the English Language 152 (3d ed. 1812) (defining "privilege" as a "peculiar advantage"); *id.*, at 105 (defining "immunity" as "privilege, exemption"); Royal Standard English Dictionary 411 (1788) (defining "privilege" as "public right, peculiar advantage").

rules and orders" that serve as "the privileges and immunities . . . of the corporation"). Writers in this country at the time of Reconstruction followed a similar practice. See, *e. g., Racine & Mississippi R. Co.* v. *Farmers' Loan & Trust Co.*, 49 Ill. 331, 334 (1868) (describing agreement between two railroad companies in which they agreed "'to fully merge and consolidate the[ir] capital stock, powers, privileges, immunities and franchises'"); *Hathorn* v. *Calef*, 53 Me. 471, 483–484 (1866) (concluding that a statute did not "modify any power, privileges, or immunity, pertaining to the franchise of any corporation"). The nature of a privilege or immunity thus varied depending on the person, group, or entity to whom those rights were assigned. See Lash, The Origins of the Privileges or Immunities Clause, Part I: "Privileges and Immunities" as an Antebellum Term of Art, 98 Geo. L. J. 1241, 1256–1257 (2010) (surveying antebellum usages of these terms).

2

The group of rights-bearers to whom the Privileges or Immunities Clause applies is, of course, "citizens." By the time of Reconstruction, it had long been established that both the States and the Federal Government existed to preserve their citizens' inalienable rights, and that these rights were considered "privileges" or "immunities" of citizenship.

This tradition begins with our country's English roots. Parliament declared the basic liberties of English citizens in a series of documents ranging from the Magna Carta to the Petition of Right and the English Bill of Rights. See 1 B. Schwartz, The Bill of Rights: A Documentary History 8–16, 19–21, 41–46 (1971) (hereinafter Schwartz). These fundamental rights, according to the English tradition, belonged to all people but became legally enforceable only when recognized in legal texts, including acts of Parliament and the decisions of common-law judges. See B. Bailyn, The Ideological Origins of the American Revolution 77–79 (1967). These rights included many that later would be set forth in our

Federal Bill of Rights, such as the right to petition for redress of grievances, the right to a jury trial, and the right of "Protestants" to "have arms for their defence." English Bill of Rights (1689), reprinted in 1 Schwartz 41, 43.

As English subjects, the colonists considered themselves to be vested with the same fundamental rights as other Englishmen. They consistently claimed the rights of English citizenship in their founding documents, repeatedly referring to these rights as "privileges" and "immunities." For example, a Maryland law provided:

> "[A]ll the Inhabitants of this Province being Christians (Slaves excepted) Shall have and enjoy all such *rights liberties immunities priviledges and free customs* within this Province as any naturall born subject of England hath or ought to have or enjoy in the Realm of England . . . ." Md. Act for the Liberties of the People (1639), in *id.*, at 68 (emphasis added).[3]

[3] See also, *e. g.*, First Charter of Va. (1606), reprinted in 7 Federal and State Constitutions, Colonial Charters, and Other Organic Laws 3783, 3788 (F. Thorpe ed. 1909) (hereinafter Thorpe) ("DECLAR[ING]" that "all and every the Persons being our Subjects, . . . shall HAVE and enjoy all Liberties, Franchises, and Immunities . . . as if they had been abiding and born, within this our Realm of *England*" (emphasis in original)); Charter of New England (1620), in 3 *id.*, at 1827, 1839 ("[A]ll and every the Persons, beinge our Subjects, . . . shall have and enjoy all Liberties, and ffranchizes, and Immunities of free Denizens and naturall Subjects . . . as if they had been abidinge and born within this our Kingdome of England"); Charter of Mass. Bay (1629), in *id.*, at 1846, 1856–1857 (guaranteeing that "all and every the Subjects of Us, . . . shall have and enjoy all liberties and Immunities of free and naturall Subjects . . . as yf they and everie of them were borne within the Realme of England"); Grant of the Province of Me. (1639), in *id.*, at 1625, 1635 (guaranteeing "Liberties Francheses and Immunityes of or belonging to any the naturall borne subjects of this our Kingdome of England"); Charter of Carolina (1663), in 5 *id.*, at 2743, 2747 (guaranteeing to all subjects "all liberties franchises and priviledges of this our kingdom of England"); Charter of R. I. and Providence Plantations (1663), in 6 *id.*, at 3211, 3220 ("[A]ll and every the subjects of us . . . shall have and enjoye all libertyes and immunityes of ffree and naturall subjects within any the dominions of us, our heires, or successours, . . . as if they, and every of them, were borne within the realme of England"); Charter of Ga. (1732),

As tensions between England and the Colonies increased, the colonists adopted protest resolutions reasserting their claim to the inalienable rights of Englishmen. Again, they used the terms "privileges" and "immunities" to describe these rights. As the Massachusetts Resolves declared:

> "*Resolved,* That there are certain essential Rights of the *British* Constitution of Government, which are founded in the Law of God and Nature, and are the common Rights of Mankind—Therefore
>
> . . . . .
>
> "*Resolved,* That no Man can justly take the Property of another without his Consent: And that upon this *original* Principle the Right of Representation . . . is evidently founded.
>
> "*Resolved,* That this *inherent* Right, together with all other, essential *Rights, Liberties, Privileges and Immunities* of the People of *Great Britain,* have been fully confirmed to them by *Magna Charta.*" The Massachusetts Resolves (Oct. 29, 1765), reprinted in Prologue to Revolution: Sources and Documents on the Stamp Act Crisis, 1764–1766, p. 56 (E. Morgan ed. 1959) (some emphasis added).[4]

---

in 2 *id.*, at 765, 773 ("[A]ll and every the persons which shall happen to be born within the said province . . . shall have and enjoy all liberties, franchises and immunities of free denizens and natural born subjects, within any of our dominions, to all intents and purposes, as if abiding and born within this our kingdom of Great-Britain").

[4] See also, *e. g.*, A. Howard, The Road from Runnymede: Magna Carta and Constitutionalism in America 174 (1968) (quoting 1774 Georgia resolution declaring that the Colony's inhabitants were entitled to " 'the same rights, privileges, and immunities with their fellow-subjects in *Great Britain*' " (emphasis in original)); The Virginia Resolves, Resolutions as Printed in the Journal of the House of Burgesses, reprinted in Prologue to Revolution: Sources and Documents on the Stamp Act Crisis, 1764–1766, at 46, 48 ("[T]he Colonists aforesaid are declared entitled to all Liberties, Privileges, and Immunities of Denizens and natural Subjects, to all Intents and Purposes, as if they had been abiding and born within the Realm of *England*" (emphasis in original)).

In keeping with this practice, the First Continental Congress declared in 1774 that the King had wrongfully denied the colonists "the rights, liberties, and immunities of free and natural-born subjects . . . within the realm of England." 1 Journals of the Continental Congress 1774–1789, p. 68 (W. Ford ed. 1904). In an address delivered to the inhabitants of Quebec that same year, the Congress described those rights as including the "great" "right[s]" of "trial by jury," "Habeas Corpus," and "freedom of the press." Address of the Continental Congress to the Inhabitants of Quebec (1774), reprinted in 1 Schwartz 221–223.

After declaring their independence, the newly formed States replaced their colonial charters with constitutions and state bills of rights, almost all of which guaranteed the same fundamental rights that the former colonists previously had claimed by virtue of their English heritage. See, *e. g.*, Pa. Declaration of Rights (1776), reprinted in 5 Thorpe 3081–3084 (declaring that "all men are born equally free and independent, and have certain natural, inherent and inalienable rights," including the "right to worship Almighty God according to the dictates of their own consciences" and the "right to bear arms for the defence of themselves and the state").[5]

Several years later, the Founders amended the Constitution to expressly protect many of the same fundamental rights against interference by the Federal Government. Consistent with their English heritage, the founding generation generally did not consider many of the rights identified in these amendments as new entitlements, but as inalienable rights of all men, given legal effect by their codification in the Constitution's text. See, *e. g.*, 1 Annals of Cong. 431–432, 436–437, 440–442 (1789) (statement of Rep. Madison)

[5] See also Va. Declaration of Rights (1776), reprinted in 1 Schwartz 234–236; Pa. Declaration of Rights (1776), in *id.*, at 263–275; Del. Declaration of Rights (1776), in *id.*, at 276–278; Md. Declaration of Rights (1776), in *id.*, at 280–285; N. C. Declaration of Rights (1776), in *id.*, at 286–288.

(proposing Bill of Rights in the First Congress); The Federalist No. 84, pp. 531–533 (B. Wright ed. 1961) (A. Hamilton); see also *Heller*, 554 U. S., at 592 ("[I]t has always been widely understood that the Second Amendment, like the First and Fourth Amendments, codified a *pre-existing* right"). The Court's subsequent decision in *Barron*, however, made plain that the codification of these rights in the Bill of Rights made them legally enforceable only against the Federal Government, not the States. See 7 Pet., at 247.

3

Even though the Bill of Rights did not apply to the States, other provisions of the Constitution did limit state interference with individual rights. Article IV, § 2, cl. 1, provides that "[t]he Citizens of each State shall be entitled to all Privileges and Immunities of Citizens in the several States." The text of this provision resembles the Privileges or Immunities Clause, and it can be assumed that the public's understanding of the latter was informed by its understanding of the former.

Article IV, § 2, was derived from a similar clause in the Articles of Confederation, and reflects the dual citizenship the Constitution provided to all Americans after replacing that "league" of separate sovereign States. *Gibbons* v. *Ogden*, 9 Wheat. 1, 187 (1824); see 3 J. Story, Commentaries on the Constitution of the United States § 1800, p. 675 (1833). By virtue of a person's citizenship in a particular State, he was guaranteed whatever rights and liberties that State's constitution and laws made available. Article IV, § 2, vested citizens of each State with an additional right: the assurance that they would be afforded the "privileges and immunities" of citizenship in any of the several States in the Union to which they might travel.

What were the "Privileges and Immunities of Citizens in the several States"? That question was answered perhaps most famously by Justice Bushrod Washington sitting as Circuit Justice in *Corfield* v. *Coryell,* 6 F. Cas. 546, 551–552 (No. 3,230) (CC ED Pa. 1825). In that case, a Pennsylvania citizen claimed that a New Jersey law prohibiting nonresidents from harvesting oysters from the State's waters violated Article IV, § 2, because it deprived him, as an out-of-state citizen, of a right New Jersey availed to its own citizens. *Id.,* at 550. Justice Washington rejected that argument, refusing to "accede to the proposition" that Article IV, § 2, entitled "citizens of the several states . . . to participate in *all* the rights which belong exclusively to the citizens of any other particular state." *Id.,* at 552 (emphasis added). In his view, Article IV, § 2, did not guarantee equal access to all public benefits a State might choose to make available to its citizens. See *id.,* at 552. Instead, it applied only to those rights "which are, in their nature, *fundamental;* which belong, of right, to the citizens of all free governments." *Id.,* at 551 (emphasis added). Other courts generally agreed with this principle. See, *e. g., Abbot* v. *Bayley,* 23 Mass. 89, 92–93 (1827) (noting that the "privileges and immunities" of citizens in the several States protected by Article IV, § 2, are "qualified and not absolute" because they do not grant a traveling citizen the right of "suffrage or of eligibility to office" in the State to which he travels).

When describing those "fundamental" rights, Justice Washington thought it "would perhaps be more tedious than difficult to enumerate" them all, but suggested that they could "be all comprehended under" a broad list of "general heads," such as "[p]rotection by the government," "the enjoyment of life and liberty, with the right to acquire and possess property of every kind," "the benefit of the writ of habeas corpus," and the right of access to "the courts of the state," among others.[6] *Corfield, supra,* at 551–552.

---

[6] Justice Washington's complete list was as follows:

"Protection by the government; the enjoyment of life and liberty, with the right to acquire and possess property of every kind, and to pursue and obtain happiness and safety; subject nevertheless to such restraints as the

Notably, Justice Washington did not indicate whether Article IV, § 2, *required* States to recognize these fundamental rights in their own citizens and thus in sojourning citizens alike, or whether the Clause simply prohibited the States from discriminating against sojourning citizens with respect to whatever fundamental rights state law happened to recognize. On this question, the weight of legal authorities at the time of Reconstruction indicated that Article IV, § 2, prohibited States from discriminating against sojourning citizens when recognizing fundamental rights, but did not require States to recognize those rights and did not prescribe their content. The highest courts of several States adopted this view, see, *e. g., Livingston* v. *Van Ingen*, 9 Johns. *507, *561 (N. Y. Sup. Ct. 1812) (Yates, J.); *id.*, at *577 (Kent, C. J.); *Campbell* v. *Morris*, 3 H. & McH. 535, 553–554 (Md. Gen. Ct. 1797) (Chase, J.), as did several influential treatise writers, see T. Cooley, Constitutional Limitations 15–16, and n. 3 (1868) (describing Article IV, § 2, as designed "to prevent discrimination by the several States against the citizens and public proceedings of other States"); 2 J. Kent, Commentaries on American Law 35 (11th ed. 1867) (stating that Article IV, § 2, entitles sojourning citizens "to the privileges that persons of the same description are entitled to in the state to which the removal is made, and to none other"). This Court adopted the same conclusion in a unanimous opinion

---

government may justly prescribe for the general good of the whole. The right of a citizen of one state to pass through, or to reside in any other state, for purposes of trade, agriculture, professional pursuits, or otherwise; to claim the benefit of the writ of habeas corpus; to institute and maintain actions of any kind in the courts of the state; to take, hold and dispose of property, either real or personal; and an exemption from higher taxes or impositions than are paid by the other citizens of the state; may be mentioned as some of the particular privileges and immunities of citizens, which are clearly embraced by the general description of privileges deemed to be fundamental: to which may be added, the elective franchise, as regulated and established by the laws or constitution of the state in which it is to be exercised." 6 F. Cas., at 551–552.

just one year after the Fourteenth Amendment was ratified. See *Paul* v. *Virginia,* 8 Wall. 168, 180 (1869).

* * *

The text examined so far demonstrates three points about the meaning of the Privileges or Immunities Clause in § 1. First, "privileges" and "immunities" were synonyms for "rights." Second, both the States and the Federal Government had long recognized the inalienable rights of their citizens. Third, Article IV, § 2, of the Constitution protected traveling citizens against state discrimination with respect to the fundamental rights of state citizenship.

Two questions still remain, both provoked by the textual similarity between § 1's Privileges or Immunities Clause and Article IV, § 2. The first involves the nature of the rights at stake: Are the privileges or immunities of "citizens of the United States" recognized by § 1 the same as the privileges and immunities of "Citizens in the several States" to which Article IV, § 2, refers? The second involves the restriction imposed on the States: Does § 1, like Article IV, § 2, prohibit only discrimination with respect to certain rights *if* the State chooses to recognize them, or does it require States to recognize those rights? I address each question in turn.

B

I start with the nature of the rights that § 1's Privileges or Immunities Clause protects. Section 1 overruled *Dred Scott*'s holding that blacks were not citizens of either the United States or their own State and, thus, did not enjoy "the privileges and immunities of citizens" embodied in the Constitution. 19 How., at 417. The Court in *Dred Scott* did not distinguish between privileges and immunities of citizens of the United States and citizens in the several States, instead referring to the rights of citizens generally. It did, however, give examples of what the rights of citizens were—

the constitutionally enumerated rights of "the full liberty of speech" and the right "to keep and carry arms." *Ibid.*

Section 1 protects the rights of citizens "of the United States" specifically. The evidence overwhelmingly demonstrates that the privileges and immunities of such citizens included individual rights enumerated in the Constitution, including the right to keep and bear arms.

1

Nineteenth-century treaties through which the United States acquired territory from other sovereigns routinely promised inhabitants of the newly acquired Territories that they would enjoy all of the "rights," "privileges," and "immunities" of United States citizens. See, *e. g.*, Treaty of Amity, Settlement, and Limits, Art. 6, Feb. 22, 1819, 8 Stat. 256–258, T. S. No. 327 (entered into force Feb. 19, 1821) (cession of Florida) ("The inhabitants of the territories which his Catholic Majesty cedes to the United States, by this Treaty, shall be incorporated in the Union of the United States, as soon as may be consistent with the principles of the Federal Constitution, and admitted to the enjoyment of *all the privileges, rights, and immunities, of the citizens of the United States*" (emphasis added)).[7]

---

[7] See also Treaty Between the United States of America and the Ottawa Indians of Blanchard's Fork and Roche De Boeuf, June 24, 1862, 12 Stat. 1237 ("The Ottawa Indians of the United Bands of Blanchard's Fork and of Roche de Boeuf, having become sufficiently advanced in civilization, and being desirous of becoming citizens of the United States . . . [after five years from the ratification of this treaty] shall be deemed and declared to be citizens of the United States, to all intents and purposes, and shall be entitled to all the *rights, privileges, and immunities of such citizens*" (emphasis added)); Treaty Between the United States of America and Different Tribes of Sioux Indians, Art. VI, April 29, 1868, 15 Stat. 637 ("[A]ny Indian or Indians receiving a patent for land under the foregoing provisions, shall thereby and from thenceforth become and be a citizen of the United States, and be entitled to all the *privileges and immunities of such citizens*" (emphasis added)).

Commentators of the time explained that the rights and immunities of "citizens of the United States" recognized in these treaties "undoubtedly mean[t] those privileges that are common to all the citizens of this republic." Marcus, An Examination of the Expediency and Constitutionality of Prohibiting Slavery in the State of Missouri 17 (1819). It is therefore altogether unsurprising that several of these treaties identify liberties enumerated in the Constitution as privileges and immunities common to all United States citizens.

For example, the Louisiana Cession Act of 1803, which codified a treaty between the United States and France culminating in the Louisiana Purchase, provided:

> "The inhabitants of the ceded territory shall be incorporated in the Union of the United States, and admitted as soon as possible, according to the principles of the Federal constitution, to the enjoyment of *all the rights, advantages and immunities of citizens of the United States;* and in the mean time they shall be maintained and protected in *the free enjoyment of their liberty, property, and the religion which they profess.*" Treaty Between the United States of America and the French Republic, Art. III, Apr. 30, 1803, 8 Stat. 202, T. S. No. 86 (emphasis added).[8]

---

[8] Subsequent treaties contained similar guarantees that the inhabitants of the newly acquired Territories would enjoy the freedom to exercise certain constitutional rights. See Treaty of Peace, Friendship, Limits, and Settlement with the Republic of Mexico, Art. IX, Feb. 2, 1848, 9 Stat. 930, T. S. No. 207 (cession of Texas) (declaring that inhabitants of the Territory were entitled "to the enjoyment of all the rights of citizens of the United States, according to the principles of the constitution; and in the mean time shall be maintained and protected in the free enjoyment of their liberty and property, and secured in the free exercise of their religion without restriction"); Treaty concerning the Cession of the Russian Possessions in North America by his Majesty the Emperor of all the Russias to the United States of America, Art. III, Mar. 30, 1867, 15 Stat. 542, T. S. No. 301 (June 20, 1867) (cession of Alaska) ("The inhabitants of the ceded territory, . . . if they should prefer to remain in the ceded territory, they,

The Louisiana Cession Act reveals even more about the privileges and immunities of United States citizenship because it provoked an extensive public debate on the meaning of that term. In 1820, when the Missouri Territory (which the United States acquired through the Cession Act) sought to enter the Union as a new State, a debate ensued over whether to prohibit slavery within Missouri as a condition of its admission. Some Congressmen argued that prohibiting slavery in Missouri would deprive its inhabitants of the "privileges and immunities" they had been promised by the Cession Act. See, *e. g.*, 35 Annals of Cong. 1083 (1820) (remarks of Kentucky Rep. Hardin). But those who opposed slavery in Missouri argued that the right to hold slaves was merely a matter of state property law, not one of the privileges and immunities of United States citizenship guaranteed by the Act.[9]

Daniel Webster was among the leading proponents of the antislavery position. In his "Memorial to Congress," Webster argued that "[t]he rights, advantages and immunities here spoken of [in the Cession Act] must . . . be such as are recognized or communicated by the Constitution of the United States," not the "rights, advantages and immunities, derived exclusively from the *State* governments . . . ."

---

with the exception of uncivilized native tribes, shall be admitted to the enjoyment of all the rights, advantages, and immunities of citizens of the United States, and shall be maintained and protected in the free enjoyment of their liberty, property, and religion").

[9] See, *e. g.*, Speech of Mr. Joseph Hemphill (Pa.) on the Missouri Question in the House of Representatives 16 (1820), as published in pamphlet form and reprinted in 22 Moore Pamphlets, p. 16 ("If the right to hold slaves is a federal right and attached merely to citizenship of the United States, [then slavery] could maintain itself against state authority, and on this principle the owner might take his slaves into any state he pleased, in defiance of the state laws, but this would be contrary to the constitution"); see also Lash, The Origins of the Privileges or Immunities Clause, Part I: "Privileges and Immunities" as an Antebellum Term of Art, 98 Geo. L. J. 1241, 1288–1290 (2010) (collecting other examples).

D. Webster, A Memorial to the Congress of the United States, on the Subject of Restraining the Increase of Slavery in New States To Be Admitted Into the Union 15 (Dec. 15, 1819) (emphasis added). "The obvious meaning" of the Act, in Webster's view, was that "*the rights derived under the federal Constitution* shall be enjoyed by the inhabitants of [the Territory]." *Id.*, at 15–16 (emphasis added). In other words, Webster articulated a distinction between the rights of United States citizenship and the rights of state citizenship, and argued that the former included those rights "recognized or communicated by the Constitution." Since the right to hold slaves was not mentioned in the Constitution, it was not a right of federal citizenship.

Webster and his allies ultimately lost the debate over slavery in Missouri, and the Territory was admitted as a slave State as part of the now-famous Missouri Compromise. Missouri Enabling Act of Mar. 6, 1820, ch. 22, § 8, 3 Stat. 548. But their arguments continued to inform public understanding of the privileges and immunities of United States citizenship. In 1854, Webster's Memorial was republished in a pamphlet discussing the Nation's next major debate on slavery—the proposed repeal of the Missouri Compromise through the Kansas-Nebraska Act, see The Nebraska Question: Comprising Speeches in the United States Senate: Together With the History of the Missouri Compromise 9–12 (1854). It was published again in 1857 in a collection of famous American speeches. See Political Text-Book, or Encyclopedia: Containing Everything Necessary for the Reference of the Politicians and Statesmen of the United States 601–604 (M. Cluskey ed. 1857); see also Lash, 98 Geo. L. J., at 1294–1296 (describing Webster's arguments and their influence).

2

Evidence from the political branches in the years leading to the Fourteenth Amendment's adoption demonstrates broad public understanding that the privileges and immunities of United States citizenship included rights set forth in the Constitution, just as Webster and his allies had argued. In 1868, President Andrew Johnson issued a proclamation granting amnesty to former Confederates, guaranteeing "to all and to every person who directly or indirectly participated in the late insurrection or rebellion, a full pardon and amnesty for the offence of treason . . . with restoration of *all rights, privileges, and immunities under the Constitution* and the laws which have been made in pursuance thereof." 15 Stat. 712 (emphasis added).

Records from the 39th Congress further support this understanding.

a

After the Civil War, Congress established the Joint Committee on Reconstruction to investigate circumstances in the Southern States and to determine whether, and on what conditions, those States should be readmitted to the Union. See Cong. Globe, 39th Cong., 1st Sess., 6, 30 (1865) (hereinafter 39th Cong. Globe); M. Curtis, No State Shall Abridge: The Fourteenth Amendment and the Bill of Rights 57 (1986) (hereinafter Curtis). That Committee would ultimately recommend the adoption of the Fourteenth Amendment, justifying its recommendation by submitting a report to Congress that extensively catalogued the abuses of civil rights in the former slave States and argued that "adequate security for future peace and safety . . . can only be found in such changes of the organic law as shall determine the civil rights and privileges of all citizens in all parts of the republic." See Report of the Joint Committee on Reconstruction, S. Rep. No. 112, 39th Cong., 1st Sess., 15 (1866); H. R. Rep. No. 30, 39th Cong., 1st Sess., p. XXI (1866).

As the Court notes, the Committee's Report "was widely reprinted in the press and distributed by Members of the 39th Congress to their constituents." *Ante*, at 772; B. Kendrick, Journal of the Joint Committee of Fifteen on Reconstruction 264–265 (1914) (noting that 150,000 copies of the

Report were printed and that it was widely distributed as a campaign document in the election of 1866). In addition, newspaper coverage suggests that the wider public was aware of the Committee's work even before the Report was issued. For example, the Fort Wayne Daily Democrat (which appears to have been unsupportive of the Committee's work) paraphrased a motion instructing the Committee to

> "enquire into [the] expediency of amending the Constitution of the United States so as to declare with greater certainty the power of Congress to enforce and determine by appropriate legislation all the guarantees contained in *that instrument*." The Nigger Congress! Fort Wayne Daily Democrat, Feb. 1, 1866, p. 4 (emphasis added).

b

Statements made by Members of Congress leading up to, and during, the debates on the Fourteenth Amendment point in the same direction. The record of these debates has been combed before. See *Adamson* v. *California*, 332 U. S. 46, 92–110 (1947) (appendix to dissenting opinion of Black, J.) (concluding that the debates support the conclusion that § 1 was understood to incorporate the Bill of Rights against the States); *ante*, at 762, n. 9, 774, n. 23, (opinion of the Court) (counting the debates among other evidence that § 1 applies the Second Amendment against the States). Before considering that record here, it is important to clarify its relevance. When interpreting constitutional text, the goal is to discern the most likely public understanding of a particular provision at the time it was adopted. Statements by legislators can assist in this process to the extent they demonstrate the manner in which the public used or understood a particular word or phrase. They can further assist to the extent there is evidence that these statements were disseminated to the public. In other words, this evidence is useful not because it demonstrates what the draftsmen of the text may have been thinking, but only insofar as it illuminates what the public understood the words chosen by the draftsmen to mean.

(1)

Three speeches stand out as particularly significant. Representative John Bingham, the principal draftsman of § 1, delivered a speech on the floor of the House in February 1866 introducing his first draft of the provision. Bingham began by discussing *Barron* and its holding that the Bill of Rights did not apply to the States. He then argued that a constitutional amendment was necessary to provide "an express grant of power in Congress to enforce by penal enactment these great canons of the supreme law, securing to all the citizens in every State all the privileges and immunities of citizens, and to all the people all the sacred rights of person." 39th Cong. Globe 1089–1090 (1866). Bingham emphasized that § 1 was designed "to arm the Congress of the United States, by the consent of the people of the United States, with the power to enforce the bill of rights as it stands in the Constitution today. It 'hath that extent—no more.'" *Id.*, at 1088.

Bingham's speech was printed in pamphlet form and broadly distributed in 1866 under the title, "One Country, One Constitution, and One People," and the subtitle, "In Support of the Proposed Amendment to Enforce the Bill of Rights."[10] Newspapers also reported his proposal, with the New York Times providing particularly extensive coverage,

[10] One Country, One Constitution, and One People: Speech of Hon. John A. Bingham, of Ohio, In the House of Representatives, February 28, 1866, In Support of the Proposed Amendment To Enforce the Bill of Rights (Cong. Globe). The pamphlet was published by the official reporter of congressional debates, and was distributed presumably pursuant to the congressional franking privilege. See Wildenthal, Nationalizing the Bill of Rights: Revisiting the Original Understanding of the Fourteenth Amendment in 1866–67, 68 Ohio St. L. J. 1509, 1558, n. 167 (2007) (hereinafter Wildenthal).

including a full reproduction of Bingham's first draft of § 1 and his remarks that a constitutional amendment to "enforc[e]" the "immortal bill of rights" was "absolutely essential to American nationality." N. Y. Times, Feb. 27, 1866, p. 8.

Bingham's first draft of § 1 was different from the version ultimately adopted. Of particular importance, the first draft granted Congress the "power to make all laws . . . necessary and proper to secure" the "citizens of each State all privileges and immunities of citizens in the several States," rather than restricting state power to "abridge" the privileges or immunities of citizens of the United States.[11] 39th Cong. Globe 1088.

That draft was met with objections, which the Times covered extensively. A front-page article hailed the "Clear and Forcible Speech" by Representative Robert Hale against the draft, explaining—and endorsing—Hale's view that Bingham's proposal would "confer upon Congress all the rights and power of legislation now reserved to the States" and would "in effect utterly obliterate State rights and State authority over their own internal affairs."[12] N. Y. Times, Feb. 28, 1866, p. 1.

---

[11] The full text of Bingham's first draft of § 1 provided as follows: "The Congress shall have power to make all laws which shall be necessary and proper to secure to the citizens of each State all privileges and immunities of citizens in the several States, and to all persons in the several States equal protection in the rights of life, liberty, and property." 39th Cong. Globe 1088.

[12] In a separate front-page article on the same day, the paper expounded upon Hale's arguments in even further detail, while omitting Bingham's chief rebuttals. N. Y. Times, Feb. 28, 1866, p. 1. The unbalanced nature of The New York Times' coverage is unsurprising. As scholars have noted, "[m]ost papers" during the time of Reconstruction "had a frank partisan slant . . . and the *Times* was no exception." Wildenthal 1559. In 1866, the paper "was still defending" President Johnson's resistance to Republican reform measures, as exemplified by the fact that it "supported Johnson's veto of the Civil Rights Act of 1866." *Ibid.*

Critically, Hale did *not* object to the draft insofar as it purported to protect constitutional liberties against state interference. Indeed, Hale stated that he believed (incorrectly in light of *Barron*) that individual rights enumerated in the Constitution were already enforceable against the States. See 39th Cong. Globe 1064 ("I have, somehow or other, gone along with the impression that there is that sort of protection thrown over us in some way, whether with or without the sanction of a judicial decision that we are so protected"); see N. Y. Times, Feb. 28, 1866, at 1. Hale's misperception was not uncommon among members of the Reconstruction generation. See *infra*, at 842–843. But that is secondary to the point that the Times' coverage of this debate over § 1's meaning suggests public awareness of its main contours—*i. e.*, that § 1 would, at a minimum, enforce constitutionally enumerated rights of United States citizens against the States.

Bingham's draft was tabled for several months. In the interim, he delivered a second well-publicized speech, again arguing that a constitutional amendment was required to give Congress the power to enforce the Bill of Rights against the States. That speech was printed in pamphlet form, see Speech of Hon. John A. Bingham, of Ohio, on the Civil Rights Bill, Mar. 9, 1866 (Cong. Globe); see 39th Cong. Globe 1837 (remarks of Rep. Lawrence) (noting that the speech was "extensively published"), and the New York Times covered the speech on its front page. Thirty-Ninth Congress, N. Y. Times, Mar. 10, 1866, p. 1.

By the time the debates on the Fourteenth Amendment resumed, Bingham had amended his draft of § 1 to include the text of the Privileges or Immunities Clause that was ultimately adopted. Senator Jacob Howard introduced the new draft on the floor of the Senate in the third speech relevant here. Howard explained that the Constitution recognized "a mass of privileges, immunities, and rights, some of them secured by the second section of the fourth article of the

Constitution, . . . some by the first eight amendments of the Constitution," and that "there is no power given in the Constitution to enforce and to carry out any of these guarantees" against the States. 39th Cong. Globe 2765. Howard then stated that "[t]he great object" of § 1 was to "restrain the power of the States and compel them at all times to respect these great fundamental guarantees." *Id.*, at 2766. Section 1, he indicated, imposed "a general prohibition upon all the States, as such, from abridging the privileges and immunities of the citizens of the United States." *Id.*, at 2765.

In describing these rights, Howard explained that they included "the privileges and immunities spoken of" in Article IV, § 2. *Id.*, at 2765. Although he did not catalogue the precise "nature" or "extent" of those rights, he thought "Corfield *vs.* Coryell" provided a useful description. Howard then submitted that

> "[t]o these privileges and immunities, whatever they may be— . . . should be added *the personal rights guarantied and secured by the first eight amendments of the Constitution;* such as the freedom of speech and of the press; the right of the people peaceably to assemble and petition the Government for a redress of grievances, [and] . . . *the right to keep and to bear arms.*" *Ibid.* (emphasis added).

News of Howard's speech was carried in major newspapers across the country, including the New York Herald, see N. Y. Herald, May 24, 1866, p. 1, which was the best selling paper in the Nation at that time, see A. Amar, The Bill of Rights: Creation and Reconstruction 187 (1998) (hereinafter Amar).[13] The New York Times carried the speech as well,

[13] Other papers that covered Howard's speech include the following: Baltimore Gazette, May 24, 1866, p. 4; Boston Daily Journal, May 24, 1866, p. 4; Boston Daily Advertiser, May 24, 1866, p. 1; Daily National Intelligencer, May 24, 1866, p. 3. Springfield Daily Republican, May 24, 1866, p. 3; Charleston Daily Courier, May 28, 1866, p. 4; Charleston Daily Cou-

reprinting a lengthy excerpt of Howard's remarks, including the statements quoted above. N. Y. Times, May 24, 1866, p. 1. The following day's Times editorialized on Howard's speech, predicting that "[t]o this, the first section of the amendment, the Union party throughout the country will yield a ready acquiescence, and the South could offer no justifiable resistance," suggesting that Bingham's narrower second draft had not been met with the same objections that Hale had raised against the first. N. Y. Times, May 25, 1866, p. 4.

As a whole, these well-circulated speeches indicate that § 1 was understood to enforce constitutionally declared rights against the States, and they provide no suggestion that any language in the section other than the Privileges or Immunities Clause would accomplish that task.

(2)

When read against this backdrop, the civil rights legislation adopted by the 39th Congress in 1866 further supports this view. Between passing the Thirteenth Amendment—which outlawed slavery alone—and the Fourteenth Amendment, Congress passed two significant pieces of legislation. The first was the Civil Rights Act of 1866, which provided that "all persons born in the United States" were "citizens of the United States" and that "such citizens, of every race and color, . . . shall have the same right" to, among other things, "full and equal benefit of all laws and proceedings for the security of person and property, as is enjoyed by white citizens." § 1, 14 Stat. 27.

Both proponents and opponents of this Act described it as providing the "privileges" of citizenship to freedmen, and defined those privileges to include constitutional rights, such as the right to keep and bear arms. See 39th Cong. Globe 474 (remarks of Sen. Trumbull) (stating that "the late slave-

---

rier, May 29, 1866, p. 1; Chicago Tribune, May 29, 1866, p. 2; Philadelphia Inquirer, May 24, 1866, p. 8.

holding States" had enacted laws "depriving persons of African descent of privileges which are essential to freemen," including "prohibit[ing] any negro or mulatto from having fire-arms" and stating that "[t]he purpose of the bill under consideration is to destroy all these discriminations"); *id.*, at 1266–1267 (remarks of Rep. Raymond) (opposing the Act, but recognizing that to "[m]ake the colored man a citizen of the United States" would guarantee to him, *inter alia*, "a defined *status* . . . a right to defend himself and his wife and children; a right to bear arms").

Three months later, Congress passed the Freedmen's Bureau Act, which also entitled all citizens to the "full and equal benefit of all laws and proceedings concerning personal liberty" and "personal security." Act of July 16, 1866, § 14, 14 Stat. 176. The Act stated expressly that the rights of personal liberty and security protected by the Act "includ[ed] the constitutional right to bear arms." *Ibid.*

(3)

There is much else in the legislative record. Many statements by Members of Congress corroborate the view that the Privileges or Immunities Clause enforced constitutionally enumerated rights against the States. See Curtis 112 (collecting examples). I am not aware of any statement that directly refutes that proposition. That said, the record of the debates—like most legislative history—is less than crystal clear. In particular, much ambiguity derives from the fact that at least several Members described § 1 as protecting the privileges and immunities of citizens "in the several States," harkening back to Article IV, § 2. See *supra*, at 832–833 (describing Sen. Howard's speech). These statements can be read to support the view that the Privileges or Immunities Clause protects some or all the fundamental rights of "citizens" described in *Corfield*. They can also be read to support the view that the Privileges or Immunities Clause, like Article IV, § 2, prohibits only state discrimination with respect to those rights it covers, but does not deprive States of the power to deny those rights to all citizens equally.

I examine the rest of the historical record with this understanding. But for purposes of discerning what the public most likely thought the Privileges or Immunities Clause to mean, it is significant that the most widely publicized statements by the legislators who voted on § 1—Bingham, Howard, and even Hale—point unambiguously toward the conclusion that the Privileges or Immunities Clause enforces at least those fundamental rights enumerated in the Constitution against the States, including the Second Amendment right to keep and bear arms.

3

Interpretations of the Fourteenth Amendment in the period immediately following its ratification help to establish the public understanding of the text at the time of its adoption.

Some of these interpretations come from Members of Congress. During an 1871 debate on a bill to enforce the Fourteenth Amendment, Representative Henry Dawes listed the Constitution's first eight Amendments, including "the right to keep and bear arms," before explaining that after the Civil War, the country "gave the most grand of all these rights, privileges, and immunities, by one single amendment to the Constitution, to four millions of American citizens" who formerly were slaves. Cong. Globe, 42d Cong., 1st Sess., 475–476 (1871). "It is all these," Dawes explained, "which are comprehended in the words 'American citizen.'" *Id.*, at 476; see also *id.*, at 334 (remarks of Rep. Hoar) (stating that the Privileges or Immunities Clause referred to those rights "declared to belong to the citizen by the Constitution itself"). Even opponents of Fourteenth Amendment enforcement legislation acknowledged that the Privileges or Immunities Clause protected constitutionally enumerated individual rights. See 2 Cong. Rec. 384–385 (1874) (remarks of Rep. Mills) (opposing enforcement law, but acknowledging, in referring to the Bill of Rights, that "[t]hese first amendments and some provisions of the Constitution of like import embrace the 'privileges and immunities' of citizenship as set forth in article 4, section 2, of the Constitution *and in the fourteenth amendment*" (emphasis added)); see Curtis 166–170 (collecting examples).

Legislation passed in furtherance of the Fourteenth Amendment demonstrates even more clearly this understanding. For example, Congress enacted the Civil Rights Act of 1871, 17 Stat. 13, which was titled in pertinent part "An Act to enforce the Provisions of the Fourteenth Amendment to the Constitution of the United States," and which is codified in the still-existing 42 U. S. C. § 1983. That statute prohibits state officials from depriving citizens of "any rights, privileges, or immunities *secured by the Constitution.*" Rev. Stat. 1979, 42 U. S. C. § 1983 (emphasis added). Although the Judiciary ignored this provision for decades after its enactment, this Court has come to interpret the statute, unremarkably in light of its text, as protecting constitutionally enumerated rights. *Monroe* v. *Pape,* 365 U. S. 167, 171 (1961).

A Federal Court of Appeals decision written by a future Justice of this Court adopted the same understanding of the Privileges or Immunities Clause. See, *e. g., United States* v. *Hall,* 26 F. Cas. 79, 82 (No. 15,282) (CC SD Ala. 1871) (Woods, J.) ("We think, therefore, that the . . . rights enumerated in the first eight articles of amendment to the constitution of the United States, are the privileges and immunities of citizens of the United States"). In addition, two of the era's major constitutional treatises reflected the understanding that § 1 would protect constitutionally enumerated rights from state abridgment.[14] A third such treatise unambigu-

[14] See J. Pomeroy, An Introduction to the Constitutional Law of the United States 155–156 (E. Bennett ed. 1886) (describing § 1, which the country was then still considering, as a "needed" "remedy" for *Barron ex*

ously indicates that the Privileges or Immunities Clause accomplished this task. G. Paschal, The Constitution of the United States 290 (1868) (explaining that the rights listed in § 1 had "already been guarantied" by Article IV and the Bill of Rights, but that "[t]he new feature declared" by § 1 was that these rights, "which had been construed to apply only to the national government, are thus imposed upon the States").

Another example of public understanding comes from United States Attorney Daniel Corbin's statement in an 1871 Ku Klux Klan prosecution. Corbin cited *Barron* and declared:

> "[T]he fourteenth amendment changes all that theory, and lays the same restriction upon the States that before lay upon the Congress of the United States—that, as Congress heretofore could not interfere with the right of the citizen to keep and bear arms, now, after the adoption of the fourteenth amendment, the State cannot interfere with the right of the citizen to keep and bear arms. The right to keep and bear arms is included in the fourteenth amendment, under 'privileges and immunities.'" Proceedings in the Ku Klux Trials at Columbia, S. C., in the United States Circuit Court, November Term, 1871, p. 147 (1872).

* * *

This evidence plainly shows that the ratifying public understood the Privileges or Immunities Clause to protect constitutionally enumerated rights, including the right to keep

rel. Tiernan v. *Mayor of Baltimore*, 7 Pet. 243 (1833), which held that the Bill of Rights was not enforceable against the States); T. Farrar, Manual of the Constitution of the United States of America 58–59, 145–146, 395–397 (1867); *id.*, at 546 (3d ed. 1872) (describing the Fourteenth Amendment as having "swept away" the "decisions of many courts" that "the popular rights guaranteed by the Constitution are secured only against [the federal] government").

and bear arms. As the Court demonstrates, there can be no doubt that § 1 was understood to enforce the Second Amendment against the States. See *ante*, at 770–780. In my view, this is because the right to keep and bear arms was understood to be a privilege of American citizenship guaranteed by the Privileges or Immunities Clause.

C

The next question is whether the Privileges or Immunities Clause merely prohibits States from discriminating among citizens if they recognize the Second Amendment's right to keep and bear arms, or whether the Clause requires States to recognize the right. The municipal respondents, Chicago and Oak Park, argue for the former interpretation. They contend that the Second Amendment, as applied to the States through the Fourteenth, authorizes a State to impose an outright ban on handgun possession such as the ones at issue here so long as a State applies it to all citizens equally.[15] The Court explains why this antidiscrimination-only reading of § 1 as a whole is "implausible." *Ante*, at 778 (citing Brief for Municipal Respondents 64). I agree, but because I think it is the Privileges or Immunities Clause that applies this right to the States, I must explain why this Clause in particular protects against more than just state discrimination, and in fact establishes a minimum baseline of rights for all American citizens.

[15] The municipal respondents and JUSTICE BREYER's dissent raise a most unusual argument that § 1 prohibits discriminatory laws affecting only the right to keep and bear arms, but offers substantive protection to other rights enumerated in the Constitution, such as the freedom of speech. See *post*, at 935. Others, however, have made the more comprehensive—and internally consistent—argument that § 1 bars discrimination alone and does not afford protection to any substantive rights. See, *e. g.*, R. Berger, Government by Judiciary: The Transformation of the Fourteenth Amendment (2d ed. 1997). I address the coverage of the Privileges or Immunities Clause only as it applies to the Second Amendment right presented here, but I do so with the understanding that my conclusion may have implications for the broader argument.

1

I begin, again, with the text. The Privileges or Immunities Clause opens with the command that "*No State shall*" abridge the privileges or immunities of citizens of the United States. Amdt. 14, § 1 (emphasis added). The very same phrase opens Article I, § 10, of the Constitution, which prohibits the States from "pass[ing] any Bill of Attainder" or "ex post facto Law," among other things. Article I, § 10, is one of the few constitutional provisions that limits state authority. In *Barron*, when Chief Justice Marshall interpreted the Bill of Rights as lacking "plain and intelligible language" restricting state power to infringe upon individual liberties, he pointed to Article I, § 10, as an example of text that would have accomplished that task. 7 Pet., at 250. Indeed, Chief Justice Marshall would later describe Article I, § 10, as "a bill of rights for the people of each state." *Fletcher* v. *Peck*, 6 Cranch 87, 138 (1810). Thus, the fact that the Privileges or Immunities Clause uses the command "[n]o State shall"—which Article IV, § 2, does not—strongly suggests that the former imposes a greater restriction on state power than the latter.

This interpretation is strengthened when one considers that the Privileges or Immunities Clause uses the verb "abridge," rather than "discriminate," to describe the limit it imposes on state authority. The Webster's dictionary in use at the time of Reconstruction defines the word "abridge" to mean "[t]o deprive; to cut off; . . . as, to *abridge* one of his rights." 1 Webster, An American Dictionary of the English Language, at 6. The Clause is thus best understood to impose a limitation on state power to infringe upon pre-existing substantive rights. It raises no indication that the Framers of the Clause used the word "abridge" to prohibit only discrimination.

This most natural textual reading is underscored by a well-publicized revision to the Fourteenth Amendment that the Reconstruction Congress rejected. After several

Southern States refused to ratify the Amendment, President Johnson met with their Governors to draft a compromise. N. Y. Times, Feb. 5, 1867, p. 5. Their proposal eliminated Congress' power to enforce the Amendment (granted in § 5), and replaced the Privileges or Immunities Clause in § 1 with the following:

> "All persons born or naturalized in the United States, and subject to the jurisdiction thereof, are citizens of the United States, and of the States in which they reside, and the Citizens of each State shall be entitled to all *the privileges and immunities of citizens in the several States.*" Draft reprinted in 1 Documentary History of Reconstruction 240 (W. Fleming ed. 1950) (hereinafter Fleming) (emphasis added).

Significantly, this proposal removed the "[n]o State shall" directive and the verb "abridge" from § 1, and also changed the class of rights to be protected from those belonging to "citizens of the United States" to those of the "citizens in the several States." This phrasing is materially indistinguishable from Article IV, § 2, which generally was understood as an antidiscrimination provision alone. See *supra,* at 819–822. The proposal thus strongly indicates that at least the President of the United States and several Southern Governors thought that the Privileges or Immunities Clause, which they unsuccessfully tried to revise, prohibited more than just state-sponsored discrimination.

2

The argument that the Privileges or Immunities Clause prohibits no more than discrimination often is followed by a claim that public discussion of the Clause, and of § 1 generally, was not extensive. Because of this, the argument goes, § 1 must not have been understood to accomplish such a significant task as subjecting States to federal enforcement of a minimum baseline of rights. That argument overlooks critical aspects of the Nation's history that underscored the need for, and wide agreement upon, federal enforcement of constitutionally enumerated rights against the States, including the right to keep and bear arms.

a

I turn first to public debate at the time of ratification. It is true that the congressional debates over § 1 were relatively brief. It is also true that there is little evidence of extensive debate in the States. Many state legislatures did not keep records of their debates, and the few records that do exist reveal only modest discussion. See Curtis 145. These facts are not surprising.

First, however consequential we consider the question today, the nationalization of constitutional rights was not the most controversial aspect of the Fourteenth Amendment at the time of its ratification. The Nation had just endured a tumultuous civil war, and §§ 2, 3, and 4—which reduced the representation of States that denied voting rights to blacks, deprived most former Confederate officers of the power to hold elective office, and required States to disavow Confederate war debts—were far more polarizing and consumed far more political attention. See Wildenthal 1600; Hardy, Original Popular Understanding of the Fourteenth Amendment as Reflected in the Print Media of 1866–1868, 30 Whittier L. Rev. 695, 699 (2009).

Second, the congressional debates on the Fourteenth Amendment reveal that many Representatives, and probably many citizens, believed that the Thirteenth Amendment, the 1866 Civil Rights legislation, or some combination of the two, had already enforced constitutional rights against the States. Justice Black's dissent in *Adamson* chronicles this point in detail. 332 U. S., at 107–108 (appendix to dissenting opinion). Regardless of whether that understanding was accurate as a matter of constitutional law, it helps to explain why

Congressmen had little to say during the debates about § 1. See *ibid.*

Third, while *Barron* made plain that the Bill of Rights was not legally enforceable against the States, see *supra,* at 806–807, the significance of that holding should not be overstated. Like the Framers, see *supra,* at 818–819, many 19th-century Americans understood the Bill of Rights to declare inalienable rights that pre-existed all government. Thus, even though the Bill of Rights technically applied only to the Federal Government, many believed that it declared rights that no legitimate government could abridge.

Chief Justice Henry Lumpkin's decision for the Georgia Supreme Court in *Nunn* v. *State,* 1 Ga. 243 (1846), illustrates this view. In assessing state power to regulate firearm possession, Lumpkin wrote that he was "aware that it has been decided, that [the Second Amendment], like other amendments adopted at the same time, is a restriction upon the government of the United States, and does not extend to the individual States." *Id.*, at 250. But he still considered the right to keep and bear arms as "an unalienable right, which lies at the bottom of every free government," and thus found the States bound to honor it. *Ibid.* Other state courts adopted similar positions with respect to the right to keep and bear arms and other enumerated rights.[16] Some courts even suggested that the protections in the Bill of Rights were legally enforceable against the States, *Barron* notwithstanding.[17] A prominent treatise of the era took the same position. W. Rawle, A View of the Constitution of the

---

[16] See, *e. g., Raleigh & Gaston R. Co.* v. *Davis,* 19 N. C. 451, 458–462 (1837) (right to just compensation for government taking of property); *Rohan* v. *Sawin,* 59 Mass. 281, 285 (1850) (right to be secure from unreasonable government searches and seizures); *State* v. *Buzzard,* 4 Ark. 18, 28 (1842) (right to keep and bear arms); *State* v. *Jumel,* 13 La. Ann. 399, 400 (1858) (same); *Cockrum* v. *State,* 24 Tex. 394, 401–404 (1859) (same).

[17] See, *e. g., People* v. *Goodwin,* 18 Johns. *187, *201 (N. Y. Sup. Ct. 1820); *Rhinehart* v. *Schuyler,* 7 Ill. 473, 522 (1845).

United States of America 124–125 (2d ed. 1829) (arguing that certain of the first eight Amendments "appl[y] to the state legislatures" because those Amendments "form parts of the declared rights of the people, of which neither the state powers nor those of the Union can ever deprive them"); *id.*, at 125–126 (describing the Second Amendment "right of the people to keep and bear Arms" as "a restraint on both" Congress and the States); see also *Heller*, 554 U. S., at 607 (describing Rawle's treatise as "influential"). Certain abolitionist leaders adhered to this view as well. Lysander Spooner championed the popular abolitionist argument that slavery was inconsistent with constitutional principles, citing as evidence the fact that it deprived black Americans of the "natural right of all men 'to keep and bear arms' for their personal defence," which he believed the Constitution "prohibit[ed] both Congress and the State governments from infringing." The Unconstitutionality of Slavery 98 (1860).

In sum, some appear to have believed that the Bill of Rights *did* apply to the States, even though this Court had squarely rejected that theory. See, *e. g., supra,* at 830–831 (recounting Rep. Hale's argument to this effect). Many others believed that the liberties codified in the Bill of Rights were ones that no State *should* abridge, even though they understood that the Bill technically did not apply to States. These beliefs, combined with the fact that most state constitutions recognized many, if not all, of the individual rights enumerated in the Bill of Rights, made the need for federal enforcement of constitutional liberties against the States an afterthought. See *ante,* at 777 (opinion of the Court) (noting that, "[i]n 1868, 22 of the 37 States in the Union had state constitutional provisions explicitly protecting the right to keep and bear arms"). That changed with the national conflict over slavery.

b

In the contentious years leading up to the Civil War, those who sought to retain the institution of slavery found that to do so, it was necessary to eliminate more and more of the basic liberties of slaves, free blacks, and white abolitionists. Congressman Tobias Plants explained that slaveholders "could not hold [slaves] safely where dissent was permitted," so they decided that "all dissent must be suppressed by the strong hand of power." 39th Cong. Globe 1013. The measures they used were ruthless, repressed virtually every right recognized in the Constitution, and demonstrated that preventing only discriminatory state firearms restrictions would have been a hollow assurance for liberty. Public reaction indicates that the American people understood this point.

The overarching goal of proslavery forces was to repress the spread of abolitionist thought and the concomitant risk of a slave rebellion. Indeed, it is difficult to overstate the extent to which fear of a slave uprising gripped slaveholders and dictated the acts of Southern legislatures. Slaves and free blacks represented a substantial percentage of the population and posed a severe threat to Southern order if they were not kept in their place. According to the 1860 Census, slaves represented one quarter or more of the population in 11 of the 15 slave States, nearly half the population in Alabama, Florida, Georgia, and Louisiana, and *more* than 50% of the population in Mississippi and South Carolina. Statistics of the United States (Including Mortality, Property, & c.,) in 1860, The Eighth Census 336–350 (1866).

The Southern fear of slave rebellion was not unfounded. Although there were others, two particularly notable slave uprisings heavily influenced slaveholders in the South. In 1822, a group of free blacks and slaves led by Denmark Vesey planned a rebellion in which they would slay their masters and flee to Haiti. H. Aptheker, American Negro Slave Revolts 268–270 (1983). The plan was foiled, leading to the swift arrest of 130 blacks, and the execution of 37, including Vesey. *Id.,* at 271. Still, slaveowners took notice—it was reportedly feared that as many as 6,600 to 9,000 slaves and free blacks were involved in the plot. *Id.*, at 272. A few years later, the fear of rebellion was realized. An uprising led by Nat Turner took the lives of at least 57 whites before it was suppressed. *Id.*, at 298–302.

The fear generated by these and other rebellions led Southern legislatures to take particularly vicious aim at the rights of free blacks and slaves to speak or to keep and bear arms for their defense. Teaching slaves to read (even the Bible) was a criminal offense punished severely in some States. See K. Stampp, The Peculiar Institution: Slavery in the Ante-bellum South 208, 211 (1956). Virginia made it a crime for a member of an "abolition" society to enter the State and argue "that the owners of slaves have no property in the same, or advocate or advise the abolition of slavery." 1835–1836 Va. Acts ch. 66, p. 44. Other States prohibited the circulation of literature denying a master's right to property in his slaves and passed laws requiring postmasters to inspect the mails in search of such material. C. Eaton, The Freedom-of-Thought Struggle in the Old South 118–143, 199–200 (1964).

Many legislatures amended their laws prohibiting slaves from carrying firearms[18] to apply the prohibition to free blacks as well. See, *e. g.*, Act of Dec. 23, 1833, § 7, 1833 Ga. Acts pp. 226, 228 (declaring that "it shall not be lawful for any free person of colour in this state, to own, use, or carry fire arms of any description whatever"); H. Aptheker, Nat Turner's Slave Rebellion 74–76, 83–94 (1966) (discussing similar Maryland and Virginia statutes); see also Act of Mar. 15,

[18] See, *e. g.*, Black Code, ch. 33, § 19, 1806 Acts of First Session of Territory of Orleans pp. 160, 162 (prohibiting slaves from using firearms unless they were authorized by their master to hunt within the boundaries of his plantation); An Act to Provide for the More Effectual Performance of Patrol Duty, 1819 S. C. Acts pp. 29, 31 (same); An Act to Amend the Sixth Section of an Act Entitled "An Act Concerning Slaves," approved 5th Feb., 1840, Tex. Laws, 3d Sess., pp. 42–43 (making it unlawful for "any slave to own firearms of any description").

1852, ch. 206, 1852 Miss. Laws p. 328 (repealing laws allowing free blacks to obtain firearms licenses); Act of Jan. 31, 1831, 1831 Fla. Acts p. 30 (same). Florida made it the "duty" of white citizen "patrol[s] to search negro houses or other suspected places, for fire arms." Act of Feb. 17, 1833, ch. 671, 1833 Fla. Acts pp. 26, 30. If they found any firearms, the patrols were to take the offending slave or free black "to the nearest justice of the peace," whereupon he would be "sever[ely] punished" by "whipping on the bare back, not exceeding thirty-nine lashes," unless he could give a "plain and satisfactory" explanation of how he came to possess the gun. *Ibid.*

Southern blacks were not alone in facing threats to their personal liberty and security during the antebellum era. Mob violence in many Northern cities presented dangers as well. Cottrol & Diamond, The Second Amendment: Toward an Afro-Americanist Reconsideration, 80 Geo. L. J. 309, 340 (1991) (hereinafter Cottrol) (recounting a July 1834 mob attack against "churches, homes, and businesses of white abolitionists and blacks" in New York that involved "upwards of twenty thousand people and required the intervention of the militia to suppress"); *ibid.* (noting an uprising in Boston nine years later in which a confrontation between a group of white sailors and four blacks led "a mob of several hundred whites" to "attac[k] and severely beat every black they could find").

C

After the Civil War, Southern anxiety about an uprising among the newly freed slaves peaked. As Representative Thaddeus Stevens is reported to have said, " '[w]hen it was first proposed to free the slaves, and arm the blacks, did not half the nation tremble? The prim conservatives, the snobs, and the male waiting-maids in Congress, were in hysterics.' " K. Stampp, The Era of Reconstruction, 1865–1877, p. 104 (1965) (hereinafter Era of Reconstruction).

As the Court explains, this fear led to "systematic efforts" in the "old Confederacy" to disarm the more than 180,000 freedmen who had served in the Union Army, as well as other free blacks. See *ante,* at 771. Some States formally prohibited blacks from possessing firearms. *Ibid.* (quoting 1865 Miss. Laws p. 165, § 1, reprinted in 1 Fleming 289). Others enacted legislation prohibiting blacks from carrying firearms without a license, a restriction not imposed on whites. See, *e. g.,* La. Statute of 1865, reprinted in *id.,* at 280. Additionally, "[t]hroughout the South, armed parties, often consisting of ex-Confederate soldiers serving in the state militias, forcibly took firearms from newly freed slaves." *Ante,* at 772.

As the Court makes crystal clear, if the Fourteenth Amendment "had outlawed only those laws that discriminate on the basis of race or previous condition of servitude, African-Americans in the South would likely have remained vulnerable to attack by many of their worst abusers: the state militia and state peace officers." *Ante,* at 779. In the years following the Civil War, a law banning firearm possession outright "would have been nondiscriminatory only in the formal sense," for it would have "left firearms in the hands of the militia and local peace officers." *Ibid.*

Evidence suggests that the public understood this at the time the Fourteenth Amendment was ratified. The publicly circulated Report of the Joint Committee on Reconstruction extensively detailed these abuses, see *ante,* at 772 (collecting examples), and statements by citizens indicate that they looked to the Committee to provide a federal solution to this problem, see, *e. g.,* 39th Cong. Globe 337 (remarks of Rep. Sumner) (introducing "a memorial from the colored citizens of the State of South Carolina" asking for, *inter alia,* "constitutional protection in keeping arms, in holding public assemblies, and in complete liberty of speech and of the press").

One way in which the Federal Government responded was to issue military orders countermanding Southern arms legislation. See, *e. g.*, Jan. 17, 1866, order from Major General D. E. Sickles, reprinted in E. McPherson, The Political History of the United States of America During the Period of Reconstruction 37 (1871) ("The constitutional rights of all loyal and well-disposed inhabitants to bear arms will not be infringed"). The significance of these steps was not lost on those they were designed to protect. After one such order was issued, The Christian Recorder, published by the African Methodist Episcopal Church, published the following editorial:

> "'We have several times alluded to the fact that the Constitution of the United States, guaranties to every citizen the right to keep and bear arms. . . . All men, without the distinction of color, have the right to keep arms to defend their homes, families, or themselves.'
>
> "We are glad to learn that [the] Commissioner for this State . . . has given freedmen to understand that they have as good a right to keep fire arms as any other citizens. The Constitution of the United States is the supreme law of the land, and we will be governed by that at present." Right To Bear Arms, Phila., Pa., Christian Recorder, Feb. 24, 1866, pp. 29–30.

The same month, The Loyal Georgian carried a letter to the editor asking, "Have colored persons a right to own and carry fire arms?—A Colored Citizen." The editors responded as follows:

> "Almost every day, we are asked questions similar to the above. We answer *certainly* you have the *same* right to own and carry fire arms that *other* citizens have. You are not only free but citizens of the United States and, as such, entitled to the same privileges granted to other citizens by the Constitution of the United States.
>
> . . . . .
>
> ". . . Article II, of the amendments to the Constitution of the United States, gives the people the right to bear

> arms and states that this right shall not be infringed. . . . All men, without distinction of color, have the right to keep arms to defend their homes, families or themselves." Letter to the Editor, Augusta, Ga., Loyal Georgian, Feb. 3, 1866, p. 3.

These statements are consistent with the arguments of abolitionists during the antebellum era that slavery, and the slave States' efforts to retain it, violated the constitutional rights of individuals—rights the abolitionists described as among the privileges and immunities of citizenship. See, *e. g.*, J. Tiffany, Treatise on the Unconstitutionality of American Slavery 56 (1849) ("pledg[ing] . . . to see that all the rights, privileges, and immunities, granted by the constitution of the United States, are extended to all"); *id.*, at 99 (describing the "right to keep and bear arms" as one of those rights secured by "the constitution of the United States"). The problem abolitionists sought to remedy was that, under *Dred Scott*, blacks were not entitled to the privileges and immunities of citizens under the Federal Constitution and that, in many States, whatever inalienable rights state law recognized did not apply to blacks. See, *e. g.*, *Cooper* v. *Savannah*, 4 Ga. 68, 72 (1848) (deciding, just two years after Chief Justice Lumpkin's opinion in *Nunn* recognizing the right to keep and bear arms, see *supra*, at 842, that "[f]ree persons of color have never been recognized here as citizens; they are not entitled to bear arms").

Section 1 guaranteed the rights of citizenship in the United States and in the several States without regard to race. But it was understood that liberty would be assured little protection if § 1 left each State to decide which privileges or immunities of United States citizenship it would protect. As Frederick Douglass explained before § 1's adoption, "the Legislatures of the South can take from him the right to keep and bear arms, as they can—they would not allow a negro to walk with a cane where I came from, they would not allow five of them to assemble together." In

What New Skin Will the Old Snake Come Forth? An Address Delivered in New York, New York, on May 10, 1865, reprinted in 4 The Frederick Douglass Papers 79, 83–84 (J. Blassingame & J. McKivigan eds. 1991) (footnote omitted). "Notwithstanding the provision in the Constitution of the United States that the right to keep and bear arms shall not be abridged," Douglass explained that "the black man has never had the right either to keep or bear arms." *Id.*, at 84. Absent a constitutional amendment to enforce that right against the States, he insisted that "the work of the Abolitionists [wa]s not finished." *Ibid.*

This history confirms what the text of the Privileges or Immunities Clause most naturally suggests: Consistent with its command that "[n]o State shall . . . abridge" the rights of United States citizens, the Clause establishes a minimum baseline of federal rights, and the constitutional right to keep and bear arms plainly was among them.[19]

III

My conclusion is contrary to this Court's precedents, which hold that the Second Amendment right to keep and bear arms is not a privilege of United States citizenship. See *Cruikshank*, 92 U. S., at 548–549, 551–553. I must, therefore, consider whether *stare decisis* requires retention of those precedents. As mentioned at the outset, my inquiry is limited to the right at issue here. Thus, I do not endeavor to decide in this case whether, or to what extent, the Privileges or Immunities Clause applies any other rights enumer-

[19] I conclude that the right to keep and bear arms applies to the States through the Privileges or Immunities Clause, which recognizes the rights of United States "citizens." The plurality concludes that the right applies to the States through the Due Process Clause, which covers all "person[s]." Because this case does not involve a claim brought by a noncitizen, I express no view on the difference, if any, between my conclusion and the plurality's with respect to the extent to which the States may regulate firearm possession by noncitizens.

ated in the Constitution against the States.[20] Nor do I suggest that the *stare decisis* considerations surrounding the application of the right to keep and bear arms against the States would be the same as those surrounding another right protected by the Privileges or Immunities Clause. I consider *stare decisis* only as it applies to the question presented here.

A

This inquiry begins with the *Slaughter-House Cases.* There, this Court upheld a Louisiana statute granting a monopoly on livestock butchering in and around the city of New Orleans to a newly incorporated company. 16 Wall. 36. Butchers excluded by the monopoly sued, claiming that the statute violated the Privileges or Immunities Clause because it interfered with their right to pursue and "exercise their trade." *Id.*, at 60. This Court rejected the butchers' claim, holding that their asserted right was not a privilege or immunity of American citizenship, but one governed by the States alone. The Court held that the Privileges or Immunities Clause protected only rights of *federal* citizenship—those "which owe their existence to the Federal government, its National character, its Constitution, or its laws," *id.*, at 79—and did not protect *any* of the rights of state citizenship,

[20] I note, however, that I see no reason to assume that the constitutionally enumerated rights protected by the Privileges or Immunities Clause should consist of all the rights recognized in the Bill of Rights and no others. Constitutional provisions outside the Bill of Rights protect individual rights, see, *e. g.*, Art. I, § 9, cl. 2 (granting the "Privilege of the Writ of Habeas Corpus"), and there is no obvious evidence that the Framers of the Privileges or Immunities Clause meant to exclude them. In addition, certain Bill of Rights provisions prevent federal interference in state affairs and are not readily construed as protecting rights that belong to individuals. The Ninth and Tenth Amendments are obvious examples, as is the First Amendment's Establishment Clause, which "does not purport to protect individual rights." *Elk Grove Unified School Dist.* v. *Newdow*, 542 U. S. 1, 50 (2004) (THOMAS, J., concurring in judgment); see Amar 179–180.

id., at 74. In other words, the Court defined the two sets of rights as mutually exclusive.

After separating these two sets of rights, the Court defined the rights of state citizenship as "embrac[ing] nearly every civil right for the establishment and protection of which organized government is instituted"—that is, all those rights listed in *Corfield.* 16 Wall., at 76 (referring to "those rights" that "Judge Washington" described). That left very few rights of federal citizenship for the Privileges or Immunities Clause to protect. The Court suggested a handful of possibilities, such as the "right of free access to [federal] seaports," protection of the Federal Government while traveling "on the high seas," and even two rights listed in the Constitution. *Id.*, at 79 (noting "[t]he right to peaceably assemble" and "the privilege of the writ of *habeas corpus*"); see *supra,* at 808. But its decision to interpret the rights of state and federal citizenship as mutually exclusive led the Court in future cases to conclude that constitutionally enumerated rights were excluded from the Privileges or Immunities Clause's scope. See *Cruikshank, supra.*

I reject that understanding. There was no reason to interpret the Privileges or Immunities Clause as putting the Court to the extreme choice of interpreting the "privileges and immunities" of federal citizenship to mean either all those rights listed in *Corfield,* or almost no rights at all. 16 Wall., at 76. The record is scant that the public understood the Clause to make the Federal Government "a perpetual censor upon all legislation of the States" as the *Slaughter-House* majority feared. *Id.*, at 78. For one thing, *Corfield* listed the "elective franchise" as one of the privileges and immunities of "citizens of the several states," 6 F. Cas., at 552, yet Congress and the States still found it necessary to adopt the Fifteenth Amendment—which protects "[t]he right of citizens of the United States to vote"—two years after the Fourteenth Amendment's passage. If the Privileges or Immunities Clause were understood to protect every conceivable civil right from state abridgment, the Fifteenth Amendment would have been redundant.

The better view, in light of the States and Federal Government's shared history of recognizing certain inalienable rights in their citizens, is that the privileges and immunities of state and federal citizenship overlap. This is not to say that the privileges and immunities of state and federal citizenship are the same. At the time of the Fourteenth Amendment's ratification, States performed many more functions than the Federal Government, and it is unlikely that, simply by referring to "privileges or immunities," the Framers of § 1 meant to transfer every right mentioned in *Corfield* to congressional oversight. As discussed, "privileges" and "immunities" were understood only as synonyms for "rights." See *supra*, at 813–815. It was their attachment to a particular group that gave them content, and the text and history recounted here indicate that the rights of United States citizens were not perfectly identical to the rights of citizens "in the several States." Justice Swayne, one of the dissenters in *Slaughter-House*, made the point clear:

> "The citizen of a State has the *same* fundamental rights as a citizen of the United States, *and also certain others*, local in their character, arising from his relation to the State, and in addition, those which belong to the citizen of the United States, he being in that relation also. There may thus be a double citizenship, each having some rights peculiar to itself. It is only over those which belong to the citizen of the United States that the category here in question throws the shield of its protection." 16 Wall., at 126 (emphasis added).

Because the privileges and immunities of American citizenship include rights enumerated in the Constitution, they overlap to at least some extent with the privileges and immunities traditionally recognized in citizens in the several States.

A separate question is whether the privileges and immunities of American citizenship include any rights besides those enumerated in the Constitution. The four dissenting Justices in *Slaughter-House* would have held that the Privileges or Immunities Clause protected the unenumerated right that the butchers in that case asserted. See *id.*, at 83 (opinion of Field, J.); *id.*, at 111 (opinion of Bradley, J.); *id.*, at 124 (opinion of Swayne, J.). Because this case does not involve an unenumerated right, it is not necessary to resolve the question whether the Clause protects such rights, or whether the Court's judgment in *Slaughter-House* was correct.

Still, it is argued that the mere possibility that the Privileges or Immunities Clause may enforce unenumerated rights against the States creates " 'special hazards' " that should prevent this Court from returning to the original meaning of the Clause.[21] *Post,* at 860 (STEVENS, J., dissenting). Ironically, the same objection applies to the Court's substantive due process jurisprudence, which illustrates the risks of granting judges broad discretion to recognize individual constitutional rights in the absence of textual or historical guideposts. But I see no reason to assume that such hazards apply to the Privileges or Immunities Clause. The mere fact that the Clause does not expressly list the rights it protects does not render it incapable of principled judicial application. The Constitution contains many provisions that require an examination of more than just constitutional text to determine whether a particular act is within Congress' power or is otherwise prohibited. See, *e. g.,* Art. I, § 8, cl. 18 (Necessary and Proper Clause); Amdt. 8 (Cruel and

[21] To the extent JUSTICE STEVENS is concerned that reliance on the Privileges or Immunities Clause may invite judges to "write their personal views of appropriate public policy into the Constitution," *post,* at 860 (internal quotation marks omitted), his celebration of the alternative—the "flexibility," "transcend[ence]," and "dynamism" of substantive due process—speaks for itself, *post,* at 871, 872, 876.

Unusual Punishments Clause). When the inquiry focuses on what the ratifying era understood the Privileges or Immunities Clause to mean, interpreting it should be no more "hazardous" than interpreting these other constitutional provisions by using the same approach. To be sure, interpreting the Privileges or Immunities Clause may produce hard questions. But they will have the advantage of being questions the Constitution asks us to answer. I believe those questions are more worthy of this Court's attention—and far more likely to yield discernible answers—than the substantive due process questions the Court has for years created on its own, with neither textual nor historical support.

Finding these impediments to returning to the original meaning overstated, I reject *Slaughter-House* insofar as it precludes any overlap between the privileges and immunities of state and federal citizenship. I next proceed to the *stare decisis* considerations surrounding the precedent that expressly controls the question presented here.

B

Three years after *Slaughter-House*, the Court in *Cruikshank* squarely held that the right to keep and bear arms was not a privilege of American citizenship, thereby overturning the convictions of militia members responsible for the brutal Colfax Massacre. See *supra*, at 808–809. *Cruikshank* is not a precedent entitled to any respect. The flaws in its interpretation of the Privileges or Immunities Clause are made evident by the preceding evidence of its original meaning, and I would reject the holding on that basis alone. But, the consequences of *Cruikshank* warrant mention as well.

Cruikshank's holding that blacks could look only to state governments for protection of their right to keep and bear arms enabled private forces, often with the assistance of local governments, to subjugate the newly freed slaves and their descendants through a wave of private violence designed to drive blacks from the voting booth and force them into peonage, an effective return to slavery. Without federal enforcement of the inalienable right to keep and bear arms, these militias and mobs were tragically successful in waging a campaign of terror against the very people the Fourteenth Amendment had just made citizens.

Take, for example, the Hamburg Massacre of 1876. There, a white citizen militia sought out and murdered a troop of black militiamen for no other reason than that they had dared to conduct a celebratory Fourth of July parade through their mostly black town. The white militia commander, "Pitchfork" Ben Tillman, later described this massacre with pride: "[T]he leading white men of Edgefield" had decided "to seize the first opportunity that the negroes might offer them to provoke a riot and teach the negroes a lesson by having the whites demonstrate their superiority by killing as many of them as was justifiable." S. Kantrowitz, Ben Tillman & the Reconstruction of White Supremacy 67 (2000) (ellipsis, brackets, and internal quotation marks omitted). None of the perpetrators of the Hamburg murders was ever brought to justice.[22]

Organized terrorism like that perpetuated by Tillman and his cohorts proliferated in the absence of federal enforcement of constitutional rights. Militias such as the Ku Klux Klan, the Knights of the White Camellia, the White Brotherhood, the Pale Faces, and the '76 Association spread terror among blacks and white Republicans by breaking up Republican meetings, threatening political leaders, and whipping black militiamen. Era of Reconstruction 199–200; Curtis

[22] Tillman went on to a long career as South Carolina's Governor and, later, United States Senator. Tillman's contributions to campaign finance law have been discussed in our recent cases on that subject. See *Citizens United* v. *Federal Election Comm'n*, 558 U. S. 310, 394–395, 433, 446, 476 (2010) (STEVENS, J., concurring in part and dissenting in part) (discussing at length the Tillman Act of 1907, ch. 420, 34 Stat. 864). His contributions to the culture of terrorism that grew in the wake of *Cruikshank* had an even more dramatic and tragic effect.

156. These groups raped, murdered, lynched, and robbed as a means of intimidating, and instilling pervasive fear in, those whom they despised. A. Trelease, White Terror: The Ku Klux Klan Conspiracy and Southern Reconstruction 28–46 (1995).

Although Congress enacted legislation to suppress these activities,[23] Klan tactics remained a constant presence in the lives of Southern blacks for decades. Between 1882 and 1968, there were at least 3,446 reported lynchings of blacks in the South. Cottrol 351–352. They were tortured and killed for a wide array of alleged crimes, without even the slightest hint of due process. Emmit Till, for example, was killed in 1955 for allegedly whistling at a white woman. S. Whitfield, A Death in the Delta: The Story of Emmett Till 15–31 (1988). The fates of other targets of mob violence were equally depraved. See, *e. g.*, Lynched Negro and Wife Were First Mutilated, Vicksburg (Miss.) Evening Post, Feb. 8, 1904, reprinted in R. Ginzburg, 100 Years of Lynchings 63 (1988); Negro Shot Dead for Kissing His White Girlfriend, Chicago Defender, Feb. 31, 1915, in *id.*, at 95 (reporting incident in Florida); La. Negro Is Burned Alive Screaming "I Didn't Do It," Cleveland Gazette, Dec. 13, 1914, in *id.*, at 93 (reporting incident in Louisiana).

The use of firearms for self-defense was often the only way black citizens could protect themselves from mob violence. As Eli Cooper, one target of such violence, is said to have explained, "[t]he 'Negro has been run over for fifty years, but it must stop now, and pistols and shotguns are the only weapons to stop a mob.'" Church Burnings Follow Negro Agitator's Lynching, Chicago Defender, Sept. 6, 1919, in *id.*, at 124. Sometimes, as in Cooper's case, self-defense did not succeed. He was dragged from his home by a mob and

---

[23] In an effort to enforce the Fourteenth Amendment and halt this violence, Congress enacted a series of civil rights statutes, including the Force Acts, see Act of May 31, 1870, 16 Stat. 140; Act of Feb. 28, 1871, 16 Stat. 433, and the Ku Klux Klan Act, see Act of Apr. 20, 1871, 17 Stat. 13.

killed as his wife looked on. *Ibid.* But at other times, the use of firearms allowed targets of mob violence to survive. One man recalled the night during his childhood when his father stood armed at a jail until morning to ward off lynchers. See Cottrol 354. The experience left him with a sense, "not 'of powerlessness, but of the "possibilities of salvation"'" that came from standing up to intimidation. *Ibid.*

In my view, the record makes plain that the Framers of the Privileges or Immunities Clause and the ratifying-era public understood—just as the Framers of the Second Amendment did—that the right to keep and bear arms was essential to the preservation of liberty. The record makes equally plain that they deemed this right necessary to include in the minimum baseline of federal rights that the Privileges or Immunities Clause established in the wake of the war over slavery. There is nothing about *Cruikshank*'s contrary holding that warrants its retention.

* * *

I agree with the Court that the Second Amendment is fully applicable to the States. I do so because the right to keep and bear arms is guaranteed by the Fourteenth Amendment as a privilege of American citizenship.

JUSTICE STEVENS, dissenting.

In *District of Columbia* v. *Heller*, 554 U. S. 570, 573 (2008), the Court answered the question whether a federal enclave's "prohibition on the possession of usable handguns in the home violates the Second Amendment to the Constitution." The question we should be answering in this case is whether the Constitution "guarantees individuals a fundamental right," enforceable against the States, "to possess a functional, personal firearm, including a handgun, within the home." Complaint ¶ 34, App. 23. That is a different—and more difficult—inquiry than asking if the Fourteenth Amendment "incorporates" the Second Amendment. The

The Right to Keep and Bear Arms In State Constitutions

As the documents presented in this book demonstrate, particularly the *Federalist Papers* and the *Anti-Federalist Papers*, there was considerable debate at the time the Constitution was being drafted over how much power and authority the federal government should have over the individual states. Since each state is an independent political entity, each state has its own, state constitution that exists alongside the federal constitution.

Just as the Constitution itself was vigorously debated, so were the various rights that came to be incorporated into the Bill of Rights. Some of the states already had constitutions with a right to keep and bear arms spelled out in them, while others were in the process of writing (or rewriting) their state constitutions. In order to better comprehend what the Second Amendment was understood to mean by the delegates who debated and adopted it, it may be helpful to refer to the corresponding provision in the constitutions of the thirteen original states.

Connecticut

Every citizen has a right to bear arms in defense of himself and the state. (*Adopted in 1818 as Art. I, § 17, subsequently renumbered to Art. I, § 15 but the text was not changed.*)

Delaware

A person has the right to keep and bear arms for the defense of self, family, home and State, and for hunting and recreational use.
(*Adopted in 1987 as Art. 1, § 20.*)

Georgia

A well-regulated militia, being necessary to the security of a free State, the right of the people to keep and bear arms shall not be infringed.
(*Adopted in 1865 as Art. I, § 4.*)

Maryland

Has no constitutional provision for the right to keep and bear arms.

Massachusetts

The people have a right to keep and to bear arms for the common defence. And as, in time of peace, armies are dangerous to liberty, they ought not to be maintained without the consent of the legislature; and the military power shall always be held in an exact subordination to the civil authority, and be governed by it.

(Adopted in 1780 as Pt. 1, art. 17.)

New Hampshire

All persons have the right to keep and bear arms in defense of themselves, their families, their property and the state.

(Adopted in 1982 as Pt. 1, art. 2-a.)

New Jersey

Has no constitutional provision for the right to keep and bear arms.

New York

Has no constitutional provision for the right to keep and bear arms.

North Carolina

That the people have a right to bear arms, for the defence of the State; and, as standing armies, in time of peace, are dangerous to liberty, they ought not to be kept up; and that the military should be kept under strict subordination to, and governed by, the civil power.

(Adopted in 1776 as Bill of Rights, § XVII. Subsequently revised in 1868 and 1875.)

Pennsylvania

The right of the citizens to bear arms in defence of themselves and the State shall not be questioned.

(Adopted in 1790 as Art. IX, § 21, subsequently renumbered Art. 1, § 21 but the text was not changed.)

Rhode Island

The right of the people to keep and bear arms shall not be infringed.

(Adopted in 1842 as Art. I, § 22.)

South Carolina

The people have a right to keep and bear arms for the common defence. As, in times of peace armies are dangerous to liberty, they ought not to be maintained without the consent of the General Assembly. The military power ought always to be held in an exact subordination to the civil authority and be governed by it.

(Adopted in 1868 as Art. I, § 28. Revised in 1895)

Virginia

That a well regulated militia, composed of the body of the people, trained to arms, is the proper, natural, and safe defense of a free state; that standing armies, in time of peace, should be avoided as dangerous to liberty; and that in all cases the military should be under strict subordination to, and governed by, the civil power.

(*Adopted in 1776 as Art. I, § 13. Revised in 1971 to insert "therefore, the right to keep and bear arms shall not be infringed"*)

About the Author

HARWOOD W. LOOMIS is a semi-retired architect, ordained minister, clinical hypnotherapist, and author whose technical articles have appeared in a number of trade magazines dedicated to architecture, engineering, and property management. A life-long automotive hobbyist, he has crewed for a stock car racing team, built his own race car for competition on the New England hillclimb circuit, and he is a former state champion in the Connecticut Council of Sports Car Clubs autocross series.

Harwood is a Vietnam veteran. His awards from his service in the United States Army include the Army Commendation Medal, Army Good Conduct Medal, Vietnam Service Medal with Two Bronze service Stars, Meritorious Unit Commendation, Republic of Vietnam Gallantry Cross Unit Citation with Palm Device, and the Republic of Vietnam Civil Actions Honor Medal Unit Citation, First Class. During his Army career he was a member of the 1814 Color Guard and a member of his battalion competition shooting team.

Harwood has served as a member of the board of directors and Vice President of Cornerstone, a mental health halfway house in New Haven, Connecticut; member of the board of directors, author, and contributing editor for the Trumbull [Connecticut] PC Users Group; member, director, Vice President and President of the International Codes Council Professional Chapter of Connecticut; member, director, Vice President and President of the New England Building Codes Council; and member of the board of directors and newsletter editor for The Phenix Society [a not-for-profit organization dedicated to improving the quality of life for senior citizens]. He currently acts as a moderator on three Internet discussion forums and writes for and serves as Senior Editor for an on-line magazine.

A widower, he lives with his family of Jeep Cherokees and Jeep Comanches in Woodbridge, Connecticut. His house stands on the last remaining portion of a larger tract of land that was granted to a maternal ancestor by King George of England before the American Revolution. He qualifies for membership in the Sons of the American Revolution as a result of service during the revolution by both maternal and paternal ancestors. He is a direct descendant of John Jay, the first Chief Justice of the Supreme Court of the United States, and a great-grandson of John Wurts, a professor of law at Yale University. As a result, his interest in the Constitution and in the Bill of Rights may be thought of as generic in derivation.